ENOCH AND THE MESSIAH SON OF MAN

# ENOCH AND THE MESSIAH SON OF MAN

*Revisiting the Book of Parables*

*Edited by*

Gabriele Boccaccini

*Associate Editor: Jason von Ehrenkrook*
*with the collaboration of J. Harold Ellens, Ronald Ruark, and Justin Winger*

WILLIAM B. EERDMANS PUBLISHING COMPANY
GRAND RAPIDS, MICHIGAN / CAMBRIDGE, U.K.

© 2007 Wm. B. Eerdmans Publishing Co.
All rights reserved

Published 2007 by
Wm. B. Eerdmans Publishing Co.
2140 Oak Industrial Drive N.E., Grand Rapids, Michigan 49505 /
P.O. Box 163, Cambridge CB3 9PU U.K.

Library of Congress Cataloging-in-Publication Data

Enoch and the Messiah Son of Man: revisiting the book of parables /
    edited by Gabriele Boccaccini.
       p.      cm.
    Includes bibliographical references.
    ISBN-13: 978-0-8028-0377-1 (pbk.: alk. paper)
    1. Ethiopic book of Enoch — Parables — Congresses.
    I. Boccaccini, Gabriele, 1958-

BS1830.E7E57   2007
229.913 — dc22

                                    2007003415

www.eerdmans.com

# Contents

Abbreviations　　　　　　　　　　　　　　　　　　　　　　　　　　　　　x

## INTRODUCTION

The Enoch Seminar at Camaldoli: Re-entering the Parables
of Enoch in the Study of Second Temple Judaism and
Christian Origins　　　　　　　　　　　　　　　　　　　　　　　　　　3
　*Gabriele Boccaccini*

Greeting to the Participants at the Third Enoch Seminar
at Camaldoli　　　　　　　　　　　　　　　　　　　　　　　　　　　17
　*Dom Emanuele Bargellini, Prior General of Camaldoli*

## PART ONE: THE STRUCTURE OF THE TEXT

Discerning the Structure(s) of the Enochic Book of Parables　　　　23
　*George W. E. Nickelsburg*

The Structure and Composition of the Parables of Enoch　　　　　48
　*Michael A. Knibb*

*Contents*

The Parables of Enoch according to George Nickelsburg and
Michael Knibb: A Summary and Discussion of Some
Remaining Questions     65
    Loren T. Stuckenbruck

The Structure of the Parables of Enoch:
A Response to George Nickelsburg and Michael Knibb     72
    Benjamin G. Wright

### PART TWO: THE PARABLES WITHIN THE ENOCH TRADITION

The Book of Parables within the Enoch Tradition     81
    James C. VanderKam

Remarks on Transmission and Traditions in the Parables of Enoch:
A Response to James VanderKam     100
    Eibert J. C. Tigchelaar

Roles and Titles of the Seventh Antediluvian Hero in the Parables
of Enoch: A Departure from the Traditional Pattern?     110
    Andrei A. Orlov

A Dead End in the Enoch Trajectory: A Response to Andrei Orlov     137
    William Adler

Exegetical Notes on Cosmology in the Parables of Enoch     143
    Jonathan Ben-Dov

### PART THREE: THE SON OF MAN

The Son of Man: The Evolution of an Expression     153
    Sabino Chialà

The Son of Man in the Parables of Enoch     179
    Helge S. Kvanvig

Enoch and the Son of Man:
A Response to Sabino Chialà and Helge Kvanvig  216
   *John J. Collins*

Questions regarding the So-Called Son of Man in the Parables
of Enoch: A Response to Sabino Chialà and Helge Kvanvig  228
   *Klaus Koch*

The Name of the Son of Man in the Parables of Enoch  238
   *Charles A. Gieschen*

"The Coming of the Righteous One" in Acts and 1 Enoch  250
   *Gerbern S. Oegema*

## PART FOUR: THE PARABLES WITHIN SECOND TEMPLE LITERATURE

Finding a Place for the Parables of Enoch within
Second Temple Jewish Literature  263
   *Gabriele Boccaccini*

The Parables of Enoch in Second Temple Literature:
A Response to Gabriele Boccaccini  290
   *Matthias Henze*

The Son of Man in the Parables of Enoch and the Gospels  299
   *Leslie W. Walck*

The Secret Son of Man in the Parables of Enoch and the
Gospel of Mark: A Response to Leslie Walck  338
   *Adela Yarbro Collins*

The Parables of Enoch and Qumran Literature  343
   *Ida Fröhlich*

Adamic Traditions in the Parables? A Query on 1 Enoch 69:6  352
   *Kelley Coblentz Bautch*

*Contents*

## PART FIVE: THE SOCIAL SETTING

"A Testimony for the Kings and the Mighty Who Possess the
Earth": The Thirst for Justice and Peace in the Parables of Enoch 363
 *Pierluigi Piovanelli*

Was the Book of Parables a Sectarian Document?
A Brief Brief in Support of Pierluigi Piovanelli 380
 *Daniel Boyarin*

The Parables of Enoch in Second Temple Jewish Society 386
 *Lester L. Grabbe*

Spatiality in the Second Parable of Enoch 403
 *Pieter M. Venter*

## PART SIX: THE DATING

Enoch in Sheol: Updating the Dating of the Book of Parables 415
 *David W. Suter*

Enoch's Date in Limbo; or, Some Considerations on
David Suter's Analysis of the Book of Parables 444
 *Michael E. Stone*

Can We Discern the Composition Date of the Parables of Enoch? 450
 *James H. Charlesworth*

The Book of Noah, the Death of Herod the Great,
and the Date of the Parables of Enoch 469
 *Darrell D. Hannah*

A Symbolic Transfiguration of a Historical Event:
The Parthian Invasion in Josephus and the Parables of Enoch 478
 *Luca Arcari*

An Allusion in the Parables of Enoch to the Acts of
Matthias Antigonus in 40 B.C.E.? 487
   *Hanan Eshel*

An Overlooked Patristic Allusion to the Parables of Enoch? 492
   *Daniel C. Olson*

## CONCLUSION

The 2005 Camaldoli Seminar on the Parables of Enoch:
Summary and Prospects for Future Research 499
   *Paolo Sacchi*

The Parables of Enoch and the Messiah Son of Man:
A Bibliography, 1773-2006 513
   *Jason von Ehrenkrook*

# Abbreviations

| | |
|---|---|
| AB | Anchor Bible |
| *ABD* | *Anchor Bible Dictionary* |
| *ABR* | *Australian Biblical Review* |
| ABRL | Anchor Bible Reference Library |
| ACW | Ancient Christian Writers |
| *ADAJ* | *Annual of the Department of Antiquities of Jordan* |
| *AER* | *American Ecclesiastical Review* |
| AGJU | Arbeiten zur Geschichte des antiken Judentums und des Urchristentums |
| *ANRW* | *Aufstieg und Niedergang der römischen Welt* |
| *Ant* | Josephus, *Antiquities* |
| *AnthA* | *Anthologia annua* |
| *AO* | *Der Alte Orient* |
| ArBib | The Aramaic Bible |
| *ASTI* | *Annual of the Swedish Theological Institute* |
| *ATR* | *Australasian Theological Review* |
| *Aug* | *Augustinianum* |
| BEHESR | Bibliothèque de l'École des Hautes Études, Sciences religieuses |
| BETL | Bibliotheca ephemeridum theologicarum lovaniensium |
| BEvT | Beiträge zur evangelischen Theologie |
| *Bib* | *Biblica* |
| *BJRL* | *Bulletin of the John Rylands University Library of Manchester* |
| BK | Bibel und Kirche |
| BKAT | Biblischer Kommentar, Altes Testament (ed. Noth and Wolff) |

*Abbreviations*

| | |
|---|---|
| *BLit* | *Bibliothèque liturgique* |
| *BN* | *Biblische Notizen* |
| *BR* | *Biblical Research* |
| *BRev* | *Bible Review* |
| *BSac* | *Bibliotheca sacra* |
| BSOAS | Bulletin of the School of Oriental and African Studies |
| BTB | Biblical Theology Bulletin |
| BWANT | Beiträge zur Wissenschaft vom Alten und Neuen Testament |
| *BZ* | *Biblische Zeitschrift* |
| BZAW | Beihefte zur Zeitschrift für die alttestamentliche Wissenschaft |
| BZNW | Beihefte zur Zeitschrift für die neutestamentliche Wissenschaft |
| *CBQ* | *Catholic Biblical Quarterly* |
| CBQMS | Catholic Biblical Quarterly Monograph Series |
| CEJL | Commentaries on Early Jewish Literature |
| *ChrEg* | *Chronique d'Egypte* |
| CJT | Canadian Journal of Theology |
| ConBOT | Coniectanea biblica: Old Testament Series |
| *CP* | *Classical Philology* |
| CRINT | Compendia rerum iudaicarum ad Novum Testamentum |
| CSCO | Corpus scriptorum christianorum orientalium |
| CSHB | Corpus scriptorum historiae byzantinae |
| *CuadT* | *Cuadernos de Teologia* |
| *DBSup* | *Dictionnaire de la Bible: Supplément* |
| DJD | Discoveries in the Judaean Desert |
| *DRev* | *Downside Review* |
| DSD | Dead Sea Discoveries |
| EJM | Études sur le Judaïsme Médiéval |
| EMML | Ethiopian Manuscript Microfilm Library |
| *EstBib* | *Estudios bíblicos* |
| ETL | Ephemerides theologicae lovanienses |
| *EvQ* | *Evangelical Quarterly* |
| *EvT* | *Evangelische Theologie* |
| *ExpTim* | *Expository Times* |
| FB | Forschung zur Bibel |
| FRLANT | Forschungen zur Religion und Literatur des Alten und Neuen Testaments |
| GCS | Die griechische christliche Schriftsteller der ersten [drei] Jahrhunderte |
| *Greg* | *Gregorianum* |
| HBT | Horizons in Biblical Theology |

*Abbreviations*

| | |
|---|---|
| HDC | Harvard Dissertations in Classics |
| *Hen* | *Henoch* |
| *HeyJ* | *Heythrop Journal* |
| *HR* | *History of Religions* |
| HSS | Harvard Semitic Studies |
| HTR | *Harvard Theological Review* |
| HTS | Harvard Theological Studies |
| HUCM | Hebrew Union College Monographs |
| IBS | *Irish Biblical Studies* |
| ICC | International Critical Commentary |
| IDB | *The Interpreter's Dictionary of the Bible* |
| *IJT* | *Indian Journal of Theology* |
| *ITQ* | *Irish Theological Quarterly* |
| *JBL* | *Journal of Biblical Literature* |
| *JBTh* | *Jahrbuch für Biblische Theologie* |
| JETS | *Journal of the Evangelical Theological Society* |
| *JHI* | *Journal of the History of Ideas* |
| *JJS* | *Journal of Jewish Studies* |
| *JNES* | *Journal of Near Eastern Studies* |
| *JPT* | *Jahrbücher für protestantische Theologie* |
| JQR | *Jewish Quarterly Review* |
| JR | *Journal of Religion* |
| JSHRZ | *Jüdische Schriften aus hellenistisch-römischer Zeit* |
| JSJ | *Journal for the Study of Judaism in the Persian, Hellenistic, and Roman Periods* |
| JSJSup | Journal for the Study of Judaism Supplement Series |
| *JSNT* | *Journal for the Study of the New Testament* |
| JSNTSup | Journal for the Study of the New Testament–Supplement Series |
| JSOTSup | Journal for the Study of the Old Testament–Supplement Series |
| *JSP* | *Journal for the Study of the Pseudepigrapha* |
| JSPSup | Journal for the Study of the Pseudepigrapha Supplements |
| JSQ | *Jewish Studies Quarterly* |
| JTS | *Journal of Theological Studies* |
| LCL | Loeb Classical Library |
| LD | Lectio divina |
| *LumVie* | *Lumière et vie* |
| *MGWJ* | *Monatschrift für Geschichte und Wissenschaft des Judentums* |
| MT | Masoretic Text |
| *Mus* | *Muséon: Revue d'études orientales* |

| | |
|---|---|
| *Neot* | *Neotestamentica* |
| NHC | Nag Hammadi Codices |
| *NIB* | *The New Interpreter's Bible* |
| NJPS | *Tanakh: The Holy Scriptures: The New JPS Translation according to the Traditional Hebrew Text* |
| *NKZ* | *Neue kirchliche Zeitschrift* |
| *NovT* | *Novum Testamentum* |
| NTL | New Testament Library |
| NTOA | Novum Testamentum et Orbis Antiquus |
| *NTS* | *New Testament Studies* |
| *NTT* | *Norsk Teologisk Tidsskrift* |
| OLP | *Orientalia lovaniensia periodica* |
| Or | *Orientalia* |
| OS | *Orientalia Suecana* |
| PAPS | *Proceedings of the American Philosophical Society* |
| PM | *Protestantische Monatshefte* |
| PTSDSSP | Princeton Theological Seminary Dead Sea Scrolls Project |
| RB | *Revue biblique* |
| RdM | Die Religionen der Menschheit |
| *RelSRev* | *Religious Studies Review* |
| *RevAug* | *Revue augustinienne* |
| *RevExp* | *Review and Expositor* |
| *RevistB* | *Revista bíblica* |
| *RevQ* | *Revue de Qumran* |
| RGG | *Religion in Geschichte und Gegenwart* |
| RHPR | *Revue d'histoire et de philosophie religieuses* |
| RSB | *Ricerche storico bibliche* |
| RSR | *Recherches de science religieuse* |
| RTL | *Revue théologique de Louvain* |
| SANE | Sources from the Ancient Near East |
| SBLDS | Society of Biblical Literature Dissertation Series |
| SBLEJL | Society of Biblical Literature Early Judaism and Its Literature |
| SBLMS | Society of Biblical Literature Monograph Series |
| SBLSP | Society of Biblical Literature Seminar Papers |
| SBT | Studies in Biblical Theology |
| *ScEc* | *Sciences ecclésiastiques* |
| *ScEs* | *Science et esprit* |
| *Schol* | *Scholastik* |
| *Scr* | *Scripture* |
| *ScrB* | *Scripture Bulletin* |

*Abbreviations*

| | |
|---|---|
| ScrTh | *Scripta theologica* |
| SCS | Septuagint and Cognate Studies |
| SE | *Studia evangelica* |
| SEÅ | *Svensk exegetisk årsbok* |
| Sem | *Semitica* |
| SHR | Studies in the History of Religions (supplement to *Numen*) |
| SIJD | *Schriften des Institutum Delitzschianum* |
| SJ | Studia Judaica |
| SJLA | Studies in Judaism in Late Antiquity |
| SJOT | *Scandinavian Journal of the Old Testament* |
| SJSJ | Supplements to the Journal for the Study of Judaism |
| SJT | *Scottish Journal of Theology* |
| SNTSMS | Society for New Testament Studies Monograph Series |
| SPAW | *Sitzungsberichte der preussischen Akademie der wissenschaften* |
| SR | Studies in Religion |
| ST | *Studia theologica* |
| StClOr | *Studi Classici e Orientali* |
| STDJ | Studies on the Texts of the Desert of Judah |
| SUNT | Studien zur Umwelt des Neuen Testaments |
| SVTP | Studia in Veteris Testamenti pseudepigraphica |
| TBei | *Theologische Beiträge* |
| TDNT | Theological Dictionary of the New Testament |
| ThPQ | *Theologisch-praktische Quartalschrift* |
| ThT | *Theologisch tijdschrift* |
| TRE | *Theologische Realenzyklopädie* |
| TRev | *Theologische Revue* |
| TRu | *Theologische Rundschau* |
| TSAJ | Texte und Studien zum antiken Judentum |
| TSK | *Theologische Studien und Kritiken* |
| TU | Texte und Untersuchungen |
| TWNT | *Theologische Wörterbuch zum Neuen Testament* |
| TZ | *Theologische Zeitschrift* |
| USQR | Union Seminary Quarterly Review |
| VC | *Vigiliae christianae* |
| VD | *Verbum domini* |
| VT | *Vetus Testamentum* |
| VTSup | Supplements to Vetus Testamentum |
| WHJP | World History of the Jewish People |
| WMANT | Wissenschaftliche Monographien zum Alten und Neuen Testament |

*Abbreviations*

| | |
|---|---|
| WUNT | Wissenschaftliche Untersuchungen zum Neuen Testament |
| *ZAW* | *Zeitschrift für die alttestamentliche Wissenschaft* |
| *ZDMG* | *Zeitschrift der deutschen morgenländischen Gesellschaft* |
| *ZDPV* | *Zeitschrift des deutschen Palästina-Vereins* |
| *ZNW* | *Zeitschrift für die neutestamentliche Wissenschaft und die Kunde der älteren Kirche* |
| *ZTK* | *Zeitschrift für Theologie und Kirche* |
| *ZWT* | *Zeitschrift für wissenschaftliche Theologie* |

# INTRODUCTION

# The Enoch Seminar at Camaldoli: Re-entering the Parables of Enoch in the Study of Second Temple Judaism and Christian Origins

*Gabriele Boccaccini*

On June 7-9, 2005, forty-four specialists in Second Temple Judaism and Christian origins met for three days in complete seclusion at the ancient monastery of Camaldoli, in the middle of a forest in the mountains between Florence and Arezzo, Italy. They came from many countries, from Belgium, Canada, England, Ethiopia, Russia, France, Germany, Hungary, Israel, Italy, the Netherlands, Norway, South Africa, and the United States of America. At their arrival they were welcomed by the prior general of the Camaldoli Order, Dom Emanuele Bargellini, and by the chief rabbi of the Florence Jewish community, Rav Joseph Levi.

All papers and responses for the conference had circulated in advance so that the entire time could be devoted to discussion in general assembly and in small groups. Every day, not without some tremor and reverence, the participants walked through the medieval cloisters of the monastery and had their sessions in the very same places that more than five centuries before, in 1468, had hosted the meetings of the Florentine Platonic Academy, led by the philosopher Marsilio Ficino.

The enchanted beauty of the monastery, the warm hospitality of the monks, the silence and peace of the surroundings fostered eight hours a day of substantive scholarly engagement and inspired an atmosphere of friendship and understanding among the participants.

The meeting was the Third Enoch Seminar, the topic "Enoch and the Messiah Son of Man."

Gabriele Boccaccini

## The 1468 Meeting of the Florentine Platonic Academy

The Camaldoli meeting in the summer of 1468 was one of the out-of-town seminars organized by the Florentine Academy. The members of the academy enjoyed meeting outdoors in the Tuscan countryside, in sacred places near sanctuaries and monasteries.

Organized and named after Plato's Academy, the Florentine Academy was a loose and informal circle of scholars and educated persons that from 1462 to 1494 gathered in Florence, at the villa of Careggi, around the philosopher Marsilio Ficino.[1]

Florence had been the center of the renaissance of Platonic studies in the West since 1438-39, when at the Council of Florence, convened by Pope Eugene IV in accord with Emperor John VIII of Byzantium, with the aim of unifying Western and Eastern Christians, the emperor came to Florence with a delegation of seven hundred sages.

Among the Greek philosophers was the old and venerable Giorgio Gemisto (known as Plètone). With his charisma, enthusiasm, and firsthand knowledge of the works of Plato and of his school (works still largely unknown to the West), the eighty-three-year-old philosopher was an overnight sensation, far beyond the walls of Florence. His teaching inspired the ruler of Florence, Cosimo de' Medici, to open a Platonic Academy in Florence.[2] The project did not gain momentum, however, until after the fall of Constantinople in 1453. Along with Venice, Florence was the city that most benefited by the influx of refugees, which guaranteed the arrival at the Medici court of Greek teachers and philosophers such as Giovanni Argiropulo and Demetrio Calcondila, as well as by the availability of hundreds of ancient Greek manuscripts, of which the Medici became voracious collectors.[3] Cosimo had now the opportunity to shape a new generation of scholars. He found in Ficino, a native of Figline Valdarno (a small town between Florence and Arezzo), a promising young scholar on whose education to invest generously. No choice could have been more felicitous: Ficino reveals himself a creative philosopher and a strong and brilliant leader. In 1462 Cosimo donated to him a villa at Careggi (in the countryside just outside the walls of Florence, not far away from

---

1. A. della Torre, *Storia dell'Accademia Platonica di Firenze* (Florence: Carnesecchi, 1902; Turin: Bottega d'Erasmo, 1960).

2. See A. Field, *The Origins of the Platonic Academy of Florence* (Princeton: Princeton University Press, 1988).

3. The Biblioteca Medicea Laurentiana in Florence rivaled the Biblioteca Marciana in Venice in purchasing and collecting Greek manuscripts. Michelangelo Buonarroti in Florence and Jacopo Sansovino in Venice made their respective libraries an artistic jewel and a symbol of the cultural pride of their cities.

the Medici villa), where the reborn Platonic Academy met and prospered for more than thirty years under the Medici's skillful patronage.

The activities of the Florentine Academy consisted in regular lectures on Platonic philosophy as well as in informal discussions and seminars. Outstanding members or associates of the academy were the Medici patrons themselves (Cosimo, and then Piero, Giuliano, and foremost, Lorenzo de' Medici, the Magnificent) and philosophers and artists such as Leon Battista Alberti, Agnolo Poliziano, Giovanni Pico della Mirandola, Benedetto Colucci, Cristoforo Landino, Donato Acciaiuoli, Alamanno Rinuccini, and others. Through its activities, the Florentine Academy sought to promote friendship, dialogue, and intellectual exchange among its members and, on the philosophical level, to show the single source and unity of the two fundamental elements in the life of Western civilization — Judaic-Christian religion, on one hand, and Greek philosophy, on the other, that is, the religious and secular components of humanistic culture.[4] The ideals of the Florentine Academy found their highest and most advanced expression in the person and work of its youngest addition, Pico della Mirandola, admirer of Plato and personal friend of Jewish and Muslim philosophers, who in the study of Latin, Greek, Hebrew, and Arabic texts found inspiration for a religious and philosophical synthesis.

The entire cultural world of Florence was profoundly affected by the Platonic renaissance. Benozzo Gozzoli celebrated the coming of the Greek philosophers to the Council of Florence as the arrival of the Magi from the East in a magnificent fresco at the Medici residence (Palazzo Medici-Riccardi); Sandro Botticelli illustrated the philosophical principles of the school in his celebrated painting *The Spring;* and Lorenzo Ghirlandaio immortalized the members of the Florentine Academy in a fresco in the church of Santa Maria Novella. Alberti paid homage to Plètone's *Hymn to the Sun* in the facade of the same church and exalted the Neoplatonic ideals of spiritual unity of humankind in the Tempio Malatestiano at Rimini (where the remains of Giorgio Gemisto would be translated as a holy relic from his native Greece).

The party that reached Camaldoli in the hot summer of 1468 included the cream of the Florentine Academy of the time: Marsilio Ficino, Leon Battista Alberti, Lorenzo and Giuliano de' Medici, Piero and Donato Acciaiuoli, Pietro and Cristoforo Landino, Alamanno Rinuccini, Marco Parenti, and Antonio Canigiani — scholars and philosophers of great doctrine ("viros litteratissimos et qui, cum a primis annis vim copiamque dicendi exactissima arte et longa exercitatione consecuti essent, vehementi deinceps ac diuturno studio maxi-

---

4. See M. Ficino, *Platonic Theology,* ed. M. J. B. Allen and J. Hankins (Cambridge: Harvard University Press, 2004).

mos in philosophia progressus fecerant"). We are provided detailed information about the meeting by the "proceedings" published in 1472 by Cristoforo Landino under the title *Disputationes Camaldulenses*.[5]

Camaldoli was chosen for its mild summer climate and its quietness, and for the beauties and holiness of its surroundings ("aestus vitandi tum animi relaxandi causa placuit in Camaldulam sylvam ascendere, regionem universae Italiae antiqua religione notissima"), but also for the cultural engagement of its monastic community.[6] At their arrival the participants were greeted by the prior general of the Camaldoli Order, Dom Mariotto Allegri, who was also an associate of the academy and a participant in the colloquium. Landino describes him as a man distinguished for religion and culture whose company and friendship Ficino and Alberti treasured ("una cum Mariotto Camaldulensi antistite, viro et religione et doctrina probato").

Under the leadership of Allegri's predecessor and teacher, the renowned Grecist and Latinist Dom Ambrogio Traversari,[7] the Camaldoli Order had already made a name for itself in the fifteenth century for religious tolerance and cultural openness. One of the protagonists of the Council of Florence and a champion of reconciliation between the Roman Catholic and the Greek Orthodox, Traversari had also initiated a dialogue with the more secular components of Florentine culture, emphasizing the compatibility (rather than the antagonism) between Christianity and modernity. The Camaldoli monastery in Florence, Santa Maria degli Angeli (now the headquarters of the College of Litera-

---

5. The Latin work in four books, modeled after Cicero's *Tusculanae disputationes*, was completed by Cristoforo Landino in 1472 and is preserved in four codices written between 1472 and 1474: (a) Vaticanus Urbinas lat. 508; (b) Mediceus Laurentianus lat. plut. 53, 28; (c) Florentinus lat. Bibl. Nat. Conv. soppr. J IX 23; and (d) Parisinus lat. Bibl. Nat. 3343$^A$. The *editio princeps* was published shortly afterward. As it was personally edited by the author, it counts as an independent source: C. Landino, *Disputationes Camaldulenses* (Florence: Nicolaus Laurentii Alamannus, 1480; 2nd ed. 1482). The work was then reprinted in several editions during the sixteenth and early seventeenth century: in Venice (1503, 1507), Strasburg (1508), Paris (1511), Basilea (1577, 1596), and Geneva (1605). See the critical edition of the Latin text edited by Peter Lohe: C. Landino, *Disputationes Camaldulenses*, ed. P. Lohre (Florence: Sansoni, 1980). Only partial portions of the work are translated into modern languages: books I and II in German by Eugen Wolf (*Camaldolensische Gespräche* [Jena: Diederichs, 1927]); book I in Italian by Eugenio Garin (*Prosatori latini del Quattrocento* [Milan and Naples: Ricciardi, 1952]); and books III and IV in English by Thomas H. Stahel in his unpublished dissertation ("Cristoforo Landino's Allegorization of the Aeneid" [Johns Hopkins University, 1968]).

6. See M. E. Magheri-Cataluccio and A. U. Fossa, *Biblioteca e cultura a Camaldoli, dal Medioevo all'Umanesimo* (Rome: Anselmiana, 1979).

7. On the figure of Ambrogio Traversari, see C. L. Stinger, *Humanism and the Church Fathers: Ambrogio Traversari (1386-1439) and Christian Antiquity in the Italian Renaissance* (Albany: State University of New York Press, 1977).

ture and Arts of the University of Florence), had become one of the centers of humanistic research in town,[8] and the monastery in the mountains served as a summer location for numerous meetings that attracted the most distinguished scholars of the time. During his term, Dom Mariotto Allegri followed in the footsteps of his predecessor with creativity, sensitivity, and great courage.[9]

Accompanied by Dom Mariotto, whose pleasant and rich eloquence was "like a vehicle along the way" ("in via pro vehiculo"), the participants walked, under the clear and most salubrious sky of Camaldoli ("verno et apprime salubri . . . horum montium contemperatissimo caelo"), from the monastery up to the hermitage ("primum ad coenobitas, inde etiam ad heremitas"), visiting the two centers of monastic life, which Romualdus, the disciple of Benedict of Norcia and founder of the Camaldoli Order, had united, side by side, in his attempt at a synthesis between the hermitic experience of the East and the cenobitic experience of the West.[10]

The Camaldoli meeting of the Florentine Academy was made of four workshops, each of them devoted to a particular topic: (1) "De vita activa et contemplativa" (the relation between active and contemplative lives); (2) "De summo bono" (the ultimate Good); and (3-4) "In P. Virgilii Maronis allegorias" (an allegorical reading of Virgil's *Aeneid,* books I-IV and IV-VI). The expressed goal of the meeting was to achieve harmony among Christian, Platonic, and humanistic thought. In his written report Landino stressed the value of dialogue and mutual understanding and singled out old Leon Battista Alberti and young Lorenzo de' Medici as the model of the encounter between the ideal teacher and the ideal student who both, although in different ways, were learned in all forms of wisdom and reached a synthesis of philosophical and political life.

## The 2005 Meeting of the Enoch Seminar

The Camaldoli meeting in the summer of 2005 was one of a series of international seminars organized in Italy by the Enoch Seminar since its constitution in 2000. The first meeting was held in June 2001 at the renaissance Villa Corsi-

---

8. See G. Farulli, *Istoria cronologica del nobile ed antico monastero degli Angioli di Firenze, del Sacro ordine camaldolese* (Lucca: Frediani, 1710).

9. See A. Giabbani, *Camaldolesi: Le figure più espressive dell'Ordine* (Camaldoli: Monastero di Camaldoli, 1944); A. Giabbani, *Menologio Camaldolese* (Tivoli: De Rossi, 1950).

10. See Saint Peter Damian, *Vita beati Romualdi,* ed. G. Tabacco (Rome: Istituto Storico Italiano per il Medio Evo, 1957); P. Ciampelli, *Vita di S. Romualdo abate, fondatore dei Camaldolesi* (Ravenna: Arti Grafiche, 1927); Centro di Studi Avellaniti, ed., *San Romualdo: storia, agiografia e spiritualità* (S. Pietro in Cariano: Il Segno, 2002).

Gabriele Boccaccini

Saviati in Sesto Fiorentino, near Careggi, Florence, and was devoted to the origins of Enochic Judaism. The members of the Enoch Seminar then moved to Venice in July 2003 for their second meeting, on "Enoch and Qumran Origins," and a conference on Jewish and Christian messianism ("Il Messia tra memoria e attesa") organized immediately afterward in collaboration with BIBLIA, the Italian Biblical Association. The third meeting of the Enoch Seminar was at the monastery of Camaldoli and was entirely devoted to the Book of Parables ("Enoch and the Messiah Son of Man").

Born by the spontaneous initiative of a group of American, European, and Israeli specialists, the Enoch Seminar is a loose and informal circle of scholars in Second Temple Judaism and Christian origins that since 2001 has gathered biennially in Italy at the invitation of the Department of Near Eastern Studies of the University of Michigan and with the support of the Frankel Center for Judaic Studies and the Michigan Center for Early Christian Studies. Through its activities the Enoch Seminar seeks to promote friendship, dialogue, and intellectual exchange among its members and, on the scholarly level, to show the common roots of Judaism and Christianity in the diverse world of the Second Temple period, and to generate understanding between different religious perspectives and dialogue with secular culture.

The renaissance of Enochic studies is undoubtedly one of the major achievements of contemporary research. In the last decades, slowly but surely, the emphasis has shifted from the study of the Enoch texts to the study of the intellectual and sociological characteristics of the movement and group(s) behind such literature. Gradually, the study of Enoch texts has overcome the canonical boundaries that restricted the research to the specialists of the Old Testament Pseudepigrapha. The presence of Enoch texts among the Dead Sea Scrolls, the literary and ideological connections with Old and New Testament documents, and the uncountable ramifications of Enochic ideas and concepts in the many Judaisms of the Second Temple period (including early Christianity) have made the study of Enoch literature a central issue for any specialist in ancient Judaism and Christian origins.

Scholars from different fields — Dead Sea Scrolls, apocalypticism, Christian origins, Old Testament Pseudepigrapha — but also from different geographical and cultural backgrounds have contributed to the success of the Enoch Seminar. The focus is on the Enoch texts, but the goal is no less ambitious than a better and more comprehensive understanding of the development of Jewish thought in the Second Temple period. Enoch is in fact an intercanonical, interdisciplinary character par excellence, and as such requires an intercanonical, interdisciplinary approach by specialists of both Judaic and Christian studies. Enoch scholars have been "forced" to go out of their "canons" of specializations and out of the boundaries of their methodologies and listen attentively to other specializations and other approaches. It is this "spirit" of sharing and dialogue that has made the meetings of the Enoch Seminar so popular and intriguing far beyond the boundaries of Enochic studies.

Not only has the Enoch Seminar offered an opportunity for meeting and discussion, it has also prompted in these last years a renewed interest in Enoch that has materialized in the writing of numerous books, articles, reviews, and dissertations. The Enoch Seminar itself has already promoted the publication of five collections of essays: *The Origins of Enochic Judaism* (Turin: Zamorani, 2002) (= *Hen* 24, no. 1-2 [2002]); *Enoch and Qumran Origins* (Grand Rapids: Eerdmans, 2005); *Il Messia tra memoria e attesa* (Brescia: Morcelliana, 2005); *The Early Enoch Literature* (Leiden: Brill, forthcoming); and now this volume, *Enoch and the Messiah Son of Man*. Lately, under the leadership of members of the Enoch Seminar, the journal *Henoch* has begun a new series focusing on the interaction of Judaism and Christianity, from Second Temple to late antiquity.

Having provided a unique experience of collaborative research and accomplished so many results, the Enoch Seminar has raised the expectation of even more to come. As long as interest and enthusiasm support the initiative, the biennial meetings and publications will continue indefinitely. The next meeting will be held at Camaldoli again in July 2007 on the topic "Enoch and the Mosaic Torah: The Evidence of Jubilees." As the meetings of the Enoch Seminar are limited to senior specialists and university professors, the first session of an "Enoch Graduate Seminar" was held at the University of Michigan in May 2006 with the participation of twenty-six Ph.D. students and postdoctoral researchers from the United States, Europe, and Israel, with James VanderKam and Gabriele Boccaccini serving as chairpersons. The Enoch Graduate Seminar will convene again in 2008 at Princeton and in 2010 at Notre Dame. What was born as the informal meeting of Enoch specialists has accomplished much more than expected — it has become the vibrant engine of studies and research for the entire field of Second Temple Judaism and Christian origins.

The party that reached Camaldoli in the summer of 2005 included, with the director Gabriele Boccaccini, many veterans from the previous sessions (Andreas Bedenbender, James Charlesworth, Sabino Chialà, John and Adela Collins, Hanan and Esther Eshel, Ida Froehlich, Lester Grabbe, Matthias Henze, Michael Knibb, Klaus Koch, Helge Kvanvig, Luca Mazzinghi, George Nickelsburg, Pierluigi Piovanelli, Paolo Sacchi, Loren Stuckenbruck, David Suter, Eibert Tigchelaar, James VanderKam, Ralph Williams, and Benjamin Wright), as well as several distinguished newcomers (William Adler, Luca Arcari, Daniel Assefa, Kelley Bautch, Jonathan Ben-Dov, Daniel and Chava Boyarin, Charles Gieschen, Darrell Hannah, Giovanni Ibba, Robert Kraft, Phillip Munoa, Hindy

Najman, Eric Noffke, Gerbern Oegema, Daniel Olson, Andrei Orlov, Michael Stone, Pieter Venten, and Leslie Walck). Six Ph.D. students from the University of Michigan (J. Harold Ellens, James Waddell, Ronald Ruark, Jason von Ehrenkrook, Aaron Brunell, and Justin Winger) served as secretaries.

Camaldoli had been chosen for its mild summer climate and its peacefulness, and for the beauty and holiness of its surroundings, but also for the cultural engagement of its monastic community.[11] After a guided tour of the city of Arezzo and the frescoes by Piero della Francesca at the Church of San Francesco, led with charm and enthusiasm by an expert and lover of Italian culture such as Prof. Ralph Williams of the University of Michigan, the participants arrived by bus at the monastery of Camaldoli where they were greeted by the doyen of Enochic studies in Italy, Paolo Sacchi (a native of Figline Valdarno), by the Italian-Israeli chief rabbi of Florence, Rav Joseph Levi, and by the prior general of the Camaldoli Order, Dom Emanuele Bargellini.

Under the leadership of Bargellini's predecessor and teacher, the renowned patristic scholar and theologian Dom Benedetto Calati,[12] the Camaldoli Order has made a name for itself in the twentieth century for religious tolerance and cultural openness.[13] One of the protagonists of the Vatican Council and a champion of ecumenical reconciliation, Calati had also initiated a dialogue with the more secular components of Italian culture, emphasizing the compatibility (rather than the antagonism) between religious traditions and modernity. The Camaldoli monastery with its large and renewed Foresteria has become one of the centers in Italy of ecumenical and interfaith meetings as well as of conferences in biblical and philosophical studies, especially in the field of Jewish-Christian relations.[14] During his term, Bargellini has followed in the footsteps of his predecessor with creativity, sensitivity, and great courage.[15]

---

11. L. Vigilucci, *Camaldoli: A Journey into Its History and Spirituality* (Trabuco Canyon, Calif.: Source Books, 1995); A. Pagnani, *Storia dei benedettini camaldolesi: cenobiti, eremiti, monache ed oblate* (Sassoferrato: Garofoli, 1949).

12. On Dom Benedetto Calati, see R. Luise, *La visione di un monaco: Il futuro della fede e della Chiesa nel colloquio con Benedetto Calati* (Assisi: Cittadella, 2000). For a bibliography of his writings, see B. Calati et al., *Sapienza monastica: Saggi di storia, spiritualità e problemi monastici* (Rome: Pontificio Ateneo S. Anselmo, 1994), 575-84.

13. See I. Gargano, *Camaldolesi nella spiritualità italiana del Novecento* (Bologna: EDB, 2000).

14. Among the many meetings held at Camaldoli is, since 1981, the annual conference of the federation of the Jewish-Christian associations in Italy — the so-called Colloqui ebraico-cristiani di Camaldoli, under the leadership of the Camaldoli theologian and scholar Dom Innocenzo Gargano.

15. See E. Bargellini, *Camaldoli ieri e oggi: L'identità camaldolese nel nuovo millennio* (Camaldoli: Monastero di Camaldoli, 2000).

Accompanied by Dom Emanuele and his passionate eloquence, the participants made the one-hour walk, under the clear and most salubrious sky of Camaldoli, from the monastery to the hermitage, visiting those that are, today as since its beginning, the two poles of the Camaldoli experience, based on the harmony and complementarity between the cenobitic and the hermitic life.

The Steering Committee of the Third Enoch Seminar (Gabriele Boccaccini, John Collins, Florentino García Martínez, Michael Knibb, George Nickelsburg, and James VanderKam) had worked hard for two years to prepare the conference in all its details, in consultation with the other senior members of the Enoch Seminar. The Camaldoli meeting was made of five workshops, each devoted to a particular aspect of the Parables of Enoch: (1) structure and composition, (2) the place of the Parables within the Enochic tradition, (3) the Son of Man, (4) the place of the Parables within Second Temple Jewish literature, and (5) dating and social setting. There were several new features to characterize our third meeting. First of all, all the material had circulated in advance among the participants so that paper presentations could be replaced by very short introductions and the entire time be devoted to discussion. The first part of each workshop was limited to an "inner circle" of from twenty-five to thirty specialists in the presence of all participants. Then the discussion broke into three small groups involving all attendees, and ended with a general assembly. The format allowed all members of the Enoch Seminar to share their views, and gave them plenty of time for deepening new perspectives and acquiring a better mutual understanding, even in the face of some major disagreements. The discussion continued far beyond the scheduled times — during the meals, the afternoon walks in the forest, and the after-dinner informal gatherings in the monastery lounge.

This volume of proceedings was not planned as a celebration. The thirty-seven specialists, who have contributed with either long or short essays, were asked to exercise constructive criticism, highlight the most controversial issues, and stress disagreement more than celebrate consensus so that the discussion could target the substance of the problems. The material is presented according to the order of discussion at the conference, except that the number of received essays has required splitting the last session into two separate parts ("Social Setting" *and* "Dating").

## Reintroducing the Parables of Enoch

The Third Enoch Seminar at Camaldoli presented some unique challenges indeed. At the center of the debate was the most controversial of all Enoch booklets, the Parables of Enoch. As Klaus Koch defines it in his essay, this is "a curious document of Jewish religion: there are no references to Israel, Moses, Abraham, or Torah!"[16] The book, on the contrary, focuses on a heavenly figure called "the Son of Man" — a title and a figure that offer some striking parallels with the development of early Christology.

The difficulty is proved by the complex history of research of the document, which since its "rediscovery" by the Scottish explorer James Bruce in 1773 (see Bruce 1790) has been at the center of a never-ending controversy.[17]

As soon as the book of Enoch was made available in modern translations (Laurence 1821 [English]; Hoffmann 1833; 1838 [German]; Dillmann 1853 [German]; Brunet 1856 [French]) as well as in its Ethiopic text (Laurence 1838; Dillmann 1851), the messianic theology of the Parables dramatically changed the terms of the then incipient scholarly debate on the meaning of the Son of Man sayings in the New Testament, which was still anchored to patristic categories (Less 1776; Scholten 1809). Since the second century C.E. with Ignatius of Antioch (To the Ephesians 20:2), there has in fact been a well-established tradition in the Christian church to interpret "son of man" as a reference to the humanity, humility, and lowliness of the divine Messiah, "Son of God" — a tradition that the flourishing of Semitic studies after the Reformation had accepted and strengthened.[18]

Now facing the idea of a seemingly heavenly, superhuman Messiah Son of Man in ancient Judaism, a passionate controversy divided philologists and theologians. For the editors and translators of 1 Enoch, the text (including the Parables) was clearly a pre-Christian Jewish text; New Testament scholars and theologians instead looked at it with suspicion and diffidence. The problem was made even more complex by the fact that, contrary to other sections of 1 Enoch, the Book of Parables did not seem to contain any explicit historical allusions, nor could it claim a clear record of quotations in ancient Jewish or Christian literature. It was relatively easy to dismiss the opinion of those early interpreters who had questioned the antiquity and Jewishness of the entire book of Enoch

---

16. See below, K. Koch, "Questions regarding the So-Called Son of Man in the Parables of Enoch: A Response to Sabino Chialà and Helge Kvanvig."

17. For the bibliographical references in this section of the introduction to studies on the Parables of Enoch, see below, J. von Ehrenkrook, "The Parables of Enoch and the Messiah Son of Man: A Bibliography, 1773-2006."

18. For a comprehensive overview of the history of research on the "Son of Man," see D. Burkett, *The Son of Man Debate: A History and Evaluation* (Cambridge: Cambridge University Press, 1999). For a survey of the history of research on the Parables of Enoch (with special emphasis on the problem of its date), see S. Chialà, *Libro delle Parabole di Enoch* (Brescia: Paideia, 1997).

(Hofmann 1852; Philippi 1868). But concerning the Parables, the debate would never reach a consensus.

Theological and apologetical concerns certainly played a major role. On one hand, the book highlights the diversity of ancient Judaism and challenges the centrality of the Mosaic Torah as the foundational and permanent element of Jewish identity. On the other hand, the idea that Jesus or his disciples could have "learned" from a noncanonical, pseudepigraphical Jewish text seemed to diminish the uniqueness and originality of the Christian message. There were exceptions, notably Heinrich Ewald and Wilhelm Baldensperger, who quite enthusiastically took the Parables as the main source for their understanding of Jesus' messianic preaching (Ewald 1857; Baldensperger 1888). But many maintained a later Christian date for the composition of the Parables (Hilgenfeld 1857), or at least for its Son of Man passages (Drummond 1877). Most New Testament scholars just ignored the document, claiming that the evidence for its pre-Christian origin was too dubious to be used.

At the turn of the century, new editions of the Ethiopic text (the real first critical editions by Flemming 1901 and Charles 1906) as well as new translations (Charles 1893; 1912; 1913 [English]; Beer 1900 [German]; Flemming 1901 [German]; Martin 1906 [French]; Riessler 1928 [German]) marked the affirmation of 1 Enoch in the field of Judaic studies. The pre-Christian date of the entire document (including the Parables) seemed to be solidly established and accepted (Gry 1909; Frey 1928), as well as the notion of the "Son of Man" as a preexistent heavenly Messiah. The idea penetrated even more conservative Christian settings, since it was suggested that Jesus using the term of himself could be taken as evidence of a clear consciousness of his own divinity or preexistence in heaven (Roslaniec 1920). Yet, ironically, the more the Book of Parables was understood as evidence of pre-Christian Judaism, the more the skepticism about the value of the text for Christian studies grew as a consequence of the rising anti-Semitism and the predominant theological tendency to dismiss the Jewish features of the preaching of the historical Jesus and of the early church as the remains of a continuity to be demythologized, in order rather to stress the elements of discontinuity. There continued to be some remarkable exceptions, notably Wilhelm Bousset and Martin Werner, who more than anybody else emphasized that the preaching and self-understanding of Jesus as well as the faith of the first Christian communities grew and developed around the concept of the Son of Man as an angel-like Messiah and explored the revolutionary implications of such a view for a reconstruction of the developments of early Christology (Bousset 1913; Werner 1941).

A new situation arose after the Second World War with the discovery of the Dead Sea Scrolls. Just when, after the shock and tragedy of the Holocaust, the conditions had become more favorable for a reappraisal of the importance of Jewish traditions for Christian origins, and the analysis of Sjöberg on the reference to the Parthians in chap. 56 seemed finally to link firmly the text to an actual historical event in the first century B.C.E. (Sjöberg 1946), the study of the Book of Parables suffered a major setback. The presence at Qumran of Aramaic fragments from all Enoch booklets *except* the Parables prompted the editor, Josef Milik, to claim in 1951 that this fact provided conclusive evidence in support of the skeptics, who had never ceased to suspect that the Book of Parables did not exist at all in pre-Christian times and had to be a later composition inspired by the Gospels (Milik 1951; 1959).

Twenty-five years passed from that dramatic announcement to the actual publication of the Aramaic Enoch fragments. Although some tried immediately to dismiss the absence of the Parables from Qumran as purely accidental and consequently devoid of significance, they were little more than voices crying in the wilderness (Thompson 1961a; 1961b). Due to the lack of conclusive data, waiting for the actual publication of the fragments was necessary — it was simply a matter of good sense. Unless one's argument could not be contradicted by Milik's assertion, nobody wished to plow the sands (Hindley 1968; Theisohn 1975).[19] For all those years, the Parables were in limbo.[20]

Even after it became apparent that the publication of the Aramaic fragments by Milik had not fulfilled his promises to provide a conclusive answer (Milik 1976), it took many years for the research in the Book of Parables to recover and regain momentum. Nobody accepted the third-century date proposed by Milik, but the absence of the book from Qumran continued to puzzle the specialists and push them toward a post-70 date (Knibb 1979; Jas 1979), although more and more scholars dared to challenge this trend (Greenfield and Stone 1977; Suter 1979; Mearns 1979; Bampfylde 1984; Black 1985). The notion of an apocalyptic Son of Man was dismissed and then reentered, back and forth in the scholarly discussion so many times that, with a few conspicuous exceptions (Charlesworth 1985; 1988; Caragounis 1986), scholars in Christian origins seemed to have lost any confidence in the possibility of using the document as a reliable source for any historical reconstruction of the earliest developments of the Jesus movement (see Burkett 1999). However, the publication of a new edition of the Ethiopic text (Knibb 1978) and numerous translations in the 1980s (Sacchi and Fusella 1981 [Italian]; Corriente and Piñero 1982 [Spanish]; Isaac 1983 [English]; Knibb 1984 [English]; Uhlig 1984 [German]; Black 1985 [En-

---

19. J. C. Hindley reviewed Sjöberg's hypothesis, arguing for early second century C.E.; in his view the Parthian-Roman war of the years 113-117 provided a more likely setting to 1 En 56.

20. See below, D. W. Suter, "Enoch in Sheol: Updating the Dating of the Book of Parables."

glish]; Caquot 1987 [French]) laid the foundation for a reevaluation of the importance of the document within Second Temple Jewish literature. Credit goes to the leadership of scholars such as George Nickelsburg in the United States and Paolo Sacchi (and his school) in Europe, who even in the darkest times kept the flame alive and did not waver but insisted on the centrality of the Parables for Second Temple Jewish and early Christian studies (Nickelsburg 1978; 1981; 1992; Sacchi 1981; 1990; cf. Boccaccini 1991).

The contemporary renaissance of Enochic studies has now vindicated their position. This new phase of research is characterized by a fresh look at the Parables within the complexity of Jewish thought and the development of Enochic Judaism (Boccaccini 1998; Nickelsburg 2001; Jackson 2004). Contemporary scholars have underlined the diversity of competing expectations and speculations about mediatorial figures and messiahs in Second Temple Judaism (Neusner 1987; Charlesworth 1992; Boccaccini 2005). By the mid-1990s scholars appeared once again comfortable in locating the Parables in pre-70 Judaism (Collins 1992; Slater 1995). The emphasis has shifted from the absence of the Parables from the Dead Sea Scrolls to the question of why the Qumran sectarians — representatives of just one of the many Judaisms of the time — might not have agreed with the theology of this Enochic booklet and thus rejected it (Boccaccini 1997; 1998; Chialà 1997; Nickelsburg 2001; Sacchi 2003). The relationship between the Enochic literature and the Dead Sea Scrolls and between the Enoch group and the Qumran community is indeed fascinating; contemporary research has just begun to explore the subject.[21]

The announced forthcoming publication of the second volume of Nickelsburg's commentary on 1 Enoch promises now to be the climax of the contemporary rediscovery of the Book of Parables and the cornerstone for future research. Nickelsburg has already made clear in the introduction to his recent English translation of 1 Enoch (coauthored with James VanderKam) what his position will be: "the Parables can be dated sometime around the turn of the era. . . . At the very least, the description of the Chosen One/son of man . . . is presumed in the gospel tradition about Jesus, the Son of Man" (Nickelsburg and VanderKam 2004, 6; cf. Olson 2004).

After the Camaldoli meeting, it can now be confidently said that the position of Nickelsburg and Sacchi is confirmed and supported by the overwhelming majority of specialists in the Enoch literature and Second Temple Judaism.

---

21. See G. W. E. Nickelsburg, "1 Enoch and Qumran Origins: The State of the Question and Some Prospects for Answers," in SBLSP (1986), 341-60; G. Boccaccini, ed., *Enoch and Qumran Origins: New Light on a Forgotten Connection* (Grand Rapids: Eerdmans, 2005); G. Boccaccini, ed., *The Early Enoch Literature* (Leiden: Brill, forthcoming).

*Gabriele Boccaccini*

Most participants passionately argued for a composition of the Parables at the turn of the era; no one suggested a date before the Roman period or after the first century C.E. Even those scholars who at Camaldoli left open the possibility that the actual composition of the book may have occurred shortly before or after 70 C.E. agreed that the traditions contained in the Parables make this text a fundamental document for understanding Second Temple Judaism and that the messianism of the Parables played an important role in the development of early Christology. It is therefore more than appropriate homage to their outstanding contribution to the research on the Parables of Enoch that this volume opens with an essay by Nickelsburg on the structure of the text and ends with Sacchi's summary and conclusions.

There are, of course, still many open questions in the interpretation of the Parables and no consensus on its place within the Enochic movement and in general within Second Temple Jewish thought. This volume, with the variety of its thirty-seven contributions, is an honest representation of our disagreements and uncertainties, not less than of our agreements and certainties. I will leave to the reader and to the skill and experience of Paolo Sacchi in his summary and conclusions the task of assessing how deeply our knowledge in the field has advanced as a result of our discussions. I can testify only of the exciting atmosphere of joy and achievement at the end of a conference, when our ways parted again in the sunny morning of June 10, 2005, at the railway station of Arezzo — the smiles, the hugs, the greetings, that common feeling shared by all participants that our meeting at Camaldoli had marked yet another fundamental turn in our research. The First Enoch Seminar in 2001 at the Sesto Fiorentino Villa will be remembered for affirming the category of "Enochic Judaism" in the international scholarly debate. The Second Enoch Seminar in 2003 in Venice demonstrated the centrality of Enoch literature for Qumran origins. After the Third Enoch Seminar in 2005 at Camaldoli, no scholar in Second Temple Judaism and Christian origins can any longer ignore the Book of Parables and its messianic theology. From their unfortunate exile, the Parables are back — with revenge.

# Greeting to the Participants at the Third Enoch Seminar at Camaldoli

*Dom Emanuele Bargellini, Prior General of Camaldoli*

Welcome to the monastery and to the monastic community of Camaldoli! A special welcome to our friend, Professor Gabriele Boccaccini. After having frequented this monastic community and this conference room for many years as a young apprentice of life and of the Christian-Jewish dialogue initiated here twenty-six years ago, Professor Boccaccini today returns, with many colleagues and friends, as director and facilitator of the Third Meeting of the Enoch Seminar on the Parables of Enoch and the Messiah Son of Man. It is a great joy for us monks to receive and welcome you as guests and as friends. My warmest wish for you all is that this seminar will provide an opportunity for both profitable academic exchange and a peaceful break in a climate of reciprocal friendship, made even more pleasurable by the beauty of the natural surroundings.

We are situated in the center of a great forest and national park that offer fascinating vistas that combine the wonder of nature itself and the sensitive intervention of human hands. We welcome you into monastic buildings marked over the centuries by the harmony and simplicity of the life of their inhabitants. They bear the evident signs of a history and culture grounded in a continuous experience of God, community life, and simple hospitality offered to guests, who according to the rule for monks written by Saint Benedict of Norcia in the sixth century, are to be recognized and received as the person of Christ himself (*Rule of Benedict* 51).

This conference room in which we now meet is dedicated to Cristoforo Landino, a great Florentine humanist of the fifteenth century. His name — together with other famous humanists: philosophers, architects, writers, and politicians — is inscribed on the marble tablet mounted on the wall as a testimony to the vital and continuous interchange between the world of monasticism and that of culture in the broadest sense of the term that has characterized the history of Camaldoli. This enriching interchange continues today with you.

You have chosen to meet in an emblematic context! The almost ten centuries of spiritual and cultural history of the monastic community here are an explicit reminder of the "humanist understanding" of the life of men and women. A humanist vision of life refers to the multiple dimensions that animate, motivate, and shape human existence understood in its full complexity and global scope, including those dimensions that remain mysterious and lie beyond parameters of valuation in terms of utility and productive efficiency.

The human person is considered and respected in his/her uniqueness as a "person in relation" in society and, as such, with rights and corresponding duties in that society. A person is a mysterious matrix of conscience, thought, and creativity, subject of cultural and economic activity and political responsibility in the country of which he/she is citizen. Today, in the context of globalization, each one of us is a citizen not only of his/her own country, but of the world itself!

Rooted in history and the concreteness of daily work, each person carries within a transcendent and spiritual dimension, like a spark of fire or light, an openness to the future and the unknown, to the extent that each person is a son or daughter of memory and the earth.

In monastic terms — if you permit me the citation, given the context in which we find ourselves — one would say that the human person reaches full realization by means of *ora et labora,* prayer and work, the concrete presence in history and openness to the divine transcendence.

This cultural horizon constitutes a reminder and a challenge for a large proportion of the modern and postmodern culture that is much in debt to scientific and technical categories, and one that often tends to isolate the individual in his/her social dimension as a "person in relation."

Welcome to Camaldoli, place of hospitality and friendly solidarity, a place that encourages interior freedom.

I hope we all, you and we, can feel not only welcome as guests, but fully at ease as if in our own homes, with the freedom and peace to listen and speak our mind, to share a search that concerns all "pilgrims" on the path to the truth of life and, as a consequence, called to cooperate and work together.

Your seminar on the Parables of Enoch is not simply a meeting at a high academic level concerning a subject whose interest is a concern for academics. It is much more than this. It is a typical example of reciprocal listening, of shared learning, of open research. The eschatological dimension of history, of which the Enoch tradition is, in its way, a significant testimony, is expressed in the monastic experience rooted in the Christian doctrine of the New Testament. This dimension is not translated into a spiritual "fleeing from the world" here at Camaldoli. Here, it has become the matrix of cultural and historical commitment, with the vision open to the mystery of man and of God recognized as present in history, as transcending history, and as the end of history.

*Listen — speak your mind — learn from each other.* It often happens that, in the light of such an exchange, one is also helped to discover and better understand oneself. The truth, also in its various historical, cultural, and religious expressions, lies beyond us all, and in its own liberty, offers itself in indeterminable ways for the benefit of humankind.

I renew my best wishes to you all that these days of collaboration will be a fruitful laboratory of mind and heart, a broadening of the interior vision of yourself and of the world. May your work proceed well and your stay be a joyful one!

*Monastery of Camaldoli*
*June 7, 2005*

PART ONE

# THE STRUCTURE OF THE TEXT

# Discerning the Structure(s) of the Enochic Book of Parables

*George W. E. Nickelsburg*

It is a well-known fact that the Book of Parables (1 En 37–71) is a pastiche of traditions. One example suffices to make the point. At 1 En 68:1, *within the Book of Parables,* Noah describes in the first-person singular *how he has received the Book of Parables* from Enoch. This verse comes at the end of a long section that focuses on the activities of Noah, sometimes relating them in the first-person singular (chaps. 65–67). In this essay I shall discuss the literary structure of the Book of Parables with a view toward two issues: How do we make sense of the book as a whole — as it now stands? To what degree can we reconstruct an earlier form of the Book of Parables, and how do we understand its redaction? The essay, which I consider a work in progress, is a way station between my understanding of the text as reflected in the recent translation published by James VanderKam and me and my ongoing work on a commentary on the Book of Parables.[1]

## The Structure of the Text as a Whole

The literary macrostructure of 1 En 37–71 is a collection of three "parables."[2] This is indicated at the end of the introduction.

---

1. G. W. E. Nickelsburg and J. C. VanderKam, *1 Enoch: A New Translation* (Minneapolis: Fortress, 2004); G. W. E. Nickelsburg and J. C. VanderKam, *1 Enoch 2: A Commentary on the Book of 1 Enoch Chapters 37–73,* Hermeneia (Minneapolis: Fortress, forthcoming). Translations in this chapter are from Nickelsburg and VanderKam, *1 Enoch.*

2. I leave open here how one should properly translate the Eth. *mesālē* (= Gk. *parabolē* = Aram. *mathlāʾ*): "parable," "similitude," "discourse."

*George W. E. Nickelsburg*

> Three parables were (imparted) to me,
> and I took (them) up and spoke to those who dwell on the earth.
> (37:5)

Furthermore, each of the three major sections begins with the designation of first, second, or third parable respectively:

> *The first parable.* (38:1)

> This is *the second parable concerning* those who deny the name of the dwelling of the holy ones and of the Lord of Spirits. (45:1)

> And I began to speak *the third parable concerning* the righteous and concerning the chosen. (58:1)

Finally, each of the three sections ends with a reference to its character as a parable. This is most evident in the second and third sections.

> *This is* the end of *the second parable.* (57:3)

> *This is the third parable* of Enoch. (69:29)

There is a similar designation one verse from the end of the first section.

> The Lord of Spirits has shown you a *parable concerning* them;
> these are the names of the *holy ones* who *dwell* on the earth. . . . (43:4)

Although the precise meaning of this text is less than clear, its wording appears to have (been) influenced (by) the wording of the superscription of the second parable: "This is the second *parable concerning* those who deny the name of the *dwelling* of the *holy ones* and of the Lord of Spirits" (45:1). The two passages appear to refer to two different things: the holy ones who presently dwell on the earth (though cf. 45:4-5); and those who deny the reality of heaven, the dwelling either of the angels or the righteous dead. In any case, the first parable ends with a reference to God's having revealed to Enoch "a parable." This may indicate that a subscript to the section has been lost or changed. The final verse of the section (44:1) dangles strangely at the end. Compared to the end of the other two sections, it is oddly anticlimactic. Perhaps it is misplaced or it is a gloss.

This evidence indicates that 1 En 37–69 was written as a work composed of three clearly delineated parts called "parables." (I shall discuss chaps. 70–71 below.) That "The Book of Parables" was a very early title for this work is evident in 68:1: "And after this, my great-grandfather gave me the explanation of all the secrets in a book, and the parables that were given to him, and gathered them for me in the words of *the Book of Parables.*" The superscription in 37:1 indicates however that this was not the author's title for the work. "[The second vision that he saw] *The vision of wisdom that Enoch saw* — the son of Jared, the son of Mahalalel, the son of Kenan, the son of Enoch, the son of Seth, the son of Adam."[3] In the next three sections I shall argue that, in composing his book, the author of the Parables has drawn on and reshaped material from the Enochic Book of the Watchers (chaps. 1–36).

## Superscription and Introduction (chap. 37)

The superscription and introduction provide a general description of the book as a whole, though not of its specific contents. It is a vision in which Enoch received basic and unprecedented wisdom consisting of three parables (37:5a).

> The beginning of (the words of) wisdom. (37:2a, 3b)

> Until now there had not been given . . . such wisdom as I have received according to my insight. (37:4ab)

The section as a whole appears to imitate the corresponding part of the introduction to the Book of the Watchers. First, the superscription:

> *The* vision *of* wisdom *that Enoch* saw . . . the beginning of *the words of* wisdom. (37:1a, 2a)

> *The words of* the blessing with which *Enoch* blessed. . . . (1:1)

Then the content:

> *The vision of* wisdom. (37:1)

> . . . *the vision of* the Holy One and of heaven. (37:2c)

---

3. The bracketed words are almost certainly a gloss that postdates the section's incorporation into the corpus, and that relates the Parables to Enoch's vision recounted in the Book of the Watchers (cf. 1:2c, "the vision of . . .").

Then the mode of speech:

> . . . *words* of wisdom, which *I took up to recount* (37:2ab)
>
> . . . *three parables.* . . . *I took up and spoke.* (37:5b)
>
> he *took up* his parable *and said* (1:2a) . . . *I speak* now. . . . *I take up my parable.* (1:3ab)

Then the double recipients, Enoch's contemporaries and those who are to come:

> *O Ancients . . . you who come after* (37:2c) . . . *at first . . . those who come after.* (37:3ab)
>
> Not for *this generation* . . . but concerning *one that is distant.* (1:2fg)

Thus, though the superscription and introduction to the Parables go their own way (especially in their use of wisdom vocabulary), important elements in them correspond to similar elements in the superscription and introduction to the Book of the Watchers.[4]

## The First Parable (chaps. 38-44)

The first parable, which — different from the second and third — has no description of its contents (38:1), concerns itself with three matters: the coming judgment, events in the heavenly throne room and its environs, and the secrets of the heavenly bodies and meteorological phenomena. Over all, it continues to parallel elements in the Book of the Watchers.

The first subsection of the first parable, written in a kind of oracular form, provides an introduction to the parable that predicts future events associated with the great judgment (chap. 38). It parallels the introductory oracle in 1:3c-9, in that it describes an epiphany that is connected with the judgment of "the sinners" and "the kings and the mighty," the enemies par excellence of "the

---

4. The introduction to the Apocalypse of Weeks (93:1-3a) also imitates chap. 1. See G. W. E. Nickelsburg, *1 Enoch 1: A Commentary on the Book of 1 Enoch 1-36, 81-108*, Hermeneia (Minneapolis: Fortress, 2001), 441, who also cites James VanderKam. However, chap. 37 indicates no knowledge of the specific features of chap. 93.

righteous and chosen." What "appears," however, is not the Great Holy One with his army (1:3b-4), but "the congregation of the righteous" and, in their midst, "the righteous one" (38:1-2), the heavenly savior and judge, who will be formally introduced in the second parable. As in 1:8-9, the judgment will result in blessings for the righteous (including the theophanic light, 38:4bc; cf. 1:8h) and, principally, the condemnation of the sinners.

This subsection is followed immediately by another allusion to the Book of the Watchers, specifically two lines that summarize chaps. 6–11:

> In those days, sons of the chosen and holy were descending from the highest heaven,
>     and their seed was becoming one with the sons of men. (39:1)

The next four lines continue to shadow the Book of the Watchers: "Enoch received *books of* jealous *wrath and rage*" (39:2), and Enoch wrote a petition in behalf of the Watchers (13:4-7), but was given *a book of reprimand* (14:1). In the sequence of the Book of the Watchers, this brief account is followed by Enoch's account of his ascent to heaven on the winds (14:8), as it is here (39:3).

What follows in the first parable, and occupies the longest section of its text, is a description of Enoch's visions of the heavenly throne room and its environs (39:4–40:10), which corresponds to Enoch's vision of the heavenly temple and throne room in 14:9–16:4, albeit with major differences. The account in 15:1–16:4 focuses on the oracle of judgment. Here, however, Enoch sees the dwelling places of the righteous dead and gets his first glimpse of the Chosen One, whose activities will dominate the second and third parables. This section climaxes in 39:9–40:10, where Enoch recounts his vision of the enthroned deity in the midst of the angelic entourage. Thus, this parable expands the relatively brief description in 14:9-23, replacing a description of the heavenly *temple* with descriptions of the *personnel* who occupy it and its environs, and the ongoing praise of God (including his own). Chap. 40 introduces a literary form familiar from the Book of the Watchers: *Enoch sees* the four archangels (vv. 2-7); *he asks the angel of peace* who is accompanying him (first mentioned here) for an explanation (v. 8); and *the angel provides an explanation* (v. 9).[5] Strikingly, the explanation does not correspond to the actions of the respective angels (vv. 3-7), and in this sense it may correspond to a later occurrence of the form, where two angels offer two explanations (52:3-9). 1 En 41:1-2 brings us back to the motif of judgment. "After that" he sees the dwelling places of the chosen and holy (repeating 39:4-5) and the process of judgment (weighing human deeds in a bal-

---

5. Cf. 1 En 21–32.

ance) and the dragging off of the sinners. The section anticipates the extensive description in chaps. 61–63.

In most of the remainder of the first parable (about three-quarters as long as the previous section), Enoch recounts his visits to the heavenly phenomena. In a general way it corresponds to chaps. 17–19 — where Enoch travels through the cosmos and sees the places of the luminaries, the stars, the thunder, the lightnings, and especially the winds (cf. 18:1-5 and 41:3-4) — and to material in the Astronomical Book (or the Book of the Luminaries, 1 En 72–82). Thus it is genuine Enochic material and not a foreign element in an eschatological book, and a comparison of its place here with the sequence in the Book of the Watchers suggests that it belongs here.

In my view, however, there is a literary problem. To lay out the problem, I divide 41:1–44:1 into five sections.

a. 41:1-2: Enoch sees the judgment.
b. 41:3-8: Enoch narrates his journeys to the places of the heavenly phenomena: the lightnings and thunders and winds (vv. 3-4); the sun and the moon (vv. 5-8).
c. 41:9: "For no angel hinders and no power is able to hinder, for the Judge sees them all and judges them all in his presence."
d. 42:1-3: A poem about the descent and ascent of Wisdom and the descent of Iniquity.
e. 43:1–44:1: Enoch narrates his journeys to "other lightnings" and the stars.

The problem in the text is twofold. First, the first section of Enoch's account of his cosmic journeys (b) separates two verses about the judgment (a) from another verse that refers to God as Judge (c). Second, sections c and d separate from one another the two sections of Enoch's narrative about his cosmic journeys (b and e).

There is a simple solution to the problem. Move a single running block of text (cd) from its present position and place it immediately after section a, creating the sequence: 41:1-2 + 41:9; 42:1-3 + 41:3-8 + 43:1–44:1 (a + cd + b + e). With this move we solve the two literary problems by creating the two thematic joins in the text that were not previously there.

*First,* immediately after hearing about the sinners being dragged away, presumably by the angels (41:2; cf. 63:1), we are told that no angel or power can hinder, and that the Judge sees them all, a typical judgment motif (41:9).[6] *Second,* we bring together the two sections about Enoch's journeys (41:3-8 + 43:1–44:1).

---

6. Cf. 1 En 9:1, 5, 11; 98:7-8; 104:7-8; Sir 16:17; Wis 1:6.

There is a bonus in this transposition, which I had not seen when I first suggested it,[7] and which, in my view, clinches my argument. It provides thematic continuities between that erratic block, the Wisdom poem (42:1-3), and the material that precedes and follows it.[8] *First,* at the front end there is a join by *Stichwort* between 42:1-3 and 41:2. Thus, 41:2 refers to *the dwelling places (maḥader)* of the chosen and *the dwelling places* of the holy ones. Similarly, 42:1-2 refers twice to Wisdom's *dwelling place.* Additionally, the references to the chosen and the holy ones (41:2) and the sinners (41:2) parallel the references to Wisdom and Iniquity in the poem. *Second,* the transposition provides an association by theme and *Stichwort* with the material that follows. The Wisdom poem, which ends by describing how Iniquity dwells among humanity "like rain in a desert and dew in a thirsty land" (42:3), is followed immediately by a verse that describes how "the clouds and the dew" "saturate the dust of the earth" (41:3). Moreover, the reference to Iniquity's "chambers" *(mazāgebt)* is followed immediately by a section in which the same noun occurs four times with reference to the "storehouses" of the hail and the winds, the mist and the clouds, and the sun and the moon.

The sequence of the whole section seems to be: (a) Enoch sees "the dwelling places" of the chosen and the holy ones and sees the sinners driven away "from there"; (b) he speaks of Wisdom's "dwelling place" in heaven and about Iniquity leaving her "chambers" and dwelling like rain in the dry land; (c) then he travels to the place of the clouds and the winds that saturate the dust of the earth and sees the "storehouses" of the elements. While the logic of this sequence is not altogether clear, the continuity of the *Stichwort* indicates that these sections belong together. I tend to ascribe these continuities to the hand of an author bringing together traditions, rather than to an interpolator who just happens to find a piece with suitable points of connection at both ends.

In summary: the first parable coheres as a single piece in which Enoch announces the judgment and describes his ascent to heaven, his visit to the heavenly throne room, and his journeys to the places of the heavenly phenomena. He accomplishes this by drawing on material in the Book of the Watchers, chaps. 1–18, and in general following its sequence. This first major part of the Book of Parables has many of its own nuances, of course, but granting one

---

7. I first suggested this in my *Jewish Literature between the Bible and the Mishnah* (Philadelphia: Fortress, 1981), 216, and I incorporated the sequence in Nickelsburg and VanderKam, *1 Enoch,* 55-58.

8. On the problem of 1 En 42:1-3 in its context, see R. H. Charles, *The Book of Enoch,* 2nd ed. (Oxford: Clarendon, 1912), 81-82, and R. H. Charles, "The Book of Enoch," in *The Apocrypha and Pseudepigrapha of the Old Testament,* vol. 2, *Pseudepigrapha,* ed. Robert Henry Charles (Oxford: Clarendon, 1913), 213; hereafter Charles, *APOT* 2.

*George W. E. Nickelsburg*

transposition, justified by the evidence, and one verse that seems to dangle at the end (44:1) and may simply be out of place, the material appears to be the work of a single author.

## The Second Parable (chaps. 45–57)

Like its predecessor, the second parable begins with a superscription and an oracular introduction that predicts events associated with the judgment. According to the superscription, "This is the second parable concerning those who deny the name of the dwelling of the holy ones and of the Lord of Spirits" (45:1). The body of the introduction alternates between descriptions of the fate of the sinners and of the blessed future of the righteous (45:2-3 | 4-5b | 5c | 6ab | 6cd). Thus, like chaps. 1–5 and chap. 38, it is an oracle of salvation and judgment.[9] Two aspects of it are significant here. First, it is cast in the first-person singular; it is God who speaks. Second, it immediately identifies the judge as "my Chosen One," the figure whose epiphany was mentioned in 38:2 ("the Righteous One") and whom and whose dwelling place Enoch saw in 39:6-8. Here the introduction anticipates his future activity, which will be described later in the book: he will sit on the throne of glory (45:3; cf. 51:3; 61:8; 62:2; 69:29), and he will dwell among the chosen ones (45:4; cf. 62:14).

The introduction is followed by a sequence of three heavenly scenes in which Enoch sees events related to the judgment (chaps. 46; 47; 48–49), two of them featuring the Chosen One (chaps. 46; 48–49). The first two are interpretations of Dan 7. In *the first scene* (chap. 46) Enoch sees "one who had a head of days" (hereafter known as "the Head of Days") and with him another "whose face was like the appearance of a man and . . . was full of graciousness like one of the holy angels" (46:1). Employing the form typical of the Parables (and of the Book of the Watchers), Enoch asks the "angel of peace" about the second figure (v. 2) and learns that he is "the son of man who has righteousness" (v. 3). For the remainder of this scene the angel describes the son of man's future activity (he will judge the kings and the mighty, vv. 4-6; cf. chap. 62), its consequences (they will be put to shame and sent into eternal darkness, v. 6; cf. 62:5, 10-12; 63:1, 11), and the reasons for this judgment (their arrogance vis-à-vis God and their persecution of the righteous, 46:7-8). *The second scene* (chap. 47) conflates motifs from both 1 En 8 and Dan 7. Enoch learns of the complaint of the persecuted righteous, hears the holy ones petitioning in their behalf, and sees the court sit in judgment. The third scene takes the heavenly action a step fur-

---

9. On this form see Nickelsburg, *1 Enoch 1*, 131.

ther (chaps. 48–49). "That son of man" is named in the presence of the "Lord of Spirits"/"Head of Days." The naming scene is, first of all, an interpretation of the naming scene of the Servant of YHWH in Isa 49, and thus the son of man is also identified as *"the Chosen One"* (1 En 49:2d; cf. 48:6a).[10] Additionally, in a phrase drawn from Ps 2:2, he is identified as God's *"Anointed One"* (1 En 48:10),[11] endowed with the kind of wisdom attributed to the Davidic king in Isa 11 (1 En 49:3; cf. Isa 11:2), and again with Second Isaiah's *Chosen One* (1 En 49:4cd; cf. Isa 42:1). Finally, the attribution of *wisdom* to the son of man and language about his preexistence (1 En 48:1, 2-3, 6) may indicate that Jewish speculation about preexistent wisdom also contributed to the Parables' description of the Chosen One.

With this series of visions complete, the author turns to a description of future events associated with the judgment (chaps. 50–51): the holy and the chosen will be glorified; having seen this, some "others" will repent and abandon their idols; the unrepentant will perish (chap. 50). Then follow the resurrection, the judgment over which the Chosen One will preside, and the transformation of the earth, where the righteous and chosen will dwell (chap. 51).

Having completed this description of future events, Enoch returns to an account of his visions, this time his journeys to the places on earth that will be the loci of eschatological punishment (52:1–56:4). This shift corresponds to the shift in the first parable, as Enoch moved from the heavenly throne room to the places of the cosmic elements. Moreover, his journeys here correspond to those depicted in 18:6–19:3 and 21:1-10 and 24:2-3. That is, the cosmic journeys here complement those in the first parable, extending the recasting of Book of the Watchers material in the first parable. The section consists of three subsections, in which Enoch visits: six mountains (52:1-9), the valley of punishment for the kings and the mighty (53:1-7; 54:2), and the valley of the rebel angels' punishment (54:1, 3-10; 55:1-4; 56:1-4). Each subsection is, for the most part, cast in the typical form: vision, seer's question, angelic interpretation of the vision.

In his first way station Enoch sees six mountains. The locative reference in 52:1 appears to place Enoch where his visions began in 39:3. The six mountains correspond roughly to six of the seven mountains in 18:6-9, 24:2-4 (the seventh mountain is the mountain of God). The mountains, however, are very different, being composed of six metals rather than of precious stones. The vision and Enoch's question are followed by a double answer, one by "the angel

---

10. For the parallels with Isa 49, see G. W. E. Nickelsburg, *Resurrection, Immortality, and Eternal Life in Intertestamental Judaism*, HTS 26 (Cambridge: Harvard University Press, 1972), 74 nn. 101-2.

11. 1 En 48:8 is the only occurrence in the Parables of the title "kings of the earth."

who went with me," to whom his question was addressed ("and he said," 52:4), and the other by "that angel of peace" (vv. 5-9). A comparison with 40:8, 54:4 ("the angel of peace who went with me") suggests that it is one and the same angel, who gives Enoch a twofold answer. The two parts, however, are complementary, the first relating to the authority of "his Anointed One" (v. 4), and the other to events associated with the judicial appearance of "the Chosen One" (vv. 6, 9). This second and longer answer indicates one of the ways the author has transformed material from the Book of the Watchers. The mountains are the high hills that will melt before the divine epiphany (52:6; cf. 1:6). This epiphany, however, is the appearance of God's "Anointed One" and "Chosen One," rather than "the Great Holy One," "the eternal God." The metals of the mountains, moreover, represent the riches of the mighty (gold and silver) and the materials employed for the weapons of war (iron, bronze, tin, and lead). That is, the judgment brings to an end the oppression of the rich and the military violence of the mighty. That the agent of judgment is God's Anointed and Chosen One is consonant with the emphasis in the Parables and ties this section to its context.

Without moving ("there"), Enoch now sees "a deep valley" that is the place of final punishment for "the sinners" who "lawlessly devour" (53:2) and "the kings and the mighty" (v. 5). This chapter is tied to the previous, both by the mention of the melting mountains in 53:7 (52:6) and by the fact that the kings and the mighty are the persons who make use of the metals of which the mountains are composed. Since 54:1 describes Enoch's journey to "another part of the earth," where the rebel angels will be punished (54:5), I have transposed 54:2 between 53:7 and 54:1. Presumably, the verse dropped from the text was subsequently collated in the margin, and then copied in at the wrong place.

Enoch's third way station, at "another part of the earth," is a deep valley, where Azazel and his host will be punished (54:1; 54:3–56:4). It corresponds to the chasm in 18:10-11, 19:1-2, and 21:7-10 with their burning fire.

> 54:1: And I looked and turned to *another part* of the earth . . . *a deep valley* with *burning fire.*
> 18:10: And *beyond these mountains, a great chasm* among pillars of heavenly *fire.*
> 21:7: I traveled to *another place* . . . a great *fire burning* . . . a narrow cleft (extending) to *the abyss.*

This section presents the only significant literary problem in the second parable. It is composed of three subsections, one of them with two parts:

a. 54:1, 3-6: Enoch's vision of the valley, his question, and the interpretation of the angel of peace.
b. 54:7–55:2: a digression about the flood, with the Head of Days speaking in the first-person singular.
c. 55:3–56:4: a return to the topic of the rebel angels.
  55:3-4: a short speech by God in the first-person singular.
  56:1-4: the second phase of Enoch's vision, his question, and the interpretation by the angel of peace.

The principal problem here is that the section about the flood (b) separates from one another (a) and (c) two sections that describe the place of punishment for the rebel angels. As the text stands now, we can explain its sequence as follows. Enoch arrives at a valley and sees "them" (some angels) preparing chains for the host of Azazel. A comparison of the wording with 10:4-5 suggests that it refers to the primordial incarceration of these angels. The next verse then predicts that the four archangels will permanently imprison them "on that great day" (v. 6). With reference still to the primordial time, 54:7-8–55:2 describes how the Lord of Spirits prepares for the flood, and "after that" how "the Head of Days," speaking in the first-person singular, announces that he will set his sign in the heavens. Still speaking in the first person, "the Lord of Spirits" announces the *future* destruction of the angels and informs the kings and the mighty that they will witness the enthronement of "my Chosen One," who will judge Azazel and his associates (55:3-4). The text then returns to the previous narrative about Enoch's visions (54:1, 3-6). With Enoch once more the first-person narrator, he describes how he sees the angels of punishment holding chains, he asks the angel of peace about the scene, and he receives an explanation (56:1-4). This section and its mode of description parallel exactly 54:1, 3-6.

Although I have made sense of the sequence between 54:1 and 56:4, I believe that 54:7–55:4 makes the best sense as an interpolation — as we shall see, the first of several Noachic additions in the Parables. With these verses removed, the remaining text (54:1, 3-6; 56:1-4) presents a pair of parallel scenes in both of which Enoch the narrator describes how he saw a particular sight relating to the punishment of the angels, asked the angel of peace, and received an explanation. The two verses 55:3-4 might be considered part of the original text. But it seems better to ascribe the first-person speech attributed to God to the interpolation, where God has already appeared, and to explain the two verses as a transition back to the subject of the punishment of the angels. It is debatable whether the interpolation is a piece of tradition or a composition by an interpolator. The divine names "Lord of Spirits" and "Head of Days" and the title "my Chosen One" are all at home in the Parables.

*George W. E. Nickelsburg*

The precise relationship between the two scenes in 54:1, 3-6 and 56:1-4 is uncertain. Perhaps it is best explained as follows. In the first, Enoch sees the angels preparing shackles for the host of Azazel. In the second he sees the angels moving off with chains that they are carrying, which they will use to imprison the "chosen and beloved ones" of the angels, evidently the offspring of the angels who continue to lead humanity astray (56:4). The passage is curious, since it is one of only two references in the Parables to the offspring of the angels.[12]

The final section of the parable comprises two subsections that describe future events (56:5-8; 57:1-3). The first depicts the eschatological war, which ends in mayhem, with parents slaughtering children (cf. 99:4-5; 100:2) and Sheol swallowing the dead. The final scene, whose sequence is indicated by "after that," depicts the return of the dispersion.

The whole ends with the notation that "this is the end of the second parable."

In summary, the second parable starts to develop the scenario hinted at in the first. The Chosen One, introduced in the first parable, is here fully explicated and his future functions as the judge anticipated. As in the first parable, Enoch narrates his journeys, but they take him not to the heavenly phenomena but to places related to the great judgment, thus providing spatial reinforcement for the announcements of the judgment, as in the Book of the Watchers.[13] In this material the author carries forward his imitation of the Book of the Watchers. Seen as a whole, the parable interlaces Enoch's heavenly visions, his journeys across the earth, and some descriptions of events related to the judgment.

## The Third Parable (chaps. 58–69)

Like the first two, the third parable begins with a superscription and an oracular introduction. Marking the beginning of a new unit, Enoch states, "I began to speak the third parable concerning the righteous and concerning the chosen" (58:1a). This superscription provides a foil to the previous one, which announced that the parable would concern itself with those who deny heaven, the dwelling of the holy ones and of the Lord of Spirits (45:1). In the same vein, the introduction here speaks only of the future blessedness of the righteous and chosen (58:1-6).

Chaps. 59–60 contain several literary disjunctions that indicate a dis-

---

12. Cf. 1 En 39:1. On the double term, cf. the use of *agapētos* in Mark 1:11, where Isa 42:1 has *eklektos*.

13. Nickelsburg, *1 Enoch 1*, 278.

placement or an interpolation in the texts, or both. The present sequence of the text is as follows:

a. 59:1-3: Enoch sees the secrets (*ḥebu'āta*, "hidden things") of the *lightning*s, the luminaries, and *the thunder*.
b. 60:1-6: in the 500th year of the life of <Noah>,[14] Enoch views a scene in the heavenly throne room, where Michael sends "another angel" to support him, and then Michael predicts how God's *"mercy and longsuffering"* will give way to *"punishment"* on the day of judgment.
c. 60:7-10: Noah (cf. v. 8) describes the separation of the *two monsters*, Leviathan and Behemoth, and queries "another (*or* the other *or* this *or* that) angel," who replies briefly that "you wish to know what is hidden."
d. 60:11-22: "the other angel who went with me and showed me what was hidden (*zabaḥebu'*)" escorts "me" through the heavens, showing him the storehouses and activities of the winds, the *thunders*, and *the lightning*.
e. 60:23: this verse places the vision near the "Garden of the righteous."
f. 60:24a: the angel of peace explains "these *two monsters*."
g. 60:24b-25 predicts the judgment and "the *punishment* of the Lord of Spirits" and after that "his *mercy and longsuffering*."

The disjunctions in the text are readily evident. (1) Two sections of material about "hidden" heavenly phenomena (a and d), one about the lightnings and the thunders (59:1-3) and the other about the winds and the thunders and the lightnings (60:11-22), are separated by a scene in the heavenly throne room (bc, 60:1-10). (2) Two sections about the two monsters (c and f; 60:7-10 and 60:24) are separated by a description of Enoch's tour of the heavens (d, 60:11-22) and a verse locating the place of Noah's vision (e, 60:23). (3) Two sections on God's mercy and long-suffering and his judgment (b and g) are separated by sections cdef.

Charles solves the problem — to the extent that he sees it — with a pair of literary moves.[15] First, he brackets 59:1-3 as "an intrusion . . . probably from a Noah-Apocalypse." Then he transposes 60:25 between 60:6 and 60:7, thus dealing with the separation of the two parts about God's long-suffering and mercy and his punishment. My difficulty with this solution is twofold. First, although Charles allows 60:11-22 to remain as an integral part of the text, he does not see

---

14. All mss. read "Enoch," which is impossible since Enoch lived on earth only for 365 years. However, see Gen 5:32 for the 500th year of Noah. My translation (Nickelsburg and VanderKam, *1 Enoch*, 75) misplaces the notation for the beginning of 1 En 60:1. The Ethiopian verse begins with "in the year 500" and ends with "were greatly disturbed."

15. Charles, *APOT* 2:223-24.

its connection with the similar material in 59:1-3, which he brackets as an intrusion. Second, he does not deal with the separation of the angel's explanation about "*these* two monsters" (60:24) from the scene to which it refers (60:7-9).

My own solution is twofold. First, to solve the main problem, I suggest that 60:11-22 has been displaced from its original place after 59:1-3. By moving this single block of text in this manner, two of our three problems are solved. The material about Enoch's journeys to the heavenly phenomena (a and d) is brought together, and the scene set in the heavenly throne room is also brought together (bc + efg). Thus the sequence is:

> ad: 59:1-3 + 60:11-22: the heavenly phenomena
> bcefg: 60:1-10 + 60:23-25: the heavenly throne room

Next I suggest that the section on the two monsters (60:7-10 + 24a) is itself an interpolation into the scene in the heavenly courtroom. Thus,

> b: 60:1-6: the throne room and the beginning of Michael's speech on the judgment
> [cef: 60:7-10 + 60:23-24a: the two monsters and the angel explanations]
> g: 60:24b-25: the completion of Michael's speech about the judgment

Thus the two parts of Michael's speech are brought together, as is the material about the two monsters.

One verse gives me trouble (60:23), and for it I have no certain answer. Does v. 23 go with v. 22 and indicate that Enoch's visions of the heavenly phenomena took place near the garden of the righteous? This seems unlikely. That it goes in general with the material about the heavenly throne room seems indicated by the reference to the garden in 60:8. In my translation I have placed it as part of the introduction to the throne room scene: 60:23 + 60:1. Here I suggest that it belongs before v. 24 as part of the interpolation about the two monsters and the garden, although it intrudes between the two angelic replies to the seer's question. Perhaps it is a gloss.

The transposition and interpolation that I have proposed raise another, related literary problem. Is the scene set in the heavenly throne room a part of the original Book of Parables, or is it itself an interpolation? I tend to think it is an interpolated interpolation. First, it is related to the figure of Noah, and in v. 8 the speaker refers to Enoch as "my great-grandfather." Thus, it appears to be part of a set of Noachic interpolations, including some near the end of this parable also being put in the mouth of Noah (see below). Thus, granting the transposition of 60:11-22, we have an interpolation within an interpolation:

*Discerning the Structure(s) of the Enochic Book of Parables*

    59:1-3 + 60:11-22: heavenly phenomena
        60:23(?) + 60:1-6: throne room part 1
            60:7-10 + 60:23(?) + 60:24a: the two monsters
        60:24b-25: throne room part 2
    61:1-5: scene relating to the resurrection

As to the placement of the material here, without (and even with) the interpolation, there is a rough chiastic relationship between the first and third parables:

Parable 1:  a: Enoch's visions of the heavenly throne room
              b: Enoch's journeys to the heavenly phenomena
Parable 3:  b: Enoch's journeys to the heavenly phenomena
              a: Enoch's visions leading up to the heavenly throne room (61:6–63:12)

This structure could explain the placement of the Noachic fragment after the astronomical material and reinforces the chiasm.

This preliminary material in place, the third parable moves toward its climax, which focuses on the great judgment and events related to it. In 61:1-5, repeating chap. 51, the author describes a scene that anticipates the resurrection of the dead. Similar to chap. 52, two angels provide Enoch with two explanations of what he has seen.

The next scene takes us to the heavenly throne room (61:6-13). The appearance of the pronoun "him" without an antecedent (v. 7) may indicate that a verse or two is missing at the beginning of the pericope. In the constitutive event in this scene, the Lord of Spirits enthrones the Chosen One and announces that he will judge the holy ones (vv. 8-9). In the verses that follow, either the Chosen One or the Lord of Spirits summons the angelic hosts (v. 10), who praise the Lord of Spirits repetitively and at length (vv. 11-13).

This sets the scene for chaps. 62–63, which describe the great judgment over which the Chosen One presides. It is the dramatic climax of the Book of Parables, and at a number of points it reprises elements that passages in the first and, especially, the second parable had anticipated. The scene focuses principally on the condemnation of the kings and the mighty: they are forced to recognize the Chosen One (whose existence they had previously denied or been unaware of), and they react in terror (62:1-8); they are condemned and will be delivered to perdition (vv. 9-12); their confession of the mighty of God and their repentance are futile, and they are taken away to darkness (chap. 63). The scene's secondary focus is on the salvation of the righteous and chosen (62:7-8,

13-16). The alternation of references to the destruction of the sinners and the salvation of the righteous parallels the pattern in the introductory material in 1:1-8, 5:5-8, and chaps. 38 and 45. With this scene the Book of Parables has reached its climax, although 202 lines of Ethiopic text intervene before we reach the four verses that conclude this scene and that are followed immediately by the subscription to the third parable (69:26-29).

We may outline the concluding material as follows:

1. Enoch sees the angels who led humanity astray. 64:1-2
2. Noachic material. 65:1–69:1
   a. Noah consults with Enoch about the tipping of the earth. 65:1–66:3
   b. God speaks with Noah about the flood and ark. 67:1-3
   c. Noah's vision about the punishment of the angels. 67:4-13
   d. Noah's concluding reference to "the Book of Parables." 68:1
   e. Conversation between Michael and Gabriel (cf. 67:12-13). 68:2–69:1
3. Lists of the fallen angels. 69:2-12
   a. First list (cf. 6:7). 69:2-3
   b. Second list. 69:4-12
4. The angels and the cosmic oath. 69:13-25
5. Conclusion of the judgment scene and subscription. 69:26-29

Three facts are noteworthy about this material. First, a large part of it is ascribed to Noah (2), and some of it relates to the flood (2ab). Second, some of the Noachic material and most of the rest of these sections relate to the sins and the punishment of the angels (1, 2cde, 3-4). All of this material separates the judgment scene in chaps. 62–63 from its conclusion and the subscript of the third parable in 69:26-29.

Section 1 of this material places Enoch in an unnamed place: "And other figures I saw hidden in that place" (64:1). In context, this means that Enoch sees the rebel angels obscured either at the place where the Chosen One has rendered judgment against the kings and the mighty (chaps. 62–63) or at the place of their punishment. The pericope is brief and perhaps a compression of a longer passage; Enoch is not said to have asked who these "figures" are, but an angel provides an explanation.

> These are the angels who descended upon the earth,
> and what was secret they revealed to human beings,
> and they led the human beings astray so that they committed sin. (64:2)

Although the passage may well be displaced,[16] from a literary and thematic point of view its presence here should not surprise us. The first parable began with reference to the descent of the angels, and this event led to Enoch's receipt of the books of wrath (39:1-2). In the second parable Enoch sees the place of punishment for both the kings and the mighty and the rebel angels (53:1–56:4). In the third parable, although we have been told that the Chosen One will judge the angels (61:8-9), the grand judgment scene mentions the condemnation and punishment of only the kings and the mighty (chaps. 62–63). Finally, the end of the parable states that the enthroned son of man will cause the sinners to perish from the earth, and "those who led the world astray will be bound in chains, and in the assembly place of their destruction they will be confined" (69:27-28). Thus, on the basis of what precedes and what follows 64:1-2, we might expect some reference to, or description of, the judgment and punishment of the rebel angels. This suggests that 64:1-2 is roughly in place, and that some of the material in 67:1–69:25 belongs to the early form of the Book of Parables. Before turning to this problem, we shall consider the Noachic material as a whole.

To begin with, it has a certain internal coherence. First comes a story in which Noah travels to the ends of the earth to inquire of Enoch why the earth had tilted and its destruction was approaching (65:1–66:3). After a narrative introduction (65:1-2), Noah narrates the story in the first-person singular and refers to Enoch in the third person.[17] The end of the story is signaled by the words "And I went forth from the presence of Enoch" (66:3). The plotline of the story parallels that of 1 En 106–107, where Noah's extraordinary appearance at the time of his birth leads his father Lamech to seek Enoch's counsel at the ends of the earth. 1 En 83–84 contains another similar story in which Enoch sees in a vision that the earth has sunk and asks his grandfather Mahalalel for an explanation. In all three cases the interpreter explains the phenomenon as a sign of the coming flood. Perhaps the writers of other essays will discuss the possible relationships between these three stories.[18]

In the next segment Noah carries the narrative a step further, describing how "the word of God" came to him, informing him that the angels were building him an ark and that he would survive the desolation of the earth (67:1-3; cf. 10:1-3). Then, in 67:4–68:1, Noah describes how his great-grandfather had shown him the valley by the six mountains mentioned in chaps. 52–53 (67:4). In

---

16. Charles, *APOT* 2:230.

17. In my translation I have transposed a few verses out of narrative necessity. See Nickelsburg and VanderKam, *1 Enoch*, 84 nn. b and c.

18. For my own comments, see Nickelsburg, *1 Enoch 1*, 541-42.

fact, the author has conflated material from 52–53 (the mountains and the valley of the punishment of the kings and the mighty) and 54–56 (the valley of the angels' punishment). Vv. 5-13 are either an account of Noah's previous vision of the valley or a fragment of an account of a subsequent vision of the valley. In either case the account ends with what appears to be the typical angelic explanation of a vision that has called forth the seer's query (67:12-13). As in 64:1-4, no such query is recorded.

The section appears to end as Noah explains that his great-grandfather had handed over to him "the Book of Parables" (68:1). This reference to the Book of Parables immediately after he has elaborated material to be found in that book indicates that this material comes from a source that was external to the Parables, but whose author knew the book.

The material in 68:2-4 presents a puzzle. In its contents, the dialogue between Michael and Raphael appears to continue the words of Michael in 67:12-13. In both cases the subject is the judgment of the angels. Was 68:1 displaced from an original position after 69:1, or was 68:2–69:1 added later without considering 68:1 as a narrative ending? Perhaps the latter is more likely since the material before 68:1 is demonstrably drawn from the Parables, but not the material that follows. In any case, the sudden unannounced appearance of Raphael indicates that we are dealing with a textual fragment.

This material on the judgment of the angels is immediately followed by two onomastica containing the names of the angels (69:2-3, 4-12). Granting a few textual corruptions, the first of these lists approximates the list in 6:7. The second corresponds in part to the list in chap. 8. All the names are different, but it is similar to chap. 8 in three respects. First, it is a second list added to a first. Second, the list has fewer names than the first, and three of its five named angels are accused of revealing secrets to humanity. Finally, as in chap. 8, two of the major issues are illicit sex and violence.

The next section (69:13-25) is obscure; however, it is linked to its previous context by the theme of the angelic revelation of heavenly secrets (69:13-16). The major part of the section (69:16-25) concerns itself with cosmological lore that has counterparts in the Parables.[19]

I doubt that it is possible to explain definitively how the material in 64:1–69:25 relates to an original form and to a redaction or redactions of the Book of Parables. The main problem, it appears, is that we are dealing with fragments of text. Having said that, I shall draw some tentative conclusions.

Three factors indicate that at least some of this material has been interpo-

---

19. Cf. 1 En 41:3-8; 43:1–44:1; and especially 59:1-3; 60:11-22. I leave aside here the question whether 69:23-24a is an interpolation between vv. 22 and 24b.

lated into an earlier form of the Book of Parables. First, in an Enochic book, the Noah narratives are placed in the mouth of Noah and refer to Enoch in the third person. Second, they refer to the book in which they are incorporated as a separate entity. Third, the whole block of material from 64:1 to 69:25 separates the great judgment scene (chaps. 61–63) from a section that is clearly a part of its conclusion and that itself is immediately followed by the superscription to the third parable (69:26-29). This last section, which begins with a pronoun that has no antecedent in its immediately preceding context, draws its language and ideas from chaps. 61, 62, and 63.

There are a few pieces of evidence, however, that suggest, or even indicate, that we cannot exclude all of 64:1–69:25 as an interpolation or a series of interpolations. First, earlier material in the Parables leads us to expect a description of a judgment and punishment not only of the kings and the mighty, but also of Azazel and his hosts. Second, there are some parallels between 64:1-2, 69:4-12, and 69:28. In 64:1-2 Enoch is told concerning what he sees:

> These are *the angels who descended* upon the earth,
> and what was secret they *revealed to the sons of men,*
> and *they led the sons of men astray,* so that they committed sin.

The second onomasticon describes precisely *angels* who are *brought down* upon the earth (lit., the dry land) and who have led humans astray. The conclusion of the parable states:

> And those *who led the world astray* will be bound in chains,
> and in the assembly place of their destruction they will be confined;
> and all their works will vanish from the face of the earth. (69:28)

This verse may indicate that 64:1-2, 69:4-12 were part of the original form of the last part of the Parables. I suggest that the second onomasticon is more integral to the Parables than the first; it describes the function of the angels as leading humanity astray, a motif that is essentially the activity of these angels according to the Parables.[20] However that may be, placing an angelic onomasticon near the end of the book enhances its chiastic structure.

> Parable 1: a: the descent of the angels
> b: Enoch's visions of the heavenly throne room
> c: Enoch's journeys through the heavens

20. 1 En 54:6; 56:4; 64:2; 69:28; cf. 67:6-7; 69:4, 5, 6, 8.

Parable 2:   c: Enoch's journeys through the heavens
           b: Enoch's visions of the heavenly throne room
         a: a list of the angels who descended and led humanity astray

## The Ending to the Book of Parables (chaps. 70–71)

Since the Book of Parables begins with an introduction that precedes the beginning of the first parable, it is reasonable to expect that there might have been a conclusion to the whole text following the conclusion of the third parable. In fact, the present text contains two and arguably three concluding sections.

The first of these is written in the third-person singular and, I think, in poetry (70:1-2). It describes how, "after this," Enoch was taken up, finally to heaven. That is, it presumes his return to earth and his transmission of the parables, and it describes his subsequent final assumption. The second unit (70:3-4), written in the first-person singular, however, carries forward the previous one, describing the location of Enoch's place in the cosmos. Charles considered it a continuation of vv. 1-2.[21] However, as Michael Knibb notes, its first-person style connects it more closely with the first-person material in chap. 71. He goes on to assert that, taken together, this ascent portion of this autobiographical account divides into three sections that correspond more or less with the three-stage ascent recounted in the Book of the Watchers.[22]

```
70:3-4     14:8-9
71:1-4     14:10-14a
71:5-11    14:14b-25
```

I am less certain about 71:3-4, which looks more like a tight summary of chaps. 17–19, or even chaps. 21ff. In any case, one can add to Knibb's list:

```
71:13-17   15:1–16:4
```

In the respective units, Enoch is commissioned as son of man who will enact God's judgment and as the prophet who announces the Watchers' judgment.

---

21. Charles, *APOT* 2:235.
22. M. Knibb, "The Translation of 1 Enoch 70:1: Some Methodological Issues," in *Biblical Hebrew, Biblical Texts: Essays in Memory of Michael P. Weitzman*, ed. Ada Rapaport and Gillian Greenberg, JSOTSup 333 (Sheffield: Sheffield Academic, 2001), 341.

*Discerning the Structure(s) of the Enochic Book of Parables*

There may be no certain resolution of the problems raised by these concluding parts of the present Book of Parables, but these are my suggestions. Regarding 70:3-4 and its use of the first-person singular, there is some difficulty in explaining how the author thought Enoch could transmit the account of his heavenly experiences (effectively the contents of the three parables) *after* his final ascent, which he recounts in vv. 3-4. For this reason I suggest that something like 70:1-2 constituted the original conclusion to the Book of Parables. Reprising the third-person singular used in the superscription (37:1), it states that Enoch, having received his revelations, was finally taken up into the presence of God. Vv. 3-4, employing the first-person voice, provides a transition to the material that follows.[23] That this material is extraneous to the Book of Parables is indicated by the content of 71:1-4 and by its opening chronological referent. "And after that" (i.e., after my final assumption), I saw all the things that I saw much earlier (the secrets of the cosmos). It seems best to me to posit that chap. 71 is a summary of the whole Enochic experience with a tendentious addition, namely, the identification of Enoch as the future eschatological judge. One could argue, of course, that for the sake of narrative vividness the author slips into the first-person singular to recount what, by all accounts, is the narrative climax of the Book of Parables in its present form. However, the fact that the author of 70:1-2 knows better than to attribute to the voice of Enoch an account that he is not in a position to transmit on earth leads me to ascribe the first-person material in 70:3-4 and chap. 71 to a later redactor or redactors.

Having said that, I believe there is narrative logic to the whole of 70–71. Enoch is taken up from the earth, he is set down first in the area of paradise, then after another tour of the cosmos he is brought into the presence of God, where he is identified and commissioned as the future judge and the protagonist of the action he had previously witnessed. That this commissioning should take place after his final rather than his first ascent to heaven makes perfect sense. For this reason, all other things being equal (which they never are), I might accept this last chapter as the climax of the original book if it were not for the first-person rhetoric that conflicts with the expected third-person rhetoric of 70:1-2.

## Reconstructing the Early Shape of the Book of Parables

On the basis of my analysis I propose that the earliest recoverable form of the Book of Parables was roughly as follows, leaving open the question as to what

---

23. Knibb, "Translation of 1 Enoch 70:1," 341.

has dropped out at the end between 63:12 and 69:26-29, and what its arrangement may have been:

| Introduction | chap. 37 |
| Parable 1 | chaps. 38–44 |
| Parable 2 | 45:1–54:6; 56:1-4 |
| Parable 3 | 58:1–59:3; 60:11-22; 61:1–63:12; 64:1-2; 69:2-12, 26-29 |
| Conclusion | 70:1-2 |

The theme of the Parables is the coming judgment that would punish the kings and the mighty as well as Azazel and his hosts, both of whom had preyed on humanity. The agent of this judgment would be "the Righteous One," "son of man," "Chosen One," "Anointed One." In creating his book, the author of the Parables drew, first of all, on traditional Enochic material from the Book of the Watchers and a source like the Astronomical Book,[24] following to some extent the order of the Book of the Watchers. In addition, he reworked non-Enochic (traditional interpretations of) biblical material about the Danielic son of man, the Davidic Anointed One (Ps 2 and Isa 11), and the Servant/Chosen One/Righteous One of Second Isaiah, and perhaps material about preexistent Wisdom.

Each of the three parables began with an oracular introduction and then featured scenes that take place in heaven, interlaced with accounts of Enoch's cosmic journeys, both in heaven and over the face of the earth. The heavenly scenes focus on the developing drama of the judgment over which the Chosen One will preside. First it is announced that "the Righteous One" will appear and then Enoch sees him in his dwelling place (parable 1). Then Enoch sees him with the deity, hears about his future functions, hears the intercession of the angels, and witnesses the convocation of the heavenly court and the commissioning of the Chosen One (parable 2). Finally, he views the enthronement of the Chosen One and the process of judgment that results in the blessedness of the righteous and, especially, the condemnation of the kings and the mighty, but also of Azazel and his hosts (parable 3). The developing drama is held together by a series of anticipatory allusions to the judgment, which are added to the descriptions of Enoch's visions.

There is a striking feature of this text that should not be overlooked. As I indicated earlier, seen from one point of view, the first two parables rewrite sections of the Enochic Book of the Watchers. Thus a partisan of the Enochic tradition would, to a degree, have felt at home in this text. However, by drawing

---

24. For the problem of identifying this source with the Astronomical Book, see below, James C. VanderKam, "The Book of Parables within the Enoch Tradition."

## Discerning the Structure(s) of the Enochic Book of Parables

other material from his religious tradition (i.e., from parts of what we call the Hebrew Bible), he has given this material a sort of Enochic "baptism." The remarkable conflated figure of biblical prophecy is authenticated by a claim of primordial Enochic revelation. This transformation of the older "biblical" material and its incorporation into an Enochic revelation, however, is not a new phenomenon. The Book of the Watchers and the Animal Apocalypse, to cite the most obvious examples, have done the same thing.[25]

## The Noachic Redaction of the Book of Parables

Following long-standing scholarly tradition, I have proposed a series of Noachic interpolations into the earliest text of the Book of Parables. Such a Noachic redaction is not surprising since the earlier Enochic traditions were associated with Noah and the flood in a variety of ways. The earliest stratum in the Book of the Watchers (1 En 6–11) is an eschatologized interpretation of Gen 6:1-4 and its Noachic context in Gen 6–9.[26] In Enoch's Dream Visions, chaps. 83–84 feature his dream about the coming flood, and the Animal Apocalypse (chaps. 85–90) contains a section about the flood that reflects chaps. 6–11 (89:1-9). The form of the Enochic corpus preserved in one Qumran manuscript (4QEnᶜ) and in a Greek manuscript of the last chapters provides early evidence for the end of the Ethiopic collection, with its account of Noah's birth that parallels 1 En 65:1-12. Since all these traditions state or imply a typology of flood and final judgment, it is understandable that a redactor would interpolate Noachic materials into the Book of Parables with its heavy emphasis on the final judgment.

The order of these interpolations and their placement may not be haphazard. The first (54:7–55:2/4) is a summary prediction of the flood and God's subsequent promise not to repeat this judgment against humanity, and it is juxtaposed with an account of the angels' punishment. In the second (60:1-10, 24-25), Noah is granted a vision of the heavenly court in session and is told about the coming judgment. The passage follows Enoch's astronomical revelations (a reverse order from the first parable) and is juxtaposed with other material about events related to the coming judgment. In the third interpolation (65:1–66:3), Noah experiences the quaking of the earth that precedes the coming judgment, and some of Enoch's revelation relates to material about the rebel angels in the second parable. In the fourth interpolation (67:1–68:1), after Noah

---

25. On the use of Scripture in 1 Enoch, see in summary Nickelsburg, *1 Enoch 1*, 57-58.
26. Nickelsburg, *1 Enoch 1*, 166-68.

has left the presence of Enoch, he receives a prophetic revelation, in which "the word of God" comes to him and informs him that the angels are preparing the ark and that he will survive the flood. Attached to this is a final vision, which builds again on material in the second parable, and in which Noah sees in detail the punishment that awaits the angels.

The provenance of the redaction is uncertain. The comment in 1 En 68:1 is suggestive. It attests a written or oral Noachic tradition that depicted the patriarch as the recipient of the Book of Parables. According to the Astronomical Book, Methuselah was the recipient of *that* book, and in 82:1-2 Enoch directs Methuselah to transmit his writings to his grandchildren and beyond. In the present case, it might be helpful if one could clarify the relationships among the stories in 65:1-12, 83–84, and 106–107. In any case, the redaction of the book reflects its ongoing life among Jews who found authority in traditions thought to have derived from Enoch and his descendants.

## Enoch as the Son of Man (1 Enoch 71): Anti-Christian or Just Jewish?

It has been maintained that 1 En 71 is a Jewish polemic against the Christian appropriation of the son of man tradition for Jesus of Nazareth. It is a fascinating possibility, but not the only one. The section may be part of a Noachic redaction. The final commissioning of Enoch as son of man is a natural extension of 1 En 14–15, based on a typology between the ancient judgment of the watchers (not explicitly the flood) and the final judgment over which the son of man/Chosen One would preside. In addition, we should note that both 2 Enoch and so-called 3 Enoch witness to the gradual glorification of the figure of Enoch and the extension of his roles. The "high Enochology" of 2 Enoch is not that far removed from the exaltation of the patriarch in 1 En 71.[27] At this point we are indulging in speculation, but further study of all the texts will prove fruitful to an understanding of the ongoing role of the figure of Enoch in Jewish theology and piety.

## Positing Sources Where There Were None

Although I have argued for the literary integrity and even artistic composition of what I consider to have been the earliest recoverable form of the Book of Parables,

---

27. A. Orlov, *The Enoch-Metatron Tradition*, TSAJ 107 (Tübingen: Mohr-Siebeck, 2005), 148-206; G. W. E. Nickelsburg, *Jewish Literature between the Bible and the Mishnah*, rev. ed. (Minneapolis: Fortress, 2005), 225.

this work as reconstructed was by no means cut from whole cloth. Rather the author has created a coat of many pieces, a pastiche of earlier traditions, drawing here on the Book of the Watchers, and using or elaborating on material like that in the Astronomical Book, and developing traditions from Daniel and the prophets. Having said that, I am suspicious of theories based on the different names for the deity or the agent of judgment. On the latter, it seems better to recognize that "son of man" derived from Dan 7, the "Anointed One" from Ps 2:2, and "the Chosen One" and "the Righteous One" from Second Isaiah, and to posit that the author of the Parables used these terms where they were appropriate to the biblical sources, and that elsewhere he alternated them where he saw fit.

## Redaction and the Dating of the Parables

I have argued elsewhere that the Book of Parables is to be dated no later than the early decades of the first century C.E. on the grounds that Mark, the Q source, and the apostle Paul knew a form of the son of man tradition that we find in the Parables but not in Dan 7.[28] Because I believe that this tradition is paralleled by a traditional interpretation of Isa 52–53 also found in the Wisdom of Solomon (early first century C.E.?), I have been cautious to allow that the Gospels and their sources could have known the son of man traditions in other than their Enochic form. I am skeptical, however — for two reasons. First, the Wisdom of Solomon seems to know parts of the Enochic tradition and allows a special place for the figure of Enoch.[29] Second, one of the son of man sayings in the Q sources draws a parallel between the days of the son of man and the days of Noah, which brings us to the Enochic typology mentioned before.[30] While it is possible that the author of that saying was aware of the Noachic elements in the earlier strata of 1 Enoch, it is simpler to suppose that the author knew the Parables in a Noachic redactional form of the book. This might push the composition of the book back a bit in the first century. There is perhaps further corroboration for this in the commonly held belief that 1 En 67:4-13 alludes to Herod the Great's retreat to the baths of Callirrhoe.[31] This might place the Noachic redaction of the Parables at a time during the late first century B.C.E. or the early first century C.E. when Herod's last days were still alive in the memory.

---

28. G. W. E. Nickelsburg, "Son of Man," in *ABD* 6 (1992), 138-49.
29. Nickelsburg, *1 Enoch 1*, 78-79.
30. Matt 24:26-27, 37-39//Luke 17:22-37. See Nickelsburg, "Son of Man," 142.
31. J. C. Greenfield and M. E. Stone, "The Enochic Pentateuch and the Date of the Similitudes," *HTR* 70 (1977): 51-65 (here 60). See also, below, D. Hannah, "The Book of Noah, the Death of Herod the Great, and the Date of the Parables of Enoch."

# The Structure and Composition of the Parables of Enoch

*Michael A. Knibb*

The Book of Parables *(maṣḥaf zamesale)*, the title used in 1 En 68:1 for chaps. 37–71 (or for an earlier version of this section), appears at first sight to have a simple structure and literary form. The overarching genre of the text is that of a report of an otherworldly journey, and the material, after an introduction (chap. 37), is clearly divided by headings and colophons[1] into three "parables" (38:1–44:1; 45:1–57:3; 58:1–69:25). Chaps. 70–71, which bring the section to a conclusion, then describe Enoch's ascent to heaven and identification as Son of Man. So much is obvious, but closer inspection suggests that the structure and literary form of the Book of Parables are not quite so straightforward.

The Book of Parables forms some of the latest material to be included in the Ethiopic Book of Enoch, and it is apparent that the authors drew their inspiration from the sections of 1 Enoch that were already in existence, particularly the Book of the Watchers, on which the Book of Parables to some extent seems consciously modeled. The text is headed "The second vision which he saw,"[2] and this suggests that the Book of Parables was intended as a continuation of the previous "vision" that Enoch had seen (cf. 1:2).[3] More particularly, the use of the term "parable" *(mesale)* to describe the contents of this section (see 37:5; 38:1; 45:1; 57:3; 58:1;

---

1. There is no colophon at the end of the first parable (chap. 44).

2. Cf. 1 En 39:4, "and there I saw another vision."

3. Josef Milik speaks of a contrast with the "first vision," but identifies the "first vision" with "the whole collection of revelations contained in the Aramaic and Greek Enochic Pentateuch in two volumes: the Book of the Watchers, the Book of Giants, the Book of Dreams, the Epistle of Enoch in the first volume, and the Astronomical Book in the second volume." See J. T. Milik, *The Books of Enoch: Aramaic Fragments of Qumrân Cave 4* (Oxford: Clarendon, 1976), 89.

*The Structure and Composition of the Parables of Enoch*

69:29) seems to have its obvious point of reference in 1:2,[4] although a wider background for its use is provided by the occurrence of the Hebrew term *mashal* in the Balaam narratives (cf., e.g., Num 23:7, 18) and in prophetic texts (cf., e.g., Ezek 17:2; 20:49; Mic 2:4). In relation to content, there are frequent references in the Parables to the story of the Watchers, whose punishment at the final judgment is associated with that of "the kings and the mighty," the opponents of the group that lies behind the Book of Parables. Above all, although the first parable reports, as if it were a new event, that clouds and a storm wind carried Enoch off to heaven (39:3; cf. 52:1), Enoch's journey around the heavenly regions and the cosmos is effectively presented as a continuation of the journey described in the second half of the Book of the Watchers (chaps. 17–36).[5] Thus the literary form of the Book of Parables continues that of the Book of the Watchers.

The account of Enoch's otherworldly journey in chaps. 17–36, which follows, without an introduction, immediately on the account of Enoch's ascent to heaven in 14:8–16:4, is characterized by repeated references to the movement of Enoch around heaven and by descriptions of the sights he sees. The narrative refers frequently to Enoch going,[6] or being taken,[7] to a different place and contains frequent descriptions of what he saw that are introduced by the phrases "and I saw (there)"[8] or "and he showed me."[9] But in addition to the widespread use of verbs referring to movement and to visionary experience, some of the individual units of which the narrative is composed have a common form,[10] which is illustrated by chap. 23: Enoch reports that he went to another place (23:1); he describes what he sees (23:2); he asks the angel who accompanies him to explain the significance of what he has seen (23:3); the angel gives him an explanation (23:4). In practice, most of the examples are more complex than this, but the fourfold pattern, notwithstanding all the variation, is used repeatedly in chaps. 17–36, and particularly in 21–36.[11]

---

4. In the Aramaic and the Greek, but not in the Ethiopic.

5. The return of Enoch to earth is not reported until the end of the Astronomical Book (81:5-10).

6. 1 En 17:5; 18:6; 21:1, 7; 22:1; 23:1; 24:1; 26:1; 28:1; 29:1; 30:3; 32:2-3; 33:1; 34:1; 35; 36:1, 2. See also 14:9, 10, 13, 25.

7. 1 En 17:1, 2, 4.

8. 1 En 17:3, 6, 7, 8; 18:1 (bis), 2 (bis), 3, 4, 5 (ter), 9, 10, 11 (bis), 12, 13; 19:3; 21:2, 3, 7 (ter); 22:5; 23:2; 24:2; 26:1, 2, 3; 28:1; 29:2; 30:1, 2, 3; 31:1, 2; 32:1, 3; 33:1, 2, 3; 34:1, 2; 35; 36:1, 2, 4; cf. 23:4; 25:3. See also 14:14, 18.

9. 1 En 22:1; 24:1; 33:3, 4.

10. Cf. M.-T. Wacker, *Weltordnung und Gericht: Studien zu 1 Henoch 22*, FB 45 (Würzburg: Echter Verlag, 1982), 101-2; G. W. E. Nickelsburg, *1 Enoch 1: A Commentary on the Book of 1 Enoch 1–36, 81–108*, vol. 1, Hermeneia (Minneapolis: Fortress, 2001), 291.

11. See 1 En 18:9b–19:2; 21:1-6; 21:7-10; 22:1-4, 5-7, 8-14; 23:1-4; 24:1–25:7; 26:1–27:5; 32:2-6.

Michael A. Knibb

The Book of Parables, as has been suggested, effectively represents a continuation of the otherworldly journey described in the Book of the Watchers, but its literary form differs in some respects from that of the latter work. Thus, although the Book of Parables clearly has the form of an otherworldly journey, it is somewhat surprising that there are virtually no explicit references, of the kind familiar from the Book of the Watchers, to Enoch moving from one place to another. In 39:3 it is said that clouds and a storm wind carried Enoch off from the earth and set him down at the end of heaven; in 52:1 that Enoch had been carried off by a whirlwind and brought to the west; and in 54:1 that Enoch "looked and turned to another part of the earth, and . . . saw there." But apart from these passages, Enoch is not explicitly said to journey to a new location, although at times it must be assumed that he does. This difference between the Book of the Watchers and the Book of Parables is no doubt linked to the different character of the two sections. In the former there is a definite narrative thread, in the latter, or at least in the core material, there is little movement (in the literary sense), and the material consists of a series of descriptions of scenes that present essentially the same events and the same themes — the enthronement of the Chosen One/Son of Man, the judgment of the wicked, the salvation of the righteous — from slightly different perspectives.

Some of the material in the Parables, like that in chaps. 17–36, consists of descriptions of what Enoch had seen that are introduced by the phrases "And (there) I saw"[12] or "And there my eyes saw"[13] (or variants of these); occasionally there are also descriptions of what Enoch had heard.[14] Again in a similar way to what applies in 17–36, in some cases these descriptions of visions have been expanded in a stereotyped way by a question from Enoch and an answer from an angel, for example, in chap. 46: Enoch describes what he sees (46:1); he asks one of the angels who accompanies him to explain the significance of what he has seen (46:2); the angel provides an explanation (46:3-8). This threefold pattern is used in eight passages (40:1-10; 43:1-4; 46:1-8; 52:1-9; 53:1-7; 54:1-6 + 55:3-4; 56:1-4; 61:1-5) that are concerned with the central themes of the Parables: the glory of the Lord of Spirits, the judgment of the Son of Man, the punishment of the kings and the mighty and the Watchers, the salvation of the righteous, and cosmic phenomena.

Although there are no accounts of otherworldly journeys in the Hebrew

12. First parable: 39:4, 7; 40:1, 2 ("I looked, and . . . I saw"); 41:1, 2, 3, 4, 5; 43:1 (bis), 2; second parable: 46:1; 47:3; 48:1; 52:1 ("in that place where I had seen"); 53:3 ("For I saw"); 54:1 ("And I looked and turned . . . and I saw"); 56:1; third parable: 59:2, 3 ("all the secrets . . . were shown to me"); 61:1; 64:1; 67:5.

13. First parable: 39:5, 6, 13: 41:2, 3; second parable: 52:2; 53:1; 54:3; third parable: 59:1.

14. First parable: 40:3, 5, 6, 7; second parable: 57:2; third parable: 67:12.

## The Structure and Composition of the Parables of Enoch

Bible, the background to the use of this genre in the Ethiopic Book of Enoch is to be found in the vision reports of the prophetic literature, and particularly in the two great vision reports preserved in chaps. 8–11 and 40–48 of the book of Ezekiel. Both sections of the book are composite, and in both a core, consisting maximally of 8:1–10:22 + 11:22-25 on the one hand, and of 40:1–43:12 + 44:1-2 + 47:1-12 on the other, has been expanded by later material that is different in character.[15] In both the hand of YHWH comes upon Ezekiel and brings him "in visions of God" to Jerusalem. In both Ezekiel is led about (see 8:7, 14, 16; 40:17, 24, 28, and frequently), and indeed the core vision that forms the basis of chaps. 40–48 was described by Zimmerli as a "guidance vision."[16] In both cases Ezekiel describes what he has been shown, in the first vision the sin of Jerusalem and its destruction, and the departure of YHWH, in the second the new Jerusalem and the return of YHWH. In chaps. 8–11 there are frequent occurrences of the verb "to see," and although this is not the case in 40–48, the section begins with the command to the prophet: "Mortal, look closely and listen attentively, and set your mind upon all that I shall show you, for you were brought here in order that I might show it to you; declare all that you see to the house of Israel" (40:4). The prophet does not ask questions about the significance of what he sees, but in the second vision there are occasional brief explanatory comments from Ezekiel's angelic guide (see 40:45-46; 41:4, 22; 42:13-14; 47:8-12) as well as two speeches by YHWH (43:7-9; 44:2).

The accounts of the two visions in which Ezekiel is carried by the hand of YHWH to Jerusalem offer the closest parallel in the Hebrew Bible to the literary genre of the otherworldly journey. However, the cycle of eight visions preserved in Zech 1–6 is also of some relevance as background in that the question and answer format that is lacking in Ezek 8–11 and 40–48 does appear in Zechariah.[17] With only one exception,[18] the brief report of each vision that Zechariah sees or is shown is followed by a request for an explanation of its significance and by an explanatory comment from "the angel who talked with" Zechariah. The pattern is present in its simplest form in 2:1-2 or 2:3-4 (Eng. 1:18-19, 20-21), but in most cases either the vision report itself or the explanation has been elaborated with further material.

---

15. Cf. W. Zimmerli, *Ezechiel,* 2 vols., BKAT XIII/1-2 (Neukirchen-Vluyn: Neukirchener Verlag, 1969), 1:201-6, 241; 2:977-80, 990-93, 1073-76, 1108-10, 1190-91, 1240-43 (ET, *Ezekiel 1,* Hermeneia [Philadelphia: Fortress, 1979], 230-34, 256; *Ezekiel 2,* Hermeneia [Philadelphia: Fortress, 1983], 327-29, 342-44, 411-13, 439-40, 508-10, 547-49).

16. See, e.g., Zimmerli, *Ezechiel,* 2:992, 1074 (ET, *Ezekiel 2,* 344, 411).

17. Wacker (*Weltordnung,* 292-94) has drawn attention to the parallels between Zech 1–6 and 1 En 21–33.

18. See Zech 3.

If a significant part of the content of the Book of Parables is cast in the form of accounts of visions, it is nonetheless the case that much of the material does not have this form. Two groups of passages in particular deserve attention. Firstly there is a series of descriptive statements concerning the enthronement of the Son of Man and the events connected with the judgment that are loosely attached to the material in visionary form, and the following passages belong in this category: 1 En 47:1-2; 48:2-7, 8-10; 49:1-4; 50:1-5; 51:1-2, 3, 4-5; 61:6-13; 62:1-16; 63:1-12. These passages are often linked to what precedes by the introductory formula "(And) in those days" that is familiar from the prophetic literature; this formula is also widely used in other contexts in the Book of Parables as a connecting device.

Secondly, there is a group of passages, partly narrative in form, that is concerned with the story of Noah and may have been taken from a preexistent book of Noah: 1 En 54:7–55:2, 60:1-25, 65:1–67:3. The Noah story has a typological function in 1 Enoch, but inasmuch as the Noah passages in the Parables do not fit naturally into their context, the question is inevitably raised as to the extent to which they are integral to the Parables. It is in any case clear that the Noah passages have attracted secondary material to themselves (for example, 60:11-23 within 60:1-25). In addition, a number of passages throughout the Book of Parables interrupt the natural sequence of the text and appear to be secondary, for example, 42:1-3 and 54:7–55:2.[19]

In the light of these general comments on the structure of the Book of Parables, I would like in what follows to consider its structure in a little more detail. One difficulty in undertaking this task should be recognized immediately, namely, that in contrast to the situation in other sections of 1 Enoch, we have only one version of the Parables, the version that the book possesses in the context of the Ethiopic Book of Enoch. We have no other version with which to compare the text, and thus any views about the structure and the composition of the Book of Parables can be based only on internal criteria.

For the purposes of what follows, I assume that the Book of Parables dates from either the end of the first century B.C.E.[20] or the end of the first century C.E.[21]

---

19. I take for granted the view that, notwithstanding the presence of some secondary material, the Book of Parables is to be regarded essentially as a unity. For a critical discussion of the two-source theory of composition advocated by Beer and Charles, see E. Sjöberg, *Der Menschensohn im äthiopischen Henochbuch*, Skrifter Utgivna av Kungl. Humanistika Vetenskapssamfundet i Lund 41 (Lund: Gleerup, 1946), 24-33.

20. Cf. G. W. E. Nickelsburg, *Jewish Literature between the Bible and the Mishnah* (Philadelphia: Fortress, 1981), 221-23; Nickelsburg, *1 Enoch 1*, 7.

21. Cf. M. A. Knibb, "The Date of the Parables of Enoch: A Critical Review," *NTS* 25 (1979): 345-59.

## Introduction (chap. 37)

The words with which the Book of Parables begins, "the second vision which he saw," present the Parables as the continuation of the Book of the Watchers, as we have seen, and were no doubt intended to facilitate the integration of the Parables into the Enochic corpus. The words that follow immediately, "the vision of wisdom which Enoch saw" (37:1), may have constituted the original title of the Book of Parables. The reference to wisdom, together with the use of wisdom terminology to describe the content of the revelation given by Enoch (see 37:2-4), is a reflection of the sapiential connections of the Parables and of the Enochic writings generally.[22]

## The First Parable (chaps. 38–44)

Each of the three parables begins with a short introductory speech spoken by Enoch,[23] in which the fate of the sinners and the righteous is foretold. The first parable begins with such a speech (38:1–39:2), and with a description of the carrying of Enoch up to heaven (39:3), and then consists of a series of vision reports that are typical of the genre of the otherworldly journey. Secondary material is relatively limited and is perhaps confined to 39:1-2a and chap. 42.

The introductory speech uses a rhetorical question — When the sinners are judged and salvation appears for the righteous, where will the dwelling of the sinners be (38:2)? — to affirm the coming judgment of the sinners and the destruction of the kings and the mighty (38:1–39:2). It thus serves to introduce one of the key themes of the Book of Parables. However, 39:1-2a breaks the connection between 38:6 and 39:2b and is widely regarded as an interpolation. The passage appears to be a fragment or a summary of the story of the Watchers, and it may be that Charles was right that the tenses in v. 1 have been adapted to their context and that at one stage the reference was to the past, not the future;[24] as such the story might offer an explanation for the behavior of the kings

---

22. Cf. M. A. Knibb, "The Book of Enoch in the Light of the Qumran Wisdom Literature," in *Wisdom and Apocalypticism in the Dead Sea Scrolls and in the Biblical Tradition*, ed. F. García Martínez, BETL 168 (Leuven: Leuven University Press and Peeters, 2003), 193-210.

23. Cf. Sjöberg, *Der Menschensohn im äthiopischen Henochbuch*, 31. In the second parable the introductory speech (chap. 45) becomes, from v. 3, a speech of God.

24. R. H. Charles, *The Book of Enoch*, 2nd ed. (Oxford: Clarendon, 1912), 74. As the Ethiopic text stands, the sequence *wayəkawwən . . . wayəwarrədu*, which comes at the end of a string of prefix tenses referring to the future (1 En 38:3-6), is most naturally translated with reference to the future: "And it will come to pass that . . . (they) will come down."

and the mighty. It may also be wondered whether 39:1-2a was originally a marginal comment intended to explain the origin of the Book of Parables in which the "books" were understood as a reference to the Parables.

The first two vision reports (39:4-14; 40:1-10) are related in that both are concerned to describe scenes in heaven, the former the dwelling of the righteous (39:4) and of the Chosen One (39:6) in heaven, the latter the divine throne room in which the heavenly hosts, and particularly the four archangels, stand before the Lord of Spirits. We may note, by way of example, the repeated use of verbs of seeing and hearing (39:4, 5, 6, 7, 13; 40:1, 2, 3-7), the use of question-and-answer in the second vision report, and the clear markers at the end of each scene (39:14; 40:10). The concern with the "dwelling" of the righteous provides a contrast with the concern with the future "dwelling" of the sinners (38:2). The attention paid to the role of the four archangels (chap. 40) perhaps reflects the influence of the Book of the Watchers (chaps. 9–10), although the name "Phanuel" (40:9) is not used there.

Chaps. 41–44 consist of a series of vision reports (41:1-9; 43:1-4;[25] 44) that are primarily concerned with astronomical and meteorological phenomena and as such are reminiscent of similar accounts in the Book of the Watchers (17:1–18:5; 33–36). As in the older material, one of the functions of these passages may be to present Enoch as the one who has knowledge of everything,[26] while the allusion to the obedience and regularity of the sun and moon to their prescribed course (41:5; cf. 43:2) is reminiscent of the stress on this theme in 2:1–5:4. However, linked to the concern with the sun, moon, and stars, and with meteorological phenomena, is a concern with mankind, and with the division between the righteous and the sinners (41:1-2, 8), and the stars of heaven, which symbolize the angelic host, are in a mysterious way connected with the righteous (43:4); the weighing of the stars (43:2) is perhaps to be linked to the "weighing" of the deeds of men (41:1). The connection between the realm of the stars and that of human beings may thus provide the explanation for the abrupt transitions in this passage — as they at first sight appear to be — that have led some scholars to question its integrity.[27]

---

25. In chap. 41 the vision report is expanded by comment from Enoch (vv. 6-9), in chap. 43 by a question from Enoch and explanation from the angel (vv. 3-4).

26. Cf. M. A. Knibb, "The Use of Scripture in 1 Enoch 17–19," in *Jerusalem, Alexandria, Rome: Studies in Ancient Cultural Interaction in Honour of A. Hilhorst*, ed. F. García Martínez and G. P. Luttikhuizen, SJSJ 82 (Leiden: Brill, 2003), 165-78 (here 171-73).

27. R. H. Charles, for example, argued that 1 En 41:3-9 is alien to its context, and that 41:9 should be read directly after 41:2; and S. Uhlig questions the relationship between 41:1-2 and 41:3-9. See Charles, *The Book of Enoch*, 79, 81; and S. Uhlig, "Das Äthiopische Henochbuch," in *JSHRZ* V.6 (Gütersloh: Gütersloher Verlagshaus Gerd Mohn, 1984), 582.

*The Structure and Composition of the Parables of Enoch*

However, chap. 42, the passage concerning the unsuccessful attempt of wisdom to dwell amongst mankind, does interrupt the natural sequence of the text and is widely regarded as misplaced. As the text stands, the passage presents the presence of wisdom in heaven on the same level as the other "secrets of heaven" (41:1) seen by Enoch.[28] But it also serves to offer an explanation of the presence of sin in the world (cf. 41:8).

## The Second Parable (chaps. 45–57)[29]

After the introductory speech (45:1-6), the second parable divides into two parts: in chaps. 46–51 there is a series of vision reports and descriptive statements concerning the Son of Man and the events connected with the judgment; in 52:1–56:4 there is a series of vision reports concerning the punishment of the sinners in which the influence of the Book of the Watchers may be detected. However, 54:7–55:2 is a Noah fragment and appears to be secondary, and 56:5–57:3a likewise may be secondary.

Three interrelated themes are touched on in the introductory speech (chap. 45): the judgment and punishment of "the sinners who deny the name of the Lord of Spirits" (v. 2); the blessed fate that awaits God's chosen ones; and the role of the individual, called in this chapter "Chosen One" and elsewhere "Son of Man," as eschatological judge. These themes are dominant throughout the second parable and hold its diverse contents together. However, there is an abrupt transition between 45:1-2 (apparently the words of Enoch) and 45:3-6 (the words of God), and it may well be that originally separate pieces of material have been brought together in chap. 45.

Chaps. 46–51 form a loosely linked sequence of passages that consist of descriptions of scenes in heaven and revolve around the three themes just mentioned; the passages are linked together only by the repeated use of the formula "And in those days" (47:1, 2, 3; 48:8; 50:1; 51:1, 3, 4). The basis (chap. 46) is a report of a vision of the Head of Days and the Son of Man that is manifestly based on the Son of Man vision of Dan 7 (see vv. 9-10, 13-14); it is presented in

---

28. Cf. Matthew Black, *The Book of Enoch, or, I Enoch: A New English Edition with Commentary and Textual Notes,* SVTP 7 (Leiden: Brill, 1985), 203; A. Caquot, "I Hénoch," in *La Bible: Écrits intertestamentaires,* ed. A. Dupont-Sommer and M. Philonenko, Bibliothèque de la Pléiade (Paris: Gallimard, 1987), 463-625 (here 512).

29. Elsewhere I have provided a brief commentary on chaps. 45–51: see M. A. Knibb, "The Ethiopic Book of Enoch," in *Outside the Old Testament,* ed. M. de Jonge, Cambridge Commentaries on Writings of the Jewish and Christian World, 200 BC to AD 200, 4 (Cambridge: Cambridge University Press, 1985), 26-55 (here 43-55).

the threefold pattern of description, question, and explanation, but it is the explanation from the angel (vv. 3-8), which describes the role of the Son of Man as eschatological judge, on which the emphasis falls.

Two further passages (47:3-4; 48:1-10) are presented as vision reports and are concerned with the Head of Days and the Son of Man. The first of these is prefaced by a comment (47:1-2) that serves to introduce a new theme — the cry for vengeance of innocent blood that has been shed — but, as the text stands, the comment continues the speech of the angel from the previous chapter. The second passage begins as a description of a vision, but from v. 3 onward becomes a statement about the attributes and functions of the Son of Man (48:3-7) and about the judgment of the kings of the earth (48:8-10). The final words of 48:10 ("May the name of the Lord of Spirits be blessed!") form a conclusion, but attached to the three vision reports is a series of statements (chaps. 49–51) that are concerned with essentially the same themes as the vision reports: the attributes and role of the Chosen One, the judgment of the sinners, the salvation of the righteous. However, some inconsistencies of viewpoint in chap. 50 (the opportunity for repentance; the role of God as judge) underline the looseness of the structure.[30]

The opening words of chap. 52 ("And after those days, in that place where I had seen all the visions of that which is secret — for I had been carried off by a whirlwind, and they had brought me to the west") clearly mark a new beginning. The following section consists of four interrelated vision reports (52:1-9; 53:1-7; 54:1-6 + 55:3-4; 56:1-4) that are all structured in the threefold pattern of description, question, explanation, and all reveal the influence of the Book of the Watchers. However, the text does raise a number of problems.

The allusion in chap. 52 to the mountains of metal in the west that serve the authority of God's messiah (v. 4) and will melt like wax before the Chosen One (v. 6) seems to have been influenced by the tradition of the seven mountains of precious stones in the northwest (18:6-9a; 24:1-3; 25:1-3), the middle one of which is the throne on which God will sit when he comes to visit the earth. However, this tradition has been transformed by its association with the tradition, familiar from theophanic passages, of the melting of the mountains at the coming of God (Mic 1:4; Ps 97:5; cf. Nah 1:5; Judg 5:4). It has further been transformed by its combination with the theme of the metals, which are no doubt to be seen, as in Dan 2:31-45, as representative of a succession of world empires. Vv. 7-9, which are introduced by "And it will come to pass in those days" and draw in v. 7 on Zeph 1:18, offer additional comment on the metals and may be secondary.

Chaps. 53 and 54 both refer to valleys that are connected with the judg-

---

30. Cf. Charles, *The Book of Enoch*, 97; Uhlig, "Das Äthiopische Henochbuch," 592-93.

ment and punishment of the kings and the powerful: in the former, apparently situated in the west near the mountains of metal[31] and to which mankind bring gifts for God, angels are preparing instruments to punish the kings and the powerful; in the latter, a burning valley situated in another part of the earth and into which the kings and the powerful are thrown, angels are making chain instruments for the hosts of Azazel who are to be thrown into the lowest part of hell. The association of the punishment of the kings and the powerful with that of the hosts of Azazel may be noted. The former valley is commonly identified with the valley of Jehoshaphat, where according to Joel 4:2, 12 (Eng. 3:2, 12) God will enter into judgment with the Gentiles, and insofar as the kings and the powerful are foreign oppressors, this identification may be right. The latter valley (chap. 54) is commonly identified with Gehenna (cf. 26:4; 27:1-3), and this is surely correct. But the passage reflects the influence of the reference in 18:11a (cf. 21:7-10) to a deep chasm full of fire at the foot of the seven mountains, and it is apparent that this valley serves as the place of punishment both for the kings and the powerful (54:2) and for the hosts of Azazel (54:5). However, the account breaks off in v. 6 and is apparently resumed in 55:3-4 (note the references to Azazel and his hosts in 54:5-6 and 55:4). The text of the beginning of 55:3-4 appears to be in some disorder, and in any case the passage is in the form of a speech of God for which there is no introduction in 54:1-6, but which continues the speech of God in 55:1-2. It is possible that some material has been lost through the insertion of the Noah fragment (54:7–55:2).

In the fourth and final vision of the sequence (56:1-4), Enoch sees angels preparing chains for the "beloved ones," that is, the offspring of the Watchers (cf. 10:12; 14:6), to throw them into "the chasm in the depths of the valley," by which the valley described in 54:1-6 is no doubt meant.

As the text stands, the sequence of four vision reports is interrupted by a fragment of the Noah story introduced by the formula "And in those days" (54:7–55:2). As elsewhere in 1 Enoch, the story of the flood followed by the divine promise of blessing has a typological function, and this was no doubt the reason for its inclusion here. Black questions the view that 54:7–55:2 is an interpolation and argues that the Parables follows the same pattern as the Book of the Watchers, in which "the account at En. 8.1–9.11 of the condemnation of the watchers [is] followed at 10.2 by an account of the deluge."[32] However, 54:7–55:2 is introduced so abruptly and seems so out of context in the sequence of visions that it is difficult not to think that it was inserted at a secondary stage.

---

31. The reference to the mountains in 1 En 53:7 indicates that chap. 53 presupposes chap. 52.

32. Black, *The Book of Enoch*, 219.

Michael A. Knibb

The final passage in the second parable (56:5–57:3a), introduced by "And in those days," takes up ideas concerning the end of the present age that are familiar from the prophetic writings: the last great assault of the Gentiles on the land of Israel (cf. Ezek 38–39), their unsuccessful attack on Zion and their destruction, and the return of the exiles to the land. The passage begins as prophetic speech, but from 57:1 becomes a report of a vision. The picture presented here of the events at the end is so out of character with the view of the rest of the Book of Parables that the passage would appear at the very least to have been taken over from elsewhere and may well have been added at a secondary stage.[33]

## The Third Parable (chaps. 58–69)

The structure of the third parable is the most complex of the three and raises the most questions about the originality of the material. The core of the parable consists of an introductory speech from Enoch (chap. 58); two vision reports (59:1-3; 61:1-5), to the second of which a series of statements concerning the enthronement of the Chosen One and the judgment of the kings and the mighty has been attached (61:6–63:12); and a concluding statement (69:26-29). All this material fits in with the ideas reflected in other parts of the Book of Parables. But the third parable also includes two substantial passages relating to the figure of Noah (60:1-25; 65:1–67:3), as well as other material (64:1-2; 67:4–69:25), and it seems clear that some at least of this has been added at a second stage.

The third parable is said at the beginning of the introductory speech to be about the righteous and the chosen (58:1), and in the remainder of the speech the author through the mouth of Enoch describes the blessed life that the righteous will enjoy (58:2-6). In practice the parable is as much about the judgment and punishment of the kings and the mighty.

The immediately following passage (59:1-3), which is presented in the form of a vision report, is concerned with the secrets of the lightning and thunder. Such a concern with meteorological phenomena is consonant with the similar concern in the first parable (chaps. 41–44) and is reminiscent of similar material in the Book of the Watchers (cf. particularly 17:3), but we may wonder why this passage was placed at the very beginning of the third parable, unless it was in the context of presenting Enoch as the one who had knowledge of all

---

33. Cf. Charles, *The Book of Enoch*, 109; Knibb, "The Date," 355. It is because the views expressed in 1 En 54:7–55:2 seem so out of character with those of the rest of the Book of Parables that it seems to me hazardous to try to hang the date of the Parables on this passage.

things to do with the heavenly realm.[34] This passage (59:1-3) may be linked with a much more extensive passage in the following chapter (60:11-23) concerned with the secrets of the cosmos, which interrupts the sequence of the text and seems to have been inserted at a secondary stage. Although it stands in the middle of a passage that belongs to a Noah tradition, it seems to be Enochic material and describes what Enoch was "shown" by the angel who went with him (60:11), what he "saw" near the Garden of Righteousness (60:23). It may have been the reference to "what is secret" in both vv. 10 and 11 that led to the insertion of 60:11-23 in its present position.

Chap. 60, which describes how Enoch was overwhelmed by the shaking of the heavens, has long been recognized as originally a Noah tradition. But Black is undoubtedly right that the person who placed it here intended it to be taken as a tradition about Enoch,[35] and the judgment that is symbolized by the quaking of heaven is not that of the flood, but of the last judgment. It is thus difficult to say whether the nucleus of chap. 60 belonged to the Book of Parables from the beginning or was added at a later stage. In any event, the Noah tradition was expanded by the attachment to it of a tradition about Behemoth and Leviathan (60:7-10 + 24-25a), into the middle of which the passage discussed above concerning the secrets of the cosmos (60:11-23) was inserted. The interpretation of the tradition about Behemoth and Leviathan is not entirely clear, and it is difficult, because of the textual problems posed by 60:24-25a, to know whether the two monsters are kept for the day of judgment to provide food for the righteous (cf. 2 Esd 6:52) or to devour the wicked. However, while the context — the judgment of the wicked — would favor the latter interpretation, the evidence of Tana 9 suggests that the former is the more original.[36]

The vision of the angels with the measuring cords (61:1-5), which draws on Zech 2:5-6 (Eng. 2:1-2); Ezek 40:3, 5, is the last passage in the Book of Parables to be cast in the threefold pattern of description of what Enoch saw, question, and explanation. According to the explanation, the angels go off to bring

---

34. Cf. above, 49.

35. Black, *The Book of Enoch*, 225.

36. On the text of 1 En 60:24-25a, see the comments in Michael A. Knibb, *The Ethiopic Book of Enoch: A New Edition in the Light of the Aramaic Dead Sea Fragments*, 2 vols. (Oxford: Clarendon, 1978), 2:170. In the light of the evidence of Tana 9, the passage should be translated: "And the angel of peace who was with me said to me: These two monsters are prepared for the great day of the Lord, and they will provide food that the punishment of the Lord of Spirits may rest upon them, that the punishment of the Lord of Spirits may not come in vain. And it will kill children with their mothers, and sons with their fathers, when the punishment of the Lord rests upon them." See also M. A. Knibb, "Commentary on 2 Esdras," in R. J. Coggins and M. A. Knibb, *The First and Second Books of Esdras*, Cambridge Commentary on the New English Bible (Cambridge: Cambridge University Press, 1979), 157-58; and Caquot, "I Hénoch," 532-33.

"the measurements of the righteous," by which is apparently meant both the measurements of the heavenly dwellings of the righteous and the extent of the righteous community itself. Attached to this is a series of descriptions of scenes in heaven, the first depicting the enthronement of the Chosen One as eschatological judge and the praise offered in heaven by the angelic host (61:6-13), the second the judgment of the kings and the mighty by the Chosen One/the Son of Man and the blessed life that awaits the righteous (62:1-16), and the third the unavailing repentance of the kings and the mighty (63:1-12). The conclusion of the third parable (69:26-29) contains similar material, and the whole of chaps. 61–63 + 69:26-29 fits naturally into the Parables in terms of both genre and content. But the status of the material in between is less clear.

Chap. 64, introduced by "And I saw other figures hidden in that place," is a fragment that refers to the punishment of the Watchers. But there is no antecedent for "in that place," which apparently refers to the place of punishment of the Watchers, and the passage comes in a little unexpectedly. However, the punishment of the kings and the mighty has already been linked with that of the Watchers in 54:1-6 + 55:3-4, and it may be that it was the concern with the fate of the kings and the mighty in chap. 63 that led to the inclusion of the fragment concerned with the Watchers in chap. 64. It may be noted that the reference to the angels revealing "what is secret" to the sons of men and leading them astray (64:2) anticipates 65:6b.

It is commonly assumed that the passage that follows (65:1–69:25) has been taken from a preexistent book of Noah or Noah apocalypse, but while this seems clearly to be the case for the first part of the material (65:1–67:3), it seems much less clear for the second and third parts (67:4–69:1; 69:2-25).[37] The first part is an autobiographical narrative about the impending flood, the destruction of mankind, and the deliverance of Noah. It was no doubt included in the Book of Parables partly because of the involvement of Enoch in the story, but more importantly because the destruction of sinful mankind at the time of the flood was interpreted in typological terms of the fate of mankind at the last judgment.

The second part of this material (67:4–69:1) describes the fate of the Watchers at the judgment; their punishment, according to 67:5-7, combines the idea of burning in Gehenna with features associated with disturbances caused by earthquakes and features associated with the flood story. The speaker in this part is still Noah (see 67:4; 68:1), but it is evident that the passage, at least in its present form, has been written or edited in the light of knowledge of other

---

37. Charles (*The Book of Enoch*, 129) makes the same divisions, but assumes the whole section belongs to a Noah Apocalypse.

parts of 1 Enoch. Thus in 67:4 reference is made to the passage about the mountains of metal in the west (chap. 52), but 67:4 also seems to refer to chap. 54 and to confuse the place where the Watchers were "shut up" prior to the judgment (cf. 10:4-6, 12-13) with Gehenna itself (cf. 54:5-6), even though the valley of chap. 54 is not in the west but in "another part of the earth." Also, as in other parts of the Book of Parables, 67:8-10, 13 link the punishment of the kings and the mighty with that of the Watchers, and 67:9b refers back to what is said about the Chosen One in 49:4.

The opening words of chap. 68 ("And after this my great-grandfather gave me in a book the explanation [lit. 'teaching,' so Tana 9] of all the secrets and the parables which had been given to him; and he put them together for me in the words of the Book of the Parables") look like a conclusion. But the theme of judgment is nonetheless continued from chap. 67 by a report (introduced by "And on the day") of a dialogue between Michael and Raphael concerning the severity of the judgment of the Watchers (68:3-4) and of Michael's subsequent decision not to plead on behalf of the Watchers before the Lord of Spirits (68:4-5). 69:1 then provides a summary statement about the punishment of the Watchers that brings the passage about their judgment and punishment to a close. However, 69:1 also serves as a bridge to a series of passages (69:2-25) that appear to be secondary, and in any case hardly form the natural continuation of the material from the book of Noah. The point of connection between 69:2-12 and 67:4–69:1 is the common concern with the fall of angels.

The additional material begins with a new heading, "And behold the names of those angels" (69:2a), which is followed immediately by a version of the list of 6:7 (69:2b-3). This list is commonly regarded as an interpolation, and it is assumed, rightly in my opinion, that the real continuation of 69:2a is to be found in 69:4-12. This latter passage provides a tradition about the fall of the Watchers quite different from that in chaps. 6–8; it is often argued that the angelic figures in this passage are satans and are superior to the Watchers, and such an interpretation is demanded once vv. 2b-3 have been inserted into the text. The list of names of angels (69:4-12) appears to continue in v. 13 with the mention of Kesbeel, but there is an abrupt transition in this verse, and 69:13-25 forms an independent section that deals with the divine oath. Even within this material 69:23-24 may be an interpolation, although there are connections with ideas elsewhere in the Parables.

Overall it would hardly appear that the material in 65:1–69:25 can be regarded as a unity. Rather it would appear that material from a book of Noah that bore on the theme of the last judgment (65:1–67:3) was successively expanded by related material concerned with the theme of the judgment and punishment of the angels and of the kings and the mighty, and with the theme of the fall of the angels who were held to be responsible for all the corruption of the earth.

## The Ending (chaps. 70–71)

Chap. 69 ends with the words "This is the third parable of Enoch," and it might be expected that the Book of Parables would end here. But there follows a further section, chaps. 70–71, in which Enoch's ascent to heaven and identification as the Son of Man, apparently the individual Enoch had previously seen enthroned in heaven, are described.[38] A good case can be made that the passage was intended as an account of Enoch's translation to heaven at the end of his earthly life.[39] The passage falls into two parts, a third-person narrative, which gives a summary account of Enoch's ascent (70:1-2), and an autobiographical report in which Enoch describes his ascent[40] and identification as Son of Man (70:3–71:17). Clear allusions are made throughout the section both to the Book of Parables[41] and to the Book of the Watchers,[42] and on any showing chaps. 70–71 belong at a late stage in the formation of the Book of Parables.

The interpretation of these two chapters raises a number of problems of translation and exegesis, particularly how 70:1 should be translated and whether it does report the elevation of Enoch's name, that is, of Enoch himself, to heaven, and whether 71:14 does refer to a real identification of Enoch as Son of Man. In relation to 70:1, I have discussed in detail elsewhere the alternative texts offered by the older manuscripts, which are represented on the one hand by British Library Orient. 485, Berlin, Petermann II, Nachtr. 29, Abbadianus 35, and to a lesser extent by Tana 9, and on the other by Abbadianus 55 (as well as

---

38. On the interpretation of these chapters, see M. A. Knibb, "Messianism in the Pseudepigrapha in Light of the Scrolls," *DSD* 2 (1995): 165-84 (esp. 170-80); Knibb, "The Translation of 1 Enoch 70:1: Some Methodological Issues," in *Biblical Hebrew, Biblical Texts: Essays in Memory of Michael P. Weitzman*, ed. A. Rapaport and G. Greenberg, JSOTSup 333 (London and New York: Sheffield Academic/Continuum, 2001), 340-54. See also the bibliographical references in both articles.

39. Cf. J. C. VanderKam, "Righteous One, Messiah, Chosen One, and Son of Man in 1 Enoch 37–71," in *The Messiah: Developments in Earliest Judaism and Christianity*, ed. J. H. Charlesworth (Minneapolis: Fortress, 1992), 169-91 (here 179).

40. According to the autobiographical report, the ascent occurred in three stages (70:3-4; 71:1-4; 71:5-11), and in broad terms the description may be compared with the account of the ascent in 14:8-25, which also occurred in three stages (14:8-9, 10-14a, 14b-25).

41. Cf. 1 En 70:2 with 39:3; 70:3 with 61:1; 71:7 with 61:10; 71:8 with 40:9; 71:10 with 46:1; 71:14 with 46:3; 71:16 with 48:7; 62:14.

42. Cf. 1 En 70:3–71:11 with 14:8-25, particularly 71:5 with 14:10-13, 15-17.

by some other manuscripts).⁴³ Here I can state only that, on balance, it still seems to me most likely that the oldest accessible text of 70:1 is represented by the former, and that 70:1-2 should be translated as follows:

> And it came to pass after this (that), while he was living, his name was lifted
> into the presence of the [or "that"] son of man
> and into the presence of the Lord of Spirits
> from among those who dwell upon the dry ground.
> And he was lifted on the chariots of the wind [or "the spirit"],
> and his name vanished among them.⁴⁴

Correspondingly, it seems most likely to me that 70:1-2 does describe the translation of Enoch to heaven. It also seems to me most likely that 71:14, which makes a connection with 46:3, does refer to his identification as Son of Man.⁴⁵ But I must refer to my earlier studies for further discussion of this issue. Here it should simply be noted that the contrast with the view of chaps. 37–69, where a clear distinction is made between Enoch and the Son of Man, and the fact that chaps. 70–71 come as something of a surprise after the end of the third parable in 69:29 point strongly to the view that chaps. 70–71 are a secondary addition to the Book of Parables.

## Conclusion

The overarching literary genre of the Book of Parables is that of an otherworldly journey, and as an account of a visionary journey it stands in a tradition that goes back to the book of Ezekiel and to Zech 1–8. The core material of the Parables consists of vision reports to which descriptions of scenes in heaven, and in particular the divine throne room, have often been attached, and this material fits naturally in the context of an account of an otherworldly journey. In two or three cases it is possible to isolate blocks of material in which the individual units are related in content (particularly 45–51; 52:1–56:4; 61–63), but throughout the Book of Parables the individual units have only loosely been

---

43. See Knibb, "Translation of 1 Enoch 70:1," 340-50.
44. Contrast the translation offered by Caquot, "I Hénoch," 549. See also Caquot, "Remarques sur les chapitres 70 et 71 du livre éthiopien d'Hénoch," in *Apocalypses et théologie de l'espérance*, ed. L. Monloubou, LD 95 (Paris: Cerf, 1977), 111-22; and D. C. Olson, "Enoch and the Son of Man in the Epilogue of the Parables," *JSP* 18 (1988): 27-38.
45. Cf. Knibb, "Messianism in the Pseudepigrapha," 177-80.

linked together, often by the formula "And in those days." This loose structure has facilitated the inclusion of other material, particularly, but not only, concerning Noah and the flood. Some of this material seems to have been interpolated or added at a secondary stage, but it seems likely that this was done on an ad hoc basis over a period of time, and the absence of alternative versions of the Parables makes it difficult to make dogmatic statements about the extent of the additions or the stages at which the additions were made. The combination of some structure and some organization of the material (three parables; some grouping of the individual units) with an overall loosely structured style of composition is reminiscent of the character of some of the prophetic collections, for example, that of the book of Isaiah.

Dependence on the Book of the Watchers, both the story of the Watchers (chaps. 6–16) and the account of Enoch's heavenly journey (chaps. 17–36), can frequently be observed. The account of Enoch's stay in heaven in the Parables can be seen as a continuation of the account of his journey in chaps. 17–36, and the judgment and punishment of the Watchers has frequently been brought into relationship with that of the kings and the mighty. The Book of Parables, the "second vision," can to a significant extent be understood as a reinterpretation of some of the themes and ideas of the Book of the Watchers in response to the circumstances of a later historical situation.

# The Parables of Enoch according to George Nickelsburg and Michael Knibb: A Summary and Discussion of Some Remaining Questions

*Loren T. Stuckenbruck*

The essays on the structure of the Parables of Enoch by George Nickelsburg and Michael Knibb (1) converge at many points, (2) disagree in other points, and (3) raise a few questions that may be worth pursuing further.[1] In my contribution I would like to identify instances from each of these areas, anticipating that some matters will need clarification while others will be explored in further detail.

## Agreements

On a significant number of points Nickelsburg and Knibb are in agreement. Here are the most important of these:

a. They share the view of most scholars in discerning for the Parables of Enoch in its present form an overall structure that consists of an introduction (37:1-5) and an appendix (Knibb: chaps. 70–71; Nickelsburg: 70:3–71:17) that frame three main sections called "parables."

b. They share the view of many others that a significant number of traditions associated with the figure of Noah were inserted by a redactor into originally Enochic material. These insertions may, above all, be found in 54:7–55:2/4; 60:1-10, 23/24-25, and in all or part of 65:1–69:1. Nickelsburg and Knibb agree,

---

1. See above, G. W. E. Nickelsburg, "Discerning the Structure(s) of the Enochic Book of Parables," and M. A. Knibb, "The Structure and Composition of the Parables of Enoch." All quotations from Nickelsburg and Knibb, unless otherwise indicated, are from these two essays.

moreover, that the Noachic insertions were subject to further editing or interpolation, whereby Enochic visionary material was either inserted into Noachic passages (so 60:11-22/23) or provided the basis for editorial activity that attempted to integrate more fully the Noachic materials into the Book of Parables (Knibb: 67:4-7; cf. chap. 52; 54:5-6). Both agree that much of chap. 69 (69:2-29), sometimes attributed to Noachic source material, is in fact Enochic, since it contains two lists of fallen angels (vv. 2-3 and 4-12), a section on angels and the divine or cosmic oath (vv. 13-25), and a concluding scene of judgment and subscription to the document (vv. 26-29). Both Nickelsburg and Knibb explain the addition of Noachic material on the basis of the flood typology: the destruction of sinful humanity and holding of the fallen angels to account in the Great Flood anticipate the eschatological reckoning of evil. On tradition-historical grounds this incorporation of Noachic material would have been inspired, for example, by already existing Noachic traditions within the early Enochic traditions, such as found in the Book of the Watchers (10:1-3, to which neither Knibb nor Nickelsburg refers) and chaps. 106–107, as well as by previously existing incorporation of Noachic motifs (relating to the Great Flood) in chaps. 83–84.[2]

c. Nickelsburg and Knibb agree that the material at the end of the Book of Parables (70:1/3–71:17) represents the product of Jewish redaction. Both think that this section, in which Enoch is commissioned as "son of man" to preside over eschatological judgment (cf. 71:14), can be explained on grounds other than as an anti-Christian polemic (i.e., against any identification of Jesus with the heavenly "son of man"). Nickelsburg, who entertains the possibility that this appendix could reflect "Noachic redaction," appeals to speculation about the figure of Enoch known through the "high Enochology" of 2 Enoch and traditions in so-called 3 Enoch. In particular, Knibb regards this section as incompatible with the foregoing chapters, according to which Enoch and the heavenly Son of Man are clearly distinguished, and therefore assigns it to "a late stage in the formation of the Book of Parables" in its present form.

d. Finally, a thesis both Nickelsburg and Knibb develop in different ways has to do with the relationship between the Parables and the Book of the Watchers. Both maintain that in addition to biblical traditions (notably Dan 7, Isaiah, Zechariah, and the Psalms), the author of the Parables of Enoch wrote under the significant influence of the Book of the Watchers (and, in places, of the Astronomical Book). They rightly add, however, that this dependence is not to be construed as static borrowing of motifs and ideas, but rather involves a creative reuse of tradition, both in structure and in how the motifs and smaller details are recast.

2. One may add, further, that the integration of the Noachic story into Enochic tradition was also known in the Book of Giants; cf. 6Q8 2; 4Q530 ii; 4Q206a.

In particular, Nickelsburg reads the first parable (38:1–44:1) largely in relation to the themes it has picked up from the Book of the Watchers: Enoch's announcement of judgment (chap. 38) and ascent to heaven (39:1-8), his visit of the heavenly throne room (39:9-14), and his heavenly tours to observe phenomena in the cosmos (40:1–44:1) are all shaped by the Book of the Watchers (esp. chaps. 1–18) and even follow its sequence. Even the formal key term "parable," which occurs throughout Parables (37:5; 38:1; 45:1; 57:3; 58:1; 69:29), reflects the influence of the book (1:2). Moreover, Nickelsburg finds a correspondence between the second parable (45:1–57:3; esp. 52:1–56:4) and Enoch's visionary journeys related in 18:6–19:3 (the mountains and deep valley of burning; cf. 52:1-9 and 54:1–56:4) and 21:1-10 (the place of the fallen angels' punishment; cf. 53:1–56:4) and 24:2-3 (the mountains). As regards the third parable, the same influence from the Book of the Watchers may be thought to apply for Nickelsburg, though his own observations are largely absorbed by a consideration of source-critical matters concerned with the place of the added Noachic sections.

Knibb, as Nickelsburg, has noted how much the Book of Parables is indebted to the Book of the Watchers. In his discussion, however, he focuses more at the outset on formalities. First, he notes how often in the Book of Parables episodes are strung together loosely by introductory phrases such as "and I saw" (Eth. *wa-re'iku*) and "he showed me" (Eth. *'ar'ayani*), picking up language from the more connected narrative in the Book of the Watchers (passim in chaps. 17–36 and 14:14, 18). Second, Knibb suggests that in giving structure to Enoch's visionary experiences, the author of the Parables has adapted a fourfold pattern of the Book of the Watchers into a threefold pattern that often leaves out any mention of Enoch moving about from one place to another.

## Disagreements

Some differences may be discerned between the views of Nickelsburg and Knibb. Here we may note only a few. One difference, which Knibb in particular does not choose to dwell on, concerns a date for the Book of Parables. Nickelsburg assigns a date sometime in the latter part of the first century B.C.E. and "no later than the early decades of the first century C.E." Knibb, on the other hand, has gone on record elsewhere to argue for a date toward the end of the first century C.E., though he does not seem to wish his comments in the essay to depend on a precise view, whether his or that of Nickelsburg. The question of date, especially if we adopt the earlier date suggested by Nickelsburg, is significant, as it raises a problem about the form and language of the Book of the Watchers used by the Parables author.

Another difference may not so much be a real difference as merely the different ways Nickelsburg and Knibb have focused their discussions. Both note that the Parables author shows a special interest in wisdom. Nickelsburg observes this as he is comparing the beginning of the Book of Parables with the beginning of the Book of the Watchers. The author of the superscription and the introduction to the parables (37:1-5) seems to borrow "important elements" from the superscription and introduction to the Book of the Watchers (the terms "parable" and "vision"; references to "taking up" and "speaking"; and the mention of double recipients from Enoch's contemporaries and a future generation). A significantly new element in chap. 37, and indeed within the first parable itself, is wisdom vocabulary (not anywhere in the Book of the Watchers). Whereas Nickelsburg — in his particular interest to focus on the indebtedness of the Parables to the Book of the Watchers — does not attempt to explain where the wisdom motif may have come from, Knibb suggests in general terms that its addition "is a reflection of the sapiential connections of the Parables and of the Enochic writings generally." Knibb's point raises the question about other parts of the early Enochic corpus to which the author of Parables may have been indebted.

Finally, a difference may be seen in the way Nickelsburg and Knibb have handled chap. 42, in which Wisdom's rejection on earth and dwelling in the heavens are contrasted with Iniquity's welcome reception on earth. Knibb regards 42:1-3 as secondary since it interrupts "the natural sequence of the text." Nickelsburg, however, in considering chap. 42 together with 41:9, suggests that 41:9–42:3 is a dislocation from an original place following 41:1-2. In this way the contrast between the heavenly and earthly realms associated with Wisdom and Iniquity, respectively, is made to stand in contrast with the "dwelling places" of the righteous and the wicked. It is one thing to regard the tradition as secondary (Knibb), but quite another to find a new location for it (Nickelsburg). In view of the fact that there is no manuscript evidence to the contrary, we may ask how much any attempt to relocate the tradition is (a) appropriate and (b) helpful in providing a better reading of the text.

## Some Remaining Questions

Given the agreements and differences between Nickelsburg and Knibb, we are in a position to note several issues that may require further attention, attention one would expect from lengthier treatments of the Parables than they have been able to offer in these essays. The issues relate to (a) the relationship between the Book of Parables and the remaining early Enochic compositions;

(b) the language of the Book of the Watchers used by the author; and (c) the choice of which level or levels of interpretation to adopt for the Parables.

a. The Book of Parables bears thematic connection with other parts of the early 1 Enoch corpus. No amount of dependence on the Book of the Watchers should vitiate the likelihood that the author and the redactors — if they were active after the other compositions were in place — knew and were influenced by the Animal Apocalypse (85:1–90:42), the Epistle of Enoch (92:1-5; 94:1–105:2), the Apocalypse of Weeks (93:1-10; 91:12-17), the story of the birth of Noah (chaps. 106–107), and perhaps even the Exhortation about the Eschatological Judgment (chap. 108). It suffices to mention two questions, for purposes of discussion: (1) To what extent may the "wisdom" language of the early part of the Book of Parables draw upon or interact with its occurrence elsewhere, for example, in the Apocalypse of Weeks? (2) There is no doubt that chaps. 70–71 come as a surprise to the reader. However, to what extent might it be possible to explain the commissioning of Enoch as the eschatological "Son of Man" in chap. 71 as the product of an inner-Enochic dynamic? Is there anything within the 1 Enoch corpus that could have propelled an author or redactor forward to make such a bold identification of Enoch with the "Son of Man"? Here I simply throw out an idea: Would, for example, the judgment scene involving a man-like, possibly enthroned,[3] *scribe* in chap. 90 (v. 20), in the Animal Apocalypse, have inspired a redactor to identify this figure with Enoch, who as a scribe in the Book of the Watchers carries out God's command to pronounce judgment against the fallen angels (12:3-4; esp. 15:1 and 16:3-4)? While the commissioning of Enoch in chap. 71 would have been difficult to reach on the basis of the Dan 7 tradition alone, the additional description of God's vice-regent in judgment as "scribe" may have made such an association, if not identification, possible.

b. The second issue is based on the probable use of the Book of the Watchers by the author of the Parables. Which version of the Book of the Watchers was being used, Aramaic or Greek? If Nickelsburg is correct, for instance, that the Book of Parables was composed during the first century B.C.E., then there would have been a greater likelihood (than, e.g., at the end of the first century C.E.) that the author was depending on an Aramaic version of the Book of the Watchers. Here Knibb's observation that the use of introductory phrases such as "and I saw" and "and he showed me" in the Book of Parables reflects the influence of the Book of the Watchers may be significant. To this we may add the active transitives "carried me" (39:3; 71:5; though see 5), "led me" (71:3), "set me"

---

3. If we are right in following here the Tanasee 9 reading for 90:20: "And I looked until a throne was built/erected in a pleasant land, and he [i.e., the man scribe of v. 17] sat on it *for* the Lord of the sheep."

(39:3), "placed me" (70:3), and "showed me" (40:3, 8; 59:2; 66:1; 71:3, 4), which likewise reflect the language of the Book of the Watchers (e.g., the Greek and Ethiopic to 14:25 [bis]; 15:1; 17:1, 2; 22:1; 24:1; 33:4). The extant verbal equivalents for Enoch's seeing in the Aramaic Book of the Watchers take two forms: they can be either (1) active (qal חזית; so the 4QEn mss. to 13:8; 22:5; 31:1) or (2) passive (hafel passive אחזית; so 31:2; 32:1, 3; 34:1; cf. possibly 14:4). In both cases the corresponding Greek in Codex Panopolitanus undifferentiatingly translates with the active τεθέαμαι. Indeed, in the Book of the Watchers the passive causatives occur with unusual frequency in relation to Enoch's activity: in addition to being "shown," he is also "brought near" (אדבקת, 14:10), "brought over" (אחלפת, 32:2, 3; and אשברת, 32:2), "brought" (אבלת, 23:1; הבלת, 32:2), "removed" (ארחקת, 30:1 and 32:2). In every single case the corresponding Greek text has an active form that makes Enoch the subject of the action, just as is invariably the case in the Ethiopic recensions to both the Book of the Watchers and the Book of Parables. Since the Ethiopic Book of Parables, unlike the Aramaic Book of the Watchers, does not retain passive forms in connective phrases concerned with Enoch the seer's movements and visions, we may assume — if the Aramaic passives in the Book of the Watchers were at hand — that the actives in the Book of Parables were the result of one of two main alternatives: (1) The original author took over, under the influence of the Book of the Watchers Aramaic, the divine passives in his own Aramaic version, so that the change to the active forms happened after composition as the Book of Parables was translated into Greek (analogous to what happens in Codex Panopolitanus), which in turn may have served as a *Vorlage* to the Ethiopic. In this case, if the Ethiopic translators were working with Aramaic as well as Greek texts in rendering the Book of Parables, the purported proclivity of the Greek for the active forms would have been preferred. (2) The original author was simply working with a Greek version of the Book of the Watchers that had already made the transition from the passive to active forms. If what we have in the Ethiopic Parables may be thought to have provided a voice for verbs that corresponded to the voice of verbs in a *Vorlage*, then it is hard to escape the possibility that the Book of Parables was either composed in Greek or, composed in Aramaic, was at least being influenced by a tendency to resolve divine passives through the use of more active forms. Though other linguistic considerations are still possible,[4] the evidence just noted makes it just as easy to derive this aspect of the Ethiopic Book of Parables from a translation tradition than to derive it directly from an Aramaic *Vorlage*. In summary, if the actives were already in use at

---

4. Such as, e.g., Knibb's vocabulary-based arguments in support of the Ethiopic Parables' use of an Aramaic *Vorlage*. See Michael A. Knibb, *The Ethiopic Book of Enoch: A New Edition in the Light of the Aramaic Dead Sea Fragments*, 2 vols. (Oxford: Clarendon, 1978), 2:41-42.

the level of composition and if it is correct that the Book of Parables was composed with the Book of the Watchers in view, then it would not be misleading to suppose that its author was writing in Greek or perhaps produced an Aramaic version that was already aware of Greek translation tradition. While this does not preclude a composition of the Book of Parables during the first century B.C.E. or early first century C.E., a later date, when a Greek translation tradition of the Book of the Watchers would more likely have been established, may be preferable.

c. Finally, as both Nickelsburg and Knibb have noted, 1 En 37–71 contains more than just an original composition called the Book of Parables. Not only a series of clearly Noachic additions was made to the document; less identifiable ones were interpolated and added as well, such as the passage on Wisdom failing to find a dwelling on earth in chap. 42 (so Knibb) and the last part in chaps. 70–71. In addition, if Nickelsburg is correct, there may have been some dislocations of original sequences in the work. This raises the question: When we refer to the Book of Parables, what are we ultimately talking about? Are we to think of an original document composed by one author, to be reconstructed on the basis of source- and tradition-historical considerations? To what extent and, more important, in what sense can we reasonably speak of the whole of chaps. 37–71 as the Parables? The failure of the material to make any direct or even indirect allusion to early Christian tradition suggests at least that the original composition *as well as* the editorial insertions and relocations may be ascribed to *non-Christian Jews.* Moreover, the lack of any allusion in the book to Christian tradition, despite the frequency of its references to an eschatological, enthroned "Son of Man" who could be worshiped alongside the Lord of the Spirits (46:5; 48:5; 61:6?), suggests that the editorial activity was carried out during a relatively short time after the original composition, that is, not much beyond the time when the Jesus movement could have begun to make its impact felt. If 1 En 37–71 as a whole reflects developments that may be explained on the basis of the early traditions associated with Enoch (alongside biblical and contemporary traditions), then this section as a whole may be interpreted as a series of texts, Enochic and Noachic, that reflect a shared interest in a preexisting Enochic corpus that was already well under way in integrating similarly different sources into a whole. The Book of Parables, built around three "parables" framed by an introduction and conclusion, is ultimately a collection of traditions that redactors, with more or less success, have woven together, inspired by a common devotion to the creative preservation and reapplication of traditions associated with Enoch.

We may be indebted to Nickelsburg and Knibb not only for providing us with an excellent framework for scholarly discussion on the structure of the Book of Parables, but also for raising issues that we may find ourselves trying to address for some time to come.

# The Structure of the Parables of Enoch:
# A Response to George Nickelsburg and Michael Knibb

*Benjamin G. Wright*

For this debate on the structure of the Book of Parables, we are fortunate to have two of the foremost authorities on 1 Enoch to guide us. In their essays George Nickelsburg and Michael Knibb have examined the structure and literary integrity of the Parables.[1] While they reach very similar conclusions about this section of 1 Enoch, their differences (and probably disagreements) highlight some important and problematic questions that affect our understanding of the Parables. Since both have more or less followed the order of the Parables, I will as well, treating both of their arguments at the same time.

This section of 1 Enoch has an obvious macrostructure — an introduction (chap. 37) with three parables (chaps. 38–44; 45–57; 58–69) and a short conclusion (chaps. 70–71), even though the first parable does not have as obvious a final subscription as do the second and third. Both Nickelsburg and Knibb emphasize that the Book of Parables is consciously modeled after already existing Enoch material, particularly the Book of the Watchers (both Nickelsburg and Knibb) and to a lesser extent "a source like the Astronomical Book" (Nickelsburg). In this light the Book of Parables constitutes some of the latest material to be included in the composite 1 Enoch. In places Nickelsburg and Knibb are remarkably concordant in their assessments of the Parables, especially in their remarks about the relationship between the Parables and the Book of the Watchers. Despite some obvious formal differences between the two Enochic

---

1. See above, G. W. E. Nickelsburg, "Discerning the Structure(s) of the Enochic Book of Parables," and M. A. Knibb, "The Structure and Composition of the Parables of Enoch." All quotations from Nickelsburg and Knibb, unless otherwise indicated, are from these two essays.

works — the virtual lack of explicit notice in the Parables that Enoch moves about, which contrasts with Enoch the peripatetic tourist in the Book of the Watchers, for example — Knibb, writing about the first parable, comments, "There are frequent references in the Parables to the story of the Watchers. . . . Thus the literary form of the Book of Parables continues that of the Book of the Watchers." Nickelsburg writes in a similar vein: "[T]he author of the Parables has drawn on and reshaped materials from the Enochic Book of the Watchers." Both scholars view the wisdom language in the introduction, to quote Knibb, as "a reflection of the sapiential connections of the Parables and of the Enochic writings generally."

## The First Parable (chaps. 38–44)

Both Nickelsburg and Knibb agree that this parable has probably the greatest literary integrity of the three. Essentially, the first parable "coheres as a single piece" and "the material appears to be the work of a single author" (Nickelsburg). Within this broader agreement, there are several places where the emphasis differs between the two scholars. Knibb accepts the conclusion that 1 En 39:1-2a is an interpolation into the text, perhaps originating as a marginal comment. Nickelsburg, when he characterizes these verses as an allusion to the Book of the Watchers that summarizes 1 En 6–11, seems to assume that they belong to the original text.

While both scholars understand the short chap. 42 on wisdom to be in the wrong place, Nickelsburg argues that this misplacement is only one aspect of a larger literary problem that encompasses 41:1–44:1. Nickelsburg's five-section division of these chapters makes good literary sense, and the solution to the problem — to reorder the text 41:1-2 + 41:9; 42:1-3 + 41:3-8 + 43:1–44:1 — does indeed have the benefit of putting the thematically similar material together. So, in Nickelsburg's rearrangement, 41:1-2, which refers to the "dwelling of the chosen," comes right before 42:1-3, which speaks of "dwelling" on at least three occasions. On the other end, 42:3 mentions rain and dew while 41:3 has "the secrets of the clouds and dew." But, as I read the text, chap. 42 still seems to sit uncomfortably in the order that Nickelsburg proposes. The chapter's description of Wisdom's failed mission undoubtedly provides a mythological "explanation of the presence of sin in the world" (Knibb), but Nickelsburg's placement still does not create an unproblematic text. In his reordering, 42:1 follows 41:1-2 + 41:9. The passage would thus move from a vision of divine judgment to the descent of mythological wisdom and then in three short verses back to Enoch's heavenly vision of cosmic phenomena. Unless one proposes a redactional attempt to smooth out the text in its present form, the "and there" that introduces 41:3 and the "there" of 41:2 — both presumably references to heaven where Enoch sees all these things — now become separated by the story of Wisdom's descent and return. The account of Wisdom's failed attempt to dwell on earth and the resultant entrance of Iniquity still seem to interrupt the passage, despite the closer connections via thematic similarities. I do not think that "the continuity of the *Stichwort*" necessarily "clinches" the argument, as Nickelsburg argues. In fact, the logic of this new arrangement still perplexes Nickelsburg, as he himself admits. For his part, Knibb only comments that chap. 42 interrupts "the natural sequence of the text." Yet, even though this passage about Wisdom might be out of place where it now stands, neither Nickelsburg nor Knibb suggests that it originates anywhere but from the hand of the author of the Parables.

## The Second Parable (chaps. 45–57)

Both Nickelsburg's and Knibb's assessments of this parable identify the same themes as operative, especially the introduction and importance of the Chosen One as eschatological judge in which the Enochic author has reshaped material taken from Dan 7. Nickelsburg notes that Isa 11 and 49 along with Ps 2 also play into this section. Both scholars outline the four vision reports of 1 En 52:1-9, 53:1-7, 54:1-6 + 55:3-4, and 56:1-4 within which appears a pattern of description/vision, question, and explanation/interpretation.

The major literary problem of the second parable concerns 54:7–55:2 (or 3-4). Both Nickelsburg and Knibb agree that this material originated as a piece of Noachic tradition. Enoch's vision of the chains being made for Azazel ends quite abruptly in v. 6, and v. 7 begins, "And in those days." Knibb contends that the section set in this context is comprehensible since "as elsewhere in 1 Enoch, the story of the flood followed by the divine promise of blessing has a typological function." Nickelsburg understands the interpolation as God's first-person speech announcing "the *future* destruction of the angels." Thus, despite slightly different variations on the theme, both scholars conclude that the passage, although a secondary intervention into the text, has a rationale where it stands.

Where Nickelsburg and Knibb disagree is about the actual extent of the interpolation. Knibb understands 55:2 to be the end of the Noachic section, and thus vv. 3-4 resume the story from 54:6, since Azazel and his hosts are mentioned in both 54:6 and 55:4. Yet he recognizes that even though the account apparently resumes in vv. 3-4, these verses are in "some disorder" and "[i]t is possible that some material has been lost through the insertion of the Noah fragment (54:7–55:2)." Nickelsburg, however, would have the insertion continue right through to v. 4. He constructs 54:1, 3-6 and 56:1-4 as parallel scenes in which Enoch, who narrates, reports his visions. The intervening verses, 54:7–55:4, are Noachic (at least through v. 2), in which God speaks in the first person. Whereas Knibb gives priority to the reference to Azazel as an indicator of the resumption of the earlier account, Nickelsburg prefers the first-person speech as the primary indicator for inclusion in the interpolation. Vv. 3-4, then, function for Nickelsburg as "a transition back to the subject of the punishment of the angels." We encounter both agreement and disagreement in the assessments of these two scholars. They both highlight the problematic nature of 55:3-4, but each assesses the verses differently when deciding whether they originally belonged to the Parables.

For the final section of the second parable (56:5–57:3a), Knibb argues that the picture given there is "so out of character" with the view of the rest of the Parables that "at the very least" the author seems to have gotten it from elsewhere, and he allows for the possibility that it might be a later addition. Nickelsburg does not comment on this issue, and so I presume he thinks that these verses do not pose the problem that Knibb does.

## The Third Parable (chaps. 58–69)

Both Nickelsburg and Knibb agree that this parable is the most complex and, as Knibb writes, "raises the most questions about the originality of the material." Several passages create difficulties here. In Nickelsburg's and Knibb's estimation, chaps. 59–60 are something of a mess. Chap. 60 clearly originates in Noachic lore, but in its context the author intends the reader to see it as part of the Enochic tradition. Knibb expresses uncertainty about whether this chapter was original to the Parables or a later insertion. Nickelsburg argues that some of the material in chap. 60 is displaced and some interpolated. He concludes that 60:11-22 originally belonged after 59:1-3 and that the section on the two monsters (60:7-10, 24a) is an interpolation into these verses. He further suggests that 60:23 goes with 60:8, part of the monster tradition. Thus, he places it before v. 24 as part of the monsters passage, describing it as a possible gloss. In addition, Nickelsburg argues that 60:1-6 + 60:24b-25, the scene in the heavenly throne room, is itself an interpolation. He, then, has an interpolation within an interpolation. According to Nickelsburg, the entire section is "part of a *set* of Noachic interpolations" (emphasis mine).

A second large insertion, 65:1–69:25 (or 69:1 in Nickelsburg's construction), interrupts the third parable. Knibb is convinced that 65:1–67:3 is Noachic; he is not so certain about 67:4–69:1 or 69:2-25 (which Nickelsburg also does not appear to think is Noachic). Nickelsburg shares the view that "some of the material in 67:1–69:25 belongs to the early form of the Book of Parables." Without rehearsing all their arguments, the important point is that Nickelsburg and Knibb agree that much of this material has been inserted into the Parables. They differ over how much and what sections were part of those interpolations and which ones belong to the original Parables. So, the third parable presents a similar situation to Nickelsburg's and Knibb's positions on the first two parables — a remarkable degree of agreement and significant points of disagreement.

## The Ending (chaps. 70–71)

Finally chaps. 70–71, which conclude the Book of Parables, offer several literary difficulties. There is no doubt that they are made up of more than one section. Reacting to Knibb's suggestions about the end of the book in his Weitzman memorial volume article,[2] Nickelsburg argues that "something like 70:1-2 constituted the original conclusion to the Book of Parables." In his article Knibb connects 70:3-4, 71:1-4, and 71:5-11 with the three-staged ascent found in the Book of the Watchers: 70:3-4//14:8-9; 71:1-4//14:10-14a; 71:5-11//14:14b-25. While Nickelsburg doubts Knibb's connection of 70:3-4 with 14:8-9 — he thinks these verses look more like a summary of chaps. 17–19 — he adds 71:13-17//15:1–16:4 to Knibb's list. He then sees vv. 3-4 as transitional to chap. 71, and chap. 71 "is a summary of the whole Enoch experience with a tendentious addition, namely, the identification of Enoch as the future eschatological judge." Again Nickelsburg and Knibb virtually agree. Knibb wants, in the end, to ascribe all of 70–71 to some secondary addition. For him Parables ends with 69:29, "Here ends the third parable of Enoch." Except for 70:1-2, where Enoch is translated into heaven, Nickelsburg also sees chaps. 70–71 as later additions.

What do we learn from the agreements between these two eminent scholars? Certainly we can have a measure of security about the basic structure of the Parables. Giving his book the form of an otherworldly journey, the author of the Parables drew on preexisting Enochic material for his work. He was heavily invested in the Book of the Watchers, and the influence of this Enochic work lies deep in the structure of this later Enochic text. The author also drew heavily on biblical sources, both for the form of his book, using Ezekiel and Zech 1-8, for example, and for specific thematic concerns. He reworked and incorporated

---

2. M. A. Knibb, "The Translation of 1 Enoch 70:1: Some Methodological Issues," in *Biblical Hebrews, Biblical Texts: Essays in Memory of Michael P. Weitzman*, ed. Ada Rapaport and Gillian Greenberg, JSOTSup 333 (Sheffield: Sheffield Academic, 2001), 340-54.

biblical material, especially about the Danielic Son of Man, the Anointed One of Ps 2 and Isa 11, the Servant of Deutero-Isaiah, and possibly traditions about preexistent wisdom. The three parables all have similar features, particularly oracular introductions, heavenly scenes, and descriptions of Enoch's cosmic journeys. Knibb notes especially that this structure is "loose," with individual units linked together with the formula "and in those days." This kind of loose linking of units has made it easier for the author or some later interpolator(s) to augment the book with additional material, such as the Noah traditions and a conclusion that identifies Enoch as the Son of Man. On all this Nickelsburg and Knibb concur, and in the face of this agreement, the differences between them about other structural matters are really quite minor.

As I see it, two basic areas of difference (or disagreement) emerge between Nickelsburg and Knibb: (a) the extent of the later inserted material; and (b) the process by which these interpolations entered the text of the Parables. The inclusion of Noachic material within an Enochic work is of course not difficult to comprehend, and both scholars suggest very plausible, and not always mutually exclusive, rationales for the insertions. The use of flood traditions in previous Enoch material together with the emphasis on judgment, an important theme in the Parables, makes the Noachic material seem almost natural, at least certainly not surprising, in its context. But while Nickelsburg and Knibb are able to construct reasonable accounts for this context, they apparently disagree about the *nature* of the Noachic insertions. Knibb thinks, although he does not elaborate much, that the interpolations were done "on an ad hoc basis over a period of time." Nickelsburg speaks of a "redactor" who inserted "a set" of Noachic interpolations. For Nickelsburg, the order and placement of the Noah material seem to indicate systematic activity on the part of a redactor. I would certainly like to hear more from Nickelsburg and Knibb on this matter.

All that said, to have such extensive agreement between two recognized experts on this text suggests to me that we really can get at the basic structure of the Parables. At this juncture, in anticipation of further work and scholarly discussion of these problems, I simply want to highlight some issues about how we work with the Parables that stem from the cautionary note that Knibb gives twice in his essay.

First of all, he reminds us that we do not have any evidence for the existence of the Parables outside of the Enochic collection we call 1 Enoch. Knibb thinks an independent existence "unlikely," and perhaps the close connections to the Book of the Watchers might suggest as much. But one could find any number of ancient Jewish texts that have very close relationships with other texts, and no one doubts their original independence. One might think immediately of the relationship between Samuel-Kings and Chronicles. Without any

*Benjamin G. Wright*

evidence outside of the Parables, we have little more at our disposal than informed scholarly intuition.

Second, unlike the other sections of the corpus we call 1 Enoch, we possess only one version of the Parables, and that one is in Ethiopic. There are simply no other versions extant for comparison. To try to unravel the structure and literary integrity of a book, and of a translation at that (or perhaps/probably even a translation of a translation?), based solely on internal criteria presents many difficult obstacles to success. We know from other ancient translations about the ways translators either intentionally impose their own agendas on their source texts or mistakenly produce target language text that effectively masks the original. Parables as we have it originally contained undeniable literary difficulties, as Nickelsburg and Knibb have described in their essays. But does translation effectively obscure any number of significant details that might provide indications of other structural problems or patterns? To what extent might a translator, whether consciously or mistakenly, have smoothed out others and thus blocked them from our view? Given the limitations of working with a translation, can we reasonably expect to discover for the Parables more than the general contours of the structure? Such methodological difficulties accompany our scholarly work on any number of ancient Jewish texts, but they seem especially acute for the Parables. In the end, we are left with the Book of Parables itself and what it can reveal to us, however opaque the lenses are through which we look. Nickelsburg and Knibb have shown us just how much we can discover about this important Enochic text using the internal evidence of the text itself. We are in their debt for the clear and concise manner in which this evidence has been presented and analyzed.

PART TWO

# THE PARABLES WITHIN THE ENOCH TRADITION

# The Book of Parables within the Enoch Tradition

*James C. VanderKam*

The evidence available today gives us reason to believe that the Parables of Enoch had a different origin and early transmission history than the other four works in 1 Enoch. In all likelihood the booklet was not copied together with other Enochic texts at Qumran, where no fragment of the Parables has been identified. Long before discovery of the Dead Sea Scrolls, the Book of Parables was thought to have a different origin than the other parts of 1 Enoch.[1] Some of the differences, noticed then and later, are these:

a. *Biography.* Deborah Dimant has adduced evidence showing that, while the earlier four Enochic booklets deal with Enoch at a particular phase of his life and clearly distinguish the phases in his career, the Book of Parables covers all of them and fails to distinguish the phases.[2]

---

1. Early in the twentieth century, Robert Henry Charles could claim that "all critics are now agreed that the Parables are distinct in origin from the rest of the book." See R. H. Charles, *The Book of Enoch, or I Enoch, Translated from the Editor's Ethiopic Text, and Edited with the Introduction, Notes, and Indexes of the First Edition Wholly Recast, Enlarged, and Rewritten* (Oxford: Clarendon, 1912), 65-66.

2. Deborah Dimant expands on the differences in this regard: "What is peculiar to the Book of Parables is its tendency to combine topics which, in the books, are kept apart. This is particularly evident in comparison with the Book of the Watchers, which precedes the Parables in the Ethiopic collection. The Book of the Watchers too is occupied with the Final Judgment and Enoch's journeys, but these topics are kept apart and it is evident that each derives from a different literary source. Significantly, also in the Astronomical Book the sojourn with the angels is not mixed, as it is in the Parables, with matters of future history. Similarly, the Book of Dream Visions confines itself to questions concerning future history." See D. Dimant, "The Bi-

b. *The extended focus on the eschatological leader.* Identified by titles that fail to appear in the other four booklets ("Chosen One," "Son of Man"), this leader is a dominant character in the Parables.[3]

c. *The eschatological foes.* The kings and the mighty are central representatives of evil, and their punishment is a prominent topic in the Parables.

d. *God's name.* The deity is called the Lord of Spirits.

The various differences that set the Parables off from the other booklets have led to the conclusion that the Book of Parables stems from another kind of Jewish group.[4]

With the failure of this lengthy text to surface at Qumran and some differences of thought or emphasis separating it as well, some questions arise. Why was it later transmitted together with the other Enochic texts (apart from its connection with Enoch himself), and why was it placed in second position, after the Book of the Watchers and before the Astronomical Book? Are there traces in the Parables of attempts by the writer or an editor to tie the work to the more ancient texts, that is, to relate it to the trajectories of these works? And

---

ography of Enoch and the Books of Enoch," *VT* 33 (1983): 14-29 (here 28). While one may not agree with all her claims, the broader claim is on target.

3. August Dillmann distinguishes the items Enoch sees in the Parables from those he sees in the Book of the Watchers. The ones he views in the Parables concern "die Geheimnisse der obersten Himmel, der Engelwelt, des Himmelreiches und des in Himmel schon vorgebildeten und mit seinen Gütern und Personen dort schon bereit liegenden künftigen messianischen Reiches, den Messias. . . ." See A. Dillmann, *Das Buch Henoch übersetzt und erklärt* (Leipzig: Vogel, 1853), ii.

4. David Suter concluded: "Examination of the heavenly ascent and the oath traditions in the Parables of Enoch leads to the conclusion that the work is Jewish rather than Christian in origin and that it belongs to an early stage of the Merkavah tradition. It might be better, perhaps, to classify the Parables as proto-Merkavah, since the throne plays more of a central role in the later mystical tradition than it does in the Parables. The apocalyptist responsible for the latter work is concerned more with a vision of order beyond the chaos of the present than in the vision of the throne itself." See D. Suter, *Tradition and Composition in the Parables of Enoch,* SBLDS 47 (Missoula: Scholars, 1979), 23. Gabriele Boccaccini understands the place of the Parables in line with his larger theory about the development of Enochic Judaism: the Book of Parables was written after the split between Qumran and Enochic Judaism, and for that reason does not appear at Qumran; see G. Boccaccini, *Beyond the Essene Hypothesis: The Parting of the Ways between Qumran and Enochic Judaism* (Grand Rapids: Eerdmans, 1998), 144. Boccaccini points to various discrepancies, including the focus on the eschatological leader and the lack of individual predestination although in a shared context of historical determinism: "While the community of the Dead Sea Scrolls engages in enforcing its doctrine of cosmic dualism and individual predestination, Enochic Judaism engages in other matters, such as conversion and deliverance from evil, which do not make good sense if good and evil are preordained by God" (149).

can we detect any reasons why it became the second element in the Enochic pentad?

We will try to tackle these problems in a somewhat manageable form by focusing on data pertinent to the relation between the Parables and two earlier Enochic works — the Book of the Watchers and the Astronomical Book. Did the author of the Parables attempt to express a relationship between his composition and these older Enochic *texts* (that is, not just with oral traditions) through borrowings of themes and formulations of ideas? The answer is clearly yes in the case of the Book of the Watchers. For it, the evidence at our disposal indicates that the attribution of the work to Enoch, indeed entitling it "The second vision that he saw, the vision of wisdom that Enoch saw — the son of Jared, the son of Mahalalel, the son of Kenan, the son of Enosh, the son of Seth, the son of Adam" (37:1),[5] was not merely window dressing but a statement regarding the tradition in which the writer saw himself standing. A note such as 37:5 articulates a similar concern: "Three parables were (imparted) to me, and I took (them) up and spoke to those who dwell on the earth" (see also 38:1; 45:1; 58:1; 69:29). These notices do not simply supply a redactional framework; they also claim a continuity with a tradition of revelation involving the seventh patriarch who, in 1:2, took up his earlier parable (cf. also 93:1, 3).[6] For the Astronomical Book, as we shall see, the evidence for a relationship is far less decisive.

In the history of commenting on the shape of 1 Enoch, several scholars have written about the placement of the Book of Parables in the second position in the collection, more specifically, about its setting between the Book of the Watchers and the Astronomical Book. They have generally been able to document a certain appropriateness of its location after the Book of the

---

5. Translations of the book are from G. W. E. Nickelsburg and J. C. VanderKam, *1 Enoch: A New Translation* (Minneapolis: Fortress, 2004). For this particular verse, Nickelsburg has omitted "The second vision that he saw" — a phrase attested in all the manuscripts but one that he considers "almost certainly a gloss that postdates the section's incorporation into the corpus and relates the Parables to Enoch's vision recounted in the Book of the Watchers" (50 n. a). Josef Milik thought the title "second vision" contrasted it with a "first vision" that incorporated "the whole collection of revelations contained in the Aramaic and Greek Enochic Pentateuch in two volumes: the Book of the Watchers, the Book of Giants, the Book of Dreams, the Epistle of Enoch in the first volume, and the Astronomical Book in the second volume." See J. T. Milik, *The Books of Enoch: Aramaic Fragments of Qumrân Cave 4* (Oxford: Clarendon, 1976), 89. As we shall see, there is a simpler explanation — the first vision is the Book of the Watchers.

6. See the discussion of this passage in G. W. E. Nickelsburg, *1 Enoch 1: A Commentary on the Book of 1 Enoch 1–36, 81–108*, vol. 1, Hermeneia (Minneapolis: Fortress, 2001), 137-39. Nickelsburg prefers to translate τὴν παραβολήν as "discourse." Yet, as Enoch was not the only ancient worthy to take up his parable, the writer of the Parables is identifying with a particular tradition here. See also D. Suter, "*Māšāl* in the Similitudes of Enoch," *JBL* 100 (1981): 193-212.

*James C. VanderKam*

Watchers, although even here some questions arise. George Nickelsburg, on the basis of the evidence from Qumran, where none of the Enochic booklets is copied with the Book of Parables and where, therefore, it almost certainly did not occupy its present position, comments: "This absence underscores the strangeness of the Parables' present placement in 1 Enoch. The book intrudes between chaps. 33–36 (esp. 33:2-4) — with their mention of Enoch's time with Uriel — and chaps. 72–82, which comprise the detailed record of the same event."[7]

## The Parables and the Book of the Watchers

While the present placement of the Parables does break up Uriel-Enoch material that appears to belong together (chaps. 33–36; 72–82), there are transparent links between the Parables and the Book of the Watchers. In fact, it looks as if someone made an effort to connect the Parables with that earlier work.[8]

A *formal* link with the Book of the Watchers is provided by the framework that undergirds the Book of Parables: it, like the second half of the Book of the Watchers, is a travelogue in which Enoch enjoys angelic guidance and enlightenment through dialogue. At several points in the work there are reminders of this situation. So, in 40:2 Enoch refers to "the angel who went with me and showed me all the hidden things."[9] Enoch poses questions to him and receives answers from him (40:8; see also 46:2; 52:1-9; 53:4; 54:4; 56:2; 60:11, 24).[10]

---

7. Nickelsburg, *1 Enoch 1*, 22.

8. The comparisons offered below are between the Book of Parables as it is now present in Ethiopic 1 Enoch and the Book of the Watchers. As Eibert Tigchelaar correctly notes in his response to this essay (see below, "Remarks on Transmission and Traditions in the Parables of Enoch"), the situation is more complex because parts of the Book of Parables (e.g., the Noachic sections) are based on other sources whose relations to the Book of the Watchers should be explored. The point is readily acknowledged. Regarding a conscious effort on the part of a writer or writers to connect the Book of Parables and the Book of the Watchers, see the suggestive comment of D. Olson, *Enoch: A New Translation* (North Richland Hills, Tex.: BIBAL, 2004), 11-12, especially: "The 'Parables' features an ingenious expansion of the twin motifs of the 'Book of the Watchers.' Noticing that the one story features angels as its main characters (the Watchers) and that the other features a human being (Enoch), the author furnishes *earthly* counterparts to the spiritual beings of the first legend and a *heavenly* counterpart to the flesh-and-blood man of the second. Thus, the 'kings and mighty' who oppress the righteous and oppose themselves to the true God are in some sense the Watchers reincarnated (chaps. 62–64; 67), while the mysterious and supernatural Messiah turns out in the end to be the heavenly double of Enoch himself (71:14)."

9. We should observe that the content of what is revealed to Enoch in the Parables is here called "all the hidden things [*wa-k"ello ḫebu'āta*]." The same term recurs throughout the passages that will be examined below. This language, beginning in 38:3, continues as far as 71:3-4.

10. The fact that in some passages the phrasing is "the angel who went with me" while in

Thus, in a formal sense, the situation appears to be the very one pictured in 1 En 17–36, although in the Parables the accompanying angel is never named.[11]

Besides the formal link, a transparent connection in *content* between the two works is the tradition about the angels who sinned, an account that in several forms seems to have been at the core of the Enochic message at least during some periods. This story surfaces in several passages in the Parables, and from them one can gain an idea of the source(s) from which the writer may have taken his formulations. They exhibit specific commonalities in wording and theme with the text of the Book of the Watchers. We should now examine the passages in the Parables where the theme of the angels who sinned makes an appearance.

## 1 Enoch 39:1

Much of chap. 39 sounds like a swift summary of the Book of the Watchers, especially vv. 1-4. There we read: "In those days, the sons of the chosen and holy were descending from the highest heaven, and their seed was becoming one with the sons of men. In those days Enoch received books of jealous wrath and rage and books of trepidation and consternation. And in those days a whirlwind snatched me up from the face of the earth and set me down within the confines of the heavens. And there I saw another vision — the dwellings of the holy ones, and the resting places of the righteous." While much of what these and the following verses say recapitulates the Book of the Watchers, there is also a new element typical of the Parables: Enoch's ancient visions are now updated to include the Chosen One who, under several titles, plays so prominent a role in the Parables. The passage also enlarges on the destiny of the righteous and chosen who are so intimately connected with the Righteous and Chosen One. As Nickelsburg says: "With respect to his functions, the Chosen One parallels and supersedes the four holy ones of chaps. 6–11. Although these four holy ones are mentioned by name in chap. 40 (with Phanuel replacing Sariel) and retain some of their functions (cf. also chap. 47), the Chosen One uniquely assumes some of their roles and thus relegates them to the background."[12]

---

others it is "the angel of peace who went with me" led Beer and Charles to posit two sources, with the first formulation associated with their Son of Man source and the second with their Chosen One source. See G. Beer, "Das Buch Henoch," in *Die Apokryphen und Pseudepigraphen des Alten Testaments,* ed. E. Kautzsch (1900; reprint, Tübingen: Mohr Siebeck, 1921), 2:227; Charles, *The Book of Enoch,* 64-65.

11. Dillmann, *Das Buch Henoch,* ii.
12. Nickelsburg, *1 Enoch 1,* 45.

*James C. VanderKam*

The brief reference to the angel story in 39:1 is located just before the words "In those days Enoch received books of jealous wrath and rage and books of trepidation and consternation. And in those days a whirlwind snatched me up from the face of the earth and set me down within the confines of the heavens" (vv. 2-3). It seems as if the writer here is referring to 1 En 12–16 and perhaps to the visions that follow.[13] If so, we would look naturally to chaps. 6–11 for the background of the précis of the angel story in 39:1.

In fact, virtually every word in 39:1 can be located in 1 En 6–16:

"the sons of the chosen and holy":[14] the term "sons" is used for the angels in 6:2 where the Watchers are said to be "the sons of heaven" (see also 13:8; 14:3).[15] The adjective "chosen" (common in the Parables) is not

---

13. See M. Black, *The Book of Enoch, or, I Enoch: A New English Edition with Commentary and Textual Notes,* SVTP 7 (Leiden: Brill, 1985), 196-97. Black finds allusions particularly to chap. 14, with 39:3 "almost a paraphrase of 14.8f" (197). A. Dillmann (*Das Buch Henoch,* 144) and R. H. Charles (*The Book of Enoch,* 74), however, thought 39:3 more reminiscent of 52:1 ("a real translation") than of 14:8, 9 ("a mere incident in a dream"). A number of commentators have argued that 39:1-2 are an addition and bracketed them (Dillmann thought only v. 2 was a gloss, noting the surprising fact that Enoch was spoken of in the third person and the lack of clarity regarding which writings were the subject of the reference). In his translation quoted above, Nickelsburg omits from the end of v. 2 the universally attested words "And there will be no mercy for them, says the Lord of Spirits" (translation of Michael A. Knibb, *The Ethiopic Book of Enoch: A New Edition in the Light of the Aramaic Dead Sea Fragments,* 2 vols. [Oxford: Clarendon, 1978], vol. 2). These he regards as "a misplaced variant of 38:6a" (cf. Nickelsburg and VanderKam, *1 Enoch,* 52 n. f). The argument is that 38:6 and 39:2b are so alike that they betray the intervening material as an addition. Although Nickelsburg does not bracket vv. 1-2a, R. H. Charles and F. Martin (*Le livre d'Hénoch traduit sur le texte éthiopien,* Documents pour l'étude de la Bible [Paris: Letouzey et Ané, 1906], 82) do. Both considered the verses an obvious interpolation, with Charles adding that they had nothing to do with their context. It is not transparently the case that they are unrelated, especially to what follows. Black writes that the verses can be retained if one assumes past tense verbs in 39:1 rather than the imperfects that are used (*The Book of Enoch,* 196, although see his next paragraph and Charles, 74 n, for a similar thought). If, however, chap. 38 serves as an introduction to the first parable, chap. 39 could be seen as an attempt to explain to the reader how Enoch himself, the recipient of the visions, came to be in the position in which he found himself. Nickelsburg's translation of the imperfects as "were descending" and "was becoming" is consistent with this suggestion. If so, we need not adopt Black's suggestion that "at the end of the days there will be fresh assaults of angelic 'watchers' on mankind" (Black, 196).

14. Many manuscripts, including those of the β family, read *daqiq* rather than *daqiqa,* yielding the meaning "chosen and holy children" (so Dillmann, *Das Buch Henoch;* Charles, *The Book of Enoch;* and Knibb, *Ethiopic Book of Enoch,* 2:126).

15. Dillmann, *Das Buch Henoch,* 143: "Darunter müssen die Engel verstanden sein; Kinder oder Söhne heissen sie als Kinder oder Söhne der Himmel. . . ." Nevertheless, he interpreted the passage as referring to a future time when the present separation between heaven and earth will disappear and the heavenly and earthly will come together as a great assembly (143-44).

attached to these angels in the Book of the Watchers,[16] but "holy" is (15:4).

"were descending": the imperfect tense form *(yewarredu)* may be surprising and has caused comment (see n. 13 above), but the idea of the angels' descent is of course well-known from the Book of the Watchers (6:6; cf. 12:4; 14:5; 15:3, 7, 10; 16:2-3).

"from the highest heaven" (or: "heavens"): the phrase is found in 12:4, 15:3 (singular in both cases; cf. 106:13).

"and their seed was becoming one with the sons of men": the exact expression does not occur in the Book of the Watchers, but some passages closely approximate it: 7:1 (Ethiopic: were mixed [*tadammaru*] with them), although the Gizeh manuscript reads μιαίνεσθαι;[17] 9:8 (Greek Gizeh); and especially 10:11 (4QEn^b 1 4 9: ]ל די אתחברו; Ethiopic: *'ella ḥabru mesla 'anest;* Greek Gizeh: ταῖς γυναιξὶν μιγέντας; Greek Syncellus: τοὺς συμμιγέντας ταῖς θυγατράσι τῶν ἀνθρώπων).

A clear implication of the way the verse is worded is that the so-called Shemihazah form of the angel story is here reflected, although that angel's name is not used. That is, according to 39:1 — and assuming the verbal tenses have been construed correctly above — the result of the angelic descent was sexual mingling with humans (in the two other forms of the story that Dimant and others have distinguished in 1 En 6–11, *teaching* is the result of angels' interaction with people).[18] Dimant has maintained that the Book of Parables uses only the form of the angel story in which angels (including Asael = Azazel) teach forbidden information to people and thus make them sin.[19] That is not

---

16. Commentators have noted, however, that the term is used in connection with angels elsewhere, citing 1 Tim 5:21 and perhaps Tob 8:15 (Dillmann, *Das Buch Henoch,* 143).

17. Nickelsburg (Nickelsburg and VanderKam, *1 Enoch,* 182) thinks the Ethiopic reading resulted from a confusion of μείγνεσθαι and μιαίνεσθαι. Charles thought a corruption in Ethiopic was the culprit *(tadammaru* for *tagammanu* or *yetgammadu);* see R. H. Charles, *The Ethiopic Version of the Book of Enoch,* Anecdota oxoniensia (Oxford: Clarendon, 1906), 16 n. 2.

18. D. Dimant, "The Fallen Angels in the Dead Sea Scrolls and in the Apocryphal and Pseudepigraphic Books Related to Them" (in Hebrew) (Ph.D. diss., Hebrew University, Jerusalem, 1974), 23-72. Dimant isolates these forms of the story: (1) Shemihazah and the angels corrupt themselves with women from whom they engender giants who are evil and violent; this version has no connection with the flood; (2) angels sin by teaching forbidden secrets to humans and in this way lead them into sin; and (3) Asael corrupts people through his teaching and thus leads them into sin.

19. Dimant, "Fallen Angels," 87-88. On p. 90 n. 29 Dimant deals with 1 En 39:1 but does not notice how it conflicts with her general conclusion about the form of the story reflected in the Parables.

true, however, for 39:1 does not mention teaching but charges them with mixing their seed with human seed.

## 1 Enoch 54:1–56:4[20]

In this passage the writer weaves motifs from the angel story into his picture of punishment on the mighty kings and his vision of the Chosen One sitting as judge upon the throne (54:2; 55:3–56:4). The occasion for introducing the angel story is Enoch's viewing "a deep valley with burning fire" (54:1). Upon inquiring about the making of heavy chains there, the angel of peace explained: "These are being prepared for the host of Azazel, that they might take them and throw them into the abyss of complete judgment, and with jagged stones they will cover their jaws,[21] as the Lord of Spirits commanded" (54:5). The text echoes features in 1 En 10,[22] and that this chapter served as a source is reinforced by the section about the four angels in 54:6. The immediate inspiration appears to be 10:4-8 — the Lord's commissioning of Raphael to pitch Asael into a dark hole in the wilderness where he was to "lay beneath him[23] sharp and jagged stones" (10:5). Asael would be confined in that uncomfortable position as a preliminary punishment until the final judgment. The Parables passage includes Azazel's host *(te'yenta 'azazē'ēl)* in his punishment — a sign that the writer knows a composite of stories regarding the angels and that he is not alluding simply to the Asael sections that modern scholars have isolated in the Book of the Watchers. Also, 10:7, still part of Raphael's orders regarding Asael, speaks of the Watchers: Raphael is to heal the earth that they have desolated, and mention is made of the mystery they had taught humans (10:7). It is noteworthy that a valley (the object of Enoch's viewing in chap. 54) does not figure in 10:4-8; instead, one appears in 10:12, part of Michael's orders with respect to Shemihazah and his band (10:11-15). The section about the flood in 54:7–55:2 — the so-called Noachic supplement or interpolation — makes some sense in this section about punishments, since in chap. 10 the flood serves to destroy the earth[24] — a punishment that makes sense if

---

20. A part of this section (54:7–55:2) is usually considered one of the Noachic fragments in the Parables (e.g., Dillmann, *Das Buch Henoch*, iii, 170; Charles, *The Book of Enoch*, 106-7).

21. The Ethiopic term *malātehihomu* is surprising here; a variant is *mal'eltihomu* = over them.

22. Dillmann, *Das Buch Henoch*, 171. Charles (*The Book of Enoch*, 106) referred more generally to chaps. 10–16.

23. Nickelsburg's translation follows the Greek ὑπὸ αὐτῷ, which Charles (*The Book of Enoch*, 23), preferring the Ethiopic, considered a mistake for ἐπὶ αὐτῷ.

24. See Black, *The Book of Enoch*, 184.

people had done something wrong, as they do in the versions (e.g., the Azazel/Asael form) of the angel story involving instruction.

It follows, then, that the writer of the Parables knew various angel stories now embedded in the Book of the Watchers, not just one of them. The words of 54:6 reinforce the point: "And Michael and Raphael and Gabriel and Phanuel will take hold of them on that great day, and throw them on that day into the burning furnace, that the Lord of Spirits may take vengeance on them, for their unrighteousness in becoming servants of Satan, and leading astray those who dwell on the earth." The phrase "that great day" refers to the final judgment, as suggested by 10:6, 13, which indicate that after the imprisonment of Asael, Shemihazah, and his angels (a confinement lasting until the final assize), they will be transferred to a fiery abyss, a conflagration (see 67:4-5). The sin for which the angels receive punishment is "their unrighteousness in becoming servants of Satan, and leading astray those who dwell on the earth" (54:6). Satan is imported by the writer (see also 65:6), but the sin of misleading comes from the Book of the Watchers (cf. 8:1-2; 9:8; 13:2; 16:3).

*1 Enoch 64–65*

The short rehearsal of angelic motifs in this chapter repeats some of the themes in chap. 54.[25] Regarding "other figures" (v. 1) he saw in a certain place, Enoch hears an angel say: "These are the angels who descended upon the earth. And what was secret they revealed to human beings, and they led the human beings astray so that they committed sin" (v. 2). Again we have a blending of traditions: the descending angels (said only of Shemihazah and his associates in 1 En 6–11) revealed secrets to humans and thus led them astray (traditions supposedly not associated with Shemihazah and company in 6–11).

Even though chap. 65 is the first chapter in the lengthiest Noachic section in the Book of Parables (65:1–69:25), it continues several of the themes introduced in chap. 64. There Enoch informs Noah, who, like Lamech in 1 En 106–107 and Genesis Apocryphon 2–5, has traveled to the ends of the earth to ask Enoch a question, that a "command has gone forth from the presence of the Lord against the inhabitants of the earth, that their end is accomplished, for they have learned all the secrets of the angels, and all the violence of the satans, and all their powers, the hidden secrets and all the powers of those who practice sorcery, and the powers of spells, and the powers of those who cast molten images in all the earth" (65:6; see also vv. 7-8, 10-11). The list of charges against the

25. See Dillmann, *Das Buch Henoch*, 199.

*James C. VanderKam*

inhabitants of the earth is in good part a rehearsal of items the angels taught in chaps. 6–16: secrets of the angels (8:3 [Greek and Aramaic]; 9:6; 10:7; 16:3; cf. 69:11); sorcery (7:1; 8:3; cf. 9:8; sorceries may be mentioned in 69:10); spells (8:3); molten images (not mentioned, although working metals are in 8:1; compare 65:7-8).[26] The satans are a contribution of the Parables. As in 65:12, in 10:1-3 Noah is assured of his righteousness (so also 67:1-3).

### 1 Enoch 69:2-3

While the sections surveyed above that recall the material about the angels in 1 En 6–16 show significant influence of the Book of the Watchers on the Parables, the most certain case of borrowing comes in the first angel list found in 69:2-3. As commentators note, the two lists — the one in 6:7 and the one in 69:2-3 — are identical (with spelling problems) apart from a scribal lapse or two. Careful comparison with the evidence from the Aramaic fragments (they attest at least parts of nineteen of the names) allows one to conclude that the list contained twenty names, with the extra one in 69:2 *(Basasā'ēl)* found in no other form of the list.[27] This list and the shorter form of it in 8:3 are closely associated, whether implicitly or explicitly, with the subjects that angels taught human beings. That point is verified by the second list in 69:4-12 (13), in which the first, Yekon, and the second, Asbe'el, are related directly to the form of the story in which the angels and women sinned (the Shemihazah form). Yekon, the first angel, "led all the children of the angels astray and brought them down upon the earth, and led them astray through the daughters of men" (v. 4). The second angel, Asbe'el, "gave evil counsel to the children of the holy angels, and led them astray so that they ruined their bodies through the daughters of men" (v. 5). The names given these angels are unexpected, but the traditions associated with them are familiar from the Book of the Watchers.[28]

There are, therefore, both formal connections and associations of content

---

26. Dillmann (*Das Buch Henoch*, 202), however, wrote that in vv. 6-8, and more so in chap. 69, a number of items not mentioned in the Book of the Watchers are enumerated.

27. Milik (*The Books of Enoch*, 152-54) sets forth the evidence of all the versions for 6:7; Black (*The Book of Enoch*, 118-19) does the same but adds the evidence from 69:2 to the list, as does Knibb (*Ethiopic Book of Enoch*, 2:70-71). Each of these scholars appends commentary to the listings in which they deal with the various problems that arise. Dillmann (*Das Buch Henoch*, 210) wondered whether the extra name resulted because the leader, Shemihazah, was numbered separately.

28. Dillmann (*Das Buch Henoch*, 210) suggested that the writer of the Parables supplied his own information in this list, but he added the first list so as not to contradict the Book of the Watchers to too great an extent.

*The Book of Parables within the Enoch Tradition*

between the Parables and the Book of the Watchers, leading one to think that the writer of the Parables used the older text as a source and tried to connect his book with it. A natural place in which to locate such a work was directly after the source text whose latter parts were also in the form of a travelogue.

## The Parables and the Astronomical Book (or Book of the Luminaries)

A more difficult question is the relation between the Book of Parables and the Astronomical Book, which follows it in our present collection. Was the author of the Parables indebted to the Astronomical Book, and is there indication of an attempt to connect the two in some sense?

On a *formal* level we can again speak of a parallel, as in most of chaps. 72–82 Enoch is again on a tour guided by an angel, in this case the angel Uriel. This means that in their basic literary form 1 En 17–36, 37–71, and 72–82 are alike.[29] There is not, however, any clear indication that an editor tailored the ending of the Parables to fit smoothly with the beginning of the Astronomical Book. As Enoch ascends in chap. 71, it is the angel Michael who "raised me up, and brought me out to all the secrets; and he showed me all the secrets of mercy, and he showed me all the secrets of righteousness. And he showed me all the secrets of the ends of heaven and all the treasuries of the stars, and all the luminaries emerge from there before the holy ones" (71:3-4). That is, we have here language familiar from other parts of the booklet (secrets, treasuries, holy ones). In the following section (vv. 5-13) the four angels mentioned earlier in 54:6 (Michael, Raphael, Gabriel, Phanuel) are seen at the house of the Head of Days. In 71:14-18 there is an unidentified angel ("That angel") who informs the patriarch that he is the Son of Man. None of this appears to have a direct connection with chaps. 72–82, which open with a statement marking the new section as a different work: "The book about the motion of the heavenly luminaries . . . which Uriel, the holy angel who was with me (and) who is their leader, showed me" (72:1). Even if an earlier form of the Book of Parables ended around the conclusion of chap. 69, as a number of scholars think, the same point would be valid. There appears to have been no effort made to fashion a literary bridge to the Astronomical Book.[30]

As for *content,* there is a series of passages in which the writer of the Para-

29. Dillmann, *Das Buch Henoch,* iv.
30. If the Book of Parables ended at 69:25, one could claim a certain relation in subject matter with the Astronomical Book, since vv. 13-25 deal with the oath that governs the working of the various parts of the creation, but, as shown below, there are important differences between the way chap. 69 presents these topics and the way they are treated in chaps. 72–82.

bles takes up subjects that remind one especially of the Astronomical Book. They are 41:3-8; 43–44; 59:1-3; 60:11-22; cf. 69:13-25; 71:4. Each of these should be examined for signs that it is based on the Astronomical Book. We should keep in mind that a comparison is rendered more uncertain by the problematic textual history leading from the Aramaic to our Ethiopic Astronomical Book. The form of the scientific book in the Ethiopic version of 1 Enoch may not be exactly like the one the writer of the Parables used, if he did in fact use such a source.

### 1 Enoch 41:3-8

The passage is set in a certain place Enoch is viewing (see vv. 1-2). Enoch mentions seeing secrets *(ḥebu'at)* and storehouses *(mazāgebt)* especially, and in the section he explains what is involved in each case. First, the secrets include:

- lightnings
- thunder
- winds (how they are divided)
- clouds and dew (the places from which they come)

The storehouses are for:

- distributing winds
- hail and winds
- mist and clouds
- sun and moon

The two great luminaries are then the subjects of the remainder of the section.

If we compare this section with the Astronomical Book, we can see that it deals with a series of items that also figure in chaps. 72–82: winds, dew, mist, sun, moon, and the fixed courses of the two luminaries. Yet, while some rather general, obvious phrasing is common to the two units, the differences between 41:3-8 and the Astronomical Book are more impressive.

First, according to chap. 41, there are two categories into which the phenomena under discussion (see above) are distributed: secrets *(ḥebu'at)* and storehouses *(mazāgebt)*. Neither of these terms is found in the Astronomical Book, which consistently uses the language of gates *(xoxt,* pl. *xāwāxew)* in connection with the sun, moon, stars, and winds.[31] In this context it is important

---

31. The gate terminology of the Astronomical Book can also be found in chaps. 33–36.

to note that the term "storehouses" could derive from the several scriptural passages that use it in a similar context. Ps 135:7, for example, declares: "He it is who makes the clouds rise at the end of the earth; he makes lightnings for the rain and brings out the wind from his storehouses (ומוצא רוח מאוצרותיו)." Or in Job 38:22 the Lord asks: "Have you entered the storehouses of the snow, or have you seen the storehouses of the hail?" (see also Deut 28:12; Jer 10:13 = 51:16; Ps 33:7).[32] The language of 1 En 41 more nearly resembles these scriptural passages than it does the vocabulary of the Astronomical Book. In addition, the expression "the storehouses of the winds" in 41:4 echoes 18:1 (*mazāgebta k"ellu nafāsāt;* τοὺς θησαυροὺς τῶν ἀνέμων πάντων).[33]

Second, several of the items that are prominent in 1 En 41 play no role in the Astronomical Book. Among these are the lightnings, thunder, and clouds. Conversely, chaps. 72–82 deal with several subjects not treated in chap. 41 (e.g., stars, calendar issues, hierarchy of stars, mountains, etc.), although this may be a product of its being far shorter. Moreover, the luminaries praise the deity in 41:7 (as in Pss 19; 148:3), and the contrasting themes of blessing and curse, and light and darkness as moral categories also receive attention in 41 (see 69:24-25); in the Astronomical Book the sun, moon, and stars are not said to offer praise, while light and darkness do not function as moral categories.

### 1 Enoch 43–44

These short chapters that conclude the first of the three parables disclose additional phenomena seen by the traveling patriarch. Specifically, he views "other lightnings and stars of heaven" that

- he calls by their names and they listen;
- are weighed in a balance according to their light, space, and day of appearing;
- have motion that produces lightning and is in agreement with the number of the angels; and
- keep faith with one another.

---

32. See Black, *The Book of Enoch*, 202, for other references.

33. See K. Coblentz Bautch, *A Study of the Geography of I Enoch 17–19: "No One Has Seen What I Have Seen,"* JSJSup 81 (Leiden: Brill, 2003), 100-101. The Greek of 1 En 17:3 reads τοὺς θησαυροὺς τῶν ἀστέρων καὶ τῶν βροντῶν. Dillmann (*Das Buch Henoch*, 149) wrote regarding the winds in chap. 41: ". . . das neue ist hier die geheimnisvolle Weise, wie sie, nachdem sie aus diesen Thoren ausgelassen sind, nun über die Erde hin sich vertheilen oder verbreiten V. 3 . . . , und die Behälter, in welchen sie aufbewahrt werden V. 4. . . ."

At this point Enoch asked what these were and received the answer: "The Lord of Spirits has shown you a parable concerning them; these are the names of the holy ones who dwell on the earth and believe in the name of the Lord of Spirits forever and ever" (43:4). Then in chap. 44 he sees that some stars become lightning but cannot leave their form.

As we have already noted, there are no references to lightning in the Astronomical Book, but the theme of stars with names (also in 69:21; see Isa 40:26; Ps 147:4)[34] is consistent generally with 72:1 ("the heavenly luminaries ... their name"), and associating each of them with an angel sounds much like 82:9-20 where, according to some, we read about the names of each angel who leads specific stars. Moreover, the subject of the motion of the luminaries appears in the title of the Astronomical Book *(maṣḥafa miṭata berhānāta samāy)*, and perhaps their keeping faith with one another (as in 41:5) expresses the enduring obedience of the stars to the divine laws imposed upon them. So there are these parallels between the two texts.

Yet these parallels should be placed in the larger context of the major differences that separate them. We have already mentioned the problem with the lightning, but the notion of weighing the stars in a balance has led Black, following other commentators, to assert that in the Book of Parables "[t]he stars and heavenly bodies are hypostatised; they are heavenly beings, with consciousness and conscience, to be assessed or 'weighed in a balance,' like mankind, and to be so judged" according to the criteria listed in 43:2.[35] The Astronomical Book, although it stresses the obedience of the sun, moon, and stars to the laws assigned to them, does not personify them. Furthermore, the parabolic correlation between the stars and the names of the holy ones in 43:4 has no counterpart in the Astronomical Book but may be an echo of a passage like Dan 12:3 where the wise shine like the stars.[36] In a weighty sense, then, one can conclude that the two works differ considerably, even where they address similar subjects.

## 1 Enoch 59:1-3

The passage resumes a number of the themes enunciated in 41:3-8.[37] So, it refers to the secrets of the lightnings and luminaries (with their laws), and it also

---

34. Dillmann, *Das Buch Henoch*, 153.

35. Black, *The Book of Enoch*, 203-4. See also Dillmann, *Das Buch Henoch*, 153; Charles, *The Book of Enoch*, 82; Martin, *Le livre d'Hénoch*, 91-92. Personified stars are familiar from Job 38:7, while stars judged for disobedience appear in 1 En 18:15.

36. The similarity to Dan 12:3 is mentioned regularly in the commentaries, e.g., Dillmann, *Das Buch Henoch*, 153.

37. See Dillmann, *Das Buch Henoch*, 180-81.

speaks of how the luminaries give their light for a blessing or curse (vv. 2-3; cf. 41:8). It reads in a similar way with respect to the secrets of the thunder (for peace, blessings, or a curse). None of these ideas is at home in the Astronomical Book. The section is consistent in its teachings with chap. 41 (and 43–44) and continues to use the language employed there.

## 1 Enoch 60:11-23

This passage, which Nickelsburg places directly after 59:1-3 and before 60:1-10,[38] is similar in several respects to the previous examples. It resumes the vocabulary of what is secret (*za-ba-ḫebu'*, v. 11) and of storehouses of the winds (v. 12),[39] but the winds or spirits play the most dominant role in the section. After referring to the thunder and lightnings in their divisions (vv. 13-14), the writer explains that the wind checks them in some fashion. Once the topic of wind *(manfasa)* has been put forward, the reader meets a listlike section that enumerates six types of winds: of the sea, frost/hail, snow (frost), mist, dew,[40] and rain (vv. 16-21; cf. Jub 2:2, where several of the same ones appear). The section concludes with a reference to the waters on the earth (compare 1 En 77). The winds are the chief topic of 1 En 76 (with 75:5), but there the term for them is *nafsāt*, not *manfas*. In addition, in chap. 76 the presentation of the winds is different than in chap. 60. In chap. 76 the writer lists the groups of three gates in each of the four directions and describes the winds that emerge from each of them (as in chaps. 33–36). That is, the Astronomical Book uses its characteristic language of gates in connection with them. In its system of twelve gates for the winds, all the items named in 60:16-21 occur,[41] except the sea, some of them several times. Despite the overlaps for the specific entities, it is not obvious that the Astronomical Book served as a source for the presentation in chap. 60.

Despite the clear differences that separate 60:11-23 and the Astronomical Book, it is of some interest that 60:21b-22, which deals with the waters on the earth, immediately precedes Enoch's summary statement: "All these things I saw toward the Garden of the Righteous. . . ." One finds the same sequence in 77:3, where the northern quarter is divided into three parts: "the second is for seas, the deeps, forests, rivers, darkness, and mist; and the other part is for the

38. 1 En 60:24-25 supplies the answer to the question asked in v. 10.
39. As we have seen, the expression is also found in 18:1; there vv. 1-5a deal with the winds.
40. The phrase *manfasa ṭall* finds its exact counterpart in 75:5.
41. See S. Uhlig, "Das äthiopische Henochbuch," in *JSHRZ* V.6, ed. Werner G. Kümmel (Gütersloh: Gütersloher Verlagshaus Gerd Mohn, 1984), 608 n. d to v. 14.

*James C. VanderKam*

garden of righteousness."[42] Nevertheless, though the sequence is the same, the descriptions are not duplicates of one another, as nothing is said in chap. 60 about divisions of the earth. Moreover, the Aramaic text for chap. 77 seems to have a different arrangement. Due to manuscript damage, most of what preceded the mention of the garden of righteousness is lost, but the only word preserved directly before it is "desert," followed by an indecipherable term.[43] So there is no evidence that words for seas and rivers immediately preceded mention of the garden in the Aramaic version.

## 1 Enoch 69:13-25

The final extended treatment of topics that, in a way, remind one of the ones examined in the Astronomical Book follows the lists of angels in 69:2-12. The first of these lists falls, as we have seen, into the category of passages in the Parables that show strong connections with the Book of the Watchers, since the angels enumerated in 69:2-3 are nearly identical with the ones in 6:7[44] (and partially present in 8:1-3). Also, the second list, which elaborates the evil actions of five angels, none of whose names appears in the first list, clearly echoes the story of the angels who sinned.

Continuing the second list of angels that began in 69:4, 69:13-25 refers to a sixth angel, Kasbe'el, who is identified as the head of the oath *(re'sa maḥālā)*, which he showed to the "holy ones when he was dwelling on high in glory" (v. 13).[45] Somehow this oath was to make the ones showing people "everything

---

42. See Charles, *The Book of Enoch*, 118.

43. 4QEnastr[b] 23 line 9 Milik reads as: למדברין ולש[ב] ע[ו]ל[פרד]ס קושטא. His reading is highly dubious and arises from his belief that the division of the world is based on the Babylonian *mappa mundi*. See Milik, *The Books of Enoch*, 289-91. It is, however, also accepted by E. J. C. Tigchelaar and F. García Martínez, "209. 4QAstronomical Enoch[b] ar," in *Qumran Cave 4.XXVI: Cryptic Texts, Miscellanea, Part 1*, ed. J. C. VanderKam and M. Brady, DJD 36 (Oxford: Clarendon, 2000), 159-61. Even if we accepted this reading, the point made above would stand: the presentation here differs from that in chap. 60.

44. As Nickelsburg (Nickelsburg and VanderKam, *1 Enoch*, 88 n. p) explains, "the first list corresponds to 6:7, except that the thirteenth name has no counterpart and the following names are pushed back one position, resulting in twenty-one rather than twenty names." We may add that the introductory and concluding statements that surround the lists in the two places are similar.

45. Dillmann did not think this angel is called the head of the oath, since in v. 15 Michael is the one who has that function. Instead, he understood the phrase *re'sa maḥālā* as a preposed object of *za-'ar'aya* ("... Kesbeêl, der das Haupt des Schwures den Heiligen zeigte . . ."). See Dillmann, *Das Buch Henoch*, 39 (translation), 213 (commentary); see also the translation of

*The Book of Parables within the Enoch Tradition*

that was in secret [*kʷello za-ba-ḫebuʾ*]" tremble at it and at the name (v. 14). The oath under discussion is the one by which creation was made and fixed according to set laws for each of its components, as vv. 16-25 show (see 41:5). In 69:16, a heading over the section about the creation claims: "And these are the secrets of this oath [*ḫebuʾātihu la-ze maḥālā*], and they are strong through this oath."

The creation section proceeds in this order: heaven, earth, sea (with deeps fixed in place). At this point it reaches the items of interest for our purposes (vv. 20-23). Through the oath

- the sun and moon complete their course *(yefeṣemu meḥwāromu)*, not violating their command;
- the stars complete their courses *(yefeṣemu meḥwārihomu)*; God calls them by name and they answer.

69:22 then provides a list of spirits or winds:

- spirits of the water
- spirits of the winds
- spirits of the breezes with their paths, from the quarters of the winds

69:23 lists several topics that are by now familiar in the Parables:

- the voices of the thunder
- the light of the lightnings
- the storehouses *(mazāgebt)* of hail, hoarfrost, mist, rain, and dew

The section concludes with a statement that all creation praises and thanks the Lord of the Spirits and that "over them this oath is mighty, and they are preserved by it, and their paths [*fenāwihu*] are preserved, and their courses [*meḥwārātihomu*] will not perish" (vv. 24-25).

If we set this section alongside the Astronomical Book, we see that two texts share the fundamental tenet that the creation runs by fixed, unchanging laws. That point is made in chap. 69 by reference to the oath and several comments to the effect that the constituents of creation do not depart from their command; it is also made in the first verse of the Astronomical Book (72:1:

---

Uhlig, "Das äthiopische Henochbuch," 627-28, with n. d to v. 13. The point is not essential to the argument here, but the verse, if it does call Kasbeʾel the head of the oath, is consistent with v. 15, which says that he put it in Michael's hand, not that he was head of the oath.

"how every year of the world will be forever"; cf. the repeated references to laws and passages such as 74:17 and chap. 79).[46]

Despite this important point of agreement (shared with wider portions of the Enoch literature such as 1 En 2–5), 1 En 69 proceeds in step with other sections of the Parables by referring to the hidden things of creation and the storehouses of various meteorological phenomena. It too uses terms that, as we have seen several times now, do not figure in chaps. 72–82 (e.g., "thunder," "lightning"). There is, however, some shared vocabulary (e.g., the courses of the luminaries, their commands, the winds [*nafāsāt* is used in both units]) — something that would have been difficult to avoid since they are talking about the same natural objects.

The upshot of comparing the several sections from the Parables with the Astronomical Book is that, though they talk about many of the same phenomena, they do so from within different frameworks and show no clear sign of a *literary* relationship, despite their taking the form of travelogues.

## Conclusion

At the end of this study some suggestions about the evolution of 1 Enoch may be in order. We do not know how our five-book arrangement arose, but some points are clear.

a. The last chapters of the Book of the Watchers (1 En 33–36) bear some relation to the Astronomical Book, with the latter seeming to be a fuller expression of material that is severely abbreviated in the former. Yet whether chaps. 72–82 ever followed 1–36 directly, we do not know. At least the data from Qumran do not allow us to say that they were combined in a single manuscript.

Nickelsburg has suggested that the original end of the Book of the Watchers can now be found in 81:1-4, which with 81:5–82:4c (the story of Enoch's return home for a year and plan for his final removal by the angels) provides a link with the Epistle of Enoch. He thinks that 81:1-3 (with v. 4) "is actually a remnant of a seventh vision, under the tutelage of the angel Remiel, which has been dropped from the journey account in chaps. 20–36, which presently records six visions."[47] On his view, this section with its sequel does not belong to the Astro-

---

46. This teaching in the Astronomical Book clashes, according to most commentators, with the poetic claim in 80:2-8 that all this will change in the days of the sinners. Hence, these verses in chap. 80 are often considered an addition.

47. Nickelsburg, *1 Enoch 1*, 23.

*The Book of Parables within the Enoch Tradition*

nomical Book. Whatever one thinks about 81:4–82:4,[48] it does not appear likely that 81:1-3 is a displaced seventh vision from the end of the Book of the Watchers.[49] At any rate, there is no reference to an angel Remiel in it.

Nickelsburg offers what he calls a rough sketch of the process through which his original Enochic testament[50] became our 1 Enoch. This is what he says about the parts under discussion here: "(1) The lengthy Astronomical Book attested in the Qumran fragments was compressed and inserted after chap. 36 in order to document the instruction that is alluded to in 33:3-4 and partly summarized in 34–36. In the process of this insertion, or at some other point, a remnant of the end of the Book of the Watchers (cf. 81:1-3) and the testamentary narrative in 81:1–82:4 came to be embedded in the Astronomical Book. (2) The Book of Parables was inserted after chap. 36 and before chap. 72 probably because it contains many overlaps with the traditions in chaps. 1–36."[51] I believe it would be simpler to say that the following step took place after the Book of the Watchers and the Astronomical Book were placed one after the other:

b. The Book of Parables, closely related in content and form to significant parts of the Book of the Watchers, was understandably placed after the book on which it is to some extent modeled and which it develops. That is, there is no need to see in 81:1-3 a part of the Book of the Watchers. In this way chaps. 33–36 were separated from the similar material in chaps. 72–82.

---

48. Many commentators agree that these sections of chaps. 81–82 (with 80:2-8) are problematic, but to call them problematic does not tell us how they got there or where they may originally have been located.

49. For some problems, including his location in 1 En 81:1-3, see J. J. Collins, "An Enochic Testament? Comments on George Nickelsburg's Hermeneia Commentary," in *George W. E. Nickelsburg in Perspective: An Ongoing Dialogue of Learning*, ed. J. Neusner and A. J. Avery-Peck, 2 vols., JSJSup 80 (Leiden: Brill, 2003), 374-75; and, in the same volume, VanderKam, "Response to George Nickelsburg: *1 Enoch: A Commentary on the Book of 1 Enoch: Chapters 1–36; 81–108*," 381-83; Nickelsburg, "1 Enoch as a Testament," esp. 415-17.

50. 1 En 1–36 + 81:1–82:4 + 91 + at least some of 92–105; later the Dream Visions or at least 85–90 were added, followed by the remainder of 92–105, and still later 106–107.

51. Nickelsburg, *1 Enoch 1*, 26 (see also 25).

# Remarks on Transmission and Traditions in the Parables of Enoch: A Response to James VanderKam

*Eibert J. C. Tigchelaar*

In his essay in the current volume, James VanderKam discusses the present place of the Parables of Enoch within the Enochic pentad that has been transmitted in the Ethiopic tradition.[1] VanderKam describes the general problem regarding the Book of Parables as follows: "Why was it later transmitted together with the other Enochic texts (apart from its connection with Enoch himself), and why was it placed in second position, after the Book of the Watchers and before the Astronomical Book? Are there traces in the Parables of attempts by the writer or an editor to tie the work to the more ancient texts, that is, to relate it to the trajectories of these works? And can we detect any reasons why it became the second element in the Enochic pentad?" VanderKam tackles these questions by focusing on data pertinent to the relation between the Book of Parables (1 En 36–71) and the two surrounding books of the Enochic pentad, the Book of the Watchers (1 En 1–36) and the Astronomical Book (1 En 72–82). In the past, scholars have discussed this issue in general terms, but VanderKam gives a more detailed comparative analysis of some traditions that are central to these books. Thus, he compares the traditions about the angels who sinned as they appear in the Book of Parables with those of the Book of the Watchers, and he studies the differences between the Astronomical Book and the meteorological sections of the Book of Parables.

I will turn to the details later, but VanderKam's conclusion posits that on the one hand there is a clear literary relationship between the Book of the Watchers and the Book of Parables, in the sense that "the writer of the Parables

---

1. See above, J. C. VanderKam, "The Book of Parables within the Enoch Tradition." All quotations from VanderKam come from this essay.

## Remarks on Transmission and Traditions in the Parables of Enoch

used the older text as a source and tried to connect his book with it." On the other hand, his comparison of the meteorological materials of the Book of Parables with the Astronomical Book shows that there is no clear sign of a literary relationship. Whereas George Nickelsburg and Michael Knibb argue for the first conclusion in their essays, the latter conclusion runs counter to the general opinion, voiced for example by Nickelsburg, who in his essay argues that "the author of the Parables drew, first of all, on traditional Enochic material from the Book of the Watchers and . . . the Astronomical Book."[2]

VanderKam's statement of the problem, as quoted above, deals with three different issues, namely, (1) the literary and/or editorial connection between the Book of Parables and the other Enochic books; (2) the transmission history of the Book of Parables in relation to the other Enochic works; (3) the present position of the Book of Parables in the Ethiopic collection. Depending on the answers to these questions, these three issues may or may not be connected. However, in discussing these issues we are dealing not merely with questions to answer, but also with a priori assumptions that determine the questions we ask and how we pose them. For example, VanderKam's first question: "why was [the Book of Parables] placed in second position, after the Book of the Watchers and before the Astronomical Book?" assumes a priori that the Book of Parables was inserted into a collection of Enochic books that already had the sequence the Book of the Watchers and then the Astronomical Book. Indeed, at the very end of his essay, in a reaction to Nickelsburg's thesis that 1 En 81:1-3 originally belonged to the end of the Book of the Watchers, VanderKam affirms explicitly this implicit assumption lying behind his question: "I believe it would be simpler to say that the following step took place after the Book of the Watchers and the Astronomical Book were placed one after the other: The Book of Parables, closely related in content and form to significant parts of the Book of the Watchers, was understandably placed after the book on which it is to some extent modeled and which it develops. . . . In this way chaps. 33–36 were separated from the similar material in chaps. 72–82."[3]

The aim of the present response is to discuss the assumptions and methodological approaches that lie behind sections of VanderKam's essay, and to suggest some alternative approaches or possibilities.

2. See above, G. W. E. Nickelsburg, "Discerning the Structure(s) of the Enochic Book of Parables," and M. A. Knibb, "The Structure and Composition of the Parables of Enoch." Cf. also J. T. Milik, *The Books of Enoch: Aramaic Fragments from Qumrân Cave 4* (Oxford: Clarendon, 1976), 91: "The author of the Book of Parables . . . was familiar with, and used cautiously, certain passages of the Astronomical Book."

3. I do not quite understand how to connect these statements with what VanderKam stated earlier, namely, that we do not know "whether chaps. 72–82 ever followed 1–36 directly."

*Eibert J. C. Tigchelaar*

## Enochic Collections

Josef Milik's presentation and interpretation of the Qumran evidence,[4] and Deborah Dimant's explanation of the Ethiopic evidence,[5] posit a more or less unified literary corpus[6] of four (Dimant: the Book of the Watchers, the Astronomical Book, Dream Visions, and the Epistle of Enoch) or five (Milik: the Book of the Watchers, the Book of Giants, the Astronomical Book, Dream Visions, and the Epistle of Enoch) Enochic booklets, and one clearly distinct booklet, the Book of Parables, which was "a later addition to the corpus."[7] With regard to the nature of the collections of Enochic booklets, literary, historical, thematical, and codicological aspects are concerned. I will argue that from most points of view the idea of a unified literary corpus should be dismissed.

First, VanderKam briefly lists the differences of content that have been taken to indicate that the Book of Parables has a different origin than the other parts of 1 Enoch. However, the distinctiveness of the Book of Parables vis-à-vis the other four books in the Ethiopic Enochic pentad does not automatically imply that the remaining four booklets form a literary corpus with the same contents, concerns, or ideology. On the contrary, apart from correspondences between the booklets, such as the Enochic pseudonymity, there are many differences, and it would be hard to find major elements that appear in each of the four other booklets but not in the Book of Parables.

Second, there is no codicological evidence of a unified literary corpus without the Book of Parables whatsoever. As for the Qumran material, Dimant justly argues that 4Q204 (4QEn$^c$) "present[s] the exception, rather than the rule."[8] The Qumran data are well-known: what we have are ten manuscripts from Qumran Cave 4 that preserve text that corresponds to any of the parts of 1 Enoch, with the exception of the Book of Parables.[9] In three of those manuscripts text has been preserved from more than one booklet: 4Q205 and 4Q206 consist of fragments preserving parts of both the Book of the Watchers and

---

4. J. T. Milik, "Problèmes de la littérature Hénochique à la lumière des fragments araméens de Qumrân," *HTR* 64 (1971): 333-78, and Milik, *The Books of Enoch*.

5. D. Dimant, "The Biography of Enoch and the Books of Enoch," *VT* 33 (1983): 14-29.

6. Dimant ("Biography," 14) poses the question "whether 1 Enoch is a mere random collection of writings or a unified literary corpus," and answers that "the Ethiopic Enoch does indeed constitute a unified corpus carefully constructed around a definite theme" (19).

7. Dimant, "Biography," 28.

8. Dimant, "Biography," 16.

9. 4Q201 (4QEn$^a$), 4Q202 (4QEn$^b$), 4Q203 + 4Q204 (4QEnGiants$^a$ + 4QEn$^c$), 4Q205 (4QEn$^d$), 4Q206 (4QEn$^e$), 4Q207 (4QEn$^f$), 4Q209 (4QEnastr$^b$), 4Q210 (4QEnastr$^c$), 4Q211 (4QEnastr$^d$), 4Q212 (4QEn$^g$).

## Remarks on Transmission and Traditions in the Parables of Enoch

Dream Visions, whereas 4Q203 + 4Q204 preserves parts of the Book of the Watchers, the Book of Giants, Dream Visions, as well as the Epistle of Enoch.[10] The latter manuscript, if accepted that 4Q203 + 4Q204 is one manuscript, also presents the exception since it would be the only manuscript in which the Book of Giants has been preserved with other compositions, against at least nine manuscripts that preserve only remnants of the Book of Giants.[11] Also, one should emphasize that there is no case where the Astronomical Book has been found in a manuscript together with another Enochic book.

The little Greek codicological evidence we have does not support the supposition of an Enochic corpus, where, in no case at all, pieces of more than one booklet have been found in one manuscript.[12] On the contrary, Enochic booklets have been collected with other, non-Enochic works. On the other hand, some secondary references to Enoch do suggest that several parts had been combined in one book.[13] In short, there may have been the notion of a collection of books of Enoch, but we have evidence only of the transmission of separate booklets.

In other words, in Qumran we have codicological evidence of a joining of the Book of the Watchers, Dream Visions, and the Epistle of Enoch (but also, in 4Q212, of the separate copying of the Epistle of Enoch) in the period before the Book of Parables was written, whereas the Greek evidence does support codicological joining of Enochic booklets with other non-Enochic texts, but not the joining of different Enochic booklets.

This means, in particular, that the literary claim of an original sequence of the Book of the Watchers and the Astronomical Book before the addition of the Book of Parables is not warranted by external evidence. VanderKam's statement that the Book of Parables "break[s] up Uriel-Enoch material that appears to belong together (chaps. 33–36; 72–82)" as well as his question quoted above

---

10. Milik's claim that two Enoch manuscripts also contained the Book of Giants has been the subject of many discussions. For a physical and preliminary codicological examination of the materials, cf. my forthcoming "Notes on Fragments of 4Q206/206a and on the Codicology of 4Q203-4Q204: With a Publication of Two IAA #359 Fragments," in which I support on physical grounds Émile Puech's claim (which he made on the basis of paleography) that 4Q206 2 and 3 do not belong with 4Q206 1 and 4. I also maintain that there are no physical or codicological reasons to argue for two manuscripts 4Q203 and 4Q204 instead of one 4Q203 + 4Q204.

11. Cf. É. Puech, *Qumrân Grotte 4.XXII: Textes Araméens, première partie*, DJD 31 (Oxford: Oxford University Press, 2001), 11, who regards as certain 1Q23, 2Q26, 4Q203, 4Q206a, 4Q530, 4Q531, 4Q532, 4Q533, and 6Q8, and as possible 1Q24 and 6Q14.

12. J. T. Milik, "Fragments grecs du livre d'Hénoch (p.Oxy. XVII 2069)," *ChrEg* 46 (1971): 343, believes that fragments 1, 2, and 4 (preserving remnants of Dream Visions) and fragments 3, 5 (part of the Astronomical Book) belong to two manuscripts written by the same scribe.

13. Cf., e.g., the reference to τὰ ἐν τῷ Ἐνὼχ μαθήματα in Eusebius, *Historia ecclesiastica* 7.32.19. Cf. also Syncellus's reference to the "*first* book of Enoch."

("why was it placed in second position, after the Book of the Watchers and before the Astronomical Book?") assume a literary sequence that may have never existed in reality.

The variant forms of the joining or nonjoining of the Enochic booklets in the extant Aramaic and Greek traditions also allow for other hypotheses. Knibb's brief remark at the Camaldoli conference that the Book of Parables never existed as an independent entity may suggest a twin-set composition consisting of the Book of the Watchers and the Book of Parables. In fact, VanderKam's reference to the lack of any "literary bridge to the Astronomical Book" as well as the absence of clear signs of literary relations between the Book of Parables and the Astronomical Book could support the hypothesis that the Book of Parables was added to the Book of the Watchers alone.[14] In that case, the question is whether the Book of Parables was added to a work consisting solely of the Book of the Watchers, or inserted into a collection that probably began with the Book of the Watchers.

If anything, the comparison of the codicological and the historical data suggests that there were different collections of books of Enoch, and there are no grounds to rule out the possibility that in between the Qumran evidence of the second and first centuries B.C.E. and the Ethiopic evidence, there were different combinations of booklets. Thus, there may have been manuscripts containing the Book of the Watchers with the Book of Parables, and perhaps other ones with the Book of the Watchers, the Astronomical Book, Dream Visions, and the Epistle of Enoch, and still another combination consisting of the Book of the Watchers and the Book of Giants.[15] In that case, the Ethiopic evidence would bear witness to the merging of several collections, rather than being the outcome of a linear process of growth of a corpus.

## Literary Dependency: Some Questions

In the essays of VanderKam, Nickelsburg, and Knibb, there seems to be a basic agreement that the Book of Parables in its present form is dependent on the Book of the Watchers, but — except for Nickelsburg — it remains unclear how these scholars see this dependence or relation. Even though they implicitly or ex-

---

14. I realize that this is not consistent with Nickelburg's views on the original Book of the Watchers including 81:1-4.

15. Apart from the exceptional manuscript 4Q203 + 4Q204, there is no direct evidence of a combination of Book of the Watchers and Book of Giants. One should note, though, that some of the fragments attributed to the Manichean Book of Giants reflect the events described in 1 En 6–11.

plicitly acknowledge different layers in the composition, they refrain from discussing to what extent the composition as such has been composed as a sequel to the Book of the Watchers, or whether the connections are to a large extent editorial. A nice example is 39:1-2a. Nickelsburg argues for the following correspondence between the first parable and the Book of the Watchers: chap. 38 cf. 1:3b-9 → 39:1 cf. chaps. 6–11 → 39:2a cf. 13:4-7 and 14:1 → 39:3 cf. 14:8 → 39:4–40:10 cf. 14:9–16:4. This would mean that 39:1-2a underlines on a macrostructural level the correspondence between the first parable and the Book of the Watchers. However, the problems of 39:1-2a are manifold,[16] and Knibb sides with the majority of scholarship in suggesting: "It may also be wondered whether 39:1-2a was originally a marginal comment intended to explain the origin of the Book of Parables." VanderKam is careful not to commit himself to one of these options, and discusses only the tradition reflected in 39:1. Yet, in this way, it remains unclear whether the contents of 39:1 are integral or alien to the Book of Parables.

On the topic of this session (sources and traditions), VanderKam focuses on the traditions of the angels who sinned, and discusses the passages where this theme makes an appearance. He argues for two related issues: first, in the passages of the Book of Parables dealing with the fallen angels, there is significant influence of the Book of the Watchers on the Book of Parables; second, the Book of Parables shows knowledge of both the Shemihazah form of the story and the Asael traditions. Any assessment of these claims should be based on both detailed study of the alleged correspondences and a consideration of assumptions and methodological issues.

VanderKam offers a synchronic intertextual comparison of the Book of Parables as a whole with the Book of the Watchers, and he refers to "the writer" or "the writer of the Parables."[17] The (historically correct) supposition is that the Book of the Watchers is older than the Book of Parables, from which VanderKam concludes that correspondences should be explained as influence of the Book of the Watchers on the Book of Parables.[18] It appears to me that there are some problems with this approach.

First, throughout scholarship on the Book of Parables it has been argued that some pieces of the book (e.g., the Noachic sections) may be units taken from older sources by the author or composer, and edited to fit into the book. On the other hand, other sections may have been interpolated or inserted later on. Thus, an essentially synchronic approach does not take full account of the

---

16. Problematic imperfect *(yewarredu)*; interruption of the narrative 38:1-6 and 39:2b; third-person reference to Enoch in 39:2.
17. Only twice does VanderKam refer to an "editor."
18. Note that VanderKam's formulation is sometimes more nuanced than at other times.

possibility of a multilayeredness of the composition. For the sections referring to the fallen angels, this may mean that sections from some layers may have been influenced by the Book of the Watchers, and other sections, from different layers, not, or to a lesser extent. Also, late editorial additions or reworkings may have attempted to relate the text closer to the Book of the Watchers. Note that these are hypothetical scenarios, but that a full investigation might also have discussed the different possibilities.

VanderKam's intertextual comparison with regard to the stories of the fallen angels strongly focuses on the points of correspondence or even agreement between the Book of the Watchers and the Book of Parables, and much less on the divergences. VanderKam is rarely explicit on the precise processes of influence, but statements such as "Satan is imported by the writer . . . but the sin of misleading comes from the Book of the Watchers" suggest that VanderKam envisages a process in which "the writer" takes over elements from the Book of the Watchers and adds elements of his own or derived from other sources or traditions. However, the relation between the Book of the Watchers and the Book of Parables is different from that between Genesis and Jubilees, for example, where we know that the latter presents a rewriting of the former. That is, even if the Book of the Watchers and the Book of Parables have elements or phrases in common, this does not necessarily indicate that the Book of Parables borrowed them from the Book of the Watchers.

## The Different Watcher Stories

There is yet another methodological problem that lurks behind the approach used in VanderKam's essay. The (ideal-typical) reconstruction of different stories or traditions of the fallen angels is primarily based on the oldest attested forms of the stories in the Book of the Watchers. However, there they are in fact already intermingled, but have been textually isolated and reconstructed by modern scholarship. The reconstructed stories consist of story elements, but one cannot argue that the presence of a specific element in a text means that the author knew the story to which scholars have attributed this specific element. Note that even if the modern scholarly reconstruction of different stories each with their own elements is correct, this does not exclude the possibility that elements of one story may have been transposed to the other story.

Only one or two of the sections discussed by VanderKam are undisputedly part of the Parables, namely, 51:4–56:4 (more specifically 54:4-6; 55:3–56:4) and 64:1. The terminology of 51:4–56:4 is reminiscent of the Asael account in 10:4-8, but VanderKam refers to two elements that do not belong to the ideal

Asael story: the reference to a host of Asael, and the mention of a valley as a place of judgment (as in 10:12). Again in 55:4 (associates of Asael) and 56:3-4 (their chosen and beloved ones) we find elements that do not belong to the ideal Asael story, but to the reconstructed Shemihazah one. The sin being attributed to Asael and his legions is very general: "leading astray." The same sin, "leading astray," occurs again in 64:1, where it is explicitly connected to the revelation of hidden things. Yet VanderKam calls attention to the fact that 64:1 mentions that these angels "descended to the earth," a motif not referred to in the Asael story of the Book of the Watchers.

With regard to these sections, we may note that only small details (e.g., the mention of a furnace of fire) are not found in the Book of the Watchers, notably 1 En 10, and that the main difference is the reference to Satan in 54:6.

Compared to these sections (51:4–56:4 and 64:1), it is striking that the idiom of the other passages, which for a variety of reasons are not universally considered as synchronic with the main body of the Book of Parables, differs to a much larger extent from the Book of the Watchers (except for the list of names of 69:2).

Thus, VanderKam argues that virtually every word in 39:1 can be located in 1 En 6–16.[19] Yet even though this may hold true for separate and very common words ("sons," "chosen," "holy," "seed," "descend," "heaven," etc.), it does not for the expressions used in 39:1. The composite phrases "the chosen and holy children" (reading *daqiq*) or "the sons of the chosen and holy" (reading *daqiqa*), or the remarkable expression "their seed will become [or: was becoming?] one with the sons of men,"[20] are not derived from 1 En 6–16. Unique expressions are also used in 39:2-3: "books of indignation and wrath," "books of agitation and disturbance,"[21] the whirlwind and "the ends of heaven."[22]

---

19. 1 En 39:1: "In those days, the sons of the chosen and holy were descending from the highest heaven, and their seed was becoming one with the sons of men. In those days Enoch received books of jealous wrath and rage and books of trepidation and consternation. And in those days a whirlwind snatched me up from the face of the earth and set me down within the confines of the heavens. And there I saw another vision — the dwellings of the holy ones, and the resting places of the righteous."

20. It is not clear whether this should be understood as a reference to "sexual mingling" (VanderKam: "mixing their seed with human seed"), or that their progeny (?) would mingle.

21. VanderKam does not elaborate on these books, but merely states that in vv. 2-3 the writer seems to be "referring to 1 En 12–16 and perhaps to the visions that follow." Nickelsburg, however, states that in 14:1 Enoch is given a book of reprimand. Of course, though the words of the reprimand have been revealed to Enoch in a vision, there is no reference to a book being given to Enoch in the Book of the Watchers.

22. The rare expression "end of the heavens" is also found in the *Cologne Mani-Codex* 59:20 (ἐκεῖνο[ι] ἐπεκάθισάν με ἐπὶ ἅ[ρ]ματος ἀνέμου καὶ ε[ἰς] τὰ πέρατα τῶν οὐρ[ανῶν] ἀνήνεγκαν).

*Eibert J. C. Tigchelaar*

Whether or not 39:1 refers to the events of chaps. 6–16, these verses use expressions that are to a large extent different from those of the Book of the Watchers.

The claim that in chap. 65 "the list of charges against the inhabitants of the earth is in good part a rehearsal of items the angels taught in chaps. 6–16" cannot be taken to mean that the author adapted these from the Book of the Watchers. In the Book of the Watchers the emphasis is on the use of the results of these secrets: mining and metallurgy resulting in the production of weapons or the production of adornments by which women seduce angels or men. Here the stress is on metallurgy per se, and the fashioning of idols. The mantic arts, as a special kind of secret described in detail in the Book of the Watchers, are absent from this section. Here the interpolation from a Noachic source runs parallel to the account in chaps. 6–11, but there are no signs of a dependence on the Book of the Watchers.

There may be different explanations of the two lists in chap. 69: the first list may have been derived from the Book of the Watchers, in order to harmonize the two accounts, or may have been included as an independent list, used in both compositions. More interesting is the second list. Of course, we have to agree with VanderKam that (some of) the traditions associated with them are familiar from the Book of the Watchers. Yet — see Knibb's essay — the list of the five angels "provides a tradition about the fall of the Watchers quite different from that in chaps. 6–8." This passage is also of interest because it shows an awareness of different stories of falls of angels, and at the same time has no problem with combining them.

This very brief overview suggests that correspondence of some items need not indicate dependence. The only cases of direct correspondence of terminology, together with an absence of other items, are the list of names in 69:2 and the section on Asael and his band in 54–56. In the crude systematization of three levels — (1) earlier materials interpolated or incorporated by a writer/editor/composer in the Parables; (2) the body text of the Parables; and (3) additions/interpolations — it would seem that there are "connections and associations of content" between the Book of Parables and the Book of the Watchers on all three levels, but no clear dependence on the first level; a close correspondence on the second level, most likely to be explained by dependence; and an ambiguous situation with regard to the third.

A comparison of the data from the Book of Parables with the ideal-typical stories on sinning angels that have been reconstructed from the Book of the Watchers shows that the elements from both stories are not strictly separated or distinguished in the different sections on sinning angels in the Book of Parables. Specific elements (the idea of "descending"; the notion of "legions" or "associates/companions" of a principal angel; imprisonment in a "valley") apparently may move from one story to the other. The second list of angels in chap. 69 is instructive in that it connects narrative elements or blocks, but not stories, to specific angels, and that these only partially fit with the stories reconstructed from the Watchers.

## Conclusion

There is no evidence that the Book of Parables was added to or inserted in an already existing Enochic literary corpus. Instead it may have been added by the author or by a later editor to the Book of the Watchers only. Second, an intertextual comparison of the Book of the Watchers and the Book of Parables may be based on a synchronical reading of the Parables, but if one wishes to draw conclusions about dependency of the Parables of Enoch upon the Book of the Watchers, then one should also include a diachronic analysis of possible different layers in the Parables. Third, when pursuing the question of originally different traditions of the fallen angels, and their transmission, one should distinguish between traditions and elements, and take into consideration that elements may wander from one tradition to another.

# Roles and Titles of the Seventh Antediluvian Hero in the Parables of Enoch: A Departure from the Traditional Pattern?

*Andrei A. Orlov*

This work rests on the premise that the clarification of the connection between the two heroes Enoch and Metatron can be achieved through analysis of the roles and titles of both figures in their respective traditions. I will argue that the various appellations of Enoch and Metatron provide the most important clues to the identities of both characters. This approach is especially promising in respect to Metatron since the bulk of information about this angel in rabbinic and Hekhalot materials appears in the form of his titles and description of his roles, as well as activities related to them.

I also contend that understanding the heavenly roles and titles of Enoch and Metatron can help explicate the enigmatic evolution of a character from a patriarch and a seer instructed by angels in the celestial secrets to a second divinity who himself is responsible for instructing visionaries and delivering to them the ultimate mysteries of the universe, including dispensing the Torah to Moses.

It will also be shown that the analysis of the evolution of the roles and titles associated with Enoch-Metatron can assist scholars in better understanding how and when this elusive transition from a diviner to a second god occurred. Examination of the conceptual development of Enoch-Metatron roles might also help clarify the difference between the influences that genuinely contributed to this

---

This essay represents, with some additional comments, excerpts from my book *The Enoch-Metatron Tradition*, TSAJ 107 (Tübingen: Mohr Siebeck, 2005). I am thankful to the editors of Mohr Siebeck Verlag for permission to reproduce parts of my book in this publication.

gradual evolution from Enoch to Metatron and other currents in the Enochic tradition(s) that, despite their promising appearance, did not directly impact this transition. An illustration can be offered to support this idea. Scholars previously noted that the sudden shift in the Book of Parables toward depicting Enoch as a highly elevated celestial being appears to signal the possible transition from Enochic to Metatron imagery.[1] Indeed, in the Parables Enoch seems to become identified with several highly elevated figures, such as the Messiah, Deutero-Isaiah's "Servant of the Lord," and Daniel's "Son of Man."[2] Despite the early date of the Parables, students of this text also pointed to the similarities of some imagery of this narrative with the Merkabah tradition.[3]

This analysis of the evolution of the celestial titles of Enoch toward their later counterparts in the Metatron lore, however, will show that the Enochic titles found in the Parables do not occur in these later beliefs about Metatron; nor do they play any formative part in the transition from the early roles and titles of the patriarch to his elevated profile in the Hekhalot literature. This illustration demonstrates that close attention to the titles occurring in Enochic and Merkabah traditions helps identify more accurately the boundaries of the evolution from Enoch to Metatron and properly outlines major factors and traditions involved in this process.

Keeping in mind these presuppositions, I now proceed to the analysis of the evolution of the roles and titles of the seventh patriarch Enoch in the early Enochic lore.

## Enoch's Roles and Titles in Early Enochic Booklets

This investigation of the patriarch's roles and titles as they appear in the early Enochic writings does not aim to give an exhaustive treatment of these concepts but rather is intended to serve as a sketch that will briefly outline several major developments pertaining to the offices and the appellations of the main hero of the Enochic writings. It is impossible within the limited scope of the in-

---

1. David Suter observed that "the closest tie between Enoch/Metatron in 3 Enoch and the role of Enoch in the earliest literature is the identification of Enoch as the 'Son of Man' in 1 En 71:14 at the conclusion of the Parables of Enoch." See D. W. Suter, *Tradition and Composition in the Parables of Enoch,* SBLDS 47 (Missoula: Scholars, 1979), 16.

2. Although the titles assigned to the patriarch in the Parables were almost completely dropped by later "Enochic" traditions, the presence of such developments shows that long before the exaltation of Enoch as Metatron in *Sefer Hekhalot* there was an apparent need of such a type of conceptual development.

3. Suter, *Tradition and Composition,* 14ff.

vestigation to trace all the evidence pertaining to the patriarch's roles and titles in early Second Temple materials. A thorough treatment of this evidence would require at least a monograph for each Enochic role or title. The task of this investigation is more modest as it concentrates only on some of the evidence pertaining to the major offices and appellations.

In this investigation of early Enochic traditions, I will deliberately avoid any in-depth treatment of Enoch's roles and titles found in 2 (Slavonic) Enoch. Although some details pertaining to this apocalypse will be occasionally mentioned, a systematic treatment of the roles and titles of the patriarch in the Slavonic apocalypse will be offered in a separate section of the study.

Several words must be said about the exposition of the Enochic roles and titles. One of the difficulties of such a presentation is that some roles of the patriarch have a composite nature, often encompassing several functions that can be linked to his other roles. Because of the composite nature of some Enochic roles, it is sometimes very difficult to delineate strictly their boundaries, as some of their functions can be interchangeable. The situation is even more complicated with the titles. The exact title used often depends on the perspectives of various subjects and parties in the texts represented by divine, angelic, and human agents who have different perceptions of the patriarch's offices and activities and, as a consequence, name them differently. Some of Enoch's titles also have a composite nature since one appellation can often include references to the patriarch's several qualities or roles. The descriptions of such complexities pertaining to the roles and titles always involve repetitive explanations. Wherever possible I will try to avoid tautologies, but it should be recognized that repetitions are inevitable in view of the highly complicated nature of the phenomena under investigation.

## Enoch as the Expert in Secrets

Helge Kvanvig observes that "in Jewish tradition Enoch is primarily portrayed as a primeval sage, the ultimate revealer of divine secrets."[4]

The patriarch's prowess in the heavenly secrets is deeply embedded in the fabric of the Enochic myth and is set against the expertise in the celestial knowledge that the fallen Watchers once possessed.[5] John Collins observes that

---

4. H. S. Kvanvig, *Roots of Apocalyptic: The Mesopotamian Background of the Enoch Figure and of the Son of Man*, WMANT 61 (Neukirchen-Vluyn: Neukirchener Verlag, 1988), 27.

5. Pierre Grelot observes that "Enoch is the originator of prophecy understood as revelation of divine secrets." P. Grelot, "La légende d'Hénoch dans les apocryphes et dans la Bible: Origine et signification," *RSR* 46 (1958): 5-26 (here 15).

"most significantly, Enoch is implicitly cast as a revealer of mysteries. The Watchers are angels who descend to reveal a worthless mystery. Enoch is a human being who ascends to get true revelation."[6]

The traditions about the patriarch's expertise in esoteric knowledge are attested in a variety of Enochic materials. In the Astronomical Book the possession and revelation of cosmological and astronomical secrets become a major function of the elevated Enoch. The origin of this role in Enochic traditions can be traced to 1 En 72:1, 74:2, and 80:1, which depict the patriarch as a recipient of angelic revelations, including the celestial knowledge of astronomical, meteorological, and calendrical lore. He remains in this capacity in the majority of the materials associated with the early Enochic circle. In 1 En 41:1 Enoch is portrayed as the one who "saw all secrets of heaven."[7]

Jub 4:17 also attests to this peculiar role of the seventh patriarch. A large portion of 2 Enoch is devoted to Enoch's initiation into the treasures of meteorological, calendrical, and astronomical lore during his celestial tour. The Slavonic apocalypse differs from the earlier materials in that it places special emphasis on the secrecy of cosmological revelations, thus demonstrating intriguing similarities with the later rabbinic developments with their stress on the secrecy of מעשה בראשית. Later Merkabah developments also underscore the role of Enoch as the "Knower of Secrets." Thus, according to *Synopse* §14 (3 En 11:2), Enoch-Metatron is able to behold "deep secrets and wonderful mysteries."[8] Martin Cohen, in his analysis of the *Shi'ur Qomah* materials, observes that this tradition depicts Metatron as "the revealer of the most recondite secrets about Godhead."[9]

Several remarks should be made about the sources of Enoch's knowledge. Collins's research points to the passage in the Apocalypse of Weeks (1 En 93:2) that succinctly summarizes the possible means by which the patriarch acquires the esoteric information.[10] In this text Enoch informs us that he received it according to that which appeared to him *in the heavenly vision,* and which he

---

6. J. J. Collins, *Seers, Sibyls, and Sages in Hellenistic-Roman Judaism,* JSJSup 54 (Leiden: Brill, 1997), 49.

7. M. A. Knibb, *The Ethiopic Book of Enoch: A New Edition in the Light of the Aramaic Dead Sea Fragments,* 2 vols. (Oxford: Clarendon, 1978), 2:128.

8. P. S. Alexander, "3 (Hebrew Apocalypse of) Enoch," in *The Old Testament Pseudepigrapha,* ed. J. H. Charlesworth, vol. 1 (Garden City, N.Y.: Doubleday, 1983), 264; P. Schäfer et al., eds., *Synopse zur Hekhalot-Literature* (Tübingen: Mohr, 1981), 8-9.

9. M. S. Cohen, *The Shi'ur Qomah: Liturgy and Theurgy in Pre-Kabbalistic Jewish Mysticism* (Lanham, Md.: University Press of America, 1983), 127.

10. J. J. Collins, "The Sage in Apocalyptic and Pseudepigraphic Literature," in *The Sage in Israel and the Ancient Near East,* ed. J. G. Gammie and L. G. Perdue (Winona Lake, Ind.: Eisenbrauns, 1990), 345.

knew from *the words of the holy angels* and understood from *the tablets of heaven.*[11] The mention of these three sources underscores the fact that the revelations to the patriarch were given on various levels and through various means of mystical perception: seeing (a vision), hearing (oral instructions of *angelus interpres*), and reading (the heavenly tablets).

It is curious that the terminology pertaining to secrets began to play an increasingly significant role in the later stages of the development of the Enochic tradition. While in the earliest Enochic booklets, such as the Astronomical Book and the Book of the Watchers, the terminology pertaining to secrets and mysteries is barely discernible, it looms large in the later Enochic materials such as the Book of Parables, 2 Enoch, and finally the Merkabah developments. The growing importance of this terminology can be illustrated by 2 Enoch. While various manuscripts of 2 Enoch are known under different titles, most of them include the word "secrets."[12] In some of these titles the term is connected with Enoch's books — "The Secret Books of Enoch." In other titles "secrets" are linked either to God ("The Book[s] [called] the Secrets of God, a revelation to Enoch") or to Enoch himself ("The Book of the Secrets of Enoch"). This consistency in the use of the term "secrets," in spite of its varied attribution to different subjects, indicates that the authors or the transmitters of the text viewed the motif of secrets as a central theme of the apocalypse.

Finally, one must note that Enoch's role as one who was initiated into the highest secrets of the universe might be implicitly reflected in his name. While several etymologies for the patriarch's name have been proposed, many scholars suggest that it might be related to the Hebrew root *ḥnk*, in the sense "to train up," "to dedicate," or "to initiate" (Deut 20:5; 1 Kings 8:63; 2 Chron 7:5).[13]

## Enoch as the Scribe

This section on the unique scribal functions of the seventh antediluvian patriarch begins with a passage found in 2 En 22 that provides a graphic picture of the patriarch's initiation into scribal activities. This initiation takes place near the throne of glory when the Lord himself commands the archangel Vereveil to give a pen to Enoch so that he can write the mysteries explained to

---

11. Knibb, *Ethiopic Book of Enoch*, 2:223.
12. ТАИНЪІ.
13. J. C. VanderKam, *Enoch: A Man for All Generations* (Columbia: University of South Carolina Press, 1995), 11. On the etymology of Enoch's name, see also Grelot, "La légende d'Hénoch," 186; Kvanvig, *Roots of Apocalyptic*, 41-43.

him by the angels. This tradition about the scribal functions of the patriarch reflected in the Slavonic apocalypse was already documented in the earliest Enochic literature.[14] The Book of Giants fragments label Enoch a distinguished scribe.[15] In Jub 4:17 he is attested as the one who "learned (the art of) writing, instruction, and wisdom and who wrote down in a book the signs of the sky."[16] In the Merkabah tradition, Enoch/Metatron is also depicted as a scribe who has a seat (later a throne) in the heavenly realm.[17] The theme of Enoch-Metatron's scribal functions became a prominent motif in the later rabbinic traditions where, according to *b. Ḥag.* 15a, the privilege of sitting beside God was accorded to Metatron alone by virtue of his character as a scribe, for he was granted permission as a scribe to sit and write down the merits of Israel. *Targum Pseudo-Jonathan* on Gen 5:24 describes Metatron as the Great Scribe (ספרא רבא).[18]

The important aspect of the early portrayals of Enoch as a scribe is that they depict him in the capacity of both celestial and terrestrial scribe, as the one who not only records messages from his heavenly guides, but also composes petitions at the request of the creatures from the lower realms, for example, the fallen Watchers/Giants who ask him for mediation. The celestial and terrestrial sides of Enoch's duties as a scribe reveal the composite nature of this important role. Indeed, the patriarch's scribal office can be seen as a mixture of various ac-

---

14. In 1 En 74:2, Enoch writes the instructions of the angel Uriel regarding the secrets of the heavenly bodies and their movements. See Knibb, *Ethiopic Book of Enoch,* 2:173. William Adler draws the reader's attention to an interesting passage from M. Glycas that refers to Uriel's instruction to Seth in a manner similar to Uriel's revelation of the calendrical and astronomical secrets to Enoch in the Astronomical Book of 1 Enoch. "It is said that the angel stationed among the stars, that is the divine Uriel, descended to Seth and then to Enoch and taught them the distinctions between hours, months, seasons, and years." See W. Adler, *Time Immemorial: Archaic History and Its Sources in Christian Chronography from Julius Africanus to George Syncellus,* Dumbarton Oaks Studies 26 (Washington, D.C.: Dumbarton Oaks Research Library and Collection, 1989), 105. For the Greek text see I. Bekker, ed., *Michaelis Glycae Annales,* CSHB (Bonn: Weber, 1836), 228.

15. 4Q203 8: "Copy of the seco[n]d tablet of [the] le[tter . . .] by the hand of Enoch, the distinguished scribe. . . ." F. García Martínez and E. J. C. Tigchelaar, eds., *The Dead Sea Scrolls Study Edition* (Leiden: Brill; Grand Rapids: Eerdmans, 1999), 1:411.

16. J. C. VanderKam, *The Book of Jubilees,* 2 vols., CSCO 510-11 (Louvain: Peeters, 1989), 2:25-6.

17. This tradition can be seen already in 2 En 23:4-6, which depicts the angel Vereveil (Uriel) commanding Enoch to sit down: "'You sit down; write everything. . . .' And Enoch said, 'And I sat down for a second period of 30 days and 30 nights, and I wrote accurately.'" See F. Andersen, "2 (Slavonic Apocalypse of) Enoch," in *The Old Testament Pseudepigrapha,* 1:141.

18. *Targum Pseudo-Jonathan: Genesis,* trans. M. Maher, ArBib 1B (Collegeville, Minn.: Liturgical Press, 1992), 36.

tivities that the Near Eastern scribe was expected to perform.[19] Besides writing, this occupation also presupposes the ability to understand various scripts and languages, since scribal duties required proficiency in copying, i.e., duplicating written materials.[20] One will see later the significance of this dimension of Enoch's scribal activities during his encounters with the celestial tablets from which he often reads and which he also occasionally copies. Another facet of the patriarch's scribal duties linked to his involvement in the Watchers/Giants' situation highlights how his scribal duties resemble the functions of the legal scribe whose activities necessarily include settling disputes and writing petitions.[21] Collins remarks that "Enoch is apparently modeled on the familiar figure of the scribe, whose skill in writing gives him importance not only in communication but also in legal proceedings."[22]

Another detail that shows the composite nature of the patriarch's scribal role is that this office cannot be separated from his initiation into the celestial lore. In early Enochic traditions these two functions appear to be conjoined. The motif of initiation into the secrets as the beginning of scribal activities occupies a substantial role in the Astronomical Book of 1 Enoch, the oldest Enochic material.[23] The same feature is discernible in the Enmeduranki mate-

---

19. On the scribes and the scribal culture in Mesopotamian and Jewish environments, see M. Bar-Ilan, "Writing in Ancient Israel and Early Judaism: Scribes and Books in the Late Second Commonwealth and Rabbinic Period," in *Mikra: Text, Translation, Reading, and Interpretation of the Hebrew Bible in Ancient Judaism and Early Christianity,* ed. M. J. Mulder and H. Sysling, CRINT 2.1 (Philadelphia: Fortress, 1989), 21-38; J. Blenkinsopp, "The Sage, the Scribe, and Scribalism in the Chronicler's Work," in *The Sage in Israel and the Ancient Near East,* 307-15; Collins, "The Sage in Apocalyptic," 343-54; P. R. Davies, *Scribes and Schools: The Canonization of the Hebrew Scriptures* (Louisville: Westminster, 1998), 74-88; L. R. Mack-Fisher, "The Scribe (and Sage) in the Royal Court at Ugarit," in *The Sage in Israel and the Ancient Near East,* 109-15; D. E. Orton, *The Understanding Scribe: Matthew and the Apocalyptic Ideal,* JSNTSup 25 (Sheffield: JSOT, 1989); A. Saldarini, *Pharisees, Scribes, and Sadducees* (Edinburgh: T. & T. Clark, 1989); C. Schams, *Jewish Scribes in the Second-Temple Period,* JSOTSup 291 (Sheffield: Sheffield Academic, 1998); E. E. Urbach, *The Halakha, Its Sources and Development,* Yad La-Talmud (Jerusalem: Massada, 1960).

20. This aspect of the scribe as a translator looms large in 2 En 23:2, where Vereveil (Uriel) teaches the elevated patriarch "every kind of language" (the longer recension) and, specifically, "the Hebrew language" (the shorter recension). See Andersen, "2 (Slavonic Apocalypse of) Enoch," 140-41.

21. Kvanvig (*Roots of Apocalyptic,* 101) draws attention to the similar role of Ezra, whose title "scribe of the law" indicates the conflation of scribal and legal duties.

22. Collins, "The Sage in Apocalyptic," 344.

23. Both R. H. Charles and M. Black argue that the possible biblical parallel to Enoch's role as the scribe could be the passage from Ezek 9 that depicts a man clad in white linen with an inkhorn by his side. See Charles, *The Book of Enoch* (Oxford: Clarendon, 1893; 2nd ed. 1912), 28; M. Black, *The Book of Enoch,* SVTP 7 (Leiden: Brill, 1985), 143.

rial, where the initiation of the practitioner is combined with the motif of the transference to him of a tablet and a stylus.

James VanderKam observes that the Astronomical Book not only expands several traits of the patriarch that are briefly mentioned in Gen 5, but also assigns an entirely new role[24] to him, that of a writer of angelic discourses.[25] VanderKam points out that the beginning of this new activity can be traced to one of the important testimonies in the Astronomical Book that reveals Enoch in his new celestial office. In 1 En 74:2[26] the patriarch is depicted as the one who writes down the instructions of the angel Uriel regarding the secrets of the heavenly luminaries and their movements: "And Uriel, the holy angel who is the leader of them all, showed me everything, and I wrote down their positions as he showed (them) to me; and I wrote down their months, as they are, and the appearance of their light until fifteen days have been completed."[27]

It can hardly be a coincidence that the text here names the angel Uriel as the one who initiates Enoch into the scribal activities; this angel is often depicted in the Enochic lore as a scribe himself.[28]

Later in the Astronomical Book (1 En 81:6), Uriel advises the patriarch to write down the knowledge received in the celestial realm, so that Enoch can share it with his children during his upcoming visitation of the earth. The patriarch's records made in heaven thus seem to play an important role in the transmission of the celestial secrets to humans in general and in particular to the patriarch's son Methuselah, who, like Enmeduranki's son in the Mesopotamian materials, occupies a special place in the mediating activities of the seventh antediluvian hero. One encounters this motif again in 1 En 82:1, when Enoch assures his son Methuselah that he wrote a book for him.

It is puzzling that despite these numerous references to the patriarch's scribal activities, the Astronomical Book does not overtly label Enoch as a scribe. This title with different variations, however, appears in other early Enochic books, including the Book of the Watchers, the Epistle of Enoch, and

---

24. In 1 En 89:62 the scribal function is assigned to Michael.

25. J. C. VanderKam, *Enoch and the Growth of an Apocalyptic Tradition*, CBQMS 16 (Washington, D.C.: Catholic Biblical Association of America, 1984), 104.

26. See also 1 En 82:1: "And now, my son Methuselah, all these things I recount to you and write down for you; I have revealed everything to you and have given you books from the hand of your father, that you may pass (them) on to the generations of eternity." See Knibb, *Ethiopic Book of Enoch*, 2:187.

27. Knibb, *Ethiopic Book of Enoch*, 2:173.

28. For example, in 2 Enoch, Vereveil (Uriel) is depicted as a scribe. The exchange in the roles between Enoch and Uriel is intriguing and goes both ways. Kvanvig (*Roots of Apocalyptic*, 239) observes that in Pseudo-Eupolemus "Enoch was placed into the same position as Uriel in the Astronomical Book."

the Book of Giants. In these writings the patriarch's scribal duties are surrounded by several titles and honorifics, including "scribe," "scribe of righteousness," "scribe of distinction," and "the most skilled scribe."

One must not forget that the great bulk of information about Enoch's scribal roles and honorifics found in Enochic literature may implicitly point to the social profile of the authors of these writings. Collins notes that the description of Enoch as "scribe of righteousness" suggests that the author and his circle may have been scribes too.[29] He observes that although we know little about the authors of the Enochic writings, the books of Enoch "often speak of a class of the 'righteous and chosen' and Enoch, the righteous scribe, must be considered their prototype."[30] He further suggests that it is possible that these people "were, or at least included in their number, scribes who were familiar with a wide range of ancient lore and who wrote books in the name of Enoch."[31]

## Enoch as the Heavenly Priest

Enmeduranki's priestly office, which is only implicitly hinted at in the text from Nineveh, finds its possible Enochic counterpart in the priestly role of the seventh patriarch. In contrast to Enmeduranki's appointments in the earthly sanctuary Ebabbara, the Enochic tradition shifts emphasis from the earthly to the celestial locale in depicting the seventh antediluvian hero, not in his terrestrial priestly role, but in the role associated with the heavenly temple. This role is attested with varying degrees of clarity by early Enochic traditions found in the Book of the Watchers, the Book of Dream Visions, and the book of Jubilees. Enoch's affiliations with the priestly office in the aforementioned texts can be seen as the gradual evolution from the implicit hints of his heavenly priesthood in the early materials to a more overt recognition and description of his celestial sacerdotal function in the later ones. While later Enochic traditions attested in Jubilees unambiguously point to Enoch's priestly role, referring to his incense sacrifice in the celestial sanctuary, the earlier associations of the patriarch with the heavenly temple hinted at in the Book of the Watchers take the form of rather enigmatic depictions. A certain amount of exegetical work is therefore required to discern the proper meaning of these initial associations of the patriarch with the celestial sanctuary.

Martha Himmelfarb's research helps us better understand Enoch's possi-

29. Collins, *Seers, Sibyls, and Sages,* 49.
30. Collins, "The Sage in Apocalyptic," 346.
31. Collins, "The Sage in Apocalyptic," 346; Collins, *Seers, Sibyls, and Sages,* 49.

ble connections with the celestial sanctuary in the Book of the Watchers, which depicts the ascension of the seventh antediluvian patriarch to the throne of glory as a visitation of the heavenly temple.[32] 1 En 14:9-18 reads:

> And I proceeded until I came near to a wall *(ṭqm)* which was built of hailstones, and a tongue of fire surrounded it, and it began to make me afraid. And I went into the tongue of fire and came near to a large house *(bēt ʿābiy)* which was built of hailstones, and the wall of that house (was) like a mosaic (made) of hailstones, and its floor (was) snow. Its roof (was) like the path of the stars and flashes of lightning, and among them (were) fiery Cherubim, and their heaven (was like) water. And (there was) a fire burning around its wall, and its door was ablaze with fire. And I went into that house, and (it was) hot as fire and cold as snow, and there was neither pleasure nor life in it. Fear covered me and trembling, I fell on my face. And I saw in the vision, and behold, another house, which was larger than the former, and all its doors (were) open before me, and (it was) built of a tongue of fire. And in everything it so excelled in glory and splendor and size that I am unable to describe to you its glory and its size. And its floor (was) fire, and above (were) lightning and the path of the stars, and its roof also (was) a burning fire. And I looked and I saw in it a high throne, and its appearance (was) like ice and its surrounds like the shining sun and the sound of Cherubim.[33]

Commenting on this passage, Himmelfarb draws the readers' attention to the description of the celestial edifices that Enoch encounters in his approach to the throne. She notes that the Ethiopic text reports that, to reach God's throne, the patriarch passes through three celestial constructions: a wall, an outer house, and an inner house. The Greek version of this narrative mentions a house instead of a wall. Himmelfarb observes that "more clearly in the Greek,

---

32. M. Himmelfarb, "The Temple and the Garden of Eden in Ezekiel, the Book of the Watchers, and the Wisdom of Ben Sira," in *Sacred Places and Profane Spaces: Essays in the Geographies of Judaism, Christianity, and Islam*, ed. J. Scott and P. Simpson-Housley (New York: Greenwood, 1991), 63-78; Himmelfarb, "Apocalyptic Ascent and the Heavenly Temple," in SBLSP 26 (Atlanta: Scholars, 1987), 210-17. Martha Himmelfarb's research draws on the previous publications of Johann Maier and George Nickelsburg. See J. Maier, "Das Gefährdungsmotiv bei der Himmelsreise in der jüdischen Apokalyptik und 'Gnosis,'" *Kairos* 5, no. 1 (1963): 18-40, esp. 23; Maier, *Vom Kultus zur Gnosis* (Salzburg: Müller, 1964), 127-28; G. W. E. Nickelsburg, "Enoch, Levi, and Peter: Recipients of Revelation in Upper Galilee," *JBL* 100 (1981): 575-600, esp. 576-82. See also Kvanvig, *Roots of Apocalyptic*, 101-2; D. J. Halperin, *The Faces of the Chariot: Early Jewish Responses to Ezekiel's Vision* (Tübingen: Mohr, 1988), 81.

33. Knibb, *Ethiopic Book of Enoch*, 1:50-52; 2:98-99.

but also in the Ethiopic this arrangement echoes the structure of the earthly temple with its vestibule (אולם), sanctuary (היכל), and the Holy of Holies (דביר)."[34]

God's throne is located in the innermost chamber of this heavenly structure and is represented by a throne of cherubim (14:18). It can be seen as a heavenly counterpart to the cherubim found in the Holy of Holies in the Jerusalem temple. In drawing parallels between the descriptions of the heavenly temple in the Book of the Watchers and the features of the earthly sanctuary, Himmelfarb observes that the fiery cherubim Enoch sees on the ceiling of the first house (Ethiopic) or middle house (Greek) of the heavenly structure represent not the cherubim of the divine throne, but images that recall the figures on the hangings on the wall of the tabernacle mentioned in Exod 26:1, 31; 36:8, 35 or possibly the figures that, according to 1 Kings 6:29, 2 Chron 3:7, and Ezek 41:15-26, were engraved on the walls of the earthly temple.[35]

Several comments must be made about the early traditions and sources that may lie behind the descriptions of the upper sanctuary in 1 En 14. Scholars observe that the idea of heaven as a temple was not invented by the author of the Book of the Watchers; the concept of the heavenly temple as a celestial counterpart of the earthly sanctuary was widespread in the ancient Near East[36] and appears in a number of biblical sources.[37] Students of Jewish priestly traditions have observed that the existence of such a conception of the heavenly sanctuary appears to become increasingly important in times of religious crises, when the earthly sanctuaries were either destroyed or defiled by improper rituals or priestly successions.[38]

Returning to the analysis of 1 En 14, one must examine the motif of the servants of the heavenly sanctuary depicted in that text. Himmelfarb argues that the priests of the heavenly temple in the Book of the Watchers appear to be

---

34. Himmelfarb, "Apocalyptic Ascent," 210.

35. Himmelfarb, "Apocalyptic Ascent," 211.

36. R. J. Clifford, *The Cosmic Mountain in Canaan and the Old Testament* (Cambridge: Harvard University Press, 1972), 177-80.

37. Himmelfarb, "The Temple," 68.

38. For an extensive discussion of this subject, see B. Ego et al., eds., *Gemeinde ohne Tempel/Community without Temple: Zur Substituierung und Transformation des Jerusalemer Tempels und seines Kults im Alten Testament, antiken Judentum und frühen Christentum*, WUNT 118 (Tübingen: Mohr/Siebeck, 1999); R. Elior, "From Earthly Temple to Heavenly Shrines: Prayer and Sacred Song in the Hekhalot Literature and Its Relation to Temple Traditions," *JSQ* 4 (1997): 217-67; Elior, "The Priestly Nature of the Mystical Heritage in Heykalot Literature," in *Expérience et écriture mystiques dans les religions du livre: Actes d'un colloque international tenu par le Centre d'études juives Université de Paris IV-Sorbonne 1994*, ed. R. B. Fenton and R. Goetschel, EJM 22 (Leiden: Brill, 2000), 41-54.

represented by angels, since the author of the text depicts them as the ones who are "standing before God's throne in the heavenly temple."[39] In her opinion, such identification can also be implicitly supported by the motif of intercession, which represents "a central priestly task." Himmelfarb also points to the possibility that in the Book of the Watchers the patriarch himself in the course of his ascent becomes a priest, similarly to the angels.[40] In this perspective the angelic status of patriarch and his priestly role are viewed as mutually interconnected. Himmelfarb stresses that "the author of the Book of the Watchers claims angelic status for Enoch through his service in the heavenly temple" since "the ascent shows him passing through the outer court of the temple and the sanctuary to the door of the Holy of Holies, where God addresses him with his own mouth."[41]

George Nickelsburg's earlier research on the temple symbolism in 1 En 14 provides important additional details relevant to this discussion. Nickelsburg argues that Enoch's active involvement in the vision of the Lord's throne, when he passes through the chambers of the celestial sanctuary, might indicate that the author(s) of the Book of the Watchers perceived him as a servant associated with the activities in these chambers. Nickelsburg points to the fact that Enoch's vision of the throne in the Book of the Watchers is "qualitatively different from that described in the biblical throne visions" because of the new active role of its visionary.[42] This new, active participation of Enoch in the vision puts 1 En 14 closer to later Merkabah accounts that are different from biblical visions. Nickelsburg stresses that in the biblical throne visions, the seer is passive or, at best, his participation is reactional. But in the Merkabah accounts, Enoch appears to be actively involved in his vision.[43] In Nickelsburg's view, the verbal forms of the narrative ("I drew near the wall," "I went into that house") serve as further indications of the active participation of the seer in the visionary reality of the heavenly throne/temple.[44]

Biblical visions are not completely forgotten by Enochic authors and provide an important exegetical framework for 1 En 14. Comparing the Enochic vision with Ezekiel's account of the temple, Nickelsburg suggests that the Enochic narrative also represents a vision of the temple, but in this case the heavenly one. He argues that "the similarities to Ezek 40–48, together with other evi-

---

39. Himmelfarb, "Apocalyptic Ascent," 211.
40. Himmelfarb, "Apocalyptic Ascent," 213.
41. Himmelfarb, "Apocalyptic Ascent," 212.
42. Nickelsburg, "Enoch, Levi, and Peter," 579.
43. Nickelsburg, "Enoch, Levi, and Peter," 580.
44. Crispin Fletcher-Louis stresses that the language of Enoch's approach ("to draw near") is cultic. C. H. T. Fletcher-Louis, *All the Glory of Adam* (Leiden: Brill, 2002), 23.

dence, indicate that Enoch is describing his ascent to the heavenly temple and his progress through its *temenos* to the door of the Holy of Holies, where the chariot throne of God is set."[45] The possibility that the author of 1 En 14 was trying to describe Enoch's celestial trip as a tour through the heavenly temple can be supported, in Nickelsburg's judgment, by three significant details:

a. the "house" (14:10) of the deity is by definition a temple;
b. both 12:4 and 15:3 speak about the eternal sanctuary; and
c. the language about the fallen Watchers and the angels approaching God indicates that some of the angels are understood to be priests.[46]

The traditions about the seventh patriarch's heavenly priesthood are not confined solely to the materials found in the Book of the Watchers, since they are attested in other materials associated with the Ethiopic Enoch, including the Animal Apocalypse. If in the Book of the Watchers Enoch's associations with the heavenly temple are clothed in ambiguous imagery, his portrait in the Animal Apocalypse does not leave any serious doubts that some of the early Enochic traditions understood the patriarch to be intimately connected with the heavenly sanctuary.

Chap. 87, vv. 3 and 4 of 1 Enoch portray the patriarch taken by three angels from the earth and raised to a high tower, where he is expected to remain until he sees the judgment prepared for the Watchers and their earthly families: "And those three who came out last took hold of me by my hand, and raised me from the generations of the earth, and lifted me on to a high place, and showed me a tower *(māxefada)* high above the earth, and all the hills were lower. And one said to me: 'Remain here until you have seen everything which is coming upon these elephants and camels and asses, and upon the stars, and upon all the bulls.'"[47]

VanderKam notes a significant detail in this description, namely, Enoch's association with a tower. He observes that this term[48] is reserved in the Animal

---

45. Nickelsburg, "Enoch, Levi, and Peter," 580.
46. Nickelsburg, "Enoch, Levi, and Peter," 580-81.
47. Knibb, *Ethiopic Book of Enoch*, 1:294; 2:198.
48. 1 En 89:50: "And that house became large and broad, and for those sheep a high tower was built on that house for the Lord of the sheep; and that house was low, but the tower was raised up and high; and the Lord of the sheep stood on that tower, and they spread a full table before him." See Knibb, *Ethiopic Book of Enoch*, 2:208. 1 En 89:73: "And they began again to build, as before, and they raised up that tower, and it was called the high tower; and they began again to place a table before the tower, but all the bread on it (was) unclean and was not pure." See Knibb, *Ethiopic Book of Enoch*, 2:211.

Apocalypse for a temple.[49] The association of the patriarch with the tower is long-lasting, and apparently he must have spent a considerable amount of time there, since the text does not say anything about Enoch's return to the earth again until the time of judgment, so the patriarch is depicted as present in the heavenly sanctuary for most of the Animal Apocalypse.[50]

Although the traditions about Enoch's associations with the heavenly temple in the Book of the Watchers and in the Animal Apocalypse do not refer openly to his performance of priestly duties, the account attested in Jubilees explicitly makes this reference. Jub 4:23 depicts Enoch as taken from human society and placed in Eden[51] "for (his) greatness and honor."[52] Jubilees then defines the Garden as a sanctuary[53] and Enoch as one who is offering an incense sacrifice on the mountain of incense: "He burned the evening incense of the sanctuary which is acceptable before the Lord on the mountain of incense."[54] VanderKam suggests that here Enoch is depicted as one who "performs the rites of a priest in the temple."[55] He further observes that Enoch's priestly duties[56] represent a new element[57] in "Enoch's expanding portfolio."[58]

In one further note, I must comment on particular details surrounding

---

49. VanderKam, *Enoch: A Man for All Generations*, 117.

50. VanderKam, *Enoch: A Man for All Generations*, 117.

51. For Enoch's place in the heavenly paradise, see TBenj 10:6; Apoc Paul 20; Clementine Recognitions 1:52; Acts Pil 25; and the Ascen Isa 9:6. C. Rowland, "Enoch," in *Dictionary of Deities and Demons in the Bible*, ed. K. van der Toorn et al. (Leiden: Brill, 1999), 302.

52. VanderKam, *The Book of Jubilees*, 2:28.

53. James VanderKam argues that there are other indications that in Jubilees Eden was understood as a sanctuary. As an example, he points to Jub 3:9-14, which "derives the law from Lev 11 regarding when women who have given birth may enter the sanctuary from the two times when Adam and Eve, respectively, went into the garden." See VanderKam, *Enoch: A Man for All Generations*, 117.

54. VanderKam, *The Book of Jubilees*, 2:28.

55. VanderKam, *Enoch: A Man for All Generations*, 117.

56. Fletcher-Louis (*All the Glory*, 24) notes that in Jub 4:7, "the patriarch's observation of the heavens and their order so that the sons of man might know the (appointed) times of the year according to their order, with respect to each of their months . . . is knowledge of a thoroughly priestly and cultic nature."

57. Scholars point to the possible polemical nature of the patriarch's priestly role. Gabriele Boccaccini observes that "Enochians completely ignore the Mosaic torah and the Jerusalem Temple, that is, the two tenets of the order of the universe." In his opinion, "the attribution to Enoch of priestly characteristics suggests the existence of a pure prediluvian, and prefall, priesthood and disrupts the foundation of the Zadokite priesthood, which claimed its origin in Aaron at the time of the exodus, in an age that, for the Enochians, was already corrupted after the angelic sin and the flood." See G. Boccaccini, *Beyond the Essene Hypothesis: The Parting of the Ways between Qumran and Enochic Judaism* (Grand Rapids: Eerdmans, 1998), 74.

58. VanderKam, *Enoch: A Man for All Generations*, 117.

the depiction of Enoch's priestly duties in early Enochic lore. The Book of the Watchers does not refer to any liturgical or sacrificial rituals of the patriarch; on the other hand, Jubilees depicts the patriarch offering incense to God. The absence of reference to any animal sacrificial or liturgical practice in Enoch's sacerdotal duties might indicate that his office may have been understood by early Enochic traditions from the divinatory angle, that is, as the office of oracle-priest, practiced also by the Mesopotamian diviners who, similarly to Enoch's preoccupation with incense, widely used the ritual of libanomancy, or "smoke divination," a "practice of throwing cedar shavings onto a censer in order to observe the patterns and direction of the smoke."[59]

## Enoch's Titles in the Book of Parables

It has been mentioned that the Book of Parables endows the seventh antediluvian patriarch with several roles and titles previously unknown in the early Enochic lore. The analysis of these roles and titles is important for this investigation of the evolution from Enoch to Metatron since in the Parables, for the first time in the Enochic tradition, the patriarch is depicted as a preexistent enthroned figure whose mission is to become an eschatological leader in the time when the wicked of this world will be punished. The reference to this highly elevated office recalls the future profile of the supreme angel Metatron known in some rabbinic and Hekhalot accounts. The relevance of the roles and titles found in the Parables as possible formative patterns for the future roles and titles of Metatron will be discussed in the later sections of this study. For now, the purpose of this investigation is to introduce and briefly describe these titles.

The enigmatic figure of the eschatological leader, possibly associated with Enoch, is designated in the Parables by four titles: Righteous One *(ṣādeq)*, Anointed One *(masiḥ)*, Chosen One *(xeruy)*, and Son of Man *(walda sab')*.[60]

---

59. M. S. Moore, *The Balaam Traditions: Their Character and Development* (Atlanta: Scholars, 1990), 43.

60. J. C. VanderKam, "Righteous One, Messiah, Chosen One, and Son of Man in 1 Enoch 37-71," in *The Messiah: Developments in Earliest Judaism and Christianity; The First Princeton Symposium on Judaism and Christian Origins,* ed. J. H. Charlesworth (Minneapolis: Fortress, 1992), 169-70. My presentation of the titles from the Book of Parables is based on the positions reflected in VanderKam's article. See also M. Black, "The Strange Visions of Enoch," *BRev* 3 (1987): 20-23; Black, "The Messianism of the Parables of Enoch: Their Date and Contribution to Christological Origins," in *The Messiah,* 145-68; J. R. Davila, "Of Methodology, Monotheism and Metatron," in *The Jewish Roots of Christological Monotheism: Papers from the St. Andrews Conference on the Historical Origins of the Worship of Jesus,* ed. C. C. Newman, J. R. Davila, and G. S. Lewis, JSJSup 63 (Leiden: Brill, 1999), 9-12.

These designations occur with various degrees of frequency in the Ethiopic text; while the first two titles are used rather sparingly, the other two designations are quite widespread and appear many times in the Parables.

## "Righteous One"

Although the expression "Righteous One" occurs at least four times in the Ethiopic text of the Parables, not all these references are equally valuable for the ongoing investigation of Enoch's titles. VanderKam suggests that one of these occurrences is "text-critically doubtful," and two of them do not constitute an individual title but rather represent collective designations. He is confident, however, that the single case in which "Righteous One" is used as an individual title of the eschatological leader is 1 En 53:6.[61]

1 En 53 describes the upcoming destruction of the wicked, including the kings and the powerful of this world, by the hands of the angels of punishment. In 53:6-7 an eschatological figure of great significance appears; the text applies two titles, "Righteous One" and "Chosen One," to this figure: "And after this the Righteous *(ṣādeq)* and Chosen One *(xeruy)* will cause the house of his congregation to appear; from then on, in the name of the Lord of Spirits, they will not be hindered. And before him these mountains will not be (firm) like the earth, and the hills will be like a spring of water; and the righteous will have rest from the ill-treatment of the sinners."[62] The title "Chosen One" will be examined in a later section. First I direct my attention to "Righteous One."

It is significant for this investigation of the provenance of the Enochic titles that this title appears to be rooted in biblical traditions. Scholars have suggested that its possible provenance is Isa 53:11.[63] In this text the epithet "the righteous one" is applied to the servant of the Lord: "the righteous one, my servant, shall make many righteous, and he shall bear their iniquities." VanderKam points out that in the Parables the title is never used alone in application to an eschatological figure; it is found only in conjunction with another title, "Chosen One."[64] This conjunction serves as a significant clue that in the Parables all four titles of the elevated messianic character are closely interconnected.

---

61. VanderKam, "Righteous One," 170-71.
62. Knibb, *Ethiopic Book of Enoch,* 1:146; 2:138.
63. VanderKam, *Enoch: A Man for All Generations,* 136.
64. VanderKam, "Righteous One," 170.

Andrei A. Orlov

### *"Anointed One"*

Another title associated with the elevated hero of the Parables is "Anointed One." This title occurs twice in the book, in chaps. 48 and 52.[65] In 1 En 48:10 it is introduced in the eschatological context in which the wicked of this world represented by rulers of the earth will fall down before the Son of Man but "there will be no one who will take them with his hands and raise them" because they "denied the Lord of Spirits and his Messiah ('anointed one')."[66] Scholars have observed that the author of this passage appears to be relying on biblical terminology, more precisely, on the expressions from Ps 2:2 that refer to rulers and kings of the earth taking "counsel together, against the Lord and his anointed."[67] Here again, as with "Righteous One," the author(s) of the Parables prefers to seek the background of the hero's titles not in Mesopotamian but in biblical sources.

The second occurrence of this title is in 1 En 52. The patriarch, carried off by a whirlwind, beholds the secrets of heaven, which include several mountains associated with particular metals: "a mountain of iron, and a mountain of copper, and a mountain of silver, and a mountain of gold, and a mountain of soft metal, and a mountain of lead."[68] Enoch is further instructed by his *angelus interpres* that these mountains are predestined to "serve the authority of his Messiah ('anointed one')."

### *"Chosen One"*

This title is used many times in the Parables, designating again, as in the previous two designations, an eschatological character.[69] The description of the

---

65. Scholars have previously questioned whether these designations belong to the original layer of the texts. See especially E. Sjöberg, *Der Menschensohn im äthiopischen Henochbuch*, Skrifter Utgivna av kungl. Humanistika Vetenskapssamfundet i Lund 41 (Lund: Gleerup, 1946), 140-41; J. Theisohn, *Der auserwählte Richter: Untersuchungen zum traditionsgeschichtlichem Ort der Menschensohngestalt der Bilderreden des Äthiopischen Henoch*, SUNT 12 (Göttingen: Vandenhoeck & Ruprecht, 1975), 55-56.

66. Knibb, *Ethiopic Book of Enoch*, 2:134.

67. VanderKam, "Righteous One," 170. James Davila ("Of Methodology," 10) observes that "the language of the passage echoes Psalm 2:2 and thus evokes the messianic traditions drawn in the Second Temple period out of the royal psalms, despite the anachronism of associating ideas with the antediluvian patriarch Enoch."

68. Knibb, *Ethiopic Book of Enoch*, 2:136.

69. The title occurs in 1 En 40:5; 45:3, 4; 49:2, 4; 51:3, 5; 52:6, 9; 53:6; 55:4; 61:5, 8, 10; 62:1.

Chosen One in the Parables paints a picture of a highly elevated celestial being. This being apparently has his own throne in the celestial realm since one of the passages, 45:3-4, depicts him as the one who has been installed on the throne of glory: "On that day the Chosen One *(xeruy)* will sit on the throne of glory, and will choose their works, and their resting-places will be without number; and their spirits within them will grow strong when they see my Chosen one *(laxeruya)* and those who appeal to my holy and glorious name. And on that day I will cause my Chosen One *(laxeruy)* to dwell among them, and I will transform heaven and make it an eternal blessing and light."[70] The significant detail in this description is that the Chosen One was set on his throne of glory by the Lord of Spirits (61:8). From this elevated seat he will then judge Asael and the angels associated with this rebellious leader (55:4).[71]

As with the previous two, this title appears to rely on imagery drawn from biblical materials. Scholars point to its possible roots in Isa 41:8, 9; 42:1; 43:10, where this designation is applied to the servant of the Lord.[72]

## *"Son of Man"*

This title is formulated in the Parables with three different Ethiopic expressions.[73] It appears multiple times and can be found in 46:2, 3, 4; 48:2; 62:5, 7, 9, 14; 63:11; 69:26, 27, 29 (twice); 70:1; 71:14; 71:17. The profile of the "Son of Man" as an elevated celestial being recalls the figure of the Chosen One analyzed in the previous section.[74] As with the Chosen One, Son of Man is a character associated with the celestial secrets who also has a throne of glory (62:5; 69:27, 29) from which he will judge sinners.

Scholars have observed that some features of the Son of Man traditions in the Parables recall details found in Dan 7, where one can find a messianic figure

---

70. Knibb, *Ethiopic Book of Enoch*, 1:126-27; 2:131.
71. The passage found in 51:3 again stresses the motif of the throne in connection with this title: "And in those days the Chosen One will sit on his throne, and all the secrets of wisdom will flow out from the counsel of his mouth, for the Lord of Spirits has appointed him and glorified him." See Knibb, *Ethiopic Book of Enoch*, 2:135-36.
72. Suter, *Tradition and Composition*, 26-27; VanderKam, *Enoch: A Man for All Generations*, 138.
73. VanderKam, *Enoch: A Man for All Generations*, 135.
74. David Suter (*Tradition and Composition*, 26) notes the interplay of the traditions about the Chosen One and the Son of Man in chap. 62 of the Parables. He observes that this "chapter begins with the Elect one being seated on the throne of his glory by the Lord of Spirits to judge the kings and mighty of the earth; however, in the midst of the passage, at 1 En. 62:5, the poet changes from 'the Elect One' to 'that Son of Man.'"

designated as "one like a son of man."[75] The parallels with the Daniel "son of man" can be illustrated by reference to 1 En 46:1-4, where the title is introduced and then repeated several times:

> And there I saw one who had a head of days, and his head (was) white like wool; and with him (there was) another, whose face had the appearance of a man, and his face (was) full of grace, like one of the holy angels. And I asked one of the holy angels who went with me, and showed me all the secrets, about that Son of Man *(walda sab')*, who he was, and whence he was, (and) why he went with the Head of Days. And he answered me and said to me: "This is the Son of Man *(walda sab')* who has righteousness, and with whom righteousness dwells; he will reveal all the treasures of that which is secret, for the Lord of Spirits has chosen him, and through uprightness his lot has surpassed all before the Lord of Spirits for ever. And this Son of Man *(walda sab')* whom you have seen will rouse the kings and the powerful from their resting-places, and the strong from their thrones, and will loose the reins of the strong, and will break the teeth of the sinners.[76]

In this passage an enigmatic character appears whose designation as "the head of days" recalls the Daniel figure of the "ancient of days."

The significant feature of the Son of Man's profile in the Parables is that the text understands this character as preexistent, even possibly a divine being who received his name before the time of creation. One sees this in 1 En 48:2-7:

> And at that hour that Son of Man *(walda sab')* was named in the presence of the Lord of Spirits, and his name (was named) before the Head of Days. Even before the sun and the constellations were created, before the stars of heaven were made, his name was named before the Lord of Spirits. He will be a staff to the righteous and the holy, that they may lean on him and not fall, and he (will be) the light of the nations, and he will be the hope of those who grieve in their hearts. All those who dwell upon the dry ground will fall down and worship before him, and they will bless, and praise, and celebrate with psalms the name of the Lord of Spirits. And because of this he was chosen and hidden before him before the world was created, and forever.[77]

---

75. Suter (*Tradition and Composition*, 26) observes that "in the Parables of Enoch, 'that Son of Man' appears largely in the context of an exegetical tradition based on Dan. 7:9-14 and derives his judicial function from 'the Elect one' as this tradition is used to amplify the latter title."

76. Knibb, *Ethiopic Book of Enoch*, 1:128-29; 2:131-32.

77. Knibb, *Ethiopic Book of Enoch*, 1:134; 2:133-34.

*Roles and Titles of the Seventh Antediluvian Hero*

One can see that, as with the previous titles from the Parables, biblical traditions play a pivotal role in inspiring the authors of this book in their portrayal of the Son of Man. For such inspiration they go not only to the prominent account found in the book of Daniel but also to other biblical materials. VanderKam observes that the reference to the fact that the Son of Man was in God's mind before the creation recalls the passage from Isa 49:1. In this text the servant of the Lord defines himself in similar terms, saying that "the Lord called me before I was born, while I was in my mother's womb he named me."[78] VanderKam argues that "there is no mistaking the author's appeal to the servant of the Lord in 2 Isaiah, in which he is to be a light to the nations (42:6; 49:6)."[79]

## *Interdependence of the Four Titles and Their Identification with Enoch in the Parables*

An important feature in the four titles is that they seem to be used interchangeably in the Parables and appear to be referring to one composite figure. Nickelsburg notes that "the identification of these figures with one another is understandable; for all their differences, their characteristics and functions can be seen to be compatible and complementary."[80] Indeed, as has been shown, the combination of the titles Righteous One and Chosen One in 1 En 53:6-7 indicates that they were used here for the same protagonist. The same interchangeability is observable in the titles Son of Man and Chosen One. Here, however, the equivalency is established not through the combination of the titles but through their separation. Scholars previously observed that "Son of Man" and "Chosen One," the two most widely used titles in the Parables, always occur in separate sections of the text, and never together.[81] Morna Hooker's research demonstrates that, while chaps. 38–45 use "Chosen One," chaps. 46–48 operate with "Son of Man." This pattern continues further as the material from 1 En 49–62:1 applies the title Chosen One, while 62:1-71 chooses to use "Son of Man."[82] The separation of these two titles appears to

---

78. VanderKam, *Enoch: A Man for All Generations*, 139.
79. VanderKam, *Enoch: A Man for All Generations*, 139.
80. G. W. E. Nickelsburg, "Son of Man," in *ABD* (1992), 6:138.
81. M. D. Hooker, *The Son of Man in Mark: A Study of the Background of the Term 'Son of Man' and Its Use in St. Mark's Gospel* (London: SPCK, 1967), 34-37; Theisohn, *Der auserwählte Richter*, 47-49; VanderKam, "Righteous One," 175.
82. Morna Hooker (*Son of Man*, 34) observes that "two sources can be distinguished, one speaking of the 'Son of Man' and the other of the 'Elect One,' and in spite of the fact that schol-

indicate that the author(s) or editor(s) of the Parables perceived them to be interchangeable.

A large group of scholars believe that all four eschatological titles found in the Parables refer to one individual, namely, the patriarch Enoch himself, who in 1 En 71 is identified[83] with the "Son of Man."[84] The crucial issue for the possible identification of the four titles with the seventh antediluvian patriarch is the status of chaps. 70–71.[85] Some scholars believe that these chapters might represent later interpolation(s) and do not belong to the original text of the Book of Parables;[86] they note that these two chapters do not appropriately correspond with the tripartite structure of the Parables. The content of these chapters also raises some critical questions. First, 1 En 70–71 exhibits repetitiveness that might indicate the attempt to expand the original material. Second, for a long time students of the Enochic traditions were puzzled by the fact that the Son of Man, who in the previous chapters of the Parables has been distinguished from Enoch, suddenly becomes identified in 1 En 71 with the patriarch. This identification seems to contradict the rest of the text since it appears impossible for a seer to fail to recognize himself in the vision. Collins points to the uniqueness of such a misidentification in the Jewish apocalyptic literature, where a visionary would scarcely fail to recognize himself in such an autovision.[87] Moreover, in view of the preexistent nature of the Son of Man in 48:2-7, it is difficult to reconcile this character with the figure of the seventh patriarch who was born from human parents in the antediluvian era.

Several explanations have been proposed to resolve this puzzling situa-

---

ars have mostly followed them in regarding the material in its present form as a mosaic, discussion of the figure of the 'Son of Man' has not generally drawn any distinction between these two titles, but has regarded passages referring to the 'Elect One' and those which speak of the 'Son of Man' as descriptive of the same figure."

83. Scholars previously observed the significance of this identification for future Metatron developments. Alan Segal points out that "this is an extraordinarily important event, as it underlines the importance of mystic transformation between the adept and the angelic vice-regent of God." See A. F. Segal, "The Risen Christ and the Angelic Mediator Figures in Light of Qumran," in *Jesus and the Dead Sea Scrolls*, ed. J. H. Charlesworth (Garden City, N.Y.: Doubleday, 1992), 305.

84. VanderKam, *Enoch: A Man for All Generations*, 140; Nickelsburg, "Son of Man," 6:138.

85. VanderKam ("Righteous One," 177) stresses that "the status of chs. 70-71 is . . . absolutely crucial to one's understanding of the phrase 'son of man' and eventually of all the other epithets."

86. Nickelsburg ("Son of Man," 6:140) observes that "the text is probably an addition to an earlier form of the Book of Parables, but an addition with important parallels."

87. J. J. Collins, "The Heavenly Representative: The 'Son of Man' in the Similitudes of Enoch," in *Ideal Figures in Ancient Judaism: Profiles and Paradigms*, ed. G. W. E. Nickelsburg and J. J. Collins, SCS 12 (Chico, Calif.: Scholars, 1980), 122-24, esp. 122.

tion. Scholars have observed[88] that the Book of Parables seems to entertain the idea of the heavenly twin (counterpart) of a visionary when it identifies Enoch with the Son of Man.[89] VanderKam suggests that the puzzle of the Parables can be explained by the Jewish belief, attested in several ancient Jewish texts, that a creature of flesh and blood could have a heavenly double or counterpart. As an example, VanderKam points to Jacob traditions in which the patriarch's "features are engraved on high."[90] He stresses that this theme of the visionary's ignorance of his higher angelic identity is observable in other Jewish pseudepigrapha, including the Prayer of Joseph.

In the light of the Jewish traditions about the heavenly counterpart of the visionary, VanderKam's hypothesis appears to be plausible, and it is possible that in the Parables the seventh antediluvian patriarch was indeed identified with the Son of Man and the other titles pertaining to this figure.

In the conclusion of this section, several observations can be offered in connection with Enochic titles attested in the Parables. First, one cannot fail to recognize that in contrast to other designations of Enoch found in the early Enochic materials, the titles from the Book of Parables exhibit strong roots and connections with the motifs and themes found in the Hebrew Bible, particularly in Isaiah, Ps 2, and Daniel. Scholars have therefore proposed that these titles might be shaped by familiar biblical characters, such as the Servant of the Lord found in Deutero-Isaiah and the Son of Man found in Dan 7. Such explicit reliance on known biblical characters demonstrates a striking contrast to the provenance of other titles of Enoch not found in the Parables (like the scribe, the expert in secrets, and the priest). It seems that these do not have explicit biblical roots but are rather based on independent Mesopotamian traditions.[91]

---

88. See VanderKam, "Righteous One," 182-83; M. A. Knibb, "Messianism in the Pseudepigrapha in Light of the Scrolls," *DSD* 2 (1995): 177-80; J. E. Fossum, *The Image of the Invisible God*, NTOA 30 (Göttingen: Vandenhoeck & Ruprecht, 1995), 144-45; C. H. T. Fletcher-Louis, *Luke-Acts: Angels, Christology, and Soteriology*, WUNT 2/94 (Tübingen: Mohr/Siebeck, 1997), 151.

89. It is important to note that in the Parables, the Son of Man is depicted as seated on the throne of glory (1 En 62:5; 69:29). Jarl Fossum (*The Image*, 145) observes that "in the 'Similitudes' the 'Elect One' or 'Son of Man' who is identified as the patriarch Enoch, is enthroned upon the 'throne of glory.' If 'glory' does not qualify the throne but its occupant, Enoch is actually identified with the Glory of God." Fossum further concludes that "the 'Similitudes of Enoch' present an early parallel to the targumic description of Jacob being seated upon the 'throne of glory.'"

90. VanderKam, "Righteous One," 182-83.

91. One must add that the later Hekhalot titles and offices of Enoch-Metatron also appear to maintain a certain independence from the imagery of the exalted figures found in the Hebrew Bible. Peter Schäfer observes that "the Hekhalot literature appears to be basically inde-

Second, the peculiar feature of the titles found in the Parables is that they can be found only in this part of Ethiopic Enoch. Other booklets of this Enochic composition, such as the Astronomical Book, the Book of the Watchers, the Book of Dream Visions, and the Epistle of Enoch, do not refer to these titles of the patriarch. It is also curious that other early Enochic materials, including the Genesis Apocryphon, Jubilees, Book of Giants, and 2 Enoch, do not provide any references either to these titles or to the features associated with them. For example, early Enochic booklets are silent about Enoch's enthronement on the seat of glory. This absence of allusions and cross-references with other Enochic writings appears to be quite puzzling and unusual since the information about other titles not found in the Parables, such as the scribe, the expert in the secrets, the priest, is typically employed as sets of recurring motifs supported by various texts, including the various booklets of 1 Enoch, Jubilees, the Genesis Apocryphon, the Book of Giants, and 2 Enoch. It is also baffling that the later rabbinic and Hekhalot materials are silent about the Enochic titles found in the Book of Parables. James Davila's research points to the fact that the titles found in the Parables, like Messiah, Son of Man, and Righteous One, are dropped almost entirely[92] in the Merkabah tradition.[93] This issue will constitute a special topic of the discussion in the following sections. Finally, another puzzling characteristic of the Parables' titles must be mentioned. In the ambiguous identification of Enoch with the "Son of Man" depicted in 1 En 71, one

---

pendent of the Bible. To formulate it even more sharply: it appears to be autonomous." See P. Schäfer, *Gershom Scholem Reconsidered: The Aim and Purpose of Early Jewish Mysticism* (Oxford: Oxford Center for Postgraduate Hebrew Studies, 1986), 14.

92. Suter (*Tradition and Composition*, 16) argues that Enoch-Metatron's identification with "an elect one" (בחיד) in *Synopse* §9 (3 En 6:3) might be related to his title in the Parables. He observes that "while it does not have the messianic sense that it does in the Parables of Enoch, there is a remote possibility of a connection between its use in the Parables as the major messianic title and in 3 En. 6:3. Greenfield does not specifically relate the identification of Enoch as the Son of Man in the Parables to Enoch/Metatron in 3 Enoch, but he may have had it in mind." H. Odeberg observes that "many of the features of the Elect One and the Son of Man in 1 Enoch are transferred to Metatron in 3 Enoch. The differences are, however, greater than the resemblances." See H. Odeberg, *3 Enoch* (Cambridge: University of Cambridge Press, 1928; New York: Ktav, 1973), 1:47. On the connections between the Parables and 3 Enoch, see also M. Black, "Eschatology of the Similitudes of Enoch," *JTS* (1952): 1-10, esp. 6-7.

93. J. R. Davila, "Melchizedek, The 'Youth,' and Jesus," in *The Dead Sea Scrolls as Background to Postbiblical Judaism and Early Christianity: Papers from an International Conference at St. Andrews in 2001*, ed. J. R. Davila, STDJ 46 (Leiden: Brill, 2003), 264. Davila observes that "in 3 Enoch — which has a close relationship of some sort with the Similitudes, whether literary, oral, or both — Enoch's role changes once again. His titles in the Similitudes — Son of Man, Messiah, Righteous One, Chosen — are dropped almost entirely (only the last is applied to him once)." See Davila, 264.

finds a unique way of introducing this Enochic title that never occurs with Enoch's other titles. In early Enochic booklets the designations are usually introduced through the gradual unfolding of the patriarch's activities pertaining to the particular title. In contrast, the Book of Parables refuses to depict in any way Enoch's participation in various offices that stand behind his titles. Nothing is said about the patriarch's messianic mission or his role in judging the mighty ones of the world. Enoch is rather depicted as a mere beholder of these deeds, which the text unambiguously associates with one or another eschatological figure. He is only named as a "Son of Man," who in no way attempts to execute the offices pertaining to this and other titles.

## Postscript

One of the important questions that William Adler raises in his stimulating response to my essay is how the potentially promising path in the Enoch trajectory attesting to the great exaltation of its hero ends up in a dead end.[94] Why do the exalted Enochic titles reflected in the Book of Parables not loom large in the later Metatron developments? What happened?

I do not have answers for these questions, but it seems to me that to approach these issues, another investigation of the hero's roles and titles is required, which will be quite different from the one reflected in my essay. This new study should be done not from the temporal angle of the past of the Enochic tradition but from its future.

When I started my research, one particular methodological question overwhelmed me: What phenomena can serve as a set of reliable indicators that would allow us to detect how and when the subtle and elusive transition from Enoch to Metatron, from the apocalyptic hero to the hero of the Hekhalot lore, from a diviner to a second god, occurred? In my book I attempted to investigate one such possible set of characteristics by focusing on the celestial roles and titles of Enoch-Metatron, which play an equally important role in early Enochic accounts and the Hekhalot materials. Each of these traditions operates with a different set of roles and titles, which make them good indicators of the transition from the Enoch tradition to the Metatron tradition. Thus, the early Enochic tradition emphasizes such roles or titles of the seventh antediluvian patriarch as diviner, scribe, sage, visionary, witness of the divine judgment in the generation of the flood, and envoy to the Watchers/Giants. Later Jewish

---

94. See below, W. Adler, "A Dead End in the Enochic Trajectory: A Response to Andrei Orlov."

mysticism reveals Enoch-Metatron in a different set of roles and titles, depicting him as the Prince of the Torah, the Prince of the Divine Presence, the Measurer of the Lord, the Prince of the World, and the Youth. Only a few titles are common to both traditions. But even in the roles that seem to be shared by both traditions, such as Enoch-Metatron's priestly role or his role as an expert in the divine secrets, one can see a significant evolution of the offices and their different functions in the Enochic and the Metatron traditions.

My investigation of Metatron's roles and titles demonstrates that Hekhalot and rabbinic materials dealing with the Metatron lore contain two clusters of his roles and titles. The first cluster appears to be connected with those already known from early Enochic traditions. These offices, in fact, represent the continuation and, in many ways, consummation of the roles of the seventh antediluvian hero. In this sense the transformation of Enoch into the principal angel Metatron represents something of a climax of the earlier Enoch traditions. In my analysis I referred to this cluster of offices and appellations as the "old" roles and titles. This cluster embraces the activities of Metatron in such offices as the heavenly scribe, the expert in the divine secrets, the heavenly high priest, and the mediator. All these roles can be seen as the development of the familiar conceptual counterparts found in early Enochic and Mesopotamian traditions about the seventh antediluvian hero. Yet, despite the recognizable similarities to these early prototypes, the roles and titles found in the Metatron tradition represent in some cases a substantial reshaping and development of the earlier Enochic sources.

The second cluster of roles and titles of Metatron embraces those that do not occur in 1 Enoch, Jubilees, and the Book of Giants. In the Merkabah tradition Enoch-Metatron appears in several new roles previously unknown in these early Enochic materials. This group of appellations and offices, in contrast to the old roles and titles, I designated as the "new" roles and titles. The offices appearing in this new cluster are related to such appellations of Metatron as the "Youth," the "Prince of the World," the "Measurer/Measure of the Lord," the "Prince of the Divine Presence," the "Prince of the Torah," and the "Lesser YHWH."

As I researched this transition from Enoch to Metatron, it became more and more clear to me that the roles and titles found in the Book of Parables do not represent a crucial link between the roles and titles of Enoch and the roles and titles of Metatron. Thus a glance at the roles and titles of the seventh antediluvian hero in the Parables from the point of view of the Metatron tradition, as with the earlier Enochic texts, indicates discontinuity rather than continuity. It is surprising that both temporal perspectives demonstrate the dissimilarities in the roles and titles of the Parables, which make the Parables a rather odd link in the chain of the Enoch-Metatron tradition. So the examination of the conceptual development of Enoch-Metatron roles and titles might help to clarify the difference between the influences that genuinely contributed to the gradual evolution from Enoch to Metatron and other currents in the Enochic tradition(s) that, despite their promising appearance, did not directly impact this transition.

However, another Enochic text of the Second Temple period seems more promising in its formative value for the later Metatron developments than the Book of Parables. This text is 2 (Slavonic) Enoch, a Jewish document traditionally dated by scholars in the first century C.E., before the destruction of the second Jerusalem temple. My inquiry into the narrative of 2 Enoch persuaded me that the conceptual developments pertaining to the roles and titles of its principal character occupy an intermediary stage between early Enochic and Metatron traditions. The evolution of the titles and roles within 2 Enoch includes two distinct processes.

One of these processes is connected with the emergence of a new imagery that demonstrates a marked resemblance to the roles and titles prominent in the Metatron lore, including the offices of the Youth, the Prince of the Presence, the Prince of the World, God's Vice-Regent, and the Measurer of the Lord. Although some designations attested in the Slavonic apocalypse, such as the Governor of the World, the Servant of the Face, among others, often do not correspond precisely to the later titles of Metatron, the peculiar features of these roles and activities show amazing similarities with their later counterparts found in the Hekhalot and *Shi'ur Qomah* materials.

The second process detected in 2 Enoch embraces an advancement of the traditional designations and offices of the seventh antediluvian hero toward their later Merkabah forms. The Slavonic apocalypse demonstrates several remarkable transitions in roles and titles. Let me briefly mention a few:

1. The transition from the office of the mantic diviner who receives his revelations in mantic dreams to the role of the seer who has his visions in the awakened state, which recalls Metatron's bodily ascent in *Sefer Hekhalot* and his bodily transformation into the luminous extent.
2. The transition from the priestly imagery of the hero detected in the early Enochic literature toward a more complex sacerdotal office, which includes Enoch's liturgical role as the leader of the heavenly worship prominent in Hekhalot and *Shi'ur Qomah* literature.
3. The transition from the early scribal imagery found in 1 Enoch, Jubilees, and the Book of Giants to the imagery of the scribe who has a seat in heaven, which demonstrates remarkable similarities with Metatron's scri-

bal profile in the *Ḥagigah Babli*, where he is depicted as a scribe who has a seat.
4. The transition from Enoch's role as the measurer of the celestial bodies and calendar in the Astronomical Book to Enoch-Metatron's office as the Measurer and Measurement of the Lord's Body, his *Shi'ur Qomah*.
5. The transition from the position of the intercessor for the Watchers and Giants prominent in the early Enochic circle toward the new role of the redeemer and the expiator of the sin of the protoplast, similar to Metatron's functions in *Sefer Hekhalot* 48C (*Synopse* §72) and the *Zohar*.
6. The transition from the office of the mediator of knowledge and judgment prominent in early Enochic lore to the new role as mediator of the divine Presence.

It must be noted that the new and old roles and titles found in 2 Enoch do not represent interpolations from the later Hekhalot macroforms, since these conceptions exist in the Slavonic text in their very early rudimentary forms, which sometimes only distantly allude to their later Hekhalot counterparts. These constructs are thus markedly different from the later Merkabah variants by their early pseudepigraphic form, which shows their close connection with the imagery and the conceptual world of Second Temple Judaism.

# A Dead End in the Enoch Trajectory:
# A Response to Andrei Orlov

*William Adler*

Andrei Orlov's essay in the current volume makes up one part of a longer study of the evolution of Enoch from a relatively obscure character in the Hebrew Bible into the complex and multifaceted figure associated with Metatron in the Merkabah literature.[1] Here Orlov compares Enoch's "titles and functions" in the Book of Parables with the other sections of 1 Enoch.[2]

The main finding of Orlov's essay is that, as in other cases, the Book of Parables is the outlier. Elsewhere in 1 Enoch, Enoch is diviner, primeval sage, expert in secrets, scribe, mediator, and heavenly priest. And the titles applied to him bear some discernible relationship to at least one of these functions (mainly that of scribe). In the Book of Parables everything is different. Here the titles "Righteous One," "Anointed One," "Chosen One" and "Son of Man" refer to a preexistent enthroned figure, only ambiguously connected with the patriarch himself. Unlike the titles found in the other parts of 1 Enoch, they do not appear to originate in Mesopotamian tradition. Rather they are connected with motifs from Jewish scriptures. Used almost interchangeably, these titles do not bear any clearly identifiable connection with the roles Enoch plays in the Parables. "The Book of Parables," writes Orlov, "refuses to depict in any way Enoch's participation in various offices that stand behind his titles." Enoch is called "Son of Man" in the Parables, but as Orlov points out, he "in no way attempts

---

1. See A. A. Orlov, *The Enoch-Metatron Tradition*, TSAJ 107 (Tübingen: Mohr Siebeck, 2005).

2. See above, A. A. Orlov, "Roles and Titles of the Seventh Antediluvian Hero in the Parables of Enoch: A Departure from the Traditional Pattern?" My comments in this response, as well as all my quotations from Orlov's work, refer specifically to this essay.

to execute the offices pertaining to this and other titles." Perhaps Orlov's most surprising finding is what he does not find, namely, a connection between the Enoch of the Parables and the exalted Enoch found in the later traditions about Enoch-Metatron.

Orlov's study demonstrates that the examination of titles and functions in Enoch can yield interesting and valuable results. Because Enoch's various titles and roles are often interconnected and overlapping, rigid systematization runs the risk of distorting more than it clarifies. But Orlov is aware of this problem, and his method is not artificial, misleading, or unduly repetitive. At places it remains a bit unclear as to when we can actually speak about a "title." This is less of a problem in the Parables. In this part of Enoch, recurring titles such as "Son of Man" seem to presuppose a fixed tradition — especially since, as Orlov observes, they are not connected with any particular function. But what about the titulature in the rest of the Enoch texts? Here, Enoch is variously called "scribe of righteousness," "scribe of distinction," even "most skilled scribe." "Scribe of righteousness" may be a formal title. It appears often, and is even used to describe Enoch in Testament of Abraham 11:2-4 [rec. B]. But in the other cases, are we speaking of formal titles or something more fluid than that (maybe just a description of what he actually does)? Since the categories of title and function are important to Orlov's approach, they might need additional clarification.

Orlov suggests that traditions about the Mesopotamian hero Enmeduranki were one of the most formative influences on the roles and titles of Enoch in the earlier portions of 1 Enoch. For guidance on the cuneiform sources about Enmeduranki and their connection with Enoch, he acknowledges the work of other scholars, especially James VanderKam and Helge Kvanvig.[3] The parallels between Enoch and Enmeduranki are in many cases striking: above all, Enmeduranki, the seventh Sumerian king, is, like Enoch, an expert in the divinatory arts. But in my view the extent and nature of this influence still need to be sorted out.

Certainly Enoch is not the only biblical figure molded into the image of the Mesopotamian sage. Orlov mentions as a parallel the figure of Daniel, represented in the first six chapters of his book as a member of a guild of sages in Babylonia. But as Orlov points out, the assimilation of Enoch to ancient Near Eastern counterparts is different from the case of Daniel. In the representation

---

3. See in particular, J. C. VanderKam, *Enoch and the Growth of an Apocalyptic Tradition*, CBQMS 16 (Washington, D.C.: Catholic Biblical Association of America, 1984), and H. S. Kvanvig, *Roots of Apocalyptic: The Mesopotamian Background of the Enoch Figure and of the Son of Man*, WMANT 61 (Neukirchen-Vluyn: Neukirchener Verlag, 1988).

of Daniel, there is not unreflective and undifferentiated borrowing, but rather adaptation and reshaping. Daniel is distinct from, in competition with, and better than his Babylonian counterparts. He beats the Chaldeans at their own game, at the same time avoiding certain techniques of Chaldean divination.[4] Writers about Enoch did sometimes attempt to demonstrate that his wisdom was either superior to or distinct from that of the Babylonians. The anonymous Samaritan writer later identified as Eupolemus ascribes the first discoveries in the celestial sciences to Enoch, from whom the Babylonians only later acquired this knowledge.[5] And in Jubilees there is a clear attempt to differentiate his discoveries from the false and demonic wisdom of the Babylonians.[6] It is true that in 1 Enoch, Enoch does not perform the full repertoire of Mesopotamian divinatory arts. But even so, we do not find the same interest in distinguishing Enoch's practice of divination (including oneiromancy and incubation rituals) from that of his Mesopotamian counterparts.[7] It thus might be useful to explore in more detail how the early traditions about Enoch both borrowed and reshaped ancient Near Eastern traditions about primordial sages and scribes.

Although the parallels with Enmeduranki are very suggestive, they may not exhaust all the possibilities. One example of this has to do with esoteric knowledge. Both Enmeduranki and Enoch are experts in secrets and mysteries. But as Orlov points out, the earlier Enoch materials (namely, the Astronomical Book and the Book of the Watchers) reveal little interest in this side of Enoch's learning. Esotericism is much more prominent, however, in the later Enoch literature (such as 2 Enoch). As he writes, "the terminology pertaining to secrets began to play an increasingly significant role in the later stages of the development of the Enochic tradition." The absence of esotericism in the earliest strata of the Enoch literature suggests that the motif of "Enoch as interpreter and revealer of heavenly secrets" does not necessarily draw upon older Mesopotamian sources, but rather reflects broader and more contemporary trends in late antiquity. Indeed, in many of the later apocalypses (as in much of the religious and theosophical literature of late antiquity), the element of secret knowledge revealed to a primordial sage seems to acquire increasing importance.

In identifying the influences on Enoch's other functions, we may also need to consider more than Mesopotamian literature. Orlov is clearly correct in

---

4. J. J. Collins, *Seers, Sibyls, and Sages in Hellenistic-Roman Judaism*, JSJSup 54 (Leiden: Brill, 1997), 46.

5. Quoted in Eusebius, *Praeparatio evangelica* 9.17.8.

6. Cf. Jub. 4:17 (Enoch's discoveries); 8:3 (on the postdiluvian discovery of the wicked teachings of the Watchers by Cainan, one of the forefathers of the Chaldeans).

7. Collins (*Seers, Sibyls, and Sages*, 46) states that although "the competitive aspect is not explicit in the case of Enoch . . . [it] is implied by the comparison with Enmeduranki."

*William Adler*

noting that Enmeduranki and Enoch play several overlapping roles. Some of Enmeduranki's functions (for example, diviner, expert in secrets, and mediator) are described in explicit language. Others are not so well defined, however. Orlov acknowledges, for example, that Enmeduranki's association with priesthood is only "implicitly hinted at in the text from Nineveh." The same observation applies to Enoch's own priestly persona. Enoch's ascension to the heavenly throne may conjure up images of the Jerusalem temple. But Enoch himself has no clearly defined sacrificial or liturgical roles.

To bolster Enoch's connection with the Mesopotamian diviner-priest, Orlov cites a passage in Jubilees, in which Enoch burns the "incense of the sanctuary" in Eden (Jub 4:25). Because Enoch is not said to perform sacrifice, Orlov proposes that Enoch is understood here as an "oracle-priest," similar to the Mesopotamian diviners who observed patterns of smoke from cedar shavings thrown upon a censer. But other early patriarchs in Jubilees perform these same priestly functions. Jub 3:27 states, for example, that when Adam went forth from Eden, he offered "frankincense, galbanum, and stacte and spices." And when Noah leaves the ark, he makes an animal offering (cf. Gen 8:20) and burns incense (Jub 6:3). We need not look beyond Jubilees itself to understand why the book represents Enoch, Adam, and Noah burning incense in a sanctuary or at an altar. According to Exod 30:34-36, God commanded Moses to "take sweet spices, stacte, and onycha, and galbanum, sweet spices with pure frankincense . . . and put part of it before the testimony in the tent of meeting where I shall meet with you." Because the author of Jubilees makes a point of establishing that even the earliest biblical patriarchs observed the Mosaic law, it was necessary to demonstrate that Enoch, like Adam and Noah, made an incense offering as well.

In the Enoch literature, Enoch's role as scribe is much less ambiguous than his role as priest. His scribal duties are both plentiful and the source of many of his titles. In his discussion of the scribal functions and titles of Enoch, Orlov observes that, although Enoch's function as scribe is amply documented in the Astronomical Book, he is never actually described here as a "scribe." The fact that the later parts of the Enoch literature regularly refer to him in this way suggests that the conferring of the title of scribe upon him is a secondary development in the tradition. It is interesting, however, that Enoch's role as scribe gets so much attention. His titles tend mainly to focus on his scribal functions. And these functions extend into many domains. In the Astronomical Book he records celestial secrets given to him by Uriel. He also records petitions from the terrestrial sphere, in this case from the Watchers and their offspring. "Enoch the scribe" is also one of the most enduring elements of the Enoch tradition. The cultic aspect of Enoch's scribal activities in the later Enoch tradition is especially notable. 2 En 22 describes how, for example, after his initiation as a scribe, he is commissioned with the task of recording heavenly mysteries.

Following his general method, Orlov links Enoch's role as scribe to Mesopotamian antecedents. But in the text from Nineveh that Orlov examines, Enmeduranki is never actually identified as a scribe. This functional asymmetry between Enoch and Enmeduranki suggests that a full understanding of Enoch's roles and titles requires us to look beyond Mesopotamian sources. Orlov himself suggests one alternative possibility in his discussion of "Enoch the scribe." He cites with favor a comment by John Collins regarding the social profile of the authors of this literature. "(I)t is possible that these people 'were, or at least included in their number, scribes who were familiar with a wide range of ancient lore and who wrote books in the name of Enoch.'"[8] Here, as elsewhere, attempts to understand Enoch's functions and titles may benefit from supplementing the analysis of Near Eastern parallels with reconstruction of the social world of the Enoch texts, especially as pertains to the scribal class.

As Orlov has clearly demonstrated, relatively late sources preserve and elaborate features of Enoch's older identity as mediator, scribe, and expert in divine secrets. They also confer upon him new titles, consistent with his increasingly exalted status: "Prince of the Presence," "Prince of the World," and "Governor of the World." If we agree that chaps. 70–71 are an integral part of the Parables, then the identification of Enoch as "Righteous One," "Anointed One," "Chosen One," and "Son of Man" in this part of Enoch would seem to put us well on the road to his exaltation in the later Enoch-Metatron tradition. But the Book of Parables disappoints. How, then, should we treat a work that seems so detached from both the rest of 1 Enoch and the later Enoch tradition?

The titles in the Book of Parables may be "a departure from the traditional pattern" of names and functions found in the Enoch literature. But they are hardly untraditional. As Orlov notes, with the exception of the Parables, the titles of Enoch reveal little or no dependence on biblical imagery and motifs. This is not the case with the Parables, however. Enoch's titles in the Parables are firmly rooted in imagery from the book of Isaiah, Ps 2, and the book of Daniel. Since these titles are not organically connected with anything that Enoch actually does in the Parables, the author apparently applied to Enoch a preexisting set of titles, already relatively fixed in the biblical tradition. Here, then, we have a case of an author "mainstreaming" the figure of Enoch by bringing him into conformity with imagery and titles better known from canonical sources. Nu-

---

8. J. J. Collins, "The Sage in the Apocalyptic and Pseudepigraphic Literature," in *The Sage in Israel and the Ancient Near East,* ed. J. G. Gammie and L. G. Perdue (Winona Lake, Ind.: Eisenbrauns, 1990), 346.

merous examples of the same thing can be found in other Jewish and Christian apocalypses.[9] But if, as seems likely, the application to Enoch of titles more familiar from biblical sources was intended to reshape and domesticate the tradition about him, it does not seem to have succeeded. As Orlov notes, the titles found in the Parables are "dropped almost entirely in the Merkabah tradition."[10] As with the older tradition, the offices of Enoch-Metatron preserve their independence from the imagery applied to exalted figures in the Bible. A potentially promising path in the "Enoch trajectory" ends up a dead end.

---

9. For one example of such domestication, see the Christian apocalypse known as the Shepherd of Hermas. The document retains the form of the apocalypse, but its contents consist mainly of exhortation to repentance and ethical instruction. For discussion, see P. Vielhauer and G. Strecker, in *New Testament Apocrypha,* ed. E. Hennecke and W. Schneemelcher, rev. ed. (Louisville: Westminster, 1992), 2:592-602.

10. Orlov also refers the reader to James Davila's study, "Melchizedek, the 'Youth' and Jesus," in *The Dead Sea Scrolls as Background to Postbiblical Judaism and the Early Christianity: Papers from an International Conference at St. Andrews in 2001,* ed. J. R. Davila, STDJ 46 (Leiden: Brill, 2003), 264.

# Exegetical Notes on Cosmology in the Parables of Enoch

*Jonathan Ben-Dov*

The first and the third parables in the Book of Parables (1 En 37–71) contain several passages on cosmology, mainly knowledge of astronomy and meteorology: 41:3-8; 43; 44; 59; 60:11-22; 69:13-25. R. H. Charles, who raised the possibility that those passages were late interpolations, then changed his mind, allowing the cosmological passages to be an original part of the Parables because "the wise in Israel were interested alike in ethical and cosmic questions."[1] However, some of the passages indeed seem to interrupt their immediate context. For example, 41:3-8 breaks the logical sequence of 41:2 and 41:9.[2] Equally, the cosmological information in 60:11-22(23?) interrupts the narrative sequence on the two creatures, 60:7-10, 23(24?)-25, which is itself sometimes considered a "Noachic" interpolation in the third parable.[3] The cosmological passages share a distinctive set of common motifs and ideas, some of them unknown from elsewhere in Enochic literature. For example, the motif of the mutual oath of

---

1. R. H. Charles, *The Book of Enoch, or I Enoch, Translated from the Editor's Ethiopic Text, and Edited with the Introduction, Notes, and Indexes of the First Edition Wholly Recast, Enlarged, and Rewritten* (Oxford: Clarendon, 1912), 82.

2. This was noted by Charles (*Book of Enoch,* 81). See above, M. A. Knibb, "The Structure and Composition of the Parables of Enoch." Generally Nickelsburg tends to solve such problems by reconstructing the suggested "original" order of the passages; see above, G. W. E. Nickelsburg, "Discerning the Structure(s) of the Enochic Book of Parables."

3. Again see the essays by Nickelsburg and Knibb in this volume.

---

I am indebted to Prof. Deborah Dimant for her valuable comments on this essay. The responsibility for the contents, however, lies on me alone.

the luminaries appears both in 41:5 and in 43:2; the idea that the luminaries (and the lightning) may appear for blessing and for curse is in 41:8 and 59:1. The composition of those passages, and their possible insertion in the text of the parables, therefore deserves a detailed study. Here I will present only some preliminary notes toward this end, exploring the tradition history of the cosmological details in the Parables.

The short reports on Enoch's journeys and revelations clearly resemble the similar reports in the latter part of the Book of the Watchers (1 En 17–36). Since much attention has been given in those passages to celestial entities like the luminaries, the winds, and the lightning, one would expect them to echo the reports of those phenomena in the Astronomical Book (1 En 72–82), a locus classicus for such descriptions.[4] However, James VanderKam, in his contribution to the present volume, concluded that the Book of Parables and the Astronomical Book, "though they talk about many of the same phenomena, . . . do so from within different frameworks and show no clear sign of a *literary* relationship, despite their taking the form of travelogues."[5] I wish to further exemplify this claim, without repeating any of VanderKam's arguments, and then offer a few reflections on the absence of Astronomical Book–type cosmology in the Parables.

## Treasures

In a recent Hebrew article I discussed the concept of "treasures of light" in Second Temple literature.[6] The point of that paper was that, while biblical authors knew the motif of heavenly treasuries (אוצר), they used it only with regard to meteorological phenomena such as winds and rain (Deut 28:12; Jer 10:13 = 51:16 = Ps 135:7; Job 38:22). This has changed in Second Temple writings, where "treasures" became more common, and were used not only for meteorology but also for various other fields of the human experience.[7] The first witness of this idea is the Septuagint version of Jer 10:13 (= 51:16). Instead of MT "He brought forth *wind* [רוח] from His treasures," LXX reads καὶ ἐξήγαγε φῶς ἐκ θησαυρῶν ἀυτοῦ, "He brought forth *light* from his treasures." As noted above, this verse

---

4. For example, Charles (*Book of Enoch,* 80) suggests such a connection.

5. See above, J. C. VanderKam, "The Book of Parables within the Enoch Tradition."

6. J. Ben-Dov, "Treasures of Light" (in Hebrew), in *On the Border Line: Literary Meets Textual Criticism,* ed. Z. Talshir and D. Amara (Beer Sheva: Ben Gurion University Press, 2005), 155-62.

7. This was already noted by A. Dillmann, *Das Buch Henoch übersetzt und erklärt* (Leipzig: Vogel, 1853), 150, and expanded in M. E. Stone, *Fourth Ezra,* Hermeneia (Minneapolis: Fortress, 1990), 96.

was widely used by biblical and postbiblical authors: it appears three times in the Bible (Jer 10:13; 51:16; Ps 135:7) and is quoted, although in a different order, in "the Hymn to the Creator" (11QPs^a XXVI 14-16).[8] 4 Ezra knows both versions of Jer 10:13, when it reports on treasures both of light (6:40) and of winds/spirits (5:37). The new usage of "treasures" is attested also in 1 En 17:3, "treasuries of the stars and of the thunders," τοὺς θησαυροὺς τῶν ἀστέρων καὶ τῶν βροντῶν, and in 1 En 41:5, "storehouses for the sun and the moon."[9]

The Book of Parables presents an interesting case in point. Here the luminaries and the meteorological phenomena are equally stored in special spaces, which are designated "treasures" and "mysteries, secrets" interchangeably. The Ethiopic terms are *mazāgebt* for the former and *ḫebu', ḫebu'āt* for the latter, and the Aramaic *Vorlage* would presumably have used אוצרין and מטמורין (see below). The interchangeability of this word pair can be seen in the two proximate verses 41:3-4, with the similar lines italicized:

> 41:3 And there my eyes beheld
> *the secrets of the lightnings and the thunder*
>   (ḫebu'at mabāraqt wanad^wadb^wād)
> *and the secrets of the winds (waḫebu'at nafāsāta),*
> how they are divided (yetkaffalu) to blow upon the earth,
> *and the secrets of the clouds and the dew*
>   (waḫebu'at dammanāt waṭall).
>
> 41:4 There I saw closed *storehouses (mazāgebt),*
>   *and from them the winds are distributed (yetkaffalu),*[10]
> the storehouses of the hail and the winds
>   (wamazgab barad wanafāsāt),[11]
> the storehouse of the mist and the clouds
>   (wamazgab dammanāt wadammana) . . .

---

8. See J. Carmignac, "Le texte de Jérémie 10:13 (ou 51:16) et celui de 2 Samuel 23:7 améliorés par Qumran," *RevQ* 7 (1969): 287-90; E. G. Chazon, "The Use of the Bible as a Key to Meaning in Psalms from Qumran," in *Emanuel. Festschrift Emanuel Tov,* ed. S. Paul et al., VTSup 94 (Leiden: Brill, 2003), 85-96, esp. 90-93.

9. Translations of 1 Enoch in this essay are from G. W. E. Nickelsburg and J. C. VanderKam, *1 Enoch: A New Translation* (Minneapolis: Fortress, 2004).

10. Since the verb *yətkaffalu* is identical in 1 En 41:3 and 41:4, I see no reason for the different translations "divide" and "distribute" in the translation.

11. This is the reading preferred also by S. Uhlig, *Das äthiopische Henochbuch,* in *JSHRZ,* ed. Werner G. Kümmel (Gütersloh: Gütersloher Verlagshaus Gerd Mohn, 1984). Several mss. lack the words "and the winds."

Several lines from those two verses are so close they seem to duplicate each other, for example, the secrets/storehouses of the winds, from which the winds are distributed. The similar lines prove the interchangeability of the terms "storehouses" and "secrets."[12] Thus we learn that the phrase "secrets of winds" in 1 En 41 does not denote the mysterious nature of the winds, but rather a place of storage, parallel to "storehouses." One must therefore conclude that the unique terminology of "mysteries" as storage places in Parables depends upon an exceptional conception of celestial geography.

But what is the source of this conception? The cosmological lists of Job 38 were suggested as a possible source.[13] However, those lists do not contain the term "secrets," so dominant in the Parables' worldview. Treasures and secrets are used as a word pair in Isa 45:3, a verse that seems to be an important source to some of the Parables' cosmology. The verse reads:

MT            ונתתי לך אוצרות חושך ומטמני מסתרים
LXX           καὶ δώσω σοι θησαυροὺς σκοτεινούς, ἀποκρύφους
              ἀοράτους ἀνοίξω σοι.[14]
Ethiopic Bible  *mazāgebt ḫebu' wakebut*, "treasures of secret and
              darkness."[15]

---

12. The two parts of the word pair are also used in 1 En 71:4: "all the secrets of the ends of heaven and all the treasuries of the stars."

13. Dillmann, *Das Buch Henoch*, 149; Charles, *Book of Enoch*, 80. In Job 37–38 a long description of the weather conditions and the luminaries appears, together with a mention of a storehouse (37:9, חדר) and of treasuries (38:22, אוצרות). On the *Nachleben* of Job 38, see M. E. Stone, "Lists of Revealed Things in the Apocalyptic Literature," in *Magnalia Dei*, ed. F. M. Cross et al. (Garden City, N.Y.: Doubleday, 1976), 414-54.

14. In this verse LXX is longer than MT. The latter does not contain any parallelism, but LXX does, filling the last semicolon with the words ἀνοίξω σοι. Seeligmann claimed that the LXX version is preferable to MT: I. L. Seeligmann, *The Septuagint Version of Isaiah: A Discussion of Its Problems* (Leiden: Brill, 1948), 60. The Greek verb ἀνοίγω in the LXX usually translates the Hebrew root פתח, but twice also the root גלה. LXX thus yields the following reconstructed Hebrew *Vorlage:* ונתתי לך אוצרות חושך/מסתרים אפתח (אגלח?) לך (cf. Seeligmann, 60). This LXX reading, especially if it represents the Hebrew גלה, possibly served as a basis for later apocalyptic readings of the same verse, sometimes combined with the vocabulary of the related verse Dan 2:22. Thus 1 En 46:3: "treasures of what is hidden he will reveal" (*mazāgebt zaḫabu' wa'atu yakaśśat*). The root *kaśata* is used in Ethiopic to translate Hebrew גלה (e.g., Lev 18:6; Deut 23:1; Dan 2:22; cf. Dillmann, *Das Buch Henoch*, 157). This is true also in cases where prophecy and revelation are involved; cp. Num 24:4, גלוי, with 1 En 1:2, ἀνεῳγμένη, *kəśutāt*, and see M. Black, *The Book of Enoch, or, I Enoch: A New English Edition with Commentary and Textual Notes*, SVTP 7 (Leiden: Brill, 1985), 104.

15. Quoted from A. Dillmann, *Lexicon Linguae Aethiopicae* (Leipzig: Weigel, 1865), 600.

*Exegetical Notes on Cosmology in the Parables of Enoch*

Isa 45:3 is important for the interpretation of the Parables because it is the only source where "treasure" and "mystery" appear as a word pair in the Hebrew Bible. Moreover, this word pair is used in this verse with regard to the darkness, a cosmological entity mentioned also in the Book of Parables (41:8). The biblical verse was originally meant as a metaphor to designate the concealed riches that will be given to the future messiah, but the diction of this verse, in particular the synonym pair of treasures and mysteries, was interpreted in the Parables as geographical data.[16] This interpretation includes not only "treasures," but also "secrets," a term hardly suitable to designate a part of the cosmos. It seems therefore that the cosmological vocabulary of the Book of Parables is dependent upon an interpretation of Isa 45:3.

Two possible examples may be presented for the use of Isa 45:3 in Second Temple writings. The Aramaic Levi Document uses the same word pair as a metaphor for the concealment of wisdom: לא יבוזזון/ולא ישכחון מטמוריה אוצרי חכמתא, "the treasure houses of wisdom they will not plunder, and they will not find its hidden places."[17] However, since the treasures of wisdom do appear in related literature (e.g., Sir 41:12; Col 2:3), the reliance of Aramaic Levi upon Isa 45:3 as a scriptural source is hard to prove. A better case is found in the cosmological hymn of the *Serekh* (1QS X 2), where a "treasure" for darkness is mentioned.[18]

To conclude this point: although "treasures" for the luminaries are common in postbiblical literature (Jer 10:13 LXX; 1 En 17:3; 41:5; 4 Ezra 6:40), the Book of Parables is unique in the cosmological twist it applies to the term "secret." The reason for this is the special interpretation given to Isa 45:3, conceiving "treasuries" and "mysteries" as geographic entities. Thus, the midrashic interpretation of a scriptural verse seems to dictate the concept of nature, so to say, the "worldview" of an author. VanderKam has recently pointed out a similar phenomenon in the Astronomical Book, where Isa 30:26 was the source for the measures of light in the sun and the moon.[19]

---

16. Isa 45:3 does not relate to a cosmological entity called "treasures of darkness," but rather uses the word חשך as a descriptive component, as in the NJPS version's "treasures concealed in the dark."

17. Aramaic Levi Document 95. For some reason this word pair is not mentioned in the list of word pairs by H. Drawnel, *An Aramaic Wisdom Text from Qumran: A New Interpretation of the Levi Document*, JSJSup 86 (Leiden: Brill, 2004), 323. Drawnel, however, gives a helpful discussion of this couplet on 340-41.

18. See the discussion and translation of this sentence by P. S. Alexander and G. Vermes, *Qumran Cave 4.XIX: 4QSerekh Ha-Yaḥad*, DJD 26 (Oxford: Clarendon, 1998), 116-17. In this passage the treasures of darkness are transformed from a metaphor (see above, n. 16) to a real geographical entity.

19. J. C. VanderKam, "Scripture in the Astronomical Book of Enoch," in *Things Revealed:*

Jonathan Ben-Dov

## Oath

An oath, *maḥalā*, of the luminaries appears several times in the Parables. First, in 41:5 the two great luminaries "keep faith with one another according to the oath that they have sworn" (cf. 43:2).[20] In the long pericope 69:13-25, many elements of nature, including the luminaries, are bound to maintain their order by oath in the great name. We should note the basic difference between the two oaths: in chap. 41 the luminaries are bound by a mutual oath, while in chap. 69 the oath is imposed on them by a superior power.

Neither of the oaths appears in the Astronomical Book,[21] thus there must be other sources or parallels. As noted by Black, the "keeping of faithfulness" (*hāymānota ʿaqaba*) of 41:5 and 43:2 stems from the Hebrew phrase אמונים שמר of Isa 26:2, LXX φυλάσσων ἀλήθειαν.[22] However, in that verse no oath is present. I suggest that a mutual commitment of the luminaries to each other appears in the cosmological hymn of the *Serekh* (1QS X 3-4): מסרותם זה לזה יחד תקופתם עם, "as well as their turning-point with their *msrt* to each other." The translation of this passage is not clear, and especially of the problematic word מסרות.[23] Milik translated this term as "positions," while Qimron, following Licht, prefers "transmitting," similar to later Hebrew מסרת, "tradition."[24] However, the nuance of commitment placed upon the luminaries in this line, as well as the biblical Hebrew traits of this text, requires an interpretation similar to that of Ezek 20:37, *massoret ha-berit*, "bounds of covenant."[25] The luminaries

---

*Studies in Early Jewish and Christian Literature in Honor of Michael E. Stone,* ed. E. G. Chazon et al., JSJSup 89 (Leiden: Brill, 2004), 89-103. David Suter has claimed that the entire composition of the Parables is dependent upon a midrash of Isa 24:17-23. See D. W. Suter, *Tradition and Composition in the Parables of Enoch,* SBLDS 27 (Missoula: Scholars, 1979).

20. The reconstruction of the last word of 1 En 41:5 is based on the correction suggested by Flemming and quoted in Uhlig, *Das äthiopische Henochbuch,* 583.

21. Pace Uhlig, *Das äthiopische Henochbuch,* 583.

22. Black, *The Book of Enoch,* 202.

23. The term תקופתם is less problematic, though not unequivocal. I prefer the meaning "turning point," with Qimron (see below).

24. J. T. Milik, *The Books of Enoch: Aramaic Fragments of Qumrân Cave 4* (Oxford: Clarendon, 1976), 187; Baruch Levine agrees with Milik: B. A. Levine, "From the Aramaic Enoch Fragments: The Semantics of Cosmography," *JJS* 33 (1982): 311-26; E. Qimron, in *The Dead Sea Scrolls: Hebrew, Aramaic, and Greek Texts with English Translations,* vol. 1, *Rule of the Community and Related Documents,* ed. J. H. Charlesworth, PTSDSSP (Tübingen: Mohr [Siebeck]; Louisville: Westminster, 1994), 43; J. Licht, *The Rule Scroll* (in Hebrew) (Jerusalem: Bialik Institute, 1965), 208-9; Alexander and Vermes, *Qumran Cave 4.XIX,* 60, agree with Licht. Licht, however, admits that this meaning of *msr* is not attested in biblical Hebrew, and depends completely on Mishnaic Hebrew.

25. M. Greenberg, *Ezekiel 1–20,* AB (Garden City, N.Y.: Doubleday, 1983), 372-73, follow-

in 1QS are bound זה לזה, "to each other," in a mutual commitment, similar to that of 1 En 41:5, 43:2. We therefore see 1QS X 3-4 and 1 En 41:5, 43:2 as witnesses of the same tradition. The difference between them is that the Book of Parables turns the covenantal obligation into an explicit oath.

Now to the second attestation of the oath in the Book of Parables (1 En 69:13-25), where the oath is not a mutual commitment but rather a duty enforced upon the luminaries by the Lord or his officers. The origin for the idea of a divine fiat imposed on the luminaries lies in Jeremiah's prophecy. Jeremiah extols the Lord, who tied the luminaries to their course either by חקות, "laws" (31:35-36),[26] or by ברית, "covenant" (33:20, 25).[27] This kind of terminology, a metaphor in Jeremiah's usage, has become quite popular in apocalyptic literature, which repeatedly describes the duty of the luminaries as a law, e.g., 1 En 2 and in the Astronomical Book passim. However, the oath enforced upon the luminaries in chap. 69 goes one step further than just "law," and is therefore a novelty. As noted above for 41:5, it is a habit in the Parables (or possibly in the cosmological additions to this composition) to augment what seem like legal commitments and depict them as taken under oath. 69:13-25 therefore continues some of the cosmological ideas of 41:5.

Oaths and the great name as elements of creation appear again in later Jewish literature such as Hekhalot and late midrash. This seems to be a clue to the *Sitz im Leben* of the (interpolated) pericope 69:13-25, as suggested by Suter.[28] Altogether, this is rather different from the worldview of the Astronomical Book.

## Conclusion

The two elements discussed here support VanderKam's conclusion, that the Book of Parables is hardly dependent upon materials from the Astronomical Book. In this the Book of Parables differs from other Enochic compositions,

---

ing the Vulgate. Contra Levine, "From the Aramaic Enoch Fragments." This reading derives *msrt* from the root *'sr*, "tie, bind." A cognate term is *riksu*, the standard term for covenant in Akkadian, which derives from *rakasu*, "tie." This covenantal term is also used in Akkadian literature to denote the installation of luminaries in their order. See W. Horowitz, *Mesopotamian Cosmic Geography* (Winona Lake, Ind.: Eisenbrauns, 1998), 265.

26. In the LXX of Jer 31:35 the word חקות is not represented, and cp. the paraphrase of this verse in 4Q392 1 6. Altogether, the entire passage Jer 31:35-37 appears in the LXX to be very different from MT.

27. The entire passage Jer 33:14-26 is not represented in the LXX.

28. Suter, *Tradition and Composition*, 19-23.

whose cosmological lore clearly depends upon the Astronomical Book. The two most prominent examples are the Book of the Watchers and the second (Slavonic) book of Enoch.[29] On the other hand, elements from the Parables show some similarity with *Serekh* and later rabbinic materials. This is an important clue for the study of the provenance of the Parables of Enoch.

---

29. On the dependence of the Book of the Watchers on the Astronomical Book, see recently K. Coblentz Bautch, *A Study of the Geography of 1 Enoch 17–19: "No One Has Seen What I Have Seen,"* JSJSup 81 (Leiden: Brill, 2003), 199-205. On the use of the Astronomical Book's traditions in 2 Enoch, see C. Böttrich, *Das slavische Henochbuch,* in *JSHRZ* V, 7 (Gütersloh: Gütersloher Verlaghaus, 1995), 864-65.

PART THREE

# THE SON OF MAN

# The Son of Man:
# The Evolution of an Expression

*Sabino Chialà*

> The crowd answered him (Jesus): "We have heard from the law that Messiah remains forever. Then how can you say that the Son of Man must be lifted up? Who is this Son of Man?"
>
> JOHN 12:34

The purpose of this essay is to try to answer the second question of the crowd: "Who is the Son of Man?" The question is actually a double one and needs to be answered in two phases. First, "What is the Son of Man?" and afterward, "Who is the Son of Man?"

In 1557 Théodore de Bèze published a study on the Son of Man,[1] and from then until the present day a steady stream of articles and monographs has kept the debate alive. Each single interpretation obviously has its own unique features, but it is possible to group them into two general categories. There are those for whom "Son of Man" is a christological title, the fruit of a particular interpretation of the book of Daniel or another text. On the other hand, for quite a few scholars the expression "son of man" is simply a redundant substitute for a personal pronoun or for the noun "man." Two articles published in

---

1. Th. de Bèze, *Annotations* in vol. 3 of *Novum D. N. Iesu Christi Testamentum* (Geneva, 1557).

---

The present essay is a revised English version of my excursus on the Son of Man published in Italian in S. Chialà, *Il libro delle Parabole di Enoc. Testo e commento* (Brescia: Paideia, 1997), 303-40.

the 1970s are prime examples: the first sides with the "minimalist" hypothesis, according to which Jesus used the expression "son of man" to refer to the weakness of his human nature.[2] The second article challenges this interpretation and is entitled, with more than a hint of polemics, "Re-enter the Apocalyptic Son of Man."[3]

It is not easy to trace the historical evolution of one of the most mysterious and debated expressions in the New Testament. I will sketch out a short comparative analysis of the texts in which the expression is used, and those in which I feel it is avoided on purpose. In doing so I will follow a rough chronology of the texts in which I date the Book of Parables as earlier than the writings of the New Testament.

In proposing to read through all these texts in a brief essay, and to revisit a topic that has already been studied in depth, I am embarking on a rather bold venture. It would take much more than a simple excursus even to discuss each of the bibliographical entries.[4] Yet, despite the risk of oversimplifying, I feel that a rapid survey of this extremely varied collection of writings is necessary if we wish to identify signs of continuity and evolution from one work to another. We will see that these texts, although each is unique, bear witness to close cultural affinities. Placed side by side, they trace out an evolutionary parabola with two key phases, or levels of reinterpretation, which I will illustrate with excerpts from the texts.

## Jeremiah, Isaiah, Psalms, Numbers, and Job

I will begin with a cursory overview of a series of texts that I have grouped together because they use the expression "son of man" in a similar way. The expression actually appears only a few times in these texts, but these few examples illustrate the most primitive meaning of "son of man," at least in the context of the Hebrew Bible.

Jeremiah uses the term *ben 'adam* four times (Jer 49:18, 33; 50:40; 51:43),

---

2. R. Leivestad, "Exit the Apocalyptic Son of Man," *NTS* 18 (1972): 243-67.
3. B. Lindars, "Re-enter the Apocalyptic Son of Man," *NTS* 22 (1975): 52-72.
4. There is a very large number of studies on our subject, and it is impossible to refer to all of them. For bibliographical details, see my book *Il libro delle Parabole di Enoc;* I cite here just a few articles that are representative of the debate and offer different points of view: J. J. Collins, "The Son of Man in First-Century Judaism," *NTS* 38, no. 3 (1992): 448-66; F. C. Burkitt, "The Nontitular Son of Man: A History and Critique," *NTS* 40 (1994): 504-21; M. Casey, "Idiom and Translation: Some Aspects of the Son of Man Problem," *NTS* 41 (1995): 168-82; T. B. Slater, "One Like a Son of Man in First-Century CE Judaism," *NTS* 41 (1995): 183-98.

and Isaiah uses the same term twice (Isa 51:12; 56:2). In the Psalms the expression *ben 'adam* appears three times (Pss 8:5; 80:18; 146:3), and the equivalent *ben 'enosh* once (Ps 144:3). The book of Numbers uses *ben 'adam* only once (Num 23:19), and Job uses the same expression three times (Job 16:21; 25:6; 35:8). In almost all these texts the expression appears in a sentence composed of two parts: in the first part the subject is "man," or a similar noun, and in the second part the subject is "son of man." "Man" and "son of man" are meant to be synonyms, and when placed in sequence, the second embellishes and accentuates the first. This narrative device is typical of the Semitic languages. In all the above occurrences of the expression, its interpretation is evident: "son of man" simply means "man," "human being," and in most cases the text seeks to emphasize the fragile and mortal nature of humanity. The Rule of the Qumran community uses the expression "son of man" in an analogous way, making it a substitute for the term "man" (1QS 11:20-21).

The plural, "sons of men," appears in a number of texts, and its meaning is the same as that of the singular form. Even when in certain contexts the expression "son of man" takes on the precise connotation we will see further on, it continues to mean "human being," and at times the two meanings are present in the same texts. The first and more primitive meaning, in fact, survived the disappearance of the second meaning: in several languages "son of man" gradually came to replace the noun "man" altogether and take on its meaning. In Syriac, for instance, *bar nasha* became the common way of saying "man," and the simple noun *nasha* was almost totally abandoned. Examples of this early use of the expression "son of man" can also be found in the Book of the Watchers, the Book of Dream Visions, the Epistle of Enoch, the book of Jubilees, the Testament of the Twelve Patriarchs, the Parables of Enoch, the Psalms of Solomon, the Testament of Abraham, the Testament of Solomon, Pseudo-Philo, and the Gospels (Mark 3:28).

## Ezekiel

I have set the book of Ezekiel apart from the above texts for two reasons: it uses the expression "son of man" amply, and its interpretation of the term is not exactly the same as the one we have just seen.

In this book *ben 'adam* appears almost a hundred times and is the form of address God typically uses in speaking to the prophet. The term does not yet represent a particular function, but it is no longer a simple linguistic device used to emphasize the fragility of human nature. Upon a first reading of Ezekiel, the expression seems absolutely neutral from a conceptual point of view, but we should note that only God or his messengers use it, and it is addressed exclusively to Ezekiel. This makes it something other than a commonly used vocative formula.[5]

A similar usage is attested in one of the Noachic fragments of the Book of Parables, in which an angel calls Enoch "son of man" (1 En 60:10), and again in the Apocalypse of Elijah (1:1), where God addresses the prophet in the same way.[6]

## Daniel

In the book of Daniel[7] the expression "son of man" receives a widely varied usage. The Aramaic plural *bene 'anasha*, which appears twice (Dan 2:38; 5:21), and the Hebrew *bene 'adam*, which appears once (10:16), are simple synonyms for "men," just as in the more ancient texts cited above. In 8:17, on the other hand, the Hebrew singular *ben 'adam* recalls the book of Ezekiel: God's messenger, Gabriel, speaks to Daniel the visionary, calling him "son of man." The last specific example we will consider here concerns the famous vision that became the basis for the repertoire of "eschatological" imagery found in later texts:

> I was watching:
> thrones were set in place
> and an Ancient of Days sat down.
> His clothing: white as snow,
> and the hair on his head: as pure wool;
> His throne: flames of fire,
> with wheels of burning fire.
> A river of fire flowed and went out
> from before him.
> Thousands upon thousands were ministering to him,

---

5. The proposed interpretations are very diverse: according to some scholars, the expression is used only to underline the fragility of the prophet; according to others, it is used in the opposite sense, to show that Ezekiel is a free man and a supernatural hero. See J. Burnier-Genton, *Ezéchiel, fils d'homme* (Geneva: Labor et Fides, 1982). In any case, what is interesting is that the expression is used only with reference to the prophet.

6. An English translation of the Apocalypse of Elijah, a text usually dated between the first and fourth century c.e., can be found in *The Old Testament Pseudepigrapha*, ed. J. H. Charlesworth, vol. 1 (Garden City, N.Y.: Doubleday, 1983), 721-53.

7. The topic "son of man in Daniel" has been widely explored. For bibliographical details, see Chialà, *Il libro delle Parabole di Enoc*, and J. J. Collins, *Commentary on the Book of Daniel*, Hermeneia (Minneapolis: Fortress, 1993).

and myriads upon myriads were standing before him.
The court was seated and the books were opened. . . .
I was watching in the visions of the night
and behold, with the clouds of heaven,
one like a son of man coming,
and he reached the Ancient of Days
and was presented before him.
To him were given dominion, honor, and kingdom,
and all peoples, nations and languages serve him.
His dominion is an everlasting dominion
that will not pass away,
his kingdom will not be destroyed. (Dan 7:9-14)

As mentioned above, this text provided most of the imagery that was used in later centuries to describe eschatological visions. The two main protagonists are already on the scene: the first one, characterized by his age (he is described as dressed in white and white-haired), is called "Ancient of Days"; in other words, old. The second protagonist, called "son of man," is characterized by his human appearance.[8] The fiery throne on which the Ancient of Days sits, the heavenly ministers, and the books of judgment — all typical eschatological images — are already present here as well.

The first of the two figures has a preeminent role, and confers upon the second figure a power that consists essentially in dominion, glory, and kingdom. The books clearly allude to a judgment, as does the court, but the "son of man" character does not seem to participate in the judgment. He enters the scene after the judgment has been pronounced, when the court is already convened and the books are open.

---

8. On this subject we need to specify that the LXX version testifies a different reading from the MT and the Greek version of Theodotion. According to the LXX reading, the Ancient of Days and the "one like a son of man" are not two separate beings, but the same one. In favor of this interpretation as the most ancient one of the Danielic text, see J. Lust, "Daniel 7,13 and Septuagint," *ETL* 54 (1978): 62-69. According to Lust, we have here the most ancient text in which the final restoration is entrusted to God himself, while the distinction between the two beings is the result of a subsequent messianic theology. The considerations of Lust are especially interesting given the fact that in the Parables of Enoch and, to a certain degree, in the Revelation of John, the elements attributed to the Ancient of Days and to the "one like a son of man" are sometimes confused. When the Book of Parables was written, this distinction was not complete, but was nearing its final degree of completion. Nevertheless, even if the reading of the LXX version shows us the most ancient text, the MT is more consistent with the explanation of the vision that is subsequently given, according to which there are two entities: the Most High and the holy ones of the Most High.

On the basis of the author's own interpretation of the vision in the verses that follow, we can be certain that here the expression *bar 'enosh*, the Aramaic equivalent of *ben 'adam*, simply means "man," "being in human form," and is meant to be a symbol for the "people of the holy ones of the Most High" (7:27). This interpretation is further confirmed by the fact that Daniel does not see "the son of man" coming, but "one *like* a son of man." What the author means is that the second figure who appears is "like" something with which his readers are familiar, a man. It is unlikely that he is attempting to explain something unfamiliar by comparing it with something even less familiar. What happens in the vision, then, is the following: an old man appears who symbolizes the Most High, judgment is pronounced on oppressors, and then a man who symbolizes the holy people approaches and is given everlasting dominion, honor, and kingdom.

Consequently, in the book of Daniel there is no trace of a particular figure with the functions that later texts were to attribute to him, as we will soon see. Nonetheless, the book contains the basic *imagistic repertoire* that was taken up and elaborated in the centuries that followed, and the expression "son of man," which Daniel uses in a totally neutral way, is part of this repertoire.

Another chapter of the book of Daniel that offers a wealth of images to later authors is the tenth. Here the author mentions a "man," whom he also describes as "one who looked like a man." This figure is accompanied a little later by another one, described as "in the image of a son of man." These expressions are all equivalent, and in later literature this figure's traits are often fused with those of the figure in chap. 7, or used alternatively. This man is dressed in linen with a gold belt around his waist, and has a body like chrysolite, a face like lightning, fiery eyes, and legs like burnished bronze pillars. His words sound like the roar of a multitude, and his function is essentially to reveal what must happen (10:1-19). The expressions "one who looked like a man" and "in the image of a son of man" do not indicate a symbolic figure, as in chap. 7, but a real one; and from Daniel's reactions we can deduce that the figure or figures in question are of a higher, probably angelic nature. Thus, even though the two expressions cited above are meant simply to emphasize that these are figures who reveal themselves in *human form*, both expressions designate real beings who belong to a higher order than that of the prophet. As early as the book of Daniel, then, we note a progression, or better, a differentiation in the way the expression "son of man" is used. The author first uses it in a symbolic sense — even if the symbol indicates a real being — to refer to a collective reality (in chap. 7, "like a son of man" simply means someone or something "like a man"), and then goes on several chapters later to refer to a real figure who speaks with the prophet, is revered by him, has a superhuman nature, and appears in human form. In this second passage, "like a man" means that even though the beings in question are not human, they show themselves in human likeness.

## The Parables of Enoch

In the Book of Parables,[9] what was only a *symbol* or *metaphor* in the book of Daniel — at least in chap. 7 — becomes a *character* to whom precise traits and functions are attributed. The Book of Parables reproduces Daniel's entire iconographic repertoire. In the text, passages of Daniel are cited almost word for word, but they are used to indicate different realities. By looking at the additions the author has made to the text of Daniel and the aspects of the text he consistently emphasizes, we can understand in which direction he is taking his reinterpretation of the text.

As we read through the key passages of the Parables, we will examine the points where the text intersects with the book of Daniel, and those places where the author has made his own additions.

A first text in which the language of the book of Daniel is clear, is chap. 46:

> In that place, I saw the One to whom belongs the beginning of days, whose head was like white wool. With him there was another individual, whose face was like that of a man, and whose face was full of grace like that of one of the holy angels.
> 
> And I asked the one from among the angels who was walking with me, and who was revealing to me all the secrets about that Son of Man: "Who is this, and from whence is he and why he is walking with the Beginning of Days?" And he answered and said to me: "This is the Son of Man, to whom belongs righteousness, and with whom righteousness dwells. He reveals all the hidden storerooms, for he is the one whom the Lord of the Spirits has chosen.... This Son of Man whom you have seen is the One who will remove the kings and the mighty ones from their seats and the strong ones from their thrones...." (1 En 46:1-4)

This scene, which is structured like Dan 7, is composed of two tableaux. In the first, a character is represented whose name is not given; it is said only that to him belongs "the beginning of days." This statement does not yet con-

---

9. I have argued that the Book of Parables was written in the last years of the first century B.C.E. or in the first years of the common era, in any case before any New Testament writings. See Chialà, *Il libro delle Parabole di Enoc*, 39-77.

tain a title, but only an attribute. Another trait attributed to this figure is hair "like white wool." The second tableau introduces another character, who is described as having a face "like that of a man," which also is "full of grace like that of one of the holy angels." The vision is followed by an explanation, which does not focus on the first character (who appears to be familiar to Enoch, as to Daniel), but on the second. It is at this point, during the interpretation of the vision, that the two texts begin to reveal considerable differences. "The One to whom belongs the beginning of days" is described as having the same traits as the "Ancient of Days" of Daniel, and these two expressions are probably equivalent to one another. Yet, when Enoch speaks to the angel, he takes the expression the text had presented as an attribute and turns it into a proper name, and thus there is a progression of meaning: Daniel's *metaphor*, which of course concealed a reality, has here become a *character*.

The second figure is presented as one "whose face was like that of a man," and it is also said that his face was "like that of one of the holy angels." This language seems to allude less to Dan 7 than to Dan 10, where two figures, probably angelic, are described with the same terminology as in the Parables. In the text we are analyzing here, the author is not using a metaphor, but is speaking of a being who is clearly not human but angelic in nature, and who walks with the Beginning of Days. Thus, Enoch's guide answers his question by saying: "This is *the* Son of Man, to whom belongs righteousness"; in other words: this is the precise figure to whom the function of righteousness is attributed.[10] The expressions "like a man," "like a son of man," and "who looked like a son of man" may be, in Dan 10 just as in this excerpt from the Parables, devices intended to convey the message that the figure being described is not actually a man but a higher being. He is only *like* a man: his face resembles that of a human being, but not completely, because it is also angelic.

Another element that Dan 7 and the Parables have in common, but that is treated differently in the two texts, is the question of power. In the Parables it is the Son of Man who strips kings of their power, while in Daniel it is the Ancient of Days who confers power upon the one who is "like a son of man."

Let us turn to a second passage of the Parables, where the language of Daniel is again vividly present:

10. Since the article here in italics does not exist in Ethiopic, the translation cannot be literal, but already involves an interpretation. Nonetheless, the translation does not seem to alter the meaning of the sentence: between the demonstrative ("this") and the noun ("son") in the text, there is a third-person singular pronoun, which acts first and foremost as a verb, but which in a certain sense also functions as a determinant of the noun: "This is he, the Son of Man." In addition, in Ethiopic a common way of indicating that a noun is indefinite is to precede it with the number "one."

## The Son of Man: The Evolution of an Expression

> In those days, I saw the Beginning of Days sitting upon the throne of his glory: the books of the living ones were open before him, and all his army of heaven above and his council stood before him. . . . At that hour, that Son of Man was called into the presence of the Lord of the Spirits. His name was in the presence of the Beginning of Days, even before the creation of the sun and of the stars. . . . He is a support for the righteous ones. . . . He is the light of the gentiles and the hope of those who suffer in their hearts. All those who dwell upon the earth shall fall and worship before him. . . . For this purpose he was chosen and hidden in the presence of (the Lord of the Spirits) prior to the creation of the world, and (he will remain) for eternity. (1 En 47:3–48:6)

The Beginning of Days is described using the same images we saw in Dan 7: the author takes up his source exactly where he had left it in the last passage. It is the hour of judgment, and the books are opened in the presence of the Beginning of Days, while his council/court stands in front of him. Yet, unlike in Daniel, the actual judgment does not take place: there is a pause in the action as the Son of Man enters. He comes on the scene sooner here than in the corresponding passage of Daniel, because, as the text goes on to tell us, it is he who is to pronounce judgment. Yet, before the author describes the Son of Man's function, he tells us about his origins, and here too the Book of Parables is entirely independent from Daniel. By giving the Son of Man certain prerogatives, the text stresses his "messianic" nature, an element absent from the book of Daniel. This Son of Man is the support for the righteous ones, the light of the Gentiles, the hope of those who suffer, the Chosen One. The language is clearly that of Isaiah, and is borrowed from those passages of Isaiah that have strongly messianic overtones. The judgment scene Daniel had described is thus interrupted here by the Son of Man's appearance, and although we do not immediately learn that he will be the one to pronounce judgment, we are told that he bears the signs of the Messiah. Yet his main function is judgment, as is clear from the images that follow. Called by a series of different names — Chosen One, Son of Man, Son of the Mother of the Living — from this point onward he is always shown seated on the throne that, in the other texts we have analyzed, belonged to the Beginning of Days, and he is always depicted in the act of judging.

The fact that the Beginning of Days yields the throne, symbol of judgment, to the Son of Man is a critical clue for dating the text. In the entire Hebrew Bible, including the book of Daniel, it is God in person who judges. In the New Testament, on the other hand, judgment is entrusted to the Son. In the Book of Parables the situation evolves within the same text: the one who is initially seated on the throne "surrenders" the throne to the Son of Man: "The

Lord of the Spirits placed the Elect One on the throne of glory; and he shall judge all the works of the holy ones in heaven above, weighing in the balance their deeds" (1 En 61:8).[11]

Moving onward, we can now turn to chap. 71, where Enoch is acknowledged as Son of Man in a vision that is once again modeled on the book of Daniel.

> Michael, Raphael, Gabriel, Phanuel, and many (other) holy angels, without number, go out of that house. With them was the Beginning of Days: his head was like white and pure wool, and his garment was indescribable. . . .
>
> That Beginning of Days came with Michael, Gabriel, Raphael, Phanuel, and thousands of myriads of angels, without number. That angel came to me, greeted me with his voice and said to me: "You are the Son of Man[12] who are born for righteousness; righteousness dwells upon you and the righteousness of the Beginning of Days will not forsake you." (1 En 71:9-14)

This excerpt narrates a new evolutionary phase. Once more the scene opens with Daniel's imagery: the Beginning of Days has his characteristic features and is accompanied by the heavenly hosts. In the second scene, though, there is a new variation: it is no longer the Son of Man who is called into the presence of the Beginning of Days, but Enoch himself who is proclaimed Son of Man and told that he is to exercise righteousness. Here the *metaphor*, initially transformed into a *character* (first level of reinterpretation), receives a *human face* (second level of reinterpretation). We have reached a new stage in the evolutionary process, and this is one of the elements that convinces us that this last chapter of the Book of Parables is a later addition.[13] During the first century

---

11. Two other texts (1 En 62:5; 69:27) also mention the Son of Man in relationship to the throne of judgment.

12. Even if the Ethiopic text does not testify here a significantly different reading, some scholars have tried to translate this passage differently, because they consider incomprehensible the normal translation: "You are the Son of Man," which is a voice addressed to Enoch. One of the other suggested translations is: "You are a son of man born for the righteousness." But I cannot understand why such a typical expression should be translated differently here than in all the other chapters. The Ethiopic expression *walda be'esi*, used here, has the same meaning as the more common *walda sabe'e*, as other passages of the Book of Parables and the Ethiopic translation of the Bible testify.

13. Some scholars have suggested that chaps. 70–71 were added as a unit to a previously existing original text of the Book of Parables, which ended with chap. 69. In my view, chap. 70 was the original conclusion and chap. 71 was a later addition, perhaps datable to the end of the first century C.E. For a discussion and arguments, see Chialà, *Il libro delle Parabole di Enoc*, 134-38, 281-85.

C.E., another series of texts bears witness to a similar phase in the evolutionary process: the New Testament, for example, gives the Son of Man the name Jesus, and the Testament of Abraham gives the name Abel (intended like another "historical" figure) to a character who is probably also the "Son of Man."

## The Gospel of Mark

Beginning with the Gospel of Mark, we can briefly survey the books of the New Testament in which the Son of Man appears and note, as before, his attributes and functions. Given the complexity of the New Testament, we run the risk of oversimplifying if we try to do more than focus on just a few points. But we will take care, as we read the texts, to remain aware of the culture that produced them and that sheds light on their interpretation, just as the texts themselves tell us much about their cultural origins.

The Synoptic Gospels are the books of the New Testament in which the expression "Son of Man" most frequently appears. In most cases the expression is spoken by Jesus himself, and, from the way he uses the title, it seems clear that it was not unknown to his contemporaries. By this era the title "Son of Man" was evidently associated with a series of characteristics that were more or less familiar, and to which Jesus added others.

New Testament exegesis traditionally groups the passages that mention the Son of Man into three categories: logia on Jesus' earthly ministry, on his passion and resurrection, and on eschatology.[14] In Mark's Gospel the most important category regards the announcement of the Son of Man's passion, death, and resurrection: into this grouping fall eight of the fourteen occurrences of the expression "Son of Man." The way Jesus presents this particular attribute of the Son of Man tells us that his listeners found it puzzling: he always has to explain it with reference to the Scriptures. Jesus' audience does not seem to be aware that the Son of Man must suffer, and that this is part of his function. There is in fact no mention of this either in the book of Daniel or in the Parables.

In another text common to the three Synoptic Gospels, the episode of the paralytic (Mark places it in chap. 2), another new feature of the Son of Man appears. As he heals the paralyzed man, Jesus speaks of "forgiveness of sins," which scandalizes the scribes who witness the scene. In response Jesus says: "That you may know that the Son of Man has authority to forgive sins on earth" (Mark 2:10). The specific mention of forgiveness of sins taking place "on earth,"

---

14. This division of the sayings into three groups has a purely conventional value, but it is still a useful means of classification.

which Luke accentuates by anticipating these words in the sentence (cf. Luke 5:24), seems to indicate that people already believed the Son of Man had the power to forgive sins — or, in the language of the Parables, to "justify" — in heaven.

Another characteristic of the Son of Man, for Mark, is that he came "to give his life as a ransom for many" (Mark 10:45). In other words, the Son of Man has a saving role, which he carries out by sacrificing his life. This typically Christian feature is absent from both Daniel and the Parables.

Lastly, we should note the three passages in which Mark speaks of the Son of Man's final coming — that is, his eschatological role. As we have seen, this theme was predominant in the Book of Parables, and Luke and Matthew also give it priority. In the first passage Mark hints at the parousia by saying that one must follow Jesus to the point of giving one's life, without being ashamed of him, or else, says the text, "the Son of Man will be ashamed of [such a person] when he comes in his Father's glory with the holy angels" (Mark 8:38). The language used here calls to mind the Parables more than it does Daniel: the Son of Man's glory is that of the Father, who has given it to the Son (cf. 1 En 61:8), and the Son comes in the company of the holy angels, a typically Enochic theme.

The second passage is found in Mark's eschatological discourse, which is much shorter here than in the other Synoptics: "And then they will see the Son of Man coming in the clouds with great power and glory, and then he will send out the angels and gather his elect from the four winds" (Mark 13:26-27).

The first part of this sentence clearly borrows from Daniel's imagery, while the second part sounds more like the Parables. Even in the sentence's first half, though, very little of Daniel remains: the Son of Man is obviously no longer a metaphor, but is clearly a character (first level of reinterpretation), and very probably already has a name (second level of reinterpretation), since Jesus himself is here claiming to be the Son of Man.

The last eschatological passage is found in the context of Jesus' interrogation before the Sanhedrin: "Again the high priest asked him and said to him: 'Are you the Messiah, the son of the Blessed One?' Then Jesus answered: 'I am; and you will see the Son of Man seated at the right hand of the Power and coming with the clouds of heaven.' At that the high priest tore his garments and said: 'What further need have we of witnesses? You have heard the blasphemy. What do you think?'" (Mark 14:61-64).

In this extremely complex passage there is a rapid succession and overlapping of christological titles, making it impossible to understand exactly how Jesus has blasphemed. What is certain is that here, for Mark, Jesus *identifies* himself with the Son of Man in glory, whom he describes with imagery that seems to be Daniel's, although in reality almost nothing of Daniel is left. In Daniel the "one like a son of man" is not seated at the right hand of the Power: when he arrives, the Ancient of Days is already seated with his court, while in the Parables the Beginning of Days is said to place the Chosen One on the throne of his glory so that he might judge (cf. 1 En 61:8). Another noteworthy aspect of this passage is the naturalness with which Mark attributes a whole series of messianic titles to the Son of Man, as if this were not a novelty. In the Book of Parables, a similar list of titles is gradually presented over the course of several chapters.

The last passage of Mark we will consider is a verse that seems to reflect the more ancient meaning of "son of man," in the singular. The other Synoptics reinterpret this verse christologically, and perhaps Mark, who seems to be quoting a traditional saying, does the same: "He said to them: 'The sabbath was made for man, not man for the sabbath. That is why the Son of Man is lord even of the sabbath'" (Mark 2:27-28).

There is no doubt that here the expression "son of man" simply means "man," at least in the source Mark is probably citing. For one thing, the "man–son of man" parallelism, which we saw in the more ancient texts, turns up again. Mark is familiar with this usage, since in the following chapter (3:28) he intends "sons of men" to mean "men," in a passage that is not a quotation but his own composition. What most helps clarify Mark 2:28, though, is the biblical text to which it alludes, Gen 1–2. Here we are told that when the world is created, man is created before the Sabbath, which means that the Sabbath is created "for" man and that man is lord not only of creation but "even" of the Sabbath (this explains the emphatic *kai*). The other two Synoptics take this sentence of Mark, eliminate the first part of it, and interpret the rest of it in a clearly christological sense.

To conclude, in the Gospel of Mark the meaning of the expression "Son of Man" is by no means unequivocal. Further, when the term is used to designate the Son of Man "character," this character is first and foremost one who must die and then rise from the dead, and who carries out an activity of justification and redemption on earth. The Son of Man's eschatological role, though already well defined in Mark, is quantitatively less important than it is in Luke and Matthew. The Son of Man is already a figure, a character, with whom Jesus identifies, but traces of the expression's primitive meaning remain.

## The Gospel of Luke

In the Gospel of Luke, as in Mark, it is possible to identify three types of contexts in which the expression "Son of Man" appears. There is a shift in emphasis, however, which is taken even further in Matthew.

The announcement of the Son of Man's passion, death, and resurrection, which was the most important category in Mark, is secondary for Luke: only seven cases out of twenty-five fall into this group. The passage on the Son of Man forgiving sins remains (Luke 5:24), as does the verse about the Son of Man having come to bring salvation (19:10). The references that are considerably more numerous here than in Mark are those concerning the Son of Man's eschatological function: there are eleven cases, whereas Mark had only three. The Son of Man's final coming is mentioned in three isolated verses (Luke 9:26; 12:8; 12:40), in a first eschatological discourse (17:20–18:8), in a second eschatological discourse (21:25-36), and finally in the context of Jesus' interrogation before the Sanhedrin (22:69).

The first eschatological discourse makes no reference to Daniel, not even on an imagistic level: the text speaks in a general way about the Son of Man's coming, but there is no mention of "clouds," Daniel's typical theme. There are, however, probable echoes of the Parables: the image of lightning, which recalls the descriptions of the various atmospheric phenomena and their corresponding angels; the comparison of the days of Noah with the days of the Son of Man; and the chosen ones who cry out to God asking that justice be done.

In the second eschatological discourse, Daniel's imagery returns, but only superficially: if we read carefully, we find that the only material that can actually be traced to Daniel is the description of the "Son of Man coming in a cloud." The rest of the dense web of apocalyptic scenes is foreign to Daniel, and once again many of the images can be found instead in the Parables: the importance of the sun, moon, and stars (which also feature in the prophecies of Isaiah and Amos), people's fearful reactions, and the Son of Man's appearance, which seems to imply a judgment.

In Luke's Gospel the influence of Daniel is very superficial, even as far as imagery is concerned, and the rare traces of Daniel we do find reveal an advanced level of reinterpretation. There seems to be an evolution in Luke with respect to Mark: by accentuating the Son of Man's eschatological function, Luke makes *his* Son of Man one who will come first and foremost to put an end to history and inaugurate the kingdom. But for Luke, just as for Mark, this Son of Man is Jesus, and so here as well we are at what we have called the second level of reinterpretation.

## The Gospel of Matthew

The process of accentuation of the Son of Man's eschatological function, already under way in Luke, continues in Matthew. The references to the Son of

Man's death and resurrection are even fewer: only eight of the thirty-one references to the Son of Man belong to this category. The passage on the forgiveness of sins and the saying about the Son of Man having come to bring salvation have been preserved (Matt 9:6; 20:28). The Son of Man's eschatological mission is described in even more verses than in either of the two preceding Gospels, and more important, it is described in greater detail. Matthew says explicitly that the Son of Man is the judge, and that he will come to exercise judgment at the end of time (cf. 13:41-42; 16:27; 19:28). In these three passages, one of the first things we should note is the total absence of Daniel's language and the obvious allusions to the Book of Parables: the angels who throw evildoers into the fiery furnace, the Son of Man coming to judge, the renewal of the world. There is also the scene in chap. 25, unique to Matthew, that describes the Son of Man's judgment at the end of time and begins: "When the Son of Man comes in his glory, and all the angels with him, he will sit upon his glorious throne, and all the nations will be assembled before him. And he will separate them from one another" (25:31-32).

In all these passages the Son of Man is accompanied by angels, who seem to have taken the place of Daniel's cloud. As far as the eschatological discourse is concerned (24:23-24) and Jesus' interrogation before the Sanhedrin (26:64), the text of Matthew does not reveal significant differences with regard to the other two Synoptic Gospels, and so what was said about these passages in Luke and Mark holds true here as well.

What is unique to Matthew can be found essentially in the four passages that describe the Son of Man as judge: here Matthew provides further detail regarding a figure and a function that were already present in Mark and developed in Luke. More than the other Synoptics, Matthew was undoubtedly influenced by the content of the Parables. Several New Testament commentators, convinced that the Book of Parables was written after Matthew but unable to deny the resemblances, have suggested that the influence took place in the opposite direction, from Matthew toward the Book of Parables. Yet a number of factors lead us to rule out this possibility, above all, the connection with the book of Daniel. In the Book of Parables Daniel is still a strongly felt presence: his language, reinterpreted though it may be, predominates in certain scenes. In the Gospels, on the other hand, and especially in Luke and Matthew, Daniel is remote. The only trace of Daniel's imagery we find in Matthew is the "clouds" that accompany the Son of Man: Matthew must have taken this image directly from Daniel, because these "clouds" are not clearly described in the Parables. The image of clouds is not completely absent from the latter work, but there are no clouds mentioned in the context of the vision of the Son of Man. Another factor that makes us tend toward Matthew's dependence on the Book of Parables, and not vice versa, is that the essential characteristics that the Book of Parables attributes to the Son of Man can be found in Matthew, but the reverse is not true. The first element in Matthew that is totally foreign to the Enochic tradition is the series of sayings about how the Son of Man must die. If the Book of Parables is a Christian text, it is hard to imagine why the author would have left out this central part of the Christian kerygma. And if it is a Jewish text that was written in the Christian era, it is hard to see why the author would have taken material from a Christian text such as the Gospel of Matthew. Furthermore, unlike the author of the Parables, the Gospels never seem to explain the nature, origin, and functions of the Son of Man, but they make a point of emphasizing those traits that are never attested in the earlier tradition, such as his power to forgive sins "even" on earth, and his passion and death.

It seems as if these developments are unique to the New Testament, and are totally absent from the sources. By the time the Evangelists were writing the Gospels, and probably already by the time of Jesus' ministry, the Son of Man was a familiar figure, but what was truly familiar about him was his role as eschatological judge. The rest belonged to developments that are attested exclusively in the Christian texts.

## The Letter to the Hebrews

The title "Son of Man" appears once in the Acts of the Apostles (7:55-56), but this passage adds nothing new to our itinerary except that it is the first time in the New Testament the expression is spoken by someone other than Jesus.

We can go on, then, to an excerpt from the Letter to the Hebrews, which is significant not primarily because of its theological content, but because it offers a concrete example of how a text can be completely reinterpreted. The author says:

> Someone has testified somewhere:
> "What is man that you are mindful of him,
> or the son of man that you care for him?
> You made him for a little while lower than the angels. . . ."
> But we do see Jesus crowned with glory and honor,
> he who for a little while was made lower than the angels. (Heb 2:6-9)

The text cited here is the Eighth Psalm, whose reference to the "son of man" was, in its own era, not meant to allude to any specific heavenly or earthly figure, but was understood to be simply a redundant way of saying "man–

human being." Yet, when the author of Hebrews reinterprets this psalm, "son of man" becomes a reference to Jesus, who in the Gospels declares himself to be the Son of Man.

This example shows how easily a normal, everyday expression could be reinterpreted and so become charged with meaning. It is very likely that the Letter to the Hebrews' reinterpretation of the psalm was inspired by texts such as the Book of Parables and the Gospels, which use the title "Son of Man" in the sense implied here, that is, with reference to a higher being who is made "a little lower than the angels" for a given mission. A similar procedure probably also guided Matthew and Luke in reinterpreting the passage about the Sabbath in Mark.[15]

## The Gospel of John

In the Gospel of John the expression "Son of Man" is less important than in the Synoptic Gospels, and the author completely transforms the Synoptics' language. Of the thirteen occurrences of the expression in John, four refer to the Son of Man being lifted up or glorified (John 3:14; 8:28; 12:23; 13:31), an event that corresponds to the passion-resurrection in this Gospel. Two occurrences are about "eating the flesh and drinking the blood" of the Son of Man (6:27, 53); three describe his unique relationship to heaven and his heavenly origins (1:51; 3:13; 6:62); one refers to his role as judge (5:27); and in the last three, two of which are found in the same verse, the author tells us about the Son of Man's identity (9:35; 12:34).

The last three types of occurrences are particularly interesting, and it is at these that we will look more closely. As far as his origins are concerned, the Son of Man is clearly a being who has an unusual relationship with heaven: angels ascend and descend upon him, and he himself came down from heaven and must return to heaven. John also tells us that judgment is entrusted to him: "He gave him the power to exercise judgment, because he is the Son of Man" (5:27). This is a very important statement, because it assumes that John's listeners were aware that judgment was a prerogative of the Son of Man, and therefore that Jesus, as Son of Man, would be the one to judge. This awareness could have come either from a familiarity with Matthew (the Synoptic Gospel that is most explicit about the Son of Man's role as judge and is generally considered to have been written before John) or directly from the Parables. In either case this statement, like Stephen's affirmation in Acts, demonstrates two things: first, the ex-

---

15. See my comments above.

pression "Son of Man" as Jesus used it was not a figure of speech, and second, in the first century c.e. this title was known and indicated a figure to whom specific functions were attributed, especially that of judge.

In the last group of references to the Son of Man in John, there are two passages about his identity. The first is found in Jesus' exchange with the man born blind: "Jesus said: 'Do you believe in the Son of Man?' He answered and said: 'Who is he, sir, that I may believe in him?' Jesus said to him: 'You have seen him and the one speaking with you is he'" (9:35-37).

The blind man does not ask about the Son of Man's traits or functions, which by now seem to be generally known. His question has to do with identity: he wants to know the "name" of the one who incarnates the Son of Man's role, and so we are at the second level of reinterpretation.

In the second passage Jesus is speaking with the crowd and trying to explain that his impending death is in conformity with what has been foreseen. The crowd replies: "We have heard from the law that Messiah remains forever. Then how can you say that the Son of Man must be lifted up? Who is this Son of Man?" (12:34).

The text assumes that the Son of Man and the Messiah are one and the same, which is why Jesus' listeners apply to the Messiah what he has said about the Son of Man. This identification of the Son of Man with the Messiah is already present in the Parables. As for the statement about the Messiah being eternal, there seems to be no trace of such a belief in the Torah. The only two texts that hint in this direction are Ezek 37:25, which says David will be "prince forever," and the Book of Parables, according to which the Son of Man–Messiah "was chosen and concealed in the presence of [the Lord of the Spirits] prior to the creation of the world, and [he will remain] for eternity" (1 En 48:6).

An interesting observation emerges from the collection of excerpts we have analyzed: by the time John was writing his Gospel, a whole series of notions about the Son of Man was quite widespread, at least in certain circles. Among these was the conviction that the Son of Man would judge, and that he would have a messianic role. The Gospel of John does not contain discourses on the Son of Man, but every so often he slips references to this figure into his narrative, presenting the things he says as if they were already known. All of this leads us to think that before the Gospel of John was written, there were texts or an oral tradition that spread these notions and allowed them to reach many people. In all likelihood these texts are the Book of Parables and the Synoptic Gospels, especially Matthew. These are the works in which we find descriptions of those features of the Son of Man that John takes for granted, especially his function as judge and his messianic role.

*The Son of Man: The Evolution of an Expression*

## The Book of Revelation

In the book of Revelation the expression "Son of Man" appears only twice, and is used in the same way as in the book of Daniel. The images that appear alongside the expression are also recognizably Daniel's, and are taken from both chaps. 7 and 10. In addition, the author of Revelation gives his "one like a son of man" those traits that the author of Daniel attributed to the Ancient of Days.

The expression first occurs at the beginning of the book, in the introduction to the seven letters (Rev 1:13-15), and it occurs for the second and last time in chap. 14 (14:14). In both cases there is no explicit reference to the Son of Man character, as there is in the Book of Parables and in the Gospels. Instead, the author has apparently chosen to return to Daniel's text. Unlike in the Gospels, where we have seen how little of Daniel remains, here Daniel's text is taken up literally, and the author even prefers Daniel's expression "like a son of man" to the Gospels' "the Son of Man."

This may well be due to the stylistic affinity of the two texts, since they were both written using apocalyptic language. But, chronologically speaking, the book of Revelation also appeared in an era in which the title "Son of Man" was falling into disuse, and so the way the author uses the term can be seen as an indication of its decline. In short, with regard to Revelation it is no longer accurate to speak of a christological title, because the expression "son of man" is simply used in accordance with the images found in the source the author quotes, or which inspired him.

It is not the author's intention to describe the heavenly figure of the Son of Man and then apply that description to Jesus. Rather, he refers directly to Jesus of Nazareth, even if in so doing he uses the sort of vocabulary that other texts had used to describe the Son of Man.

In Revelation, then, the "Son of Man" character is no longer explicitly evoked, and we can say that in this respect there is a "recession" toward Daniel, from both a semantic and a conceptual point of view. Yet there is a difference: the one "like a son of man" is no longer a symbol of the holy people of the Most High, as he was for Daniel, but a symbol of Jesus of Nazareth.

## Fourth Book of Ezra

The Fourth Book of Ezra (chap. 13) offers yet another elaboration of the concepts and images we have seen in the previous texts. The basis for this chapter is once again the vision described by Daniel, which the author of Ezra embellishes with a variety of new features. The structure of the entire chapter recalls Daniel:

there are an account of the dream, a request for an explanation, and then the giving of the explanation:

> I looked, and behold, this wind made something like the figure of a man come up out of the heart of the sea. And I looked, and behold, that man flew with the clouds of heaven; and wherever he turned his face to look, everything under his gaze trembled, and whenever his voice issued from his mouth, all who heard his voice melted as wax melts when it feels the fire....
>
> This is the interpretation of the vision: as for your seeing a man come up from the heart of the sea, this is he whom the Most High has been keeping for many ages, who will himself deliver his creation; and he will direct those who are left....
>
> And he, my servant (or son), will reprove the assembled nations for their ungodliness....
>
> No one on earth can see my servant or those who are with him, except in the time of his day. (4 Ezra 13)[16]

This text is heavily reworked, which makes its possible sources difficult to isolate, but the allusions to Daniel and the Parables are fairly easy to spot. The expression "something like the figure of a man" is derived from Daniel and recalls his "like a son of man." Also from Daniel are the accompanying clouds, which, as we have seen, are one of the few elements of the book of Daniel that recur in almost all the texts that adopt the "Son of Man" imagery in some way.

Yet a critical question arises: Why has "son of man" become "man"? A first explanation is that this may have to do with the phenomenon of the different versions of 4 Ezra: we do not know in which language the book was originally written, although a Semitic language seems likely. Only translations have survived, the most important of which seem to be those in Latin and Syriac. The Latin version of the book clearly refers to a "man," indicating that the Latin translator worked from a text in which the term used was "man," and not "son of man." As for the Syriac translation, the question is more complex. Here the term used is *barnasha*, which literally means "son of man" but is used in Syriac Christian literature to mean "man."[17] Several scholars, commenting on the Syriac text of 4 Ezra, have suggested that the Semitic original must have contained the expression "son of man." In that case, though, it is hard to explain the

---

16. About the dating of this text and its relationship with contemporary writings, see especially P. M. Bogaert, "Les apocalypses contemporaines de Baruch, d'Esdras et de Jean," in *L'Apocalypse johannique et l'Apocalyptique dans le Nouveau Testament*, ed. J. Lambrecht (Leuven: Leuven University Press, 1980), 47-68.

17. See my comments above.

Latin translation. If, on the other hand, the original text contained the word "man," we can explain both the Syriac and the Latin versions.

Given the complexity of the problem, we must look for another solution. The author may have varied the text intentionally so as to avoid using an expression that had become problematic. The Fourth Book of Ezra was written around the turn of the second century C.E., by which time all speculation about the "Son of Man" had been rejected. This can be seen in the book of Revelation and in the Jewish and Christian traditions, which had stopped using the expression. It seems that in both the Jewish and Christian worlds, the "son of man" imagery was abandoned fairly quickly, and although a few elements of the ancient traditions were conserved, they were completely reinterpreted and recontextualized.

In 4 Ezra we can also identify several parallels with the Book of Parables: the mention of how those who hear the voice of this figure "melt as wax melts" before him (an image already used in the Hebrew Bible to refer to the coming of the day of the Lord, but used in both 4 Ezra and the Parables to refer to the coming of the Messiah); the expression "the Most High has been keeping (him) for many ages," which recalls the concealment of the Son of Man by the Lord of the Spirits; the judgment that this figure is to exercise, still present in 4 Ezra even if only timidly announced; and last, the fact that no one can see this "servant" before his day.

If 4 Ezra contains echoes of both Daniel and the Parables, this does not mean that the three authors had the same conception of what they described. We have already seen the distance between Daniel and the Parables, even though the latter text imitates the former, and now we are at a new level. In 4 Ezra the Son of Man has been replaced by a messianic figure. This figure comes with the clouds (Daniel's language), delivers the people and is called "my servant" by the Most High (Isaiah's terminology), will carry out judgment and will not be revealed before his day (expressions found in the Parables). Even in those passages where, given the context, one would expect the Son of Man to be mentioned, the author prefers to avoid the term and speaks simply of a human figure.

## Testament of Abraham

The last text we will analyze is the Testament of Abraham, where we have what appears to be an intriguing — and perhaps polemical — reinterpretation of the Son of Man theme.

This is an unusual text: for one thing, it attributes the role of judge to

Abel, and it does so by taking up and incorporating a series of elements that recall the Son of Man, especially as he is portrayed in the Parables and in Matthew. What catches the reader's attention are the expressions that appear alongside the name of Abel, who is called "the son of Adam, the first-formed" (TestAbr [A] 13:2).[18]

Here are the key verses of this long scene:

> Behold (there were) two angels, with fiery aspect and merciless intention and relentless look, and they drove myriads of souls, mercilessly beating them with fiery lashes. . . . Between the two gates there stood a terrifying throne with the appearance of terrifying crystal, flashing like fire. And upon it sat a wondrous man, bright as the sun, like unto a son of God. Before him stood a table like crystal, all of gold and byssus. On the table lay a book. . . . On its right and on its left stood two angels holding papyrus and ink and pen. In front of the table sat a light-bearing angel, holding a balance in his hand. . . . And the wondrous man who sat on the throne was the one who judged and sentenced the souls. . . .
>
> And Abraham said: "My lord Commander-in-chief, who is this all-wondrous judge? . . ." The Commander-in-chief said: "Do you see, all-pious Abraham, the frightful man who is seated on the throne? This is the son of Adam, the first-formed. His name is Abel, whom Cain the wicked killed. And he sits here to judge the entire creation, examining both righteous and sinners, for God said: 'I do not judge you, but every man is judged by man.'" (TestAbr [A] 12:1–13:3)

There are evident linguistic affinities here with the judgment described in the Parables: the angels who drive the souls, the book, the balance, the judgment throne, and the man seated upon it, who is described as a "wondrous man" and "like unto a son of God." Beyond these features, which can be considered typical aspects of a judgment scene even if they do not always appear in the parallel texts, what is striking is the person of the judge. In the vision he is presented as having the Son of Man's characteristics, but in the explanation that follows he is interpreted differently. He is described as seated on the judgment throne, with a balance in front of him, while angels guide into his presence the souls he is to judge and is already in the act of judging. As for his appearance, he is said to resemble a "wondrous man" — an expression that suggests, more than

---

18. An English translation of both recensions A and B of the Testament of Abraham can be found in *The Old Testament Pseudepigrapha*, ed. J. H. Charlesworth, vol. 1 (Garden City, N.Y.: Doubleday, 1983), 871-902.

## The Son of Man: The Evolution of an Expression

beauty, the extraordinary nature of the image — and immediately afterward he is said to be "like unto a son of God," that is, like an angel. This last description seems to echo the Book of Parables, which says of the Son of Man: "His face was full of grace like that of one among the holy angels" (1 En 46:1). Yet, just as in 4 Ezra, the expression "son of man" is avoided here, although its context is reproduced. 4 Ezra mentions "something like the figure of a man," and the Testament of Abraham speaks of one "like unto a son of God"; Daniel had called his character "like a son of man" in chap. 7, and one "who looked like a son of man" in chap. 10. Here the author seems to take pains to avoid the expression "son of man," and as we read ahead, this impression persists up through the explanation given to Abraham by the guide. The attribution of the role of judge to Abel, which enjoyed a certain success in later literature, seems to be unattested in any text prior to the Testament of Abraham. But Abel, according to the above excerpt, is "the son of Adam" — in Hebrew *ben 'adam,* the same expression that, translated, yields "Son of Man." At this point the question arises as to whether the Testament of Abraham was originally written in Hebrew or Aramaic, as some scholars have argued, or in Greek.[19] Actually, for the purposes of our study the problem is marginal, because in any case the Greek in the text that has survived — whether it be the original or a translation — reinterprets and assigns a precise meaning to a Semitic expression that was both familiar and debated. The words that follow the expression "son of Adam" seem to confirm that we are on polemical ground: the author insists that the judge-son of Adam (or "of man") is none other than "Abel," the one "whom Cain the wicked killed," and that the Adam in question is "the first-formed."

Another trace of polemics can be glimpsed in chap. 11 (recension B), where the author not only assigns to Abel the role of judge but places at his side Enoch, who is *reduced* to a mere "scribe of righteousness" (TestAbr [B] 11:3). And when Abel asks the angel Michael, who is with him, if Enoch can give sentence or take part in the judgment, he is given the answer: "It is this one's [Enoch's] task only to write" (TestAbr [B] 11:7). Reading on, we learn that Enoch had told the Lord he did not want to judge souls so as not to have to condemn them, and the Lord had granted his request, but had kept him as a scribe.

What we have in this text is another reinterpretation, in a polemical context, of an earlier tradition regarding the Son of Man–judge figure, a tradition supported by the Parables. Our author's reinterpretation can be considered what we have called a second-level reinterpretation, since the figure-function of

---

19. On the original language of the Testament of Abraham, see F. Schmidt, "Testament d'Abraham," in *La Bible. Écrits intertestamentaires,* ed. A. Dupont-Sommer and M. Philonenko (Paris: Gallimard, 1987), 1676.

the "son of man" is given a human face, that of Abel. As we have seen, reinterpretations of this type are found in the last chapter of the Book of Parables, where Enoch is called Son of Man, and in the Gospels, where the Son of Man is Jesus of Nazareth. These texts, which can all be dated to the second half of the first century C.E., are products of cultural trends that were probably at odds with one another as far as the interpretation of the Son of Man–eschatological judge was concerned, and each text attributes this role to a different "historical" figure.

## Conclusion

With this brief excursus we have revisited the most important stages in the evolution of an expression that changed meaning substantially over the course of just a few centuries. In doing so, we have been able to do no more than skim the surface of the relevant passages of the New Testament, without delving into its complex problematics. From the most ancient books, which can be dated around the era of the exile, to the last text we analyzed, written at the end of the first century C.E., we have seen that the expression "Son of Man" has received a wide spectrum of usages, and above all, has been reinterpreted and viewed from one angle after another.

In the first series of texts we examined, the expression "son of man" was a simple figure of speech meaning "man," and was often coupled with the word "man" in the same sentence. This usage persisted over the centuries, especially in the plural form, "sons of men." Even when several texts began to speak of the "Son of Man" as a character with precise traits, the original meaning of the expression remained, and survived the disappearance of the more recent developments in its usage.

Ezekiel's use of the expression should be considered alongside that of the most ancient texts, allowing for a certain difference. Here "Son of Man" is the expression with which the deity, or one of his messengers, addresses the prophet. This usage is also attested in Daniel, in a passage of the Book of Parables, and in the Apocalypse of Elijah.

With the book of Daniel a new phase began, not primarily because of how Daniel used the expression, but because of the way his work was to be reinterpreted in the centuries that followed. In chap. 7 the author introduced an expression to which he gave a purely symbolic value, but later authors took it and transformed it, along with the rest of Daniel's iconographic repertoire. Chap. 10 received the same treatment. The meaning Daniel gives his "son of man" terminology is clear: in the first case, the "one like a son of man" is a symbolic entity in human form, and in chap. 10 Daniel seems to indicate a character who is not human, which is why this figure is presented as one "like" a son of man. Yet, even if the expression is meant to designate a *nonhuman figure,* it is clear that it is still an exact equivalent of "man." If anything, it is the word "like" that suggests we are dealing with a character whose appearance conceals another reality.

We can begin to speak of the Son of Man as eschatological judge — that is, as a character with a specific function — only with the Book of Parables and later with the New Testament, especially the Gospels. In these texts we witness an initial reelaboration of Daniel's vocabulary, a transition we have called "first-level reinterpretation." The expression "Son of Man," which has the generic meaning of "man" and is used in a purely symbolic way in Daniel, comes to indicate a *function.* Daniel's "son of man" is merely a "man" who is a symbol of another reality — the holy people of the Most High — but in the Book of Parables the expression is given a new meaning.

In the last chapter of the Book of Parables, in the New Testament, and in the Testament of Abraham we witness the "second level of reinterpretation." Here the Son of Man *function* receives the name of a *historic individual,* past or present: Enoch, Jesus, Abel.

This evolution was accompanied by a reactionary tendency, represented by the Revelation of John and the Fourth Book of Ezra, in which much of the previously used "apocalyptic" imagery was reproduced, but all references to the Son of Man were actively avoided. Throughout the entire controversy there is a voice that never makes itself heard and stays entirely out of the debate: that of Paul. The silence of a corpus as important as the Pauline letters on the Son of Man is unquestionably an eloquent silence that deserves to be considered. Paul never mentions the "Son of Man," even though he wrote in an era in which this title had not yet become problematic; nor does he engage in polemics with those who use it.

By the end of the first century C.E., it seems that all "Son of Man" language is attentively avoided, and this should weigh as a critical factor in dating the Book of Parables. Once the Christian era had begun, there was no longer any mention of the Son of Man in Judaism,[20] not even among the specific

---

20. The one exception is a passage of the Palestinian Talmud that is highly enigmatic. I quote: "R. Abbahu said: If a man says to you: 'I am God,' he is lying; (if he says): 'I am the Son of Man,' he will later repent of it; (if he says): 'I am going up to heaven,' he says it but does not do it" (*y. Ta'anit* 65b, 68-70). The text appears to betray signs of a controversy with those who still referred in some way to the Son of Man, but it is hard to say who they were or what they intended to affirm. On this subject and on several other rabbinic texts that refer to Daniel's "son of man," see J. Coppens, *La relève apocalyptique du messianisme royal* (Leuven: Peeters, 1983), 2:175-83.

group of Jews who wrote the Second Book of Enoch, and later the Third Book of Enoch. Christian literature also abandoned the title, and Christology developed around the titles of Messiah and Son of God. The term "Son of Man" remained only in those texts in which Christian authors quoted the New Testament — as a question of faithfulness to their source — and in a certain apologetics that opposed the Son of Man to the Son of God to show Christ's dual nature. In this last context the title is interpreted in a completely different way from how it is interpreted in the Book of Parables and the New Testament. The only cultural context in which the christological title Son of Man continued to be used similarly to how it was used in the New Testament was that of gnosticism. The expression appears frequently in the Gospel of Thomas, and even more so in the Gospel of Philip, perhaps because, being so enigmatic, it opened the door to gnostic speculations.

The reasons for this loss of interest in the "Son of Man," especially on the part of Christians — given the fact that Jesus himself seems to prefer "Son of Man" to all the other christological titles — will, I hope, be discussed in one of the next convocations of the Enoch Seminar. I want just to point out some ideas or questions: Did Christians abandon this title because of its use in gnostic circles? Was the loss of interest due to the weakening of eschatological tension in most of Christianity, given that the title is linked in a particular way to eschatological functions? Or perhaps the reason for this decline was a practical one: in a missionary context, this title was useful neither in the Jewish milieu — which at that time was not Essenic or Enochic but Pharisaic — nor in the Gentile milieu, where the title "Son of Man" was not evocative of any particular function or power of Jesus, whereas the title "Son of God" was more useful and clear.

# The Son of Man in the Parables of Enoch

*Helge S. Kvanvig*

## The Parables and the Book of the Watchers

### The Second Vision of Wisdom

The Book of Parables presents itself as *rā'y za-rĕ'ya kālĕ' rā'ya tĕbab za-rĕ'ya henok*, "the vision that he saw, the second, a vision of wisdom which Enoch saw."[1] The document is further designated as *rā'ya tĕbab*, "vision of wisdom," and *nagara tĕbab*, "speech of wisdom" (1 En 37:2), seen and spoken by Enoch, the seventh patriarch. The words recorded by Enoch are, according to most of the manuscripts, *nagara qĕdus*, "speech of the Holy One." This speech concerns

---

1. In their new translation George Nickelsburg and James VanderKam assume that the three first words "the vision that he saw, the second" almost certainly are to be regarded as a gloss, inserted to relate the Parables to the Book of the Watchers within the larger Enochic corpus. They make this assumption despite the presence of these introductory words in all the Ethiopic manuscripts. Whether this assumption can overturn the manuscript evidence depends on whether there are other significant links between the Parables and the Book of the Watchers that make a succession of first and second vision likely. See G. W. E. Nickelsburg and J. C. VanderKam, *1 Enoch: A New Translation* (Minneapolis: Fortress, 2004), 50 n. a.

---

This article is based on my written presentation distributed before the Third Enoch Seminar. I have in some places considered the responses given by John Collins and Klaus Koch, but have not followed all their remarks, as can be seen in their final responses to this paper. See below, J. J. Collins, "Enoch and the Son of Man," and K. Koch, "Questions regarding the So-Called Son of Man in the Parables of Enoch." I have also included some aspects of other written and oral contributions in the seminar when appropriate.

not only Enoch, but also coming generations. It surpasses in wisdom what has been revealed to mankind before, and it is revealed by Enoch, who is given the lot of *ḥĕywat za-laʿālam*, "life which is forever" (37:4). The vision and speech came to Enoch as three "parables, discourses," *mĕshālīm*, with the Aramaic equivalent מתל, *mĕtal*, and Hebrew משל, *māshal* (37:5). Although the root of these nouns in most Semitic languages implies a sort of comparison, the translation "simile" or "parable" is too narrow, since they may also include other kinds of utterances intended to convey wisdom.[2]

The closest parallels to this introduction to the Parables are found in the Apocalypse of Weeks and the Book of the Watchers. In the Apocalypse the revelation is described as "a vision of heaven" and Enoch has learned everything from the speech of the Watchers and holy ones (4Q212 III 21 = 1 En 93:2). The whole Apocalypse is twice characterized as *mĕtal* (line 18:23 = 93:1, 3). It seems clear then that the Apocalypse in this introduction draws on the introduction to the Book of the Watchers.

In the Book of the Watchers the revelation is described as "a vision of the Holy One and of heaven" according to the Greek version (1 En 1:2 Gr$^{Pan}$). The divine name "the Holy One" is here the same as in the Parables, and it is seldom used in the Enochic writings (93:11; 104:9). The revelation is further described as the words of the Watchers and holy ones (4Q201 I 3 = 1, 2). It emphasizes that the revelation is given to distant generations, as in the Parables: "Not for this generation, but for a distant generation I speak" (line 4 = 1, 2). The divine revelation is given to Enoch as *mĕtalīn* (line 2 = Gr$^{Pan}$ 1, 2). In the Parables the vision of wisdom clearly refers to visions of God in his heavenly glory, which form the backbone of this text (cf. 1 En 39:7ff.; 40:1ff.; 46:1; 47:1ff.; 49:2ff.; 51:3; 61:8ff.; 62:3ff.; 69:29; 70:1; 71:5ff.). This is also the case in the vision of the Holy One in 1 En 1:2. The introductory phrases "vision of the Holy One and of heaven" and "words of the Watchers and holy ones" paraphrase the visionary part of the Book of the Watchers, the throne vision in 1 En 14–16, and the visionary journeys accompanied by angels in 1 En 17–36.

Thus it seems that the introduction to the Book of Parables is analogous to the introduction to the Book of the Watchers. Parables is made the second set of visions, speeches and wisdom discourses, Aramaic *mĕtalīn*, based on the first set in the Book of the Watchers. They are intended to reveal a secret that

---

2. Assuming that "comparison" is an essential aspect of the word, David Suter finds three kinds of comparisons crucial for the Parables: the fate of the righteous compared to the fate of the wicked, the order of cosmos compared to the order of the end-time, the heavenly reality compared to the earthly reality. From this perspective Suter certainly highlights three important features of the composition. See D. W. Suter, "*Māšāl* in the Similitudes of Enoch," *JBL* 100 (1981): 193-212.

*The Son of Man in the Parables of Enoch*

was not revealed in the first parables, and therefore they surpass this revelation in wisdom.

### Enoch's Heavenly Vision

In both the Greek and Ethiopic versions of 1 En 1:2 there is an unusual change in personal pronoun in the middle of the sentence. The discourse is introduced as direct speech — "Enoch said" — and is followed by Enoch's words "I heard everything." However, a third-person reference to Enoch as "a righteous man whose eyes were opened by God, who had a vision of the Holy One and of heaven" separates the introduction and direct discourse. Enoch is presented in the third person as someone known, as the distinguished protagonist of these visions. The reference is clearly to Enoch's vision of his ascent to heaven in 1 En 13–16. Since this vision plays an important role in the Parables, it is necessary to consider more carefully its content.

Enoch's vision in 1 En 13–14 is not formulated as a journey with heavenly companions as 1 En 17–36 is. The ascent takes place in a dream. The dream report has a rather complex literary structure. First there is a narration in 13:7-10, then the actual report of the content of the dream follows in detail in 14–16. The first narration tells the whole succession of events: Enoch arrives at the waters of Dan, he reads the petition from the Watchers, he falls asleep, dreams come to him, in a dream he is commissioned to go back to the Watchers and to reprimand them, and then he wakes up and goes to the Watchers to carry out this mission. The report of the content of the dream in 14–16 opens as a new section with the Aramaic ספר מלי קושטא, *sĕfar milāh qūshṭ'ā,* "the book of the words of truth" (4Q204 VI 9 = 1 En 14:1). This section concentrates solely on Enoch's dream experience of ascent to the heavenly temple, and it ends with Enoch still in the divine realm. The dream is thus told by Enoch from two perspectives. The first tells the whole series of events, emphasizing that Enoch stays on the earth during the entire dream. This is clearer in the Aramaic text than in the Ethiopic translation. Enoch reports: לשכני עיני לתרעי ה]יכל שמיא, "I lifted my eyelids to the portals of the pa[lace of heaven" (VI 4), and then hears the commission to go to the Watchers. The second perspective focuses on Enoch as the protagonist of the dream itself, and he is actually carried away to the heavenly temple. The two perspectives thus constitute two ways of reporting a dream experience where the dreamer sees himself. In the first the dreamer reports what happened in retrospect, depicting how he sees himself acting in the dream; in the second he remains in the dream experience itself, where only one of the figures is involved, the figure seen in the dream.

Helge S. Kvanvig

There is accordingly a difference between these dream reports and other reports about Enoch staying in the divine realm. In 1 En 12 it is presumed that Enoch actually remained with the holy ones. This is also the case in the Parables when Enoch's final translation to heaven is reported in 1 En 70–71. This section of the Parables certainly draws on 1 En 14, but in this case the ascension is reported differently. In 1 En 13–14 Enoch sees himself as a visionary counterpart in heaven. In 70–71 Enoch is actually taken to heaven to be identified as the Son of Man. Most of the manuscripts to 71:5 of the Eth I group read that *manfas waenok*, "the spirit and Enoch," was taken to heaven.[3] Here Enoch actually disappears from the earth.[4]

In the vision Enoch sees himself passing through three stages. He first comes to a wall (14:9). He goes through the wall and comes to a great house (14:10). He enters the house (14:13) and sees a door open to an even greater house (14:15). In this house he sees the lofty throne (14:18) on which the Great Glory is seated (14:20). Martha Himmelfarb has identified these three stages as the three parts of the temple, first the *'ūlām*, "the hall," then the *hēkal*, "the sanctuary," and finally the *dĕbīr*, "the inner sanctuary," where the throne of God is placed.[5] It even appears that Enoch enters "the inner sanctuary." In 14:24 he is brought to the door, and in 15:1 God says to him, "Come here, and hear my voice," which would indicate that he enters the inner house. Himmelfarb has further observed that in the Second Temple period scribes could serve as priests, as had Ezra (4 Ezra 7:6).[6] This apparently is the case with Enoch, who seems to be depicted both as scribe and as priest.[7] Enoch's role as intercessor in

---

3. The Ethiopic manuscripts are labeled according to M. A. Knibb, *The Ethiopic Book of Enoch 2* (Oxford: Clarendon, 1978), 21-27.

4. In his response to the paper I presented for the seminar (see below, "Enoch and the Son of Man"), Collins had doubts whether this understanding of the dream report could be correct: "Enoch was a participant in his own dream and presumably thought that he was actually experiencing what he saw. There is no visionary counterpart." Collins's argument is here in accordance with the second perspective in the dream reports; in 1 En 14 Enoch is certainly experiencing what he saw. It drops, however, the oddity of the dream reports contained in the first narration: Enoch tells how he as a dreamer sees himself ascending in the dream.

5. M. Himmelfarb, "Apocalyptic Ascent and the Heavenly Temple," in SBLSP 26 (Atlanta: Scholars, 1987), 210-17, here 210f.; Himmelfarb, *Ascent to Heaven in Jewish and Christian Apocalypses* (Oxford: Oxford University Press, 1993), 14-20.

6. Himmelfarb, *Ascent to Heaven*, 24f.

7. In Collins's response to my seminar paper (see below, "Enoch and the Son of Man") he doubted that there was evidence for seeing Enoch as a priest: "[I]t does not seem to me that entering a temple, earthly or heavenly, automatically makes one a priest." I would rather twist the argument: Who are allowed according to the Jewish tradition to cross the line between *'ūlām*, "the hall," and *hēkal*, "the sanctuary"? Only those persons ordained as priests. It even appears that Enoch enters *dĕbīr*, "the inner sanctuary." Nevertheless, the question of how close Enoch

the vision is traditionally priestly. His priestly role is made explicit in Jubilees, where Enoch burns incense in the sanctuary of the Garden of Eden (Jub 4:25). His mission in the vision is remarkable; he functions as a human mediator between God and angels. Enoch's priestly function at this point overlaps with the role of a prophet, since he is included in God's heavenly council, is addressed by God "with his own mouth" (1 En 14:24), and is commissioned to go to the Watchers with the word of judgment.

At this point it is important to highlight the literary relationship between the two main parts of the Watcher story (1 En 6–16) — the rebel story in 6–11 and the Enoch story in 12–16. Similar to the relationship between 1 En 13 and 14, the literary structure here is complex. Even though the texts are placed in a linear order, they function as narrative doublets in the sense that what is reported in 12–16 is something that takes place within the framework of what is told in 6–11. 1 En 12:1 starts by dating Enoch's stay with the holy ones before *kwĕllu nagar*, "the whole account," or before "everything," according to the Ethiopic version, and πρὸ τούτων λόγων, "before these words" or "matters" according to the Greek version. The phrase must be read as antedating Enoch's stay to a time before everything, which is then recounted in the Watcher story. The entire Enoch story begins in heaven, just as the Watcher story does, with the emphasis that Enoch's stay antedated the story of the Watchers.

The rebellion of the Watchers and the destruction caused by the giants are then repeated in the divine speech in 12:3-6. In the rebel story the four archangels are sent to the earth, to Noah, the Watchers, and the giants, to carry out a mission on behalf of the Most High: Noah will be saved, the Watchers chained in the abyss, and the giants destroyed (10:1–11:2). This mission of the archangels parallels Enoch's mission in 12:3–13:3. Enoch is sent to the Watchers, not to carry out the judgment like the archangels, but nevertheless to pronounce the judgment. In response the Watchers ask Enoch to write a petition on their behalf and to bring it to the Most High.[8] In the narrative structure of the two parts (6–11 and 12–16), this event occurs prior to the judgment of the archangels. The two parallel story lines are made possible because the story in 6–11

---

comes to a priestly role is not central to my argument. The most important issue is Enoch's commission as mediator between God and the angelic Watchers.

8. The role of Enoch as an intercessor is similar to the description of Atra-Ḫasīs as intercessor in the Sippar Library version of the *Epic of Atra-Ḫasīs*, V rev. See H. S. Kvanvig, "Gen 6:3 and the Watcher Story," *Hen* 25 (2003): 277-300 (esp. 297-99). This seems to be the oldest layer of tradition behind 1 En 13, which is taken up and elaborated in 1 En 12–16, where the whole scenery is much more transcendent than in *Atra-Ḫasīs*. The adoption of this tradition in 1 En 13 would explain the complexity in the literary structure between 1 En 13 and 14.

shifts from narration of past events in 6:1–9:11 to direct speech of future events in 10:1–11:2. In this gap Enoch could intervene.

Enoch's role here is thus parallel to the archangels — he is sent in the same manner to carry out a mission between the Most High and the divine Watchers. In both cases this is a mission of judgment, and the only difference is that Enoch pronounces judgment instead of executing it.

## The Book of the Watchers as a Point of Departure

In the Watcher story (1 En 6–16) *prōton* and *eschaton* are woven together. The story is placed in primeval time, but the events are highly significant for the end time.[9] It is this aspect of the narrative that is stressed in the introduction to the Book of the Watchers (1 En 1–5). Enoch's throne vision and his announcement of judgment for the Watchers in primeval time are transposed to the eschatological time when God appears with myriads of holy ones to execute judgment on the wicked and to save the righteous and chosen (1:3-9). This interpretation of the Enoch vision is the point of departure for the Parables. They record a set of additional visions seen by Enoch and related to the fate of the chosen and the wicked in the end time.

The first parable (1 En 38–44) contains the basic themes of the teaching of Enoch in successive order: the judgment of the wicked (38:1-6), the descent of the angels (39:1-2), the ascent to heaven (39:3), the dwellings of the righteous (39:4-5), the dwelling of the chosen ones (39:9–40:10), and the final judgment of humanity (41:1-2). The sequences are introduced either through the visionary formula *rĕ'iku,* "I saw," connected to a statement of location, or through a statement of time, using *mawā'ĕl,* concrete "days," indicating a period of time.

A closer examination of the structure of these sequences shows that they are based on the structure of the Book of the Watchers. The introduction in 38:1-6 elaborates on the introduction to the Book of the Watchers in 1 En 1–5. Then follows a brief record of the descent of the angels in 39:1, referring to the narrative in 1 En 6–11. After this comes a direct reference to 13:8, "vision of wrath," and to 14:1, "books of the words of righteousness (*qūshṭ'ā,* 4Q204 VI 9) and of reproof for the Watchers." 39:2 mentions "books of jealous wrath and rage and books of tumult and confusion." The reference to the books is followed by Enoch's ascent in 39:3, drawing on 14:8. All that happens next in the Parables is based on this ascent to the heavenly realm, i.e., Enoch does not re-

---

9. H. S. Kvanvig, "Cosmic Law and Cosmic Imbalance," in *The Early Enoch Tradition,* ed. G. Boccaccini (Leiden: Brill, forthcoming).

turn to the earth again. This is one way to read the Book of the Watchers as well, because when we follow the story line, there is no report of Enoch returning to the earth. He ascends to the divinity and goes on to journey with the angels in 1 En 17–36. Thus it is possible to conclude that both in the introduction and in the formative structure of the first part of the Parables we observe a considerable influence from the Book of the Watchers. The most central motif in this influence is Enoch's dream where he sees himself ascending to heaven and is commissioned to bring the word of judgment to the Watchers.

## The Revelation of the Divine Name

Since Parables is so rooted in the Book of the Watchers, it comes as a surprise that the divine name constantly used, the Lord of Spirits, has no antecedents in this book. The revelation of this name is the core of the first parable where Enoch makes his first journey to the heavenly temple. Here he encounters the heavenly praise of the divinity. The section 39:12–40:1 clearly draws on both 1 En 14 and Isa 6. It is, however, not 1 En 14 that is the point of departure for the revelation of the divine name, but Isa 6:3.

This verse reads: קדוש קדוש קדוש יהוה צבאות מלא כל־הארץ כבודו, "holy, holy, holy is the YHWH of hosts; the whole earth is full of his glory." The rendering in the parable is highly significant: *qĕddus qĕddus qĕddus 'ĕgzi'a manāfĕst yĕmal'ĕ mĕdra manfasāta,* "holy, holy, holy, the Lord of Spirits, he fills the earth with spirits" (1 En 39:12). The divine name in Isa 6:3 is *YHWH Ṣĕbā'ōt*. As is commonly known, the Tetragram was increasingly pronounced *'adonay,* "Lord," in Second Temple Judaism.[10] The epithet צבאות, *ṣĕbā'ōt*, is based on the noun צבא, *ṣābā'*, "army, host." Used together with the Tetragram, it is open to multiple interpretations. One can stress the abstract aspect of the feminine plural *ṣĕbā'ōt* in the meaning "might, power." This is reflected in the common Greek translation in LXX as κύριος παντοκράτωρ, "Lord Almighty." But there is also the possibility of maintaining a more concrete plural aspect, as in the common translation "Lord of Hosts," "hosts" being all the living beings of the universe, as in Gen 2:1. This is reflected in another translation of the epithet in the LXX, κύριος τῶν δυνάμεων, "the Lord of Powers."[11]

This understanding is attested in Jubilees in two ways. In Jub 10:3 we find

---

10. Cf. M. Rösel, "Names of God," in *Encyclopedia of the Dead Sea Scrolls II*, ed. L. H. Schiffman and J. C. VanderKam (New York: Oxford University Press, 2000), 600-602, esp. 601.

11. Cf. A. S. van Woude, *ṣābā'*, in *Theologisches Handwörterbuch zum Alten Testament*, ed. E. Jenni and C. Westermann (Munich: Kaiser, 1976), 498-507.

the divine appellation *'amlāk manāfĕst za-wĕsta k<sup>w</sup>ellu za-šĕgā*, "Lord of the Spirits who are in all flesh."[12] The creation narrative as recorded in Jubilees provides the broader background for this appellation. The spirit from Gen 1:2 and the host from Gen 2:1 are seen together in Jub 2:2. The רוח אלהים in Gen 1:2 is read as the spirit of the angels, with the result that the whole universe is animated with spirits "in heaven, on earth and every place."[13]

Here we find the context for what occurs in 1 En 39:12. The divine epithet *YHWH Ṣĕbā'ōt*, "Lord of Hosts," is rendered in the Ethiopic *'ĕgzi'a manāfĕst*, "Lord of Spirits."[14] One of the reasons for this may be that the Aramaic, supposedly the original language of the Parables, does not have the root צבא, *ṣābā'*, with the meaning "army, host" or the like.[15] The Hebrew *YHWH Ṣĕbā'ōt* could have been read in Aramaic מרא רוחין, *māre' rūḥīn*, "Lord of the Spirits," similar to the Greek κύριος τῶν δυνάμεων, within the interpretative context attested in Jubilees.

In 1 En 39:12 the Hebrew of Isa 6:3, "the earth is full of his glory" (כבוד, *kābōd*), is rendered "he fills the earth with spirits." There is a passage from the *Hodayot* that comes close to this interpretation. In 1QH<sup>a</sup> XVIII 8 the Lord is described as ruler of the universe in the following way: "You are the prince of the gods and the king of the glorious ones, lord of every spirit, ruler of every crea-

---

12. Cf. the discussion in K. Berger, *Das Buch der Jubiläen*, in *JSHRZ* II/3 (Gütersloh: Mohn, 1981), 378 n. 3c.

13. Cf. J. T. A. G. M. van Ruiten, *Primeval History Interpreted: The Rewriting of Genesis 1–11 in the Book of Jubilees*, JSJSup 66 (Leiden: Brill, 2000), 25.

14. The same is argued by M. Black, who comments: "It seems on the whole very unlikely that the Ethiopic translator of the Parables should invent for himself an entirely new name of God, especially since everyone agrees he is drawing on traditional Jewish (or Jewish-Christian sources)." This argument does not only relate to the Ethiopic translator, but it also relates to the scribe(s) of Parables in its original language. See M. Black, *The Book of Enoch, or, I Enoch: A New English Edition with Commentary and Textual Notes*, SVTP 7 (Leiden: Brill, 1985), 189-93 (here 191).

15. In his response to my paper in the seminar, Koch remarked that the Hebrew term *ṣb'* is kept and transliterated in other Aramaic traditions, for instance, in the Targums (e.g., Amos 3:13; 4:13) and the Christian traditions. My statement was based on the absence of the word in the Aramaic section of *The Dead Sea Scrolls Concordance I*, Non-Biblical Texts from Qumran (Leiden: Brill, 2003). The absence here is of course not conclusive for all Aramaic dialects, but still interesting when we are dealing with a manuscript so rooted in the Enochic traditions. Koch's decisive point at this place is of importance. It is not necessarily a lexical deficiency that created the basis for the new rendering of the *YHWH ṣĕbā'ōt* as the Lord of Spirits; rather the name change depends on the sophisticated pneumatology in the Parables. The spirits cause the movements in the astral and meteorological realm (1 En 60:11ff.), and they also act in the minds of angels (68:2) and humans (41:8). The spirit is not only a holy spirit acting in the community of believers, but the spirit sustaining the cosmos as God's good creation. All such spirits are directed by the Lord of Spirits as his extensions.

ture."[16] The king of the נכבדים, *nikbadīm*, "glorious ones," of the same root as *kābōd*, is here parallel to "the Lord of every רוח, *rūaḥ*, spirit."

Parables adopts the most central passage from Isaiah's vision in Isa 6 and from it derives the divine epithet used throughout, certainly knowing that YHWH Ṣĕbā'ōt is likewise used repeatedly in the book of Isaiah. This text thus creates the basis for the frequent allusions to Isaiah in the portrait of the eschatological savior seen by Enoch in the next two parables (especially Isa 9; 11; 42; 49; 52–53).

## The Heavenly Representative

### The Chosen One and the Son of Man

Whereas the first parable opens by presenting Enoch (1 En 37:1-5), the second parable starts by introducing the second main figure of the book, the Chosen One, *xĕruy* (45:3-6).[17] He is introduced through a formula well known from the introduction of prophetic oracles in the Hebrew Bible, especially the book of Isaiah — "on that day," ביום ההוא, *bayōm hahū*',[18] Ethiopic *bayĕ'ĕtu 'ĕlat* (45:3, 4). The presentation of the Chosen One is in the first person like the presenta-

---

16. F. García Martínez and E. J. C. Tigchelaar, *The Dead Sea Scrolls: Study Edition I* (Leiden: Brill, 2000), 186.

17. There is the possibility that the individual eschatological figure does not appear, or is only briefly referred to, in the first parable. In 1 En 38:2 there is a better textual basis for reading *ṣedeq*, "righteousness," than reading *ṣādĕq*, "the righteous one" (cf. the old manuscripts BM 485, Berl, Abb 35, Abb 55, and Tana 9). Cf. R. H. Charles, *The Book of Enoch* (Oxford: Clarendon, 1912), 70; J. C. VanderKam, "Righteous One, Messiah, Chosen One, and Son of Man in 1 Enoch 37–71," in *The Messiah: Developments in Earliest Judaism and Christianity*, ed. James H. Charlesworth (Minneapolis: Fortress, 1992), 169-91 (here 170).

In 1 En 39:6 the manuscripts of the Eth II group read *makāna xĕruyān*, "the place of the chosen ones," instead of the simple *xĕruy*, "the Chosen One," of the Eth I group of manuscripts. In 39:7 manuscripts from the Eth I group are added to the Eth II group in reading the plural "their dwelling" instead of "his dwelling" (Berl, Abb 35, Abb 55). The plural here is an indication that 39:6 originally referred to the plural chosen ones and not to the individual Chosen One.

The third place the individual figure appears in the first parable is in 1 En 40:5: "The second voice I heard blessing the Chosen One and the chosen ones." Here the textual evidence is clear. Nevertheless, there is the possibility that *xĕruy* was a later addition. The sequence 40:2-10 deals with the blessings of the four archangels. If the Chosen One should appear here, I find it strange that Enoch should make no further notice of him. He is concerned only about the identity of the archangels. If the Chosen One really is included here, it must be a literary device. Enoch is allowed a glimpse of this most central figure in the heavenly visions as an anticipation of his presentation in the second parable.

18. For instance, Isa 11:10, 11; 17:7; 24:21; 25:9; 26:1; 27:1, 2.

tion of "my Servant," עבדי, 'abdī, and "my Chosen One," בחירי, bĕḥīrī, in Isa 42:1. The Chosen One is presented as the representative in heaven for the chosen ones among humans. The appearance of the Chosen One coincides with the appearance of the chosen ones (1 En 45:3); the Chosen One and the chosen ones shall together dwell on the renewed earth (45:4-5). The designation "heavenly representative" thus indicates the common fate of the Chosen One and the chosen ones, and identifies the Chosen One as a warrant of the salvation of the chosen ones (51:1-5; 61:4-5).[19]

The designation "Chosen One" is together with the "Son of Man" the most used title for the eschatological judge and savior in the Parables. Other, less frequent titles are the Righteous One (53:6) and the Anointed One (48:10; 52:4).[20] The use of various titles with differing backgrounds does not mean that there are several figures involved. They all refer to the same eschatological figure.[21] The most likely background for "Chosen One" and "Righteous One" is the oracles about the Servant of the Lord in the book of Isaiah (cf. especially Isa 42:1 and 53:11), which present the Servant as a representative of Israel (49:3).[22]

After the presentation of the heavenly representative as the Chosen One, the parable continues to present him in a vision as *walda sab'*, "son of man" (or "son of mankind"), drawing on Dan 7:9-10, 13-14. The Danielic vision is quoted in the Parables and given a new context in 1 En 46:1–51:5. Within this section the vision from Daniel is included in 46:1–48:7, and the parallels to Daniel are most clear in 46:1-3, 47:3, 48:2.[23] The figure is first introduced as someone with the face like *rĕ'yata sab'*, "the appearance of a human," in 46:1 and is later given the designation *walda sab'*, "son of humankind," in 46:3, both drawing on כבר אנש, *kĕbar 'ĕnāsh*, "someone like a son of man," in Dan 7:13. Besides the designation *walda sab'* (plural), Parables uses two other designations rendered as "son of man" in modern translations, *walda bĕ'si* (singular) and most frequently *walda 'ĕgʷāla 'ĕmma-ḥĕyāw*, "the son of the offspring of the mother of the living,"

---

19. Of all the designations for the heavenly figure, the idea of the heavenly representative permeates the parables. Cf. J. J. Collins, "The Heavenly Representative: The 'Son of Man' in the Similitudes of Enoch," in *Ideal Figures in Ancient Judaism: Profiles and Paradigms*, ed. John J. Collins and George W. E. Nickelsburg, SCS 12 (Chico, Calif.: Scholars, 1980), 111-33 (here 112-16).

20. VanderKam, "Righteous One," 169-76.

21. VanderKam, "Righteous One," 185f.; G. W. E. Nickelsburg, "Son of Man" and "The Parables of Enoch," in *ABD*, s.v.; Nickelsburg, *Ancient Judaism and Christian Origins: Diversity, Continuity, and Transformation* (Minneapolis: Fortress, 2003), 104-6.

22. VanderKam, "Righteous One," 187-90.

23. J. Theisohn, *Der auserwählte Richter: Untersuchungen zum traditionsgeschichtlichem Ort der Menschensohngestalt der Bilderreden des Äthiopischen Henoch* (Göttingen: Vandenhoeck & Ruprecht, 1975), 15-23; VanderKam, "Righteous One," 188; VanderKam, *Enoch: A Man for All Generations* (Columbia: University of South Carolina Press, 1995), 138-40.

which is also the Ethiopic translation "son of man" in the Bible. These designations are used several other places in the Parables, although the reference to Dan 7 is not as clear in these instances (1 En 62:5, 7, 9, 14; 63:11; 69:26, 27; 70:1; 71:14, 17).

On the question of the identity of this figure, Enoch receives an answer that clearly demonstrates that the Son of Man outshines all the previous eschatological models in the Hebrew Bible. He is given four characteristics: (1) he is the one who has righteousness; (2) he reveals the treasures of what is hidden; (3) he is the chosen one by God; (4) his lot is preeminent before the divinity (46:3).[24] The first two characteristics place him above all in judicial and revelatory matters, the next two underscore his uniqueness.

## The Heavenly Judge

There is, however, one feature that is not covered in the Servant oracles or in Dan 7. The Chosen One and Son of Man are placed on the throne of glory to execute judgment (1 En 45:3; 51:3; 55:4; 61:8; 62:2, 3, 5; 69:27, 29). The vision in Dan 7 could have invited the scribe to include this feature, but it is not sufficient to explain why it receives such a dominant place in the Parables. In this vision "thrones," כרסון, kārsāwān, were set in place for the Ancient of Days (Dan 7:9). There was accordingly an empty throne next to the divinity, which was meant for the Son of Man. But this throne was in Daniel not a throne of judgment, since the judgment is definitely carried out before the Son of Man appears (7:11-12). The Son of Man comes to rule, not to judge (Dan 7:14). There must have been other traditions that caused the scribe of the Parables to elevate the Chosen One and the Son of Man to the supreme judge in heaven.

Johannes Theisohn, followed by Matthew Black, has called attention to the only text that contains this motif in the Hebrew Bible — Ps 110.[25] This psalm contains the elements of enthronement, judgment, and polarization between the enthroned and his enemies, which is also combined in the passages about the Chosen One and the Son of Man.

The psalm itself is a riddle, and the MT is not intelligible without emenda-

---

24. M. Casey, "The Use of the Term 'Son of Man' in the Similitudes of Enoch," *JSJ* 7 (1976): 11-29 (here 22f.). According to Casey, these characteristics of the Son of Man have close links to the description of Enoch in Second Temple Judaism; cf. also Casey, *Son of Man: The Interpretation and Influence of Daniel 7* (London: SPCK, 1979), 103f.

25. Theisohn, *Der auserwählte Richter*, 92-98; M. Black, "The Messianism of the Parables of Enoch: Their Date and Contribution to Christological Origins," in *The Messiah: Developments in Earliest Judaism and Christianity*, ed. James H. Charlesworth (Minneapolis: Fortress, 1992), 145-69 (here 150-55).

tions. Traditionally the psalm has been read as part of an enthronement ritual for the Davidic king.[26] It is quite possible that the psalm contains preexilic elements.[27] For instance, the placement of the king on the right hand of the divinity (Ps 110:1) on a double-seated throne is represented in an Egyptian sculpture.[28] This does not mean, however, that the psalm in its present form is preexilic. The passage in v. 4, "You are priest forever according to the order of Melchizedek," does not necessarily contain an old reference to the Jebusite priesthood in Jerusalem, as is often presumed. It may just as well refer to the Melchizedek traditions evolving in Second Temple Judaism, later attested in the Melchizedek midrash 11Q13 and in the New Testament (Heb 4–8). The Melchizedek midrash at Qumran dates from the end of the second century B.C.E. In this text Melchizedek is identified as *'elohīm* from Ps 82:1 and placed as judge among the angels (11Q13 II 10).[29] The nature of this figure is still under discussion, but he is presented in a heavenly environment, portrayed as a high priest, acting as judge for the wicked and eschatological savior for the righteous.[30]

At least the LXX version of Ps 110 comes close to the imaginations found in 11Q13. The text of v. 3, which in the MT is readable only with emendations, is in LXX smooth: "With you is dominion on the day of your power, in the splendour of the holy ones. I have begotten you from the womb before the dawn." In the context of the whole psalm, this is not far removed from what is said about Melchizedek in 11Q13: "for it is the year of grace of Melchizedek, and of [his] arm[ies, the pe]ople of the holy ones of God, of the rule of judgment, as it is written about him in the songs of David, who said: '*'elohīm* will [s]tand in the assem[bly] of God, in the midst of *'elohīm* he judges.' And about him he said: 'And above [it] to the heights return: God will judge the peoples'" (11Q13:9-11). There is also a convergence of messianic and priestly traditions in 11Q13. In lines 15-21 the anointed of the spirit of Dan 9:25 is depicted. This figure is either meant to be Melchizedek himself, or more likely a close companion.

When we read Ps 110, especially in the LXX version, together with the Melchizedek midrash of 11Q13, a series of motifs connected to the Chosen One

---

26. H.-J. Kraus, *Psalmen*, 4th ed., BKAT XV/2 (Neukirchen-Vluyn: Neukirchener Verlag, 1972), 754-56.

27. K. Koch, "Rituelle Bezüge in den Königpsalmen?" in *Ritual und Poesie*, ed. E. Zenger (Freiburg: Herder, 2003), 211-49 (here 214-19).

28. O. Keel, *Die Welt der altorientalischen Bildsymbolik und das Alte Testament* (Neukirchen-Vluyn: Neukirchener Verlag, 1984), 240, 246f.

29. For text, see García Martínez and Tigchelaar, *The Dead Sea Scrolls*, 1206.

30. J. J. Collins, *The Scepter and the Star: The Messiahs of the Dead Sea Scrolls and Other Ancient Literature* (New York: Doubleday, 1995), 161-63; A. Steudel, "Melchizedek," in *Encyclopedia of the Dead Sea Scrolls* (New York: Oxford University Press, 2000), 1:535-37 (here 536).

and the Son of Man emerges: the enthronement on the throne of glory, the royal title Messiah (1 En 48:10; 52:4), the location in the heavenly council (40:5; 61:10), the judgment carried out on behalf of God, the polarity between this heavenly figure and the mighty kings (46:1-6), the liberation of the righteous.

It is also possible to see an analogy to what seems to be a notion of the preexistence of the Son of Man (cf. esp. 48:3, 6; 62:7). In the LXX version of Ps 110:3, the royal figure is described as begotten from the womb before the morning. The closest parallel to this motif is the description of the origin of Wisdom in Prov 8:22-26, here quoted according to the MT: "The Lord created me at the beginning of his work, the first of his acts of long ago. Ages ago I was poured out, at the first, before the beginning of the earth. When there were no depths I was born, when there were no springs abounding with water. Before the mountains had been shaped, before the hills, I was born, when he had not yet made earth and fields, or the world's first bits of soil." Wisdom was begotten, poured out (from the womb) before the beginning of the earth, in the same manner that the figure in the LXX version of Ps 110:3 was begotten from the womb before the morning. This parallel in imagery is significant because there are features that connect both the notion of Wisdom in 1 En 42 and the preexistence of the Son of Man to Prov 8.[31] We will return to this issue later.

There is another text, the so-called Self-Glorification Hymn, with features similar to the Melchizedek midrash of 11Q13.[32] It was published as a part of the War Scroll cycle, but the exact relation to this cycle is not clear.[33] In this text the poet describes himself as sitting on the mighty throne in the congregation of the gods (4Q491c, frag. 1,5). He is alone in exaltation (line 6), counted among the gods (line 7), and no one is like him in glory (line 8). His teaching and judgment are incomparable (lines 10-11). John Collins contends that the figure should be associated with the eschatological priest known from 4Q541, frag. 9, and that the Self-Glorification Hymn was placed in the War Scroll because the figure in this text was associated with the high priest described there.[34]

The elevated position of the figure parallels Melchizedek's in 11Q13, and the heavenly figure in both texts is presented as a judge.[35] In 4Q491c, frag. 1:9-11

---

31. For the relationship between the preexistence of the Son of Man and Prov 8, cf. Theisohn, *Der auserwählte Richter*, 130-35.

32. García Martínez and Tigchelaar, *The Dead Sea Scrolls*, 978-81, 4Q491c.

33. Cf. the discussion in P. R. Davies, "War of the Sons of Light against the Sons of Darkness," in *Encyclopedia of the Dead Sea Scrolls*, 2:965-68 (here 965f.).

34. J. J. Collins, *Scepter and the Star*, 146-49 (here 148).

35. In his response to my paper presented at the seminar, Collins claimed that he saw no evidence that the figure of the Self-Glorification Hymn was imagined as a judge. I have therefore attempted to deepen this aspect of my argument.

we read: "I have been instructed, and there is no teaching comparable [to my teaching . . .]. And who will attack me when [I] op[en my mouth]? And who will endure the flow of my lips? And who will confront me and retain comparison with my judgment[?]" (ידמה במפטי, *yĕdameh bĕmishpaṭī*). Even though *mišpaṭ* has a wider use than simply describing the act of judgment in both the Hebrew Bible and Second Temple Judaism, this activity nevertheless belongs to the core meaning of the word. Moreover, these lines seem to allude to the messianic oracle in Isa 11:2-4, where the act of judgment twice is described through the verb *šāfaṭ*. The passage reads as follows in Isa 11:2-4: "The spirit of the LORD shall rest on him, the spirit of wisdom and understanding, the spirit of counsel and might, the spirit of knowledge and the fear of the LORD. His delight shall be in the fear of the LORD. He shall not judge by what his eyes see, or decide by what his ears hear; but with righteousness he shall judge the poor, and decide with equity for the meek of the earth; he shall strike the earth with the rod of his mouth, and with the breath of his lips he shall kill the wicked." There are three similar elements in the two texts: (a) the notion that the figure is instructed by the Lord, (b) the act of judgment, and (c) the reference to the powerful breath from the figure's lips. If this echo of Isa 11 is found in the Self-Glorification Hymn, then there is also another interesting similarity to Ps 110 and 11Q13 — the incorporation of messianic traditions in the notion of the heavenly judge.

The three texts examined show that there existed a "high" messianic eschatology in Second Temple Judaism prior to the Parables with many of the same features as the heavenly figure described there — the seating on the divine throne or location among the angels in the divine assembly; partaking in the divine judgment and equipment with divine wisdom; and even, as it seems with the figure in Ps 110, an origin prior to the creation of ordinary humans. This observation does not confirm the view often advanced in earlier scholarship that there existed a concept of the Son of Man in Second Temple Judaism that was utilized in Jewish and Christian sources. Such a conclusion moves us well beyond what can be determined from the "high" eschatology attested in the texts examined here. Instead, these texts point toward a development from earthly, "low" messianic expectations to more transcendent expectations in Second Temple Judaism. The believers on earth seemingly needed one focal figure in heaven that could represent their cause before the Most High. This must be taken into account when we observe how the passages about a future savior, especially in the book of Isaiah, are transposed to a heavenly Chosen One and Son of Man in the Parables.

The variety of designations and notions connected to the eschatological figure in the Parables seems intentional. The scribes have made him the focal point of a wide spectrum of expectations in the Hebrew Bible and in their contemporary Judaism. Thus they could express their belief that this figure was the only supreme Chosen One who represented humankind in heaven.

### The Son of Adam and Eve

The variety of notions connected to the heavenly representative could be even larger than presumed in the modern translations of the Ethiopic text, as K. Koch suggested in his response to my paper in the seminar.[36] The question can be raised whether modern translators are correct in subsuming the differing Ethiopic terms into one single phrase, "the Son of Man." We cannot take it for granted that the differing terms were only translation variants of *bar 'enāsh* from Dan 7:13.[37]

The Ethiopic text uses *walda sab'* (plural) in 46:2, 3, 4;[38] 48:2; *walda bĕ'si* (singular) in 62:5; 69:29 (twice); 71:14; *walda 'ĕgʷāla 'emma-ḥĕyāw* in 62:7, 9, 14; 63:11; 69:26, 27; 70:1; 71:17. The three terms could go back to three Aramaic notions: *walda sab'* should be translated "son of mankind," i.e., a particular member of the human race, referring back to *bar 'enāsh* in Dan 7:13. In the singular *walda bĕ'si*, there could be a notion similar to the Aramaic Targum to Ezekiel, which uses *bar 'ādām* in the addresses to Ezekiel, keeping the *'ādām* from the Hebrew *ben 'ādām*. Whereas in Hebrew the phrase simply denotes an emphasis on the human character of Ezekiel, in Aramaic the meaning is different. The term *bar 'ādām* means "son of Adam," and Ezekiel is accordingly made the son of the primeval man. In a similar way *walda bĕ'si* could go back to the Aramaic *bar 'ādām*, referring to Adam as the primeval man.[39] This would imply an eschatological interpretation of the first man — he reappears at the end of time.

---

36. In this paragraph I am greatly indebted to K. Koch's response to my paper presented at the seminar. The idea of pursuing these differing notions behind the three phrases translated as "Son of Man" was his. The underlying material was also presented by him. The way it is done in this article is, however, my responsibility.

37. Cf. the discussion in Casey, "Use of the Term," 17f., who concludes in this way.

38. The reading *walda sab'* is not as certain as the oldest one in 1 En 46:2; cf. below.

39. The Ethiopic term *walda bĕ'si* is a strange designation for the heavenly figure, since it directly means "son of a man," i.e., male. This caused embarrassment for the Ethiopic translators, since they interpreted the oracles in the Parables as prophecies about Christ. "Son of a male" would thus imply that Jesus was the biological son of Joseph. There is accordingly confusion in the manuscripts in an attempt to avoid this term, especially in 1 En 62:5 and 69:29. In 71:14, where Enoch is identified as *walda bĕ'si*, the term has clearly been interpreted as "a son of man," keeping Enoch distinct from the prophecies about the coming Christ; see D. Olson, *Enoch: A New Translation* (North Richland Hills, Tex.: BIBAL, 2004), 139f.

This notion is not new in Enochic Judaism. The Animal Apocalypse ends by describing how humanity is transformed into the image of a white bull (1 En 90:37-38). The white bull is clearly Adam redivivus. History reaches its goal by turning back to its initial state where Adam comes forth from the earth as a white bull (85:3).[40]

The last Ethiopic phrase is *walda 'ĕgʷāla 'ĕmma-ḥĕyāw*, "the son of the offspring of the mother of the living." This phrase echoes Gen 3:20, where the first woman is given the name חוה, *ḥawwāh*, "life," because she will be כל־חי אם, *'em kōl ḥāy*, "the mother of all living."[41] The Aramaic phrase could thus be *bar 'em kol ḥay*, since *'ĕgʷāl* belongs together with *'ĕmma-ḥĕyāw* as a designation for humankind in Ethiopic. This would mean an eschatological parallel to the "son of Adam," only with the primeval mother as the point of departure. Such a notion is well-known in the Christian exegesis of Gen 3:15, where the struggle between the offspring of Eve and the serpent is given a victorious outcome in Christ (i.e., the "Protoevangelium").[42] There are early marks of an analogous kind of exegesis in the Targums to Gen 3:15.[43] In *Targum Onkelos* the address to the serpent in Gen 3:15 is commented on in the following way, taking the subject of the clause as an individual: "He will remember what you did in primeval time, and you will see him at the end."[44] In *Targum Pseudo-Jonathan* the biblical verse receives the following additional comment about the fate of the descendants of the first mother: "And they are destined to create peace in the end time, on the day of the king Messiah."[45] Both of these translation commentaries see the serpent as a demonic power that will be conquered in the end time. The first in *Targum Onkelos* implies a direct reference to one person of the offspring of Eve who will eradicate the power of evil at the end.

In the use of these terms in the Parables, it is important to keep in mind first that *walda sab'* is always used in connection with Dan 7:13 (1 En 46:1-3, 4; 48:2). The other two terms have no such connection, except in 1 En 71:14 where

---

40. See also K. Koch, "Messias und Menschensohn. Die zweistufige Messianologie der jüngeren Apokalyptik," *JBTh* 8 (1993): 73-102; reprinted in K. Koch, *Vor der Wende der Zeiten* (Neukirchen-Vluyn: Neukirchener Verlag, 1996), 235-66 (here 247-50).

41. The same kind of argumentation is found in J. Michl, "Der Weibsame (Gen 3,15) in Spätjüdischer und Früchristlicher Auffassung (I)," *Bib* 33 (1952): 371-401 (here 383-86).

42. C. Westermann, *Genesis 1-11*, 3rd ed., BKAT I/1 (Neukirchen-Vluyn: Neukirchener Verlag, 1983), 354f.

43. See also K. Koch, "Adam, was hast Du getan? Erkenntnis und Fall in der zwischentestamentlichen Literatur," in *Glaube und Toleranz. Das theologische Erbe der Aufklärung*, ed. T. Rendtorff (Gütersloh: Mohn, 1982); reprinted in Koch, *Vor der Wende der Zeiten*, 181-218, esp. 198-202.

44. The English translation is based on the text in Michl, "Der Weibsame," 375.

45. See also Michl, "Der Weibsame," 379f.

the divine epithet Head of Days is used when Enoch is identified with *walda bĕ'si*.

Second, the figure called *walda* is presented through Dan 7:13 and the term *walda sab'* is the only *walda* term used for this figure in the introduction (1 En 46–48). In the second parable only this term is used, while in the third parable it is exchanged for *walda bĕ'si* and *walda 'ĕgʷāla 'ĕmma-ḥĕyāw*. These two terms are often used in pairs in this parable: *walda bĕ'si* in 1 En 62:5 in conjunction with *walda 'ĕgʷāla 'ĕmma-ḥĕyāw* in 62:7; *walda 'ĕgʷāla 'ĕmma-ḥĕyāw* in 69:26, 27 with *walda bĕ'si* twice in 69:29; *walda bĕ'si* in 71:14 with *walda 'ĕgʷāla 'ĕmma-ḥĕyāw* in 71:17.

It thus seems as if the term taken from Dan 7:13, *walda sab'* from *bar 'enāsh*, in the third parable is understood more distinctly as the son of the primeval mother and father. There is then a paradox here. If the figure is the son of Adam and Eve — Eve is certainly referred to in the Ethiopic term — how then could he at the same time be preexistent? We will return to this issue below. At this point we can infer that the diversity of "messianic" expressions in the Parables could be even larger than the use of titles like the Chosen One, the Anointed One, the Righteous One, and the Son of Man. It seems likely that there could be added two more, the Son of Adam and the Son of the Mother of the Living, both drawing a line from *prōton* to *eschaton*.

This diversity of designations for the eschatological figure seems already signaled in the first presentation of the Son of Man in 1 En 46:1-3. He is first introduced as someone with "the appearance of a human" in 46:1, the context clearly drawing on Dan 7. Then Enoch asks about the identity of this figure (1 En 46:2). According to the majority of Ethiopic manuscripts, Enoch asks who the *walda sab'* is. This seems to be an anticipation, since this title is introduced in the angelic response in 46:3: "This is the Son of Man," *walda sab'*. The Ethiopic manuscript Tana 9 seems preferable here. Maintaining the suspense, Enoch asks "concerning the one who was born of humans," *za-tawalda 'ĕm-sab'*.[46] Accordingly this first presentation combines the *kĕbar 'enāsh* from Dan 7:13 with the notion of someone with human ancestors as we find it in the idea of the "son of Adam" and the "son of the mother of the living." When the identity is explored in the angelic answer, this *walda sab'* is the one who has righteousness, i.e., he is the Righteous One, and he is the Chosen One by God (46:3). The Book of Parables thus really collects multiple imaginations about a coming eschatological savior and bestows them on the Son of Man. He occupies the whole horizon of hope.

---

46. Thus Olson, *Enoch*, 88f.

Helge S. Kvanvig

## Core Texts to the Chosen One and the Son of Man

The Chosen One and the Son of Man have the dominant role in two sections: in the second parable in 45:3–51:5 and in the third parable in 61:8–63:12. In both places the double naming occurs — the Chosen One from Isa 42:1 and 49:7 and the Son of Man from Dan 7. The first section opens with a presentation of the two designations. First the Chosen One is introduced in a divine speech resembling the presentation of the Servant in Isa 42:1-9 (1 En 45:1-6), and then the Son of Man is presented in the language from Dan 7 (1 En 46:1-8). The second section contains only oracles. The main focus of the two sections is the seating of the Son of Man on the throne of glory and the judgment of the mighty ones on earth. The sections contain no cosmological or angelic material.

The first section (1 En 45:3–51:5), which opens the second parable, is followed by a section with cosmological and angelic material extending to the end of this parable. There is a clear break in the text between the two sections, and there is no attempt to bridge the gap. In the cosmological section Enoch is on a visionary journey, and there is considerable influence here from the Book of the Watchers. The second core section to the Son of Man in the third parable (61:8–63:12) is framed by cosmological and angelic material (58:1–61:7; 64:1–69:25). These sections likewise contain substantial influence from the Book of the Watchers. In the angelic and cosmological section following the second core section, there is no reference to the Chosen One or the Son of Man. In the other sections encompassing the core sections, the heavenly figure is combined with typical Enochic material. In the material traditionally characterized as Noahitic (54:7–55:2; 60; 65:1–69:1), there is no interest in the Chosen One or the Son of Man.

What we observe is that those texts that contain the most typical Enochic material do not belong to the core sections of the Chosen One and the Son of Man.[47] This basically demonstrates two kinds of sources for the Parables, one

---

47. In his presentation of the structure and composition of the Parables in the present volume, Michael Knibb carefully demonstrates how clearly the structure of the Parables followed the Book of the Watchers. From a different angle this is also the conclusion of J. C. VanderKam's examination of the Parables within the Enochic traditions. This does not, however, apply to all the material in the Parables. G. W. E. Nickelsburg could thus conclude his presentation of the structure of the Parables by arguing that the book contained two kinds of material, one drawing especially on the Book of the Watchers and the other containing non-Enochic interpretations of biblical material about an eschatological savior figure. It is significant that both Knibb and VanderKam in their presentations came to the same result without paying attention to its significance: there were no Enochic traces in the two sections 45:3–51:5 and 61:8–63:12.

coming from biblical and Jewish oracles and visions of an eschatological messianic figure, the other coming from Enochic traditions, above all the Book of the Watchers. The basic framework of the book is taken from the Book of the Watchers. Into this framework is incorporated what we broadly can designate as messianic material. This is most clearly done in two blocks that are so concentrated on the heavenly figure that the Enochic framework is lacking. This may indicate that these two blocks are based on discrete strands of traditions about a heavenly judge and savior. We have previously shown that these kinds of imaginations existed in contemporary Judaism.

On the basis of this analysis we can infer that Parables has sections with four characteristics:

1. Proper Enochic material drawing on the Book of the Watchers:
    First Parable (37–44)
    Second Parable (45:1-2; 54:1-6; 56:1–57:3)
    Third Parable (58–59; 64:1-2; 69:2-25)
2. Core texts to the Chosen One and the Son of Man:
    Second Parable (45:3–51:5)
    Third Parable (61:8–63:12)
3. Texts that mix Enochic and "messianic" patterns:
    Second Parable (52:1–54:6; 55:3-4)
    Third Parable (61:1-7; 69:26-29; 70–71)
4. Texts that contain Noahitic traditions:
    Second Parable (54:7–55:2)
    Third Parable (60; 65:1–69:1)

## The Heavenly Representative and Enoch

### The Basic Problems in the Identification

The interpretation of the Son of Man in the Parables is closely connected to the understanding of 1 En 71:14, where Enoch is taken to heaven and greeted with the words: "You are that Son of Man *('anta wĕ'ĕtu walda bĕ'si)* who was born for righteousness and righteousness dwells with you. And the righteousness of the Head of Days will not forsake you." The problem arising out of this address concerns both how to understand the identification between Enoch and *walda bĕ'si* and how to regard 1 En 70–71 (or 70:3–71:17, if 70:1-2 is taken as the epilogue) in relation to the Parables. Is this end section the final conclusion or a later addition?

*Helge S. Kvanvig*

John Collins has suggested a tempting solution to the understanding of the identification that would ease the tension. He suggests that the address to Enoch as *walda bě'si* could be read in the same manner as the address to Noah as *walda sab'* in 60:10.[48] The solution is not impossible grammatically. Collins proposes the translation: "You are a son of man," since Ethiopic has no definite or indefinite article and the word *wě'ětu* could function as a copula rather than as a demonstrative.[49] If this is the case, a more direct translation would be: "You are he who is a son of man."[50] According to Collins, there is a close resemblance in this announcement to the presentation of the Son of Man in 46:3: "This is the Son of Man who has righteousness, and righteousness dwells with him." This means for Collins that "Enoch is not being greeted simply as a human being, but as a very specific human being, in a language closely related to that used for the heavenly Son of Man."[51] And further: "Enoch, then, is a human being in the likeness of the heavenly Son of Man, and is exalted to share his destiny."[52] But even though Enoch is transfigured into the image of the heavenly figure, there are for Collins still two figures in heaven, the Son of Man and his earthborn image, Enoch.

This interpretation is appealing, but hardly convincing. There are two main problems. The first is that it is not only 1 En 71:14 that resembles what is said about the Son of Man earlier in the Parables. The rest of the section ties the fate of humans to Enoch in the same manner as is done earlier to the Son of Man (71:15-17). The second is that the term "Son of Man," this time in the form of *walda 'ěg"āla 'ěmma-ḥěyāw*, occurs once more in the section, in v. 17. Here also it refers to Enoch, and there is apparently no other Son of Man in heaven besides him. Thus we are left with a dilemma — the scribe of 71:14 really meant that Enoch in his final removal to heaven was identified as the Son of Man. The remaining question is whether this was the intention throughout the Parables, or whether the identification took place at a later stage in the transmission of the book.

This is one of the most debated issues in the interpretation of the Parables. Among scholars there are both points of agreement and points of dis-

---

48. We think that Noah and not Enoch must be meant here, since we are in a Noachic section of the book; cf. Olson, *Enoch*, 106.

49. J. J. Collins, "The Son of Man in First Century Judaism," *NTS* 38 (1992): 448-66 (here 456f.).

50. T. O. Lambdin, *Introduction to Classical Ethiopic*, HSS 24 (Missoula: Scholars, 1978), 29, also referred to by Collins; see also A. Dillmann and C. Bezold, *Grammatik der äthiopischen Sprache* (Leipzig: Tauchnitz, 1899), 440.

51. Collins, "The Son of Man," 457.

52. Collins, "The Son of Man," 457.

agreement. Some are quite obvious, but nevertheless important to keep in mind. In the following I have sorted out some of the basic issues in the scholarly debate.

1. Most scholars agree that at one stage in the growth of the Parables the Son of Man and Enoch were identified.
2. Scholars may disagree what this identification meant for the whole understanding of the Parables.
3. Scholars certainly disagree at what stage in the growth of the book the identification took place.
4. There is an obvious consensus that the Son of Man originally had nothing to do with Enoch.
5. Scholars agree that the identification between the two protagonists, wherever it took place, creates a demanding reading of the book as a complex literary structure.

We may begin by discussing points 1-3, which are closely related. If we regard 1 En 70:3-4 and 71 as an addition to the composition structured as three parables, how then do we consider this addition in relation to the larger composition? Most scholars consider the Noahitic sections as later additions to the book. Is the addition of the end in 70:3-4 and 71 of a similar kind as the Noahitic additions, which contribute new material to the book without changing its basic meaning? I do not think the section 70:3-4 and 71 functions in the same way. The section not only adds new material, but it alters the basic meaning of the book; what is said about the Son of Man throughout the book must now also relate to Enoch.

If we presume that the ending is an addition, then we must imagine an influence of the book on later readers in two stages instead of one: one stage where Enoch and the Son of Man were two separate figures, and a second stage where they were identified. After stage two, I hardly think that the readers of the book thought according to the methods of modern literary criticism, namely, that the ending is only a secondary addition with no relevance for the meaning of the book. I rather think they considered the ending as the climax of the whole. This is in fact the function of the ending. Scholars who assume a later addition cannot escape the troublesome question that at one stage in the growth of the book readers actually were invited to identify Enoch and the Son of Man.

The Son of Man originally had nothing to do with Enoch. Therefore the identification of the two figures creates a demanding reading of the book as a complex literary structure. Assuming 70:3-4 and 71 is an addition, the complexity of the parables appears when the ending is taken as an interpretative key. If we assume that the identification was intended already in the composing of the three parables, then the complexity occurs when the underlying sources to the Chosen One and the Son of Man, as they appear in Isaiah, Daniel, and other places, are made to be descriptions of Enoch. In this case the tension between the Chosen Son of Man and Enoch appears in the composition itself, because the underlying sources are quoted or explicitly referred to.

### *Enoch as the Son of Man — Obstacles and Interpretations*

If we assume that the scribes of the three parables composition wrote the final part as the climax of the whole, as James VanderKam does,[53] then they had to join two different traditions. On the one hand they were firmly rooted in the Book of the Watchers, which contains no sort of messianism, but on the other hand they incorporated messianic traditions, either based on blocks, as indicated in the core texts to the Chosen One and the Son of Man, or more directly from the biblical texts themselves. The merging of the two kinds of traditions was by no means easy. The combination demanded on the one hand that the scribes in one way or another found support for the identification between Enoch and the Son of Man in the Book of the Watchers, a support that originally was not intended in this book, but was nevertheless a possible interpretation when the identification was taken for granted. On the other hand they had to bridge the ending and the parables proper in a way that was meaningful, even though they deliberately created an ingenious literary design.

The question is, however, whether the obstacles to such a reading of the Book of the Watchers are so great that we must suppose that the scribes of the three parables composition never intended identification. There could be too many gaps between the ending and the parables proper, and the basis in the Book of the Watchers could be too weak. Accordingly it could be better to suppose that the identification was done by a later scribe with greater distance from the text of the parables proper. Three issues have been especially discussed where the obstacles to an identification seem severe.

Collins has called attention to the odd phenomenon that Enoch sees himself in the visions as the Son of Man without recognizing himself.[54] VanderKam responded by applying the idea attested in several other Jewish sources that a human being could have a supernatural double in heaven. What Enoch sees is

---

53. VanderKam, "Righteous One," 177-85.
54. J. J. Collins, "The Heavenly Representative," 122.

the Son of Man as the supernatural double of himself.⁵⁵ VanderKam's second explanation seems more convincing: that Enoch sees the Son of Man in visions of the future, not in disclosures of the present. He is seeing what he will become.⁵⁶

This suggests the following pattern. The scribes of the Parables adopted a wide range of expectations known from the Hebrew Bible and other Jewish sources into their work. They placed these within the framework of 1 En 13–14, which originally contained two perspectives. In chap. 13 Enoch's role as visionary is emphasized, and in chap. 14 the stress is on the content of the vision, namely, how he entered the heavenly temple to be installed as a heavenly intermediary. The scribes of the parables utilized both perspectives. In the first usage they placed Enoch in the role of a visionary, being the one who received these revelations about the heavenly judge and savior long before any other prophet or sage in history. He sees what will take place at the end of time when the Son of Man will be revealed to the chosen. In the second usage Enoch is himself made the protagonist. He ascends to heaven in order to remain there forever identified as the Son of Man seen in the vision. There are of course differences between the concept of the Watcher story and the Parables, but there is one important common trait that could function as the point of departure for the scribes of the parables: in both cases Enoch sees himself in a heavenly location in a role related to the judgment of the sinners and the salvation of humankind. He is called to deal with the root causes of evil.

The second obstacle is that the introduction to the final section clearly keeps Enoch and the Son of Man apart: "And after this, while he was living, his name was raised into the presence of that Son of Man and into the presence of the Lord of Spirits" (1 En 70:1). Until quite recently one could argue that this translation was based on the oldest Ethiopic manuscripts and that the different reading of the old manuscript *u* was too isolated to have any bearing.⁵⁷ Daniel Olson has however called attention to a series of old manuscripts with the same textual variant as *u*.⁵⁸ These manuscripts allow a different translation: "And it happened after this, while he was living, that the name of that Son of Man was raised into the presence of the Lord of Spirits." The difference between the two

---

55. VanderKam, "Righteous One," 182-84.
56. VanderKam, "Righteous One," 184.
57. The labeling *u* is according to R. H. Charles. Michael Knibb labels the manuscript as Abb 55 and dates it to the fifteenth or sixteenth century. See Knibb, *Ethiopic Book of Enoch 2*, 23. Cf. the list of signs in S. Uhlig, *Das äthiopische Henochbuch*, in *JSHRZ* V.6, ed. Werner G. Kümmel (Gütersloh: Gütersloher Verlagshaus Gerd Mohn, 1984), 474, with the same dating.
58. D. C. Olson, "Enoch and the Son of Man in the Epilogue of the Parables," *JSP* 18 (1998): 27-38 (here 30-33).

variants is nothing more than the absence of the prepositional term *baxabehu*, "into his presence," in the second variant. This makes it possible to read *sĕmu la-wĕ'tu walda 'ĕg"āla 'ĕmma-ḥĕyāw* as a genitive, "the name of that Son of Man," and to make the whole genitive the subject of the sentence. If we consider the theology connected to Ethiopic text transmission, where the Son of Man was considered a *typos* of Christ and therefore separate from Enoch, the confusion of the two in 1 En 70:1 is certainly *lectio difficilior*.

The third obstacle may be the most difficult. Several passages seem to indicate that the Chosen One and the Son of Man were held to be preexistent, while Enoch explicitly is listed as the seventh after Adam (1 En 37:1). 1 En 48:2-3, 6 is particularly difficult, because it asserts that the name of the Son of Man was proclaimed in the presence of the Lord of Spirits before the sun and constellations were created and the stars of heaven were made (vv. 2-3), and that he was chosen and hidden in God's presence before the world was created (v. 6). VanderKam considers these passages to be an echo of the Servant oracle in Isa 49:1, but this does not seem convincing.[59] Both the Hebrew and the LXX texts of Isa 49:1 state that the Servant was "called" and "remembered" (MT) in his mother's womb, and this is different from being "named, chosen" and "hidden" before the creation.

The tension exists not only in the relationship between Enoch and the Son of Man, but also in the naming of the Son of Man. In the context, 1 En 48:2 belongs together with v. 1, which describes the dwelling places of the righteous and chosen. In this context v. 2 begins with *wa-bayĕ'ti sa'āt*, "and at this time," and continues: "this Son of Man was proclaimed in the presence of the Lord of Spirits and his name before the Head of Days." This looks like the eschatological enthronement of the Son of Man. The next verse, recounting that his name was proclaimed before creation, turns the eschatological proclamation into a precreational event.

The best explanation for this double proclamation is that the text includes another tradition in 48:3, 6 — the birth of Wisdom before creation in Prov 8:22-31. In the Parables the Chosen One is intimately connected to wisdom (1 En 49:1-4; 51:1-3). In 1 En 42:1-3 Wisdom appears as an independent figure, as in Prov 8. In fact, the descent of Wisdom and the increase of iniquity in this Enoch passage seem like a parody of Proverbs. In Prov 8:31 Wisdom is rejoicing in the inhabited world and has her delight in the sons of men. In 1 En 42:1-2, after Wisdom did not find any place to stay among the sons of men and went back to heaven, iniquity came forth. It is easier to read this parody as a concealed reference to Enoch than to the Son of Man. Coming from the realm of

---

59. VanderKam, "Righteous One," 180.

God, Wisdom sought a dwelling on earth, but she did not find any and thus returned to the place in heaven among the angels.

This agrees with the portrait of Enoch in the Book of the Watchers (1 En 12–16). In 1 En 12:1 Enoch is introduced for the first time in the Watcher story (1 En 6–16). The text of the Greek version (Gr$^{Pan}$) differs from most of the Ethiopic manuscripts. The Greek version clearly reads the introduction in the light of Gen 5:24: "Before these things Enoch was taken," ἐλήφθη, reflecting the Hebrew לקח, lāqaḥ. Most of the Ethiopic manuscripts read: wa-'ĕmqĕdma k$^w$ellu nagara takabta henok, "And before everything Enoch was hidden." Uhlig, Black, and Nickelsburg/VanderKam all prefer the Greek text in their translations,[60] thinking that Ethiopic takabta refers to Gen 5:24 in the same manner as Greek ἐλήφθη. The basic argument is the use of the same Ethiopic verb in Enoch's translation to heaven in 1 En 71:1, 5. But the situations in chap. 71 and in chap. 12 are different. 1 En 71 may draw on Enoch's final translation in Gen 5:24. This is, however, not the case in 1 En 12:1. This passage does not describe Enoch's final translation to heaven in the Watcher story, but introduces him as someone living among the Watchers and holy ones.[61] The relationship to the short biography in Gen 5:21-24 is in fact quite obscure.[62] According to Jub 4:21-23, which records Enoch's biography, Enoch testified against the Watchers when he stayed with the angels for six jubilees, or 294 years. After this incident he stays on the earth before he is finally taken from the human world and led into the Garden of Eden (Jub 4:23). Jubilees attempts to read the

---

60. Uhlig, *Das äthiopische Henochbuch*, 533; Black, *The Book of Enoch*, 141; Nickelsburg and VanderKam, *1 Enoch*, 31.

61. Charles, *The Book of Enoch*, 27f.

62. Gabriele Boccaccini thinks 1 En 12:1-2 describes the period of 300 years when Enoch according to Gen 5:22 walked with hā'elohīm, either "God" or "the angels"; see G. Boccaccini, *Roots of Rabbinic Judaism* (Grand Rapids: Eerdmans, 2002), 98f. This accords with the sequence of events in Genesis and in the Watcher story, and it is the interpretation of the book of Jubilees, but it does not suit the content of the events as understood in the Watcher story. According to 1 En 12:1, no human being knew where Enoch was hidden. This conflicts with the Genesis statement that Enoch in this period "begot sons and daughters" (Gen 5:22). It might be that the Enochic scribes dropped this statement because it was not in accord with their image of Enoch staying with the Watchers and holy ones. But there is also the possibility that the Enochic scribes did not use the genealogy in Gen 5 as their source. They could have known the same genealogical framework as the Genesis scribes, since some of the names from Genesis occur in the Watcher story: Jared (6:5), Lamech and Noah (10:1-2; the name of Noah only explicitly mentioned in Gr$^{Syn}$). This does not necessarily mean that they used the genealogy in the actual form it was given in Genesis. This could explain why the years counted in Gen 5 are not reflected in the Watcher story. As a whole the relationship between Genesis and the Watcher story seems more complex than the idea that the Enochic scribes simply used Genesis as source. See H. S. Kvanvig, "The Watcher Story and Genesis: An Intertextual Reading," *SJOT* 18 (2004): 163-83.

Watcher story and Gen 5:21-24 together, and in so doing, places Enoch's stay with the angels during the 300-year period that according to Gen 5:22 Enoch walked with *ha'elōhīm*.

Even though *kabata* in 1 En 71:1, 5 is used with reference to translation, the basic meaning of the verb is "to hide." Accordingly, what most of the Ethiopic manuscripts to 1 En 12:1 indicate is that Enoch, before everything, was hidden among the heavenly beings, and from this position he came to the earth and met the Watchers, after which he ascended to heaven. This is the movement we also find in the description of Wisdom in 1 En 42:1-2. She came from heaven and visited humans on earth, and then "she returned to her place and sat down among the angels." Enoch in the Watcher story is not preexistent in relation to creation, because no creation event is recorded, but he is preexistent, i.e., residing in heaven, before everything that is recounted took place.

There are common traits between Enoch and the Proverbial Wisdom as well, when we look into the background of the two figures. In Prov 8:30 Wisdom is called אָמוֹן, *'āmōn*, "craftsman." This word is attested with this meaning in the Hebrew of Jer 52:15 and Song of Songs 7:2. In Aramaic the equivalent is אומנה, *'ōmmanah*,[63] closer to the Akkadian *ummiānu*, which could mean both "craftsman" and "scholar, expert." In the same manner that *'āmōn* could be used about Wisdom as a primeval figure in Prov 8:22-31, *ummiānu* could be applied to the primeval sages, *apkallus*, in a Mesopotamian context.[64] Jonas Greenfield has argued that the Mesopotamian concept of the seven primeval *apkallus* is also underlying the reference to Wisdom and the seven in Prov 9:1. He suggests the following translation: "Wisdom has built her home, the Seven has set its foundation."[65]

In the Mesopotamian setting the seven *apkallus* are most extensively dealt with in the incantation series *Bīt Mēseri*.[66] The text contains two lists of primeval sages: first the list of seven, then a list of four. At the end of the lists their characteristics are summarized. About the seven *apkallus* it is stated: *sebet apkallu ša ina nāri ibbanû muštešīrū uṣurāt šamê u erṣeti*, "the seven *apkallus* engendered in

---

63. Cf. the Beth Shean synagogue inscription ggBS 2 and the Alma synagogue inscription ggAL 1, in K. Beyer, *Die aramäischen Texte vom Toten Meer* (Göttingen: Vandenhoeck & Ruprecht, 1984), 378 (here 373).

64. Cf. the Epic of Erra I, 147, in L. Cagni, *The Poem of Erra*, SANE 1 (Malibu, Calif.: Undena, 1977), 32.

65. J. C. Greenfield, "The Seven Pillars of Wisdom (Prov 9:1) — a Mistranslation," *JQR* 76 (1985): 13-20 (here 20).

66. E. Reiner, "The Etiological Myth of the Seven Sages," *Or* 30 (1961): 1-11; R. Borger, "Die Beschwörungsserie *Bīt Mēseri* und die Himmelfahrt Henochs," *JNES* 33 (1974): 183-96; H. S. Kvanvig, *Roots of Apocalyptic* (Neukirchen-Vluyn: Neukirchener Verlag, 1988), 197-207.

*The Son of Man in the Parables of Enoch*

a river who keep in order the plans of heaven and earth."[67] About the four *apkallus* it is stated: *ilitti amēlūti ša Ea bēlum uzna rapašta ušaklilušunuti,* "of human descent whom the Lord Ea had endowed with broad wisdom."[68] We may observe first the different origins of the sages in the lists. The first group of seven is engendered, or "created," Akkadian *banû,* in the river, which is the abode of the god of wisdom and civilization Ea.[69] This means that although they appeared on earth among humans, their origin was from Ea in his abode. This is different from the group of four, which were of human descent.

A second observation concerns the function of the sages. The last four were endowed with "broad wisdom," while the first seven had an even higher position. They are described as cosmic architects responsible both for the cosmic order and for the founding knowledge of civilization, expressed in the phrase "keep in order the plans of heaven and earth."[70] The same characteristic is underlined for the first *apkallu,* U-Anna, "light of heaven."[71] Berosus describes this function in the following way in his *Babyloniaca:*[72]

> In the first year a beast named Oannes appeared from the Erythraean Sea in a place adjacent to Babylonia. Its entire body was that of a fish, but a human head had grown beneath the head of the fish and human feet likewise had grown from the fish's tail. It also had a human voice. A picture of it is still preserved today. He (Berosus)[73] says that this beast spent the days with the men but ate no food. It gave to the men the knowledge of letters and sciences and crafts of all types. It also taught them how to found cities, establish temples, introduce laws and measure land. It also revealed to them seeds and the gathering of fruits, and in general it gave men everything which is connected with the civilized life. From the time of that beast noth-

---

67. Reiner, "The Etiological Myth," 1, 8-9; cf. also Borger, "Die Beschwörungsserie *Bīt Mēseri* und die Himmelfahrt Henochs," 192, for both lists.

68. Reiner, "The Etiological Myth," 1, 10-11.

69. On the relationship between Ea and the *apkallus,* cf. J. Bottéro, *Mesopotamia: Writing, Reasoning, and the Gods* (Chicago: University of Chicago Press, 1992), 246-50.

70. Cf. Kvanvig, *Roots of Apocalyptic,* 199ff.; Bottéro, *Mesopotamia,* 237ff.

71. Cf. Borger, "Die Beschwörungsserie *Bīt Mēseri* und die Himmelfahrt Henochs," 192.

72. Text: Euseb. (Arm.) Chron. p. 6,8–9,2, and Syncellus p. 49,19, in F. Jacoby et al., *Die Fragmente der griechischen Historiker III, C, Band I-II* (Leiden: Brill, 1958), 1B, sequences 4-5, 369f. Translation in S. M. Burstein, *The Babyloniaca of Berossos,* SANE 1/5 (Malibu: Undena, 1978), 13f. Berosus the Chaldean wrote his work in 282 B.C.E., and it contains a fairly exact rendering of earlier Mesopotamian traditions; see G. Komoróczy, "Berosos and the Mesopotamian Literature," *Acta Antiqua* 21 (1973): 125-52.

73. It is Eusebius or his antecedents in traditions who record this from *Babyloniaca* by Berosus.

ing further has been discovered. But when the sun set this beast Oannes plunged back into the sea and spent the nights in the deep, for it was amphibious. Later other beasts also appeared. He says that he will discuss these in the book of the kings. Oannes wrote about birth and government and gave the following account to men:[74]

Thus the first *apkallu*, like Wisdom in Prov 8, was engendered by a god in his abode, was the cosmic architect, and appeared among humans to provide them with the basic knowledge of civilization.

There seems to be a growing consensus that the figure of Enoch is modeled partly on the seventh antediluvian king Enmeduranki, as he is described in the composition labeled "Enmeduranki and the Diviners."[75] I have argued in several places that the Mesopotamian background of Enoch also included the *apkallu* tradition. This concerns especially the seventh *apkallu*, who ascended to heaven, like Adapa in the myth,[76] and it concerns the first *apkallu*, who brought humanity the basic knowledge and wrote astronomical and other important compositions under divine inspiration.[77]

If this is the case, there is a double background for the figure of Enoch. He is the seventh patriarch, patterned on the seventh antediluvian king Enmeduranki, who was of human descent. He is, however, also a Jewish counterpart of a primeval *apkallu*, sage and priest. The primeval *apkallu* had its origin in the divine realm and visited mankind. When we first meet Enoch in the Book of the Watchers, he stays with the Watchers and holy ones and is sent to the human world. Thus there are multiple links between the preexistence of the Son of Man in the Parables, the precreational existence of Wisdom in the Proverbs and the Parables, the divine origin of the *apkallus*, and the transcendent abode of Enoch.

---

74. The text continues with a summary from Enuma Elish.

75. P. Grelot, "La légende d'Hénoch dans les Apocryphes et dans la Bible: Origine et signification," *RSR* 46 (1958): 5-26, 181-220; J. C. VanderKam, *Enoch and the Growth of an Apocalyptic Tradition*, CBQMS 16 (Washington, D.C.: Catholic Biblical Association of America, 1984), 23-51; Kvanvig, *Roots of Apocalyptic*, 160-342; A. A. Orlov, *The Enoch-Metatron Tradition*, TSAJ 107 (Tübingen: Mohr Siebeck, 2005), 23-78.

76. For the Myth of Adapa and the *apkallu* tradition, see S. Dalley, *Myths from Mesopotamia* (Oxford: Oxford University Press, 1991), 182-88.

77. Cf. Kvanvig, *Roots of Apocalyptic*, 191-213; Kvanvig, "Origin and Identity of the Enoch Group," in *The Origins of Enochic Judaism*, ed. G. Boccaccini (Turin: Zamorani, 2002), 207-12; Kvanvig, "Cosmic Law and Cosmic Imbalance," in *The Early Enoch Tradition*, ed. G. Boccaccini (Brill: Leiden, forthcoming). See also Greenfield, "Seven Pillars of Wisdom," 19f.

*The Son of Man in the Parables of Enoch*

## Key Points in the Identification

One question is seldom raised in the debate about the identification: Why was Enoch identified as the Son of Man and not as the Chosen One? Since the designation Chosen One has the clearest representative function in relation to the chosen ones on earth, it would not have been unusual to make Enoch as the Chosen One the supreme leader in heaven. The identification as the Son of Man could be accidental — one had to choose the one or the other — or it could contain the clue to the whole dilemma. I think there are two basic reasons why the Son of Man was preferred.

One reason relates to the way the Parables' two most important sources, 1 En 12–16 and Dan 7, are intertwined. At this point we should remember that there are two different chronologies involved. The first is the historical chronology to which the scribes of the Parables belonged; they quoted Dan 7 as an earlier text. The second is the fictional chronology of the Book of Parables itself. The historical chronology has the succession 1 En 12–16, Dan 7, Parables, the fictional 1 En 12–16, Parables, Dan 7. In the last chronology Dan 7 comes after the revelations given to Enoch as an imitation of Enoch, as in the other biblical texts alluded to in the Parables.

Historically an examination of the relationship between 1 En 14 and Dan 7 shows that Dan 7 was patterned on 1 En 14. This concerns above all the throne imagery in Dan 7:9-10.[78] The question is whether there are more correspondences. A closer examination of the vocabulary used about the monsters in Dan 7 and the Watchers and giants in the Watcher story indicates that some of the traits of the monsters are similar to the Watchers and giants.[79] There are also similarities connected to the protagonists of the two visions, Enoch and the Son of Man. When Enoch is included in the heavenly council, he is called in Greek: ὁ ἄνθρωπος ὁ ἀληθινός ἄνθρωπος τῆς ἀληθείας ὁ γραμματεύς, "true man, man of truth, the scribe" (1 En 15:1).[80] In Aramaic this would be איש קושטא, *'īsh qūshṭ'ā*, or אנש קושטא, *'enāsh qūshṭ'ā*, as a part of the phrase. The figure coming to the throne in Dan 7:13 is described as כבר אנש, *kĕbar 'enāsh*, "someone like a son of man."

There are more similarities between the two protagonists of the visions. When Enoch is taken to heaven, he records: "clouds were summoning me" (1 En

---

78. Cf. H. S. Kvanvig, "Henoch und der Menschensohn. Das Verhältnis von Hen 14 zu Dan 7," *ST* 38 (1984): 101-33; Kvanvig, *Roots of Apocalyptic*, 558-64; Kvanvig, "Throne Visions and Monsters: The Encounter between Danielic and Enochic Traditions," *ZAW* 117 (2005): 249-72.

79. Kvanvig, "Throne Visions and Monsters."

80. The Ethiopic *bĕ'si ṣādĕq wa-ṣaḥāfi ṣĕdq*, "righteous man and scribe of righteousness," looks like an abbreviation.

14:8). The Son of Man in Dan 7:13 arrives "with the clouds of heaven." In 1 En 14:24 it is said: "one of the holy ones . . . brought me near." I think we here can suppose the Aramaic verb קרב, qĕreb, in hafel הקרבני, haqrebnī, "brought me near." This is the verb used in Dan 7:13: קדמוהי הקרבוהי, qĕdamōhī haqrĕbōhī, "they brought him near to him."

Accordingly we observe two visionary protagonists with some similar descriptions appearing in throne visions where the one, Dan 7, is dependent on the other, 1 En 14–15. It appears that the scribe of Dan 7 borrowed the language from 1 En 14–15 to create a transcendent scene for the enthronement of his eschatological figure, the Son of Man. From the point of view of the Danielic scribe, this did not mean that his Son of Man was Enoch. The Son of Man in Dan 7 is described with royal features and has in this respect little in common with the Enoch of 1 En 14–15. But for the scribe of the Parables, this must have looked different. Daniel in fact saw much of what Enoch saw, including a figure designated "man" coming on a cloud and approaching near to the divinity.

In the fictional chronology of the Parables, the succession is different. First, Enoch has a dream vision (1 En 13–15). In this vision he sees himself brought to the heavenly throne chamber as the man of truth to be commissioned as heavenly intermediary. Then Enoch had a second set of visions in the Parables, which revealed what this really meant. In these visions he saw the Son of Man enthroned in heaven, and learned that this Son of Man was himself. Much later Daniel had a vision confirming the Parables. Daniel saw Enoch coming with the clouds of heaven like the Son of Man.

The second reason why the Son of Man was preferred presupposes different concepts subsumed under the designations "Son of humankind," *walda sab'*, from Dan 7 in the second parable, and "Son of the primeval man," *walda bĕ'si*, and "the primeval mother," *walda 'ĕg"āla 'ĕmma-ḥĕyāw*, paired in the third parable. In the Book of the Watchers Enoch is actually portrayed as the son of Adam and Eve. In his visionary journeys he comes to Paradise with the tree of life from which Adam and Eve ate. They are characterized as follows in Aramaic: אבוך רבא ו[אמך רבתא, *'ābūk rab'ā wĕ-'emāk rabĕt'ā*, "your father of old and your mother of old" (4Q206, frag. 4, 9-10 = 1 En 32:6).[81]

This is the only genealogical information for Enoch in the Book of the Watchers. At this place Parables is more informative — Enoch is at the very beginning placed in a genealogical line (1 En 37:1). The structure of the genealogy is strange, since it is counted from Enoch backward with the word *wald* placed in construct before each of the ancestors ("son of"). The result is that Enoch

---

81. Cf. García Martínez and Tigchelaar, *The Dead Sea Scrolls*, 426; J. T. Milik, *The Books of Enoch: Aramaic Fragments of Qumrân Cave 4* (Oxford: Clarendon, 1976), 235f.

twice is designated in Hebrew/Aramaic as "son of man," *bar 'enosh* and *ben 'adām*, as VanderKam has argued.[82] Of special interest here is the last designation, which in Aramaic would be the term used for Ezekiel in the Targum, and could be supposed to stand behind *walda bĕ'si*, בר אדם, *bar 'ādām*.

This would give meaning to the literary design of the Parables. Enoch is at the very beginning declared *bar 'ādām*. When he has the first vision of the *bar 'enāsh* from Dan 7 in 1 En 46:1-3, he sees "someone born of humans" (Tana 9 to 46:2). At the end he is declared to be *walda bĕ'si, bar 'ādām* (71:14). Thus the identification of Enoch as the *bar 'enāsh* from Dan 7:13 was not necessarily based only on the reading of 1 En 14 and Dan 7 together, identifying the two protagonists. It could have been facilitated by the reading of 1 En 32:6, where Enoch is declared to be the son of the primeval father and mother, and thus *bar 'ādām* and *bar 'em kol ḥay*.

The last question to consider is why the identification of Enoch as the Son of Man was necessary within the theology of the Parables. There can be no doubt that the scribes of the Parables were deeply impressed by the most influential Enochic composition, the Book of the Watchers. The Book of Parables is presented as supplementary visions to the visions in this book. Through these supplementary visions the Book of the Watchers is reinterpreted with a new eschatological outlook. This way of dealing with the earlier tradition is not very different from what occurred in the development of Enochic compositions in earlier history. Both the Apocalypse of Weeks and the Apocalypse of Animals are deeply influenced by the Book of the Watchers, even though they have their distinct features in form and content.

There is another similarity to earlier Enochic compositions. The Enochians throughout their history have been in dialogue with other branches of Second Temple Judaism. Of special interest here is the relation to the Judaism centered on the Mosaic Law. The Apocalypse of Weeks and the Animal Apocalypse both deal with the same history of humanity and Israel that we find in the Hebrew Bible, but in the Enochic materials wisdom and revelation are the focal points and not Moses and the law. This feature is especially clear in the book of Jubilees, where the Mosaic Law is reinterpreted in an Enochic fashion.[83] In a similar way the scribes of the Parables were in dialogue with religious beliefs of their own time. In their case the focus was, however, not Moses and the law, which is not mentioned at all, but the eschatological expectations. The scribes of the Parables adopted the eschatological horizon of contemporary Ju-

---

82. VanderKam, "Righteous One," 178f.
83. H. S. Kvanvig, "Jubilees — between Enoch and Moses: A Narrative Reading," *JSJ* 35 (2004): 243-61.

daism and gave it a new Enochic interpretation in the same manner as Enochians earlier reinterpreted history. But by doing so they approached a serious problem.

Only once before did the Enochians advance the idea that a distinct individual figure would be crucial in the end-time. This was at the end of the Animal Apocalypse, where a white bull appears as an eschatological counterpart to Adam, the first white bull, and all humanity is transformed into his image (1 En 90:37-38; 85:3). This eschatological white bull can hardly be considered a messianic figure in the traditional way, because he appears after the eschatological turn (crisis, judgment, and new creation) where the Messiah traditionally had a crucial role, and there is no link to David described earlier in the Apocalypse. There is a closer analogy to the Son of Man in Dan 7, who also appears after the great judgment.[84] The description of the bull is quite colorless, and the emphasis of this final section of the Apocalypse is not on this figure in itself, but on its symbolic value as the goal of history, namely, the transformation of humanity into the image of man as originally created by God.

This is the only place such an individual appears in the Enochic traditions before the Parables. The most obvious reason why the Enochians had no place for messianism was the prominent role of Enoch himself. He was from the very beginning portrayed as something far more than a visionary sage. He was crossing the borders between the human and the divine and between the earthly and heavenly realms. He was not only describing what should take place, he was also an actor within his own visions. He appeared in an intermediary role similar to the angels. He was, in the minds of the Enochians, still alive in this prominent position in heaven when they received his wisdom on earth.

Therefore the inclusion of the eschatological horizon and the concentration of this horizon on one supreme figure in heaven, the Chosen One and the Son of Man, threatened the coherence of Enochic theology. The occurrence of another representative in heaven, taking part in the final judgment relating to the root causes of evil, and bestowing his believers with wisdom, did not allow any space for Enoch. He remained in heaven, but was deprived of any eschatological significance. Without the final identification, the believers would not any longer be followers of Enoch, but followers of the Son of Man.

---

84. See the discussion in Koch, "Messias und Menschensohn," in *Vor der Wende der Zeiten*, 247-50; Nickelsburg, *1 Enoch 1: A Commentary on the Book of 1 Enoch 1–36, 81–108*, vol. 1, Hermeneia (Minneapolis: Fortress, 2001), 406f.

## The Enoch Myth and the Christian Son of Man

We can now reflect on the relationship between the Son of Man in the Parables and some aspects of the Christology derived mainly from the Gospels. At this point it is necessary to underscore that these reflections are limited, because Christology involves a broad spectrum of problems and the literature to the field is vast.[85] Moreover, it is impossible in this context to discuss the authenticity of the Jesus sayings in the Gospels. Therefore our discussion concentrates on two points. The first is a comparison between the oracles and visions of the Son of Man and Chosen One in the Parables and the eschatological sayings about the Son of Man in the Gospels. The second concerns what was intended with the Enochic and Christian identification of their protagonists as the Son of Man.

We may first consider the emphasis in the oracles on the Son of Man (and Chosen One in the Parables). In the Parables the emphasis is clearly on the appearance of the Son of Man and Chosen One sitting on the throne of glory in heaven (1 En 45:3; 51:3; 55:4; 61:8; 62:2, 5; 69:27). There is a movement toward this throne, because he was from the beginning hidden in God's presence, even from before creation (48:6; 62:7). From this position he was installed in glory (48:2) and revealed for the chosen ones (48:7; 62:8). This exaltation is described in the following terms: "take his stand" (49:1), "arise" (51:5a), "appear" (59:2). The sitting on the throne is throughout combined with the act of judgment. The emphasis on the appearance and exaltation is, however, not exclusive. In the first presentation of the Chosen One in 45:3-6, two distinctive features are described in successive order. First the Chosen One will sit on the throne of glory to judge (45:3), and then he will dwell among the chosen ones on a renewed earth (45:4-5). The same idea seems to be present in 62:13-16 where the righteous and chosen, with newly created everlasting bodies, will eat together with the Son of Man.

There is more emphasis on the coming of the Son of Man in the central eschatological sayings in the Gospel of Mark. The Son of Man "comes in the glory of his Father with the holy angels" in 8:38; he is "coming in clouds with great power and glory" in 13:26. In the last saying there is a clear reference to the "coming with the clouds of heaven" in Dan 7:13, a feature neglected in the Parables. When the Son of Man is seated in heaven, the reference is clearly to Ps 110:1. Interestingly this text is placed before Dan 7:13: "You will see the Son of

---

85. Important issues in the discussion up to the end of the nineties are reviewed by D. Burkett, *The Son of Man Debate: A History and Evaluation*, SNTSMS 107 (Cambridge: Cambridge University Press, 1999).

Man seated at the right hand of the Power, and coming with the clouds of heaven" (1 En 14:62). The Son of Man is not coming to be seated on the throne as we could have expected from Dan 7:13-14; rather he is seated on the throne, and then from this position he is coming. This emphasis on the parousia is accordingly more clear in Mark than in the Parables. This does not mean, however, that "the Son of Man seated at the right hand" is not meant as an exaltation in Mark, only that the coming to earth is added as a distinct feature.

In Luke there seems to be a combination of the two aspects. Luke has sayings that refer to the coming of the Son of Man: "When the Son of Man comes, will he find faith on earth?" (Luke 18:8); "then they will see the Son of Man coming in a cloud with power and great glory" (21:27). In the central Sanhedrin saying, however, Luke excludes the prediction of the parousia contained in Mark and Matthew ("and coming with the clouds of heaven"): "But from now on the Son of Man will be seated at the right hand of the power of God." Here the emphasis is clearly on the exaltation of the Son of Man, as in the Parables.

Furthermore, Matthew describes the coming of the Son of Man in the same manner as Mark (10:23; 16:27-28; 24:30). But in one of the two sayings in Matthew that comes closest in wording to the Parables,[86] he reverses the Markan order: "When the Son of Man comes in his glory, and all the angels with him, then he will sit on the throne of his glory" (Matt 25:31). This may also be the case in the other saying that is particularly close to the Parables. At least there is a special emphasis on the appearance of the Son of Man on the throne of glory: "Truly I tell you, at the renewal of all things, when the Son of Man is seated on the throne of his glory, you who have followed me will also sit on twelve thrones, judging the twelve tribes of Israel" (19:28). These two sayings sound very similar to the Parables, particularly the reference to sitting upon the throne of his glory (cf. 1 En 61:8; 62:2) and the renewal of all things (cf. 45:4; 62:13-16).

These observations demonstrate two things. First, there is more emphasis on the parousia, the coming of the Son of Man to the earth, in the Gospels than in the Parables, although this feature is also present in the latter.[87] Second, there are more clear similarities to the Parables in the two sayings from Matthew than in Mark. This relates also with the first point, namely, the emphasis on the appearance and exaltation of the Son of Man before his coming to the earth.

---

86. Theisohn, *Der auserwählte Richter*, 153-61.

87. Adela Yarbro Collins considers the interpretation of Dan 7:13 as an epiphany where a manlike figure is coming to the earth in Mark to go back to Jesus' own teaching, and that Jesus was the first to understand Dan 7:13 in this way. As shown above, the idea is present in the Parables, but not as a direct interpretation of Dan 7. See Adela Yarbro Collins, "The Apocalyptic Son of Man Sayings," in *The Future of Early Christianity*, ed. B. A. Pearson (Minneapolis: Fortress, 1991), 220-28 (here 228).

The discussion of the literary relationship between the Parables and the Gospels still continues. If there has been any kind of diffusion, the direction from the Parables to the Gospels seems most likely, since there are no traces of a Christian influence in the Parables. We have observed earlier that there existed different concepts in Second Temple Judaism of a heavenly judge. The Parables and the Gospels could both be variants of these concepts. On the other hand, we must admit that no other texts from the Hebrew Bible or Second Temple Judaism come closer to the Gospels in these eschatological sayings than the Parables, when the oracles there are read in context.[88]

In the Parables the Son of Man was identified as Enoch. We have argued that this most likely was intended in the composition of the Parables, not as a later addition. Nevertheless, those who argue for a later addition also need to take more seriously this identification as a new interpretation of the Parables. This identification created a complex picture of the protagonists in the Parables. We find two biographical lines that meet. Enoch is described as a human, born as the seventh from Adam. He sees visions and utters oracles about the Chosen One and Son of Man, seen as someone different from himself. Enoch is a human figure, and he tells about the Son of Man as a heavenly eschatological figure. This eschatological figure is even said to be preexistent, which is hard to reconcile with the birth of Enoch. First, when Enoch finally is taken to heaven, the two seemingly different figures are unified.

This paradox resembles the paradox of Jesus as he is described in the Gospels and Acts. There is no explicit identification between Jesus and the eschatological Son of Man in the Synoptic Gospels before the scene in the Sanhedrin, which is recorded in Mark. The relationship between the earthly Jesus and the heavenly Son of Man is an enigma throughout the Gospels.

In the Sanhedrin, according to Mark and Matthew, Jesus quotes the familiar combination of Ps 110:1 and Dan 7:13 — seated at the right hand and coming with the clouds of heaven (Mark 14:62; Matt 26:64). The Son of Man is enthroned in heaven and will come to judgment accompanied by the clouds. When Luke drops the last part of the saying and refers only to the enthronement — "but from now on the Son of Man will be seated at the right hand of the power of God" (Luke 22:69) — he does so to create a bridge to the ascent of Jesus in Acts 1:4-11. Here Jesus is lifted up, "and a cloud brought him out of their sight" (Acts 1:9). The disciples are told that he will return in the same manner. Dan 7:13 is thus used in two ways: first to describe the ascent of Christ, then to describe his coming in glory (for the last, cf. Luke 21:27). Jesus ascends to heaven to become the heavenly Son of Man who will return in glory. The two

---

88. See the discussion of Black, "Messianism," 161-68.

figures are identified after the ascent, as seen by Stephen in the vision before his death: "I see the heavens opened and the Son of Man standing at the right hand of God" (Acts 7:56).

In the Gospel of John we see that the heavenly Son of Man and Jesus are explicitly identified already at the beginning. Christ is preexistent as *logos* from the start, drawing on Prov 8. He is born as the incarnated wisdom. He has descended from heaven to live on earth, and he will ascend to heaven again. He is lifted up, not through a special ascent like the one reported in Luke, but through the death on the cross and his resurrection (John 3:13; 6:62; 12:23; 13:31). The Son of Man title is used here to describe Jesus' exaltation, preexistence, descent and ascent, and role as king and judge.[89] When the Son of Man title is introduced in John, it is used to bridge the gap between two seemingly contradictory statements about Jesus: he is the son of Joseph (1:45), and he is the Son of God (1:49). These two statements are brought together in Jesus' own self-affirmation: he is the Son of Man (1:51). Thus this title functions to unify Jesus' terrestrial and heavenly origins, because it contains both elements.[90]

I find this development in the Christian theology about Jesus very close to what takes place in the Parables. There are two different figures, the earthly visionary and the heavenly eschatological Son of Man. The burning issue is how to unify them. The unification takes place when the earthly figure is taken up to the heavenly throne of God. Through this unification it also appears that even though the earthly figure is born on earth, he is bestowed with the qualities of the heavenly Son of Man. Thus he is a manifestation of the preexistent wisdom of God.

There is only one huge gap in this comparison — the violent death of Jesus. This incident was not prefigured in any earlier writings connected either to the visionary or to the eschatological Son of Man. The incident was so grave that it threatened to destroy all reasonable theology. Nevertheless, the early Christian theologians tried to bridge the gap. Luke did so by concluding the resurrection with the ascent and the identification with the Son of Man. John went one step further — the death itself was the exaltation of Jesus to glorification.

The assumption that the eschatological Son of Man sayings form the foundation of early Christology has been advanced earlier in New Testament scholarship.[91] The identification of Jesus as the Son of Man presupposed a res-

---

89. J. Painter, "The Enigmatic Johannine Son of Man," in *The Four Gospels III*, ed. F. Van Segbroeck et al. (Leiden: Brill, 1992), 1869-87.

90. W. O. Walker, Jr., "John 1.43-51 and 'the Son of Man' in the Fourth Gospel," *JSNT* 56 (1994): 31-42.

91. B. Lindars, "Re-enter the Apocalyptic Son of Man," *NTS* 22 (1975): 52-72 (here 61f.); C. L. Mearns, "Dating the Similitudes of Enoch," *NTS* 25 (1979): 360-69 (here 364-69).

urrection that was interpreted as his exaltation.[92] If we presuppose a date of the Parables contemporaneous with the New Testament,[93] there might be another explanation. At the time early Christology was developing, there existed a theology of the Son of Man that contained most of the elements of this Christology, but without his violent death and resurrection. The crucial point in the Son of Man theology was the identification of a terrestrial revelatory figure as the heavenly Son of Man through the ascent and exaltation of this terrestrial figure. The crisis, challenge, and foundation of Christian theology would accordingly be to unify this Son of Man theology with the violent fate of Jesus.

---

92. B. Lindars, *Jesus Son of Man: A Fresh Examination of the Son of Man Sayings in the Gospels in the Light of Recent Research* (London: SPCK, 1983), 110 — with different arguments than in his previous article; cf. also Mearns, "Dating," 365.

93. Milik's suggestion that Parables was a late (ca. 270 C.E.) Christian composition has not gained wide acceptance (*The Books of Enoch,* 89-98). Typically the composition is dated to the first century C.E.; thus J. C. Greenfield and M. E. Stone, "The Enochic Pentateuch and the Date of the Similitudes," *HTR* 70 (1977): 51-65, and D. W. Suter, "Weighed in the Balance: The Similitudes of Enoch in Recent Discussion," *RelSRev* 7 (1981): 217-21. Michael Knibb has suggested a date late in the first century; see M. A. Knibb, "The Date of the Parables of Enoch: A Critical Review," *NTS* 25 (1979): 345-59. At the Third Enoch Seminar, many argued that the Parables had to be dated before 70 C.E.

# Enoch and the Son of Man:
# A Response to Sabino Chialà and Helge Kvanvig

*John J. Collins*

The essays of Sabino Chialà and Helge Kvanvig in the current volume are nicely complementary.[1] Chialà takes the broad view, reviewing the whole tradition through the New Testament period. Kvanvig provides in-depth analysis of problems in the Parables of Enoch. Since the relation between the Parables and the New Testament is the subject of another section of this volume, I do not propose to address that issue here, except to say that I agree with Chialà on the relation between the Parables and the Gospel of Matthew. I will focus primarily on the Parables, but first it is necessary to say something about two passages on which the author of the Parables evidently drew, Dan 7 and 1 En 14.

## "One Like a Son of Man" in Daniel 7

The interpretation of Dan 7 is the only area where I have substantive disagreement with Sabino Chialà. He writes: "On the basis of the author's own interpretation of the vision in the verses that follow, we can be certain that here the expression *bar 'enosh*, the Aramaic equivalent of *ben 'adam*, simply means 'man,' 'being in human form,' and is meant to be a symbol for the 'people of the holy ones of the Most High.'"

The first part of this statement is certainly correct: "one like a son of man" means "one like a human being," and is not a title in any sense. It is also true

---

1. See above, S. Chialà, "The Son of Man: The Evolution of an Expression," and H. S. Kvanvig, "The Son of Man in the Parables of Enoch."

that this figure represents in some way the people of the holy ones of the Most High (presumably the Jewish people). But to speak of the "one like a son of a man" as a symbol is misleading, especially when Chialà goes on to distinguish rather simplistically between "a symbolic figure" and "a real one," in the context of Dan 10, or of a *metaphor* as distinct from a *character*. He recognizes that in chap. 10 the Hebrew expressions "a man," "one in the likeness of sons of men," and "one like the appearance of a man" are all equivalent, and refer to an angel. Other examples of angels in human form can be added, from chaps. 8 and 12. Chialà then argues for a progression, or differentiation, within Daniel for the way the expression "son of man" is used. But there is no basis for this differentiation. Daniel consistently uses human imagery to depict angelic figures, and varies the expression from one passage to another. As becomes clear in chap. 10, in the symbolic world of Daniel, Israel is represented on the heavenly level by the angelic "prince," Michael. He is regarded as "real," or, from a modern perspective, as "mythic realistic." The interpretation in Dan 7 equates the beast from the sea with kings or kingdoms, but it does *not* say that "the one like a son of man" is "the people of the holy ones." Rather, he receives the kingdom on their behalf, and on behalf of the "holy ones," or the angelic host. As I have argued, along with many scholars before and after me, the "one like a son of man" in Dan 7 should be identified with the archangel Michael, who represents Israel explicitly in chaps. 10 and 12.[2] In short, the world imagined in Dan 7 is more complex and multilayered than is suggested by those modern interpretations that speak of "mere symbols" or distinguish between "real" and "symbolic" figures in a visionary context.

The understanding of Daniel's "one like a son of man" is important for the Parables. Parables still reinterprets Daniel's vision, but the conception of the "Son of Man" is more directly continuous with Dan 7 than Chialà's interpretation would suggest. In fact, all the early interpretations or adaptations of Daniel's vision through the New Testament period, and arguably down to the Middle Ages, understand the "one like a son of man" as an individual, not as a corporate symbol.

## Enoch's Ascent in 1 Enoch 14

Also important for understanding the Parables is the account of Enoch's ascent in 1 En 14. There are some important points of similarity between this passage

---

2. See further J. J. Collins, *Daniel: A Commentary on the Book of Daniel*, Hermeneia (Minneapolis: Fortress, 1993), 304-10.

and Dan 7, as Kvanvig, among others, has pointed out.³ The descriptions of the divine throne and its surroundings are especially close, and there is a further important parallel in the Book of Giants.⁴ It may well be that Daniel is dependent on the Enochic vision at this point, as Kvanvig has argued. At the least, the two works draw on a common tradition. Kvanvig has also noted the similarity between the "one like a son of man" and Enoch, insofar as both are accompanied by clouds and are presented before the divine throne. Kvanvig is quite clear that the one like a son of man in Daniel is not to be identified as Enoch, in the original context. But he raises the intriguing possibility that the author of the Parables may have made this identification. This suggestion may help explain how Enoch might be identified with the Son of Man. Whether this identification was made by the author of the Parables is a more complex question to which we shall shortly return.

But first, a few other issues relating to 1 En 14 must be addressed. Kvanvig has rightly noted that the ascent takes place in a dream. But he goes on to say that in this dream vision he "sees himself as a visionary counterpart in heaven," and that he "sees himself passing through three stages." These statements imply that Enoch maintained a distinction between himself as the perceiving subject and the visionary counterpart in the dream. I do not see any textual basis for his implication. Rather, it seems to me, Enoch was a participant in his own dream, and presumably thought (if we may so speak about a fictional character) that he was actually experiencing what he saw. There is no visionary counterpart. Kvanvig counters by distinguishing between the summary narrative in 1 En 13:12-10 and the actual report of the content of the dream in chaps. 14–16. He then claims that these two passages "constitute two ways of reporting a dream experience where the dreamer sees himself. In the first the dreamer reports what happened in retrospect, depicting *how he sees himself acting in the dream*,⁵ in the second he remains in the dream experience itself, where only one of the figures is involved, the figure seen in the dream." But in fact, the summary narrative does not imply a distinction between the perceiving subject and the visionary counterpart any more than the longer account of the content of the dream. He does not say, "I saw a man being taken up to heaven on clouds," or even "I saw myself being taken up." He merely says "dreams fell upon me, and visions fell upon me, and I saw visions of wrath." Kvanvig is eager to make a dis-

---

3. H. S. Kvanvig, *Roots of Apocalyptic: The Mesopotamian Background of the Enoch Figure and of the Son of Man*, WMANT 61 (Neukirchen-Vluyn: Neukirchener Verlag, 1988), 558-71.

4. L. T. Stuckenbruck, "Daniel and Early Enoch Traditions in the Dead Sea Scrolls," in *The Book of Daniel: Composition and Reception*, ed. J. J. Collins and P. W. Flint, VTSup 83 (Leiden: Brill, 2001), 368-86.

5. Emphasis mine.

tinction, because in the Parables Enoch sees a figure called "that Son of Man," who is clearly distinct from the perceiving subject, and Kvanvig wishes to argue that they are identical, in short, that the Son of Man is a "visionary counterpart" of Enoch. But there is no such distinction in 1 En 14, and so Kvanvig's interpretation of the Parables derives no support from the older passage on this point.

Also without textual basis in 1 Enoch, as far as I can see, is the claim that Enoch is installed as priest when he ascends to heaven in chap. 14. Martha Himmelfarb is certainly right that the heavenly house of God that Enoch enters is viewed as a temple.[6] But it does not seem to me that entering a temple, earthly or heavenly, automatically makes one a priest.[7] Neither does the fact that scribes *could* be priests mean that all scribes were priests, or that Enoch was a priest because he was a scribe. The fact remains that Enoch is called a scribe in this passage and is *not* called a priest, and it is possible that the implication of the text is that the traditional function of priests might be better exercised by scribes. In the book of Jubilees, Enoch is said to offer incense in the Garden of Eden (Jub 4:25). But must we assume that whatever is said of Enoch in Jubilees is implied in the Book of the Watchers? Not necessarily.[8] We could perhaps argue that the author of the Parables would have read the older Enochic book in light of Jubilees, but it is not clear to me that anything said about Enoch in the Parables implies a priestly function. The commissioning of Enoch in 1 En 15 seems to be prophetic rather than priestly.[9] He is given a job to do. He is *not* installed in heaven at this point, and the passage surely does not describe a priestly installation. Even if Enoch is identified with the Son of Man in the Parables, there again I do not see that there is anything peculiarly priestly about his function as judge.

The supposed priestly character of Enoch is important for Kvanvig's argument as a bridge to traditions about Melchizedek, and also to the self-glorification hymn from Qumran. I find this part of Kvanvig's essay intriguing,

---

6. M. Himmelfarb, *Ascent to Heaven in Jewish and Christian Apocalypses* (Oxford: Oxford University Press, 1993), 14-20.

7. Leif Carlsson goes so far as to say that Enoch takes on the role of high priest, because he enters the Holy of Holies. See L. Carlsson, *Round Trips to Heaven: Otherworldly Travelers in Early Judaism and Christianity*, Lund Studies in History of Religions 19 (Lund: Almqvist and Wiksell, 2004), 43.

8. Andrei Orlov thinks the priesthood of Enoch is implied in the Book of the Watchers, but he grants that it is only explicit in Jubilees. See A. A. Orlov, *The Enoch-Metatron Tradition*, TSAJ 107 (Tübingen: Mohr Siebeck, 2005), 70-75.

9. See G. W. E. Nickelsburg, *1 Enoch 1: A Commentary on the Book of 1 Enoch 1–36, 81–108*, vol. 1, Hermeneia (Minneapolis: Fortress, 2001), 30.

and I would like to see his argument developed at greater length. I agree that these texts are indeed relevant to the interpretation of the Parables, and that they show "that there existed a 'high' messianic eschatology in Second Temple Judaism prior to the Parables with many of the same features as the heavenly figure described there." My initial impression, however, is that the points of contact between these texts and Enoch are not very secure. Kvanvig writes that Melchizedek, in 11QMelchizedek, is "presented in a heavenly environment, portrayed as a high priest, acting as judge for the wicked and eschatological savior for the righteous." The text speaks of the Day of Atonement, when atonement shall be made for the men of the lot of Melchizedek. It does not actually say that Melchizedek is a high priest, and it does not describe him as doing what a high priest is supposed to do according to Leviticus. The claim that he is portrayed as a high priest rests on a number of (reasonable) inferences about the relation of this text to Gen 14 and Ps 110. Also, while Ps 110 provides a precedent for someone being enthroned in heaven, Melchizedek is not enthroned in 11QMelchizedek. There is certainly similarity between Melchizedek and the Son of Man in the Parables, insofar as both are heavenly judges. I think we should hesitate, however, to infer from these similarities that the Son of Man is installed as priest, or that he must have a human pedigree. It is not even clear whether or how Melchizedek in 11QMelchizedek is identified with the king of Salem, honored by Abraham, or whether he is regarded as an exalted human being.

As for the self-glorification hymn, Kvanvig has presented a very interesting argument that the self-presentation of the speaker is influenced by the messianic prophecy in Isa 11. He finds three points of similarity: "(a) the notion that the figure is instructed by the Lord, (b) the act of judgment, and (c) the reference to the powerful breath from the figure's lips." He offers the following translation of the passage in the self-glorification hymn (4Q491c, frag. 1:9-11): "I have been instructed, and there is no teaching comparable [to my teaching . . .]. And who will attack me when [I] op[en my mouth]? And who will endure the flow of my lips? And who will confront me and retain comparison with my judgment."[10] But the passage has also been translated "never have I been instructed?"[11] The motif of judgment *(mishpaṭ)* arguably relates to the teaching function, and the verbal usage is not especially close to Isa 11 ("flow" rather than "breath" of the lips). This is not to disqualify the parallel proposed by Kvanvig, but just to say that it is by no means certain.

10. Following M. Baillet, *Qumrân Grotte 4. III*, DJD 7 (Oxford: Clarendon, 1982), 28.
11. So E. Eshel, "The Identification of the 'Speaker' of the Self-Glorification Hymn," in *The Provo International Conference on the Dead Sea Scrolls*, ed. D. W. Parry and E. Ulrich, STDJ 30 (Leiden: Brill, 1999), 622. Maurice Baillet takes the negative as the answer to the preceding question: "et il n'y en a pas."

Both the Melchizedek text and the self-glorification hymn are important parallels to the Son of Man in the Parables in some respects, and Kvanvig has rendered an important service by bringing them into the discussion. But we need a good deal more clarification both of the texts themselves and of their relation to the Enoch tradition before further inferences can be drawn from the relationships.

## Enoch and the Son of Man

The most intriguing question about the Son of Man in the Parables, however, is undoubtedly that of his relation to Enoch. Controversy has centered on the concluding chapters, 70–71. It is usually assumed that Enoch is identified with the Son of Man in 1 En 71:14. Nickelsburg and VanderKam translate: "you are that son of man who was born to righteousness." There is no consensus, however, on whether this identification is implied throughout the Parables, or indeed on how it should be understood.

These chapters constitute an epilogue to the Parables, or rather a succession of epilogues. 70:1-2 tells of the translation of Enoch in the first person. 70:3-4 switches to the third person and refers to Enoch's journey to the abode of the righteous dead. 71:1 signals a new unit by beginning again in the first person: "and after that, my spirit was taken away and it ascended to heaven." From a literary point of view, one has the impression that 70:3-4 and chap. 71 are appendices, added after 70:1-2 has brought the Parables to a satisfactory conclusion.[12] There is good reason, then, to suppose that the passage that contains the apparent identification of Enoch and the Son of Man is a secondary addition.

Kvanvig, however, refuses to accept redaction as a solution. We must still ask how the book would have been read in its final form. "I hardly think," he writes, "that the readers of the book thought according to the methods of modern literary criticism, namely, that the ending is only a secondary addition with no relevance for the meaning of the book. I rather think they considered the ending as the climax of the whole," and started to ponder on the whole composition once more. But the kind of holistic reading that Kvanvig advocates is very much a product of "modern literary criticism," more so indeed than the redaction-critical reading. The only evidence we have of how Parables was read is in the Ethiopic tradition. And there, as we might expect in a Christian context, the Son of Man was assumed to be Christ, and Enoch was not

---

12. See, above, the essays of George Nickelsburg and Michael Knibb on the literary structure of the Parables.

thought to be identified with him at all.[13] In fact, it is possible to construe the Ethiopic text of 1 En 71:14 so that it does not require that the two figures be identified. One can translate "you are a son of man," taking the Ethiopic word *we'etu* as a copula rather than as a demonstrative adjective, and I take it that it has been read that way in Ethiopic tradition.[14] This is one of only two passages in the Parables where "son of man" is used in direct address. The other passage is 60:10, where the Ethiopic is *walda sab'*, and this passage is universally understood as being in the manner of Ezekiel. Kvanvig objects that the whole rest of the section (71:15-17) ties the fate of humans to Enoch in the same manner as is done earlier to the Son of Man. He also assumes that 71:17, "and thus there will be length of days with that son of man," also refers to Enoch.[15] This is not necessarily so. The text can be understood to mean that Enoch is "a son of man" (i.e., a man) who has modeled himself on the righteousness of the heavenly Son of Man. Other human beings may attain a heavenly afterlife by modeling themselves on Enoch. We may compare Paul's exhortation to his readers to "be imitators of me as I am of Christ" (1 Cor 11:1). In that case, those who share an afterlife with Enoch will also share it with the Son of Man. Enoch is preeminent among human beings in his similarity to the heavenly Son of Man, but still distinct from him.

This reading of 1 En 71 is not invalidated by Kvanvig's objections. There is, however, another consideration that weighs against it. In the much later Hebrew text, Sefer Hekhalot, or 3 Enoch, Enoch is enthroned in heaven as Metatron.[16] Enoch was eventually, indisputably, identified with a heavenly figure, and this lends plausibility to the view that such an identification is made in 1 En 71. But while it is attractive to posit a trajectory leading from the Parables to Sefer Hekhalot, it is remarkable that the titles applied to the Son of Man in the Parables (Son of Man, messiah, Righteous One, Chosen One) are almost entirely absent from the later text.[17]

The issue is complicated by the fact that the Book of Parables is not pre-

---

13. I am dependent here on oral information supplied by Daniel Assefa, who kindly checked two traditional Ethiopic commentaries but has not checked all that are extant. See also D. C. Olson, "Enoch and the Son of Man in the Epilogue of the Parables," *JSP* 18 (1998): 27-38 (here 36).

14. Olson, "Enoch," 36.

15. In this case the Ethiopic is *walda eguala emma-heyaw*.

16. P. Alexander, "3 (Hebrew Apocalypse of) Enoch," in *The Old Testament Pseudepigrapha*, ed. James H. Charlesworth, 2 vols. (Garden City, N.Y.: Doubleday, 1983, 1985), 1:258.

17. Only the title "chosen" is applied to Metatron, once. See J. R. Davila, "Melchizedek, The 'Youth,' and Jesus," in *The Dead Sea Scrolls as Background to Postbiblical Judaism and Early Christianity: Papers from an International Conference at St. Andrews in 2001*, ed. J. R. Davila, STDJ 46 (Leiden: Brill, 2003), 254; Orlov, *The Enoch-Metatron Tradition*, 85.

served in the original Aramaic. On the basis of the Ethiopic translation, it is possible, but not inevitable, that 71:14 was taken to mean that Enoch was identified with the Son of Man. If this was a secondary expansion of the Parables, as I think highly likely, it is then possible that the identification would be read back into the Parables, as indeed it is by many modern scholars. The identification was presumably not introduced by the Ethiopic translator, and so the expansion of the text would be dated relatively early, perhaps in reaction to the Christian identification of Jesus with the Son of Man. But none of this requires that Parables was originally composed with the identification in mind, and many of us would still argue that the composition of the text is more easily explained if chap. 71 is recognized as an addition.

Kvanvig sides with those who think the identification with Enoch is implied throughout, but he acknowledges that there are problems, and tries to address them.

The first "obstacle" he acknowledges is the one I myself have pointed out, that it is odd that Enoch should fail to recognize himself in his vision.[18] Kvanvig does not seem to be convinced by James VanderKam's suggestion that the Son of Man is Enoch's heavenly "double."[19] After all, Enoch is not told in 71:14, "this is your heavenly double," but "you are the Son of Man." Kvanvig entertains VanderKam's secondary suggestion, that "Enoch sees the Son of Man in visions of the future, not in disclosures of the present." This suggestion seems problematic in light of the preexistence of the Son of Man, to which we will return. (He is not entirely future.) Kvanvig's main suggestion, however, is that there is a parallel in the account of Enoch's ascent in 1 En 12–14. "In both cases Enoch sees himself in a heavenly location. . . ." As we have seen, however, it is misleading to say that Enoch "sees himself" in the Book of the Watchers. At no point in the earlier account is Enoch described in a way that could be taken to distinguish him from the visionary.

The second obstacle concerns the evident contradiction between 1 En 71:14 and the majority text of 1 En 70:1. 1 En 70:1-2 is translated as follows by George Nickelsburg: "And after this, while he was living, his name was raised into the presence of that son of man and into the presence of the Lord of Spirits from among those who dwell on the earth. He was raised on the chariots of the wind, and his name departed from among them."

This translation, based on the majority reading in the manuscripts,

---

18. J. J. Collins, *The Apocalyptic Imagination,* 2nd ed. (Grand Rapids: Eerdmans, 1998), 188.

19. J. C. VanderKam, "Righteous One, Messiah, Chosen One, and Son of Man in 1 Enoch 37–71," in *The Messiah: Developments in Earliest Judaism and Christianity,* ed. James H. Charlesworth (Minneapolis: Fortress, 1992), 182-83.

*John J. Collins*

makes a clear distinction between Enoch and the Son of Man. In 1976 Maurice Casey proposed a different understanding of the passage based on one important manuscript, Abbadianus 55 (U), and two late manuscripts, which lack the word *baxaba* (or *baxabehu* in some manuscripts), "into the presence," before "that son of man."[20] The text could then be rendered: "the name of that son of man was raised into the presence of the Lord of Spirits," thus permitting an identification of Enoch with the Son of Man.[21] (The translation "to the son of man" is also possible.) Since this proposal relied primarily on one manuscript, which was known for capricious omissions, there was little reason to regard it as anything but a scribal mistake. In the meantime, however, four, and possibly five, other manuscripts have come to light that support the minority reading.[22] Whether this reading is to be preferred, however, remains very doubtful. Kvanvig argues that it should be preferred as the *lectio difficilior* since Enoch was not identified with the Son of Man in Ethiopic tradition. But even the minority reading here does not require the identification; it only allows it. The simplest explanation is still that a word was omitted by scribal error. If the majority reading of this verse were a correction, to eliminate the possibility of the identification, we should expect that 71:14, which lends itself even more readily to the identification, would also be corrected.

VanderKam, who accepts the majority reading, or at least accepted it in 1992, argues that it is "unlikely that this passage draws a line between Enoch and the son of man" on the grounds that this passage is the introduction to all of chaps. 70 and 71, and "it would be remarkable if, at the beginning of this artistically structured unit, there was a statement that contradicted what the unit itself forthrightly declared."[23] But as we have noted already, chaps. 70 and 71 are not a unit at all. Chap. 71 constitutes a second, or third, epilogue, and in my view, is most readily explained as a secondary addition.[24] Even if the identification of Enoch with the Son of Man is accepted in chap. 71, the first epilogue in chap. 70 should not be harmonized with it. If the majority reading of 70:1 is accepted, as I think it should be, then the distinction it makes between Enoch and the Son of Man cannot be explained away.

20. M. Casey, "The Use of the Term 'Son of Man' in the Similitudes of Enoch," *JSJ* 7 (1976): 11-29.
21. Compare Matthew Black, who translates: "the name of a son of man (i.e. Enoch) was raised up to the Lord of Spirits." See M. Black, *The Book of Enoch, or, I Enoch: A New English Edition with Commentary and Textual Notes*, SVTP 7 (Leiden: Brill, 1985), 67.
22. Olson, "Enoch," 30-31.
23. VanderKam, "Righteous One," 184.
24. So also Nickelsburg and Knibb in their respective essays in the present volume. See also Chialà, *Libro delle Parabole di Enoc* (Brescia: Paideia, 1997), 287.

The third obstacle is the one that Kvanvig regards as the most difficult. This is the preexistence of the Son of Man. 1 En 48:2-3 reads: "And in that hour that son of man was named in the presence of the Lord of Spirits, and his name before the Head of Days. Even before the sun and the constellations were created, before the stars of heaven were made, his name was named before the Lord of Spirits." The passage continues in 48:6: "For this (reason) he was chosen and hidden in his presence before the world was created and forever." While the context of 48:2 is either eschatological or the time of Enoch's ascent, 48:6 seems to state unequivocally that the Son of Man existed before the world was created. Similarly, in 62:7 we read:

For from the beginning the son of man was hidden,
and the Most High preserved him in the presence of his might,
and he revealed him to the chosen.

It is sometimes suggested that preexistence here means only "a project in the mind of God,"[25] or that what was hidden was merely his identity.[26] But it is difficult to see why his identity would need to be hidden if he did not yet exist. The clearest parallel for a preexistent figure in pre-Christian Judaism is the portrayal of wisdom in Prov 8:22-31, as Kvanvig has recognized.[27] It would seem that Parables here developed the identity of the Son of Man well beyond anything that we found in Daniel, by applying to him language that is elsewhere used of wisdom.

Kvanvig claims that the parallel with wisdom is relevant not only to the Son of Man but also to Enoch: "In 1 En 42:1-2, after Wisdom did not find any place to stay among the sons of men and went back to heaven, iniquity came forth. It is easier to read this parody as a concealed reference to Enoch than to the Son of Man. Coming from the realm of God, Wisdom sought a dwelling on earth, but she did not find any and thus returned to the place in heaven among the angels. This agrees with the portrait of Enoch in the Book of the Watchers (1 En 12–16)."

But does it? Kvanvig's argument is that according to 1 En 12:1, "Enoch, before everything, was hidden among the heavenly beings, and from this position

---

25. T. W. Manson, "The Son of Man in Daniel, Enoch and the Gospels," *BJRL* 32 (1949-50): 183-85.
26. VanderKam, "Righteous One," 180.
27. Kvanvig notes that wisdom is also associated with the Son of Man in 1 En 49:1-4 and 51:3. See also Theisohn, *Der auserwählte Richter: Untersuchungen zum traditionsgeschichtlichem Ort der Menschensohngestalt der Bilderreden des Äthiopischen Henoch* (Göttingen: Vandenhoeck & Ruprecht, 1975), 126-39.

*John J. Collins*

he came to the earth and met the Watchers, after which he ascended to heaven." He relies on the Ethiopic translation of this verse ("before all")[28] rather than the Greek ("before these things"), which is preferred by Nickelsburg/ VanderKam and Uhlig.[29] But even the Ethiopic text does not necessarily mean that Enoch originated in heaven. He was "hidden," presumably after he had been born on earth. According to Gen 5, he was the son of Jared. Kvanvig doubts whether the Book of the Watchers presupposes the biblical account of Enoch.[30] I do not doubt that the statement that Enoch "walked with elohim" (Gen 5:22, 24) is understood differently in Genesis and in 1 Enoch, but this hardly requires that the Book of the Watchers did not presuppose Genesis at all. In any case, it is quite possible, with the Greek, to interpret the passage to mean that Enoch was hidden before the events described in chaps. 6–11. It should be noted that some of the *apkallus* also were of human descent.

It does not seem to me that there is any real analogy between Enoch's emergence from hiddenness in 1 En 12:1 and wisdom's futile search for a place to live on earth. Neither, it seems to me, does the story of Enoch in the Book of the Watchers imply that Enoch was preexistent. A clear distinction remains between the transcendent preexistent Son of Man and Enoch, seventh from Adam. In the body of the Parables there is no suggestion at all that the Son of Man ever had an earthly career.

It seems to me, then, that the identification of Enoch with the Son of Man in 1 En 71:14, if that is indeed how this passage should be understood, is most satisfactorily explained as a secondary addition, which stands in unresolved tension with the main body of the Parables, and with the original epilogue in 70:1.

Kvanvig observes, accurately, that the older Enoch tradition had no place for a messiah.[31] He makes the interesting argument that the reason for this phenomenon was the prominent role of Enoch himself, who was more than a visionary sage, and already in the Book of the Watchers took on an intermediary role similar to the angels. In Kvanvig's view, a separate "Son of Man" would threaten the coherence of Enochic theology, and not leave any space for Enoch. In my view, this argument misunderstands the nature of mediation in ancient

---

28. Cf. Michael Knibb's translation of the Ethiopic, *The Ethiopic Book of Enoch: A New Edition in the Light of the Aramaic Dead Sea Fragments*, 2 vols. (Oxford: Clarendon, 1978), 92 ("and before everything").

29. S. Uhlig, *Das äthiopische Henochbuch*, in *JSHRZ* V.6, ed. Werner G. Kümmel (Gütersloh: Gütersloher Verlagshaus Gerd Mohn, 1984), 461-780.

30. See H. S. Kvanvig, "The Watcher Story and Genesis: An Intertextual Reading," *SJOT* 18 (2004): 163-83.

31. The only possible exception is the "white bull" in the Animal Apocalypse.

Judaism. The prominence of Michael or the Prince of Light in the Dead Sea Scrolls did not mean that there was no room for a messiah.[32] The apocalyptic literature envisions a layered, hierarchical universe, where agents on different levels act in synergy with each other. The Son of Man complements Enoch on the heavenly level, and does not obviate the need for a human revealer to bridge the gap between heaven and earth. In an analogous (but also different) way, the preeminence of Christ still left room for saints, who could also serve as subordinate mediators, in Catholic and Orthodox Christianity.

None of this is to deny that the eventual exaltation of Enoch to a heavenly throne, which is explicit in 3 Enoch and possible in a secondary recension of the Parables, was continuous with his role in the earlier Enochic books in important ways. Kvanvig's learned essay helps us think about that continuity, and I look forward to a continuing conversation about it.

---

32. J. J. Collins, *Apocalypticism in the Dead Sea Scrolls* (London: Routledge, 1997), 82.

# Questions regarding the So-Called Son of Man in the Parables of Enoch: A Response to Sabino Chialà and Helge Kvanvig

*Klaus Koch*

The Book of the Parables of Enoch is a curious document of Jewish religion: there are no references to Israel, Moses, Abraham, or Torah! The three titles of its main figure and mediator of eschatological salvation are usually translated "son of man," a term that has no antecedent in Torah and Nebiim, but probably has a prototype in Dan 7 and christological parallels in the Gospels.

Chialà as well as Kvanvig agree with the equation "the Messiah Son of Man" as the title of the Third Enoch Seminar at Camaldoli and of this volume. However, I am not yet convinced. In the translations of 1 Enoch, "Son of Man" occurs fifteen/sixteen times, but "the Anointed One" only twice. In other apocalypses the two terms refer to different constellations in different periods: the Messiah belongs to a national, Davidic perspective, the Son of Man has "international" competence as son of Adam (cf. below).[1]

## Chialà's Essay

Chialà's essay is an important attempt to reconstruct the historical evolution of the expression "Son of Man," a notion that has certainly not remained unchanged in different literatures through the centuries. His results are:

---

1. Cf. Dan 9:26 versus 7:13f.; 1 En 90:9-19 versus 5:37f.; 4 Ezra 12:31-34 versus 13:2, and my article "Messias und Menschensohn," in K. Koch, *Vor der Wende der Zeiten. Beiträge zur apokalyptischen Literatur*, Gesammelte Aufsätze 2 (Neukirchen-Vluyn: Neukirchener Verlag, 1996), 235-66.

I must thank Charlotte Hempel for improving my English.

1. The colloquial Hebrew or Aramaic nouns *'adam/'enash* with or without the addition *ben-/bar* are "simple synonyms for men."
2. The expression gets a specific meaning in Dan 7, where *bar 'enash* signifies "a symbol for the holy people of the Most High."
3. In Enoch "Daniel's metaphor, which of course concealed a reality, has . . . become a character." Whereas in Daniel the Ancient of Days pronounces the eschatological judgment and installs the Son of Man afterward, in Enoch this figure comes on the scene before the final trial over the rulers of the earth, and acts as the decisive judge. This extension of his function is taken over by the New Testament.
4. A new level is reached in the Parables, the New Testament, and the Testament of Abraham, where "the Son of Man *function* receives the name of a historical individual . . . Enoch, Jesus, Abel."
5. Around 100 C.E. the specific use of the expression begins to disappear.

This line of development makes explicit what may be the presumption of many biblical scholars today. The separation of the apocalyptic and christological use from everyday language is certainly true. Convincing also is the differentiation between the speech in Daniel, which paraphrases the regent of the coming aeon, and the function of an eschatological judge in later literature, as well as the identifications with a historical or legendary person in some apocalyptic texts.

There remain, nevertheless, some severe problems regarding a short-circuited equation of the Hebrew and the Aramaic nouns and constructions in question. The Hebrew language presents two expressions, *'adam* and the more poetical *'enôsh*. Both may be used in a generic or a collective sense, meaning "human being(s), humankind"; but the former also provides the proper name of the *Urmensch*, and the latter has the connotation of a weak and mortal being. The Aramaic language knows only the noun *'enash*, which sounds much more neutral.

Another crucial question is the assumed synonymity of the simplex and the construct-phrase with the *nomen regens ben-/bar* in both languages. Regarding Aramaic, a look at the book of Daniel seems informative to me.

1. In Daniel the compound *bar 'enash* appears only once; however, the simplex *'e/anash(a)* appears twenty-three times. Contrary to the *bar 'enash* as eschatological ruler (Dan 7:13), the lion-bird as symbol of the first dominion in a global history is described only as "like an *'enash*" standing on his feet and receiving "the heart of an *'enash*" (7:4; cf. 4:13: "his heart from humankind [*min 'anashâ*, with article]). The fourth beast appears with "eyes of *'anashâ*" (7:8 with article); this may be meant as the attrib-

ute "human eyes"; but if the determination is missing as in Dan 7:4, the sense may rather be "some man." The undetermined simplex refers to a single figure. The determined noun, however, has a general meaning: there is one "kingdom (= system of rulership?) of the humankind *(malkût 'ana/osha)* on earth" (4:14, 22, 29; cf. 4:13). The compound with *bar* in Dan 7:13 probably accentuates the specification: "(like) one *single* human being."

2. The dominion of *bar 'enash* corresponds to the rule of the *qaddishê 'elyonîn* (Dan 7:18), which is commonly translated "the holy ones of the Most High." This rendering is problematic. *'elyonîn* is clearly plural and probably denotes (the holies among) the highest class of angels (cf. *qdwshy qdwshm*, 4QShirShab I 2.3.29), certainly not God himself, who in Dan 7:25 and nine times elsewhere is called *'illayâ*. Apparently "the one like a son of man" does not designate a human collectivity but the leader of that angelic group.[2] Dan 7 describes an angel (probably Michael) as God's eschatological delegate on earth,[3] ruling in a manner that is much more humanlike than the rule of the former human superpowers on earth (Dan 7:4-8).

Let me add a side glance at the Aramaic of the Targum to the Latter Prophets, which seems to me a rather old version.[4]

1. Here the undetermined Aramaic *'enash* mostly corresponds to Hebrew *'ish* (seventeen times), and only thrice to *'adam*.

2. The determined *'enashâ* appears three times instead of Hebrew *'enôsh* and thirteen times for *ha'adam* (with article!), but mostly for the undetermined *'adam*. The compound *benê ('e)nashê* (always with article) occurs three times for *benê 'adam* (without article) and nine times for the simplex *'adam*. Apparently the Hebrew expression has a broader meaning than the Aramaic one.

3. The singular *bar 'enash* (undetermined) is restricted to four occurrences in Jeremiah, always negated in parallelism with the simplex *'enash*, representing total destruction: not a single human being will survive. The determined construction *bar 'enasha* appears only twice, in both cases rendering the different Hebrew roots *'enôsh* and *ben 'adam* with one and the same Aramaic

---

2. The mention of an "*am* of the holy ones of the highest (angels)" may refer to Israel as the elect people under the special care of this upper group of angels (v. 27).

3. J. J. Collins, *A Commentary on the Book of Daniel*, Hermeneia (Minneapolis: Fortress, 1993), 304-13; K. Koch, *Die Reiche der Welt und der kommende Menschensohn. Studien zum Danielbuch*, Gesammelte Aufsätze 2 (Neukirchen-Vluyn: Neukirchener Verlag, 1995), 140-72.

4. The text is from A. Sperber, *The Bible in Aramaic*, vol. 3, *The Latter Prophets according to Targum Jonathan* (Leiden: Brill, 1962).

*Questions regarding the So-Called Son of Man*

noun. Again a negation is stressed: no one, not even a single individual, will remain (Isa 51:12; 56:2).

The supplement *bar/benê* to the generic notion *'enash* is very rare in these Aramaic texts. Where it does occur it underlines the singularity of an individual's behavior or destiny. There is no evidence that the simplex and the *compositum* are simply interchangeable in Aramaic, as often is maintained.[5]

As Chialà rightly remarks, Ezekiel is to be set apart regarding this notion in Hebrew, because this prophet is addressed by his God as *ben 'adam* around eighty times (cf. Dan 8:17). The Aramaic version is somewhat unusual, addressing him as *bar 'adam*. Since *'adam* is unknown as a generic noun in Aramaic, the construction must mean "Son of the (primeval) Adam." Thus, the prophet is understood as an outstanding Adamite, perhaps as the representative of a new divine start with humankind. In his translation of the Targum, S. H. Levey has remarked that in distinction from the *Vorlage* the phrase is now "an expression of laudation and commendation, rather than a derogatory designation"; it reveals within the Targum and its interest in Merkabah mysticism, "the key to the proper understanding." It seems to present an early parallel to the praise of Jesus Christ as the second Adam (1 Cor 15:45), although I am not convinced that we have here "an indirect polemic thrust against the Pauline view," as Levey supposes.[6]

No other person is called *bn 'dm* in the Targum. Is Ezekiel imagined as a posthumous descendant of the primeval ancestor in spite of a direct father (Ezek 1:3)? According to the *Targum Neofiti* and the *Fragmentary Targum*, Adam was gathered from the earth (*'tknysh mn gw' 'lm*) after his death (Gen 5:5); does this mean that he was elevated into a heavenly surrounding with the ability to connect directly with specific descendants?

As I argued some years ago,[7] the Enochic Animal Apocalypse already knew such an Adam typology and applied it to the eschatological savior, who is certainly seen as a second Adam with a universal function. The final scene at the beginning of the new aeon is described in 1 En 90:37f.:

> And I saw how a *white bull* was born, and its horns were large. And all the wild beasts and all the birds of heaven were afraid of it and made petition to it continually.
> 
> And I saw until their species were changed, and *they all became white cattle*.
> 
> And the first one became >leader< among them . . . and there were large

---

5. Cf. the differentiation with K. Beyer, *Die aramäischen Texte vom Toten Meer* (Göttingen: Vandenhoeck & Ruprecht, 1984), 517f.

6. S. H. Levey, *The Targum of Ezekiel*, ArBib 13 (Wilmington, Del.: Glazier, 1987), 6-9.

7. Koch, *Vor der Wende der Zeiten*, 247-50.

black horns on its head. And the Lord of the sheep rejoiced over it and over all the cattle.

According to the symbolic dream, the first white bull had been Adam as the first man, and from him came forth white bulls as the pious branch of humankind until Shem at the time between creation and flood (85:3–89:1). With the eschatological bull as the father of a renewed humankind, God will regenerate the good creation of the human race at the time of Adam. All human beings will henceforth be as white and righteous as their primeval ancestors.

Perhaps a similar typology provided the background for the curious title in the last chapters: "that/this son (of?) the offspring of the mother of living." This is the regular Ethiopic rendering (in both Testaments, including Dan 7) of *bn 'dm*.[8] Concerning Hebrew *ben 'adam*, the second noun could refer to the name of the first primeval man (cf. 90:37f. and Ezekiel) and to the time of creation. Do we have here a surprising parallel, but with a change of perspective from the masculine to the feminine representative of humankind, to the Eve of Gen 3:20?[9] If we presuppose a double *status constructus* in the Ethiopic expression (with Matthew Black), does the "offspring" refer to Seth as the "righteous" son after Abel's death?[10] As far as I can see, there is scarcely any debate among scholars about this curious circumscription. Was Eve in the view of the Parables the mother of living not only for the people of the disappearing aeon but also of life in the aeon to come? Whereas at the turn of the era in Jewish and Christian writings Eve as *Urmutter* is mostly condemned as the first cause of sin among humankind and Adam excused (Sir 25:24; 1 Tim 2:14), a contrary tradition appears here: the life of the first woman has remained the nucleus for eschatological liberation. *Targum Onkelos* pursues a similar track in the rendering of Gen 3:15. The famous sentence about the enduring fight between the seed of Eve and the serpent, which is conceived as Satan, will end with an eschatological victory: "The son of the woman will remember all, what you (the serpent) have done until the end, the day of the king Messiah."[11] As the Messiah here, so also in Enoch the Son of Man is conceived as the victorious descendant of the first wife!

---

8. Black, *The Book of Enoch, or, I Enoch: A New English Edition with Commentary and Textual Notes*, SVTP 7 (Leiden: Brill, 1985), 206f.

9. The general statement "mother of life" (*hy* in Hebrew) is specialized in *Targum Onkelos*: "mother of all human beings" (*bny 'nsh'*).

10. A parallel tradition may be found among the Mandeans: from Adam and Eve originated a "Stamm des Lebens" with Abel, Seth, and Enosh; see K. Rudolph, "Mandäer, Mandäismus," in *TRE* 22 (Berlin: De Gruyter, 1992), 21.

11. Koch, *Vor der Wende der Zeiten*, 198-202.

## Kvanvig's Essay

Kvanvig presents some important observations. Under his first heading, "The Parables and the Book of the Watchers," Kvanvig demonstrates that the Book of Parables was written as a "second vision" with the intention of providing further explanations of the Book of the Watchers over and above the first vision. The Book of Parables elaborates upon the eschatological separation of the destiny of the righteous and the wicked, taking up chap. 14, where we find an account of Enoch's ascent to heaven installed as heavenly priest, mediator, and intercessor between God and the angels.[12] He states: "The Book of the Watchers is reinterpreted with a new eschatological outlook." We may add: with a more positive and less mythological one. Not the watchers, but the kings and mighty ones are the recognizable cause of evil.

Without any antecedent in the Book of the Watchers, however, a divine title, "Lord of the Spirits," dominates in the Parables. Kvanvig explains it as an originally Aramaic rendering *(marê ruhîn?)* of the Hebrew name YHWH Zeba'ot, especially with reference to Isa 6:3. The hosts, a kind of divine attribute in the Hebrew original, are now conceived as God's creative manifestations in heaven and on earth. Kvanvig finds this interpretation already in Hebrew in the *Hodayot* of Qumran (1QH XVIII 8; he could also add *sb' rhym*, 1QH V 14). This is a very convincing explanation, and I wonder why nobody has suggested it before.[13] Already in the Astronomical Book the sun takes its course in the care of the spirits. In the Parables this conception is generalized. According to 1 En 60:10ff., Enoch is told what is hidden as the first and the last in heaven, on earth, and in the abyss: primarily there are the spirit-winds and their divisions as the last causes of the movements in the astral and meteorological realm. But spirit-winds are also acting in the minds of angels (68:2) and men (41:8; 61:1; 62:1). Thus the Book of Parables teaches a sophisticated *pneumatology* that is not restricted to a holy spirit within the community of believers, but further reckons with a background force sustaining the cosmos as God's good creation. All of them are directed by the Lord of the spirits and are his extensions.[14] Does the rendering with "spirits" testify to a decisive change of the worldview of this Enochian group — mirrored throughout in the Book of Parables — from the outward and visible phenomena as the fundamental

---

12. For the relationship of the Parables with the Book of the Watchers, see the essays of George Nickelsburg, Michael Knibb, and James VanderKam in the present volume.

13. In other Aramaic traditions, however, the Hebrew expression *şĕbā'ôt* is kept and transliterated (thus in the Targums — e.g., Isa 6:3; Amos 3:13; 4:13 — and the Christian traditions).

14. Alongside them, however, are bad spirits; cf., e.g., 67:8.

forces of movement in nature and society to invisible forces as the God-given motor of change and development in the course of times?

Kvanvig's second major heading is "The Heavenly Representative." Along with other commentators he postulates in the Parables a single mediator between the divine and the human realm despite the use of a range of different titles such as the Chosen One, the Son of Man, the Anointed One, and the Righteous One, which were taken from Daniel and the Servant Songs (Isa 42–53),[15] but extended to the description of an eschatological figure who will sit on a throne of glory and execute a general judgment.

A crucial issue here is the generalizing translation "Son of Man,"[16] which is usual in all modern translations for three different combinations in Ethiopic. Can it be philologically justified? Kvanvig remarks on the difference and the variant references. Specifically, there are differences in their usage:

1. "The son of humankind" *(walda sab')* occurs four times, only in 1 En 46–48, interpreting Dan 7,[17] certainly with the Aramaic *bar 'enash* as background. He will be the universal judge on a throne of his own.[18]
2. "The son (of) the offspring of the mother of living" *(walda 'eg*ʷ*ala 'emaḥeyāw)* is mentioned much later on, eight times to be exact (1 En 62; 69:26-71), probably relating to Eve as "mother of living" and her offspring; cf. Gen 3:15-20, understood as *protoevangelion*.[19]
3. "The son of a man" *(walda be'si)* appears three/four times[20] in 1 En 69–71, surely referring to a second Adam.

The identity of these three actors is probably intended. Dan 7 is not the only source; Kvanvig remarks that preexistence and coming for judgment of the Son of Man are lacking in Daniel and taken from Ps 110 and Prov 8. According to Ps 110:3, God has "begotten you (Messiah) from the womb before dawn"; and in Proverbs Wisdom was created by God "at the beginning of his work." Therefore

---

15. The servant is taken as an individual as in the Targum and the New Testament.

16. Although I do not know a preferable rendering, the English "son of man" is misleading in two regards. First, the term "man" awakens the connotation of a masculine restriction, whereas the Aramaic noun *'enash(a)* includes female persons also (the German language has a closer equivalent, *Mensch, Menschenkind*). Second, "son," instead of the singular *bar*, necessarily suggests a direct genealogical relation. The Aramaic correspondence (and the Hebrew *'adam* as well) has a wider meaning: an "exemplar" of the genre humankind.

17. Cf. moreover 1 En 60:10.

18. Beside the throne of God there is a second throne; cf. the plural *krsn* in Dan 7:9.

19. On parallel expressions in Gen-Targums and the New Testament, see Koch, *Vor der Wende der Zeiten*, 199-202.

20. Is feminine to be preferred in 62:5 (Eve)?

Kvanvig sees the Son of Man as personified wisdom, which is also demonstrated in 1 En 42. However, could the womb of Ps 110 (whose? of a deity?) have been preexistent? And is it possible in Hebrew to identify the male Son of Man with a feminine *ḥokhmâ*, which "did not find a dwelling on earth"? Regarding preexistence, the Targum to Mic 5 seems to me a closer parallel: "[The coming ruler in Israel] whose name was called from the beginning, from the days of eternity."

More than a Son of Man, as attested in three forms, "the Chosen One *(heruy)*" occurs fifteen/sixteen times. In the second parable this figure is mentioned first as the heavenly representative. From a throne of glory he strengthens the chosen ones on earth and condemns the sinners (chap. 45). After a son-of-humankind passage he appears again in the text as arising before the Lord, installed with the messianic spirits (based on Isa 11) and saving the righteous and holy. Before him the metal mountains of worldly empires will smelt, and then he will cause the house of his congregation to appear and judge Azazel and his host (chaps. 49–56). In the third parable (1 En 58–69:25) his enthronement and his presiding over the great judgment are prophesied anew.[21]

Like Nickelsburg, VanderKam, and others, Kvanvig takes "the Righteous One" to be a further title of the savior in dependence on Isa 42:6, 49:6, 53:11. However, this title is certain only in 1 En 53:6 as an attribute of the Chosen One; whereas elsewhere the singular is used (only in some Ethiopic manuscripts), it may have a collective meaning, especially in the phrase "the blood of the righteous" (1 En 47:1, 4).[22]

As Deutero-Isaiah attributed the notable name "Israel" (Isa 49:3) to the

---

21. The term "chosen" as the main title of the human-superhuman savior is not unique among the Aramaic-speaking religions of that time. In Hebrew it is used in the scripture for the Servant of the Lord as well as for David (Isa 42:1; Ps 89:4). Nevertheless, the outstanding role of this single predicate goes beyond any Hebrew source. It has a close parallel in Mandean, i.e., Aramaic, texts. There the personified divine source of life sends his Chosen One of righteousness *(bhiria kushta)* to the chosen human righteous (he sends "den Boten, Gesandten, Helfer, den Sohn des Lebens als den Auserwählten"). The title is referred to as Anos (= Enosh) as well as the Hibil (= Abel). Through his activity righteousness takes place in the heart of the chosen ones on earth, the members of the Mandean community. From Adam and Eve emerged "das Geschlecht des Lebens," and a hidden Adam remains in the world of light as support for the human beings who are living in a world of darkness and demons. See K. Rudolph, "Die Religion der Mandäer," in H. Gese, M. Hoefner, and K. Rudolph, *Die Religionen Altsyriens, Altarabiens und der Mandäer*, RdM 10.2 (Stuttgart: Kohlhammer, 1970), 421-25; E. S. Drower and R. Macuch, *A Mandean Dictionary* (Oxford: Clarendon, 1963), 53. The address "my chosen one" is the *Hauptgebrauch* in Mandean writings; see G. Schrenk, "Auserwählt in den mandäischen Schriften," in *TWNT* 4 (Stuttgart: Kohlhammer, 1942), 190.

22. Black, *The Book of Enoch*, 209; M. A. Knibb, *The Ethiopic Book of Enoch: A New Edition in the Light of the Aramaic Dead Sea Fragments*, 2 vols. (Oxford: Clarendon, 1978), 1:132.

servant of the Lord as the spiritual center of the nation, so also according to Enoch the Chosen One is acting as the central figure of his congregation. Whereas the *walda sab'* predicates primarily have to do with external affairs, foremost the defense against the kings and mighty ones, the acts of the (Righteous and) Chosen One are orientated to the inside, to his congregation. The different functions of each of them — in spite of a certain amount of harmonization — support Kvanvig's conclusion of a different origin of these traditions (cf. already Beer and Charles). As he says, the notion of a heavenly representative as the result of merged traditions has arisen "most likely before the date of the Parables."

A further title could have been "the Anointed One," an ancient biblical title of the Messiah. It occurs only twice in the Parables. According to 1 En 48:8-10, "in those days" the kings and the mighty ones on earth will be given into the hand of "my chosen ones" and will burn before the face of the holy, because "they have denied the Lord of the Spirits and his Anointed One." But the identification with the titles mentioned above is questionable. If the last noun means a Son of Man who was hidden in the presence of the Lord of the Spirits since creation and only revealed to the righteous as their staff and (invisible) hope, how could unbelievers have become aware of him during their lifetime on earth and denied him? Does the term refer to a (royal or priestly) messiah of Israel in the last epoch of this aeon, distinct from the universal judge of all people and savior of the righteous (as in 4 Ezra and 2 Baruch)? In chap. 52 Enoch describes how he has seen six mountains of metal as secrets of heaven, which apparently symbolize the great kingdoms of this aeon as in Dan 2. After the eschatological turn the corresponding people "will serve the authority of the Anointed One, so that he may be powerful and mighty on earth" (1 En 53:4). Before that time, however, the mountains will melt like wax before the Chosen One when he appears before the Lord of the Spirits. Is this Chosen One the heavenly organizer who takes care of the future authority of a coming Messiah? Nowhere in the Parables is the Chosen One combined with a special earthly power in succession of human kingdoms.[23]

"The Heavenly Representative and Enoch," the heading over the last and longest of Kvanvig's sections, considers the final chapters as a "climax." After ascending to heaven, Enoch seems to meet the son of the man as another figure, but afterward he himself is greeted: "You are that son of the man, who was born for righteousness" (1 En 71:1, 14). Usually scholars consider chaps. 70–71 as a late addition, revealing an identification between Enoch and the Son of Man, who was previously hidden. Collins contradicts this in his essay in the present vol-

---

23. In the Noah insertion (1 En 65:1–69:25) no heavenly representative is mentioned.

ume: "The distinction . . . between Enoch and the Son of Man cannot be explained away." Kvanvig finds an elegant solution: Enoch "is seeing what he will become," because the earthly life of Enoch is on the one hand a manifestation of the preexisting wisdom, enthroned in heaven from everlasting time, and on the other hand it appears that he is the Son of Man that the chosen ones have for ages longed for. The problem remains that we have no other Aramaic allusion to an otherworldly doppelgänger of earthly beings, as is probably presupposed in this interpretation.[24]

Finally, Kvanvig compares the Enoch myth and the Christian Son of Man. He detects an influence of the Parables on the Jesus narrative in the Gospels, especially in Matthew. But the message of the violent death and resurrection reveals a "huge gap." Kvanvig's suggestion of an older origin of the Parables, which will be important for further exegesis of the Gospels, is certainly convincing.

---

24. Does the Jesus of the Synoptic Gospels offer a parallel? Some scholars suppose that he spoke of a Son of Man as distinct from himself, but was identified with him after the resurrection; e.g., R. Bultmann, *Theologie des Neuen Testaments* (Tübingen: Mohr, 1953), 25-33.

# The Name of the Son of Man in the Parables of Enoch

*Charles A. Gieschen*

There is significant scholarly interest in the numerous designations ascribed to the mysterious figure who has a central role in many of the scenes found in 1 En 37–71, especially the "Son of Man" designation.[1] Interest in the identification of this figure with the "one like a son of man" of Dan 7:13 has largely come from biblical scholars searching for background to Jesus being identified with a similar designation in Gospel traditions. Much less interest has been shown in the testimony of these chapters concerning the hidden name of this Son of Man figure.[2] This study will demonstrate that references to the "name" of the Son of Man in 1 En 37–71 indicate that he shares the Divine Name of the Ancient of Days, the Tetragrammaton, which is a profound assertion that reflects a complex understanding of Jewish monotheism. Furthermore, it will be suggested that this evidence is related to the Divine Name angel traditions of the Pentateuch as well as later traditions about the one who shares in possessing the Divine Name as found in some literature of Second Temple Judaism and first-century Christianity.

---

1. These designations include: Elect One, His Messiah, Chosen One, Righteous One, and Son of Man. The latter one, without doubt, has generated more secondary literature than the rest combined; for an introduction, see G. W. E. Nickelsburg, "Son of Man," in *ABD* 6 (1992), 137-50. See also J. C. VanderKam, "Righteous One, Messiah, Chosen One, and Son of Man in 1 Enoch 37–71," in *The Messiah: Developments in Earliest Judaism and Christianity*, ed. James H. Charlesworth (Minneapolis: Fortress, 1992), 169-91.

2. For a broad discussion of these traditions and their impact on early Christology, see C. A. Gieschen, "The Divine Name in Ante-Nicene Christology," *VC* 57 (2003): 115-58. The discussion below draws heavily on this earlier research.

## "The Name" in 1 Enoch 37–71

Before discussing the name of the "Son of Man," it is important to observe that the Parables of Enoch gives significant attention to the other primary figure from Dan 7: the "one who was ancient of days" (Dan 7:9). This one is often identified in these chapters of 1 Enoch with the designation "the Lord of the Spirits," which reflects the Hebrew title יְהוָה צְבָאוֹת ("YHWH Sabaoth"; see Isa 6:3).[3] These chapters also testify repeatedly that the Lord of the Spirits has a special and unique name.[4] Two examples will suffice to illustrate this point. 1 En 38:2 asserts that "sinners" deny this name: "Where will the dwelling of the sinners be, and where the resting place of those who denied the name of the Lord of the Spirits?" 49:7 notes, however, that the righteous know and praise this name: "Their lips will praise the name of the Lord of the Spirits." This "name" of the Lord of the Spirits is self-evident for any Jewish reader; it is יהוה, the revered Divine Name (hereafter YHWH).[5] Unlike Elohim and the many other titles or names used to identify God in the Hebrew Scriptures, YHWH was understood to be the personal name of God.[6]

The Lord of the Spirits is not the only one to possess the Divine Name according to the Parables. Beginning with the second parable, Enoch is given a vision that serves as the reader's introduction to the "Son of Man":

> [46:1] And there I saw one who had a head of days, and his head (was) white like wool; and with him (there was) another, whose face had the appearance of a man, and his face (was) full of grace, like one of the angels. [2] And I asked one of the holy angels who went with me, and showed me all the secrets, about that Son of Man, who he was, and whence he was, (and) why he went with the Head of Days. [3] And he answered me and said to me: "This is the Son of Man who has righteousness, and with whom righteousness dwells; he will reveal all the treasures of that which is secret, for the Lord of

---

3. M. Black, "Two Unusual Nomina Dei in the Second Vision of Enoch," in *The New Testament Age: Essays in Honor of Bo Reicke*, ed. William C. Weinrich, 2 vols. (Macon, Ga.: Mercer University Press, 1984), 1:53-59.

4. See the phrase "the *name* of the Lord of Spirits" in 1 En 38:2; 39:7, 9, 14; 40:4, 6; 41:2, 8; 43:4; 45:1, 2, 3; 46:7; 47:2; 48:7, 10; 50:2, 3; 53:6; 55:4; 61:3, 9, 11, 13; 63:7; 67:8.

5. Concerning the significance and use of the Divine Name in first-century Judaism, see S. M. McDonough, *YHWH at Patmos: Rev 1:4 in Its Hellenistic and Early Jewish Setting*, WUNT II.107 (Tübingen: Mohr Siebeck, 1999), esp. 58-122.

6. K. van der Toorn, "Yahweh," in *Dictionary of Deities and Demons of the Bible*, ed. K. van der Toorn, B. Becking, and P. W. van der Horst (Leiden: Brill, 1995), 1711-30.

Spirits has chosen him, and through uprightness his lot has surpassed all before the Lord of the Spirits forever."[7]

Although the characters are those of Dan 7, the setting of eschatological triumph in Daniel is not the scene here; that setting inspired the depiction of the Son of Man in 1 En 69:26-29. This scene is emphasizing the existence of the hidden Son of Man as the Chosen One long before he will be revealed to all in the latter days. Furthermore, the language of this text makes it clear that the author understood the "one like a son of man" in Dan 7 to be none other than the Glory of YHWH who was seen by Ezekiel (1:26-28): "whose face had *the appearance of a man*" (1 En 46:1).

Crucial for this study is the depiction of the Son of Man that follows in 1 En 48. Far from being a scene of eschatological triumph inspired by Dan 7, this scene depicts the Son of Man as a preexistent being who was given a special name by the Lord of the Spirits in the primal "hour" *before* creation began: "At that hour, that Son of Man *was named by the name,* in the presence of the Lord of the Spirits, the Before-Time; even before the creation of the sun and the moon, before the creation of the stars, he *was named by the name* in the presence of the Lord of the Spirits" (48:2-3).[8]

Although this scene is certainly related to the naming of the servant in Isa 49:1, the Isaiah text has been reinterpreted by changing the setting of the naming: it does not take place at the calling of the servant from the womb, but is done *prior to creation.*[9] In 1 Enoch "the name" by which the Son of Man "was named" appears to be the Divine Name of the Lord of the Spirits because there are numerous references to "the name of the Lord of the Spirits" throughout the Parables.[10] Especially noteworthy is the description that follows in this scene: "All those who dwell on earth *shall fall and worship before him* [the Son of Man]; they shall *glorify, bless, and sing the name of the Lord of the Spirits*" (48:5). They will use the name of the Lord of the Spirits in worshiping the Son of Man because *both* possess the same Divine Name.

---

7. This translation is that of M. A. Knibb, *The Ethiopic Book of Enoch: A New Edition in the Light of the Aramaic Dead Sea Fragments,* 2 vols. (Oxford: Clarendon, 1978), 2:131-32.

8. This translation is that of E. Isaac in *The Old Testament Pseudepigrapha,* ed. James H. Charlesworth, 2 vols. (Garden City, N.Y.: Doubleday, 1983, 1985), 1:35, but incorporates his literal rendering "named by the Name" in place of "was given a name"; see n. 48b.

9. Similar to Isa 49:1, Micah states that the eschatological deliverer will feed his flock "in the majesty of the Name of YHWH, his Elohim" (5:4).

10. Although there is clear testimony that this name is possessed before creation by the Son of Man, it should be noted that an enigmatic discussion about the Evil One revealing this name to Michael and placing it in his hand (69:14-15) introduces the verses that describe this name as the source of creation (69:16-26).

## The Name of the Son of Man in the Parables of Enoch

The fulfillment of this bold promise is depicted in the eschatological enthronement scene near the conclusion of 1 En 69: "And they [the righteous] blessed, glorified, and extolled (the Lord) on account of the fact that the name of that (Son of) Man was revealed to them" (69:26). The significance of the revealing of the name of the Son of Man becomes readily apparent when one sees the relationship between the Divine Name, the oath used in creation, and the name of the Son of Man in 1 En 69.[11] Immediately preceding the dramatic revelation of the name of the Son of Man to the righteous, 1 Enoch elaborately ascribes the creation and its sustenance to this "powerful and strong" oath (69:14):

[16]  And these are the secrets of this oath [i.e., the Divine Name]:
Through his oath the firmament and the heavens were suspended before the world was created and forever.
[17]  And through it the earth was founded upon the waters; and from the secret recesses of the mountains comes sweet water, for the creation of the world and unto eternity.
[18]  And through that oath the sea was created and its foundations; for the time of its wrath he placed for it the sand as a barrier, and it does not pass beyond its boundary from creation of the world to eternity.
[19]  And through that oath are the depths made firm and abide and do not move from their place from eternity to eternity.
[20]  And through that oath the sun and the moon complete their course, and do not deviate from their ordinance from eternity to eternity.
[21]  And through that oath the stars complete their course, and he calls them by their names, and they answer him from eternity to eternity.
[22]  And likewise with regard to the waters, to their winds, and to all spirits and their course from all regions of spirits.
[23]  And there are kept the storehouses of the thunder-peals and the flashes of the lightning; and there are kept the storehouses of the hail and of the hoar-frost, and the storehouses of the storm-cloud, and the storehouses of the rain and of the dew.
[24]  And all those who give thanks and praise before the Lord of the Spirits, and glorify (him) with all their power; and their sustenance is in all (their) thanksgiving; they will praise and glorify and extol the Name

---

11. Regarding the relationship of this chapter to mystical contemplation of the Divine Name, see D. C. Olson, *Enoch: A New Translation* (North Richland Hills, Tex.: BIBAL, 2004), 128-31 (esp. 270-73).

of the Lord of the Spirits for ever and ever.
[25] And this oath is binding upon them;
And by it they will be kept, and they will keep to their paths,
And their course will not be spoiled.[12]

This description of the cosmogenic power of the Divine Name reflects similar understandings of the Divine Name as power in contemporary Jewish and Christian literature, even as the word used in creation.[13]

There is one other text in 1 En 37–71 that discusses the name of the Son of Man: "[70.1] Afterwards it came to pass that the immortal name of that Son of Man was exalted in the presence of the Lord of Spirits above all those who live on earth. [2] He was raised aloft on a chariot of wind, and his name became a household word."[14] This text serves as a prologue to Enoch's transformative ascent and identification as the Son of Man described in chap. 71. Here the ascent of Enoch is described as the exalting of "the immortal name of that Son of Man." As 1 En 69:26 states, the eschatological revelation of the identity of the Son of Man includes the revelation of his true name.

Three conclusions from the evidence presented above are especially important. First, although Dan 7 and Ezek 1 are foundational to the description of the Son of Man in the Parables, 1 Enoch takes the Son of Man's presence with the Ancient of Days back to before creation. Second, 1 Enoch strengthens the identification of the Ancient of Days and the Son of Man within the mystery of the one YHWH by teaching that they share the one Divine Name. Third, the understanding of the significance of this name is greatly enhanced by the elaborate description of the power of the Divine Name ("oath") given in 1 En 69.

## The One Who Shares the Divine Name in the Literature of Ancient Israel, Second Temple Judaism, and First-Century Christianity

The testimony concerning the Divine Name of the Son of Man found in the Parables of 1 Enoch is by no means unique, but is visible in other literature of

---

12. This is the translation of M. Black, *The Book of Enoch, or, I Enoch: A New English Edition with Commentary and Textual Notes*, SVTP 7 (Leiden: Brill, 1985).

13. For example: Ps 124:8; Pr Man 2-3; Jub 36:7; 3 En 13:1; Heb 1:3; 1 Clem 59:8; Herm Sim 9.14.5; see also J. E. Fossum, *The Name of God and the Angel of the Lord: Samaritan and Jewish Concepts of Intermediation and the Origin of Gnosticism*, WUNT 36 (Tübingen: Mohr Siebeck, 1985), 77-84.

14. This is the translation of Olson, *Enoch*, 132-33; see his note on the challenges of the manuscript tradition here. For an argument supporting chaps. 70–71 as an original part of the Parables (and not a later appendix), see VanderKam, "Righteous One," 182-83.

## The Name of the Son of Man in the Parables of Enoch

the period.[15] If the Divine Name cannot be separated from the reality of YHWH, then how could Jews who confessed the Shema identify a second figure with this name? Significant antecedents of this phenomenon are the Pentateuch traditions where the Divine Name is the possession of the visible image of YHWH in various theophanies.[16] One of the places where this is made very clear is when YHWH promises Moses that he will send "an angel" before Israel on their journey from Sinai to Canaan: "Behold, I send an angel in front of you, to guard you on the way and to bring you to the place that I have prepared. Be attentive to him and listen to his voice; do not rebel against him, for he will not pardon your transgression; for *my name is in him*. But if you listen attentively to his voice and do all that I say, then I will be an enemy to your enemies and an adversary to your adversaries" (Exod 23:20-22).

The need for some distinction between YHWH and his visible form arises from the paradox that YHWH appears in some form on many occasions, yet one cannot see YHWH and live (Exod 33:20). A delicate distinction between YHWH and his visible form is often expressed in theophanic texts by the use of another title, such as מַלְאָךְ ("angel" or "messenger") in Exod 23:20. The status and authority of the various theophanic forms of YHWH are usually expressed in the description of his appearance, words, or actions. Exod 23:20-22 communicates the identity of this "angel" especially through noting his possession of the Divine Name; YHWH says, "my name is in him." This text testifies that a figure that has some independence from YHWH can still share in his being through the possession of the Divine Name (i.e., a divine hypostasis).[17] If this "angel" has the name YHWH in him, he can be understood to be YHWH in a visible form. The divine identity of this "angel" is further communicated by mention that he has the authority to absolve and speak as YHWH (23:21-22).[18]

This phenomenon is not limited to isolated texts in the Pentateuch that

---

15. For a more extensive discussion, see Fossum, *The Name of God and the Angel of the Lord*, and the essays collected in J. E. Fossum, *The Image of the Invisible God: Essays on the Influence of Jewish Mysticism on Early Christology*, NTOA 30 (Göttingen: Vandenhoeck & Ruprecht, 1995).

16. Even when there is not an overt reference to the Divine Name (e.g., Exod 23:20-22), the question about the name of the visible manifestation of YHWH is asked in several OT theophanies (e.g., Judg 13:17-18).

17. Exod 23:20-22 is a very significant text among the so-called Angel of the Lord traditions because of this overt mention of the possession of the Divine Name. Most texts that refer to the Angel of the Lord figure depict him as a brief manifestation that is indistinguishable from God. For further discussion of these traditions, see C. A. Gieschen, *Angelomorphic Christology: Antecedents and Early Evidence*, AGJU 42 (Leiden: Brill, 1998), 51-69. For a defense of "hypostasis" nomenclature, see esp. 36-45.

18. See Fossum, *Name of God*, 86.

Charles A. Gieschen

mention YHWH appearing as an angel. Another example of a divine hypostasis in the OT possessing the Divine Name is שֵׁם ("the Name") or שֵׁם יהוה ("the Name of YHWH") who dwelt in the temple as mentioned especially in Deuteronomy, the so-called Deuteronomistic History, and Jeremiah.[19] Contrary to Gerhard von Rad's modern abstraction of this Name theology as a "theologically sublime idea" that "is replacing the old crude idea of Jahweh's presence," the texts themselves depict the Name as a theophanic form who manifested the presence of YHWH in a manner similar to the Angel of YHWH, the Glory of YHWH, and the Word of YHWH.[20] These traditions may have contributed to biblical writers using "the Name" as the subject of divine actions in other texts (e.g., Isa 30:27 and Prov 18:10). Furthermore, הַשֵּׁם is often used in rabbinic literature as a substitute for the Tetragrammaton rather than Adonai.[21]

Second Temple Jewish literature evinces considerable interest in the Divine Name and the theophanic figure who possesses it.[22] A significant aspect of the understanding of the Divine Name in this literature is an emphasis on its power. This name is not another word among the myriad of words in the human language, but is the most powerful word of the world, even the very word that God spoke to bring the world into existence (Ps 124:8). Jubilees, a second century B.C.E. Jewish text, testifies to the cosmogenic power ascribed to the Divine Name as it describes Isaac calling his sons to swear an oath by the name that is responsible for all creation: "And now I will make you swear by the great oath — because there is not an oath which is greater than it, by *the glorious and honored and great and splendid and amazing and mighty name* which created heaven and earth and everything together — that you will fear and worship him" (Jub 36:7).

A similar tradition is found in 3 Enoch, a fifth or sixth century C.E. Jewish mystical text preserved in Hebrew that purports to be a record of the mystical ascent visions of Rabbi Ishmael, one of the second-generation Tannaim (120-140 C.E.). 3 Enoch contains an account that depicts "the Holy One" (God) writ-

---

19. See O. Grether, *Name und Wort Gottes im Alten Testament*, BZAW 64 (Giessen: Toepelmann, 1934), 1-58, and T. Mettinger, *The Dethronement of Sabaoth: Studies in the Shem and Kabod Theologies*, ConBOT 18 (Lund: CWK Gleerup, 1982), 129-32. For a summary of research on Name theology, see I. Wilson, *Out of the Midst of Fire: Divine Presence in Deuteronomy*, SBLDS 151 (Atlanta: Scholars, 1995), 1-15.

20. G. von Rad, *Studies in Deuteronomy*, trans. D. Stalker (London: SCM, 1953), 39. Wilson defends Deuteronomy's presentation of a tangible divine presence conveyed by the Name dwelling in the temple; see his *Out of the Midst*, esp. 199-217. For further discussion of the interrelationship of these theophanic traditions in later interpretation, see Gieschen, *Angelomorphic Christology*, 51-123.

21. H. Beitenhard, "ὄνομα," in *TDNT* 5:269.

22. See Fossum, *Name of God*, 239-338, and Gieschen, *Angelomorphic Christology*, 124-86.

ing "the letters by which heaven and earth were created" upon a crown (13:1) that he places upon Metatron: "He set it upon my head and he called me, *'the lesser YHWH'* in the presence of his whole household in the height, as it is written, *'My name is in him'*" (12:5). The overt reference to Exod 23:21 demonstrates the ongoing influence of the Divine Name angel tradition: Metatron is depicted as the theophanic angel who possesses the Divine Name that is responsible for all creation and is even called "the Lesser YHWH."[23]

The depiction of Yahoel in the Apocalypse of Abraham, usually dated to the late first century C.E., is another striking example of the powerful Divine Name possessed by a theophanic figure:[24]

> And while I was still face down on the ground, I heard the voice speaking, "Go, Yahoel of the same name, *through the mediation of my Ineffable Name*, consecrate this man for me and strengthen him against his trembling." (10:3)

> I am Yahoel and I was called so by him who causes those with me on the seventh expanse, on the firmament, to shake, *a Power through the medium of his Ineffable Name in me.* (10:8)

This undeniable identification of Yahoel with the angel who bears the Divine Name is made even more obvious with his doubly divine name (YH + EL). His significance in this document is augmented by an elaborate physical description that identifies him with the Glory of Ezek 1:26-28 (Apoc Ab 11:2-3). Another important depiction of a named angel that possesses the Divine Name is Israel in the extant fragments of the Prayer of Joseph.[25] This angel is "the firstborn of every living thing" who "tabernacles among men" as the man Jacob.

Philo of Alexandria, writing in the first half of the first century C.E., also evinces considerable interest in the theophanic angel of Exod 23:20-22 who possesses the Divine Name, and even uses him as the foundation of his teaching about ὁ λόγος ("the Word"). Note especially how closely "Name" and "Word" are related: "But if there be any as yet unfit to be called a son of God, let him press to take his place under God's First-born, *the Word,* who holds the eldership among the angels, an archangel as it were. And many names are his for he is called: the Beginning, *the Name of God, Word (of God),* the Man after His Im-

---

23. 3 En 48:1 (rec. B) records the contrasting title, "the Greater YHWH," as one of the seventy "divine names"; see *The Old Testament Pseudepigrapha,* 1:310.

24. See further Fossum, *Name of God,* 318-21, and Gieschen, *Angelomorphic Christology,* 142-44.

25. See esp. Gieschen, *Angelomorphic Christology,* 137-42.

245

age, and 'the One that sees,' namely Israel" (*De confusione linguarum* 146). Nor should it be assumed that this identification of the Divine Name angel traditions of the OT as the Word is the invention of Philo under the influence of Hellenistic philosophy. Other pre-Christian Jewish evidence of this includes the identification of the theophanic Angel of YHWH who speaks to Moses from the burning bush in Exod 3:4 as θεῖος λόγος ("Divine Word") by Ezekiel the Tragedian in the second century B.C.E. (*Exagoge* 96-99) and the identification of the Destroying Angel of the Tenth Plague as ὁ παντοδύναμός σου λόγος ("your all-powerful Word") in the first century B.C.E. Wisdom of Solomon (18:14-16; cf. 1 Chron 21:15-16).

The Gospel of John, which identifies Jesus frequently as the Son of Man, also depicts him as the embodiment of the Divine Name of the Father, to the extent that Jesus even prays: πάτερ, δόξασόν σου τὸ ὄνομα ("Father, glorify *your Name*"; 12:28).[26] This is not simply a pious prayer that God's name be glorified through Christ's sacrifice; it is the identification of Jesus as the one who possesses the Divine Name. This indicates that he can simply be identified as "the Name," much like the visible manifestations of YHWH of Deuteronomy and Jeremiah. This personal identification of the Name as Jesus is supported by the parallel announcement that comes shortly before this prayer: "The hour has come *for the Son of Man* to be glorified" (12:23). The "Son of Man," therefore, is also known as "Your [the Father's] Name."[27] That "Your Name" could be understood in this way by the intended readers of this Gospel is apparent from the use of "the Name" as a title — indeed, the *only* title — of Jesus in 3 John: "For they departed on behalf of the Name [ὑπὲρ γὰρ τοῦ ὀνόματος ἐξῆλθον] and have accepted nothing from the heathen" (v. 7).

The Gospel of John most clearly presents him as the possessor of the Divine Name in the prayer of Jesus at the close of the farewell discourse (John 17):

> I revealed *your name* to those you gave me from the world. (v. 6a)

> Holy Father, protect them in *your name* that you have given me, in order that they be one, as we are one. While I was with them, I protected them in *your name* that you have given me. (vv. 11b-12a)

---

26. John identifies Jesus as the Son of Man at crucial places in his narrative: 1:51; 3:13-14; 5:27; 6:27, 53, 62; 8:28; 9:35; 12:34; and 13:31.

27. The relationship between this Divine Name tradition and the prominent Son of Man sayings in John can be understood in light of traditions like those in 1 En 37–71 discussed above. It is apparent that this Gospel challenges some of the Jewish understandings of the Son of Man figure in its portrait of Jesus; see R. Bauckham, *God Crucified: Monotheism and Christology in the New Testament* (Grand Rapids: Eerdmans, 1998), 63-79.

*The Name of the Son of Man in the Parables of Enoch*

I made *your name* known to them and will continue to make it known. (v. 26)

A few conclusions can be drawn from these petitions in John. First, the repeated use of the personal pronoun makes it evident that the name discussed here is the Divine Name of the Father, to whom this prayer is directed.[28] Second, the Divine Name was given to the Son (17:11b). Based upon the testimony in this prayer that the Son received the Father's Glory before the foundation of the world (17:24), the giving of the Divine Name is probably also understood to have taken place before creation.[29] Third, Jesus has made the Divine Name, normally a hidden mystery in this world, known to his disciples. Fourth, the Divine Name that was revealed to the disciples by Jesus has protecting power (17:11b). This power is especially reassuring to the disciples because earlier in the farewell discourse Jesus gives some emphasis to how much they will suffer "on account of my name" (15:21), a theme also found in Acts (5:41; 9:16; 15:26; 21:13).

The book of Revelation, which uses the "one like a son of man" designation twice for Christ (1:12; 14:14), also identifies Christ as the possessor of the Divine Name in the description of the triumphant warrior on the white horse in 19:11-16.[30] This text presents Christ as the possessor of a mysterious name that only he knows: "He has *a name written on him that no one except he himself knows.* He is dressed in a robe dipped in blood and *his name is called the Word of God*" (19:12b-13). Several Jewish texts speak of the Divine Name as the hidden or secret name.[31] Support for interpreting the mysterious name in 19:12 as the Divine Name is found in the next sentence where John notes that the (known) name of the rider is ὁ λόγος τοῦ θεοῦ ("the Word of God"). Texts noted above

---

28. Many commentators argue mistakenly that here "name" denotes the "revealed character and nature of God" rather than the Divine Name; see C. H. Williams, *I Am He: The Interpretation of 'Anî Hû' in Jewish and Early Christian Literature*, WUNT II.113 (Tübingen: Mohr Siebeck, 2000), 280 n. 85.

29. This conclusion is also based upon the identification of the preexistent Word as the Divine Name in both the prologue and the farewell prayer; see Gieschen, *Angelomorphic Christology*, 271-80. The tradition of giving the Divine Name to the Son of Man prior to creation is already found in 1 En 48:2-3, as discussed above.

30. For a more complete discussion, see Gieschen, *Angelomorphic Christology*, 252-56.

31. For example, see Gen 32:29; Judg 13:17; 1 En 69:14; Jos Asen 15:12; Prayer of Joseph; Gos Thom 13; Gos Truth 38:7-40:29; and Gos Phil 54:5. The assertion that the name written on him "no one except he himself knows" is hyperbolic "insider" language, since Revelation states the saints are sealed with the name of Christ and bear it on their foreheads. As in John 17 where Jesus states that he revealed his (hidden) name to his disciples, the enlightened reader of Revelation is expected to know (by revelation) this secret name that only Christ knows (by nature).

testify that "the Word" or "the Word of God" was a title sometimes given to the theophanic angel who possesses the Divine Name.[32] The understanding that Christ is called "the Word of God" here because he possesses the Divine Name responsible for creation is substantiated by the observation that the "faithful and true witness" (19:11; 3:14) is earlier given the title "the Beginning of God's Creation" (3:14).[33]

Further support for interpreting the mysterious name of Rev 19:12 as the Divine Name is found in the other references to the name(s) of God in Revelation:

> He who conquers, I will make him a pillar in the temple of my God; never will he go out of it, and I will write on him *the name of my God*, and *the name of the city of my God*, the new Jerusalem that comes down from my God out of heaven, and *my own new name*. (3:12)

> Then I looked, and behold, on Mount Zion stood the Lamb, and with him a hundred and forty-four thousand who had *his name* and *his Father's name* written on their foreheads. (14:1)

> There will no more be anything accursed, but the throne of God and of the Lamb will be in it, and his servants will worship him; they will see his face, and *his name* will be on their foreheads. (22:3-4)

On the basis of these texts, some assert that the saints receive three names.[34] A much simpler answer to the portraits painted here is to see that the name of God and the name of the new Jerusalem is the same name possessed by the Son.[35] Therefore, the saints have *one* name on their foreheads: the Divine Name.[36]

---

32. See esp. Wis 18:14-25 and Isa 63:1-14.
33. Gieschen, *Angelomorphic Christology*, 255 n. 36.
34. For example, R. C. H. Lenski, *Revelation* (Columbus, Ohio: Lutheran Book Concern, 1935), 152.
35. For the church as a manifestation of the Holy Spirit, see the Shepherd of Hermas, especially Sim 9.1.1.
36. This understanding that Jesus possesses the Divine Name is also affirmed by the sharing of divine titles between Christ and God (the Father) that are closely related to the Divine Name; see R. Bauckham, *The Climax of Prophecy: Studies in the Book of Revelation* (Edinburgh: T. & T. Clark, 1993), 30-35.

## Conclusion

This brief overview of related traditions, therefore, points to several things that are helpful for our understanding of "the Name" of the Son of Man in the Parables of Enoch. First, there is testimony that the Divine Name was the possession of YHWH's visible image, such as the divine hypostasis who is identified as the Angel of YHWH or the Name of YHWH in the Pentateuch. Second, the Divine Name angel tradition provided some influence on figures in later Jewish literature like the Word and Wisdom. Third, there is evidence that the Divine Name is a potent reality, even the word that brought the world into existence and sustains it. Finally, both the Gospel of John and the book of Revelation provide contemporary first-century evidence of Christian groups who saw the importance of identifying the Son of Man as the possessor of the Divine Name.

Why is there testimony in the Parables about the Son of Man's possession of the Divine Name? The presence of a "second" divine figure in Dan 7 posed challenges for later interpreters.[37] The possession of the Divine Name was a theological category that became vital to faithful depictions of YHWH; by it a clear — and complex — monotheism is confessed. If the Son of Man shares the Name of the Lord of the Spirits, he can be identified within the mystery of the one God even though he has distinct personhood, especially as evident in the eventual revelation that the patriarch Enoch is the Son of Man (1 En 71:14). Without the clear identification of the Son of Man within the mystery of YHWH by means of his possession of the Divine Name, his enthronement and worship depicted in 1 En 69 could have been considered idolatry.[38]

---

37. See esp. A. Segal, *Two Powers in Heaven: Early Rabbinic Reports about Christianity and Gnosticism*, SJLA 25 (Leiden: Brill, 1977).

38. For further discussion, see R. Bauckham, "The Throne of God and the Worship of Jesus," in *The Jewish Roots of Christological Monotheism: Papers from the St. Andrews Conference on the Historical Origins of the Worship of Jesus*, ed. C. C. Newman, J. R. Davila, and G. S. Lewis, SJSJ 63 (Leiden: Brill, 1999), 57-60.

# "The Coming of the Righteous One" in Acts and 1 Enoch

*Gerbern S. Oegema*

This paper aims at a study of the tradition- and reception-historical context of the expression ἡ ἔλευσις τοῦ δικαίου, "the coming of the Righteous One," found in Acts 7:52, the only passage in the New Testament where it appears — by comparing it to a similar expression found in 1 En 89:52, and in other Jewish and Christian writings of the same period. Whereas the expression as such is a hapax legomenon in both writings, the broader tradition-historical context reveals quite an interesting range of connotations, which may also throw more light on the latter-day figures found in the Parables of Enoch. With this in mind, the following essay has been written.

The context or framework in which the expression ἡ ἔλευσις τοῦ δικαίου appears is in that of a literary genre. Acts 7:52 is found in one of the two main historical accounts in Luke-Acts, namely, in Acts 7:2b-53, where the *Auctor ad Theophilum* takes up the well-known literary genre (or subgenre) of the "summary of the history of biblical Israel." It is also found in such texts as 1 Sam 12:8-13, Deut 26:5-10, Ps 105:7-44, Ezek 20:5-29, and 1 En 85:3–90:38 as well. Therefore, also the framework of the most important parallel to Acts 7:52, namely, 1 En 89:52, appears to be a summary of the history of Israel.

As for the relation between Acts 7:2-53 and 1 En 89, Luke has used, according to Joachim Jeska,[1] the Greek version of 1 En 89:10-53 as a model for his "summary of the history of Israel" by adopting its structure and sequence of

---

1. J. Jeska, *Die Geschichte Israels in der Sicht des Lukas: Apg 7,2b-53 und 13,17-25 im Kontext antik-jüdischer Summarien der Geschichte Israels,* FRLANT 195 (Göttingen: Vandenhoeck & Ruprecht, 2001).

events and especially by placing the killing of the prophets after the building of the temple, which is found only in 1 En 89:50-52 and Acts 7:50-52, but not in any other contemporaneous writings. Luke then has further edited his model in such a way that it fits into the overall theology of his work, especially by replacing Elijah with Jesus. Central in both passages is the expression and concept of "the coming of the Righteous One."[2]

## The "Righteous One" in Acts 7:52 and 1 Enoch 89:52

Acts 7:52 reads in English according to the NRSV: "Which of the prophets did your ancestors not persecute? They killed those who foretold *the coming of the Righteous One,* and now you have become his betrayers and murderers." The problem with the expression ἡ ἔλευσις τοῦ δικαίου is that ἡ ἔλευσις is a hapax legomenon in the New Testament and that only ὁ δίκαιος occurs more often. Therefore, the whole expression as a combination of the two parts appears nowhere else in the New Testament.[3] If we therefore want to look for parallels, we have to look, first of all, for all possible early Jewish and Christian parallels of the whole expression ἡ ἔλευσις τοῦ δικαίου outside of the New Testament.

According to Matthew Black, the whole verse of Acts 7:52 is an example of one of the many cases of asyndeton in the Gospels and Acts, the lack of a connecting particle between sentences being far more characteristic of Aramaic than of Greek. For this reason, it is mostly found in the sayings and parables of Jesus, as well as here in the speech of Stephen.[4] In Aramaic the phrase "the coming of the Righteous One" may have been: ביאת הצדיק (and in Syriac: דזדיקא מאתיתה), although the Aramaic word for "(the) righteous (one)" is קשיט/

---

2. Our main observation is therefore to be related to the end of Acts 7, which has parallels to 1 Enoch but not to Pseudo-Philo, the other main parallel to Acts 7, although all three passages offer a remarkably similar summary of the history of Israel. The social, religious, and political setting of Pseudo-Philo may explain why it has no eschatological figure at the end of the history of Israel; the existence and partial similarity of an eschatological figure in Acts and 1 Enoch, however, ask for further investigation. See further Jeska, *Die Geschichte Israels in der Sicht des Lukas.* See E. Reinmuth, *Pseudo-Philo und Lukas: Studien zum Liber Antiquitatum Biblicarum und seiner Bedeutung für die Interpretation des lukanische Doppelwerks,* WUNT 74 (Tübingen: Mohr-Siebeck, 1994).

3. See W. Bauer, *A Greek-English Lexicon of the New Testament and Other Early Christian Literature,* 2nd ed. (Chicago and London: University of Chicago Press, 1979), 195-96.

4. M. Black, *An Aramaic Approach to the Gospels and Acts: With an Appendix on the Son of Man by Geza Vermes,* 3rd ed. (Oxford: Clarendon, 1967; reprint, 1979), 55-61.

קשטה (Ethiopic: *sadqa*).[5] We will therefore also have to look for parallels to the Aramaic phrase.[6]

The Ethiopic rendition of 1 En 89:52 reads in an English translation: "However, one of them was not killed but escaped alive and fled away; he cried aloud to the sheep, and they wanted to kill him, but the Lord of the sheep rescued him from the sheep and caused him to ascend to me and settle down."[7]

The "one of them" is Elijah; the "Lord of the sheep" is God; and the "I," to whom the "one of them" ascends, is Enoch. That the "one of them" can be identified only with Elijah is (1) because according to the biblical account Elijah ascended into heaven, where God and Enoch also are, according to the book of 1 Enoch, and (2) this Elijah is furthermore characterized as one of the prophets, whom (3) the "sheep" (= the people of Israel) wanted to kill, but who (4) could escape alive and flee away, and who (5) cried aloud to the sheep, which tried to kill them, but who (6) is rescued by the Lord.

If one compares this narrative account with the one in Acts 7:52, it is obvious that the author of Luke-Acts could easily identify this Elijah figure with Jesus, who (1) according to Acts 1:9-11 ascended into heaven, (2) was inter alia understood to be the last of the prophets (see Luke 7:16-26), whom (3) some of the people of Israel wanted to kill (see Luke 22–23), but who (4) was resurrected from the dead, (5) spoke to his followers, and (6) ascended to his Father in heaven (see Luke 24). For this reason, not because of the use of the expression itself, but because of the similarity of the concept behind it, a comparison of both passages will be of special interest.

## Similar Concepts in Acts and 1 Enoch

Even though 1 Enoch, especially the Animal Apocalypse (1 En 83–90) as well as the Book of Parables (1 En 37–71), offers the largest and most impressive number of parallels to the New Testament[8] in a general way, this also holds true in

---

5. See the Aramaic-Greek-Ethiopic glossary in J. T. Milik, *The Books of Enoch: Aramaic Fragments of Qumrân Cave 4* (Oxford: Clarendon 1976), 392 and 402.

6. See on this my forthcoming article, "The Coming of the Righteous One in 1 Enoch, Qumran and the New Testament."

7. Translation according to E. Isaac, "1 (Ethiopic Apocalypse of) Enoch," in *The Old Testament Pseudepigrapha*, ed. J. H. Charlesworth, 2 vols. (Garden City, N.Y.: Doubleday, 1983, 1985), 1:5-89 (here 67).

8. See G. S. Oegema, *Apokalypsen*, in *JSHRZ* VI.1.5 (Gütersloh: Gütersloher Verlagshaus, 2001), on 1 Enoch, and G. W. E. Nickelsburg, *1 Enoch 1: A Commentary on the Book of 1 Enoch 1–36, 81–108*, vol. 1, Hermeneia (Minneapolis: Fortress, 2001); see here for further literature.

*"The Coming of the Righteous One" in Acts and 1 Enoch*

many details. One of the main characteristics and names of the eschatological figure in the Parables of Enoch is "Son of Man," and precisely this title is also found in the book of Acts, the only instance outside the Gospels, namely, Acts 7:56.[9]

Therefore, the whole of Acts 7:52-56 should be seen in the light of the influence of the Enochic "Son of Man" with special attention for Jesus' elevation and enthronement, which Luke, according to Jeska, may very well have conceptualized in analogy or competition with 1 Enoch.[10] Other expressions or possibly equivalents of or associations with "the Righteous One" are "the Beloved One" and, of course, Elijah himself.

Nevertheless, if one looks for parallels in the commentaries on Acts, only very few give a clue of the possible tradition-historical background of Acts 7:52.[11] Many do refer to ὁ δίκαιος in Acts 3:14 (ὑμεῖς δὲ τὸν ἅγιον καὶ δίκαιον ἠρνήσασθε καὶ ᾐτήσασθε ἄνδρα φονέα χαρισθῆναι ὑμῖν).[12] From there further parallels to the "Holy and Righteous One" (as a well-known biblical and later also messianic title) are easily found, so, for instance, in Gen 6:9 (αὗται δὲ αἱ γενέσεις Νῶε. Νῶε ἄνθρωπος δίκαιος τέλειος ὢν ἐν τῇ γενεᾷ αὐτοῦ τῷ θεῷ εὐηρέστησεν Νῶε) and 2 Kings 4:9 (καὶ εἶπεν ἡ γυνὴ πρὸς τὸν ἄνδρα αὐτῆς ἰδοὺ δὴ ἔγνων ὅτι ἄνθρωπος τοῦ θεοῦ ἅγιος οὗτος διαπορεύεται ἐφ' ἡμᾶς διὰ παντός), as far as the Tanakh is concerned.

From the Apocrypha, Pseudepigrapha, and New Testament one should mention Sir 44:17, Mark 6:20, as well as 1 En 51:3, 61:5, and 62:7.[13] However, references to ἡ ἔλευσις or ἡ ἔλευσις τοῦ δικαίου are almost never mentioned in the commentaries, although they do exist in various forms and places, as will be shown in the following.

---

9. "'Look,' he said, 'I see the heavens opened and the Son of Man standing at the right hand of God!'"; cf. the logion in Luke 22:69. See outside of the Gospels and Acts also Rev 1:13; 14:14; Heb 2:6; as well as 1 Enoch.

10. Jeska, *Geschichte*, 286-92.

11. The commentaries on Acts investigated are C. K. Barrett, *A Critical and Exegetical Commentary on the Acts of the Apostles* (Edinburgh: T. & T. Clark, 1994-98); J. A. Fitzmyer, *The Acts of the Apostles: A New Translation with Introduction and Commentary* (New York: Doubleday, 1998); E. Jacquier, *Les Actes des Apôtres* (Paris: Victor Lecoffre, 1926); and R. C. Tannehill, *Luke* (Nashville: Abingdon, 1996). The commentary with the promising title by Hilary Le Cornu, *A Commentary on the Jewish Roots of Acts* (Jerusalem: Academon, 2003), offers little new material. Barrett, 377, and Fitzmyer, 385, both give a reference to the article of Kilpatrick (see below).

12. In Fitzmyer, *Acts, ad loc.;* Jacquier, *Actes,* 234; Le Cornu, *Commentary,* 368; et al.

13. Jacquier, *Actes,* 234, and Fitzmyer, *Acts,* 285-86. Nickelsburg, *1 Enoch 1,* however, offers neither parallels to nor comments on 1 En 89:52 and does not mention Acts 7:52.

*Gerbern S. Oegema*

## "The Righteous One" in 1 Enoch and in the Qumran Writings

If one looks for examples of the expression הצדיק in the sectarian writings found in Qumran, one finds numerous passages, such as CD 4:7; 20:20; 1QpHab 1:12; 11Q11 5:11-12; et al., whereas for the expression of הצדק one finds in total forty-two examples in many further fragments. In addition, a limited number of Qumran writings use the expression בא or בוא for the coming of an eschatological figure, so, for instance, 1QS 9:11 (בוא נביא) and 4QPatr 1:1-3/ 4Q252 5:1-7 (בוא משיח הצדק).[14]

These and other passages in the Qumran writings, such as 4Q161 (4QpIs$^a$) 11-21 and 4QFlor (4Q174) 1:12, refer then to an expectation among the Qumran Essenes, namely, of the coming of one or more messiahs, a royal and a priestly messiah, who is sometimes accompanied by a latter-day prophet and/or Teacher of Righteousness/Righteous Teacher.[15]

However, the combination of הצדק and בוא is found only in 4Q252 5:3 and in 4Q215a fiii 6 and 10. Especially 4QPatr 1:1-3, now identified as 4Q252 5:1-7 with a script dating from the Herodian period, is of interest, as it contains the three central expressions "coming," "anointed," and "righteous." The passage is part of a longer text, which retells parts of Genesis, and is, one may state, the beginning of a summary of the history of Israel:

4Q252 5:3-4: ואל]פי ישראל המה הדגלים [[ ]] עד בוא משיח הצדק צמח
דויד. כי לו ולזרעו נתנה ברית מלכות עמו
עד דורות עולם אשר

In 4Q252 5:3-4 we are dealing with an eschatological setting of the coming of the Righteous One, who is furthermore called the shoot of David. An interesting parallel to the latter is found in 4QFlor (4Q174) 1:12 and 4QpIs$^a$ 11-21 as well as in the formulation "through it [the Shoot] will arise the rod of righteousness" in TJud 24:5-6, while PsSol 17:32 uses the three expressions "righteous," "king" and "anointed."[16]

The expression found in 4Q252: בוא משיח הצדק, also has a parallel in the Targum of Gen 49:10: בוא מלכה משיח, which replaces the Masoretic read-

---

14. See J. H. Charlesworth, *Graphic Concordance to the Dead Sea Scrolls* (Tübingen: J. C. B. Mohr; Louisville: Westminster John Knox, 1991).

15. See for this G. S. Oegema, *The Anointed and His People: Messianic Expectations from the Maccabees to Bar Kochba*, JSPSup 27 (Sheffield: Sheffield Academic, 1998), 98.

16. See for details G. S. Oegema, "Tradition-Historical Studies on 4Q252," in *Qumran-Messianism: Studies on the Messianic Expectations in the Dead Sea Scrolls*, ed. J. H. Charlesworth and G. S. Oegema (Tübingen: J. C. B. Mohr/Paul Siebeck, 1998), 170-72.

ing שילה עד כי־בוא in Gen 49:10.[17] It points to a clear messianic understanding as the tradition-historical context, in which the expression "the coming of the Righteous One" has to be placed.

This also holds true of the text known as 4QTime of Righteousness (4Q215a), where one reads in fragment ii, lines 6 and 10, about the coming of righteousness in the following formulation: "the age of peace has *arrived,* and the laws of truth, and testimony *of justice*" and "the dominion [of *justice*] of goodness *has arrived*" (בא קץ השלום וחושי האמת ותעודת [ה]צדק and [ — כיא בא ממשל הצדק הטוב וירם כסא ה]).

This text speaks about the coming of the dominion of justice or goodness, an age in which "he" "will raise the throne of ... and knowledge, etc." We are therefore clearly dealing with an ideal period (at the end) of history, called "the age of righteousness," a concept found both in the prophetic writings of the Hebrew Bible, such as Jer 46–51 and Ezek 7; in Qumran writings, such as 4Q252 and 4QSapiential Work A; as well as in 1 Enoch and Jubilees, but which, as far as the expression עד הצדק is concerned, is unparalleled.[18]

## 1 Enoch

| | |
|---|---|
| 1 En 89:52 | However, one of them was not killed but escaped alive and fled away; he cried aloud to the sheep, and they wanted to kill him, but the Lord of the sheep rescued him from the sheep and caused him to ascend to me and settle down. |

This passage is one of many passages in 1 En 1–36 and 81–108 in which a "Righteous One" plays a prominent role in an eschatological context. Other passages identify him with Noah (10:3-4), the sons of men (10:21), Elijah (89:52), someone risen (91:10), Enoch (92:1), the sons of righteousness (93:2), or a witness of righteousness (93:2). In all cases the authors speak about the future, or the eschaton, which itself — as eighth and ninth week — is also called the "time of righteousness" (as in 4Q215a).

Looking at the Qumran fragments of 1 Enoch, one can only confirm the above findings and thus the popularity of the expressions הצדיק and הצדק or

---

17. See Oegema, *Anointed,* 120-21.
18. See E. G. Chazon, "A Case of Mistaken Identity: Testament of Naphtali (4Q215) and Time of Righteousness (4Q215ᵃ)," in *The Provo International Conference on the Dead Sea Scrolls,* ed. D. W. Parry and E. Ulrich (Leiden: Brill, 1999), 113-21.

of derivations of the verb קשׁט in the Enochic literature (the righteous man; to become righteous; ways, paths, plant, and week of righteousness; scribe, witness, and sons of righteousness). One finds them in the Aramaic fragments of 1 En 10:3-4; 10:21–11:1; 12:4-6; 91:10, 11-17, 18-19; 92:1-2; 92:5–93:4; 93:9-10.[19]

Whereas the copies of 4Q252 date from the Herodian period and the date of 4Q215a is approximately the same (late Hasmonean–early Herodian),[20] 1 En 89:52 as part of 1 En 85–90 is dated by George Nickelsburg between the third century B.C.E. and 163 B.C.E.[21] We can say little about a possible reception of 1 En 89 in 4Q252 and 4Q215a, although the age of righteousness referred to in 4Q215a 10 may very well have an analogy in the eighth and ninth week of righteousness (שׁבוע קשׁוט) in 1 En 93:12-17.

Therefore, we can conclude only in a very general way that there exist tradition-historical links between all three writings and that parts of the book of 1 Enoch were well-known and often used in Qumran, as it was copied and interpreted there. This tradition-historical context of a number of expressions found in 4Q252 and 4Q215a can be dated between the second third of the first century B.C.E. and the first third of the first century C.E.,[22] thus bringing it in close proximity to the speech of Stephen, assuming the latter to be pre-Lukan. All three passages, 4Q252, 4Q215a, and 1 En 89:52, predate Acts 7:52 and can very well have been part of the tradition-historical background of Acts 7, and therefore have influenced it.

## ἡ ἔλευσις τοῦ δικαίου and Its Messianic Connotation

In returning to the central expression in Acts 7:52, it is important to refer to a much-quoted article from 1945, in which G. D. Kilpatrick gives a number of important parallels to ἡ ἔλευσις τοῦ δικαίου.[23] The author looked for parallels to the Greek word ἔλευσις, and found that in the New Testament the expression is found only in Acts 7:52. It is absent from the Septuagint, the other Greek versions of the Old Testament, 1 Enoch in its Greek fragments, the Psalms of Solomon, the Testaments of the Twelve Patriarchs, the Greek Apocalypse of Baruch, and the Apocalypse of Sedrach.

---

19. See Milik, *The Books of Enoch*.
20. See Chazon, "Case of Mistaken Identity," 110-23.
21. See *1 Enoch 1*, 360-61. See also P. Sacchi, *The History of the Second Temple Period* (Sheffield: Sheffield Academic, 2000), 174-80.
22. See Oegema, "Tradition-Historical Studies," 165-85, esp. 171.
23. G. D. Kilpatrick, "Acts VII.52 Ἔλευσις," *JTS* 46 (1945): 136-45.

*"The Coming of the Righteous One" in Acts and 1 Enoch*

However, early Christian literature frequently uses the expression, as in 1 Clem 17:1, Polycarp's To the Philippians 6:3, Irenaeus's *Against Heresies* 1.2, and Acts Phil 78. One also finds it in the Codex Bezae of Luke 21:7 and 23:42,[24] and, not mentioned by Kilpatrick, in Acts Thom 28.[25] Kilpatrick's overall conclusion is that "In all early Christian examples of ἔλευσις the word is used of the messianic coming and in four out of the six instances up to Irenaeus appears as one of a certain group of terms, indicated by spaced letters in the quotations given above, (1) a reference to the prophets, (2) a word denoting proclamation, usually some form or compound of κηρύσσειν, (3) ἔλευσις in a messianic sense, (4) a messianic title."[26]

To find an explanation for this phenomenon of an obviously messianic understanding of ἔλευσις in the second century C.E., Kilpatrick rules out the possibilities of the *testimonia,* suggested by Otto Michel in his book *Paulus und seine Bibel* of 1929,[27] and instead looks for another kind of Jewish or Christian source written in Greek and prior to Acts and 1 Clement. This he finds in two recensions of the Lives of the Prophets, namely, *Epiphanii Recensio Prior* (E') and *Dorothei Recensio* (D).[28]

It is clear now where we have to look for parallels of ἡ ἔλευσις and its tradition- and reception-historical context, namely, in the Pseudepigrapha from the period up to the beginning of the second century C.E. written or translated in Greek. Kilpatrick mentions the Hebrew and Coptic Apocalypse of Elijah (1:5-6), which refer to the coming of the Messiah, as well as the Ascension of Isaiah (3:13) and 4 Baruch (3:8), which speak about ἡ ἐξ-/συνέλευσις τοῦ ἀγαπητοῦ or τοῦ ἠγαπημένου.[29] Furthermore, ἡ ἔλευσις also appears in TestAbr (rec. A) 16, TJob (rec. M) 29, the Septuagint version (in some manuscripts) of 2 Sam 15:20 (ἡ ἐξέλευσίς σου), and Acts Phil 137, although in the latter examples without a messianic connotation.[30]

As far as the possible equivalent of ἔλευσις is concerned, namely, παρουσία, Kilpatrick mentions TJud 22:3, TLevi 8:14, TestAbr (A) 13 (bis), and

---

24. Kilpatrick, "Acts," 136.
25. Referred to by Jacquier, *Actes,* 234.
26. Kilpatrick, "Acts," 137.
27. Otto Michel, *Paulus und seine Bibel* (Gütersloh: Gütersloher Verlagshaus, 1929).
28. See also A.-M. Schwemer, *Vitae Prophetarum,* in *JSHRZ* I.7 (Gütersloh: Gütersloher Verlagshaus, 1997). However, the recensions are clearly tendentious and may not reflect the original text of the *Vitae Prophetarum.* Recension E contains "durchgehend einen sprachlich verbesserten und christlich redigierten Text," and recension D is characterized by a "Voranstellung von messianischen Testimonien zu den jeweiligen Schriftpropheten"; see 540-41.
29. Kilpatrick, "Acts," 140.
30. Kilpatrick, "Acts," 141. All references according to Kilpatrick. I was not able to see the Acts Phil 137. 4 Baruch = Paralipomena Jeremiou.

TSol (rec. C) 13:8, and concludes that the expression is mainly used in Jewish apocalyptic writings written or preserved in Greek and often denotes the advent of the Messiah (see also 3 [= 2] Baruch — the Syriac Apocalypse — 30:1 and 1 Thess 2:19).

Two additional remarks have to be made here. First, it should be noted that ἡ ἔλευσις in general means "the (first) coming (of the Messiah)," whereas ἡ παρουσία mostly refers to "the (second) coming (of Christ)." Second, assuming that the Hebrew בא and אתה are the Semitic equivalents of the expression ἡ ἔλευσις, we may furthermore refer to a number of examples in the Qumran writings (see below).

## Concluding Remarks

Although the expression ἡ ἔλευσις τοῦ δικαίου as such, as found in Acts 7:52, does not appear in 1 En 89:52, there are a number of reasons to conclude that 1 En 89:52 indeed has formed the background — or in its Greek version was even the source — from which the author of Luke-Acts has drawn. Firstly, both Acts 7:2-53 and 1 En 89:10-53 belong to the genre "summary of the history of Israel," in which the eschatological figures Jesus and Elijah play a central role.

Secondly, both figures share a number of common features: (1) both ascended into heaven, (2) both were understood as the last of the prophets, (3) both spoke to their followers, (4) the people of Israel wanted to kill both, and (5) both would return in the future. Although 1 Enoch in this passage does not use the technical expression the "Righteous One," a similar expression is often found in many other passages in 1 Enoch, and their author(s) knew of these expressions. It can easily be explained that the expression itself did not fit in the animal imagery of sheep used in chap. 89.

Thirdly, also the other parallels mentioned clearly indicate that there was a widespread expectation of the "coming of (the Messiah as) the Righteous One" in the decades before and after Luke wrote his Acts of the Apostles, both in the earlier and contemporaneous Jewish writings and in the contemporaneous and later Christian writings, although the examples mentioned here also display a certain variety in the use of associations to "Righteous One," such as "Beloved One," "Elect One," and "Anointed One."

This interconnectedness of meanings and connotations of the different aspects of latter-day figures not only constitutes an important element of early Christian Christology as found in the Gospels and Acts, but is also a defining moment in the Parables of Enoch, in which "Enoch," the "Son of Man," and the

"Elect One" are interrelated in a unique way, as is the case in other parts of the Enochic literature as well.

And finally, Luke has taken over the narrative framework of 1 En 89 (the summary of the history of Israel), has adapted it in such a way that Elijah was identified with or replaced by Jesus, and thus has Christianized its meaning. Whether this expectation of "the coming of the Righteous One," a hapax legomenon in the New Testament, was totally Luke's own formulation, whether he edited an older source, or whether it goes back to the speech of Stephen himself — and thus expresses the beliefs of the earliest community of the Jewish followers of Jesus — has to remain open here.

PART FOUR

# THE PARABLES WITHIN SECOND TEMPLE LITERATURE

# Finding a Place for the Parables of Enoch within Second Temple Jewish Literature

*Gabriele Boccaccini*

## The Archaeology of Ideas

Can we identify conceptually and chronologically an ancient document as an archaeologist identifies an ancient building from its remains? Does the archaeology of ideas have the means and the capability of tracing back the place and time of composition of a document even in the absence of a narrative that describes the author, origin, and goal of that document?

Intellectual historians have indeed often compared a document to a building. Whereas a building is made of bricks and stones, a document can be properly described as a complex of ideas. Intellectual historians like to depict themselves as archaeologists engaged in unearthing and studying the remains of ideological edifices.

With the Parables of Enoch we face a most difficult challenge. The document is a relatively well preserved "building" that has survived the ages, but no ancient source describes its social setting and the time and place of its composition, and the document seems to have little to say about itself and its author and social setting.

The most obvious starting point seems to be to examine the constituent parts of its system of thought, the many bricks of which every intellectual building is made (what the American philosopher Arthur O. Lovejoy, one of the fathers of modern intellectual history, would define as its "unit-ideas"),[1] and compare them with similar material found in other documents.

---

1. A. O. Lovejoy, *The Great Chain of Being: The Study of the History of an Idea* (Cambridge: Harvard University Press, 1936).

*Gabriele Boccaccini*

Disassembling the texts and searching for "parallels" is after all a methodology that biblical scholars have been applying since the seventeenth century to the study of ancient Jewish and Christian documents.[2] Identifying a system of thought by studying its unit-ideas, however, may be very tricky to the point of being misleading. The same ideas often happen to play completely different roles in different documents. Conversely, ideologically related documents can use different ideas and traditions to express the continuity of the same ideological system. This has been well stated by E. P. Sanders: "One may consider the analogy of two buildings. Bricks which are identical in shape, color, and weight could well be used to construct two different buildings which are totally unlike each other."[3] Ideas are not systems of thought, but inert material used for the construction of a great diversity of ideological buildings.

Trying to establish the chronology of a "building" on the basis of the chronology of its constituent parts may turn into a nearly impossible task. Obviously, a system of thought cannot be earlier than the latest of its constituent parts. The rule, however, does not apply, in a building as well as in a document, to the presence of later additions (or interpolations), *provided they have not reshaped the entire building*. Sometimes there is no obvious answer: Is the cathedral of Syracuse, Sicily, a pagan temple with some architectural additions, or a Christian building that has completely reshaped the ancient pagan structure? Are the Testaments of the Twelve Patriarchs a Jewish text with some Christian additions, or a Christian text that has totally reshaped the previous material?

On the other hand, the presence of some very ancient elements does not mean that the entire system is as ancient as the earliest of its constituent parts. A Christian basilica cannot be dated before Constantinian times because its actual columns, if not the entirety of its structural elements, were taken from a preexisting Roman building. Furthermore, even when all the elements of a system of thought were proved to be available, it is only their assembly in a coherent whole that marks the birth of a new subject. This rule, which is valid in the history of architectural structures, works as well in the history of systems of thought. Later ideological systems, like the ones testified in medieval Jewish mysticism, cannot be anachronistically transferred back and imposed on Sec-

---

2. This methodological approach first emerged when Christian scholars began to use Jewish "postbiblical" literature to gain a better understanding of the New Testament. J. Lightfoot, *Horae Hebraicae et Talmudicae*, 6 vols. (Cambridge: J. Field, 1658-74), provides the most successful, early example of this methodology. The climax was reached in the first half of the nineteenth century with the publication of H. S. Billerbeck, *Kommentar zum Neuen Testament aus Talmud und Midrasch*, 6 vols. (Munich: Beck 1922-61), and the launching of Gerhard Kittel et al., eds., *Theologisches Wörterbuch zum Neuen Testament*, 10 vols. (Stuttgart: Kohlhammer, 1933-73).

3. E. P. Sanders, *Paul and Palestinian Judaism* (Philadelphia: Fortress, 1977), 13.

ond Temple Jewish sources, only because some of their constituent parts were generated there. Hunting ideas means entering the fascinating and capricious universe of synchronic relations, cultural influences, and dependencies from a common heritage. As Lovejoy used to say: "Ideas are the most migratory things in the world."[4] Ideas are the raw ingredients that are borrowed, exported, adapted, recycled within different systems of thought, and cooked according to the most diverse recipes.

This is certainly true also in the case of the Parables of Enoch. There is virtually no element in the document that cannot be found elsewhere in Second Temple Jewish and early Christian and rabbinic literature. The mere listing of parallels seems to lead us in different, if not opposite, directions. Sapiential texts (like Sirach and the Wisdom of Solomon), Christian texts (from Matthew to Revelation and beyond), apocalyptic texts (like Daniel, 2 Baruch, and 4 Ezra), early Jewish mystical literature (like 3 Enoch) — all are good mines for "parallels." Emphasizing one set of "parallels" over against the others would only mean that the elements have been drafted into an inconclusive "parallelomania," what Samuel Sandmel denounced as "that extravagance among scholars which first overdoes the supposed similarity in passages and then proceeds to describe source and derivation as if implying literary connection flowing in an inevitable or predetermined direction."[5] The many "parallels" only tell us that the bricks used by the author of the Parables belong to the common heritage shared by different Judaisms in late antiquity.

However, Lovejoy also reminds us that "many unit-ideas . . . have long life-histories of their own. . . . Until these units are first discriminated, until each of them which has played any large role in history is separately pursued through all the regions into which it has entered and in which it has exercised influence, any manifestation of it in a single region of intellectual history, or in an individual writer or writing, will, as a rule, be imperfectly understood — and will sometimes go unrecognized altogether."[6] We may then usefully trace the history of some of the key concepts and try to figure out with some degree of certainty to which stage of development the Book of Parables testifies. Sabino Chialà's and George Nickelsburg's articles on the history of the concept of the Son of Man are outstanding samples of the history of ideas applied to the term and concept of the Son of Man.[7] It is only desirable that similar compre-

---

4. A. O. Lovejoy, "Reflections on the History of Ideas," *JHI* 1 (1940): 3-23 (here 4).

5. S. Sandmel, "Parallelomania," *JBL* 81 (1962): 1-13.

6. A. O. Lovejoy, "The Historiography of Ideas," *PAPS* 78 (1938): 529-43.

7. G. W. E. Nickelsburg, "Son of Man," in *ABD* 6 (1993), 137-50; S. Chialà, "Il Figlio dell'Uomo: Evoluzione di un'espressione," in *Libro delle parabole di Enoc* (Brescia: Paideia, 1997), 303-40 (see now his contribution to the present volume).

hensive studies will be done about some other significant "unit-ideas" in the Book of Parables.

However, to locate the place of the Parables within Second Temple Jewish literature, to identify "unit-ideas," and to search for "parallels" and the writing of their history are still preliminary stages. We have to look at the entire building, not only at its constituent parts, however distinctive they may be. In other words, what is distinctive in the Book of Parables is not as much the presence of any of its constituent parts, but the unique way in which the parts are combined, and the hierarchy that the text establishes among them.

## From Unit-Ideas to Paradigms

Being aware of the limitations in the study of the history of ideas, intellectual historians have turned to the identification and study of more complex units, or "paradigms."[8] Paradigms are not "unit-ideas," but "belief-systems," macrostructures, conglomerates of unit-ideas. They are the equivalents of styles in the architecture of buildings. In Second Temple Judaism a large variety of "paradigms" coexisted and interacted in various ways. Among the many paradigms that played a structural role in the building of the Parables of Enoch, I will focus here on only five of them, which appear to be the most relevant for the purpose of comparative analysis.[9] These paradigms are so well established in contemporary scholarship that only a few words will be necessary here to introduce them.

### The Wisdom (Sapiential) Paradigm of Revelation

The recognition of the presence in ancient Judaism of a Wisdom tradition is a well-established paradigm in the history of research. Scholars such as Ronald

---

8. The term "paradigms" is taken from the work of Thomas Kuhn (*The Structure of Scientific Revolutions* [Chicago: University of Chicago Press, 1962; 2nd ed. 1979]), which Ian G. Barbour then applied to the field of religion (*Myths, Models and Paradigms: The Nature of Scientific and Religious Language* [London: SCM, 1974]). See a discussion in D. R. Jackson, "Paradigms and Paradigm Exemplars," in *Enochic Judaism: Three Defining Paradigm Exemplars* (London: T. & T. Clark, 2004), 15-28.

9. In his perceptive essay, Matthias Henze draws attention to the phenomenal wealth of intertextual echoes, quotes, paraphrases, and allusions in Second Temple literature and points to some other "paradigms" that would also be relevant for the study of the Parables of Enoch. See below, M. Henze, "The Parables of Enoch in Second Temple Literature: A Response to Gabriele Boccaccini."

*The Parables of Enoch within Second Temple Jewish Literature*

Murphy and James Crenshaw have traced its origins in Judaism and the ancient Near East since the earliest times; John Collins has studied the development of the tradition in the Hellenistic and Roman period.[10]

*The Apocalyptic Paradigm of Reversal*

Since the rediscovery of the Pseudepigrapha at the end of the nineteenth century, studies in Jewish apocalypticism have flourished. Authors like R. H. Charles, H. H. Rowley, D. S. Russell, K. Koch, and J. J. Collins have made the paradigm of "apocalypticism" an indispensable tool in contemporary research.[11]

*The Messianic Paradigm of Power*

Studies on Jewish messianism and the origins of Christology are a classic in Second Temple Judaism and Christian origins, from the groundbreaking studies of J. Klausner and S. Mowinckel to the more recent collections of articles edited by Jacob Neusner and James Charlesworth to the studies on the Jewish roots of early Christology by James Dunn and Larry Hurtado.[12]

---

10. R. E. Murphy, *The Tree of Life: An Exploration of Biblical Wisdom Literature*, 2nd ed. (Grand Rapids: Eerdmans, 1996); J. L. Crenshaw, *Old Testament Wisdom: An Introduction* (Atlanta: John Knox, 1981); L. G. Perdue et al., eds., *In Search of Wisdom* (Louisville: Westminster John Knox, 1993); J. J. Collins, *Jewish Wisdom in the Hellenistic Age* (Louisville: Westminster John Knox, 1997); cf. B. L. Mack and R. E. Murphy, "Wisdom Literature," in *Early Judaism and Its Modern Interpreters*, ed. R. A. Kraft and G. W. E. Nickelsburg (Atlanta: Scholars, 1986), 371-410.

11. K. Koch, *Ratlos vor der Apocalyptic* (Gütersloh: Gütersloher Verlaghaus, 1970); J. J. Collins, *The Apocalyptic Imagination: An Introduction to Jewish Apocalyptic Literature*, 2nd ed. (Grand Rapids: Eerdmans, 1998); cf. J. J. Collins, "Apocalyptic Literature," in *Early Judaism and Its Modern Interpreters*, 345-70.

12. J. Klausner, *The Messianic Idea in Israel: From Its Beginning to the Completion of the Mishnah*, translated from the third Hebrew edition by W. F. Stinespring (New York: Macmillan, 1955); S. Mowinckel, *He That Cometh: The Messiah Concept in the Old Testament and Later Judaism*, trans. from the Norwegian edition by G. W. Anderson (New York: Abingdon, 1956); J. Neusner et al., eds., *Judaisms and Their Messiahs at the Turn of the Christian Era* (Cambridge: Cambridge University Press, 1987); J. H. Charlesworth, ed., *The Messiah: Developments in Earliest Judaism and Christianity* (Minneapolis: Fortress, 1992). See also G. S. Oegema, *Der Gesalbte und sein Volk* (Göttingen: Vandenhoeck & Ruprecht, 1994); J. J. Collins, *The Scepter and the Star: The Messiahs of the Dead Sea Scrolls and Other Ancient Literature* (New York: Doubleday, 1995); and G. Boccaccini, ed., *Il Messia tra memoria e attesa* (Brescia: Morcelliana, 2005).

Gabriele Boccaccini

## The Covenantal Paradigm of Law

The importance of the Mosaic Torah in Second Temple Judaism is obviously a datum that comes from the tradition, even before the emergence of critical scholarship. Credit goes to E. P. Sanders, however, for having transformed this traditional element into a scholarly paradigm.[13]

## The Enochic Paradigm of Corruption

Thanks to the work of specialists in Enoch literature, such as George Nickelsburg and Paolo Sacchi, the paradigm of the demonic origin of evil has established itself in recent years as one of the most important keys for the interpretation of Second Temple Jewish thought.[14] A paradigm of deviation from the divinely created order of the cosmos appears in fact to be shared by a large number of Second Temple Jewish texts, even outside the Enochic corpus.[15]

None of these paradigms is unique to the Parables, or common to all Second Temple Jewish texts.[16] As the diagram on page 269 shows, the Book of Parables (P) shares all these paradigms, with the conspicuous exception of the Covenantal Paradigm. Each of these paradigms connects the Parables to a different set of documents:

a. The Enochic Paradigm connects the Parables not only to the other Enoch books but also to the Dead Sea Scrolls, some Pseudepigrapha (significantly Jubilees, the Testaments of the Twelve Patriarchs, the Apocalypse of Abraham, and the Fourth Book of Ezra), and the early Christian literature (which is exactly what makes it so difficult in the case of the Parables and the Testaments to decide whether these documents were "Jewish or Christian," or better, whether they were Christian or were composed by a Jewish group other than Christian).

---

13. Sanders, *Paul and Palestinian Judaism;* Sanders, *Judaism: Practice and Belief, 63 BCE–66 CE* (Philadelphia: Trinity, 1992); cf. D. A. Carson et al., eds., *Justification and Variegated Nomism,* vol. 1, *The Complexities of Second Temple Judaism* (Tübingen: Mohr, 2001).
14. G. W. E. Nickelsburg, *1 Enoch: A Commentary* (Minneapolis: Fortress, 2001); P. Sacchi, *Jewish Apocalyptic and Its History* (Sheffield: Sheffield Academic, 1997). Cf. the Proceedings of the Enoch Seminar that biennially gathers the specialists of the Enoch literature: G. Boccaccini, ed., *The Origins of Enochic Judaism* (Turin: Zamorani, 2002 = Henoch 24 [2002]); Boccaccini, ed., *Enoch and Qumran Origins: New Light on a Forgotten Connection* (Grand Rapids: Eerdmans, 2005).
15. Jackson, *Enochic Judaism.*
16. *Pace* Sanders, who made the Covenantal Paradigm the axis of his "common Judaism."

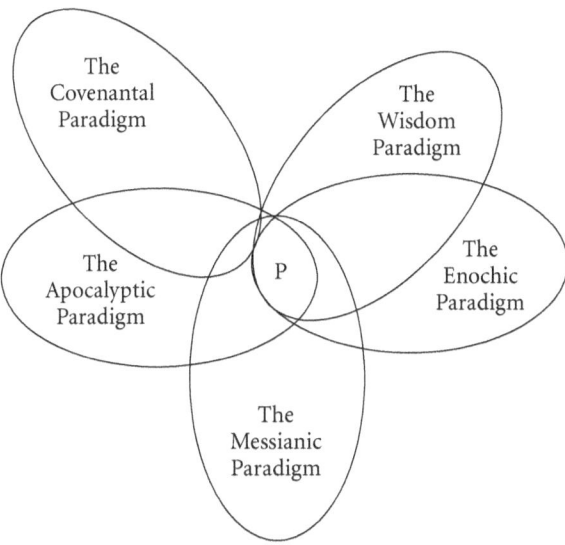

b. The Apocalyptic Paradigm connects the Parables to an even larger corpus of apocalyptic literature that overlaps yet is not coincidental with the Enochic Paradigm, as the latter is not clearly apparent in apocalyptic texts like Daniel, the Psalms of Solomon, 2 Baruch, or the Sibylline Oracles.
c. The Messianic Paradigm makes the Parables an important part in the history of early Jewish messianism, connecting the text back, on the one hand, to Davidic traditions and ancient prophetic texts like Isaiah and, on the other, to several apocalyptic texts, but it also distinguishes the Parables from a significant number of Second Temple Jewish documents where the figure of the eschatological Messiah is absent.
d. Even more intriguing is the relevance of the Wisdom Paradigm, which seems to connect the Parables to a completely different set of non-Enochic, nonapocalyptic, and nonmessianic texts that explore how God's Wisdom makes herself present on earth and accessible to human beings — ancient sapiential texts such as Proverbs or Job, and Second Temple texts like Sirach, Baruch, and the Wisdom of Solomon.
e. The Covenantal Paradigm is the only major paradigm of the five we have singled out that is absent in the Parables, and in fact this is the major reason why the Book of Parables was not included in Sanders's analysis as representative of "Palestinian Judaism." The unique features of the document did not fit his construct of "covenantal nomism," as the all-inclusive label for first-century "common Judaism." And as everybody knows: "If

they do not fit, you must acquit."[17] Sanders judged that the Book of Parables had to be promptly released from serving in the house of Second Temple Judaism and set free as a later Christian text.

If we take these paradigms one separated from the other, each will locate the Parables within a different trajectory of thought and within a different "chain (or family) of documents," without providing a clear conceptual and chronological framework for this document. We have to resist the temptation to pick up just one paradigm, which will simply make us replace a "parallelomania" with an equally arbitrary "paradigmania." Paradigms in fact are not "intellectual movements," or Judaisms (even less the product of a single social group), but complex material used by different Judaisms or social groups for the construction of ideological buildings. Paradigms (like the less complex "unit-ideas") can be combined in various ways to form different systems of thought, exactly as architectural styles (no less than identical bricks) have been used by different social groups in different ages to produce different buildings (the ancient Parthenon of Athens as well as the modern "temples" of Washington, D.C., the White House and the Capitol). To understand the structure of the entire building, therefore, we have not only to identify its "bricks" and "styles," or its "unit-ideas" and "paradigms," but also (and mostly) to look at the distinctive *combination* of *all* of them to form a coherent system. A comparative study, which focuses on the synchronic relations of various paradigms, can help us locate the place of the Parables of Enoch within Second Temple Jewish literature better than any study in the history of any single idea or paradigm, and can contribute significantly to the ultimate goal of our research, which is not the identification of "unit-ideas" and "paradigms" but the study of the many parallel and competing systems of thought (or Judaisms) that were active in Second Temple Judaism. The complexity of Jewish thought cannot be reduced to a single line of development; a variety of Judaisms coexisted and interacted side by side, each of them playing with the same "bricks" and "styles" to construct their distinctive systems of thought.

## The Merging of Paradigms (the Hellenistic Period)

The second century B.C.E. signals a crucial time in Jewish thought when these different paradigms, which originated apart from each other, finally came together in the most diverse and creative fashion.

---

17. Probably the most famous line in the O. J. Simpson trial has become proverbial in the United States.

## Sirach

At the beginning of the second century B.C.E., Ben Sira provided the example of a text where for the first time the Sapiential and Covenantal Paradigms were merged. A few decades before, the book of Tobit had already stated that the faithful Jew had to live according to both the teaching of the Mosaic Torah and the sayings of the Wisdom tradition (Tob 1:8). Yet, no explanation was there provided about the relationship between these two sets of traditions.[18] Sirach proposed what would prove to be an ingenious and fortunate solution. According to Sirach, Wisdom is not a goddess or a divine attribute, as it was in the ancient sapiential tradition (Ahiqar; Job 28; Prov 1–9), but a heavenly being created by God (Sir 1:4) and used by God as a tool in creation (1:7-8). Wisdom lived in heaven with the angels, but asked God for a dwelling place on earth (24:1-7). This dwelling place is the temple of Jerusalem (24:8-12), where Wisdom embodied herself in the cultic service of the high priest,[19] and more specifically in the priestly Torah, "the book of the covenant of the Most High God, the Law that Moses commanded us as an inheritance for the congregations of Jacob" (24:23). Such a concept would later be reiterated in similar terms by the book of Baruch (3:9–4:4).[20] This does not mean that Wisdom and Torah are identical, as some commentators have claimed.[21] Identity is a transitive relation, in which the two elements bear the same properties. In Sirach and Baruch, Wisdom and Law are not interchangeable and their relationship is still conceived in strongly asymmetrical terms.[22] The connection between Wisdom and Torah is the result of a one-way process. Wisdom manifested herself in the Torah. It is not the other way around. The heavenly Wisdom does not lose her autonomy and the Torah does not gain either the autonomy or the cosmic functions of the heavenly and preexistent Wisdom.

---

18. See G. Boccaccini, "An Unexpected Supporter of Zadokite Judaism: Tobit," in *Roots of Rabbinic Judaism* (Grand Rapids: Eerdmans, 2002), 124-31.

19. C. H. T. Fletcher-Louis, "Wisdom Christology and the Partings of the Ways between Judaism and Christianity," in *Christian-Jewish Relations through the Centuries,* ed. S. E. Porter and B. W. R. Pearson (Sheffield: JSOT, 2000), 52-68.

20. Cf. C. A. Moore, *Daniel, Esther, and Jeremias: The Additions,* AB 44 (Garden City, N.Y.: Doubleday, 1977), 255-316.

21. *Pace* E. J. Schnabel, *Law and Wisdom from Ben Sira to Paul* (Tübingen: Mohr, 1985).

22. G. Boccaccini, "The Problem of Knowledge: Wisdom and Law," in *Middle Judaism: Jewish Thought, 300 BCE to 200 CE* (Minneapolis: Fortress, 1991), 81-99; Boccaccini, "The Preexistence of the Torah: A Commonplace in Second Temple Judaism or a Later Rabbinic Development?" *Hen* 17 (1995): 329-50; see also Collins, *Jewish Wisdom,* 61; R. E. Murphy, "The Personification of Wisdom," in *Wisdom in Ancient Israel,* ed. J. Day et al. (Cambridge: Cambridge University Press, 1995), 227.

Gabriele Boccaccini

## Daniel and Enoch

In merging the Sapiential and Covenantal Paradigms, Ben Sira had consciously and polemically rejected the Enochic and Apocalyptic Paradigms.[23] From his viewpoint this perspective was a threat, but despite his efforts and polemical arrows, it was not something he could successfully oppose. The recent publication of presectarian wisdom texts from Qumran has demonstrated how strong the tendency of the Wisdom Paradigm to assimilate to these other paradigms was in the second century B.C.E. As M. J. Goff has pointed out, "If Ben Sira can be said to merge the sapiential and covenantal traditions, 4QInstruction combines the sapiential and apocalyptic traditions."[24]

The attraction between the Sapiential Paradigm and the Apocalyptic Paradigm was mutual. In spite of their differences, the apocalyptic traditions of both Daniel and Enoch witness to an increasing presence of sapiential elements. They reject Sirach's attempt at removing Wisdom from the divine sphere and to restrict its manifestation to the Mosaic Torah and the temple cult. The Book of Dream Visions makes it explicit: "Wisdom never departs from you, nor does she turn aside from your throne or from your presence" (1 En 84:3).

However, both Enoch and Daniel are presented as wise men and their teaching as wisdom.[25] But this wisdom differs radically from that of Sirach. It is a special revelation given by God to a mediator, to remain hidden and only "addressed to an elect group, not to Israel at large and certainly not to humanity at large in the manner of the older wisdom texts."[26]

Within the apocalyptic framework, wisdom belongs at the same time to the past and to the future of humankind. According to the Enochic tradition, the ancient patriarch, who lived with the angels, has already handed down to

---

23. On Ben Sira as an anti-apocalyptic, anti-Enochic text, see G. Boccaccini, "Ben Sira, Qohelet, and Apocalyptic: A Turning Point in the History of Jewish Thought," in *Middle Judaism*, 77-123; R. A. Argall, *1 Enoch and Sirach: A Comparative Literary and Conceptual Analysis of the Themes of Revelation, Creation, and Judgment* (Atlanta: Scholars, 1995); B. G. Wright, "Fear the Lord and Honor the Priest: Ben Sira as Defender of the Jerusalem Priesthood," in *The Book of Ben Sira in Modern Research*, ed. P. C. Beentjes (Berlin: De Gruyter, 1997), 189-222.

24. M. J. Goff, *The Worldly and Heavenly Wisdom of 4QInstruction* (Leiden: Brill, 2003), 217; cf. D. Harrington, "Two Early Jewish Approaches to Wisdom: Sirach and Qumran Sapiential Work A," in *The Wisdom Texts from Qumran and the Development of Sapiential Thought*, ed. C. Hempel et al. (Leuven: Leuven University Press, 2002), 263-75.

25. R. A. Coughenour, "The Wisdom Stance of Enoch's Redactor," *JSJ* 13 (1982): 47-55.

26. J. J. Collins, "The Eschatologizing of Wisdom in the Dead Sea Scrolls," in *Sapiential Perspectives: Wisdom Literature in Light of the Dead Sea Scrolls*, ed. J. J. Collins et al. (Leiden: Brill, 2004), 49-65.

his children a secret knowledge that generation after generation has reached the present-day community: "Wisdom I have given to you and to your children and to those who will be your children so that they may give this wisdom which is beyond their thought to their children for the generations" (1 En 82:2). On the other hand, the fullness of wisdom is an eschatological gift, when "wisdom will be given to the chosen and they will live" (5:8) and "the righteous will arise from sleep, and wisdom will arise and be presented to them" (91:10).

The Apocalypse of Weeks links past and present by associating the inheritance of wisdom with the beginning of the end of times and with the emergence of the Enochic community of the wise within the people of Israel, as a special group of chosen among the chosen: "In the seventh week . . . the chosen from the eternal plant of righteousness will be elected to serve as witnesses to righteousness: and sevenfold wisdom and knowledge will be given to them" (93:10). This secret wisdom is apart from the Mosaic Torah and is rather embodied in the Enoch literature: "To the righteous and pious and wise my books will be given for the joy of righteousness and much wisdom" (104:12-13).

Unlike the Enochic tradition, the tradition of Daniel makes some efforts to save some link with the Covenantal Paradigm, by introducing its hero as a pious and righteous person, who has received the gift of divine wisdom in virtue of his faithfulness to the Mosaic covenant (Dan 1:17), and rejecting (or at least downplaying) the Enochic Paradigm of corruption.[27] Yet ultimately the wisdom given to Daniel does not identify with the Torah. On the contrary, as the prophecy of Jeremiah shows, even in Scripture and prophecy there is a secret and hidden meaning that is not immediately manifest and can be understood only through a special revelation from above (Dan 9). And as in Enoch, the wisdom given to Daniel "has to remain secret and sealed until the time of the end" (Dan 12:9).

In both traditions the Messianic Paradigm does not yet play an important role. Neither Daniel nor Enoch is presented as messiah. At this stage the traditions of Enoch and Daniel know an eschatological leader: the angelic "Son of Man" of Daniel (Dan 7) and the "snow-white cow" of Dream Visions (1 En 90:37), but they remain quasi-messianic figures, who are not given all the titles and attributes (including wisdom) that the Davidic traditions associated with the Messiah. Daniel closely united "wisdom and power"; they are both gifts from above: "Wisdom and power are His. . . . He deposes kings and sets up kings, He gives wisdom to the wise" (Dan 2:20-21). Yet, interestingly, the "Son of Man" (like its Enochic counterpart) receives "power and dominion" (Dan 7:14)

---

27. G. Boccaccini, "The Covenantal Theology of the Apocalyptic Book of Daniel," in *Enoch and Qumran Origins*, 39-44.

at the end of time, but no wisdom, nor is he a revealer or source of divine wisdom. The eschatological leaders do not have any revelatory function, which is restricted exclusively to the mediators Daniel and Enoch. The functions of leader and revealer remain separated; the eschatological, Sapiential, and Messianic Paradigms have not merged yet.

## Lady Wisdom Meets the Messiah (the Early Roman Period)

A second stage (which corresponds to the early Roman period) is characterized by an unprecedented merging of the Wisdom and Messianic Paradigms (both within and outside the apocalyptic framework). The Messianic Paradigm, which did not play an important role in the Hellenistic period, now takes center stage.

### *Psalms of Solomon*

Even more radically than Daniel, the Psalms of Solomon reject the Enochic Paradigm (cf. PsSol 18:10-12 and Sir 16:24-30) and anchor the Apocalyptic Paradigm to the Covenantal Paradigm. But what is more remarkable is that the Messianic and Apocalyptic Paradigms are now solidly connected in a way that was unknown even in the Danielic and Enochic traditions. The end of time will see the manifestation of an Elect One, who is the Messiah Son of David foretold by the ancient prophets. This implies a connection between the Messianic and Wisdom Paradigms. It was in fact part of the ancient Davidic tradition (Isa 11:2) that the Messiah would be full of wisdom. According to PsSol 17, the Messiah will drive out the sinners "in wisdom and righteousness" (17:23), "will rule peoples and nations in the wisdom of his righteousness" (17:29), and "will bless the Lord's people with wisdom and happiness" (17:35). The reference is explicitly to Isa 11:2: "God made him . . . wise in the counsel of understanding with strength and righteousness" (17:37); "those born in these days . . . (will live) in wisdom of spirit and of righteousness and of strength" (18:7). Significantly, the Psalms of Solomon even ignore any connection between Wisdom and Torah, which played such an important role in Sirach and Baruch.

Contrary to Daniel and Enoch, however, the Psalms of Solomon do not know any mediator, or revealer of secret knowledge (the "hidden things") besides and before the eschatological Messiah. The wise Solomon, the hero of sapiential Judaism, neither is an apocalyptic seer nor is destined to be the leader of the world to come. Both wisdom and power are given to the future Messiah, the Son of David.

## The Wisdom of Solomon

With the Wisdom of Solomon, we see a sapiential text in which the Wisdom and Messianic Paradigms are merged in a noneschatological, non-Enochic context, to emphasize the manifestation of wisdom on earth. The document shares with Sirach and Baruch the priestly idea of the universe as an orderly cosmos, yet it also shows that many, even outside apocalyptic and Enochic circles, were not convinced by the transformation of the divine Wisdom into a heavenly being created by God, and by the view that the Mosaic Torah is the embodiment of Wisdom on earth.

According to the Wisdom of Solomon,[28] Wisdom "is a kindly spirit . . . the spirit of the Lord" (Wis 1:6-7); she is "an aura of the might of God and a pure effusion of the glory of the Almighty . . . she is the refulgence of eternal light, the spotless mirror of the power of God, the image of His goodness" (7:25-26). Unlike Sirach, for whom Wisdom is heavenly, the Wisdom of Solomon speaks of a divine *sophia,* who, as in the tradition of Enoch, "sits" on the throne by God (9:2). Unlike the tradition of Enoch, however, Wisdom is not relegated to heaven, but "comes from God" (9:6). She is not at all an eschatological gift, whose presence is enjoyed in this world only by a group of chosen, but is rather a constant salvific agent in the history of Israel. "Through the devil's envy death entered the world" (2:24), and Wisdom — it is said — "will flee from deceit" (1:5), but the document rejects the Enochic Paradigm of corruption — the iniquity of this world is not strong enough to stop her way and action in a world that is solidly under God's control ("The dominion of Hades is not on earth," 1:14). So Solomon can confidently pray God to send Wisdom from the divine throne: "Send her forth from the holy heavens, and from the throne of your glory send her, that she may labor at my side, and that I may learn what is pleasing to you" (9:10).

Unlike the Psalms of Solomon, the Davidic traditions are not associated with a future Messiah, the Son of David, but are used to describe "a typical figure who is persecuted and put to death by rich and powerful opponents but vindicated in the heavenly court"[29] — a symbol in the chain of the children of Wisdom on earth. This is the way Wisdom reveals herself — not secretly, not indirectly, but acting in the first person, directly, in human history. There is not one particular mediator, not even Solomon, but a series of mediators. "In every generation she passes into holy souls and makes them friends of God and prophets" (7:27). Wisdom is not remote but easily accessible to humankind:

---

28. Cf. D. Winston, *The Wisdom of Solomon* (Grand Rapids: Eerdmans, 1979).
29. Nickelsburg, "Son of Man," 140.

"she is easily discerned by those who love her, and is found by those who seek her" (6:12).

### The Parables of Enoch

This scenario of integration among Sapiential and Messianic Paradigms seems to be the most likely setting for the composition of the Parables of Enoch. Here we have an apocalyptic text that rejects any conception of an active presence of Wisdom on earth: "Wisdom could not find a place in which she could dwell; but a place was found for her in the heavens. Then Wisdom went out to dwell with the children of the people, but she found no dwelling place. So Wisdom returned to her place and she settled permanently among the angels. Then Iniquity went out of her rooms . . . and dwelt with them" (1 En 42:1-3). The text is an explicit rebuttal not only of Sirach and Baruch's conception of the relation between the heavenly Wisdom and the Mosaic Torah, but also of the Wisdom of Solomon's view of direct intervention of the divine Wisdom in history. The passage takes up the myth that Wisdom searched for a dwelling place, but denies its happy ending. The disappointing outcome of Wisdom's search fits the Enochic Paradigm that the world has become the place of evil as a consequence of a cosmic rebellion of angels. There is no room in this world for the salvific role of Wisdom, both directly (as for the Wisdom of Solomon) or indirectly through the priestly Law (as in Sirach or Baruch).

Dwelling in heaven, Wisdom is connected with the eschatological judge of the Parables of Enoch, the "Son of Man," a heavenly creature who shares — at least ideally — the same preexistent nature as Wisdom.[30] As the Messiah announced in the Davidic traditions of Isaiah, the Son of Man has a special relation with Wisdom ("in him dwells the spirit of Wisdom," 1 En 49:3). Consistently, he would be her revealer at the end of times, sitting with her on God's throne: "In those days, the Elect One shall sit on my throne, and all the secrets of wisdom will go forth from the counsel of his mouth, for the Lord of the Spirits has given them to him and glorified him" (51:3). Then "the springs of wisdom" will become accessible to humankind (48:1) and "wisdom will be poured out like water" (49:1).

At the same time, the Book of Parables preserves the idea of the earlier Enochic tradition that Enoch is the recipient of revelation and the messenger of revealed wisdom for the chosen. The revealed parables are "the beginning of the words of wisdom. . . . It is proper to declare such things to those of former

---

30. Cf. Chialà, *Libro delle parabole di Enoc*; Nickelsburg, "Son of Man," 137-50.

times, but even those of later times will not be denied the beginning of wisdom. Until the present day the Lord of the Spirits has never given me such wisdom as I have now received" (37:2-4). This creates an internal tension within the Enochic system, due to the presence of two mediators (Enoch and the Messiah) who are both in heaven and are both recipients and revealers of wisdom. This tension (and the danger of a disruptive competition between the two revealers) is finally resolved by identifying Enoch with the Son of Man (71:14).[31] Now we can have a better understanding why Enoch received and will reveal wisdom — it is because he is the Messiah.

Although the language of wisdom may have influenced the concept of the preexistence and role of the Son of Man, in the Parables neither the Messiah Son of Man nor Enoch is identified with the divine Wisdom of God.[32] The heavenly Enoch is the herald and messenger of the divine Wisdom, not its incarnation.

### The Earliest Christian Traditions

It is widely recognized by scholars that the earliest Christian traditions present Jesus not as the embodiment of the divine Wisdom, but as the messenger and teacher of wisdom.[33] With language reminiscent of the Wisdom of Solomon, Q introduces Jesus, along with John the Baptist, in a series of children of wisdom, maintaining that "Wisdom is vindicated by all her children" (Luke 7:35; cf. Matt 11:19). Yet Jesus is claimed to be the greatest revealer, wiser than Solomon (Q: "Something greater than Solomon is here!" Matt 12:42; Luke 11:31).

The superiority of Jesus does not derive, as in the case of the early Enoch literature or Daniel, simply from his being chosen by God as the mediator of a secret knowledge, but primarily from his messianic status. As in the Psalms of Solomon, the Messiah is the recipient of both wisdom and power. Not unexpectedly, people wonder about the origins of *both* Jesus' wisdom and Jesus' power. "From where *(pothen)* did these things come to him? What is this wis-

---

31. The point is emphasized also by Helge Kvanvig in his contribution to the present volume: "Therefore the inclusion of the eschatological horizon and the concentration of this horizon on one supreme figure in heaven . . . threatened the coherence of Enochic theology. . . . Without the final identification, the believers would not any longer be followers of Enoch, but followers of the Son of Man." See above, H. S. Kvanvig, "The Son of Man in the Parables of Enoch."

32. "Although the son of man is not identified *as* Wisdom, aspects of the Wisdom myth have colored the Parables' eclectic portrait of this heavenly figure" (Nickelsburg, "Son of Man," 139).

33. J. D. G. Dunn, *Christology in the Making: An Inquiry into the Origins of the Doctrine of the Incarnation,* 2nd ed. (London: SCM, 1989), 197-240.

dom that has been given to him and these deeds of power that are done through his hands?" (Mark 6:2; cf. Matt 13:54: "From where [*pothen*] did this wisdom and deeds of power come?").

Like Enoch in the Parables, Jesus also has a mission to accomplish on earth before the end of times — to be the revealer of the secrets of the kingdom of God. "You have been given the secret [*mysterion*; Matt 13:11 and Luke 8:10, *mysteria*, secrets] of the kingdom of God" (Mark 4:11). Before the end of times, this knowledge is reserved to a group of chosen among the chosen: "God has hidden these things from the wise . . . and revealed them to the little ones . . . through his Son" (Q: Matt 11:25; Luke 10:21).

The earliest Christian tradition presents a combination of Sapiential, Messianic, and Apocalyptic Paradigms very similar to that found in the Parables of Enoch.

The identification of Jesus with the Messiah Son of Man is a result of the same dynamics that produced the identification between Enoch and the Messiah Son of Man, namely, the idea that the eschatological Messiah is the most proper revealer of Wisdom and that such a function cannot be divided among two different and equally important mediators.

## The Christian Assimilation of Wisdom to the Messiah

In the Parables of Enoch, as well as in the earliest Christian traditions, the Messiah Son of Man is at the same time the messenger and (part of) the message of God's Wisdom. "The Wisdom of the Lord of the Spirits has revealed him to the holy and the righteous" (1 En 48:7), in heaven as well as on earth. If the manifestation of the Messiah is the center of the hopes of the righteous, then the Messiah may be understood as the core of revealed Wisdom. This idea would have an extraordinary and unexpected development within the Christian tradition.

### The Letters of Paul

Paul never uses the *term* "Son of Man," yet his view of the Messiah Jesus as the *kyrios* so closely resembles the *concept* of the Messiah Son of Man of the Parables that one could look at the term *kyrios* as a convenient translation and development in Hellenistic terms of the Enochic concept.[34]

---

34. See G. Boccaccini, "Uomo, angelo o Dio? Alle radici del messianismo ebraico e cristiano," in *Il messia tra memoria e attesa*, 15-48.

As is the "Son of Man" of the Parables, Paul's *kyrios* is preexistent and belongs to the heavenly realm, but he is at the same time distinct and subordinated to the Father (1 Cor 15:28). Significantly, unlike the later Christian tradition, in the entire Pauline corpus the Son never receives the title of *theos*, "God" (which is reserved for the Father only). At least in one passage (which almost verbatim is reminiscent of the Gospel sayings on the Son of Man), *kyrios* replaces "Son of Man" almost as if they were interchangeable terms. "The *kyrios* himself, with a cry of command, with the archangel's call and with the sound of God's trumpet, will descend from heaven" (1 Thess 4:16).

Yet, in spite of the many parallels, conceptually Paul testifies to a further stage of development. The theology of Paul presupposes not only the Enochic concept of the Son of Man but also its earliest Christian reinterpretation, and raises both to a higher and more complex level of elaboration. In the Psalms of Solomon, the Parables of Enoch, the Wisdom of Solomon, and the earliest Christian tradition, the Messianic and Sapiential Paradigms merged in the sense that the Messiah is full of Wisdom and the revealer of God's "secrets." Even when in the Parables the coming of the Messiah is presented as one of the contents of God's wisdom revealed to the chosen, this knowledge is not exclusive. Also in the earliest Christian tradition, Jesus is primarily the revealer of something greater than himself — the mystery of the kingdom of God.

Now in Paul, the coming of the Messiah becomes the *exclusive* content of God's wisdom. Jesus is not even the revealer (such function is rather entrusted to "the Spirit," 1 Cor 2:10-13). Jesus is the message rather than the messenger; he is the very content of the Wisdom of God. Hence, Wisdom is not the knowledge of God's hidden things, but specifically — and exclusively — the revelation of the mystery of the person of Christ.

In the First Letter to the Corinthians, Paul contrasts the revealed Wisdom to the wisdom of this world. The wise consider the Christian message as foolishness; but "God chose what is foolish in the world to shame the wise" (1:27), and "God's foolishness is wiser than human wisdom" (1:25). There is in fact another kind of wisdom, "which is not a wisdom of this age or of the rulers of this age, who are doomed to perish" (2:6). This is "God's wisdom, secret and hidden, which God decreed before the ages for our glory" (2:7). This knowledge from above is "Christ, power of God and wisdom of God" (1:24). Paul falls short of saying that Jesus is *the* Wisdom *incarnata;* but his statement goes in the direction of tying even more closely the Messiah and God's Wisdom, and so the Sapiential and Messianic Paradigms.

The same combination of "Power and Wisdom" within the messianic figure — a phenomenon that, as we have seen, is characteristic of the merging of the Sapiential and Messianic Paradigms — is apparent in the Letter to the

Ephesians. Paul first states that Jesus is the full manifestation of God's power and wisdom: "With all wisdom and insight, [God] has made known to us the mystery of his will, according to his good pleasure that he set forth in Christ.... [God] put this power to work in Christ when he raised him from the dead and seated him at his right hand in the heavenly places, far above all rule and authority and power and dominion, and above every name that is named, not only in this age but also in the age to come" (1:8-9, 20-21). Paul goes on by illustrating the content of his preaching, which is the eschatological revelation of the eternal and preexistent plan of God's Wisdom. "Grace was given to me to bring to the Gentiles the news of the boundless riches of Christ and to make everyone see the plan of the mystery hidden for ages by God who created all things, so that through the church the wisdom of God in its rich variety might now be made known to the rulers and authorities in the heavenly places. This was in accordance with the eternal purpose that [God] has carried out in Christ Jesus our *kyrios*" (3:8-11). The resemblance with 1 En 48:7, where the Book of Parables announced Wisdom's revelation of the Son of Man to the holy and the righteous in heaven as well as on earth, could not be more striking. Paul's parenesis ends with the invitation to "be wise ... and not foolish," which in his vision means only one thing — to "understand what the will of the *kyrios* is" (5:15-17).

## From Paul to John

By making Jesus primarily not the mediator but the object of God's revelation, Paul lays the foundations for a theological revolution. If Jesus is the message of God's preexistent wisdom, then Jesus the messenger is more than the Son of Man full of Wisdom of the Parables of Enoch and of the earliest Christian tradition.

Scholars have noticed in some passages of the Gospels of Matthew and Luke the tendency to modify the received tradition in order to make Jesus himself the subject of acts that were previously attributed to God's Wisdom. Jesus does the deeds of Wisdom (Matt 11:19) and speaks the words of wisdom (Luke 11:49).[35] If not evidence of a "full blown expression of Wisdom Christology" (as James Dunn has claimed),[36] the Gospels of Matthew and Luke signal however a

---

35. See for the Gospel of Matthew in particular, C. Deutsch, "Jesus as Wisdom: A Feminist Reading of Matthew's Wisdom Christology," in *A Feminist Companion to Matthew*, ed. A.-J. Levine (Sheffield: Sheffield Academic, 2001), 88-113; Deutsch, *Lady Wisdom, Jesus, and the Sages: Metaphor and Social Context in Matthew's Gospel* (Valley Forge, Pa.: Trinity, 1996).

36. Dunn, *Christology in the Making*, 201.

shift, which is confirmed in contemporary Christian sources, toward a closer identification between Jesus and the divine Wisdom.

The Letter to the Hebrews still locates Jesus in the line of the children of Wisdom, but he is now singled out as the most perfect manifestation of Wisdom, a manifestation to whom the very same features of Wisdom can be applied. "Long ago God spoke to our ancestors in many and various ways to the prophets, but in these last days he has spoken to us by a Son, whom he appointed heir of all things, through whom he also created the worlds. He is the reflection of God's glory and the exact imprint of God's very being, and he sustains all things by his powerful word" (1:1-3a). This view translates into a higher status for the Messiah, who is now claimed to stand far above the angels. Jesus is indeed the Son of Man announced by Ps 8, who "for a little while was made lower than the angels" (Heb 2:9), but now "he sat down at the right hand of the Majesty on high, having become as much superior to angels as the name he has inherited is more excellent than theirs" (1:3b-4).

In similar sapiential terms, Colossians describes Jesus as "the image of the invisible God, the firstborn of all creation, for in him all things in heaven and on earth were created, things visible and invisible, whether thrones or dominions or rulers or powers — all things have been created through him and for him. He himself is before all things and in him all things hold together" (1:15-17). A comparison with the above-mentioned passage of Ephesians is revealing in terms of the progress made toward an identification of Jesus with the divine Wisdom. While in Ephesians Jesus is the content of God's Wisdom and the apostle Paul announces the mystery regarding Jesus, in Colossians Jesus himself is God's mystery. "I want you . . . to have the knowledge of God's mystery, that is, Christ himself, in whom are hidden all the treasures of wisdom and knowledge" (Col 2:2-3).

If Christian sources still appear very cautious, almost reluctant, to transform the sapiential metaphor into an ontological reality, it is because they were fully aware of the theological implications on Jewish monotheism as well as of the difficulty of overcoming the gender barrier between the male Jesus and the female Wisdom. Eventually, toward the end of the first century C.E., the *logos* theology provided the answer.

The *logos*-Word was an equally uncreated and powerful divine hypostasis whose creative power was recognized by the ancient Jewish tradition (Ps 33:6: "By the Word of the Lord the heavens were made"; cf. Gen 1).[37] Particularly in the early targumic tradition, the concept of the Word *(memra)* of God had de-

---

37. On the concept of Word *(logos)* in Second Temple Judaism and its cultural environment, see A. Dubrunner et al., "λέγω, λόγος," in *TWNT* 4 (1942), 69-198.

veloped from being a way to obviate anthropomorphism into a quite sophisticated theology. While in the protorabbinic traditions no relation could be established between the divine Word and the heavenly Wisdom, in Hellenistic Judaism the two equally divine hypostases soon became interchangeable ("You have made all things by your Word, and by your Wisdom have formed humankind," Wis 9:1-2; "The *sophia* of God is the *logos* of God," Philo, Legum allegoriae 1.65). For the second-generation Christians, the masculine *logos*, with his well-established parallelism with the Wisdom of God, was the key for assimilating the Sapiential Paradigm into the Messianic Paradigm. The change of terminology (from "Son of Man–*kyrios*" to *logos-theos*) betrays a revolution: the Christian Messiah from heaven has become divine.

The prologue of the Gospel of John is a masterpiece synthesis. It identifies the Messiah Jesus with the uncreated, divine *logos* ("In the beginning was the *logos*, and the *logos* was with God, and the *logos* was divine," 1:1), which in turn is identified with Wisdom,[38] as the tool used by God in the act of creation ("He was at the beginning with God. All things came into being through him, and without him not one thing came into being," 1:2-3).[39]

While stressing the divinity of the *logos-sophia*, John however retained the Sirach-Baruch model in order to explain the incarnation of the preexistent *logos* ("And the *logos* became flesh and lived among us," 1:14), with Jesus taking the place of the Torah. This stance dismisses any claim by the Torah to be the perfect manifestation of Wisdom: Jesus, not the Torah, is the earthly embodiment of God's Wisdom ("The Law was given through Moses; grace and truth came through Jesus Christ," 1:17).

The prologue of John finally alludes to the Enochic Paradigm in its insistence on the rejection of the *logos* ("He [the *logos*] came to what was his own and his own people did not accept him," 1:11). Jesus-*logos-sophia*, however, did not go back to heaven empty-handed. The first coming of Jesus marks the beginning of redemption, as forgiveness of sin is assured to those who believe in his heavenly power ("But to all who received him, who believed in his name, he gave power to become children of God," 1:12).

For some time Christian theology would still struggle to make sense of the once-separated concepts of wisdom and *logos* (and Son of Man), but eventually the solution provided by the prologue of John (the assimilation of *logos*-

---

38. M. Scott, *Sophia and the Johannine Jesus* (Sheffield: JSOT, 1992).

39. Compared to *sophia*, the *logos* had also the advantage, in Christian eyes, to refer to a divine hypostasis that unlike Wisdom had never been turned into a heavenly creature. With the term *logos* (instead of *sophia*), the divinity of Jesus and the masculinity of the incarnated Messiah were unambiguously stated and clearly understood by both the Jewish and Gentile readers of the Gospel of John.

*sophia*-messiah to Jesus) would prove to be the most effective. The Johannine identification between *kyrios* and *theos* (20:28) will penetrate Christian faith, so much so that in his letters even such an imitator of Paul as Ignatius will commonly refer to Jesus as "our *theos*" (something Paul would have never dared). Wisdom would become nothing more than poetic imagery, a metaphor for the divine *logos*-Christ. Generated, not created, preexistent, the Christ is, as Justin says, "the beginning," the *re'shit/arche* of Prov 8:22a:

> God has begotten as a Beginning *(arche)* before all His creatures a kind of Reasonable Power from Himself, which is also called by the Holy Spirit the Glory of the Lord, and sometimes Son, and sometimes Wisdom *(sophia)*, and sometimes Angel, and sometimes God, and sometimes Lord and Word *(logos)*. . . . [Jesus is] the *logos* and *sophia* and Power and Glory of God who begat and spoke as follows by Solomon: The Lord made me the beginning *(arche)* of His ways for his works [Prov 8:22]. (*Dialogue with Trypho* 61.1-3)

## The Downfall of Wisdom in Apocalyptic Literature and the Rise of the Torah

The Christian identification of the Messiah and Wisdom caused the rapid collapse of the Sapiential Paradigm, which now appears to be in retreat on all fronts as an autonomous paradigm. The phenomenon is apparent in the apocalypses composed after the first half of the first century C.E.

### The Second and the Third Book of Enoch

In 2 Enoch, Wisdom still has some autonomy. She is said to be the tool used in God's creation ("I commanded my wisdom to create man," 30:8), and is the source of Enoch's knowledge: "Everything that I have explained to you . . . by my supreme wisdom I have contrived it all" (33:3). Enoch wrote "360 books" (23:6), and God commanded him to "deliver these books to your children, and the children to the children, and to (all) your relatives, and to all your generations, who have the wisdom and who will fear the Lord" (48:6-7). Enoch's books (and wisdom) will be preserved forever within the group of the chosen: "They will not be destroyed until the final age" (33:11).

Enoch is therefore the recipient and the revealer of wisdom, a wise man, as he was in the earliest Enoch tradition. As in the Book of Parables and in the later Enoch traditions (cf. 3 Enoch), the patriarch is transformed in heaven into an angelic being, but the Messianic Paradigm has almost completely vanished. There is no eschatological Messiah in 2 Enoch. Enoch is anointed, but his anointment indicates his angelification (22:6-10; 56:2), not his appointment as the ruler or judge in the world to come. Only much later, in 3 Enoch, a Messiah will resurface in the Enochic tradition — in a marginal role, as Son of David and not as Son of Man and, even more remarkably (but not unexpectedly), as a completely autonomous character from Enoch-Metatron (3 En 48:10).

### The Fourth Book of Ezra

The protagonist of 4 Ezra also shares many similar features with wise revealers like Enoch, Daniel, or the Jesus of the earliest Christian tradition.[40] Ezra is chosen by God to be the recipient of a wisdom to be written and kept hidden and taught only to the wise: "And you alone were worthy to learn the secret of the Most High. Therefore write all these things that you have seen in a book, and put it in a hidden place; and you shall teach them to the wise among your people, whose hearts you know are able to comprehend and keep these secrets" (12:36-38).

But if the Messianic Paradigm still plays an important role in 4 Ezra, any link between the Sapiential and the Messianic Paradigms is lost. On one hand, while Ezra is the revealer and recipient of hidden wisdom, unambiguously he is *not* the eschatological Messiah. On the other hand, 4 Ezra drops the idea of any association between Wisdom and the Messiah. The absence in 4 Ezra of any reference to wisdom in relation to the Messiah is conspicuous when considering how, within the Christian perspective, the contemporaneous apocalyptic book of Revelation reiterates the foundational belief of the Messianic Paradigm that "wisdom and power," which belong to God (Rev 7:2), will be given to the Messiah: "Worthy is the Lamb . . . to receive power . . . and wisdom" (5:12). 4 Ezra is clearly moving in the opposite direction. The document consciously transfers even the Wisdom imagery associated with the messianic age to the knowledge of the mediator. "The spring of understanding and the fountain of wisdom" are not to be expected, as in the Parables of Enoch, as a gift from the Messiah, but are to be found in the secret books revealed to Ezra (4 Ezra 14:47).

Another new element in 4 Ezra is the reemergence of the Covenantal Paradigm, an even more remarkable phenomenon when one considers the influence that the Enochic Paradigm of corruption plays in the document. The secret knowledge given to Ezra is presented not in opposition to but side by side

---

40. See M. A. Knibb, "Apocalyptic and Wisdom in 4 Ezra," *JSJ* 13 (1982): 56-74.

with the Mosaic Torah. As Daniel also before him, Ezra is righteous according to the Torah and is devoted to the Torah: "And you alone have been enlightened about this, because you have forsaken your own ways and have applied yourself to mine, and have searched out my law; for you have devoted your life to wisdom and called understanding your mother" (13:53b-55). But 4 Ezra goes much further. Unlike Daniel, Ezra is the one to whom both the Mosaic Torah and the secret, additional knowledge contained in the apocalyptic texts were revealed. "Make public the twenty-four books that you wrote first and let the worthy and the unworthy read them; but keep the seventy that are written last, in order to give them to the wise among your people. For in them is the spring of understanding, the fountain of wisdom, and the river of knowledge" (14:45b-47).

### The Second Book of Baruch

In 2 Baruch any residual link between the Messianic, Sapiential, and Apocalyptic Paradigms vanishes. Wisdom is no longer associated either with an apocalyptic revealer or with the eschatological Messiah, but only with the Torah. Baruch's only concern is with the Mosaic Law, which is the exclusive source and premise of any knowledge: "O Lord, you are the one who has always enlightened those who conduct themselves with understanding. Now show me the explanation of this vision. You know that my soul has always been associated with your Law and I did not depart from my earliest days" (38:2-4).

Any reference to a secret knowledge or additional books disappears; the Torah is the wisdom revealed to Baruch. In the parallelism, the two terms appear now to be interchangeable rather than complementary: "Your law is life and your wisdom is the right way" (38:2); "the Law that is among us will help us, and that excellent wisdom which is in us will support us" (48:24); "look upon the Law and [be] intent upon wisdom" (77:15).

## The Assimilation of the Heavenly Wisdom to the Torah

A document like 2 Baruch testifies to the presence of two opposite forces that came to clash in the second century C.E. On one hand, Christianity pushed to the limit the merging of the Sapiential and Messianic Paradigms, which eventually led to the complete assimilation (and disappearance) of the Sapiential Paradigm within the Messianic Paradigm. On the other hand, in protorabbinic traditions the Sapiential Paradigm was undergoing an equally spectacular metamorphosis in its encounter with the Covenantal Paradigm, which eventually would lead to the complete assimilation (and disappearance) of the Sapiential Paradigm within the Covenantal Paradigm.

Sirach and Baruch had closely associated Wisdom and Torah, making the Torah an inferior, earthly, and quite late manifestation of the heavenly Wisdom on earth. Echoes of this position can still be found in rabbinic literature, most explicitly in a saying attributed to R. Amin: "The incomplete form of the heavenly light is the orbit of the sun; the incomplete form of the heavenly Wisdom is the Torah" (Gen Rab 17:5; 44:7).

But this is no more than the last, inert relic of what used to be the predominant position in protorabbinic traditions. The second century C.E. was the turning point. Facing the Christian challenge of the identification between the preexistent divine Wisdom and the preexistent divine Messiah, protorabbinic traditions explicitly identified the preexistent heavenly Wisdom with the preexistent heavenly Torah. A passage in *Targum Neofiti*[41] may well be the earliest surviving evidence of the idea that "two thousand years before the world was created, [God] created the Torah" (*Tg Neof Gen* 3:25). The figure "two thousand years" is the result of a subtle reading of Prov 8:30 in light of Ps 90:4,[42] based on the assumption that Wisdom is nothing more than poetic imagery, a metaphor for the preexistent Torah. *Neofiti* still grants both Wisdom and the *logos-memra* a central role in creation and the function of hypostases ("From the beginning with Wisdom <the Word of> God created and perfected the heavens and the earth," *Tg Neof Gen* 1:1), but soon even this residual homage to the once glorious status of Wisdom will be lost. For the post-Mishnaic treatise *Aboth*, the Torah, not Wisdom, is "the precious instrument by which the world was created" (*m. 'Abot* 3:14). This approach would then become normative and exclusive in later rabbinic texts:

> The Torah says, I was the instrument of the Holy One, blessed be He. As a rule when an earthly king builds a palace, he does not build it by himself, but calls an architect; and the architect does not plan the building in his

---

41. Cf. A. Díez Macho, *Neophyti I*, 5 vols. (Madrid and Barcelona, 1968-78); R. Le Déaut, *Targum de Pentateuque*, 4 vols. (Paris: Cerf, 1978-80); cf. G. Boccaccini, "Targum Neofiti as a Proto-Rabbinic Document: A Systemic Analysis," in *The Aramaic Bible: Targums in Their Historical Context*, ed. M. McNamara and D. R. G. Beattie (Sheffield: Sheffield Academic, 1995), 260-69.

42. In Prov 8:30 Wisdom claims that before creation she "was beside [God] . . . and was daily [His] delight." "Daily" implies the succession of at least two days, and since from Ps 90:4 we learn that "one thousand years in [God's] sight are like yesterday," it means that the Torah-Wisdom had to be created at least "two thousand years" before the creation of the world in order to have stood "daily" before God.

head, but he makes it of rolls and tablets. Even so the Holy One, blessed be He, looked in the Torah and created the world. And the Torah declares: By means of the *re'shit (en arche, bᵉre'shit)* God created and *re'shit* means no other than the Torah as it is written: The Lord made me the *re'shit* of his work [Prov 8:22a]. (Gen Rab 1:1)

## Conclusion

In the end, the Sapiential Paradigm vanished and Christ and the Torah replaced Wisdom, superseding her role, each within its own system of thought. The (almost ironical) reference to the same proof text of Prov 8:22a in both traditions shows that their divergent theologies were not the consequence of a direct replacement. Christianity was not born from rabbinic Judaism, nor rabbinic Judaism from Christianity.[43] They parted from each other; neither ever parted from its ideological roots in Second Temple Judaism.[44]

The Christians developed the Enochic idea that divine Wisdom had her dwelling place in the heavens and the Messiah Son of Man stood side by side with her on the divine throne, first identifying their revealer Jesus with the heavenly Son of Man and then replacing the divine Wisdom with the preexistent and divine Christ. The rabbis, on the other hand, developed the idea of Sirach and Baruch that the Torah was the earthly embodiment of the heavenly, preexistent Wisdom, first making the Torah stand side by side with the heavenly Wisdom and then replacing Wisdom with the preexistent and heavenly Torah.

In the process, both Christianity and rabbinic Judaism exploited the potential of the Sapiential Paradigm. The Christians merged and then assimilated the Sapiential Paradigm with the Messianic Paradigm by giving the Christ all the attributes (preexistence, heavenly status, creative role, etc.) of Wisdom, *including* her divine nature. On the other hand, the rabbis merged and then as-

---

43. On Christianity and rabbinic Judaism as "fraternal twins," see A. F. Segal, *Rebecca's Children: Judaism and Christianity in the Roman World* (Cambridge: Harvard University Press, 1986); H. Shanks, ed., *Christianity and Rabbinic Judaism: A Parallel History of Their Origins and Early Developments* (Washington, D.C.: American Archaeological Society, 1992).

44. The "parting of the ways" was between Christianity and rabbinic Judaism; see J. D. G. Dunn, *The Partings of the Ways between Christianity and Judaism and Their Significance for the Character of Christianity* (London: SCM, 1991); Dunn, ed., *Jews and Christians: The Partings of the Ways, AD 70 to 135* (Grand Rapids: Eerdmans, 1992). The ways between Christianity and Judaism never parted; see A. H. Becker and A. Y. Reed, eds., *The Ways That Never Parted* (Tübingen: Mohr, 2003).

similated the Sapiential Paradigm with the Covenantal Paradigm, by giving to the Torah all the attributes of Wisdom *except* her divine nature.

In this titanic clash of wills, little room was left for a third way. By the end of the first century, in the apocalyptic traditions the Wisdom Paradigm lost all autonomy and appeal.

A study that moves away from a mere reckoning of ideas and parallels to focus on the way more complex paradigms were creatively combined, allows us to locate the Parables of Enoch in its proper context within Second Temple Jewish literature. The Book of Parables (including chaps. 70–71) ignores the identification between Wisdom and Torah that will become normative in rabbinic Judaism as well as the identification between Wisdom and the Messiah, which will become normative in early Christianity. The document as a whole therefore testifies to a stage in which the encounter and merging of the Sapiential, Messianic, and Apocalyptic Paradigms were still at their inception — a stage that parallels the earliest origins of the Jesus movement and is the logical premise for the theological developments in Paul and the later Christian tradition. It was in fact the association between God's Wisdom and the eschatological Messiah that opened the path to the Pauline idea that the Messiah is the primary (and even exclusive) content of God's wisdom. Consistently, the Christian tradition will apply to its mediator, Jesus, with more and more conviction the language and the metaphor of Wisdom, until Jesus himself came to be seen as the embodiment of the Wisdom-Word of God.

It is difficult to imagine that someone, either Christian or Jew, could "forge" so well after the year 50 a text like the Parables of Enoch that so well fits in this quite distinctive (and chronologically well confined) stage in the development of Second Temple Jewish thought.[45] For some time the heavenly Jesus of the earliest Christian tradition (including Paul's *kyrios*) and the heavenly Enoch of the Book of Parables remained competitors in the diverse world of Second Temple Jewish messianic figures. The Gospel of John still reflects such a tension in its search for a decisive score: "No one has ascended into heaven except the one who descended from heaven, the Son of Man" (John 3:13). But in the very moment that Jesus was claimed to belong to the divine sphere and identified with the divine *logos,* the game was over. Enoch had lost his battle; his retreat from any messianic ambition turned into an irreparable defeat.

Having failed to succeed as an autonomous movement, the Book of Para-

---

45. Strikingly enough, my comparative analysis of "paradigms" confirms and strengthens the dating of the Parables that both Nickelsburg ("Son of Man") and Chialà (*Libro delle parabole,* 303-40) have determined based solely on the study of the history of the "Son of Man" idea. See also, above, Chialà, "The Son of Man: The Evolution of an Expression."

bles now faced a destiny of oblivion. Because of its rejection of the Covenantal Paradigm, the document had no chance of survival within rabbinic Judaism. In Christianity too, the intensity of competition between Enoch and Jesus made difficult a smooth transition of the Parables into an old, revered prophetic text. The disappearance of Wisdom and the decline of the theology of the heavenly Messiah Son of Man were consequences of the same dynamics. It was certainly no accident but a deliberate act of censorship, which the Christians and the rabbis perpetrated consciously in order to stress the centrality of their own mediator.[46] That, against all odds, the Book of Parables has survived, is a little, precious miracle.

---

46. Boccaccini, "The Preexistence of the Torah."

# The Parables of Enoch in Second Temple Literature: A Response to Gabriele Boccaccini

*Matthias Henze*

Reading through the Parables of Enoch, one cannot but be impressed with the numerous ways in which this intriguing book is connected to its surrounding literature. Even a casual reader will immediately spot numerous points of connection of the Parables with the other books of 1 Enoch, primarily with the Book of the Watchers from which it derives much, but also with the literature of Second Temple Judaism and nascent Christianity in general. In the words of Gabriele Boccaccini, "There is virtually no element in the document that cannot be found elsewhere in Second Temple Jewish and early Christian and rabbinic literature."[1]

Boccaccini's assertion that any attempt to locate the Parables within Second Temple literature needs to begin with an acknowledgment of the book's extensive intertextuality reflects a larger effort currently under way in the field to uncover the intertextual nature of the Pseudepigrapha more generally. In recent years a number of studies have been devoted to this endeavor. Especially successful in this regard is Dale Allison's new commentary on the Testament of Abraham. One of the principal contributions of the commentary is the attention Allison gives to a phenomenal wealth of intertextual echoes, quotes, paraphrases, and allusions he finds throughout the Testament.[2] The operating as-

---

1. All quotations from Boccaccini's work, unless otherwise noted, refer to his contribution to the present volume. See above, G. Boccaccini, "Finding a Place for the Parables of Enoch within Second Temple Jewish Literature."

2. D. Allison, *Testament of Abraham,* CEJL (Berlin: De Gruyter, 2004); the commentary of about 400 pages is followed by an index of ancient texts, broadly conceived, of another 115 pages.

*The Parables of Enoch in Second Temple Literature*

sumption here is that intertextuality cannot easily be dismissed as that which modern scholars detect with their sophisticated search engines but no ancient reader — or hearer — would have noticed, but rather that ancient Jewish (and Christian) audiences would have been keenly aware of such literary connections. Perhaps it is time to give ancient authors and their audiences more, and modern scholars less, credit. To uncover the links between these ancient texts and their cognate literature is a pivotal part of a modern reading of the Pseudepigrapha, especially when they are read against their original setting.

The renewed emphasis on intertextuality for the study of the Pseudepigrapha is immediately relevant for the Parables of Enoch as well. Like so many other texts composed during the late Second Temple period, Parables stands at the literary intersection of multiple intellectual avenues. Hardly anyone will dispute the claim that we find in the Parables "the creative development and mutual modification of complementary traditions,"[3] which, in turn, have roots and parallels in cognate literature. Indeed, the Book of Parables, like few other pseudepigraphic texts, has the character of a storehouse of diverse pieces of traditions — one might think, for example, of the Son of Man texts, or of the Noachic material — which are not always well integrated, at least for our modern sensitivities. However, while the intertextuality of the Parables is undisputed, it is a different matter altogether to determine exactly how to make sense of these diverse points of filiation. The potential pitfalls are considerable. One only needs to think of Josef Milik's claim, now widely rejected, and rightfully so, that the Book of Parables is a Christian text composed in the late third century C.E., an assertion Milik based on alleged "parallels" between the Parables and the Christian parts of the Sibylline Oracles.[4]

Boccaccini takes a different route. To explain the complex terrain of interrelated texts and shared traditions, he offers an evolutionary model of the "history of ideas," spanning some four hundred years, from Sirach in the early second century B.C.E. up to the end of the second century C.E. The place of the Parables within that time frame, Boccaccini concludes, is the late 30s and 40s of the first century C.E., "a stage that parallels the earliest origins of the Jesus movement and is the logical premise for the theological developments in Paul and the later Christian tradition."

Boccaccini's essay is a tour de force that manages to cover an impressive amount of textual material. The scope of his article is impressive, as is the rigor with which it is developed. Boccaccini deserves our gratitude for drawing a

---

3. G. W. E. Nickelsburg, "Son of Man," in *ABD* 6 (1992), 139.

4. J. T. Milik, *The Books of Enoch: Aramaic Fragments from Qumrân Cave 4* (Oxford: Clarenden, 1976), 96-98.

large picture of the intellectual history of the last four hundred years of the Second Temple period, a picture that is at once concise and provocative. It is imperative to notice, however, that the model he presents rests on a number of broader assumptions regarding the nature of Second Temple Judaism and nascent Christianity, as well as their early histories and diverse modes of interaction, that underlie and thus shape his argument. It is to these assumptions that I now turn. Specifically, I will focus on three aspects: first, on what Boccaccini calls the "paradigms"; second, on his reconstruction of the "intellectual history" of Second Temple Judaism; and third, on a subject that the Parables more than any other Enochic book forces upon us, the question of the place of Enochic Judaism in the Jewish-Christian encounters in the first and second century C.E.

I begin with the paradigms. Here Boccaccini takes his lead from the twentieth-century Anglophone historiographer Arthur O. Lovejoy. Lovejoy argued that historians of ideas ought to dismantle systems of thought into "unit-ideas," which are then traced through various eras and disciplines.[5] Lovejoy's sweep of disembodied ideas through time has not always been met as favorably as in Boccaccini's reading. Mindful of the obvious problems in Lovejoy's model, Boccaccini does not leave it with the concept of "unit-ideas," but moves on to the next larger unit, which he calls "paradigms."[6] These he describes as the "conglomerates of unit-ideas." Of these Boccaccini finds five in Second Temple literature — the Wisdom, Apocalyptic, Messianic, Covenantal, and Enochic Paradigms. All originated independently of one another in biblical times. Only in the second century B.C.E., according to Boccaccini's reconstruction, did they begin to merge in diverse and creative ways to form new coherent systems of thought. They all can be found in the Parables of Enoch, "with the conspicuous exception of the Covenantal Paradigm." To determine the book's place within Second Temple literature, the intellectual historian ought not to look for the trajectory of any single paradigm but at the combination of them all, the unique way in which they are combined in each text, and the hierarchy that the text under consideration establishes among them.

Boccaccini's choice of paradigms is helpful, but it is not self-evident. One could, for example, think of additional paradigms. One could conceivably make a case for a Cosmological Paradigm, concerned with astronomical mat-

---

5. A. O. Lovejoy, *The Great Chain of Being: A Study of the History of an Idea* (Cambridge: Harvard University Press, 1936; New York: Harper and Row, 1960); see the recent critique by E. A. Clark, *History, Theory, Text: Historians and the Linguistic Turn* (Cambridge: Harvard University Press, 2004), 106-13.

6. This term is borrowed from D. R. Jackson, *Enochic Judaism: Three Defining Paradigm Exemplars* (London and New York: T. & T. Clark International, 2004), 14-28.

ters. After all, astronomical calculations, precise observations of the stars, and issues pertaining to the calendar lie at the heart of Enochic literature. The Cosmological Paradigm originated in the Wisdom literature of the Hebrew Bible, with deep roots in Mesopotamian astronomy. It is attested most prominently in two of the earliest compositions now collected in 1 Enoch, the Apocalypse of Weeks (1 En 93:1-10; 91:11-17; 4QEn$^g$) and the Book of the Luminaries (1 En 72–82). Cosmology also plays a role in the Parables.[7] Or one could think of a Prophetic Paradigm. Prophets who play a particularly prominent role in the Parables of Enoch are Isaiah, Ezekiel, and Zechariah. The author of the Parables draws extensively on these prophetic texts, not least in his description of the central messianic figure, alternatively called "Son of Man" and "Chosen One." After being named (1 En 48), the Chosen One is endowed with heavenly wisdom "poured out like water" (49:1; 51:3), an attribute derived from Isaiah's depiction of the ideal Davidic king in Isa 11:1. The description of the naming scene is modeled on the second Servant Song in Isa 49:1-6. There the servant is also named in the presence of God, even before he was born, much like the Son of Man in 1 En 48:1-3.[8] All these biblical texts, particularly Isa 11, are frequently invoked in messianic texts of Second Temple Judaism,[9] and the Servant Songs figure prominently in New Testament descriptions of Jesus. In short, we are justified to speak of a Prophetic Paradigm.

It is to be regretted that Boccaccini does not provide an even more detailed definition of what constitutes a paradigm, as it remains somewhat unclear what exactly the term "paradigm" stands for — conglomerates of texts, related literary genres, biblical interpretive traditions, or theological ideas without any fixed organization that are developed in cognate literature? While in some cases we can assume with some confidence what a particular paradigm entails — the Apocalyptic Paradigm would be an example where one could come to an agreement, even though the literature subsumed under this rubric differs significantly in both form and content — in other cases the parameters of the paradigms are less clear. What constitutes the Messianic Paradigm, for example, or what is implied by the Enochic Paradigm? How is the Enochic Paradigm different from the Apocalyptic Paradigm? Boccaccini's division of the

---

7. J. C. VanderKam, *Enoch: A Man for All Generations* (Columbia: University of South Carolina Press, 1995), 17-25.

8. On the use of Isa 49 in the Parables, see G. W. E. Nickelsburg, *Resurrection, Immortality, and Eternal Life in Intertestamental Judaism,* HTS 26 (Cambridge: Harvard University Press, 1972), 74; see also, above, his contribution to the present volume, "Discerning the Structure(s) of the Enochic Book of Parables."

9. References to Isa 11:1-9 in an explicitly messianic context are found in 1QSb 5; 4Q285; 4QpIs$^a$; TLevi 3:2; 18:2-7; and 4 Ezra 13.

material into clearly distinct paradigms seems somewhat strained, and it is not always clear how the paradigms relate to one another. Is there some element that connects all Enochic literature, an element not found in the Apocalyptic Paradigm and that therefore makes the Enochic Paradigm distinct? Also, according to Boccaccini's current arrangement, it is the Enochic Paradigm that connects the Book of Parables with 4 Ezra, but the Apocalyptic Paradigm that connects it with 2 Baruch, so that these two closely related sister apocalypses end up in opposing paradigms. Finally, if a text like the Book of Parables does not explicitly mention the Torah of Moses, does this automatically imply that the Covenantal Paradigm is not attested in that text? I find it difficult to conceive of any Jewish group during the Hellenistic and early Roman periods for which Mosaic Torah would not have been an established authority.

At times Boccaccini's paradigms seem broad and appear to include rather diverse materials. Does each reference to wisdom in a text imply, for example, that its author made use of the Sapiential Paradigm? Clearly, subsumed under the umbrella term "Wisdom" is a range of materials and divergent worldviews.[10] Even within the Book of Parables itself, the term "Wisdom" has different connotations. In 1 En 42, a parody on Sir 24 — and possibly on early Christian claims to identify wisdom with Jesus, at least for those who date the Parables to the first century C.E. — wisdom is personified as a female mediator, an obvious reference to Prov 8. In 1 En 49:3 "the spirit of wisdom and the spirit of insight" are said to dwell in the Chosen One. There the reference is not to the personified wisdom of the hymns, but, as we saw above, to the royal ideology of Isa 11.

The second and perhaps central aspect of Boccaccini's essay I wish to highlight is his reconstruction of the intellectual history from 200 B.C.E. to 200 C.E. Following a broad consensus Boccaccini divides the period into two stages, the Hellenistic and the early Roman period. A basic premise that underlies Boccaccini's model is the notion that all these texts are linked by a *common* intellectual history that unfolds in a single, linear progression. As ancient authors were aware of each other and constantly responded to one another through their texts (e.g., Boccaccini writes that the Psalms of Solomon "reject" the Enochic Paradigm; early Christians "developed" the Enochic concept of divine wisdom dwelling in heaven with the Son of Man; the prologue of John "alludes to" the Enochic rejection of the *logos*), the modern interpreter delineates one text in comparison and contrast with another. Yet Boccaccini's assertion that all these texts are ultimately reducible to a linear chain of development, a develop-

---

10. The pluriform connotations of Wisdom are nicely illustrated in the volume by J. J. Collins, G. S. Sterling, and R. A. Clements, eds., *Sapiential Perspectives: Wisdom Literature in Light of the Dead Sea Scrolls* (Leiden: Brill, 2004).

ment that can be reconstructed in the form of an intellectual stemma of pure strands or, as he has it, "paradigms," runs the risk of imposing an evolutionary model on the material that is not integral to the texts and that ultimately leads, I submit, to systemic problems in Boccaccini's reconstruction of Second Temple intellectual thought. Of these problems I mention two.

It remains unclear to me what leads Boccaccini to argue that the eschatological figures in the book of Daniel and in Enoch's Dream Visions are any less messianic than the Son of Man in the Parables of Enoch. Boccaccini points out that they lack the titles and attributes the Davidic tradition typically associates with the Messiah. In particular, he notes that the Son of Man has "power and dominion" (Dan 7:14), but no wisdom. We should bear in mind, however, that the description of the Son of Man in Dan 7:13-14 is extremely terse and does not provide an exhaustive list of messianic attributes beyond those required by the scene, i.e., the transfer of power from the beasts to the Son of Man. Early interpreters clearly were not irritated by the missing sapiential attributes. The enormous impact these two verses had on later messianic depictions is well-known, with the Book of Parables taking center stage in the reception history of Dan 7. Also, why should Daniel's Son of Man "remain quasi-messianic," only because the text does not mention explicitly that wisdom was given to him? To say, then, that the Messianic Paradigm "does not yet play an important role" in Daniel and 1 Enoch is misleading.

My second concern has to do with the alignment of the New Testament material. Boccaccini argues that, whereas the earliest Christian tradition, which he associates with Q, presents Jesus only as the messenger and teacher of wisdom, it is in the later tradition, tentatively already in Paul and then explicitly in the prologue to John (John 1:1-18), that Jesus the *logos* is identified with Wisdom and, in effect, declared divine. It is certainly true that Paul is already the recipient of emerging Christian traditions, handed down to him in creeds and brief confessional statements (e.g., 1 Cor 11:2, 23; 15:3). But what evidence is there to suggest that pre-Pauline Christian traditions were similar in form and content to Q? Little can be said about where these earliest traditions came from (the church in Damascus?) and how we are to compare them to the canonical material. Moreover, I have also some concern about the chronological sequence in which Boccaccini aligns the material. Paul probably composed his epistles in the late 40s and 50s. Boccaccini appears to suggest that Q represents the earliest Christian traditions, which were then further developed by Paul. But is it clear that Q is older than Paul? What is the evidence in support of that assumption? In general I remain skeptical of evolutionary theories that hold that the earliest Christian traditions were somehow primitive and only later developed to become increasingly complex.

*Matthias Henze*

One problem with Boccaccini's reading, as I see it, arises from his attempt to arrange the texts in a *linear* fashion, presupposing that they all are part of a *single* history, one text building on the other. But should we not allow for the possibility of parallel and potentially independent developments and chains of transmission, intersecting with one another at times and evolving independently at others? In her review of Nickelsburg's monumental commentary on 1 Enoch, Annette Reed calls into question Nickelsburg's reconstruction of the redactional growth of 1 Enoch. "What interests me most about N.'s theory, however, is the presupposition that he shares with Milik, namely, that there must be a single, unilinear development connecting the collection of Enochic materials at Qumran with the Ethiopic collection of 1 Enoch." The textual evidence, Reed concludes, suggests otherwise. Rather than viewing the compilation of Enochic writings as a linear process that began with a core text, say the Book of the Watchers, to which other Enochic writings were subsequently added, Reed proposes "a broader and more variegated phenomenon, whereby Enochic books were collected together in different configurations, even as they also continued to circulate independently."[11] If we should no longer think of the transmission of individual texts in a strictly linear fashion, and here I think Reed's point is well taken, how much more so is this true for the transmission of ideas, or "paradigms." To return to Boccaccini's essay, instead of arguing that Daniel's Son of Man is "quasi-messianic" because he lacks distinct signs of wisdom, and that 4 Ezra has again "lost" or "dropped" the Messianic Paradigm, would it not be easier to assume that we are dealing with parallel strands of messianic expectations, in this particular case with a sapiential strand in the Parables and a nonsapiential strand in Daniel that was continued in 4 Ezra? This would lead us to a model of the intellectual history at the turn of the era that differs markedly from Boccaccini's concept and that renders any attempt to reconstruct a unilinear stemma highly problematic.

Third, and finally, I want to comment briefly on Boccaccini's sketch of the intellectual history as it culminates in the late first century in a "competition" between two "Jewish messianic figures," the "heavenly Jesus" and the "heavenly Enoch." Is Enoch considered a messiah in the Parables, as Boccaccini implies? The only indication comes from 1 En 71:14, one of the conclusions to the Parables, which directly identifies Enoch with the Son of Man: "You are that Son of Man who was born for righteousness, and righteousness dwells on you, and the righteousness of the Head of Days will not forsake you." But chap. 71 is widely

---

11. A. Y. Reed, "The Textual Identity, Literary History, and Social Setting of 1 Enoch: Reflections on George Nickelsburg's Commentary on 1 Enoch 1–36; 81–108," *Archiv für Religionsgeschichte* 1 (2003): 289.

considered to be a secondary addition to — and quite possibly the earliest interpretation of — the original Book of Parables, and so the claim that the identification of Enoch and the Son of Man is implied throughout the book is far from certain. Throughout the Parables the two figures are clearly distinct individuals, and Enoch does not play the role of a messianic figure.

Boccaccini continues to explain that the Book of Parables was forgotten largely because the branch of Enochic Judaism responsible for the Parables lost the competition to Christianity. The fate of the Parables was sealed once Jesus — and not Enoch! — was declared Son of Man. But competing and mutually exclusive claims regarding the identity of venerated figures in Scripture were by no means uncommon in Second Temple Judaism. A prominent example would be the anonymous voice of Isa 40 calling out in the desert to prepare the way of the Lord, a prophecy the Qumran community readily applied to itself (1QS 8:12-16) but that Mark understood to be a prediction of John the Baptist (Mark 1:3). Different appropriations of the same biblical text or figure such as Isaiah's anonymous voice were very common and hardly led to the demise of the competing interpretive communities. Similarly, several prominent Jewish figures of the early second century C.E. thought Bar Kokhba was the Messiah. They were wrong, of course, but this did not mean that they somehow disappeared or that their memory was blotted out as a consequence of their mistaken belief.

Moreover, it seems doubtful that early Christianity really had the impact on the fate of the Parables Boccaccini claims it did. Had there ever been an intense competition over the identity of the Messiah, as Boccaccini alleges, would one not expect to find at least some reference to Jesus in the Enochic material, or to Enoch in the early Christian sources beyond a few fleeting references in Luke 3:37, Heb 11:5, and Jude 14 (cf. Sir 44:16; 49:14)? Much is made in modern scholarship of the absence of the Parables from the Qumran library. But it is equally remarkable that Enoch and Enochic literature, generally speaking, play so small a role in early Christianity. There we find some references to the fallen angels in the Book of the Watchers, but these references do not amount to a competition between Enochic Judaism and early Christianity, let alone over the identity of the Messiah.[12]

In his story of the parting of the ways of Judaism and Christianity, Boccaccini assigns the *logos* theology one of the lead roles. I am in full agreement with his double assertion, first that the *logos* theology derives from the Sapiential Paradigm as inspired by the hymns about personified wisdom as we find them in Prov 8 and Sir 24, and secondly that an examination of the *logos* theology leads us straight to a core issue in first century C.E. religious discourse,

---

12. VanderKam, *Enoch*, 169-82.

both Jewish and Christian. In Boccaccini's reading, however, the *logos* theology, as found most famously in the prologue to John (John 1:1-18), was a divisive element that pushed Judaism and Christianity apart from each other and ultimately turned out to be one principal reason why the Book of Parables was largely forgotten. Here, of course, Boccaccini is not alone, as several New Testament exegetes, some of considerable acumen and standing, have found in John's prologue clear signs that early Christianity drew away from Judaism.

Alternatively, the case has been made that *logos* theology was a conjunctive rather than disjunctive element in first-century Jewish-Christian encounters, a shared rather than divisive *theologumenon*. Most recently Daniel Boyarin has argued eloquently, and, I think, altogether persuasively, that "nothing in *logos* theology as a doctrine of God indicates or even implies a particularly Christian as opposed to generally Jewish, including Christian, kerygma."[13] In other words, what we find in John 1 is the ingenious combination of Jewish messianic soteriology with an equally Jewish *logos* theology. What makes this text distinctively Christian is not its messianism or *logos* theology, both of which are inherited Jewish traditions, but the fact that these are now applied to the figure of Jesus. Moreover, it remains difficult to see how divergent renditions of the *logos* theology could have contributed to the alleged demise of the Parables. The Book of Parables was not forgotten. It may be that the book has not fared well, but some of its core ideas survived for centuries and subsequently resurfaced in both rabbinic and, at a later point, Hekhalot literature.[14]

Gabriele Boccaccini is to be applauded for his comprehensive assessment of the place of the Enochic Parables in Second Temple literature. Even though I take issue with some of the presuppositions of his approach, his essay raises important questions, which are most timely, and which are certain to command our attention for some time to come.

---

13. D. Boyarin, *Border Lines: The Partition of Judeo-Christianity* (Philadelphia: University of Pennsylvania Press, 2004), 95.

14. See below, D. Boyarin, "Was the Book of Parables a Sectarian Document? A Brief Brief in Support of Pierluigi Piovanelli."

# The Son of Man in the Parables of Enoch and the Gospels

*Leslie W. Walck*

The occurrence of the figure of a "Son of Man" in the Parables of Enoch raises fascinating questions about the possible influence of the Parables on the Christian Gospels.[1] In the Parables the term "Son of Man" is one of several used of the eschatological, judicial figure that is central to the three visions.[2] The figure is unknown to the kings and the powerful, but is the hope of the elect and righteous. Most interesting is the role the Son of Man plays as judge at the eschatological judgment. In the Gospels the term "Son of Man" occurs only on the lips of Jesus and is nonrevelatory to the narrative audience.[3] The Son of Man sayings in the Synoptic Gospels can be divided among Bultmann's three categories of earthly, suffering, and future sayings.[4] The future sayings, which are the sayings

---

1. The portions of this paper relating to the Parables of Enoch and the Gospel of Matthew are based on my dissertation, "The Son of Man in Matthew and the 'Similitudes of Enoch'" (Ann Arbor: UMI Dissertation Services, 1999).

2. J. C. VanderKam, "Righteous One, Messiah, Chosen One, and Son of Man in 1 Enoch 37–71," in *The Messiah: Developments in Earliest Judaism and Christianity*, ed. James H. Charlesworth (Minneapolis: Fortress, 1992), 174-75.

3. These characteristics have been noted by all the commentators, including J. A. Fitzmyer, *The Gospel according to Luke (I–IX)*, AB 28 (New York: Doubleday, 1979), 208; G. Vermes, "The Use of *bar-nash/bar-nasha* in Jewish Aramaic," in *An Aramaic Approach to the Gospels and Acts*, ed. M. Black (Oxford: Clarendon, 1967), app. E, 310-30; J. Kingsbury, *Matthew as Story*, 2nd ed. (Philadelphia: Fortress, 1988), 95-103; and G. W. E. Nickelsburg, "Son of Man," in *ABD* 6 (1992), 137-50.

4. R. Bultmann, *Theology of the New Testament*, trans. K. Groebel (London: SCM, 1952), 30; he is followed by P. Vielhauer, "Gottesreich und Menschensohn in der Verkündigung Jesu," in *Aufsätze zum Neuen Testament* (Munich: Kaiser, 1965), 57-58; N. Perrin, *A Modern Pilgrimage*

with eschatological content, are the sayings most likely to reveal similarities to and the possible influence of the concept of the Son of Man in the Parables.

Some have seen a clear dependence of Matthew upon the Parables for the concept of the figure called the Son of Man,[5] while others have argued against such a dependence.[6] This study will examine the concept of the Son of Man in the Parables and in each of the Gospels to discern any possible influence.

The dating of the Parables, while tentative, is important.[7] If the Book of Parables postdates the Gospels, then it could not have had an influence on the Gospels. But if it can be shown to predate them, then its possible influence is worthy of study.

Most likely, in my view, the Book of Parables can be dated to the end of or shortly after the reign of Herod the Great, toward the end of the first century B.C.E. or early first century C.E. Herod, a vassal king of the Romans, the Romans, and their generals fit the characterization in the Parables of the kings and mighty ones.[8] The Parthians' hand in Herod's accession and Herod's visit late in life to healing springs, probably Callirrhoe, also fit the allusions in the

---

in *New Testament Christology* (Philadelphia: Fortress, 1974), 60-77; H. E. Tödt, *The Son of Man in the Synoptic Tradition*, trans. D. M. Barton (London: SCM, 1965); A. J. B. Higgins, *The Son of Man in the Teaching of Jesus*, SNTSMS 39 (Cambridge and New York: Cambridge University Press, 1980), 2; B. Lindars, *Jesus Son of Man: A Fresh Examination of the Son of Man Sayings in the Gospels and in the Light of Recent Research* (Grand Rapids: Eerdmans, 1983), vii.

5. For example, D. R. Catchpole, "The Poor on Earth and the Son of Man in Heaven: A Re-appraisal of Matthew XXV.31-46," *BJRL* 61 (1979): 355-97; and J. Theisohn, *Der auserwählte Richter: Untersuchungen zum traditiongeschichtlichem Ort der Menschensohngestalt der Bilderreden des Äthiopischen Henoch* (Göttingen: Vandenhoeck & Ruprecht, 1975), 149-201.

6. Such as M. Casey, *Son of Man: The Interpretation and Influence of Daniel 7* (London: SPCK, 1979), and D. R. A. Hare, *The Son of Man Tradition* (Minneapolis: Fortress, 1990).

7. A discussion of the wide variety of dates for the Parables can be found in my dissertation, 19-39, including a review of the views of a number of scholars: R. H. Charles, *The Book of Enoch, or I Enoch, Translated from the Editor's Ethiopic Text, and Edited with the Introduction, Notes, and Indexes of the First Edition Wholly Recast, Enlarged, and Rewritten* (Oxford: Clarendon, 1912), liv-lv, 67. See also the summary of the positions in C. L. Mearns, "Dating the Similitudes of Enoch," *NTS* 25 (1979): 360; J. C. Greenfield and M. E. Stone, "The Enochic Pentateuch and the Date of the Similitudes," *HTR* 70 (1977): 51-65; J. J. Collins, *The Apocalyptic Imagination: An Introduction to the Jewish Matrix of Christianity* (New York: Crossroad, 1984), 142f.; J. T. Milik, *The Books of Enoch: Aramaic Fragments of Qumrân Cave 4* (Oxford: Clarendon, 1976), 89-107; D. W. Suter, "The Measure of Redemption: The Similtudes of Enoch, Non-violence, and National Integrity," in SBLSP 22 (1983), 167-76; J. C. Hindley, "Toward a Date for the Similitudes of Enoch: An Historical Approach," *NTS* 14 (1968): 551-65; M. A. Knibb, "The Date of the Parables of Enoch: A Critical Review," *NTS* 25 (1979): 344-59.

8. For a profile of the kings and mighty ones in the Parables, locating them in their sociological setting, see my dissertation, 56-88.

Parables. Further, the bloodshed, for which the righteous and elect desire vindication (1 En 47), fits the conflict of the times.

## The Son of Man in the Parables of Enoch

The Son of Man in the Parables can be discerned by examining the passages in which the Son of Man plays a part: the second and third visions and the epilogue.

The term "Son of Man" deserves some comment.[9] As is well known, in Hebrew and Aramaic the term *ben-adam* or *bar-nasha* is an idiomatic way of referring to a member of the human race.[10] As many have pointed out,[11] the rendering of this term into other languages has resulted in the appearance of nonidiomatic expressions, as in Greek, where the odd expression "the son of the man" was coined, betraying itself as "a translation or a mistranslation of a Semitic idiom."[12] Since Ethiopic is a Semitic language, however, the translation of the construct term carries the same idea of a member of the human race.

In the Parables, however, there is an added dimension. This human figure is also a particular figure, with a particular function in the heavenly court, as seen in the vision. The term in the Parables carries messianic overtones. Adela Yarbro Collins argues that already in Dan 7:13, the concept of the son of man is an allusion to the son of man in Ps 8 and related psalms, where the term was interpreted messianically at the time Daniel was composed and read.[13] She goes on to point out that even though the Parables and 4 Ezra 13 are literarily independent, they both treat the Son of Man messianically. Further, the Book of Parables uses four terms for the messianic figure, the "Righteous One," the "Anointed," the "Elect One," as well as "that Son of Man," but these terms are used to refer to the same figure.[14] Collins then concludes that the independent uses of Dan 7:13 in 4 Ezra and the Parables indicate that "a tradition had devel-

---

9. John Collins discusses the various theories of the origins of the term, including Iranian, Babylonian, and Canaanite influences. Collins sees the Baal cycle of Canaanite mythology as the most likely source for the origins of the concept of the Son of Man in Dan 7. See J. J. Collins, *Daniel: A Commentary on the Book of Daniel*, Hermeneia (Minneapolis: Fortress, 1993), 280-94.

10. In the Parables the plural form appears in 69:6, 14, for example, referring to humanity in general.

11. C. Colpe, "Ho huios tou anthropou," in *TDNT* 8:401-2; Adela Yarbro Collins, "The Origin of the Designation of Jesus as 'Son of Man,'" *HTR* 80 (1987): 391-92.

12. Yarbro Collins, "The Origin," 394.

13. A. Yarbro Collins, "The Apocalyptic Son of Man Sayings," in *The Future of Early Christianity*, ed. B. Pearson (Minneapolis: Fortress, 1991), 221-24.

14. Yarbro Collins, "Son of Man Sayings," 224; see also VanderKam, "Righteous One," 185-86.

oped prior to the composition of both works that the 'one like a son of man' in Daniel 7 should be understood as the messiah."[15] If that is true, it must also be asserted that, not only had the interpretive tradition developed that the figure of Dan 7 should be understood messianically, but also the concept of the Son of Man as a heavenly, messianic figure had developed. It was no longer just a symbolic metaphor for an angelic being or for the saints of God, but had become an individualized member of the heavenly court, who was the subject of such interpretations. Both the Son of Man in the Parables and the figure in 4 Ezra are manifestations of that developing concept of the Son of Man.

## 1 Enoch 46:1-5

This scene unfolds in heaven, to which the seer has been transported in his vision, with the "Lord of Spirits," and "another, whose face had the appearance of a man," *walda sab'*.[16] The seer asks the accompanying, interpreting angel[17] about "that Son of Man" and is told that the Son of Man is righteous,[18] that he

---

15. Yarbro Collins, "Son of Man Sayings," 224.

16. Vanderkam ("Righteous One," 174-75) notes that three terms for the Son of Man are used in the Parables: *walda sab'*, *walda be'si*, and *walda 'eg"ala 'emma-ḥeyaw*. See also Colpe, "Ho huios tou anthropou," 400-477 (esp. 423-26), for its appearances in 1 Enoch. The terms occur in the following locations: *walda sab'* occurs only in the second parable, at 1 En 46:2, 3, 4; and 48:2; *walda be'si* occurs in the third parable and the concluding chapters, at 62:5; 69:29 (twice); and 71:14; *walda 'eg"ala 'emma-ḥeyaw* occurs most frequently (eight times), also in the third parable and the concluding chapters, at 62:7, 9, 14; 63:11; 69:26, 27; 70:1; 71:17. The three terms appear to be synonymous, for the components of each term seem to be used in synonymous ways in the translation into Ethiopic of the Hebrew Bible and the New Testament. Together with the "Righteous One," the "Anointed," and the "Elect One," they refer to the messianic figure, who is the final judge.

17. Michael J. Davidson notes that the function of the interpreting angels is that as they "move around the universe, confidently explaining its mysteries," they convey to the reader an awareness "that the world and its future are firmly under divine control," and that derivatively, Enoch's word is also trustworthy. See M. J. Davidson, *Angels at Qumran: A Comparative Study of 1 Enoch 1–36, 72–108, and Sectarian Writings from Qumran*, JSPSup 11 (Sheffield: JSOT, 1992), 77.

18. He is righteous, and righteousness dwells with the Son of Man, insuring just judgments (1 En 46:3). In Scripture righteousness is imagined in a variety of metaphors. Righteousness can kiss, look down on and go before someone (Ps 85:10, 11, 13); righteousness sometimes is an article of clothing worn by a priest (Ps 132:9), a belt (Isa 11:5), a breastplate (Isa 59:17), or a robe (Isa 61:10; Job 29:14); the image of a ruler also is used of righteousness (Isa 60:17), as well as the image of a plant springing up (Isa 61:11). While righteousness does not seem to have been objectified or personified to the extent that Wisdom was, these passages are examples of metaphorical images used of righteousness in a way similar to what is done here with the image of righteousness dwelling with the Son of Man.

will reveal secret treasures,[19] and that he has been chosen by the Lord of Spirits. The Son of Man has a standing of top priority eternally before the Lord of Spirits, and will confront the kings and mighty ones, casting them down from their thrones and their places of power,[20] for they do not acknowledge or honor him.

The scene is a concise but precise allusion to Dan 7:9, 13, and in it the reader is transported to the heavenly scene where God and God's judicial partner are ready to pass judgment on the enemies of the community. God and the humanlike figure are described in ways to emphasize the purity, innocence, venerableness, fairness, and absolute power and authority of those in charge of the judicial process, while at the same time affirming the eventual positive outcome of the judgment for the faithful community. Despite indications in the real world to the contrary, the message is that God is in charge and will save and restore the righteous and faithful.

The scene depicted in 1 En 46 brings out several attributes of the Son of Man:

a. heavenly status (although without the motion of coming as is noted in Dan 7:13);
b. the status and quality of righteousness;
c. a revelatory function;
d. the status of being chosen for a special purpose by the Lord of Spirits; and
e. opposition to the kings and the mighty. The Son of Man is described opposing the current ruling elite and has the power to overthrow them. Im-

---

19. Davidson (*Angels at Qumran*, 93) notes that angelic control of the meteorological and cosmological secrets implies an "orderliness and integration of the cosmos." See also M. E. Stone, "Lists of Revealed Things in the Apocalyptic Literature," in *Magnalia Dei: The Mighty Acts of God; Essays on the Bible and Archaeology in Memory of G. Ernest Wright*, ed. F. M. Cross, W. E. Lemke, and P. D. Miller, Jr. (New York: Doubleday, 1976), 414-52, who notices that meteorological and cosmological secrets form part of traditional materials that appear in several different apocalypses.

20. Several themes in this passage have similarities with the taunt against the king of Babylon in Isa 14. In Isa 14:9 the prophet says that even Sheol will raise the kings from their thrones to taunt the king of Babylon, while the seer in 1 En 46:4 envisions the kings and the powerful being roused from their resting places and the strong from their thrones by the Son of Man. The uncomfortable vision of maggots and worms covering their beds is common to both (Isa 14:11; 1 En 46:6), while the Babylonian king's aspiration to rule above the stars (Isa 14:13) is similar to the kings' claim to rule the stars (1 En 46:7). The king of Babylon is foreseen to be laid low (Isa 14:5, 11-12), and similarly the kings of the Parables are cast down from their thrones and kingdoms (1 En 46:5). These similarities indicate that the taunt against the king of Babylon in Isa 14 may have provided some of the ideas for the author of the Parables in envisioning the Son of Man overthrowing the kings and the mighty ones in 1 En 46.

plicit in this power is the verdict that the kings and the mighty are corrupt, and that the Son of Man is acting with divine authority in overturning them.[21]

## 1 Enoch 48:2-7

This is a poem[22] proclaiming that the Son of Man was named in the presence of the Lord of Spirits even before the sun and the constellations were made. He will be a staff of support for the righteous, the light of the nations, the hope of the grieving, and mortals will worship him, praising the Lord of Spirits. Even though he has been hidden since before creation, the Lord of Spirits chooses to reveal him to the holy and the righteous, for they have rejected evil and so are saved and restored by the Son of Man. The poem is very encouraging, comforting, and uplifting for the implied audience, as it highlights the Son of Man's eternity and his redemptive, restorative power.[23]

The poem also alludes to the preexistence of the Son of Man (1 En 48:2-7; 62:7). He is named in the presence of the Lord of Spirits before the sun, the constellations, and the stars were created (48:2-3). He was both chosen and hidden from everlasting (48:6). These characteristics reveal the author's belief that the Son of Man enjoyed a premundane existence.[24] Manson, followed by

21. Colpe, "Ho huios tou anthropou," 425-26.
22. See the outline of this poem with its structure of seven tripartite verses in my dissertation, 140-41.
23. Theisohn (*Der auserwählte Richter*, 119-21) has shown that there are extensive similarities on two levels between 1 En 48 and Isa 49.
24. Mowinckel, *He That Cometh: The Messiah Concept in the Old Testament and Later Judaism*, trans. G. W. Anderson (New York: Abingdon, 1956), 370-73; M. Casey, "The Use of the Term 'Son of Man' in the Similitudes of Enoch," *JSJ* 7 (1976): 12-13, 28, and *Son of Man*, 99-112; C. C. Caragounis, *The Son of Man: Vision and Interpretation*, WUNT 38 (Tübingen: Mohr Siebeck, 1986), 114-15; R. G. Hamerton-Kelly, *Pre-existence, Wisdom, and the Son of Man: A Study of the Idea of Pre-existence in the New Testament* (Cambridge: Cambridge University Press, 1973), 17-18. Sjöberg, *Der Menschensohn im äthiopischen Henochbuch*, Skrifter Utgivna av kungl. Humanistika Vetenskapssamfundet i Lund 41 (Lund: Gleerup, 1946), 83-101, and Theisohn, *Der auserwählte Richter*, 128-39, also discuss the issue and favor the ontological preexistent understanding.

Messel (*Der Menschensohn in der Bilderreden des Henoch*, BZAW 35 [Giessen: A. Töpelmann, 1922], 52-55), however, takes the position that v. 3 is an interpolation, and that v. 6 is so corrupt that all that can be gleaned from v. 6 is that the Son of Man was hidden from the beginning. He suggests that the "beginning" is not the beginning of time (i.e., premundane existence) but the beginning of Israel's memory. Further, the naming of the Son of Man refers not to his premundane appointment but to the angels in the kingly court refreshing the memory of the

VanderKam, posits an existence for the Son of Man in the mind of God,[25] a view that understands the naming to be concerned more with purpose and mission than with ontology. As Morna Hooker notes, "apocalyptic (literature) by its very nature held together what was at once present and future, that which was already in existence, but yet still had to take place."[26] The Son of Man's preexistence occurs in a poetic, multivalent,[27] honor-bestowing mode of discourse that fits well with the apocalyptic concern to show that the representative of the righteous is powerful enough to reverse the oppression that the righteous and elect ones are suffering.

1 En 48:2-7, then, reveals that the Son of Man has the role and function of the chosen servant. This figure is developed in 1 En 48 in the following ways:

a. named from eternity,
b. named before the Lord of Spirits,
c. a support for the righteous,
d. the light to the Gentiles,
e. a source of hope,
f. worthy of worship and celebrated with great joy,
g. hidden,
h. revealed to his followers, and
i. his followers are called "righteous/elect/holy."

## 1 Enoch 62–63

This unit deals with the theme of the judgment of the kings and the mighty ones and their reaction to their condemnation. The ones who were used to

---

supreme king as to the Son of Man's availability. Thus Messel, in a dubious way, defines preexistence out of the passage altogether.

25. Manson ("The Son of Man in Daniel, Enoch and the Gospels," *BJRL* 32 [1950]: 171-95) points out that the Hebrew and Jewish mind had no qualms about believing in the premundane existence of Israel either. He cites BerR 1.2b, where six things were thought to have preceded creation: some were actually created, e.g., the Torah and the throne of glory, while others were only planned, e.g., the patriarchs and the nation of Israel, which then existed only in the mind of God. See also VanderKam, "Righteous One," 179-82.

26. M. D. Hooker, *The Son of Man in Mark: A Study of the Background of the Term "Son of Man" and Its Use in St. Mark's Gospel* (Montreal: McGill University Press, 1967), 43.

27. J. J. Collins (*The Apocalyptic Imagination*, 39, 11-17) used the term "multivalent" in discussing "the allusive and evocative power of apocalyptic symbolism," and this, it seems to me, is a very helpful way of expanding our concepts to grasp what the ancient writers were seeking to convey.

commanding others, trusting in their own power, will respectfully stand in the presence of the Lord of Spirits and the Son of Man. They will recognize and acknowledge the Son of Man on the throne of his glory.[28] Their pain is compared to that of a woman giving birth, as they bow down in worship, hoping for and petitioning the Son of Man for mercy. Nonetheless, it will be too late, for no mercy is forthcoming. The angels of punishment, then, will take them, ashamed and dismayed, to be punished for all their wrongdoing against the righteous and elect. The kings and mighty ones plead for mercy, acknowledging their guilt and their misplaced trust, but must accept the appropriateness of the judgment against them and their ultimate fate. In the middle of the vision (62:13-16), however, the blessedness of the righteous and elect in the everlasting presence of the Son of Man is portrayed. They will enjoy safety, protection, sumptuous feasting, and garments of life that will not wear out. All this is made possible because of the reversal of fortunes that will be effected.

Several more features are revealed about this Son of Man in this passage:

a. that he is seated upon the throne of his glory;
b. that he is finally revealed to, recognized, and acknowledged by the kings and the mighty;
c. that he has power to inflict pain, terror, and shame, so that darkness fills the faces of the kings and the mighty;
d. that the righteous will enjoy salvation, which entails dwelling and feasting with this Son of Man and receiving glorious, nonfading garments;
e. that a request is made to him by the kings and the mighty ones;
f. that the judged will plead for mercy;
g. that no mercy will be forthcoming; and
h. that his judgment is fair, which is acknowledged even by the condemned kings and the mighty ones.

The function of a passage like this is to bring comfort and hope to the narrative audience. It illustrates graphically and vividly to the righteous and elect that their oppression will end, and that they will enjoy salvation in the presence of the Son of Man. Their oppressors, however, will be shamed in everlasting, nonreversible condemnation.

---

28. George Nickelsburg notes the importance of recognition in the judgment scene. Since the Son of Man was not known to them before, Nickelsburg argues, they must have recognized him in the righteous and elect who have been aligned with him. See G. W. E. Nickelsburg, *Resurrection, Immortality, and Eternal Life in Intertestamental Judaism*, HTS 26 (Cambridge: Harvard University Press, 1972), 72.

*The Son of Man in the Parables of Enoch and the Gospels*

## 1 Enoch 69:26-29

These four verses form the conclusion of the third parable,[29] and they gather together many key characteristics of the concept of the Son of Man in the Parables. The name of the Son of Man has been revealed and has brought great joy (69:26). He is described as sitting upon the throne of his glory (69:27, 29), and is given total authority for judgment over the wicked, becoming the cause of their destruction (69:27-28). "The throne of his glory"[30] is quite a rare phrase. It is the throne of the Head of Days (47:3; 60:2), but in several places the Elect One or the Son of Man is placed upon the "throne of his glory" for the kings and mighty ones to acknowledge and be judged by (55:4; 61:8; 62:2, 3, 5; 69:27, 29). These characteristics are significant to the implied readers, because they reassure them of their eventual vindication and the punishment of their current oppressors. Three new characteristics of the Son of Man are added from this passage:

a. that the word of the Son of Man before the Lord of Spirits is strong and incontrovertible;
b. that the Son of Man is the means for the destruction of evil; and
c. that this judge has worldwide jurisdiction.

## 1 Enoch 70–71

These chapters, forming an epilogue,[31] draw the reader back to the narrative frame of Enoch's translation. The vehicle for his ascent to heaven is the chariots of the spirit, and he is presented to the Lord of Spirits.[32] A brief allusion is made to

---

29. Black (*The Book of Enoch, or, I Enoch: A New English Edition with Commentary and Textual Notes*, SVTP 7 [Leiden: Brill, 1985], 249) and Charles (*The Book of Enoch*, 140) note how these verses do not fit smoothly into the narrative.

30. This phrase, "the throne of his glory," apparently is quite rare, appearing here in 1 Enoch and in the Gospel of Matthew.

31. See the section entitled "Literary Integrity" in my dissertation, 216-19, in which I follow Vanderkam, "Righteous One," 178-79. Casey ("Use of the Term," 26) has a similar position. I argue against Black, *I Enoch*, 250; J. J. Collins, *The Apocalyptic Imagination*, 151-53; J. J. Collins, *Daniel*, 81; Colpe, "Ho huios tou anthropou," 426; and Theisohn, *Der auserwählte Richter*, 234 n. 80, 211 n. 17.

32. I argue in my dissertation, in the section on the textual problem of 1 En 70:1, 212-16, and on the significance of the Son of Man, 219, that the term "son of man" in that verse is used in a general sense and refers to the human being, Enoch, rather than to the heavenly figure of the visions, adding rich irony to the identification of the seer with the heavenly subject of the visions. This reading depends on three factors. (1) The phrase "to the presence of," *ba-xabehu* ("to the presence

cords for measuring the righteous (cf. 61:1-7) and to the holding place for the spirits of the ancient righteous ones (22:9). In chap. 71 the ascent of Enoch is narrated,[33] with a vision of the fiery, crystal palace and myriads of angels. The Head of Days, together with the archangels and the whole angelic host, approaches the seer, who reacts with terror and praise. Then in the final, climactic scene, the seer, the human being Enoch, is informed that he is the Son of Man of the visions, the instrument who accomplishes righteousness and peace for the implied audience.

Three new features are added in the epilogue to the portrayal of the Son of Man:

a. angels are in the presence of the Son of Man;
b. those angelic attendants have bright garments; and
c. everlasting blessedness is in store for the righteous.

### Tabulated Characteristics of the Son of Man

Twenty-seven characteristics relating to the Son of Man in the Parables have been identified and are tabulated in table 1 on page 251. They are listed in the order in which they appear, and we note in which portion of the text they appear.

---

of the Son of Man"), in 70:1 can be argued to be a scribal insertion. It is missing in Abb 55 (according to Charles, *The Ethiopic Version of the Book of Enoch* [Oxford: Clarendon, 1906], p. xxiv, Abb 55 can be characterized as quite reliable prior to chap. 83, although after that it is unreliable). (2) Grammatical oddities can be resolved by following Abb 55. An extra preposition, "to," *la-* ("to the Son of Man"), is redundant if "to the presence of," *ba-xabehu*, is original (some manuscripts do omit *la-*), and the conjunction "and," *wa-*, is missing between "Son of Man" and "to the presence of the Lord of Spirits" (some manuscripts do include it). (3) Understanding this occurrence of "son of man" as a general reference to the human being, Enoch, is the *lectio difficilior*. The previous passage refers to the heavenly Son of Man. Scribal emendation would likely "correct" the current instance to indicate that "Son of Man" here also refers to the heavenly being. Therefore the reading of Abb 55 that understands a son of man, i.e., a human being, being lifted up is the more difficult reading. Casey, "Use of the Term," 25-27, argues along these same lines. Black (*I Enoch*, 67, 250) concludes the same thing and translates the text this way. In a recent article Daniel C. Olson ("Enoch and the Son of Man in the Epilogue of the Parables," *JSP* 18 [1998]: 27-38) comes to the same conclusion, drawing into the evidence some new manuscript support.

33. See the comparison of ascent accounts in 1 Enoch in my dissertation, 221-27. There I suggest that the author of the Parables has alluded concisely yet precisely to the ascent account in 1 En 14, and yet has altered that allusion to fit the purposes of the Parables of offering hope to the righteous and elect, and of elevating Enoch to a favored status as a heavenly, judicial figure, which reflects the promised, future status of those righteous and elect. This manner of precise but concise allusion is characteristic of this author as noted in his treatment of Dan 7 and other biblical passages.

*The Son of Man in the Parables of Enoch and the Gospels*

Table 1
Characteristics of the Son of Man in the Parables of Enoch

| Characteristic or Feature | 1 En 46 | 48:2-8 | 62–63 | 69:26-29 | 70–71 |
|---|---|---|---|---|---|
| 1. heavenly status* | • | • | • | • | • |
| 2. righteousness | • | (implied) | • |  | • |
| 3. revelatory function | • |  |  |  |  |
| 4. chosenness | • |  |  |  |  |
| 5. judicial role | • |  | • | • |  |
| 6. named from eternity |  | • |  |  |  |
| 7. named before the Lord of Spirits |  | • |  |  |  |
| 8. a support for the righteous |  | • |  |  |  |
| 9. a light to the Gentiles |  | • |  |  |  |
| 10. source of hope for the righteous |  | • |  |  |  |
| 11. worthy of worship |  | • | • |  |  |
| 12. hidden |  | • | • |  |  |
| 13. revealed to followers |  | • | • | • |  |
| 14. followers called "righteous/holy/elect" | • | • |  |  |  |
| 15. seated upon the throne of his glory |  |  | • | • |  |
| 16. inflicts pain, terror, and shame |  |  | • |  |  |
| 17. finally revealed to and recognized by the kings and the mighty |  |  | • |  |  |
| 18. request by kings and mighty |  |  | • |  |  |
| 19. no mercy forthcoming |  |  | • |  |  |
| 20. righteous to enjoy salvation |  |  | • |  | • |
| 21. fairness in judgment |  |  | • |  |  |
| 22. the Word of the Son of Man is strong and incontrovertible |  |  |  | • |  |
| 23. means of destruction of evil |  |  |  | • |  |
| 24. worldwide jurisdiction |  |  |  | • |  |
| 25. angels in presence of Son of Man |  |  |  |  | • |
| 26. bright garments of angelic attendants |  |  |  |  | • |
| 27. everlasting blessedness for the righteous |  |  |  |  | • |

*but without the motion of coming

The judgment scene in 1 En 62–63 contains thirteen of the characteristics, the greatest number of all the scenes, while nine characteristics are shared by more than one passage. The heavenly status of the Son of Man and the righteousness associated with him are the most broadly reported characteristics.

Leslie W. Walck

*Other Features in the Pattern of Relationships*

Complementing the portrait of the Son of Man are other features describing those who interact with the Son of Man.

The vindicated will be radiant in heavenly brightness and glory, shining like the sun (38:4; 39:7; 51:5; 58:3-6). The kings and mighty ones, however, are condemned and consigned to a fiery fate, in a deep burning valley that had been prepared for Azazel and his host (54:1, 5; 63:10; cf. also 67:7, 12-13 in the Noachic section). Fetters were also prepared to bind them.

Resurrection, for the purpose of facing judgment, is also foreseen. The earth will give back those who have died, and the righteous and holy will then be chosen out from among them to enjoy a satisfying life with the Elect One (51:1-5). The elect will be gathered by the angels from wherever they had been lost, in the desert, at sea, or slain by wild beasts. But they will return and find security in the Elect One, for "none can be destroyed" (61:1-5). Resurrection is envisioned for those aligned with the Son of Man, for they will be gathered to enter into a life of satisfaction and joy, which contrasts markedly with their current oppressed status.

At the same time, a clear dichotomy exists between the righteous and the oppressors. Before the judgment the righteous are downcast and oppressed, while the kings and the mighty enjoy wealth, power, and prestige. After judgment, however, their fortunes are reversed. Judgment is executed against the kings and mighty ones because of their denial of the Lord of Spirits (46:7) and because of their treatment of the righteous, who are aligned with the judge (46:8; 47:2). They will lose their power and status (38:4-5; 45:6) and will be given over to the righteous and elect, so that no trace of them will survive (48:9-10). They will be filled with shame, handed over to the angels of punishment (62:9-12; 63:11), consigned to eternal destruction, imprisoned (69:27-28), in fetters (53:4-5), in a deep, burning valley (chap. 54). On the other hand, the vindicated will be blessed, to enjoy everlasting life with the Son of Man and to take over the earth and live on it in peace, free from the oppression of the kings and mighty ones (45:5-6; 48:7-10). Glory and honor and life shall return to them (50:1-2; 62:13-16), and they are promised fortunes, power and prestige, in effect a reversal of fortunes, signifying the judicial power of the Son of Man.[34]

Table 2 on page 311 presents other salient features of the portrait of the Son of Man.

---

34. J. C. VanderKam, *Enoch: A Man for All Generations* (Columbia: University of South Carolina Press, 1995), 134.

## Table 2
## Other Features Relating to the Son of Man in the Parables of Enoch

| | Characteristic or Feature | Passages Where Found |
|---|---|---|
| 28. | fiery fate of the condemned | 54:1, 5; 63:10; cf. also 67:7, 12-13 in the Noachic section |
| 29. | fate was prepared for Azazel | 54:5 |
| 30. | fetters for the condemned | 53:4-5 |
| 31. | radiance of the vindicated | 38:4; 39:7; 51:5; 58:3, 5-6 |
| 32. | resurrection | 51:1 |
| 33. | the elect will be gathered | 61:5 |
| 34. | gathered from widely scattered areas* | 61:5 |
| 35. | clear dichotomy between the righteous and the condemned | passim |
| 36. | basis of judgment** | 62:11; cf. 46:8 |
| 37. | reversal of fortunes | 38:4-5; 45:5-6; 48:7-10; 50:1-2; 62:9-16; 63:11; 69:27-28 |

*they will be gathered from the depths of the earth, the desert, and the sea
**the treatment the righteous have received at the hands of the kings and mighty ones

## The Son of Man in the Gospels

The concept of the Son of Man in the Gospels continues to be baffling. No longer can it be assumed that there existed a unified, comprehensive concept of an eschatological, judicial figure known as "the Son of Man,"[35] which can be reconstructed from Daniel, the Parables of Enoch, the Wisdom of Solomon, 4 Ezra, and 2 Baruch. But not to discern any influence of that earlier literature on the content of the term is to go to the other extreme.[36] Perhaps wiser is to recognize the development of several overlapping concepts of the Son of Man,[37] one or another of which may have influenced the Gospel writers.

To evaluate the influence of the Parables on the Gospels, I will begin with Q and the Synoptic Gospels. I will again identify the characteristics associated with the Son of Man in those texts. The sayings referring to the earthly presence and authority of the Son of Man will be examined first, followed by the sayings in which the suffering of the Son of Man is prevalent, and then finally the say-

---

35. E.g., Bultmann, *Theology*, 1:29-33; and Tödt, *Son of Man*, 22.
36. E.g., Hare, *Son of Man Tradition*, 4.
37. Nickelsburg, "Son of Man," 137-50.

ings in which the future, eschatological, judicial Son of Man is in focus. Following the study of the Son of Man sayings in the Synoptic Gospels, I will examine those from the Gospel of Saint John.

### Earthly Sayings from Q

Three sayings from Q clearly refer to the earthly presence of the Son of Man. Luke 6:22//Matt 5:11, the final beatitude in both Luke and Matthew, refers to the blessedness of those who are persecuted on account of Jesus (Matthew) or on account of the Son of Man (Luke).[38] Hatred, exclusion, revulsion, and defamation all may besiege followers of Jesus as the Son of Man. Matthew's removal of the term "Son of Man" here may be due to his concern to elevate Jesus' status as the Son of Man, and to distance negative effects from him and his followers. These negative effects of hatred, exclusion, revulsion, and defamation are comparable to the oppression experienced by the righteous and elect in the Parables. The righteous in the Parables have been persecuted by the kings and mighty ones (1 En 46:8); their blood has been shed (47:2, 4); they have rejected the ways of the mighty and powerful (48:7); and they have experienced the shame of downcast faces (62:15) due to exclusion and hatred by the kings and the mighty ones. Thus oppression and persecution are common to both the blessed of the Beatitudes and the righteous and elect of the Parables. We may be tempted to see this as evidence of the influence of the Parables on the wording of the Beatitudes, but more likely it may simply be from the general, apocalyptic attributes of the oppressed that were current at the time.

Secondly, Luke 7:34//Matt 11:19 refers to the Son of Man who was celebrating life through table fellowship rather than fasting as John the Baptist's disciples did. The Son of Man is criticized for being a "glutton and a drunkard."[39] In the Parables no such accusation is leveled against the Son of Man. This is due to the narratological setting of the Parables: it is located in the Son of Man's judgment and condemnation of the oppressors, the kings and the mighty ones, rather than in the period of their oppressive activity prior to the final judgment. Their misdeeds are described as trusting in their own power and wealth rather than recognizing the authority of their judge, the Son of Man. However,

---

38. C. M. Tuckett, "The Son of Man and Daniel 7: Q and Jesus," in *The Sayings Source Q and the Historical Jesus*, ed. A. Lindemann (Leuven: University Press; Sterling, Va.: Peeters, 2001), 373 n. 12. Tuckett believes that the term "Son of Man" was original in this saying, as preserved in Luke's Gospel, and that Matthew's Gospel introduced a change to "on my account."

39. Tuckett, "Son of Man," 386, believes this saying is from the redactional stage of Q, rather than the first stage.

the blessedness of the reversal of fortunes to be brought about by the Son of Man is described in terms of eternal feasting in the presence of the Son of Man (1 En 62:13-15). The feasting motif also occurs in Isa 25:6, where God will make a feast of rich foods and well-aged wine. God will destroy the shroud cast over all people and death will be swallowed up. It also appears in Rev 19:9, which refers to the marriage feast of the Lamb, who is the Son of Man (Rev 5:6, 9, 12), and where only the redeemed will be present. Feasting in the presence of the Son of Man, then, is a quality of the reversal of fortunes shared by both Q and the Parables. The similarities in feasting for the righteous are general, however, and too minimal to suggest direct influence. Nonetheless, it is in keeping with the patterns of relationship surrounding the Son of Man in both the Parables and Q.

Luke 9:58//Matt 8:20 is a third saying from Q referring to the earthly presence of the Son of Man. While the foxes and birds have protective places of refuge and rest, "the Son of Man has nowhere to lay his head."[40] Referring to the itinerant nature of Jesus' activity in this context, it is a response to a would-be follower. Nickelsburg points to a possible reflection of the contrast between the beasts and the "one like a son of man" in Dan 7:3, 13, as well as to the uses of Ps 8:4-8 as bringing out "an ironic contrast between present lowliness and future glory."[41] This may be similar to the contrast between the hiddenness and the glorious status of the Son of Man in the Parables, but the similarity is conceptual and general rather than precise and direct.

Two further sayings from Q overlap two of the categories of the Son of Man sayings.[42] Luke 11:30//Matt 12:40 compares Jonah as a sign to the Ninevites with the Son of Man as a sign to the generation being addressed.[43] Jonah's journey to Nineveh was for the purpose of proclaiming God's judgment. It had the result that the Ninevites repented. Similarly the Son of Man's presence reveals God's judgment on the present generation. The words are a call to repentance before the judgment takes place.[44] The Son of Man as a warning sign is conceived of as being a future event, for both the queen of the South and the

---

40. Tuckett, "Son of Man," 386, believes this saying is also from the redactional stage of Q.

41. Nickelsburg, "Son of Man," 143.

42. Contrast M. E. Boring, "Matthew," in *NIB* 8:360, who refers to the three categories as remaining "distinct."

43. Cf. Nickelsburg, "Son of Man," 143. Tödt (*Son of Man*, 52-54) treats this saying as a "coming saying."

44. While the Lukan version of this saying refers to a "sign," the Matthean version interprets the sign as being the three-day sojourn in the belly of the whale. This three-day sojourn parallels Jesus' burial, and so the saying is transformed by Matthew into a prediction of the resurrection. Even so, the judgment of the queen of the South and of the Ninevites remains. In effect, Matthew's version overlaps with the "suffering" category of sayings as well, since the resurrection followed on the terrible suffering of Jesus.

Ninevites arising in judgment are in the future. But Jesus' contemporaries are being addressed, and so the earthly presence of the Son of Man is also in focus. In Luke 11:31-32 Jesus asserts that something greater than Solomon or Jonah is here, and this also locates the saying in the earthly presence of Jesus. From the context of these verses, it is the Son of Man who is that "something" greater than Solomon or Jonah. Thus both a future aspect and a present aspect are contained in this saying as well. It overlaps the "future" category and the "present" category of Son of Man sayings.

The Book of Parables does not include the possibility of repentance. When repentance does occur in the oppressors' plea for mercy, it is too late, for the Son of Man's judgment has already taken place and is incontrovertible. In Q repentance and forgiveness are possible, while in the Parables they are not. Further, in Q the Son of Man is parallel to Jonah, and thus is conceived of as a witness at the judgment, rather than judge, as in the Parables. Thus it can be surmised that this saying was not influenced in a direct verbal way by the Parables. But on the level of a theological dynamic, both Q and the Parables envision the presence of the Son of Man as a revelation of judgment on behalf of an omnipotent God against unrepentant earth dwellers. This is an interesting similarity on the level of patterns of relationships surrounding the figure of the Son of Man.

Luke 12:10//Matt 12:32 again is a saying that overlaps the earthly and the future Son of Man sayings. Forgiveness for speaking against the Son of Man lies in the future, with the future tense being used. But the offense occurs during the earthly presence of the Son of Man. Thus both the "earthly" and the "future" aspects are present. Here, however, since the Book of Parables does not envision the forgiveness of sinners, the direct influence of the Parables on this saying is improbable.[45]

Beyond these five sayings, Q also reports the temptation of Jesus in Luke 4:1-13//Matt 4:1-11.[46] This description in Q gives a fuller account than that in Mark, and reflects the opposition between good and evil. Among other things, Jesus' being in the wilderness may reflect the status of his followers in a societal

---

45. See also Boring, "Matthew," 8:286 n. 266, for his understanding of the tradition history of this saying. He refers to "The Unforgivable Sin Logion Mark 3:28-29/Matt 12:31-32/Luke 12:10: Formal Analysis and History of the Tradition," *NovT* 17 (1976): 258-79; *The Continuing Voice of Jesus: Christian Prophecy and the Gospel Tradition* (Louisville: Westminster John Knox, 1991), 219-21. He argues that the unforgivable sin logion was originally a pronouncement concerning divine forgiveness toward human beings who are referred to in the Aramaic phrase *bar-nasha*. Early Christian prophetic activity reworked it to refer to sins against the Son of Man as being forgivable and those against the Holy Spirit as being unforgivable.

46. Nickelsburg, "Son of Man," 143.

*The Son of Man in the Parables of Enoch and the Gospels*

wilderness, and thus also may compare to the societal wilderness in which the righteous and elect find themselves in the Parables. The devil in the temptation story claims to be able to bestow power and dominion over all the kingdoms of the earth, and this may be comparable to the power and authority the kings and mighty ones claim in the Parables. The power struggle between the devil and Jesus, who recognizes that God alone holds that power, may be comparable to the power and authority the Son of Man exerts in the judging of the kings and mighty ones in the Parables. As Nickelsburg acknowledges, the title "Son of God" is explicit in the temptation story, not "Son of Man." These similarities are on the level of the patterns of relationship, and they are intriguing, even though direct verbal influence seems unlikely.

The earthly sayings in Q, then, do not seem to reflect any direct verbal influence from the Parables on the character of the Son of Man, but interestingly some of the same theological dynamics seem to be present.

*Earthly Sayings in Mark*

Mark reports two sayings that refer to the Son of Man's earthly presence. These two sayings claim and establish the present authority of Jesus and his disciples over against the Jewish authorities.[47] Both sayings are taken over by Matthew and Luke, and are used as a form of self-reference.

Mark 2:10//Matt 9:6//Luke 5:24,[48] in the story of the healing of the paralytic, refers first to Jesus and then to the Son of Man as having authority on earth to forgive sins. This authority to forgive sins is a divine authority and raises the charge of blasphemy against Jesus. It is problematic for his antagonists. In response, Jesus utters the Son of Man statement about having authority to forgive sins and then he heals the man, eliciting astonishment from the onlookers. Since the term "Son of Man" elicits no comment from the other characters in the story, it functions as a self-referent.

In the Parables the Son of Man is portrayed as having divine authority. That authority is conveyed in the heavenly context for the visions, of being named before the Lord of Spirits (1 En 48:2-8), as seated on the "throne of his glory" (1 En 62–63; 69:26-29), and in the incontestable nature of his judicial role (1 En 46; 62–63; 69:26-29), which is recognized even by the kings and mighty ones (62–63). The authority of the Son of Man is judicial and is exercised in his judging against the kings and mighty ones. In this judicial authority, forgive-

---

47. P. Perkins, "Mark," in *NIB* 8:550.
48. The ordering of the phrases in Matthew and Luke is slightly different.

ness must be assumed as a possibility, but it is not exercised. Thus the point of similarity between the Markan saying and the concept of the Son of Man in the Parables is divine, judicial authority. However, there is a significant contrast. In the Markan saying the Son of Man's authority is exercised on earth in a specific, contemporaneous situation, while in the Parables his authority is associated with his heavenly status in an eschatological setting. And yet this authority is exercised against the earthly kings and mighty ones. The Markan saying is in the context of exercising the authority to forgive, while in the Parables the authority to forgive is not acknowledged nor exercised. Authority to forgive must be assumed as part of the depiction in the Parables, whereas it is explicitly claimed in the Markan saying. In both cases divine authority has been attributed to the Son of Man. Thus while direct verbal dependence cannot be claimed, the Markan saying seems to reflect a theological dynamic similar to that of the Parables.

Mark 2:28//Matt 12:8//Luke 6:5 also refers to the Son of Man's earthly authority, this time as "lord of the sabbath." The term "lord" *(kurios)* implies authority, and again it is an authority over a divine matter, the observance of the Sabbath. Exercising divine authority on earth may be somewhat similar to the authority the Son of Man wields in the Parables in an eschatological setting. While this is not enough to suggest direct, verbal influence from the Parables, it may reflect a similar theological understanding of the authority of the Son of Man.

### Lukan Earthly Sayings

Luke reports one further Son of Man saying that refers to present, earthly activity and authority. Luke 19:10 shows Jesus' assertion that the Son of Man came to seek and to save the lost. Using the self-referent to describe Jesus' purpose, the saying is appended to Luke's story of Jesus' encounter with Zacchaeus, and is given in response to the crowd's criticism of Zacchaeus's being a sinner. The "lost" in Luke's Gospel are those outside the bounds of the mainstream society, as illustrated by the parables of the lost coin, the lost sheep, and the lost son in Luke 15. Thus, this saying in 19:10 characterizes Jesus' ministry to those outside the mainstream. It expresses the Son of Man's salvific purpose.[49]

---

49. The saying conveys a similar purpose to that found in Mark 10:45//Matt 20:28, where seeking and saving the lost is expressed in terms of giving his life as a ransom for many. While the purpose expressed is the same, the imagery used to express that purpose is different. The ransom imagery places the Markan/Matthean saying in the category of the suffering of the Son of Man, while Luke's seeking and saving imagery places it in the category of earthly sayings. A similar purpose is expressed in the variant added to Luke 9:56. This addition is not strongly supported

## The Son of Man in the Parables of Enoch and the Gospels

When the Son of Man in the Parables is compared to this Lukan saying, two points of conceptual similarity can be noted: the authority of the Son of Man, and seeking and saving the lost. In the Parables the authority of the Son of Man is evident, and as a part of the judgment the angels gather the scattered righteous ones (1 En 61:5) to restore them to their rightful place. These scattered ones were oppressed by those in power. They were not a part of the society controlled by the kings and mighty ones, and so they may be comparable to the "lost" in Luke's Gospel. Thus seeking and saving the lost is similar to gathering the scattered righteous ones in the Parables. While verbal similarities between Luke 19:10 and the Parables are absent, on the level of the theological dynamics and the pattern of relationships, the concept is similar. Here it can be seen that the Son of Man in both has the purpose of saving the righteous on the margins of society.

### An Earthly Saying in Matthew

An earthly Son of Man saying has been created by Matthew in Matt 16:13. This verse reports Jesus' first question regarding who the people think he is, and the term "Son of Man" is used where the parallel passages simply have the personal pronoun "me" (Mark 8:27//Luke 9:18). In Matt 16:21, however, a continuation of the same episode and the first passion prediction, the personal pronoun "him" is used instead of "Son of Man" (Mark 8:31//Luke 9:22: "it is necessary for the Son of Man to suffer many things"). The insertion of the term in v. 13 and its replacement in v. 21 indicates that for Matthew, Jesus is the Son of Man.[50] John Meier sees the use of the term in Matt 16:13 and its absence in Matt 16:21 as very significant to

---

textually. The added words note the purpose of the Son of Man as not destroying life but as saving it, and are part of Jesus' response to the suggestion by James and John to bring fire down on a certain Samaritan village that had turned them away. A further Lukan addition that refers to Jesus' earthly presence with the self-referent of the Son of Man is his question to Judas in the Garden of Gethsemane, "Is it with a kiss that you are betraying the Son of Man?" (Luke 22:48). Because the betrayal is in focus, and the saying is embedded in the passion story, it is better to consider it among the suffering sayings rather than the earthly sayings.

50. J. D. Kingsbury, *Matthew: Structure, Christology, Kingdom* (Minneapolis: Fortress, 1975), 115, and *Matthew as Story*, 2nd ed. (Philadelphia: Fortress, 1988), 95-103, where he argues that "Son of man" is a public title used in the context of opposition, and the personal pronoun is used with regard to insiders such as Peter, whose "evaluative point of view . . . is in accord with the evaluative point of view of God." Cf. W. D. Davies and D. C. Allison, Jr., *A Critical and Exegetical Commentary on the Gospel according to Saint Matthew*, 3 vols., ICC (Edinburgh: T. & T. Clark, 1988, 1991, 1997), 2:51, who agree with Kingsbury's emphasis on the "Son of man" as a public title.

Matthew's development of Christology.[51] Narratively, in Peter's confession (16:16) Matthew has brought together two titles, "Messiah" and "Son of the living God," in close proximity with the concept of the Son of Man (16:13). The Son of Man, then, has a powerful transcendence hidden in deprivation and service, and embodies the mystery of the dying and rising servant, as well as being the judge who will come in glory.[52] Meier then connects this revelation to Peter with the revelation of the hidden Son of Man by the Most High to the elect and righteous ones in 1 En 62:7, 46:1, 48:1-7. Further, as Nickelsburg has argued, Caesarea Philippi had an ancient reputation for being a place where revelations took place, and both Peter's confession and the Enochic revelations are associated with Caesarea Philippi as well.[53] Here, then, we observe several characteristics in common with the Parables: transcendence, hiddenness, the judicial role, future glory, revelation by God, as well as the narrative location near Caesarea Philippi. This is an intriguing set of similarities on the level of theological dynamics and the pattern of relationships.

### Suffering Sayings

Q does not preserve any sayings that refer to the suffering Son of Man.[54] They appear only in Mark and the literature dependent on Mark. These sayings are evidently a development of the early church. While scholars generally argue for the originality of either the "earthly" sayings or the "future" sayings, the "suffering" sayings are generally agreed to be derivative, for they can readily be seen to be a development out of the identification of Jesus with the Son of Man, an identification that already exists in Q, the Synoptics, and John. Suffering and the Son of Man, however, were combined already before the composition of Mark's Gospel, though this combination is not reflected in Q.[55]

The suffering sayings can be seen as a paradox challenging the conventional views of power,[56] arising out of Dan 7:13, in which the "one like a son of man" identifies with the righteous of Israel in their suffering.[57] Alternatively,

---

51. J. P. Meier, *The Vision of Matthew: Christ, Church, and Morality in the First Gospel* (New York: Paulist, 1979), 109-20.

52. Meier, *The Vision of Matthew*, 110.

53. G. W. E. Nickelsburg, "Enoch, Levi, and Peter: Recipients of Revelation in Upper Galilee," *JBL* 100 (1981): 575-600.

54. Tuckett, "Son of Man," 391.

55. E.g., Boring, "Matthew," 8:361, and Perkins, "Mark," 8:550.

56. Perkins, "Mark," 8:550.

57. Perkins, "Mark," 8:631, 703, where she also refers to J. Marcus, *The Way of the Lord: Christological Exegesis of the Old Testament in the Gospel of Mark* (Minneapolis: Fortress, 1992),

the suffering Son of Man sayings may arise out of the development of the "conflation of servant and Son of Man materials in the Parables of Enoch."[58] The author of the Parables, however, did not assimilate suffering to the Son of Man along with the other servant characteristics, and so the Book of Parables does not portray a suffering Son of Man. On the other hand, the suffering sayings show the Son of Man identifying with those who do suffer, the oppressed, just as the Son of Man in the Parables identifies with the righteous and elect who suffer at the hands of the oppressive kings and mighty ones.

Scholars have identified three passion predictions:

- Mark 8:31//Matt 16:21//Luke 9:22[59]
- Mark 9:31//Matt 17:22-23//Luke 9:44
- Mark 10:33-34//Matt 20:18-19//Luke 18:31-33

These passion predictions refer to suffering, rejection, mockery, scourging, betrayal, being killed and rising on the third day, or after three days. Persons associated with bringing about this suffering are the elders, chief priests, scribes, and Gentiles. In the second and third predictions, all three Gospels employ the term "Son of Man," where it functions as a self-referent.

*Other Markan Suffering Sayings*

The other suffering sayings in Mark's Gospel all appear after the first passion prediction. Jesus admonishes his disciples after the transfiguration not to speak of the event until after the Son of Man was raised from the dead (Mark 9:9; Matt 17:9; but Luke 9:36 omits the reference to the Son of Man). In relation to the coming of Elijah (Mark 9:12; Matt 17:12), reference is made to written predictions of the suffering Son of Man (omitted by Luke). In Mark 10:45//Matt 20:28 Jesus asserts that the suffering of the Son of Man is a ransom for many, while in Mark 14:21//Matt 26:24//Luke 22:22 the fate of the Son of Man is re-

---

174-75. Marcus's research brings out the parallels between Mark's passion narrative and the suffering of the righteous in the Psalms, which can be seen as prophecies of Jesus' suffering.

58. Nickelsburg, "Son of Man," 144.

59. As noted above, Matt 16:21 does not include the term "Son of Man," where Mark 8:31 and Luke 9:22 do. The absence of "Son of Man" in Matthew may be due simply to Matthew's identification of Jesus with the Son of Man, or it may reflect a pattern in Matthew of Jesus using the term in confrontational situations and the personal pronoun in intimate settings with his disciples. See Kingsbury, *Matthew: Structure, Christology, Kingdom*, 115, and *Matthew as Story*, 95-103.

ferred to as having been written beforehand, while the betrayer is mourned. In the Garden of Gethsemane (Mark 14:41//Matt 26:45) Jesus announces the hour of betrayal for the Son of Man.

### Lukan Suffering Sayings

Luke has added a "Son of Man" saying. Even though he has shortened and streamlined the episode in the garden, omitting the announcement of the betrayal of the Son of Man, a question to Judas about betrayal with a kiss (Luke 22:48) is inserted, using the term "Son of Man." This question is not present in Mark 14:45, while in Matt 26:50 Jesus' question is to his "friend," Judas, asking why he is there.

Luke has created two further suffering Son of Man sayings. One is in the midst of the discussion on the day of the Son of Man (Luke 17). Among those "future" sayings is Luke 17:25, which echoes the first passion prediction (Mark 8:31//Matt 16:21//Luke 9:22). It appears to be a reminder added to the passage in which the coming day of the Son of Man is compared to lightning flashes, and its intent is to point out that the future Son of Man is the same one who endured much suffering and rejection (Luke 17:25; cf. 9:22).[60] Another reminder of the prediction of suffering is found in the story of the resurrection appearance to the two walking to Emmaus (24:7). The unrecognized, risen Jesus reminds them that the Son of Man had to be handed over and crucified, and rise on the third day. Here the use of the term and the reference to his suffering are dependent on the earlier narrative.

### A Matthean Suffering Saying

Similarly, Matthew has added a reference to the Son of Man's suffering in the reminder about the nearness of the Passover (Matt 26:2). No reference to the Son of Man is included in the parallel passages of Mark 14:1-2 and Luke 22:1-2.

### Comparison with the Parables

It is interesting to note that in these sayings, Jesus' suffering is at the hands of the elders, chief priests, scribes, and Gentiles, who are members of the ruling

---

60. R. A. Culpepper, "Luke," in *NIB* 9:331.

elite. In the Parables the oppressors also are the ruling elite. Further, whereas the Book of Parables does not portray a suffering Son of Man, the figure does identify with the oppressed righteous and elect. In a similar way, the suffering Son of Man in the Gospels identifies with the oppressed by joining them in their suffering and by dying on their behalf. Thus the suffering sayings reflect three similarities between the Gospels and the Parables: identification with the oppressed; the ruling elite being the oppressors; and the divine intention to act on behalf of the oppressed. Rather than indicating dependence or influence, however, these similarities may simply reflect the reality that the ruling elite have the power to cause suffering. Nonetheless, the similarities just noted cohere with the patterns of relationship reflected in the Parables.

## The Future Son of Man

### Q and the "Future" Son of Man

Four passages about the "future" Son of Man can be found in Q. In Luke 12:8-9// Matt 10:32-33 the Son of Man is envisioned in a future courtroom scene as acknowledging or denying those who acknowledge or deny Jesus on this earth. Matthew has used the first-person pronoun instead of the term "Son of Man," because for Matthew the identification of Jesus with the Son of Man is so complete.[61] Describing this saying as a "promise," Tödt sees the form of the saying that includes the term "Son of Man" as more likely to be original, and since it distinguishes between Jesus and the Son of Man, he considers it to be an authentic saying of Jesus.[62] This saying casts the Son of Man as a guarantor, savior, and rescuer, rather than as a judge,[63] which would be expected if the Book of Parables had directly influenced this passage. The saying and the Parables share only a judicial context for the Son of Man, because his role differs.

In the admonition to readiness, Luke 12:40//Matt 24:44, also considered by Tödt to be authentic, the Son of Man is compared to a thief coming at an unexpected hour. The quality of unexpectedness in this saying may be compared to the unexpected judgment by the Son of Man, which produces the surprise on the faces of the kings and mighty ones when they recognize their judge in the Parables (1 En 62:5). Thus the unexpectedness of the judgment is a similarity.

---

61. Boring, "Matthew," 8:261; Culpepper, "Luke," 9:253.
62. Tödt, *Son of Man*, 55.
63. Tödt, *Son of Man*, 60.

*Leslie W. Walck*

Preserved in Q are some comments about the future Son of Man as compared to natural and biblical events. Luke has incorporated these sayings into a passage on the day of the Son of Man (Luke 17:22-37), while Matthew has included them in the Synoptic Apocalypse (Matt 24:26-28, 37-41). The day of the Son of Man, or the parousia of the Son of Man, is compared to lightning flashes, vultures gathering around a carcass, the flood of Noah's time, or the destruction of Sodom from which Lot escaped. The point of these comparisons is that even though unexpected, the world would not fail to recognize that sudden day. Tödt argues that these sayings reflect the concern of the early church, believing that the day would come, but without being concerned for describing it, or differentiating successive stages. Their belief was that it would come, it would come suddenly, it would be recognized, and therefore the world must heed the warning to be prepared.[64]

These images are not found in the Parables, although one of the Lukan sayings (Luke 17:30) refers to the day of the Son of Man being "revealed." In a general but precise sense, the revealing of the Son of Man and his recognizability are shared by both.

Another passage from Q, Luke 22:28-30//Matt 19:28, refers to sitting in judgment. In the Lukan version the disciples who have endured Jesus' trials will be sitting at table, eating and drinking in his kingdom, and sitting on thrones judging the twelve tribes of Israel. In this passage Jesus refers to himself with the first-person pronoun, not as the "Son of Man." For Q this is apparently the climactic "last word," indicating that not only Jesus but also those who have followed him will act as judges over Israel,[65] which can be seen as a concern and perspective of the early church.[66] Luke includes this image in the last words of Jesus at the last supper on the night of his arrest and trial. Matthew's version has a different setting. It is part of the conversation with the disciples following the encounter with the rich young ruler. No mention is made of eating and drinking, but in response to the disciples' query about their rewards for having given up so much to follow him, Jesus promises that at the renewal of all things (*palingenesia*),[67] when the Son of Man is seated on the throne of his glory, they

---

64. Tödt, *Son of Man*, 48-52.
65. Tuckett, "Son of Man," 380.
66. R. Bultmann, *History of the Synoptic Tradition* (New York: Harper & Row, 1963), 163; Tödt, *Son of Man*, 63-64; Francis Wright Beare, *The Gospel according to Matthew* (San Francisco: Harper and Row, 1981), 400; Boring, "Matthew," 8:391.
67. For *palingenesia*, see Theisohn, *Der auserwählte Richter*, 165; Tödt, *Son of Man*, 91; Robert H. Gundry, *Matthew: A Commentary on His Handbook for a Mixed Church under Persecution*, 2nd ed. (Grand Rapids: Eerdmans, 1994), 392; E. Schweizer, *The Good News according to Matthew*, trans. D. E. Green (Atlanta: John Knox, 1975), 389-90; H. Geist, *Menschensohn und*

## The Son of Man in the Parables of Enoch and the Gospels

too will be sitting on twelve thrones judging the twelve tribes of Israel, as "the most important persons among the Jewish people" at the eschaton.[68] Not only does Matthew use the term "Son of Man," but he also depicts him sitting on "the throne of his glory" along with the image of his followers sitting on their thrones and sharing in judgment.

When compared with the Parables, one similarity can be noted. The image of eating and drinking in his kingdom in the Lukan passage bears some similarity to the image of feasting and dwelling under the benevolent rule of the Son of Man in 1 En 62:15. Outside of the Parables, the image of being seated on thrones participating in judgment is similar to 1 En 108:12. Here those envisioned as being given thrones are not only leaders, but also all the restored righteous, placed on thrones one by one. In the Parables, only the Lord of Spirits and the Elect One/Son of Man are seated on thrones. The righteous and elect do not pass judgment, although they enjoy the benefits of vindication.

The Matthean treatment of this passage in Matt 19:28, however, reveals very close similarities to the Parables. A very strong similarity, perhaps even a direct quotation,[69] is the description of the Son of Man's throne as the "throne of his glory." Found also at Matt 25:31, the image of a "throne of his glory"[70] has been shown by Theisohn not to have been developed out of Christian sources.[71] Rather, this image, while rare, is present in pre-Christian literature.[72] This same Semitic construct form is preserved in Ethiopic, *manbara sebhatihu*,

---

*Gemeinde: Eine redaktionskritische Untersuchung zur Menschensohnprädikation im Matthäusevangelium* (Würzburg: Echter Verlag, 1986), 239; Davies and Allison, *Matthew*, 3:57-58; Burnett, "*Palingenesia* in Matt. 19:28," JSNT 17 (1983): 60-72; J. D. M. Derrett, "Palingensia (Matthew 19.28)," JSNT 20 (1984): 51-58; D. C. Sim, "The Meaning of *Palingenesia* in Matthew 19:28," JSNT 50 (1993): 3-12.

68. D. J. Harrington, *The Gospel according to Matthew* (Collegeville, Minn.: Liturgical Press, 1982), 281. Burnett ("*Palingenesia* in Matt. 19:28," 63-64) notes that this scene of the disciples on thrones seems to be in tension with the request for preeminent positions in Matt 20:20-28, especially with Jesus' claim that he cannot grant a seat at his right hand to anyone. Burnett believes that Matt 19:28 was included to reduce tensions over hierarchy among the disciples in his own community, to equalize the status of all twelve, and to emphasize the future, eschatological nature of their function.

69. See my dissertation, 285-87.

70. A throne is mentioned five times in Matthew: at 5:34 and 23:22, it is God's throne; at 19:28 and 25:31, the Son of Man is depicted as sitting upon a throne; at 19:28, the disciples are on thrones judging the twelve tribes of Israel.

71. Theisohn, *Der auserwählte Richter*, 153-58.

72. For the "glorious throne," see, for example, 1 Sam 2:8; Isa 22:23; Jer 14:21; 17:12; Sir 47:11; Wis 9:10; and TestAbr 8:5; 12:4. See D. Burkett, *The Son of Man Debate: A History and Evaluation*, SNTSMS 107 (Cambridge: Cambridge University Press, 1999), 78 n. 20, and Davies and Allison, *Matthew*, 3:54.

the throne of his glory (1 En 62:5; 69:27, 29).[73] In Dan 7 the Ancient of Days is on the throne, but even though plural thrones are envisioned (Dan 7:9), neither the "one like a son of man" nor members of the court are explicitly described as sitting on thrones. The Book of Parables has made it explicit that the Son of Man is seated on the "throne of his glory," and this has been followed by Matthew. The inclusion of the personal possessive pronoun "his," qualifying "glory," is a further indication that Matthew has the Parables in mind, not Dan 7. This precise image of the Son of Man seated on the "throne of his glory" is rare, and since it appears in both documents in association with the same figure, the influence of the Parables on Matt 19:28 is quite likely.

## Mark and the "Future" Son of Man

Three statements regarding the future Son of Man are first reported in Mark and incorporated by Matthew and Luke.

In Mark 8:38–9:1//Matt 16:27-28//Luke 9:26-27, Jesus warns that whoever is ashamed of him, of them the Son of Man will also be ashamed when he comes in the glory of his Father and the holy angels. Then he assures some of his listeners that they will see the coming kingdom of God. Luke is fairly similar to Mark, but omits the mention of the adulterous and sinful generation. Luke adds that the Son of Man will come in his own glory, as well as that of his Father, but omits the qualification of great power at the end of the verse.

Matthew has reworked these verses significantly.[74] The idea of being ashamed has been dropped.[75] In Mark and Luke this reciprocal shame gives the Son of Man the role of a witness. Matthew, however, removing the idea of being ashamed, adds a clear reference to the coming judgment, warning that the Son of Man will repay everyone for what they have done. In Matthew the Son of Man is not a witness, but a judge imposing repayment. Another significant feature of Matthew's rendition is to attribute the entourage of angels to the Son of Man, calling them "his angels." This suggests that they are under his authority, in contrast to Mark and Luke, who simply envision the angels as participants in

---

73. The Elect One is also depicted on a throne in 1 En 45:3; 51:3; 55:4; 61:8. See table 2 in my dissertation, 199.

74. Meier, *The Vision of Matthew*, 119-20; Meier, *Matthew*, New Testament Message 3 (Wilmington, Del.: Michael Glazier, 1980), 186-88; Beare, *Matthew*, 360; Gundry, *Matthew*, 340; Casey, *Son of Man*, 164; Davies and Allison, *Matthew*, 2:674-75.

75. But cf. Matt 10:33//Luke 12:9, where Jesus' being denied on earth is reciprocated by a heavenly denial, although the term "Son of Man" is not used.

*The Son of Man in the Parables of Enoch and the Gospels*

the heavenly scene, contributing to the glory of the Father. Further, in the Matthean version the coming kingdom is ruled by the Son of Man, not described simply as the "kingdom of God," but as "his kingdom," thus further elevating the role and status of the Son of Man.

Matthew, then, has developed the tradition he received in three ways. Placing the angels under the authority of the Son of Man is a development not only from Mark, but also from Dan 7:13, 4 Ezra 13, and the Parables. Secondly, exercising judgment through exacting repayment according to what they have done is not explicit in Dan 7, 4 Ezra 13, or the Parables. But in the Parables a huge step has been made toward connecting the judgment of the kings and mighty ones with repayment for their behavior. Their condemnation is based on their denial of the Lord of Spirits (1 En 46:6-7; 63:7) and their oppression of the righteous and elect (46:8). While the idea of repayment for sins may not be explicit in the Parables, it is implicit. Matthew has taken it a step further, then, by making implicit authority explicit, thus shaping his conception of the Son of Man in the direction of the Parables. Thirdly, Matthew envisions the coming kingdom as under authority of the Son of Man, thus elevating the Son of Man's status from witness or advocate to judge.

The qualities of coming in the glory of the Father and the presence of the angels, as found in Mark and Luke, are shared with Dan 7, 4 Ezra 13, and the Parables. These qualities then are insufficient to see an exclusive influence from the Parables. Matthew's treatment of the passage, however, does reveal those redactional developments that shape the conception of the Son of Man in the direction of the Parables, indicating Matthew's familiarity with the concepts expressed in the Parables.

The second statement regarding the future Son of Man that is found in Mark and incorporated by Matthew and Luke is Mark 13:26-27//Matt 24:30-31//Luke 21:27. Part of the apocalyptic chapter, these verses describe the Son of Man as coming on the clouds with great power and glory. Then follows a great ingathering of the elect, carried out by the angels.

Luke 21:27 is almost identical with Mark 13:26, except that Luke envisions a single cloud rather than multiple clouds, as in Mark. Luke, however, omits the ingathering of Mark 13:27 and encourages positive anticipation of that redemptive day (Luke 21:28).

Again Matthew has edited these two verses significantly.[76] Matthew ex-

---

76. Most would say that Matthew has followed his Markan source, but altered it in significant ways; e.g., Harrington, *Matthew,* 336; Tödt, *Son of Man,* 80; and R. H. Gundry, *The Use of the Old Testament in St. Matthew's Gospel* (Leiden: Brill, 1967), 52-54. France (*Matthew: Evangelist and Teacher* [Grand Rapids: Zondervan; n.p.: Paternoster, 1989], 41-49) claims to be less certain about the two-source hypothesis, although the Griesbach Theory is also untenable. He be-

pands the vision of the future Son of Man to include the sign of the Son of Man in heaven[77] and the mourning on the part of earth's tribes (cf. Zech 12:10-14) because of the judgment the Son of Man will enact.[78] Accompanying the sending out of the angels is a trumpet call as the elect are gathered from the four winds. Further, Matthew adds a possessive pronoun to both the "angels" and the "elect," indicating that the Son of Man has authority over them.[79] The sign, the mourning, the addition of "his," and the trumpet call are all Matthean expansions.

The Book of Parables also envisions a judging Son of Man. The righteous and elect will rejoice at the judgment of the Son of Man (1 En 62:13-16), while the condemned, like the mourning tribes in Matt 24:30, will be dismayed, with faces downcast and filled with shame (1 En 46:6; 48:8; 62:4, 5, 10; 63:11).

The image of the gathering of the elect from the four winds is shared by Mark and Matthew, and its origin may have been Dan 7:13.[80] But it is also consistent with the image portrayed in the Parables.[81] However, for Matthew, em-

---

lieves that a more complex process must be understood, allowing for the introduction of oral material in the composition of the Gospel.

77. T. F. Glasson, "The Ensign of the Son of Man (Matt. XXIV, 30)," *JTS* 15 (1964): 299-300; Harrington, *Matthew*, 338. Colpe, "Ho huios tou anthropou," 437, argues that the sign was a banner; Davies and Allison, *Matthew*, 3:359-60, outline the various views, and then argue for the cross. Beare, *Matthew*, 471, notes that patristic interpretation favored an appearance of the cross and that in iconography Jesus often is envisioned as arising from the dead brandishing a cross. Others see the sign *as* the Son of Man: Tödt, *Son of Man*, 80; Meier, *Matthew*, 287; Gundry, *Matthew*, 488; Beare, *Matthew*, 471; Hare, *Son of Man Tradition*, 173; J. Lambrecht, *Out of the Treasure: The Parables in the Gospel of Matthew* (Louvain: Peeters; Grand Rapids: Eerdmans, 1992), 258; Boring, "Matthew," 8:444.

78. Lambrecht (*Out of the Treasure*, 259) notes that Matthew's universality is apparent in the reference to all the tribes being judged. This universality also appears in the description of the last judgment in Matt 25:31-46, as all people are to appear before the throne. See also Meier, *Matthew*, 287, and Boring, "Matthew," 8:444. Tödt (*Son of Man*, 81) also sees that the judgment is for everyone in the omission of the use of the concept of the "pierced one" from Zech 12:10. Jesus' enemies who pierced him are not the only ones who will be judged, but everyone. The absence of the allusion to the "pierced one" also emphasizes the Son of Man's authority to judge, according to Tödt.

79. In Mark 13:27, "his" is also present in some witnesses after "angels," but it is probably not original. After "elect" in this same verse, "his" is questionable, even though Nestle-Aland[27] includes it in the text, but in square brackets. It may have been added in both locations due to the influence of this verse, Matt 24:31.

80. Perkins, "Mark," 8:692.

81. The idea of gathering the elect from the four winds is consistent with the image portrayed in the Parables, where in 1 En 61 the angels with measuring cords are sent off to "reveal all that is hidden in the depths of the earth, Those who have been destroyed by the desert, And those who have been devoured by the fish of the sea and by wild beasts." They will return to the

phasizing judgment and subsuming the angels under the authority of the Son of Man can be seen as bringing the Matthean depiction of the Son of Man closer to that of the Parables.

The third Markan saying about the future Son of Man, which is also included by Matthew and Luke, is Mark 14:62//Matt 26:64//Luke 22:69. In response to a question from the high priest regarding his divine sonship, Jesus responds in the affirmative, and announces the Son of Man seated at the right hand of power and coming with the clouds (quoting Dan 7:13 and Ps 110:1). The Matthean addition, "from now on," claims that the Son of Man is being revealed, not only to the followers of Jesus, but now also to the opponents as well. This is very similar to the dynamic in the Parables (1 En 62–63), where the kings and mighty ones, who are the opponents of the righteous and elect and the Son of Man, have their judge, the Elect One/Son of Man, revealed to them. The day of the revelation of the Son of Man in the Parables is the Day of Judgment, when the righteous and elect from that time on will enjoy peace, rest, and prosperity under the rule of the Son of Man, and when the kings and mighty ones from that time on will experience condemnation, punishment, shame, and guilt. The whole tenor of the vision in the Parables is to announce how things will be different from the day of the Son of Man on into the future, and Matthew has captured that sense in two words, *ap' arti*, "from now on."

Ironically, where the kings and mighty ones in the Parables are being condemned by the Son of Man, in the Gospels the Son of Man is being condemned by those in authority who will condemn him to death. This, however, coheres with the suffering servant motif that is combined with the Son of Man in the Gospels. Through suffering and death, the Son of Man accomplishes God's will of redemption.

While the Markan saying is derived from Dan 7:13 and Ps 110:1, the Matthean adaptation of adding "from now on . . ." reflects the dynamic of the revelation of the Son of Man in the Parables and the continuing effect of that revelation into the future.

### Future Son of Man Sayings Unique to Luke

There are two "future" Son of Man sayings unique to Luke. Luke 18:8b forms the conclusion of the parable of the persistent widow, and it may serve as a con-

---

presence of the Elect One. The exact terminology is not repeated by Matthew, but the concept of being gathered from the whole world is the same.

clusion also to the discourse on the day of the Son of Man (17:20-37).[82] Jesus wonders whether the Son of Man will find faith when he comes. The faith in focus is as powerful as a mustard seed, is prayerful and persistent, and demands justice. The only explicit quality of the Son of Man in this passage is his future coming. But in association with the unjust judge, a connotation regarding the Son of Man is that he will be just, vindicating the righteous. The second Lukan "future" Son of Man saying, 21:36, is the conclusion to the eschatological discourse, and is an admonition to stay alert, to pray for strength to endure, in order to stand before the Son of Man at the final vindication. Here the Son of Man has a position of some power and authority as intercessor and advocate, although probably not of judge.[83]

The similarities of these two passages to the depiction of the Son of Man in the Parables are general in nature. They share the concept of this figure coming in the future to play a role in the vindication of the righteous. But because this is quite general, it is unlikely to be evidence for direct influence of the Parables.

## Future Son of Man Sayings Unique to Matthew

Two passages in Matthew contain references to the future Son of Man, Matt 13:37-43, the interpretation of the parable of the weeds, and Matt 25:31-46, the description of the last judgment.

The interpretation to the parable of the weeds, Matt 13:37-43, is a Matthean creation,[84] in which the term "Son of Man" appears twice, and it reveals many features that can be traced back to the Parables. The angels are the agents of the Son of Man in Matt 13:37-43. They are called "his angels" and are at his disposal, for he sends them out to collect all causes of sin, which will be disposed of in fiery furnaces with weeping and gnashing of teeth, while the righteous will be radiant. The conception of the Son of Man surrounded by angels, who are also agents of judgment, betrays strong similarity with the Parables. The angels being in the presence of the Head of Days and surrounding the throne are expressed most explicitly in 1 En 40:1, in which a vision of the Lord of Spirits and the four archangels is introduced, and in the vision of the final ascent in 1 En 71, where myriads of angels populate the scene. The angels acting as

---

82. J. A. Fitzmyer, *The Gospel according to Luke (X–XXIV)*, AB 28A (New York: Doubleday, 1985), 1175; Culpepper, "Luke," 9:338.

83. Tödt, *Son of Man*, 98, 109. Fitzmyer (*Luke X–XXIV*, 1350), however, combines the two roles, summarizing the role of the Lukan Son of Man as judgment and deliverance of the Christian disciple.

84. See my dissertation, 265-71, for a fuller discussion.

agents of judgment appear in 1 En 56:1-5, in which angels with scourges are foreseen to gather the wicked and cast them into the abyss of the valley where they will suffer with the kings and the mighty ones (cf. 62:11-12). The angels in 61:1-9 gather the righteous and elect, even from their deaths in the sea, the desert, and the wilderness, and restore them to the presence of the Elect One and the Lord of Spirits, where they praise God forever, are clothed in radiant garments, and feast in joy and peace (62:13-16). Included in the Parables are the themes of the radiance of the righteous, the fiery fate of the condemned, and the angels being involved in carrying out the punishment. This set of features is common only to Matt 13:40-43 and to the Parables, and does not occur elsewhere.[85] While precise quotations may not be evident, nonetheless the pattern of relationships is clearly the same, and it points to the fact that a precise and concise allusion is being made to the Parables of Enoch in the interpretation of the parable of the weeds. Another striking feature of the Parables is that a blatant dichotomy exists between the righteous and the wicked. Their fates in the final judgment are clear and opposed to each other. This is evident in 1 En 63 where the kings and the mighty ones put themselves at the mercy of the Lord of Spirits, but no mercy is forthcoming. Similarly in Matt 13:42-43 the wicked are thrown into the furnace to perish and the righteous are assured that they will shine like the sun. The Son of Man in Matt 13:36-43, as he does in the Parables, executes a mercy-less judgment.

The last judgment in Matt 25:31-46 also reveals many themes that fill out Matthew's conception of the Son of Man. Glory, his angels, the throne of this glory, separating the righteous from the accursed, no hope of forgiveness and mercy, the treatment of the righteous as the criterion for condemnation, the fiery fate, the devil and his angels for whom that fiery fate was prepared but which the accursed will suffer — all are themes that highlight the omnipotent, judicial role of the Son of Man.[86]

Many close similarities exist between Matthew and the Parables regarding the Son of Man. Both depict the Son of Man sitting on the "throne of his glory," with the authority to judge (1 En 69:27, 29; the "throne of his glory" may be a direct quotation, as noted above). In both the condemned will be terrified (1 En 62; 55:4) and will be consigned to eternal punishment (62:11) as the Son of Man exercises an all-inclusive judgment. This judgment results in an everlasting separation to eternal reward or eternal condemnation, with no possibility of crossover from one group to the other (62:9-11; 69:27). A further feature is the surprise of the judged and their ignorance of the judge and his decisions, whether

---

85. Theisohn, *Der auserwählte Richter*, 197.
86. See my dissertation, 300-338, for a fuller discussion.

they are righteous or condemned. In Matt 25:31-46 both groups ask where they had ever seen the judge, which suggests that the judgment is also the revealing of the judge. In the Parables the kings and mighty ones are surprised to see the one on the throne, and they plead for mercy, although none is available. The righteous and elect, however, are not noted as being surprised, since the Son of Man, and presumably the criterion for judgment, has already been revealed to them. The criterion for judgment in both Matthew and the Parables is the treatment of the ones with whom the judge identifies. Finally, a close similarity is the fiery fate in each work and for whom it was prepared: in the Parables, Azazel and his rebellious angels (1 En 54:5; 55:4; 67:4-7), in Matthew, the devil and his angels (Matt 25:41).

It can be seen, then, that both Matt 13:37-43 and 25:31-46 reveal many characteristics of the Son of Man that are shared with the Parables. These two passages are unique to Matthew, containing the bulk of the traits attributed to the Son of Man. Of all the passages in Matthew containing "Son of Man," these two exhibit the most traits shared with the Parables, which suggests that Matthew's concept of the Son of Man was significantly influenced by the Parables.

Table 3 below notes passages from all of Matthew's Gospel that display specific similarities to the Parables.

### Table 3
### Specific and Detailed Characteristics of the Son of Man
### Shared by the Parables and Matthew

| Characteristic or Feature | 1 Enoch | Matthew |
| --- | --- | --- |
| 1. heavenly status | 46; 48:2–8; 62–63; 70–71 | 13:36-43; 16:24-28; 19:28; 24:30; 25:31-46 |
| 2. judicial role | 46; 62–63; 69:26–29 | 13:36-43; 16:27; 19:28; 24:30; 25:31 |
| 3. followers called "righteous" | 48:2–8; 62–63 | 13:36-43; 25:31-46 |
| 4. followers called "elect" | 48:2–8; 62–63; and passim | 24:30-31 |
| 5. seated upon throne of his glory | 62:5; 69:27, 29 | 19:28; 25:31 |
| 6. no mercy for condemned | 62–63 | 13:36-43; 25:31-46 |
| 7. promise of eternal bliss for the righteous | 62:13–16; 71:16–17 | 13:43; 25:34, 46 |
| 8. worldwide jurisdiction | 69:27 (cf. 46:1-3; 48:2-8; 62:3, 5, 9) | 24:30; 25:32 |
| 9. brightness of inhabitants of heaven | 71:1; cf. 58:1, 4, 6 | 13:43 |

## Conclusions from the "Future" Son of Man Sayings

As noted above, the Matthean treatment of the future Son of Man sayings and the passages unique to Matthew that incorporate the depiction of the future Son of Man reveal a significant awareness of the concept of the Son of Man in the Parables. The quantity and scope of these similarities together with the precise phrase "the throne of his glory" strongly suggest the influence of the Parables on Matthew's conception of the Son of Man.

By way of contrast, the future Son of Man sayings in Q, Mark, and Luke do not betray a direct verbal influence from the portrayal of the Son of Man in the Parables. Shared characteristics do exist. They could be explained as deriving from Dan 7, or from the general conceptions of an eschatological judge and deliverer current in the milieu of the first century C.E. as well as in the Parables.

Table 4 on page 332 presents the patterns of relationship shared by the Parables and Matthew.

## The Son of Man in the Gospel of John

The "Son of Man" sayings are used quite differently in the Gospel of John than in the Synoptics.[87] John even departs from the convention of reserving the term "Son of Man" to Jesus' own words, for in John 12:34 the term appears twice on the lips of the questioning crowd. For John the term is infused with incarnational theology.[88] I have distinguished three groups of Son of Man sayings in John: ascending/descending, exaltation/glorification, and sayings relating to the Son of Man's authority.

### Ascending/Descending Son of Man Sayings

Three sayings, John 1:51, 3:13, 6:62, refer to the Son of Man ascending or descending, or both. In 1:51, apparently a detached saying,[89] and in an apparent al-

---

87. C. K. Barrett, *The Gospel according to St. John: An Introduction with Commentary and Notes on the Greek Text* (London: SPCK, 1955), 60; L. Morris, *The Gospel according to John*, rev. ed. (Grand Rapids: Eerdmans, 1995), 150-52; G. R. O'Day, "The Gospel of John," in *NIB* 9:493; N. Perrin, "Son of Man," in *IDB* 4:386.

88. Barrett, *John*, 62; O'Day, "John," 9:352; J. Painter, "The Enigmatic Johannine Son of Man," in *The Four Gospels, 1992: Festschrift Frans Neirynck* (Leuven: Leuven University Press, 1992), 1869; W. Walker, "John 1.43-51 and 'The Son of Man' in the Fourth Gospel," *JSNT* 56 (1994): 31.

89. R. E. Brown, *The Gospel according to John (i–xii): Introduction, Translation, and Notes*, AB 29 (Garden City, N.Y.: Doubleday, 1966), 88; O'Day, "John," 9:352; Walker, "John 1.43-51," 38.

## Table 4
## Patterns of Relationships of the Son of Man and Other Similarities Shared by the Parables and Matthew

| | Characteristic or Feature | 1 Enoch | Matthew |
|---|---|---|---|
| 1. | righteousness | 46:3; 48:2-8 (implied); 62:2-3; 71:14, 16 | 13:41-43; 16:27; 25:37, 46 |
| 2. | revelatory role | 46:3 | 13:36; 25:31-46 |
| 3. | chosenness | 46:3; 48:6 | cf. 12:18, quoting Isa 42:1 |
| 4. | named from eternity (i.e., purpose and preexistence) | 48:2-8 | 25:34; cf. 1:18-25; 12:18-21, quoting Isa 42:1-4 |
| 5. | support for the righteous | 48:4 | cf. 11:28-29 |
| 6. | light for the Gentiles | 48:4 | cf. 5:14, 16 |
| 7. | worthy of worship | 48:5; 62:6 | cf. 2:2, 11; 8:2; 9:18; 14:33; 15:25; 20:20; 28:9 |
| 8. | hiddenness | 48:6; 62:7 | 16:13-15 (implied); 25:31-46 |
| 9. | revealed to insiders | 48:7; 62:7; 69:26 | 16:13-15; 25:31-46 |
| 10. | inflicts pain, terror, and shame | 62:4-5, 10 | 8:12; 13:42, 50; 22:13; 24:51; 25:30; 24:30 (cf. Zech 12:10-14) |
| 11. | finally revealed and recognized by the kings and the mighty | 62:3; 63:4 | 25:31-46 |
| 12. | request by the condemned | 62:9; 63:5 | 25:44 |
| 13. | fairness of judgment | 63:8-9 | 25:31-46 |
| 14. | word is strong and incontrovertible | 69:26-29 | 13:36-43; 24:30-31; 25:31-46 |
| 15. | causes the destruction of evil | 69:26-29; cf. 48:8; 63; 53:3-5; 54:1-5 | 13:36-43; 25:31-46; cf. 13:47-50 |
| 16. | angels in presence of Son of Man ("his" in Matthew) | 71:8-14 | 13:41; 16:27; 24:31; 25:31 |
| 17. | fiery fate of the condemned | 54:1, 5; 53:4-5; 63:10; cf. also 67:7, 12-13 in the Noachic section | 13:42; cf. also 13:50; 25:41 |
| 18. | fate prepared for Azazel/ the devil | 54:5 | 25:41; cf. Rev 20:10 |
| 19. | clear dichotomy between righteous and condemned | passim | 13:36-43; 25:31-46; cf. 19:28 |
| 20. | basis of judgment: treatment of righteous by oppressors | 62:11; cf. 46:8 | 25:31-46 |
| 21. | anticipated reversal of fortunes | 38:4-5; 45:5-6; 48:7-10; 50:1-2; 62:9-16; 63:11; 69:27-28 | 13:36-43; 16:27-28; 25:31-46; implied in 10:23; 19:28; 24:30-31 |

lusion to Jacob's dream of angels ascending and descending (Gen 28:12), the Son of Man is depicted with angels ascending and descending on him.[90] Again, in justifying his ability to speak of heavenly matters with Nicodemus, Jesus appeals to the heavenly origins of the Son of Man (John 3:13). Thirdly, when responding to the shock of the listeners over comments regarding eternally enduring food, his flesh and blood, Jesus raises the shock level by asking how they would react to seeing the Son of Man ascending to where he was before (6:62). These ascending/descending Son of Man sayings emphasize the heavenly origins of the Son of Man, which authenticates both the teacher and the teachings being presented. But assumed in this characterization of the Son of Man is his temporary, earthly presence. He "bridges the distance between heaven and earth,"[91] and he is the "point of contact between heaven and earth."[92] The Son of Man is temporarily on earth to reveal God's power and desire to impart abundant life. Thus heavenly origins, earthly activity, and revelation of God are characteristics of the Son of Man.

### Exaltation/Glorification Sayings

The ascending/descending Son of Man is also the one to be lifted up and glorified. A second group of Son of Man sayings refers to his being lifted up and to glorification both for himself and for God. The Son of Man being lifted up is compared to the bronze serpent lifted up in the wilderness (John 3:14; cf. Num 21:9), and he is lifted up for the purpose of offering eternal life. Again in John 8:28, the lifting up of the Son of Man will convince the people of his identity and purpose, for he does only what God wills. Finally in John 12:34 the crowd questions precisely the identity and purpose of the Son of Man who must be lifted up. This exaltation of the Son of Man is a thinly veiled reference to his crucifixion. Its content is the passion of the Christ, his suffering and death on the cross. The exaltation of the Son of Man is accomplished in his suffering and death, and so has an ironic double meaning. The same is true of the sayings regarding the glorification of the Son of Man. In response to Andrew's report of the Greeks who wish to see him, Jesus announces that the hour has come for the Son of Man to be glorified (12:23). The very next statement compares death with a grain of wheat, which must "die" to produce much fruit (12:24). Again in

---

90. The plethora of allusions and connotations are drawn out, for example, by Barrett, *John*, 156; Brown, *John*, 88-91; J. C. O'Neill, "Son of Man, Stone of Blood (John 1:51)," *NovT* 45 (2003): 374-81.
91. O'Day, "John," 9:532.
92. Brown, *John*, 91.

13:31, between his predictions of betrayal by Judas and denial by Peter, Jesus refers to the time for the Son of Man to be glorified, through which God is also glorified. Glorification includes physical death for Jesus, even as it reveals God's glorious, redemptive grace and power. Both concepts of exaltation and glorification include the suffering and death of the Son of Man (and, by extension, his resurrection). The suffering and the revelation of God's means of grace through suffering are characteristics of the Son of Man.

### The Son of Man's Authority on Earth

Further, the ascending/descending Son of Man has authority while on earth, for a third group of sayings refers to the Son of Man's authority to judge and his authority over the forces of nature. John 5 revolves around the theme of authority to judge, and specifically 5:27 refers to the authority to execute judgment because he is Son of Man (the term is used without definite articles). This authority is delegated to him by the Father (5:22) and will result in eternal life or eternal condemnation (5:24, 29), depending on one's belief in the one who was sent by God. Further, his judgments are just, since they are guaranteed and authorized by the will of the one who sent him. Ultimately they are comparable to and fulfill Moses' authority (5:45-47).

The theme of the Son of Man's authority to execute judgment follows the story of the healing of the sick person at the pool of Bethesda on the Sabbath (5:1-17). Thus the Son of Man's authority to judge is closely connected to and undergirds his authority to heal. It applies not only to the healing of the sick man on the Sabbath, but also to the man born blind, who is invited to believe in the Son of Man (9:35). In this latter passage the Son of Man is explicitly identified for the reader as Jesus (9:37), the main focus of the Gospel.[93]

The Son of Man's authority, which is delegated from the Father and undergirds his power to judge and to heal by reversing the natural power of disease, is also, then, extended further to other forces of nature. With divine authority Jesus multiplies bread and fish (6:1-15), walks on water (6:16-21), and changes water into wine (2:1-11, even though the term "Son of Man" does not appear there). The multiplication of the bread and fish gives rise to the extended discourse, with its sacramental overtones, about the food that endures, given by the Son of Man (6:27), and the flesh and the blood of the Son of Man that gives eternal life (6:53-54). Here again, the authority of the Son of Man to do something physical gives rise to the underlying authority to restore and

---

93. Cf. the healing of the official's sick son in John 4:46-54.

strengthen spiritual life. Thus judgment resulting in life or condemnation, incontrovertible justice, and power to heal, to multiply food, and to still the storm are characteristics of the Son of Man's authority, which he exercises on behalf of God.

These three groups of Johannine sayings reveal some points of similarity to the three groups of sayings identified in the Synoptic Gospels, although they do not dovetail neatly into them. The ascending/descending group is somewhat similar to the "future" sayings, in that both refer to the heavenly status of the Son of Man. The exaltation/glorification sayings also touch on the "suffering" and the "future" sayings. John's Gospel, however, does not refer to the eschatological return of the Son of Man to execute final judgment. However, the authority sayings have points of similarity with the "future" sayings as well as the "earthly presence" sayings. Especially interesting is that the authority to execute judgment in John 5:27 follows the healing of the sick man by the pool of Bethesda, just as the Son of Man's authority to forgive sin is a part of the healing of the paralytic in the Synoptics (Mark 2:10; Matt 9:6; Luke 5:24).[94] While there is some overlap, the similarities are minimal.

Some points of similarity with the Parables can also be noted. John's Son of Man has heavenly origins, as does the Son of Man in the Parables. Both have the authority to execute judgment. The Son of Man in the epilogue (1 En 70–71) is the ascended Enoch, and not far in the background is the descended Enoch in the Book of the Watchers, returning to report God's judgment on the fallen angels. John's Son of Man speaks of himself as ascending and descending. Thus both John and the Parables have strong connotations of the Son of Man being both heavenly and earthly, divine and human. Angels are associated with both. In both the Son of Man plays a role in restoring people to wholeness: in John's Gospel in healing the sick, and in the Parables in gathering in the lost and the scattered, even from death. In both the Son of Man also provides food, in John by multiplying the loaves and in the Parables by providing feasting in the reversal of fortunes.

Significant contrasts also exist. Where the exaltation and glorification of John's Son of Man include suffering, the Son of Man in the Parables does not suffer, but rather acts as judge on behalf of the suffering righteous and elect. Where John's Son of Man functions as a link between heaven and earth, upon which the angels ascend and descend, in the Parables the angels are functionaries in the heavenly court and therefore are under the authority of the Son of

---

94. This is one example of an incident suggesting that John was familiar with Mark at some level, or that he was aware of some of the same traditions. See Barrett, *John*, 34-45; Brown, *John*, 84; O'Day, "John," 9:501-4.

Man. While the righteous and elect in the Parables will enjoy feasting in the presence of a reigning Son of Man, their food is not miraculously multiplied as it was by Jesus, nor is what they eat put in terms of the flesh and blood of the Son of Man, as is found in John's sacramental description. And where the righteous and elect in the Parables are restored from the various places of being lost, in John health is restored to the sick.

The similarities, then, are somewhat general, but the dynamic of the Son of Man's authority is the same in both works. Further, the contrasts of suffering, the angelic function, and the sacramental terminology are stark. The contrasts of suffering and sacramental terminology, it would seem, are necessary to the Christian, theological framework. Thus while precise, verbal similarities are few, the similarities in the pattern of the relationships are striking. This suggests that possibly John knew the concepts and some of the characteristics of the Son of Man in the Parables, but he does not use them in such a way as to posit the direct influence of the Book of Parables on the Gospel of John.

## Conclusions

This study of the features of the Son of Man in the Parables and the Christian Gospels reveals that some similarities and contrasts can be noted. For Q, Mark, Matthew, and Luke, the "earthly" sayings and the "suffering" sayings show some similarities in the pattern of relationships to those in the Parables, but they are not precise enough to suggest direct, literary influence. For Q, Mark, and Luke, some similarities to the Parables can be noted in the "future" sayings, and these similarities are of a broad and general nature, not being specific enough to posit direct, verbal influence. The sayings of John's Gospel show similarities in heavenly origins, authority, and the power to restore, but they are exemplified in ways different from the Parables. While these are fascinating similarities in the theological dynamics associated with the Son of Man and those he judges, they do not admit of direct, literary dependence.

In Matthew, however, specific similarities with the Book of Parables exist, and strongly suggest significant influence from the Parables on the Matthean concept of the Son of Man. These strong similarities are found in the "future" Son of Man sayings unique to Matthew: the interpretation of the parable of weeds (Matt 13:37-43) and the description of the last judgment (25:31-46). Strong similarities can also be found in Matthew's reworking of "future" sayings from Q (Luke 22:28-30//Matt 19:28, sitting on the throne of his glory) or Mark (Mark 8:38–9:1//Matt 16:27-28, coming with the angels, to exact repayment; Mark 13:26-27//Matt 24:30-31, coming on the clouds; and Mark 14:62//

Matt 26:60, the response to the trial question from the high priest). Thus it can be concluded that Matthew's redaction of his source materials reveals his particular conception of the Son of Man, and it strongly suggests that he was shaping that concept in the direction of the Parables of Enoch.

# The Secret Son of Man in the Parables of Enoch and the Gospel of Mark: A Response to Leslie Walck

*Adela Yarbro Collins*

Leslie Walck's essay is a model of thoroughness and sound judgment.[1] In his analysis of the Son of Man sayings in the Gospels, he uses Rudolf Bultmann's categorization of these sayings into three groups: the earthly sayings, the suffering sayings, and the eschatological sayings. Although, as he notes, not all the sayings fit well into these categories, they are nonetheless useful. The aim of his essay is to determine whether the Parables of Enoch have had any influence on the Son of Man sayings in the Gospels. As he recognizes, the date of the Parables is crucial in determining the direction of influence, if any. He dates the Parables to the late first century B.C.E. or to the early first century C.E., a date that fits the internal evidence reasonably well.

In a number of places Walck uses the phrase "narrative audience," and in the discussion of 1 En 48:27 he states that this "poem is very encouraging, comforting, and uplifting for the implied audience."[2] It is not clear whether this phrase refers to the audience to which the narrative actually addresses itself, that is, to an audience within the narrative, or to the implied or actual audience of the Parables. The audience within the narrative seems to be "those who dwell on the dry ground," to whom Enoch directs his second vision (37:2, 5). The implied audience would seem to be "the righteous and holy," who are mentioned in the poem itself (48:4, 6). It seems that Walck takes the designation of the implied audience, "the holy and the righteous," to be the self-understanding of the actual audience. This move is evident in the conclusion to the discussion of 1 En

---

1. See above, L. Walck, "The Son of Man in the Parables of Enoch and the Gospels."
2. Walck, "The Son of Man in the Parables of Enoch and the Gospels."

62–63, in which he equates "the narrative audience" with "the righteous and the elect" who experience actual oppression. But in his discussion of 1 En 69:26-29, he speaks of "the implied readers."

In his discussion of 1 En 62–63, Walck presupposes George Nickelsburg's translation of 62:1, "Open your eyes and lift up your horns if you are able to recognize the Elect One."[3] He follows Nickelsburg in explaining what "recognize" means here. Since the kings and the mighty ones had not known the Son of Man beforehand, "they must have recognized him in the righteous and elect who have been aligned with him."[4] Michael Knibb translates "Open your eyes, and raise your horns, if you are able to acknowledge the Chosen One."[5] Nickelsburg conjectured that the Greek verb in question was ἐπιγιγνώσκειν. Now that verb can also have the sense "to indicate that one values the person of another: acknowledge, give recognition to."[6] Since Walck describes the scene as involving the kings and mighty ones "acknowledging their guilt," it would seem simpler and appropriate to the context to translate the verb as "acknowledge" rather than "recognize." Since the Chosen One is sitting on the throne of his glory, they quickly realize that he is their judge and acknowledge him as such.

Walck rightly concludes that most of the Son of Man sayings in the Gospels are not dependent on the Parables. He has made a good case, however, for the conclusion that there is a relationship of literary dependence between the Matthean redaction of certain Son of Man sayings from the Synoptic sayings source (Q) and the Parables. It is more likely that the author of Matthew is dependent on the Parables than vice versa. The link between the epithet "Son of Man" and the precise phrase "the throne of his glory" in Matt 19:28 and 25:31 probably derives from 1 En 62:5, 69:27, and/or 69:29.

Walck argues that the image of the gathering of the elect from the four winds in the Gospel of Mark may have derived from Dan 7:13, although it is consistent with the Book of Parables (1 En 61:1-5). It should be noted that the

---

3. Walck, "The Son of Man in the Parables of Enoch and the Gospels." Cf. G. W. E. Nickelsburg, *Resurrection, Immortality, and Eternal Life in Intertestamental Judaism*, HTS 26 (Cambridge: Harvard University Press, 1972), 72. In G. W. E. Nickelsburg and J. C. VanderKam, *1 Enoch: A New Translation Based on the Hermeneia Commentary* (Minneapolis: Fortress, 2004), 79, the title is translated "the Chosen One" rather than "the Elect One."

4. Walck, "The Son of Man in the Parables of Enoch and the Gospels"; see also Nickelsburg, *Resurrection*, 72.

5. M. A. Knibb, *The Ethiopic Book of Enoch: A New Edition in the Light of the Aramaic Dead Sea Fragments*, 2 vols. (Oxford: Clarendon, 1978), 2:150.

6. F. W. Danker, *A Greek-English Lexicon of the New Testament and Other Early Christian Literature* (based on the work of Bauer, Arndt, and Gingrich) (Chicago and London: University of Chicago Press, 2000), s.v. ἐπιγινώσκω, 4.

motif of the four winds may come from Dan 7:2, the description of the four winds of heaven stirring up the great sea.

In his essay Walck offers a list of "close similarities" between Matthew and the Parables of Enoch regarding the Son of Man. His fifth similarity is expressed as follows: "the surprise of the judged and their ignorance of the judge and his decisions, whether they are righteous or condemned." It is true that both the righteous and the condemned are surprised in Matt 25:31-46. But Walck does not cite any evidence that the righteous are surprised by the judge and his decisions in the Parables. It would seem that in the latter work, the revelation of the Son of Man to the elect beforehand implies that the judge and the criteria for his decisions are also revealed to them.

Apart from the minor points mentioned so far, I am in substantial agreement with Walck's essay. In the rest of my response I would like to pursue the question of the relationship between the Gospel of Mark and the Parables of Enoch. The idea that the Son of Man is hidden from the world, but revealed to the chosen (1 En 62:7), is useful in interpreting the so-called messianic secret in Mark. The author of Mark may know this idea from reading the Parables, or the two works may be dependent on common tradition.

The theme of secrecy in Mark is best understood as a literary device meant to impress upon the audience of the Gospel the great importance of certain things with which it deals.[7] The Gospel of Mark, like other texts from antiquity, creates tension between the narrative process of revelation, on the one hand, and the commands to secrecy, on the other. Martin Dibelius noted this tension and expressed it in his aphorism that the Gospel of Mark is a series of secret epiphanies.[8]

The dialogue between Jesus and the disciples in Mark 8:27-30 explicitly takes up the theme of Jesus' identity, which was introduced by the unclean spirit's declaration in 1:24, "I know who you are, the Holy One of God," and especially by the narrator's remark in 1:34, "he would not allow the demons to speak, because they knew him." Peter's answer in 8:29, "You are the Messiah," is clearly superior to those mentioned in v. 28 from the point of view of the implied author, since Jesus is declared to be the Messiah in the introductory titular sentence of the Gospel. The subsequent unfolding of the narrative (and the

---

7. H. J. Ebeling, *Das Messiasgeheimnis und die Botschaft des Marcus-Evangelisten*, BZNW 19 (Berlin: Töpelmann, 1939), 167-69, 170-72, 177-78. See also Heikki Räisänen's summary and criticism of Ebeling's interpretation, in H. Räisänen, *The 'Messianic Secret' in Mark* (Edinburgh: T. & T. Clark, 1990), 60-62.

8. Ebeling, *Das Messiasgeheimnis*, 221-24; M. Dibelius, *Die Formgeschichte des Evangeliums* (Tübingen: Mohr Siebeck, 1919; 2nd ed. 1933); English ed., *From Tradition to Gospel* (New York: Scribner, 1935), 230.

symbolic import of the preceding healing of a blind man in 8:22-26), however, indicates that Peter's response, although true, is ambiguous and thus in need of clarification.

The initial response of the Markan Jesus to Peter's answer, rebuking the disciples so that they would speak to no one about him, is the same as his response to revelations of his identity by the demons, which are also called unclean spirits.[9] This rebuke does not signify that the answer is wrong. It signifies first and foremost that the identity of Jesus as Messiah must be kept secret for the time being. Why that identity must be kept secret is illuminated by the use of the epithet "Son of Man" in the second response of Jesus, the teaching described in v. 31. The use of this epithet as a synonym for "Messiah" indicates that the author and audience have a shared understanding of the Davidic or royal messiah and a shared assumption that "Messiah" in this sense and "Son of Man" are equivalent.[10]

The command to keep silent about Jesus' identity as the Son of Man is at least analogous to, if not dependent on, the portrayal of "that Son of Man" in the Parables of Enoch, which itself is based on the "one like a son of man" in Dan 7:13. One of the most distinctive characteristics of the Son of Man in the Parables is his hiddenness. He is revealed to the community that will be redeemed, but his revelation on the day of judgment will surprise the kings and the mighty. The Son of Man is revealed secretly to the righteous and later publicly to the rest of humanity, in particular, on the day of judgment. A difference between the Book of Parables and the Gospel of Mark is that, according to the former, the Son of Man is a heavenly being, whereas in Mark, Jesus walks the earth as Son of Man. Nevertheless, one factor in the secrecy of Jesus' messiahship may be the idea that the Son of Man is revealed in a secret and anticipatory way to the elect.[11]

This interpretation of the secret of Jesus' identity explains the apparent giving away of the secret in 14:62. Wrede argued that the key to the secret was the saying in 9:9, that the three disciples who witnessed the transfiguration were not to speak of it until "the Son of Man had risen from the dead." Critics of Wrede argued that Jesus' remark to the high priest, "you will see the Son of Man sitting on the right of the Power and coming with the clouds of heaven,"

9. Mark 1:34; 3:11-12.

10. That Peter's answer refers to the Davidic or royal messiah is implied by the rejection of the theory that Jesus is a prophet in the first answer.

11. The epithet "Son of Man" in Mark 2:10, 28 may already have been in the source that the Evangelist used in composing 2:1–3:6. Furthermore, these occurrences of the epithet do not give away the "messianic secret" because they are so ambiguous. They conceal as much as they reveal about the identity of Jesus.

revealed the secret *before* Jesus had risen from the dead. The saying in 9:9, however, should be interpreted as a signal that the transfiguration serves as a preview of the resurrected state of Jesus. The Gospel of Mark offers this account instead of a description of an appearance of the risen Jesus later on. Analogously, the saying in 14:62 is a preview of the parousia, the day of the return of Jesus, on which his identity as the Son of Man will be revealed to all of humanity. That Jesus is the Son of Man will come as a surprise to the high priest and his allies, who rejected Jesus' claim to be the Messiah (expressed in the first part of 14:62). The saying hints at a scenario like that described in 1 En 62:3-12, in which the kings and the mighty react with pain and terror at the sight of the Son of Man on the throne of his glory and petition him for mercy.[12]

---

12. John P. Meier, as Walck points out in his essay, mentions 1 En 62:7, 46:1ff., and 48:1-7 in connection with the statement in Matt 16:17 that Jesus' identity as "the Messiah, the son of the living God" has been revealed to Peter. See J. P. Meier, *The Vision of Matthew: Christ, Church, and Morality in the First Gospel*, Theological Inquiries (New York: Paulist, 1979), 111 n. 108. Meier, however, contrasts the revelation of Jesus as Messiah and Son of God with the revelation of the Son of Man in the Parables.

# The Parables of Enoch and Qumran Literature

*Ida Fröhlich*

In his essay in the current volume, Gabriele Boccaccini employs the metaphor of an "archaeology of ideas," comparing a document to a building constructed of bricks and stones.[1] Just as a building consists of a complex of different materials, so also a document can be properly described as a complex of ideas.[2] The problem is that the same ideas often happen to play completely different roles in various documents. Using the language of archaeology and architecture, the same types of bricks may result in different buildings. Applying this methodology to the Book of Parables (1 En 37–71), Boccaccini states: "There is virtually no element in the document that cannot be found elsewhere in Second Temple Jewish and early Christian and rabbinic literature. The mere listing of parallels seems to lead us in different, if not opposite, directions."

Boccaccini suggests a new method to locate the Parables within Second Temple Jewish literature. Instead of focusing on the constituent parts (unit-ideas), interpreters should look at the "unique way in which the parts are combined, and the hierarchy that the text establishes among them." Boccaccini proposes to introduce a new category, that of "paradigm."

The Greek word *paradeigma* has multiple meanings: it can be a pattern, model (e.g., an architect's model), precedent, example; lesson, warning; argu-

---

1. See above, G. Boccaccini, "Finding a Place for the Parables of Enoch within Second Temple Jewish Literature." All quotations from Boccaccini, unless otherwise indicated, come from this essay.

2. Arthur Lovejoy worked with "unit-ideas" as the constituent parts of intellectual buildings; A. O. Lovejoy, *The Great Chain of Being: The Study of the History of an Idea* (Cambridge: Harvard University Press, 1936).

ment. The basic meaning of the word is "to show something through another thing." Boccaccini singles out five paradigms: the Wisdom Paradigm, the Apocalyptic Paradigm, the Messianic Paradigm, the Covenantal Paradigm, and the Enochic Paradigm. These thus constitute the basic elements from which the "building" of the Book of Parables is supposedly constructed.

Without question these elements are all present in the text, with the conspicuous exception of the Covenantal Paradigm. However, they are not commensurate. Specifically, they do not all have the same background and function in a text. They belong to various concepts like literary genre (wisdom) or means of communication (revelation); they may represent an idea, a group of texts, a biblical tradition, etc. To remain with the building imagery, some of the above "paradigms" are not building bricks, but mortar. The sole paradigm which in my opinion can be treated as a real *paradeigma,* a model or an example, is one of the Enochic paradigms, the story of the Watchers (1 En 6–11). It is a real paradigm, a coherent story consisting of various motifs and conveying a special message to its readers. The use of the category of paradigm with the above meaning will lead us in a different direction — or, to remain with the building metaphor, a different building will be constructed from the same bricks.

The story of the Watchers is a foundational element in the Enochic tradition. According to paleographic and philological analyses, and in agreement with the results of the study of the literary tradition of the Enochic collection, it belongs (together with the whole of the Book of the Watchers) to the earliest Enochic tradition and represents the oldest layer of the Qumran manuscript tradition.[3] On the basis of references from Qumran literature, we may conclude that it was widely known in the Essene tradition and influenced other writings like the book of Jubilees.[4]

Two threads are entwined in the story of the Watchers (1 En 6–11). The narrative of Shemihazah and his companions (6:1–7:6) is a coherent tale of the deeds of the Watchers and antediluvian mankind. The Asael story is thus a short supplement to the Shemihazah story (8:1-2). The Asael narrative does not mention the deeds of the Watchers; it presents only an alternative tradition of Asael's teachings. This narrative is located between the Shemihazah story and a supplement to the teachings of Shemihazah's companions (8:3-4).

1 En 9–10 relates the aftermath of the deeds of the Watchers. Humankind

---

3. The oldest Qumran manuscript of the Aramaic Enoch containing the story of the Watchers may be dated to the beginning of the second century B.C.E., which indicates an earlier time for the origin of the tradition. See J. T. Milik, *The Books of Enoch: Aramaic Fragments of Qumrân Cave 4* (Oxford: Clarendon, 1976), 140.

4. The author of Jubilees incorporated the story of the Watchers into his narrative, which is otherwise based on the biblical tradition; see Jub 5:1-19.

was misled by the Watchers' teaching of magic and sorcery. The heavenly angels saw it and reported it to God (9:1-11), who sent Raphael to chastise them (10:1-4). Raphael bound Asael hand and foot, and threw him "into the darkness" in the desert until the great day of judgment (10:4-7).

Additions and commentaries to the Shemihazah story appear early; they are present already in the collection of the Book of the Watchers itself. Although the traditions in the Book of the Watchers about the teachings of Shemihazah and Asael differ in places, they are not inconsistent. The narrative on Shemihazah and his companions is a paradigm of the origin of evil. The basic meaning of the story is that evil came into existence because of the sin of the Watchers, which resulted in further corruption — sins that infected the earth with impurity. Thus the primary cause of evil is impurity. According to the Shemihazah story, sins resulting in impurity are magic arts (7:1). The author of the Asael story contends that sins resulting in impurity are the production of cosmetics and weapons made of minerals and metals (8:1). Additions to the Shemihazah story attach to the above types of sins the interpretation of *omina* (8:3-4). The earliest layer of the Enochic tradition thus reflects a strong Mesopotamian influence.[5]

Using the language of archaeology and architecture, the Book of the Watchers can be defined as a building designed by a Jewish architect and built of Mesopotamian bricks with Jewish mortar. The Book of the Watchers may have been written before the establishment of a separate community at Qumran, and the text does not seem to reflect a sectarian outlook.[6] On the other hand, the concepts expressed in this particular paradigm constitute the evidence for the assumptions of the Qumran community. The story had become a basic metaphor for the Qumran community as a separate group with its strict observance of purity laws. It could (and even now can) serve as a basic paradigm for any distant group.

The question is how the paradigm of the story of the Watchers is used in the later Enochic tradition, and what its function is in the formation of later ideas. Primary heirs of the tradition of the Watchers are 1 En 72–108 (the Astro-

---

5. R. Borger, "Die Beschwörungsserie BIT MESERI und die Himmelfahrt Henochs," *JNES* 33 (1974): 183-96; J. C. VanderKam, *Enoch and the Growth of an Apocalyptic Tradition*, CBQMS 16 (Washington, D.C.: Catholic Biblical Association of America, 1984); H. S. Kvanvig, *Roots of Apocalyptic: The Mesopotamian Background of the Enoch Figure and of the Son of Man*, WMANT 61 (Neukirchen-Vluyn: Neukirchener Verlag, 1988).

6. As mentioned above (n. 4), the tradition of the Watchers may go back at least to the third century B.C.E. There is a scholarly consensus that a separate community in Qumran may have been established about the middle of the second century B.C.E.; see J. Magness, *The Archaeology of Qumran and the Dead Sea Scrolls* (Grand Rapids: Eerdmans, 2002), 49-50.

*Ida Fröhlich*

nomical Book and Dream Visions), which survives in the Aramaic manuscripts of the Qumran collection, and 1 En 37–71 (the Book of Parables), which exists only in the later Ethiopic version. These two collections contain genres different from that of the narrative of 1 En 6–11. 1 En 72–108 is a collection of several genres: letter, vision, narrative, etc. The so-called Animal Apocalypse (1 En 85–90) is a revelation of world history in which the biblical tradition is interwoven with the story of the Watchers (86:3–87:1). The parables of 1 En 37–71 refer repeatedly to the tradition of the Watchers.

The visions of the Book of Parables merge the elements of the Enochic paradigm with imagery originating from other traditions, first of all from the vision of Dan 7 together with the prophetic and wisdom tradition. The book of Daniel and other Danielic traditions were well-known, together with Enoch, in Qumran.[7]

The background of the visions of the Book of Parables is the story of the Watchers and the visions and heavenly journeys of the Book of the Watchers. The Parables are firmly rooted in this material, especially in the paradigm of the Watchers. The following outline attempts to offer a short (and consequently incomplete) list of themes from the Book of the Watchers, the sectarian literature of Qumran, and Daniel that are present in the Book of Parables.

## Themes from the Narrative of the Book of the Watchers in the Parables

The idea of the opposition of the holy ones and sinners in the Parables originates undoubtedly from the Book of the Watchers. In the Parables the *typos* of the sinners is represented by the Watchers and the humans who were misled by them, while the holy ones are represented by the heavenly angels who chastise sinners (1 En 41:2).

Another reference to the tradition of the Watchers in the Parables is an indirect allusion to the Asael tradition in the pronouncement against the metal mountain: "there will be neither iron for war, nor material for a breastplate" (52:1-8). This is a reference to Asael's instruction in metal weaponry (8:1). The Parables refers again to the Asael tradition (8:1-2) when mentioning the secret

---

7. Besides the fragments of eight copies of the book of Daniel, several fragments categorized as pseudo-Danielic were found in the Qumran caves together with the Prayer of Nabonidus (4Q242), which elaborates on a Danielic theme. Enoch was represented in Qumran by seven Aramaic manuscripts. References to Enochic traditions, especially to the story of the Watchers, are found in several Qumran works; e.g., Jub 5:1-19, the historical overviews of the Damascus Document (CD 2:2–3:12) and 4Q180, and the wisdom text 4Q510-11.

powers of the angels, such as the magic arts, enchantments, alchemy, and the making of molten images (65:6-9). The deeds of the Watchers related to metallurgy are here combined with alchemy and the making of molten images. Elsewhere the Parables mentions Azazel's host and their iniquity, "in that they became servants of Satan" (54:5-6). The name Azazel here clearly refers to the Asael in the Watcher narrative.

The punishment of the Watchers (10:4-7) is echoed in the Parables in a scene depicting the judgment of the stars of heaven (46:7), although the Watchers are not depicted as stars in the Book of the Watchers.[8] The "angels of punishment" preparing the chains of Satan in the Parables (53:3-4) similarly alludes to the Watchers' punishment. Enoch's vision of a deep valley with burning fire, the future abode for the hosts of Azazel, may also be viewed as an allusion to the Watcher story (54:1-6). Traditions from the Book of the Watchers and Dan 7 are combined in the scene of the Parables where the Elect One sitting on the throne judges Azazel and his army, in the name of the Lord of the Spirits (55:4).

The theme of the fallen angels becomes the central focus in 1 En 64–69, which interprets and expands the narrative of the Book of the Watchers. Chap. 64 recounts the teaching of heavenly secrets by "the angels who came down from heaven on to the earth, and revealed what is secret to the sons of men, and led astray the sons of men so that they committed sin" (64:2). Chap. 65 then records Noah's dialogue with Enoch regarding the coming flood, which is interpreted as a punishment for the Watchers' deeds (65:10-11). Chap. 67 includes Noah's monologue on the punishment of "the angels who showed iniquity" (67:4).

The tradition on the punishment of the Watchers in the Parables reflects many changes. The binding of the Watchers is not mentioned here, and the scene of their punishment occurs not in an underground dark place but in a burning valley near the metal mountains (67:4), recalling the Asael tradition. In addition to fire, the tool of their chastisement is water (67:5-8). The Watchers' deeds are not mentioned here, only the particulars of their chastisement (67:10-13). 1 En 68:2 refers to a coming judgment because "they act as if they were the Lord," which may again allude to the story of the Watchers. Chap. 69 deals in its entirety with the story of the Watchers, informing the reader of the names and misdeeds of the fallen angels according to the Shemihazah tradition. Six further names are added to the list, which are not known from any previous tradition

---

8. Later sections of the Enochic collection, such as the Animal Apocalypse, explicitly represent the Watchers as stars (1 En 86:1-3).

(69:4-16). Commentaries added to the names indicate rich exegetical and folkloristic material behind the texts.

Finally, heavenly travels of Enoch and cosmic mysteries revealed to him through angels during his journeys are a main theme of the Book of the Watchers (1 En 17–20; 21–36). These themes likewise resurface with commentary in the Parables: 41:3 (secrets of lightning and thunder, winds, etc.), 1 En 43–44 (storerooms of the wind, hail, sun, moon), and 1 En 52 (the six metal mountains).

## Themes Known from Qumran in the Parables

Opposition of the righteous and sinner, an idea that possibly originates in the Book of the Watchers, is an important theme also in Qumran literature. The concept of the "two spirits" is found in the Community Rule (1QS 1-5). Similarly, according to the Parables, the spirit of the people belongs either to righteousness or to sin, and is associated with light and darkness (1 En 41:8-9). Furthermore, secret ways and conduct are mentioned in 1 En 61:9.

Watering is used as a metaphor for knowledge and wisdom in both the Parables and Qumran texts. The Book of Parables speaks of wisdom that came from heaven and dwelt among mankind, "like rain in the desert, and like dew on parched ground" (42:3). This metaphor is used several times in the Damascus Document (CD 1:14 and passim). Note also that the name Teacher (מורה) comes from the root ירה, which has a double meaning: "to teach, instruct" and "to water." Furthermore, both the Parables and Qumran texts employ a chosen mediator to transmit divine knowledge. In the Parables this mediator is the Elect One (1 En 51:3); in Qumran the Righteous Teacher is authorized to interpret the words of the prophets (1QpHab 2:7-10).

The special importance of the oaths is highlighted in the Parables: the fallen angel Kasb'el is mentioned as the chief of the oaths, empowering him over the secrets of the creation (1 En 69:13-26). Josephus underscores the importance of oaths among the Essenes (*Bellum judaicum* 2.8.2-13), and the Temple Scroll likewise deals in great length with the subject (11QT$^a$ 53-54). It is also noteworthy that oath is important in the Book of the Watchers, specifically when the Watchers take an oath on Mount Hermon[9] before descending to the daughters of men (1 En 6:4-6).

The theme of obtaining the land as the result of observance of the Mosaic Law (or loss of the land for nonobservance) appears in the Parables. Enoch is

---

9. Pun based on the similarity of the Aramaic word חרם and the place-name Hermon.

shown in a vision "the righteous who dwell on the dry ground and believe in the name of the Lord of Spirits for ever and ever" (43:4). The Deuteronomistic idea that sinners will be destroyed from the face of the earth is a recurring motif at the scenes of the judgment. The Temple Scroll focuses on the conditions for obtaining or losing the land. The same ideas are also in the background of several Qumran exegetical works (e.g., 4Q252-254).

In fact, the correlations between the Qumran literature and the Parables are significant, requiring a detailed analysis that exceeds the limitations of this essay. As such, we may simply add to the above list several other examples that demonstrate my point. The idea of predetermined history appears in 1 En 46:1-6, which states that the Son of Man's activity in history is preordained. The same idea is expressed in several works of Qumran literature (1QS 1-5; 1QpHab 8:12-14; etc.). The theme of the end of evil occurs in the Parables: with the appearance of the Elect One wisdom will flow like water, and "oppression will vanish like a shadow" (1 En 49:2). The same theme emerges in Qumran texts 4Q474 and 4Q215a with similar wording. The city of God's righteousness, an obstacle to the enemy in an apocalyptic war (1 En 56:7), parallels the Temple Scroll's "city of the sanctuary," which has a unique status with special prescriptions concerning purity. Finally, revelation of antediluvian patriarchs at the extreme ends of the world is a theme in both the Parables (1 En 65:1) and the Genesis Apocryphon (1QapGen 2:19-26).

## Themes from Daniel 7 (and Other Sources) in the Parables

The idea of historical eschatology, the end of the earthly kingdoms and the scene of the heavenly judgment with Danielic symbolism, is a recurring theme of the Parables (1 En 41:1; 45:3-6; 46:5-7; 47:3-4; 48:8-10; 62; 63). But Daniel is not the only source for images of judgment in the Parables; judgment is also present in the Book of the Watchers in two forms. The first is the punishment of the rebellious Watchers who are bound and cast into the depths of the earth. Their final judgment will take place at the end of time; the prefatory words of the Book of the Watchers connect the story of the Watchers with final judgment. Enoch takes his parable to the righteous elect, "who will be present on the day of tribulation to remove all the enemies and the righteous will be delivered" (1:1). The Book of Parables adopts both the binding of the Watchers and their judgment at the eschaton. Sin, punishment, and judgment receive cosmic *and* historical perspectives in the Parables. The punishment of heavenly evil is now extended to humanity — kings, landlords, *and* fallen angels are all subject to the eschatological judgment.

Other motifs in the Parables clearly originate outside the Enochic tradition. The proper character of the Watchers is not clear in the Book of the Watchers. Originally, their figures are likely related to the heavenly bodies (1 En 80–85, the Animal Apocalypse, symbolizes them by stars). The Book of Parables seems to know of a larger tradition on the Watchers than what we find in the Book of the Watchers. In the Parables the Watchers are identified with Satan, a figure originating outside of Enochic literature. The visions are often joined with other Enochic themes: heavenly journey and revelations on the cosmos. Additionally, the figure of the Son of Man, and the theme of the judgment in heaven, may have originated from Dan 7, and the connections between the traditions of Dan 7, written on the eve of the Maccabean revolt, and the Enochic collection should be investigated more thoroughly in the future.

## Conclusion

The traditions behind the visions and revelations of the Parables come from three main literary circles of the Second Temple period. The parables of 1 En 37–71 are based on a tradition from the Book of the Watchers, which deals with the origin of evil and the doom of the sinners. The judgment in the Parables is depicted with apocalyptic imagery derived from the tradition of the vision of heavenly judgment in Dan 7. Finally, there are in the Parables ideas and themes known from Qumran, for example, the duality of the righteous and sinners. In addition to these sources, elements of the wisdom genre are also present in the Parables. Concepts of natural history prevalent in wisdom circles appear in the Parables' description of the nature of dyes and metals.[10] The only theme without parallel from Second Temple Jewish literature is righteousness and light of the eternal life (1 En 58:6).

Whose tradition is the Book of Parables? The authors of the Parables belong to a group that is heir to the spiritual tradition of the Book of the Watchers. They rethought, reworked, and actualized this tradition, adding to it new elements from the riches of a much wider intellectual background. They reshaped the tradition into new forms with new genres. However, it is not the use of a certain tradition that makes a community. Communities are heirs of certain traditions, but they use those traditions in unique ways. They pick up a parable that they feel reflects their world, reshape it, and add to it elements originating from other works, employing new genres in the process. The same

---

10. The preface of the Book of the Watchers (chaps. 1–5) similarly contains a scientific taxonomy, in its catalogue of trees.

process is at work in Jubilees when the tradition of the Watchers is merged with the tradition of the patriarchal narratives, not an easy task since the tradition on the Watchers and the Genesis narrative hold radically different views on the origin of evil. Nevertheless, in spite of the disparity of the two traditions, the author of Jubilees merges them in his narrative.[11]

Boccaccini claims that Enochic Judaism lost its competition with Christianity and rabbinic Judaism. I doubt there ever was any distinctive form of Judaism we could call Enochic. Belonging to any religious group is determined by many factors, most importantly by religious practice. It is not even the attitude toward any single literary tradition that determines a religious group. The readers of the Book of the Watchers, including the authors of the Book of Parables, were a postexilic pious Jewish group whose self-determination was based on the ideas and vocabulary of the tradition of the Book of the Watchers. Besides the tradition of the Book of the Watchers, they had access to a broader spiritual and intellectual background containing apocalyptic and wisdom traditions. They actualized the basic Enochic idea of the judgment over sinners and expressed it with the help of apocalyptic imagery. Their work reflects a dualistic worldview similar to Qumran thinking.

Why then was the Book of Parables not present in any Qumran manuscript of 1 Enoch? There are two possible reasons: either the Qumran community rejected the Parables and its ideas, or the community no longer physically existed when the text was composed. In my opinion, there are no convincing reasons for the first possibility. On the other hand, neither do we have conclusive evidence for the second. Thus the question remains open. However, even if there is no strong positive evidence proving that the Book of Parables was written by a Jewish group that was heir to the Qumran tradition, it is not unreasonable to suppose that this was the case. I think we should not even rule out the possibility that the authors of the Parables might have been Jewish Christians. This fact would explain the presence of Christian elements in the text. It also would explain the fact that the Enochic collection, finalized with the material of 1 En 37–71, found its way into the Christian tradition.

---

11. On merging of traditions, see I. Fröhlich, "From Pseudepigraphic to Sectarian," *RevQ* 21, no. 3 (2004): 395-406.

# Adamic Traditions in the Parables?
# A Query on 1 Enoch 69:6

*Kelley Coblentz Bautch*

For literature set in the antediluvium period, the Book of the Watchers and the Book of Dream Visions make few references to the first couple. When they do (1 En 32:6; 85:3, 6-8), the texts betray knowledge of the Gen 2–4 narrative. The Book of the Watchers shows awareness of Gen 3, in which Adam and Eve eat from the tree and are expelled from the garden.[1] In this third-, possibly fourth-century Enochic work, Adam and Eve, here described as the "aged father" and "aged mother," take from the tree of wisdom (τὸ δένδρον τῆς φρονήσεως) and acquire wisdom (1 En 32:6).[2] The first couple, upon realization of nakedness, is

---

1. So also J. C. VanderKam, *Enoch: A Man for All Generations,* Studies on Personalities of the Old Testament (Columbia: University of South Carolina Press, 1995), 59, who observes numerous parallels between Gen 2–3 and 1 En 32. Though Ben Sira may contain the earliest datable allusion to the story of Adam and Eve, the earliest reflections of Gen 2–3 occur most likely in the Book of the Watchers, as John Collins observes; see J. J. Collins, "Before the Fall: The Earliest Interpretations of Adam and Eve," in *The Idea of Biblical Interpretation: Essays in Honor of James L. Kugel,* ed. H. Najman and J. Newman, JSJSup 83 (Leiden: Brill, 2004), 293-308 (here 296).

2. On recent efforts to date the Book of the Watchers, see J. H. Charlesworth, "A Rare Consensus among Enoch Specialists: The Date of the Earliest Enoch Books," *Hen* 24, no. 1-2 (2002): 225-34. Josef Milik reconstructs the Aramaic of En$^e$ I 27 thus: [ די ערתליין ואתבוננו] [אבוך רבא] [ו]אמך רבתא ויד[עו מנדע ואתפתחו עיניהון] . . . . See J. T. Milik, *The Books of Enoch: Aramaic Fragments of Qumrân Cave 4* (Oxford: Clarendon, 1976), 235-36. Perhaps the reference to the first couple gaining wisdom from the tree in 1 En 32:6 recalls Gen 3:6, where Eve discerns that the tree of the knowledge of good and evil is good for wisdom.

---

I wish to acknowledge St. Edward's University for a Presidential Excellence Grant that allowed me to devote time to research of Adamic traditions in the Parables and, in turn, led to this paper.

*Adamic Traditions in the Parables?*

subsequently driven from the paradise of righteousness; this recounting of events would seem to recall the reproving tenor of Gen 3. Yet, one notes that the portrayal of the couple is softened in the Book of the Watchers; like "the holy ones" mentioned in 1 En 32:3, they eat from the tree and are made wise (cf. Gen 3:6).[3] No references are made to the serpent, deception, the reproach of God, and additional punishments that figure prominently in the Genesis account. In a text concerned with judgment and accountability, Adam and Eve do not appear as actors in the eschatological drama, unlike their murderous offspring Cain (cf. 1 En 22:7).[4]

The Animal Apocalypse from the Book of Dream Visions seems even more favorable in its depiction of the first couple. The Animal Apocalypse opts to recast exclusively events familiar from Gen 2 and 4. The protoplast's creation from Gen 2:7 is recalled as Adam is presented as a white bull fashioned out of earth (1 En 85:3). Eve, depicted as a heifer to signal her virginity, is created from the bull (cf. Gen 2:21-24),[5] and with her come black and red bullocks, respectively Cain and Abel (cf. Gen 4:1-2). After recounting the fratricide of Gen 4, the Animal Apocalypse presents the first woman mourning the loss of Abel. She must be consoled by her mate but then eventually gives birth to another white

---

3. George Nickelsburg rightly observes that since the description of the couple gleaning wisdom from the tree interrupts the flow of the Genesis tradition, there is great investment in identifying the tree as a source of wisdom. See G. W. E. Nickelsburg, *1 Enoch 1: A Commentary on the Book of 1 Enoch 1–36, 81–108,* vol. 1, Hermeneia (Minneapolis: Fortress, 2001), 32. The gaining of knowledge would presumably be esteemed, for we read in 1 En 32:3 that the "holy ones" (ἅγιοι) too eat of the same tree and become wise. I follow the emendation here of R. Argall, *1 Enoch and Sirach: A Comparative Literary and Conceptual Analysis of the Themes of Revelation, Creation, and Judgment,* SBLEJL 8 (Atlanta: Scholars, 1995), 33 n. 80. So also Nickelsburg and VanderKam, *1 Enoch: A New Translation* (Minneapolis: Fortress, 2004), 48. Randall Argall hypothesizes that the tradition may be rooted in a particular reading of Gen 3:5. There the serpent tells Eve that when she eats of the tree she will be like *'elohim*. The reference to *elohim* may have been understood by the Enochic author to be to angelic beings, those who eat of the tree of wisdom and share their great wisdom with Enoch. See Argall, 33 n. 81. As Nickelsburg (*1 Enoch 1,* 50, 52-53) observes, Enochic literature is founded upon wisdom revealed to the patriarch of Gen 5 and the elect (cf. 1 En 5:8; 82:1-3; 92:1; 93:10; 98:9; 99:10; 104:12–105:2). Thus, it is significant in a text that so greatly esteems revealed wisdom that Adam and Eve acquire it as well.

4. Nickelsburg (*1 Enoch 1,* 328) makes a similar point regarding the tree of wisdom. Unlike the tree of life in 1 En 24–25, which is to be replanted by the temple in the end times, the tree of wisdom merits mention only in relation to the first couple, and we are not informed as to its having any eschatological function.

5. As noted by R. H. Charles, *The Book of Enoch, or I Enoch, Translated from the Editor's Ethiopic Text, and Edited with the Introduction, Notes, and Indexes of the First Edition Wholly Recast, Enlarged, and Rewritten* (Oxford: Clarendon, 1912), 186.

bull (Seth) and ends her lamentation (1 En 85:6-8).⁶ The second century B.C.E. Animal Apocalypse does not offer a recitation of the fall in the garden.⁷ There is no tree, forbidden or otherwise, no illicit gain of knowledge, no expulsion from Eden, and no recapitulation of any part of Gen 3; rather than serving as the grounds for disobedience and death (cf. Rom 5:12-14), Adam becomes a prototype for the Animal Apocalypse's messianic figure, also a white bull (1 En 90:37; cf. 85:3).⁸ As has been noted, the Animal Apocalypse amplifies instead the descent of the angels (the sons of God from Gen 6:1-4; cf. 1 En 6–11) in 1 En 86–88.⁹

Whatever these early Enochic authors thought of the first couple, their retellings of the biblical account seem to improve the lot of Adam and Eve substantially from Gen 3, especially when one considers the approaches taken in other expansions of Genesis from the Second Temple period and late antiquity (e.g., Life of Adam and Eve). Indeed, discussion of the Enochic corpus frequently takes up the literature's distinctive view of evil. As is commonly asserted, Enochic texts posit that evil originates with the rebellious watchers who descend to earth: their prohibited union with women and teaching of forbidden arts lead to the contamination of the human sphere (for example, 1 En 6–11). This observation has led contemporary scholars to delineate two contrast-

---

6. Charles (*The Book of Enoch*, 186) calls attention to a comparable tradition in Jub 4:7, where Eve mourns with Adam for twenty-eight years.

7. Thus VanderKam (*Enoch: A Man for All Generations*, 74) remarks: "The fact that the author omits this incident shows that thinkers in the Enoch tradition placed little emphasis on the Gen. 3 story for explaining the growth of sin on the earth. The first sin is the murder of Abel, and the narrative of the serpent, the temptation, and the fruit finds no place in this Apocalypse. It is safe to say the writer knew about it, but he chose not to symbolize it."

8. While it is possible to argue that the white bull of the new age may be associated with Seth (so VanderKam, *Enoch: A Man for All Generations*, 84-85) or Abraham (Nickelsburg, *1 Enoch 1*, 407), there is a strong case for thinking, as do Milik (*The Books of Enoch*, 45), Matthew Black (*The Book of Enoch, or, I Enoch: A New English Edition with Commentary and Textual Notes*, SVTP 7 [Leiden: Brill, 1985], 279-80), and Patrick Tiller (*A Commentary on the Animal Apocalypse of 1 Enoch* [Atlanta: Scholars, 1993], 383-84; cf. also 19-20), that the bull represents a new Adam. Tiller especially views Adam, both the first man and the eschatological figure, in the Animal Apocalypse as patriarch of a restored humanity. With the transformation of humans in a manner like that of the new Adam, primitive Eden is restored. The association of the white bull, or eschatological figure, with a new Adam seems especially probable since other animals can attain the pristine state of the first man *by becoming white bulls as well*. Nickelsburg (407) describes the soteriological imagery of the second century B.C.E. author of 1 En 90 as "daring and perhaps without parallel in pre-Christian Jewish literature."

9. Thus VanderKam (*Enoch: A Man for All Generations*, 74) remarks: "The relative amount of space give to the Gen. 3 account (no mention) and the watcher story (more than virtually any other episode) underscores the fact that in the Enoch tradition Gen. 6:1-4, not Gen. 3, was the primary narrative about sin."

ing trends within Second Temple Judaism: one rooted in early Enochic texts like the Book of the Watchers where evil develops as a result of the angels' sins, and the other that understands sin to be the consequence of human failings (e.g., Gen 3).[10]

It is curious, then, to find in the Parables, the latest work in the collection we refer to as 1 Enoch, a single reference to Eve that seemingly diminishes Enochic literature's neutral-to-favorable view of at least one member of the first couple. Among the list of fallen angels and their leaders, 1 En 69:6 describes a chief named Gadre'el. He is credited not only with teaching humankind about the blows of death and weaponry, but also with leading Eve astray. This trifling comment provokes many questions. Who is this Gadre'el? How is Eve misled and where is her partner Adam, who appears with her in other Enochic works? How does the deception of Eve relate to the other offenses of Gadre'el, namely, the creation of weapons? Finally, is this tradition meant to recall the account of Gen 3, and if so, does that rest awkwardly with the Enochic tradition of evil originating with the angels' descent?

As provocative as these questions are, 1 En 69:6 has received little sustained attention in the history of scholarship. In contrast to the Book of the Watchers (where the first woman is known only as the "aged mother") and to the Animal Apocalypse (where she appears as a heifer to comport with the allegory), the Book of Parables speaks of Eve by name *(hewa)*. Adam also appears in the Parables, where he too is finally given a proper name. The Book of Parables is unique, however, in depicting Eve without her partner Adam. Adam is included in Enoch's genealogy (1 En 37:1). Of the Enochic texts that allude to the first couple, the Book of Parables provides the most spartan presentation. While the Book of Parables relates Adam to Enoch's genealogy (cf. Gen 5:1-21), we do not read of the protoplast's creation (cf. Gen 1:27; 2:7) or time in the garden (Gen 3). While Eve is presented in the Parables as misled (so Gen 3:1-5, 13),

---

10. See, for instance, M. E. Stone, "The Axis of History at Qumran," in *Pseudepigraphic Perspectives: The Apocrypha and Pseudepigrapha in Light of the Dead Sea Scrolls: Proceedings of the International Symposium of the Orion Center for the Study of the Dead Sea Scrolls and Associated Literature, 12-14 January 1997*, ed. E. Chazon and M. E. Stone (Leiden: Brill, 1999), 133-49 (esp. 144-49); M. De Boer, "Paul and Jewish Apocalyptic Eschatology," in *Apocalyptic and the New Testament: Essays in Honour of J. Louis Martyn*, ed. J. Marcus and M. L. Soards, JSNTSup 24 (Sheffield: JSOT, 1989), 169-90 (esp. 174-80); and R. Penna, "Enochic Apocalypticism in Paul: The Idea of Sin," *Hen* 21 (1999): 285-306; esp. 296-97. Romano Penna elaborates on Martinus De Boer's "two tracks concerning the origin and nature of evil in Jewish apocalypticism." Enochic works may in fact preserve and combine up to three stories concerning the origin of evil. For further discussion of these stories and their merger, see J. C. VanderKam, *Enoch and the Growth of an Apocalyptic Tradition*, CBQMS 16 (Washington, D.C.: Catholic Biblical Association of America, 1984), 122-25, and also Nickelsburg, *1 Enoch 1*, 171-72.

the text betrays no knowledge of her creation (Gen 1:27; 2:18-22), her connection with Adam (Gen 2–3), or the nature of her deception in the Garden of Eden (Gen 3).

In other Second Temple period and late antique works, Eve is depicted as misled or betrayed in contrast to Adam — Satan discerns that he can get to the keen Adam only through Eve (Apoc Mos 7:2-3; 16:3) — drawing on the biblical tradition that has the serpent address Eve alone (for example, 2 En 30:18; 31:6; Prot Jas 13:1; LAE 18:1; 26:2; 35:2, 38; 44:2; cf. Gen 3:1-6). As if to underscore this point, Satan deceives the penitent Eve again in LAE 9–10; 18:1. Such a reading of Genesis that emphasizes Eve's culpability also accords with 2 Cor 11:3 and 1 Tim 2:14.[11] While the biblical account is unclear about Adam's whereabouts during Eve's deception, these later traditions underscore that Eve alone is deceived. Is 1 En 69:6 influenced by traditions like these that emphasize the blamelessness of Adam by exaggerating Eve's role in disobedience? Or, might we view Adam's absence in light of the polemical trend that Andrei Orlov identifies in 2 Enoch in which Adamic motifs and themes are transferred to Enoch?[12] That is, as Enoch's standing increases (from "scribe of righteousness" in the Book of the Watchers [1 En 12:4] to exalted "son of man" [62:5]), Adam's role is subsequently minimized.

As for Gadre'el, the name of this malevolent being is not so well-known. The list of the fallen watchers and their leaders in 1 En 69:2-12 is understood to be comparable to those of 1 En 6:7 and 8:1-3, yet Gadre'el does not appear in the Book of the Watchers, nor is the name to be found elsewhere in the Enochic corpus.[13] Apart from the reference in 1 En 69:6, the name has also been observed in an Aramaic incantation bowl from Nippur, the *Sefer HaRazim* (1:214), and the *Zohar* (*Vayaqhel* 202a).[14] In this last source, which Daniel Olson suggests may have been influenced by the Parables, Gadre'el is responsible for wars that occur among nations, reminiscent of his role in 1 En 69:6 as the one who

---

11. Perhaps also Sir 25:24-26. Levison makes a strong case that Ben Sira does not refer to Eve in 25:24 but instead to the evil wife, a common trope, in fact, in this book; see Levison, "Is Eve to Blame? A Contextual Analysis of Sirach 25:24," *CBQ* 47 (1985): 617-23 (here 622). Further, for Ben Sira to suggest a connection between the first woman and death would conflict greatly with Sira's interpretation of Gen 1–3; see Levison, 618.

12. A. A. Orlov, *The Enoch-Metatron Tradition*, TSAJ 107 (Tübingen: Mohr Siebeck, 2005), 211-53.

13. See David Suter's thorough study on this topic: *Tradition and Composition in the Parables of Enoch*, SBLDS 47 (Missoula: Scholars, 1979), esp. 73-102. Suter argues that the lists of 1 En 69:2-12 are traditions independent of 1 En 6–11.

14. See J. A. Montgomery, *Aramaic Incantation Texts from Nippur*, University of Pennsylvania: The Museum, Publications of the Babylonian Section 3 (Philadelphia: University Museum, 1913), no. 14, 183.

introduces weapons to humanity.[15] While the names of the angels and their leaders betray something of the function or role of the celestial beings, the name Gadre'el continues to elude. While Robert Henry Charles and Michael Knibb suggest that the name Gadre'el derives from עדריאל (= "God is my helper" or "God has helped"),[16] Matthew Black remarks that none of the derivations proposed, including this one, has proved convincing.[17]

Though it is seemingly the debut of this particular leader, Gadre'el in fact shares with Azazel, the prominent fallen watcher of the Book of the Watchers (cf. 1 En 8:1; 9:6; 10:4, 8; 13:1), some interesting characteristics. Notable is that Gadre'el oversees activities — the making of weaponry, specifically — that are assigned to Azazel in 1 En 8:1.[18] In the narrative of the Book of the Watchers that concerns the angels' descent, there is no mention of the first woman. Rather the text is interested in the watchers' misdeeds and offers expansions of Gen 5–6. We learn of the first couple in the Book of the Watchers only in a retrospective on the paradise of righteousness, and lest there be any confusion, they are further identified in the Greek and Ge'ez as the ones "who were before you (Enoch)." Thus, there is no connection between the first humans and the fallen angels made by the Book of the Watchers. Yet outside of the Enochic corpus, Azazel *is* linked with the deception of Eve in Apoc Ab 22:5–23:12, just as we observe with Gadre'el in 1 En 69:6.

Olson suggests that as the deceiver of Eve, Gadre'el "must be the one who spoke through the serpent in Genesis 3."[19] Indeed, the association is easy to imagine: the motif of misleading Eve brings to mind the account in Genesis where the serpent entices Eve to eat from the tree of the knowledge of good and evil (Gen 3). Hence, Charles is wont to conclude that Gadre'el must be a satan as he led astray Eve.[20] Anticipating that some may be quick to identify the serpent from Genesis with Satan, Olson notes that the earliest association of the two may be Rev 12:9.[21] Yet Gadre'el, not merely an angel, belongs to a distinctive class of celestial being in the Parables. Along with four others (Yeqon,

---

15. See D. Olson, *Enoch: A New Translation; The Ethiopic Book of Enoch, or 1 Enoch, Translated with Annotations and Cross-References* (North Richland Hills, Tex.: BIBAL, 2004), 272.

16. Charles, *The Book of Enoch*, 137, and Knibb, *The Ethiopic Book of Enoch: A New Edition in the Light of the Aramaic Dead Sea Fragments*, 2 vols. (Oxford: Clarendon, 1978), 161.

17. Matthew Black (*The Book of Enoch*, 246) is correct in my estimation in asserting that the derivation of Gadre'el from עזר or עדר seems inappropriate for a malevolent being. Various etymologies for the name are also suggested by L. Gry, "Mystique gnostique (juive et chrétienne) en finale des Paraboles d'Hénoch," *Le Muséon* 52 (1939): 337-78 (esp. 340 and n. 11).

18. So Black, *The Book of Enoch*, 246.

19. Olson, *Enoch*, 126.

20. Black, *The Book of Enoch*, 137.

21. Olson, *Enoch*, 126.

Asbe'el, Penemue, and Kasdeya), Gadre'el is a leader to the watchers or angels (1 En 69:3) familiar from the Book of the Watchers and other Enochic texts.[22] In fact, Gadre'el is typically classified as one of the satans described in 1 En 40:7.[23]

As for Gadre'el's activities, when he is not teaching humankind how to deliver deathblows or how to craft shields, breastplates, and swords, he is misleading Eve. What is meant, though, by "misleading"? We have no allusions in the Parables to Gen 3 or the fall of humanity, and in the earlier texts, 1 En 32:6 and 85:3, 6-9, the first couple is not described as misled in any respect. Further, in Enochic literature the sins of the angels (paralleled in the Parables by the misdeeds of their rulers; cf. 1 En 69:3-12) are defined by two broad categories: the watchers mate with mortal women and spur fornication among humankind (a result of the union is offspring that give rise to violence, demons, and idolatry), and the watchers teach humanity about crafts (from metallurgy and cosmetics to folk remedies) forbidden to them. In this context, how might Gadre'el corrupt Eve?

In the exegesis of 1 En 69:6 there are at this point more questions than answers. Nonetheless, our observations thus far suggest a different perspective on the first couple in the trajectory of Enochic literature. Moreover, Gabriele Boccaccini has seen in this passage a transformation in Enochic Judaism.[24] The text, he observes, provides an example of how Enochic Judaism has developed from the Book of the Watchers, where sin and evil seem to derive from outside the human sphere, to the Parables, where superhuman agents, such as satans, influence people, like Eve, and humans have free will to act. In Boccaccini's words, we see in the Parables, especially through the lens of 1 En 69:6, "the psychologization of the ancient myth of the fallen angels. The emphasis is not on the universe's contamination, of which human beings are passive victims, but overwhelmingly on the spread of secret knowledge passed on to human beings by the angels (1 En 64:1-2; 69:1-26). This revelation, aimed to mislead hu-

---

22. Black, *The Book of Enoch*, 245-46. The satans occupy several roles in the Parables: they command watchers, but also accuse humans (1 En 40:7, as in the Hebrew Bible; cf. Zech 3:1-2), lead others astray (1 En 54:6; 69:6), and play a role as agents of punishment (1 En 53:3; 56:1; 62:11; 63:1). While the angels or watchers corrupt humans as well as the earth in the Book of the Watchers and the Book of Dream Visions, it is the satans in the Parables who lead astray angels as well as humans.

23. Charles (*The Book of Enoch*, 136-37) thinks 1 En 69:3 to have read originally "the names of the satans" instead of "the names of the angels." Satan is featured in 1 En 54:6, and there seems to occur as a proper name. He is there described as ultimately in charge of the satans and watchers. Olson (*Enoch*, 138 n. 13) does not regard this reference to Satan as a Christian interpolation but sees it as comparable to Jub 10:11.

24. See G. Boccaccini, *Beyond the Essene Hypothesis: The Parting of the Ways between Qumran and Enochic Judaism* (Grand Rapids: Eerdmans, 1998), 145-46.

man beings, is described as a process of temptation that started at the beginning of humankind. The angel who taught human beings the art of making instruments of war is the same who first 'misled Eve' (69:6)."[25] Boccaccini goes on to describe this later manifestation of Enochic Judaism as seeking a balance "between the superhuman origin of evil and human responsibility." He sees this balance as newly possible with the Enochic writers embracing the tradition that employs Satan, Eve, and Adam to depict evil now entering the world through the human heart.

An important test of his thesis is available through exegesis of 1 En 69:6 and through the study of the first couple in this context. Scholars, including participants of the 2005 Enoch Seminar in Camaldoli, have noted the extent to which the Book of Parables resembles the Book of the Watchers, especially in its literary structure and through repetition of key motifs. While some suggest that traditions in the Parables develop independent of the Book of the Watchers, others maintain that the work is positioned as a sort of continuation of the earlier work in the collection of booklets we have come to call 1 Enoch.

Even so, we notice many points of discontinuity between the Book of the Watchers (as well as the second century B.C.E. Book of Dream Visions) and the Parables. Most notable are the Parables' characterizations of angels and humankind (1 En 69:11; cf. 15:4-7) and its distancing itself from wisdom traditions and revealed knowledge (42:1-3; 69:8-10; cf. 5:8; 32:3; 34:4). These differences affect, in fact, the depiction of the primordial couple in the Parables; Adam and Eve in this later booklet no longer resemble the first couple of the Book of the Watchers, figures associated with wisdom, and of the Animal Apocalypse, where the protoplasts are connected with a messianic figure of some sort. Chap. 69 of the Parables in particular highlights, rather, the different approaches taken by later Enochic communities, especially in interpreting Genesis.

If one is of the opinion, and not all are, that the Book of Parables self-consciously summons the Book of the Watchers, the former has the effect of rehabilitating earlier traditions.[26] In this scenario the points of dissimilarity signal development in an Enochic community; the community must be conservative to the degree that it clings to the Book of the Watchers, perhaps demonstrating the extent to which the booklet is a source of authority for a contemporaneous circle of followers. At the same time, the Book of Parables (e.g., 41:8-9), like the Epistle of Enoch (cf. 98:4), challenges key insights of the earliest Enochic literature. We see through study of Adamic tradition either evi-

---

25. Boccaccini, *Beyond the Essene Hypothesis*, 145-46; see also 187. In this respect the Epistle of Enoch, e.g., 1 En 98:4, is also comparable in its view of human culpability.

26. A sentiment to this effect was shared by Andrei Orlov at the Enoch Seminar 2005.

dence of transformation in Enochic Judaism, as Boccaccini posits, or witness to distinctive traditions associated with Enoch that enigmatically come to circulate together. In either event, we can at least maintain that Enochic literature is not univocal in its understanding of the first couple.

PART FIVE

# THE SOCIAL SETTING

# "A Testimony for the Kings and the Mighty Who Possess the Earth": The Thirst for Justice and Peace in the Parables of Enoch

*Pierluigi Piovanelli*

Dedicated to the memory
of André Caquot (1923-2004)
and Pierre Geoltrain (1929-2004)

The Book of Parables (1 En 37–71) represents an excellent test case for any socio-rhetorical analysis of late Second Temple apocalyptic discourse. In spite of the inclusion of some Noachic traditions (54:7–55:2; 60; 65:1–69:1), the narrative of the Book of Parables is reasonably well constructed and homogenous.[1] From an intertextual perspective, it is a sort of midrashic rewriting of the Book of the Watchers (1 En 1–36) with the addition of many new motifs resonating with dif-

---

1. For a short description of its narrative texture, see G. W. E. Nickelsburg, *Jewish Literature between the Bible and the Mishnah: A Historical and Literary Introduction*, 2nd ed. (Minneapolis: Fortress, 2005), 250-54, 399-400. Curiously enough, one of the most insightful judgments on the literary structure of the Book of Parables is to be found in a highly polemical and debatable monograph of the Canadian historian Donald Harman Akenson, who dares to compare the Book of Parables to James Joyce's *Finnegans Wake*, "not only because each starts before human time, but because each is a cyclical composition. Indeed, Joyce would argue that *Finnegans Wake* doesn't start or end; it just keeps going round and round. And that's also the way the Book of Similitudes works. . . . The several visions ascribed to Enoch in the Book of Similitudes can neither be taken as forming a sequential series of events, nor as happening coterminously; and one cannot declare them to be either mutually incompatible or to be capable of harmonization. At one moment they are one thing, then, another." D. H. Akenson, *Saint Saul: A Skeleton Key to the Historical Jesus* (Montreal and Kingston: McGill-Queen's University Press, 2000), 30-31.

*Pierluigi Piovanelli*

ferent parts of the Tanakh (especially Genesis, Isaiah,[2] and Daniel). Embedded in the narrative are different social realities and values that can be used as invaluable clues to reconstruct the profile of the implied audience and community. Having already studied these complementary aspects of the Book of the Watchers in a previous essay,[3] in the present study I would like to transfer such an approach à la Vernon K. Robbins to the Book of Parables and its "sociotext," i.e., the social perspectives inscribed into the text.[4]

To be effective, socio-rhetorical analyses need to be carried out on the original texts. This raises the question of the degree of accuracy not only of the Ethiopic translation — the only ancient version to have preserved the Book of Parables — but also of its modern editions and translations. The 1 Enoch collection, including the Parables, was translated together with the rest of the Holy Scriptures — the canonical and apocryphal texts as well — from Greek into Ethiopic[5] between about 340 and 525 C.E., more probably earlier (i.e., 340-400)

---

2. Concerning this Isaian intertextuality, George W. E. Nickelsburg, in his seminal study, *Resurrection, Immortality, and Eternal Life in Intertestamental Judaism*, HTS 26 (Cambridge: Harvard University Press, 1972), 70-74, has persuasively demonstrated that passages like 1 En 46; 62–63 use a narrative pattern of persecution, vindication, and (heavenly) exaltation of the righteous based on the Servant Song in Isa 52–53. While David W. Suter, *Tradition and Composition in the Parables of Enoch*, SBLDS 47 (Missoula: Scholars, 1979), has argued that 1 En 54:1–56:4; 64:1–69:12 is a midrash of Isa 24:17-23.

3. P. Piovanelli, "'Sitting by the Waters of Dan,' or the 'Tricky Business' of Tracing the Social Profile of the Communities That Produced the Earliest Enochic Texts," in *The Early Enoch Tradition*, ed. Gabriele Boccaccini (Leiden: Brill, forthcoming). The reader will refer to this article for all the methodological issues involved in my approach as well as the relevant bibliography.

4. For a similar approach, see L. W. Walck, "The Son of Man in Matthew and the Similtudes of Enoch" (Ph.D. diss., University of Notre Dame, 1999), 55-87 (I would like to thank the author for providing me with a copy of the relevant pages of his unpublished dissertation). Leslie Walck identifies there the social setting of the Book of Parables with the help of Richard L. Rohrbaugh's relational understanding of ancient cultures, Amy-Jill Levine's model of social and temporal axes embedded in biblical narratives, Vernon K. Robbins's analysis of the implied author's competencies in different social arenas, and Gerhard Lenski's description of social stratification of advanced agrarian societies. A more classical but still fruitful sociological path is now taken by Lester L. Grabbe; see below, his contribution to the present volume, "The Parables of Enoch in Second Temple Jewish Society."

5. See P. Piovanelli, "Sulla *Vorlage* aramaica dell'Enoch etiopico," *StClOr* 37 (1987): 545-94; Piovanelli, "Nouvelles perspectives dans l'étude des 'apocryphes' éthiopiens traduits du grec," in *Études éthiopiennes: Actes de la X$^e$ conférence internationale des études éthiopiennes. Paris, 24-28 août 1988*, ed. C. Lepage et al. (Paris: Société française pour les études éthiopiennes, 1994), 323-30 (here 326-27); J. C. VanderKam, "The Textual Base for the Ethiopic Translation of 1 Enoch," in *"Working with No Data": Semitic and Egyptian Studies Presented to Thomas O. Lambdin*, ed. D. M. Golomb (Winona Lake, Ind.: Eisenbrauns, 1987), 247-62 (reprinted in J. C. VanderKam, *From Revelation to Canon: Studies in the Hebrew Bible and Second*

than later (400-525). Clearly, we have no means of retrieving the text of the Greek model of the Book of Parables, not to mention its original text, presumably written in Hebrew or Aramaic.⁶ This is the first major obstacle to any scientific study of the Parables.

One should think of the occurrences of the generic expression *walda sab'/ be'esi*, "son of men (collective)⁷/of (a single) man," instead of the titular periphrasis *walda 'eg"āla 'emaḥeyāw*, "Son of the offspring of the Mother of the Living." The latter is more inclusive and originally refers to the common descent of humankind from Eve, "the mother of all the living" (Gen 3:20). It is the normal rendition of the Greek υἱὸς ἀνθρώπου in the Ethiopic version of Ps 80:18 (79:17 LXX) and Dan 7:13, in all the addresses of Ezekiel, and in the Son of Man passages of the New Testament.⁸ Leaving aside the interesting but too speculative

---

*Temple Literature*, JSJSup 62 [Leiden: Brill, 2000], 380-95). An eloquent example that points to the use of a Greek *Vorlage* is the Ethiopic reading *'eska manfaqa 'elat*, "until the middle of the day" (1 En 57:1), almost certainly based on a too-literal rendering of the Greek μεσημβρία that means both "midday" and, what the context requires here, "the South." One should be reminded that there is no evidence for any translation of biblical and parabiblical texts from Hebrew, Aramaic, Syriac, or Coptic into Ethiopic. Cf. M. A. Knibb, *Translating the Bible: The Ethiopic Version of the Old Testament* (Oxford and New York: British Academy and Oxford University, 1999), 35, 40.

6. In spite of many insightful studies devoted to the question of the original language of the Book of Parables — see, for example, the influential essay of A. Caquot and P. Geoltrain, "Notes sur le texte éthiopien des Paraboles d'Hénoch," *Sem* 13 (1963): 39-54 — it is practically impossible to decide whether it was written in Hebrew, Aramaic, or (according to Caquot and Geoltrain) Syriac. To posit an Aramaic *Urtext* is to stress the continuity existing between the Enochic writings found in Qumran and the Book of Parables, which is, after all, an integral part of the 1 Enoch collection. Conversely, to opt for a Hebrew text would emphasize its affinity with the 3 Enoch writings, as if the Book of Parables was the forerunner of the Hekhalot literature.

7. Cf. *weluda sab'*, "sons of men, human beings" (1 En 39:5; 40:7; 42:2; 64:2 [twice]; 69:6 [twice], 12, 14, and Tana 9 variant readings in 48:2; 62:5).

8. A. Dillmann, *Lexicon linguae Aethiopicae cum indice Latino* (Leipzig: Weigel, 1865), 803, 886, gives the examples of Matt 8:20; 9:6; 10:23; 11:19; 12:8; 25:31. In the present essay, the Ethiopic words and expressions are transliterated according to the Ethiopian traditional pronunciation as recorded in W. Leslau, *Comparative Dictionary of Geʻez: Geʻez-English/English-Geʻez* (Wiesbaden: Harrassowitz, 1987); Leslau, *Concise Dictionary of Geʻez (Classical Ethiopic)* (Wiesbaden: Harrassowitz, 1989). The Ethiopic readings are taken from the editions of R. H. Charles, *The Ethiopic Version of the Book of Enoch* (Oxford: Clarendon, 1906), and M. A. Knibb (in consultation with E. Ullendorff), *The Ethiopic Book of Enoch: A New Edition in the Light of the Aramaic Dead Sea Fragments*, 2 vols. (Oxford: Clarendon, 1978). Additional readings from unpublished manuscripts can also be found in the translations of S. Uhlig, *Das äthiopische Henochbuch*, in *JSHRZ*, ed. Werner G. Kümmel (Gütersloh: Gütersloher Verlagshaus Gerd Mohn, 1984), 5:461-780, and D. C. Olson (in consultation with M. Workeneh), *Enoch: A New Translation* (North Richland Hills, Tex.: BIBAL, 2004).

question of the Gnostic overtones of such an expression,[9] what is rather surprising in the Book of Parables is not the presence of *walda 'eg"āla 'emaḥeyāw*, but the use of *walda sab'/be'esi*.

| 1 Enoch | Ethiopic Expression | Character Addressed |
|---|---|---|
| 46:2 | *zekku walda sab'* | someone "whose face is |
|  | *zatawalda 'emsab'* Tana 9 | like the appearance of |
|  |  | men *(sab')*" (46:1) |
| 46:3 | *we'etu* | idem |
|  | *walda sab'* |  |
| 46:4 | *zentu walda sab'* | idem |
|  | *walda sab'* Tana 9 |  |
| 48:2 | *zekku walda sab'* | idem |
|  | *walda sab' zekku* BM 485, BM 491, Berl, Abb 35 |  |
|  | *weluda sab' zekku* Tana 9 |  |
| 60:10 | *'anta walda sab'* | Noah |
| 62:5 | *zekku walda be'esit* | the "Chosen One" (62:1) |
|  | *zekku walda be'esi* Berl, Abb 35, Abb 55 (BM 485) |  |
|  | *zekku weluda sab'* Tana 9 |  |
| 62:7 | *walda 'eg"āla 'emaḥeyāw* | idem |
| 62:9 | *zekku walda 'eg"āla 'emaḥeyāw* | idem |
| 62:14 | *zekku walda 'eg"āla 'emaḥeyāw* | idem |
| 63:11 | *zekku walda 'eg"āla 'emaḥeyāw* | idem |
| 69:26 | *we'etu walda 'eg"āla 'emaḥeyāw* | idem |
|  | *we'etu 'eg"āla 'emaḥeyāw* Tana 9, BM 491, Abb 35, Abb 55 |  |
| 69:27 | *walda 'eg"āla 'emmaḥeyāw* | idem |
| 69:29 | *we'etu walda be'esi* | idem |
|  | *walda be'esi* BM 491, Berl |  |

9. It is true that in Gnostic cosmogonic texts "the Mother of the Living" is the epithet given to the spiritual Eve/Zoe (Apocryphon of John, NHC II, 23:23-24//III, 30:13-14//IV, 36:15-16// BG, 60:14-16; Hypostasis of the Archons, NHC II, 89:11-15) or to the Holy Spirit/Sophia (Apocryphon of John, NHC II, 10:17-18//III, 15:19-21//BG, 38:10-12) that is "the first woman" (Irenaeus, *Against Heresies* 1.30.1-2). Similarly, according to the Manichean primeval myth, the Great Spirit projected the Mother of the Living, who projected, in turn, the First Man. However, some "orthodox" authors used to apply the same title to Mary the Mother, the new Eve (Epiphanius, *Refutation of All Heresies* 78.9.18; Peter Chrysologus, *Sermons* 140; John Damascene, *Sermons* 2), or to the church (Tertullian, *The Soul* 43). On Gnostic pneumatology, see W.-D. Hauschild, *Gottes Geist und der Mensch. Studien zur frühchristlichen Pneumatologie*, BEvT 63 (Munich: Kaiser, 1972), 228-31. For Mary as the second Eve, see J. Pelikan, *Mary through the Centuries: Her Place in the History of Culture* (New Haven and London: Yale University Press, 1996), 39-52, 235-36. For a critical assessment of "Gnostic" influences on Ethiopian Christendom, see P. Piovanelli, "Connaissance de Dieu et sagesse humaine en Éthiopie. Le traité *Explication de la Divinité* attribué aux hérétiques 'mikaélites,'" *Le Muséon* 117 (2004): 193-227.

"A Testimony for the Kings and the Mighty Who Possess the Earth"

| 69:29 | we'etu walda be'esi | idem |
|---|---|---|
| | we'tu walda be'esit EMML 2080, BM 485, BM 492 | |
| 70:1 | we'etu walda 'eg"āla 'emaḥeyāw | idem |
| 71:14 | 'anta we'etu walda be'esi | Enoch |
| 71:17 | we'etu walda 'eg"āla 'emaḥeyāw | the "Chosen One" |

The distribution of the three expressions apparently follows a regular pattern. At the beginning *walda sab'* refers to someone who has the appearance of a human being, while later on the Chosen One is either described as *walda be'esi,* a true human being, or identified with the *walda 'eg"āla 'emaḥeyāw,* the son of Mary, the Mother of the Living.[10] It seems to me that this pattern corresponds to a rhetorical effect of progressive disclosure: in the second parable the heavenly character previously introduced as the Chosen One is but a mysterious creature — an ambiguity consonant with the nature of the "one like a son of man" of Dan 7:13 — while in the third parable, after the Lord has officially enthroned the one "who was hidden," thus revealing him to "the kings, the mighty, and all who possess the earth" (1 En 62:5-7),[11] the true humanity and special filiation of the Chosen One are clearly suggested to the reader in a perfectly post-Nicene Christian way.[12] Not so surprisingly, we can see here the hand(s) of the Axumite translator(s) at work.[13]

---

10. See the previous footnote. Olson, *Enoch,* 139-40 n. 22, notes that normally the expression *walda be'esi* is never applied to Jesus Christ in Ethiopian literature (but contrast the case of the Amharic version quoted below, n. 12). This could explain the introduction of a slightly modified reading — *walda be'esit,* "son of a woman" (cf. Gal 4:4) — in such embarrassing passages as 1 En 62:5; 69:29. Conversely, Noah and Enoch are exclusively addressed, respectively, as *walda sab'* (60:10) and *walda be'esi* (71:14), two expressions that make clear that, according to the Ethiopian translator(s), scribes, and exegetes, these patriarchs were *not* to be identified with the heavenly Son of Man.

11. Unlike what is related in the second parable, where the future exaltation of the supernatural "son of men" creature does not correspond to a scene actually seen by the narrator, but is part of a prophetic announcement (1 En 48:4-5).

12. In this connection one should notice that the Ethiopian scholars who produced the targumic Amharic version of 1 Enoch printed in the great bilingual Bible of Emperor Haile Selassie (*Maṣḥaf qeddus bage'ezennā ba'amāreññā yataṣāfa,* 4 vols. [London?, 1935?], 3:59v-82v [EMML 673]), systematically referred the three expressions to the Christ. Thus, *walda sab'* and *walda be'esi* become "the Christ born of man" (cf. Tana 9 reading in 1 En 46:2), while *walda 'eg"āla 'emaḥeyāw* corresponds to "the Christ, son of Adam" (not Eve!). See the passages translated in the footnotes of L. Fusella and P. Sacchi, "Libro di Enoc," in *Apocrifi dell'Antico Testamento,* ed. Paolo Sacchi, vol. 1 (Turin: UTET, 1981), 413-667.

13. Theoretically, this could also be the case for the historically relevant reference to the *Pārtē waMēd* (*Parātē waMudē* Tana 9), "Parthians and Medes" (1 En 56:5; cf. Acts 2:9), because we know that the Ethiopian translators did not hesitate to actualize the biblical names of some

In spite of this hermeneutical solution, the initial difficulty is only partially removed because we are still unable to determinate if (1) two or more Ethiopian translators and/or correctors rendered the same Greek expression in three different ways, or (2) if a single Ethiopian translator interpreted it in different ways according to the context — this is the solution I would be personally inclined to adopt — or (3) if he or she tried to faithfully reproduce different Greek expressions, such as υἱὸς ἀνθρώπου (as in the Septuagint) versus ὁ υἱὸς τοῦ ἀνθρώπου (as in the New Testament) — that is another intriguing possibility. If this were the case, we could also legitimately ask (4) what the underlying Aramaic (and not Hebrew) expressions were looking like, hesitating between *bar 'enāsh* and *bar nasha'*. Perhaps it would be wiser to avoid translating all of them as "Son of Man" in order to make the readers aware of the variety and the complexity of these terminological and exegetical issues.[14]

As the presence of many variant readings in the previous example tellingly demonstrates, there also is, to a certain extent, a degree of uncertainty in our reconstructions of the Ethiopic text of the Book of Parables. However, even if it is true that we don't dispose of up-to-date and reliable critical editions of the Ethiopic version, we are lucky enough to have some useful and complementary translations — the old ones of Luigi Fusella, Ephraim Isaac, Michael A. Knibb, Siegbert Uhlig, André Caquot, and the new ones of George W. E. Nickelsburg and James A. VanderKam or Daniel C. Olson[15] — to which we can also add Matthew Black and Sabino Chialà's excellent commentaries.[16] If we ju-

---

bordering peoples, replacing, for example, the Assyrians and the Chaldeans with the Persians. See Dillmann, *Lexicon linguae Aethiopicae*, 1424. As a matter of fact, however, the mention of the Parthians is here a *lectio difficilior* because, among other considerations, the Parthian regime was no longer topical after the establishment of the Sassanid dynasty, in 228 C.E. Accordingly, this reading should be maintained as it is.

14. This is what Fusella and Sacchi, "Libro di Enoc," and S. Chialà, *Libro delle parabole di Enoc: Testo e commento*, Studi biblici 117 (Brescia: Paideia, 1997), wisely did.

15. Fusella and Sacchi, "Libro di Enoc"; E. Isaac, "1 (Ethiopic Apocalypse of) Enoch," in *The Old Testament Pseudepigrapha*, ed. J. H. Charlesworth, vol. 1 (Garden City, N.Y.: Doubleday, 1983), 5-89; M. A. Knibb, "1 Enoch," in *The Apocryphal Old Testament*, ed. H. F. D. Sparks (Oxford: Clarendon, 1984), 169-319; Uhlig, *Das äthiopische Henochbuch*; A. Caquot, "I Hénoch," in *La Bible. Écrits intertestamentaires*, ed. A. Dupont-Sommer and M. Philonenko, Pléiade 337 (Paris: Gallimard, 1987), 463-625; G. W. E. Nickelsburg and J. C. VanderKam, *1 Enoch: A New Translation; Based on the Hermeneia Commentary* (Minneapolis: Fortress, 2004); Olson, *Enoch*. The translations made in the eighties were reviewed by P. Piovanelli, "Il testo e le traduzioni dell'Enoch etiopico, 1976-1987," *Hen* 10 (1988): 85-95.

16. M. Black (in consultation with J. C. VanderKam and O. Neugebauer), *The Book of Enoch, or, 1 Enoch: A New English Edition with Commentary and Textual Notes*, SVTP 7 (Leiden: Brill, 1985); Chialà, *Libro delle parabole di Enoc*. After his impressive and exhaustive *1 Enoch 1: A Commentary on the Book of 1 Enoch 1–36, 81–108*, vol. 1, Hermeneia (Minneapolis: Fortress,

"A Testimony for the Kings and the Mighty Who Possess the Earth"

diciously combine the information provided in these works, we can obtain a more satisfactory picture, not of the Hebrew or Aramaic original text or its Greek translation, but at least of the Ethiopic version of the Book of Parables.

With these limitations in mind, we can begin to detect the social and cultural values that have left their imprints on the text and pinpoint the narrative strategies used to foster the socioreligious program of the Book of Parables.

The first observation to be made is that the use of Enochic characters and motifs already sets this work apart as belonging to a specific cluster of Jewish apocalyptic texts. Even if the original Semitic language of the Book of Parables is presently impossible to determine, its narrative point of departure can also be found in other Enochic literature, that is to say, the role that the seventh patriarch played in the crisis of the fallen angels, the eschatological events he foresaw, and the special cosmological knowledge he acquired during his visionary travels fully described, for the first time, in the third century B.C.E. Book of the Watchers. This primeval myth was subsequently reenacted at different turning points of the history of the Jewish people in the late Second Temple period. Each time, every rewriting addressed different social and religious questions, providing new solutions and perspectives to its audience. The most perceptible feature of this process is perhaps the constant reactualization of the prophecies concerning the end of the days. Thus the Epistle of Enoch (1 En 91–105) includes an apocalyptic discourse known as the Apocalypse of Weeks (93:1-10; 91:11-17) that was probably written around 170 B.C.E., and the Dream Visions (1 En 83–90) ends with a longer Animal Apocalypse (85–90), whose author was apparently unaware of Judas Maccabeus's death in the spring of 160 B.C.E.[17] The Enoch speaking in the Apocalypse of Weeks promises a violent inauguration of "the week of righteousness" and the beginning of the restoration of Israel (91:11-13) as a prelude to the true eschaton (91:14-17), while his alter ego in the Animal Apocalypse locates the dawn of the messianic era in the aftermath of the Maccabean insurrection (90:28-39). Needless to say, both seers were too hasty or optimistic in their judgments,[18] and it is only understandable that subsequent Enochic authors

---

2001), George W. E. Nickelsburg is now preparing with James VanderKam a second volume devoted to the Book of Parables and the Astronomical Book to be published in the same series.

17. On these two Enochic booklets and apocalypses, see especially J. C. VanderKam, *Enoch and the Growth of an Apocalyptic Tradition,* CBQMS 16 (Washington, D.C.: Catholic Biblical Association of America, 1984), 141-78; VanderKam, *Enoch: A Man for All Generations* (Columbia: University of South Carolina Press, 1995), 60-101; P. A. Tiller, *A Commentary on the Animal Apocalypse of I Enoch,* SBLEJL 4 (Atlanta: Scholars, 1993); Nickelsburg, *1 Enoch 1,* 345-535; Olson, *Enoch,* 183-253.

18. Their ideas certainly contributed to the growth of a feeling of frustration among the

had to bring these announcements up to date. It is such a chain of reactualizations that betrays the existence of a specifically Enochic tradition, school, group, or movement engaged in what we could describe, in sociological terms, as a series of attempts to reduce the cognitive dissonance provoked by disconfirmation of prophecy.[19] The Book of Parables seems to be the last link in this Enochic chain.

If the Book of Parables really is a literary production of the Enochic movement, we could wonder about the nature of the actual or ideal communities portrayed in its text. We could also try to detect the indicators of a strong group-identity disseminated through it, not to mention the evidence of an eventual sectarian stance. Surprisingly, this does not seem to be the case. Human beings and societies[20] share the common destiny of being submitted to the two incoming retributions, the flood in the past and the last judgment in the future. Nonetheless, they are not described as enemies of Judaism or of the Enochic community. On the contrary, before glorifying the Lord of Spirits all the inhabitants of the earth will bow down to the Chosen One, who is appropriately called "the light of the nations" (1 En 48:4-5). Moreover, at the moment of the judgment the Lord of Spirits will spare non-Jewish peoples — or more improbably, Jewish apostates — that witnessed the triumph of the righteous and, consequently, repented and abandoned idolatry (50:2-4). The same benevolent and nonsectarian attitude is shown toward Israel and Jerusalem, which are referred to as the land and the city of the Lord of the Spirit's chosen ones (56:6-7). Different from what we find in the Apoc-

---

Jewish faithful when the policies of the Hasmonean government did not meet their enthusiastic expectations, as A. I. Baumgarten, *The Flourishing of Jewish Sects in the Maccabean Era: An Interpretation*, JSJSup 55 (Leiden: Brill, 1997), has cogently argued.

19. This phenomenon was at first recognized and studied by L. Festinger, H. W. Riecken, and S. Schachter, *When Prophecy Fails: A Social and Psychological Study of a Modern Group That Predicted the Destruction of the World*, 2nd ed. (New York: Harper and Row, 1964); Leon Festinger, *A Theory of Cognitive Dissonance* (Stanford: Stanford University Press, 1957). For the application of their model to Second Temple Judaism and early Christianity, see J. G. Gager, *Kingdom and Community: The Social World of Early Christianity* (Englewood Cliffs, N.J.: Prentice-Hall, 1975), 37-49, 62-64 (the spread of Christian mission); P. F. Esler, *The First Christians in Their Social Worlds: Social-Scientific Approaches to New Testament Interpretation* (London and New York: Routledge, 1994), 92-130 (Dan 7 and 4 Ezra). One should note that B. J. Malina, "Normative Dissonance and Christian Origins," *Semeia* 35 (1986): 35-59, has — in my opinion, unconvincingly — disputed the usefulness of such an approach. For a good overview of the contemporary debate, see the studies collected in J. R. Stone, ed., *Expecting Armageddon: Essential Readings in Failed Prophecy* (New York and London: Routledge, 2000).

20. Men (1 En 41:1; 41:8; 68:5; 69:9, 10, 11); sons of men (39:5; 40:7; 42:2; 64:2 [twice]; 69:6 [twice], 12, 14); those who dwell on the earth (40:6, 7; 48:5; 54:6, 9; 55:1, 2; 60:5; 65:6, 10, 12; 66:1; 69:1, 7; 70:1) or on the land, the sea, and the islands (53:1); the nations (48:4).

## "A Testimony for the Kings and the Mighty Who Possess the Earth"

alypse of Weeks (93:9) and the Animal Apocalypse (89:73-74), in the Book of Parables no criticism is openly expressed against the Second Temple or its official clergy.[21]

The text only rarely and obliquely refers to the socioreligious group from which it emanates — the "community" *(māḫbar)* of the righteous (1 En 38:1), of the holy ones (45:1 Tana 9), of the chosen and the holy (62:8) — and to the places where they meet — the "house(s) of the assembly" *(bēta/'abyāta mesteguba')* of the Lord of Spirits (46:8; 53:6).[22] More frequently the ideal readers to whom the Book of Parables is addressed are simply designated as "righteous" (37 times), "chosen" (26 times), and "holy ones" (11 times).[23] The works of the righteous depend on the Lord of Spirits (38:2); they believe in the name of the Lord of Spirits (43:4), and have hated this age of unrighteousness (48:7). They are associated with light (38:2, 4; 39:7; 41:8; 50:1; 58:3), and their temporary resting places are with the angels (39:4, 5). In the end they will be saved (62:13), obtain glory and honor (50:1; 62:15, 16), receive a new covenant (60:6), inherit the earth (45:5-6), live in peace (58:4), and accede to everlasting life (40:9; 58:3; 62:14). The entire text is a hymn to the glory of "the children and the chosen ones" of the Lord of Spirits (62:11), an invitation to take courage and not abandon the hope (cf. 104:4).

The obvious antagonists of the righteous are the sinners (mentioned 15

---

21. On the anti-Zadokite stance adopted by many early apocalyptic texts (including Daniel), see M. A. Knibb, "The Exile in the Literature of the Intertestamental Period," *HeyJ* 17 (1976): 253-72; G. Boccaccini, *Beyond the Essene Hypothesis: The Parting of the Ways between Qumran and Enochic Judaism* (Grand Rapids: Eerdmans, 1998), 85-86, 139-40; Boccaccini, *Roots of Rabbinic Judaism: An Intellectual History, from Ezekiel to Daniel* (Grand Rapids: Eerdmans, 2002), 92. The priestly role that Enoch plays as an intermediary between heaven and earth and the references to his knowledge of the astronomical secrets (1 En 41:3-8; 43:1–44:1; 59:1-3; 60:11-22; 69:20-25) are of course constitutive elements of the Enochic narrative cycle and socioreligious identity, but they do not seem to be used in a polemical way in the Book of Parables.

22. In 1 En 46:8, the oldest Ethiopic manuscripts display an interesting variety of readings. Thus, BM 485 and Abb 35*: "They persecute/banish *(yesaddedu)* the houses of his assembly . . ."; BM 491 and Abb 55: "Are persecuted/banished *(yessaddadu)* the houses of his assembly . . ."; Tana 9: "They desire *(yefaqqedu)* to meet in his houses. . . ." Even if "[i]t does not seem likely that the idol-worshipping kings and mighty [heavily criticized in 46:4-8] would also be hypocritical co-religionists of the persecuted people of God in the 'Parables'" (Olson, *Enoch*, 90), this could actually be the case of the Hasmonean and Herodian kings.

23. The righteous (1 En 38:1, 2, 3; 39:4; 41:8 [twice]; 45:6; 47:1; 47:2 [twice], 4; 48:4, 7, 9; 53:7; 61:3 [twice]; 71:17 [twice]); the chosen ones (45:5; 48:9; 56:8; 60:6; 61:4 [twice]; 62:8); the holy ones (who dwell on the earth) (43:4; 45:1; 50:1); the righteous and the chosen ones (38:2, 3; 39:6, 7; 58:1, 2, 3; 60:8; 61:13; 62:12, 13, 15; 70:3); the children and the chosen ones of the Lord of Spirits (62:11); the righteous and the holy ones (38:5; 48:7; 51:2); the chosen and the holy ones (41:2; 50:1; 62:8); the holy, the righteous, and the chosen (38:4; 48:1).

times) and their associates (5 times).[24] The sinners are guilty of denying (the name of) the Lord of Spirits (1 En 38:2; 41:2; 45:1, 2), the community of the holy ones (45:1 Tana 9), and even the existence of a judgment (60:6). They oppress the righteous (53:7) and their deeds are wicked (53:2). They are associated with darkness (41:8), and their final destiny is to be ill treated (46:4), judged (38:3; 41:1, 2; 45:6; 60:6, 24), punished (60:24), expelled into a netherworld (45:2), and eventually destroyed (45:6; 53:2; 62:2).

However, the real bad guys and girls of the Book of Parables belong to a more specific category of sinners living at the summit of ancient Jewish and Greco-Roman societies. The kings (cited 15 times), the mighty (13 times), the exalted (6 times), those who possess the earth (6 times), and the strong ones (2 times) are the main target of the work.[25] The powerful of this world too do not praise (the name of) the Lord of Spirits (46:5, 6), and they deny him, his name, and his messiah (46:7; 48:10; 67:8, 10). Their deeds manifest unrighteousness (46:7; 63:9, 10), their spirits are full of lust (67:8, 10, 13), and they persecute the faithful (46:8; 62:11). They are associated with darkness (46:6; 62:10; 63:6, 11), and at the arrival of the Son of Man they will be overturned (46:4, 5; 48:8), terrified (62:5), humiliated/ashamed (46:6; 62:10; 63:11), and punished (62:11). They will ask in vain for a little respite (63:1, 5, 6, 8) and will finally burn (48:9) and perish (38:5, 6; 53:5).

This explicit and uncompromising attack against the political leaders of the day is a novelty in the Enochic tradition. Thus, for example, even if some scholars interpret the myth of the fallen angels in the Book of the Watchers (1 En 6–11) as a metaphoric response to persecution by the Hellenistic kings,[26] the text never suggests such identification. On the other hand, even if the Epistle of Enoch contains many woes against the rich (94:6–95:2; 96:4-8; 97:7-10) that cruelly oppress the righteous (103:9-15), kings and mighty ones are never accused of being guilty of such a crime. As David W. Suter has eloquently shown, the justification for their presence in the eschatological, grandiose

---

24. The sinners (1 En 38:2, 3; 41:2; 43:8; 45:2, 6; 50:2; 53:2 [twice]; 53:7; 56:8; 60:6); the wicked (38:3); those who commit sin and error (45:5); the strong and the sinners (46:4); the sinners and the unrighteous (62:2, 13).

25. The kings (1 En 46:5); the mighty kings who dwell on the earth (55:4); the kings and the mighty (of this earth) (38:5; 46:4; 53:5; 54:2); the kings and the strong who possess the earth (48:8); the mighty and exalted who possess the earth (38:4); the mighty and the kings who possess the earth (63:1; 67:12); the kings, the mighty, and all who possess the earth (62:6); the kings, the mighty, the exalted, and those who possess (rule/dwell on) the earth (62:1; 62:3, 9; 63:12; 67:8); the strong (46:6); the rulers (67:13?).

26. See especially G. W. E. Nickelsburg, "Apocalyptic and Myth in 1 Enoch 6–11," *JBL* 96 (1977): 383-405.

fresco offered by the Book of Parables is primarily scriptural, to be found in an Enochic midrashic interpretation of a key passage of the Isaiah Apocalypse (Isa 24:17-23).[27] However, in apocalyptic literature, as elsewhere, images and symbols are not gratuitously interchangeable, and such a shift from economic to political injustice demonstrates that some changes had occurred in the social world of the circle that produced the Book of Parables.[28] In this connection we can quote in full Suter's still relevant conclusion.

> While the lack of concrete details in the Parables makes it difficult to translate the symbolism into history, a study of the symbolism illuminates the social situation in which the work was produced. The kings and mighty are seen as part of a cosmic rebellion against the power of God, while the present sufferings of the righteous servants of an omnipotent God are sanctioned by reference to the eschatological reversal that will take place. The symbolism of the Parables functions as a means of integrating the present experience of the righteous of a world that does not seem to be structured according to the laws of their God with their belief in a God who, as the divine lawgiver, rewards in concrete ways the community of his chosen ones when it is faithful to his law. While a collective representation of a social order generally functions as a means of sanctioning the structure and authority of that order, in an apocalyptic system such a representation must sanction the overthrow or fall of the oppressive order and the establishment of a new society.[29]

Before addressing the final and fatidic question of the historical setting of the Book of Parables, we could ask, once more, if this opposition to the dominant — and actually perceived as oppressive — social order is not an indicator of religious sectarianism. After all, according to the typology elaborated by Bryan R. Wilson, the basic prerequisite for sectarianism is the rejection of the existing society.[30] But even if we are ready to ascribe such a countercultural and

---

27. Suter, *Tradition and Composition*, 52-61, 181-83. According to Isa 24:21-22, "On that day the LORD will punish the host of heaven, in heaven, and the kings of the earth, on the earth. They will be gathered together as prisoners in a pit; they will be shut up in a prison, and after many days they will be punished" (RSV).

28. The latter's condemnation of the kings and the mighty is not to be confused with a criticism of the monarchic institution per se, because among Noah's righteous and glorious descendants the Book of Parables does not hesitate to mention the biblical sovereigns (1 En 65:12).

29. Suter, *Tradition and Composition*, 163-64.

30. See especially B. R. Wilson, *Religious Sects: A Sociological Study* (London: Weidenfeld and Nicolson, 1970), 26-34. Wilson "characterises the sect as a voluntary association with a

antisocial attitude to the Book of Parables, where are the traces left in the text by typically sectarian "boundary marking mechanisms" — to use the terminology of Albert I. Baumgarten — that allow us "to distinguish between its own members and those otherwise normally regarded as belonging to the same national or religious entity"? Where are "the social means of differentiating between insiders and outsiders"? Who are the righteous, a sectarian rest or the anonymous and silent majority of the Jewish faithful? Who are the sinners, a hostile majority or some black sheep that seem to act against the mitzvoth of the Jewish Torah?

In other words, if the Book of Parables is the expression of a sectarian group that we could qualify — according to Wilson's typology — as "revolutionist" (waiting for a supernatural intervention that will change the world), "manipulationist" (claiming to possess special or esoteric knowledge that enables them to influence the world), "thaumaturgical" (believing in oracles and miracles dispensed by supernatural agencies), and "spiritualistic" (emphasizing communication with the dead), the tone used in the narrative is more consensual and ecumenical than exclusivist and elitist. It seems to me that the intended audience to whom the Book of Parables addresses its message of solace

---

strong sense of self-identity. Membership depends upon merit or some kind of qualification such as knowledge or acceptance of doctrine or of conversion evidenced by some form of religious experience. The sect is exclusive and regards itself as an elite in sole possession of the truth. It is separated from the wider society and at odds with prevailing orthodoxy. Certain standards of behaviour are required of members and expulsion may follow any serious or persistent failure to live by them. Regular procedures for expulsion will exist. The commitment of the sectarian is always more total than that of the non-sectarian and he or she is always more distinctly characterised in terms of religious affiliation. The sect has no distinct or professional ministry" (M. B. Hamilton, *The Sociology of Religion: Theoretical and Comparative Perspectives* [London and New York: Routledge, 1995], 197-98). Compare Anthony Saldarini's synthetic definition: "Sect: a religiously based group which is either actively involved against society or withdrawn in reaction to it. Such groups are often political forces. In its classical Christian definition sect is contrasted with the dominant religious force, church"; see A. J. Saldarini, *Pharisees, Scribes, and Sadducees in Palestinian Society: A Sociological Approach* (Wilmington, Del.: Glazier, 1988), 313. Contrast Baumgarten's broader — and perhaps too encompassing — description: "I would therefore define a sect as a *voluntary association of protest, which utilizes boundary marking mechanisms — the social means of differentiating between insiders and outsiders — to distinguish between its own members and those otherwise normally regarded as belonging to the same national or religious entity*. Ancient Jewish sects, accordingly, differentiated *between Jews who were members of their sect and those not*" (Baumgarten, *Flourishing of Jewish Sects*, 7). For an application of Wilson's categories to Second Temple religious movements and groups, see P. Piovanelli, "Was There Sectarian Behavior before the Flourishing of Jewish Sects? A Long-Term Approach to the History and Sociology of Second Temple Sectarianism," in *Sectarianism in Early Judaism: Sociological Advances*, ed. David Chalcraft (London: Equinox, forthcoming).

and hope is but the ensemble of the Jewish people fallen under the domination of a new and merciless dynasty.

Obviously enough, these findings are of some import when we try to provide a rational explanation of the absence of the Book of Parables from the shelves of the Qumran libraries. Besides the fact that the latest booklet of the Enochic collection was probably written after the creation of the Community of the Renewed Covenant, here at stake is the issue of its religious perspectives that are, in a certain way, more universalistic, pacifist, and tolerant than what can be found in the writings authored by the most radically "introversionist" Jewish sect of the Second Temple period.[31]

The most plausible historical setting in which the Book of Parables is to be located is, in my opinion, the reign of Herod the Great (37-4 B.C.E.), more exactly, sometime after the momentous parenthesis of the Parthian occupation of the Roman provinces of Asia, Pamphylia, Cilicia, and Syria under the joint leadership of Pacorus I and Quintus Labienus, in 40-37 B.C.E., and before the death of the Idumean king.[32] On one hand, the Book of Parables explicitly projects into the eschatological future the memory of Parthians and Medes invading Judea, even if, at the end of the days, Jerusalem will resist their powerful cavalry (1 En 56:5-7).[33] As for Herod's unsuccessful attempts to recover by going to hot

---

31. For a sociological understanding of the Qumran community, see Esler, *The First Christians*, 70-91; J. Marcus, "Modern and Ancient Jewish Apocalypticism," *JR* 76, no. 1 (1996): 1-27; S. Walker-Ramisch, "Graeco-Roman Voluntary Associations and the Damascus Document: A Sociological Analysis," in *Voluntary Associations in the Graeco-Roman World*, ed. John S. Kloppenborg and Steven G. Wilson (London and New York: Routledge, 1996), 128-45; M.-F. Baslez, "Recherches sur le *yahad* des manuscrits de Qumrân dans l'environnement associatif sémitique et grec," in *Les communautés religieuses dans le monde gréco-romain: Essais de définition*, ed. N. Belayche and S. Mimouni, BEHESR 117 (Turnhout: Brepols, 2003), 75-92; E. Regev, "Comparing Sectarian Practice and Organization: The Qumran Sects in Light of the Regulations of the Shakers, Hutterites, Mennonites and Amish," *Numen* 51 (2004): 146-81; A. Sivertsev, "Sects and Households: Social Structure of the Proto-Sectarian Movement of Nehemiah 10 and the Dead Sea Sect," *CBQ* 67 (2005): 59-78. Also see the methodological caveat of J. M. Jokiranta, "'Sectarianism' of the Qumran 'Sect': Sociological Notes," *RevQ* 20, no. 2 (2001): 223-39, and the comments of P. Piovanelli, "Some Archeological, Sociological and Cross-Cultural Afterthoughts on the 'Groningen' and the 'Enochic/Essene' Hypotheses," in *Enoch and Qumran Origins: New Light on a Forgotten Connection*, ed. G. Boccaccini (Grand Rapids: Eerdmans, 2005), 366-72.

32. In a similar vein, see P. Sacchi, "Qumran e la datazione del Libro delle Parabole di Enoc," *Hen* 25 (2003): 149-66. The different proposals are reviewed by David W. Suter in his contribution to the present volume, "Enoch in Sheol: Updating the Dating of the Book of Parables."

33. Then follows an enigmatic description of a column of noisy chariots arriving from the east and the west (1 En 57:1-2) that could represent either the returnees from the Diaspora or another foreign army.

springs, they are brilliantly ridiculed and interpreted as a foretaste of the fiery punishments in store for him and the tyrants like him (67:5-11).[34] On the other hand, the text is apparently silent about the circumstances of the king's death; the troubles that disrupted his succession; the Roman occupation of Judea, Samaria, and Galilee; the military resistance that ensued; Caligula's attempt to have his own statue introduced in the temple, and more significantly, the destruction of Jerusalem in 70 C.E., not to mention the hope to rebuild the Holy City before the tragic epilogue of the Second Jewish War, in 135 C.E.

We can only guess about the arguments used by Herod's propagandists to convince their Jewish coreligionists to acknowledge the legitimacy of the monarch's authority. If their arguments were based on the grandeur of Herod's achievements — military, diplomatic, and architectural as well — they probably did not impress too much a large number of Jewish faithful. If they echoed some motifs of Roman imperial propaganda as — at least after Octavian's victory at Actium, in 31 B.C.E. — the instauration of the Pax Augustea and the return of the Golden Age,[35] the group behind the Book of Parables was definitively not convinced and prepared to reply in a typically Enochic way.

In this connection, it is perhaps useful to compare Virgil's famous "messianic" *Fourth Eclogue*, written in 41 or 40 B.C.E.,[36] to the slightly more recent Book of Parables. The Roman poet supposedly reports a prophecy by the Sibyl of Cumae that announces the coming of the *ultima aetas*, the "last age" (v. 4), corresponding to the mythical reign of Saturn (v. 6); "a new generation now descends from heaven" (v. 7) and the birth of a boy is imminent, "with whom the iron age will cease and the golden race arise" (vv. 8-9); he will be Jupiter's offspring (v. 49), and under his leadership "the memories of our past crimes

---

34. The historical evidence is now discussed by Darrell Hannah in his contribution to the present volume, "The Book of Noah, the Death of Herod the Great, and the Date of the Parables of Enoch."

35. One should be reminded that the Jewish historian Nicolaus of Damascus actually wrote an encomiastic biography of the young Octavian. Its fragments have been translated by C. M. Hall, *Nicolaus of Damascus' Life of Augustus* (Menasha, Wis.: Banta, 1923). Also see B. Z. Wacholder, *Nicolaus of Damascus* (Berkeley: University of California Press, 1962); Wacholder, "Josephus and Nicolaus of Damascus," in *Josephus, the Bible, and History*, ed. L. H. Feldman and G. Hata (Leiden: Brill, 1989), 147-72.

36. See W. Clausen, "Virgil's Messianic Eclogue," in *Poetry and Prophecy: The Beginnings of a Literary Tradition*, ed. J. L. Kugel (Ithaca, N.Y., and London: Cornell University Press, 1990), 65-74; J. B. Van Sickle, *A Reading of Virgil's Messianic Eclogue*, HDC (New York and London: Garland, 1992); C. Habicht, "Messianic Elements in the Prechristian Greco-Roman World," in *Toward the Millennium: Messianic Expectations from the Bible to Waco*, ed. M. R. Cohen and P. Schäfer, SHR 77 (Leiden: Brill, 1998), 47-55; C. G. Perkell, "The Golden Age and Its Contradictions in the Poetry of Vergil," *Vergilius* 48 (2002): 3-39.

## "A Testimony for the Kings and the Mighty Who Possess the Earth"

will vanish and traditional fears will disappear" (vv. 13-14); to this child the earth, untilled, will give her gifts and the goats will spontaneously offer their milk, while the flocks will not be afraid of the lions (vv. 18-22); the serpent and "the treacherous poison-plant" will disappear, and Assyrian spices will blossom everywhere (vv. 24-25); after a series of new wars that will send another "great Achilles to Troy" (vv. 34-36), the truly messianic era will coincide with the infant's adult age: all the human activities that go against the natural course of things, as sea trade and agricultural labors, will come to an end (vv. 38-41), and there will be no need to "learn wool to lie with different colors" because the ram himself will be able to change the color of his fleece (vv. 42-45); thanks to this divine child, "the great order of the centuries begins anew" (v. 5).

If we leave aside the tricky and insoluble question of the messianic child's identity, both the *Fourth Eclogue* and the Book of Parables share the same expectation for a better world that will restore, after too many internecine conflicts, the primordial goodness of the original creation. Especially noticeable is the almost ecological longing for a planet earth released from the bondage of any unnatural craft present in both texts.[37] Nonetheless, the major difference between them lies in the way they construct their main characters. Thus, Virgil's poem is entirely devoted to the glorification of a future great ruler — a motif that would soon be redirected and applied by the poet himself, in the *Aeneid* (6.791-793), to the person of the Divus Augustus — whereas the Book of Parables is more concerned with the incoming rehabilitation of an oppressed community and/or nation through the agency of a divine savior. The first celebrates the birth of a strong man and the beginning of an authoritarian regime, while the second condemns any form of human despotism. The first — in Suter's words — "functions as a means of sanctioning the structure and authority" of a new social order, while the second "sanction[s] the overthrow or fall of the oppressive order and the establishment of a new society." The perspectives of the *Fourth Eclogue* correspond to the point of view of the colonizer, those of the Book of Parables to the perception of the colonized.

Be that as it may, a final point of interest to be raised concerns the eventual survival in the Book of Parables of some early features that were already present, from the beginning of the Enochic trajectory, in the Book of the Watchers. This is apparently not the case of the Galilean geographical frame-

---

37. In the Book of Parables the industries of gold and silver (1 En 52:7) are negatively viewed, as are those of silver, lead, and tin (65:7-8; 67:4). Equally condemned are iron weapons and breastplates (52:8); shields, breastplates, and swords (69:6); bronze, tin, and lead objects (52:8), to be destroyed (52:9); pen, ink, and paper (69:9-10). But contrast the iron chains made to take hold of the rebel angels (54:1) or the chains of iron and bronze in store for the spirits of the giants (56:1).

work in which the Book of the Watchers originally staged the myth of fallen angels (1 En 12–16).[38] Actually, to the best of my knowledge the Book of Parables does not make any reference to such an Upper Galilean landscape. However, this is certainly true for what I labeled "the magico-therapeutic possibilities of Enoch's teachings," that is to say, the positive evidence that points to the involvement of the people beyond the Enochic texts in some kind of "magic" or "shamanic" activities.[39] The Book of Parables not only provides two detailed lists of the names and functions of the fallen angels that are of great utility for any "manipulationist" reader (69:2-12),[40] it also ends by describing the heavenly apotheosis of the narrator, the patriarch Enoch (70–71), who is identified with the heavenly Son of Man (71:14).[41] This is the supreme reward that the Book of

---

38. See G. W. E. Nickelsburg, "Enoch, Levi, and Peter: Recipients of Revelation in Upper Galilee," *JBL* 100 (1981): 575-600 (reprinted in *George W. E. Nickelsburg in Perspective: An Ongoing Dialogue of Learning*, ed. J. Neusner and A. J. Avery-Peck, 2 vols., JSJSup 80 [Leiden: Brill, 2003], 2:427-57); Nickelsburg, *1 Enoch 1*, 238-47; D. W. Suter, "Revisiting 'Fallen Angels, Fallen Priests,'" in *The Origins of Enochic Judaism: Proceedings of the First Enoch Seminar (University of Michigan, Sesto Fiorentino, Italy, June 19-23, 2001)*, ed. G. Boccaccini (Turin: Zamorani, 2002), 137-42; Suter, "Why Galilee? Galilean Regionalism in the Interpretation of 1 Enoch 6–16," *Hen* 25 (2003): 167-212; P. M. Venter, "Spatiality in Enoch's Journeys (1 Enoch 12–36)," in *Wisdom and Apocalypticism in the Dead Sea Scrolls and in the Biblical Tradition*, ed. F. García Martínez, BETL 168 (Leuven: Peeters, 2003), 211-30; Piovanelli, "'Sitting by the Waters of Dan,' or the 'Tricky Business' of Tracing the Social Profile of the Communities That Produced the Earliest Enochic Texts."

39. See P. Piovanelli, "A Theology of the Supernatural in the Book of the Watchers? An African Perspective," in *The Origins of Enochic Judaism*, 87-98; Piovanelli, "'Sitting by the Waters of Dan,' or the 'Tricky Business' of Tracing the Social Profile of the Communities That Produced the Earliest Enochic Texts." Concerning shamanism in late antique Jewish mystical circles, see the groundbreaking monograph of J. R. Davila, *Descenders to the Chariot: The People behind the Hekhalot Literature*, JSJSup 70 (Leiden: Brill, 2001). Davila adopts as a working definition Åke Hultkrantz's description of the shaman as "a social functionary who, with the help of guardian spirits, attains ecstasy in order to create a rapport with the supernatural world on behalf of his group members" (44). The main features of Hultkrantz's model include: the "Means of becoming a shaman" (generally, election by the spirits); "Ecstasy or trance and ascetic techniques"; "Initiatory disintegration and reintegration"; "The otherworldly journey"; "Control of the spirits"; "Serving a community" (healing, divination, psychopompy, propitiation, addressing various social problems) (45-48).

40. Especially noteworthy is the description of Kasdyā' (i.e., the "Chaldean"?), who "is the one who showed the sons of men the blows of each evil (provoked) by the spirits and the demons, the blows of the foetus in the womb so that it aborts, the blows of the soul, the bites of the serpent, the blows that come about at noonday, and the son of the serpent whose name is Tabā'et" (1 En 69:12).

41. In spite of the present conditions of the Ethiopic text that do not permit such identification (see above, n. 10), Enoch's "deification" can be inferred from the analogous transformation he experiences in 2 En 39 and in the so-called 3 Enoch Hekhalot literature. See P. S. Alexan-

*"A Testimony for the Kings and the Mighty Who Possess the Earth"*

Parables promises to any practitioner who would engage in Enoch's mystical path.[42]

In conclusion, even if it seems plausible that the Enochians progressively evolved from "magic" to "the millennium," we can safely assert that in the Book of Parables "a magic still dwells."

---

der, "From Son of Adam to Second God: Transformations of the Biblical Enoch," in *Biblical Figures outside the Bible*, ed. Michael E. Stone and Theodore A. Bergren (Harrisburg, Pa.: Trinity, 1998), 87-122; A. A. Orlov, *The Enoch-Metatron Tradition*, TSAJ 107 (Tübingen: Mohr Siebeck, 2005), 165-76.

42. Some years ago Alan F. Segal (*Two Powers in Heaven: Early Rabbinic Reports about Christianity and Gnosticism*, SJLA 25 [Leiden: Brill, 1977], 213-14 n. 87) quoted an interesting saying of Rabbi Abbahu of Caesarea, a third-century contemporary of Origen: "If a man says to you, 'I am God,' he is a liar; if (he says,) 'I am the Son of Man,' in the end people will laugh at him; if (he says,) 'I will go up to heaven,' he says so, but shall not perform it" (*y. Ta'an.* 65b, slightly modified). Now even if it is plausible to imagine that "in Abahu's time, Christianity of the gnostic or even Johannine type, [was] the most likely referent for the heresy [sic]" (Segal, 213-14 n. 87), the Book of Parables eloquently demonstrates that Christians did not invent or have a monopoly on ascents to heaven.

# Was the Book of Parables a Sectarian Document?
# A Brief Brief in Support of Pierluigi Piovanelli

*Daniel Boyarin*

The second booklet of the Ethiopian Enoch, known as 1 Enoch, namely, the Parables (or Similitudes) of Enoch, may provide important clues for unlocking the mysteries of that nexus.[1] This is a text, apparently originally written by a Jew or Jews in either Hebrew or Aramaic sometime in the first century C.E., translated into Greek in some form of a Greek Bible, and known to us only from a late-ancient translation into Ethiopic. While some parts of the text of 1 Enoch as a whole are known from other sources (either Aramaic ones or Greek), the Book of Parables has survived only in the Ethiopic version. Its provenance (at the level of generality in which I have given it) seems relatively secure. In his essay, Pierluigi Piovanelli uses rhetorical analysis "to reconstruct the profile of the implied audience and community" of the Parables and compellingly argues that the producers of this document did not belong to an embattled and oppressed sect but identified themselves, in fact, in some important sense with Israel as a whole. His interpretative assumption is that the "kings and the mighty" who are the declared enemies of the author(s) of the Parables are Gentile (probably Roman) rulers.[2] What I wish to do here is explore some potentially highly significant implications of this argument for the investigation of rabbinic literature and for the history of the rabbinic movement as part and parcel of a much larger phenomenon we might call Judaism. Piovanelli

---

1. For an excellent translation and introduction to the scholarly issues surrounding this work, see G. W. E. Nickelsburg and J. C. VanderKam, *1 Enoch: A New Translation* (Minneapolis: Fortress, 2004). The Book of Parables itself is there on pp. 50-95.

2. See above, P. Piovanelli, "'A Testimony for the Kings and Mighty Who Possess the Earth': The Thirst for Justice and Peace in the Parables of Enoch."

## Was the Book of Parables a Sectarian Document?

posits two alternative possibilities for conceiving of the place of the Parables of Enoch, writing: "To posit an Aramaic *Urtext* is to stress the continuity existing between the Enochic writings found in Qumran and the Book of Parables, which is, after all, an integral part of the 1 Enoch collection. Conversely, to opt for a Hebrew text would emphasize its affinity with the 3 Enoch writings, as if the Book of Parables was the forerunner of the *hekhaloth* literature."

While I am less than convinced of the necessary ties between language and affinity, I do find that the distinction between Qumranic connections and Hekhalot connections is a deeply compelling one. (I must say, however, that I am rather unimpressed with the arguments offered, on all fronts, for a particular, specific historical background for the text; my own suggestions here are not in any way dependent on any specific dating for the text.) It seems to me that Piovanelli is right to stress these different alternatives, not only as mere matters of literary history but also as powerful and significant indicators of the social location of the group that formed the text.

Piovanelli's observations on the relatively nonsectarian (or nonsectlike) character of the Parables suggest, in fact, a disjunction between them and Qumran, as there may be no doubt but that the Qumran community is sociologically a kind of sect. As Gabriele Boccaccini has written, at Qumran we find "the first example of an underground trend of thought that would often resurface in the history of Christianity and Rabbinic Judaism. The outside world is the dominion of Belial.... The one who does not join the community 'will not become clean by the acts of atonement, nor shall he be purified by the cleansing waters, nor shall he [be] made holy by the seas or rivers, nor shall he be purified by all the water of ablutions.'"[3] Aharon Shemesh has, moreover, argued in two closely reasoned articles that from a halachic standpoint, the members of the Qumran community understood themselves as Israel, and all others, including other Israelites, as Gentiles.[4] This is, of course, consistent with other aspects of the ideology of the sectarian scrolls that seem to imply such an identification of the Community with Israel *tout court*.[5] Indeed, Albert Baumgarten has proposed that this is the very definition of Jewish sectarianism: "Ancient Jewish sectarians... turned the means of marking separation normally applied against

---

3. G. Boccaccini, *Beyond the Essene Hypothesis: The Parting of the Ways between Qumran and Enochic Judaism* (Grand Rapids: Eerdmans, 1998), 67.

4. A. Shemesh, "The Origins of the Laws of Separatism: Qumran Literature and Rabbinic Halacha," *RevQ* 18, no. 2 (1997): 223-41; A. Shemesh, "The One Who Divides between the Children of Light and the Children of Darkness, between Israel and the Nations," in *Atara l'Haim: Studies in the Talmud and Medieval Rabbinic Literature in Honor of Professor Haim Zalman Dimitrovsky*, ed. Daniel Boyarin et al. (Jerusalem: Magnes, 2000), 209-20.

5. Boccaccini, *Beyond the Essene Hypothesis*, 66.

non-Jews against those otherwise regarded as fellow Jews, as a way of protesting against those Jews, and/or against Jewish society at large. As a result of these actions all Jews were no longer on the same footing: *sectarian Jews treated other Jews as outsiders of a new sort.*"[6] At the same time, however, Baumgarten makes clear that there were significant differences in this respect between the "introvertionist" and "greedy" Qumranite sectarianism that allowed virtually no value at all to any other form of Judaism and the "reformist" sects of the Pharisees and Sadducees. The latter groups "hold hopes of reforming the larger society, and have not given up on it or renounced it totally, still perceiving themselves as members of the whole," while the "introvertionist sort of sect, by contrast, has so finally rejected the institutions of the society as a whole as to turn in on itself completely, and to rank those outside its bounds as irredeemable."[7] One way to think of this is that a sect describes itself as having left the larger group, owing to the corruption of that larger group, while a church, as it were, describes the others as having left (or been pushed out of) it, owing to their defection from the true way and concomitant corruption, or even as representing a contaminating force that comes from the outside. This does not necessarily represent a difference in "reality," but it does constitute an important difference in representation and self-fashioning. In terms of discourse, one distinction will be with respect to legitimation. While the "church" will frequently present itself as the heir to an apostolic succession, the "sect" will as frequently present itself as the heir to a new revelation. As Moshe Herr has written, "Rabbinic thought projects a definite attitude regarding *continuum* and *continuity* in the chain of Torah transmission. In direct contrast to this approach the writings of the Dead Sea Sect (CD 5:2) contend that the Torah was not known at all from the era of the Judges until the end of the First Temple period. Even after the destruction, they maintain, the Torah was not really understood until the founding of the sect."[8]

As has been frequently pointed out, the sociological situation of the Qumran group answers precisely to the description of a sect in the sense of a group that has broken off from the main part of a religious community in search of greater purity or stringency. In a sense the rhetoric of Qumran in this respect is similar to that of the Gospel of John. Indeed, following Boccaccini, it seems more attractive to find the roots of supersessionism, *Verus Israel*, rather than the roots of heresiology in Qumran. This point comes out very clearly in

---

6. A. I. Baumgarten, *The Flourishing of Jewish Sects in the Maccabean Era: An Interpretation*, JSJSup 55 (Leiden: Brill, 1997), 9, emphasis in original.

7. Baumgarten, *Flourishing*, 12-13.

8. M. D. Herr, "Continuum in the Chain of Torah Transmission" (in Hebrew with English summary), *Zion* 44 (1979): x.

another discussion by Shemesh.⁹ Certain members of the house of Israel, owing to their righteousness, have been vouchsafed additional revelation, and they — the Dead Sea community — now constitute Israel. The structure is, then, seemingly analogous to Pauline thought, whereby a new revelation has taken place and, whether voluntarily or involuntarily, only some of Israel have heard it, and these constitute a new Israel. Piovanelli, on the other hand, convinces at least this reader that the Parables of Enoch is not the product of a sect, that indeed it shows none of the signs of the particular apocalyptic imagery that characterize such groups, that rather the Parabolists, if I may coin yet another term, speak for Israel against a common outside oppressor, the Romans, of course. As he concludes, "the intended audience to whom the Book of Parables addresses its message of solace and hope is but the ensemble of the Jewish people fallen under the domination of a new and merciless dynasty." Whether or not we need speak of a full-blown parting of the ways, it seems nevertheless compellingly the case that Qumranic sectarianism and the ethos behind the Parables of Enoch represent distinct forms of Jewish religious imagination and distinctly different types of community. It becomes even less plausible than previously thought to seek to date the Book of Parables on the basis of its absence from the Enoch of Qumran.

Piovanelli's comments anent the social background of the Parables of Enoch strongly support, in my opinion, the notion that the best way to interpret early Christianity (and by this I mean, right to the end of ancient Christianity) is as a form of Judaism, *in some ways* as a more conservative form than rabbinic Judaism. The famous statement at the end of the narrative of the four who went into Pardes to the effect that Rabbi Aqiva came out safely (literally, in peace) while *Aḥer* died in infamy, would, on this possible but by no means proven interpretation, then represent a Rabbi Aqiva who turned away from "heresy" to orthodoxy and an Elisha who remained adamant in the old traditions. The drama of *this* parting of the ways *within* Enochic Judaism, as it were, surely is to be set in late antiquity and not before. There is no reason to assume that we are talking about the real Rabbi Aqiva and the real Elisha ben Abuya here, nor about early second-century realities, and everything in fact that we know of rabbinic literature and its practices of ascription militates against such a conclusion. What we have before us, in my view, is a virtual allegory of different historical trends within historical Judaism, those who remained faithful to the old ways, continuing to believe in the Son of Man and being declared heretics, and those who turned from such beliefs and adopted

---

9. A. Shemesh, "Expulsion and Exclusion in the Community Rule and the Damascus Document," *DSD* 9, no. 1 (2002): 44-74.

the new, improved, "purer" rabbinic Judaism. It should be noted, however, that both groups are apparently observers of the same basic halachic norms, at least by late antiquity, and this is, after all, precisely what the Hekhalot literature would lead us to expect.[10]

If the Enochic traditions, as they extend from the Parables forward into 3 Enoch and into Metatron literature, represent indeed the common religious heritage of much of Israel and not particular sectarian formations, as I am convinced they do, then the evidence just offered for such theology in the heart of the rabbinic sociocultural world is rendered even more cogent. As Pogo would have put it, we have met the heresy and it is us. I would go so far as to suggest (but in a very tentative and preliminary fashion) that on the basis of the rabbinic material adduced, it is the Son of Man, Enoch, Metatron, Christ who is always at issue when "Two Powers in Heaven" is broached in rabbinic literature. It is, however, not the continuing fact of these traditions themselves that so mobilized the later Babylonian rabbis to expel from within their own hearts such "heresies," but the way the Son of Man was taken up in Christianity, beginning of course with the gospel itself that explains the horror these late Babylonian rabbinic texts express at the very thought of a messianic figure in human shape sitting at the right hand of the Lord. Rather than being the product or the origin of a Jewish Christianity, *pace* Mearns, but also not the product of a Judaism that is *not* Christian, the Son of Man, i.e., the Parables of Enoch and the later avatars of this tradition, such as 3 Enoch (the Hebrew Enoch), becomes a touchstone precisely in the institution of such a Judaism (and, moreover, an unsuccessful one to boot, as Metatron and even the Son of Man by this name[11] become the very heart of later kabbalistic speculation).[12]

This approach quite obviates, I think, some traditional forms of posing the question as represented in David Suter's formulation:

> Black calls for a reassessment of the question of the influence of the Parables on the gospels and indicates that he has committed himself to the proposition that there are pre-Christian Jewish traditions in the Parables, including the Son of Man passages, that have exercised an influence on Christian usage, although we cannot also rule out Christian editing of those traditions. Even so, exercising an influence upon Christian usage is a

---

10. I will explore the implications of this point for the history of so-called Enochic Judaism in an expanded version of this essay.

11. As I am informed by Moshe Idel with respect to work of his yet to be published.

12. D. Abrams, "The Boundaries of Divine Ontology: The Inclusion and Exclusion of Metatron in the Godhead," *HTR* 87, no. 3 (1994): 291-321.

far cry from when the Parables was taken as *prima facie* evidence for the apocalyptic Son of Man in ancient Judaism.[13]

Once we fully take in that "Christianity" is simply part and parcel of ancient Judaism, this very way of posing the issue becomes immaterial, in my humble opinion.

---

13. See below, D. Suter, "Enoch in Sheol: Updating the Dating of the Book of Parables."

# The Parables of Enoch in Second Temple Jewish Society

*Lester L. Grabbe*

The present article attempts to do something different from simply putting the Parables of Enoch in the context of other Second Temple Jewish writings. It tries to find a social setting for the book, a task that is much harder than has sometimes been thought. To do so, it will need to consider how to go about asking questions with regard to the social setting of the book, since methodology lies at the heart of the enterprise.

## Methodology

Trying to determine the social context of an ancient document is an extremely difficult task. The standard procedure among anthropologists and sociologists is to observe a society in operation, to look at the social interactions among people, and to see how their beliefs and mental outlook are translated into the acts of daily living. In short, the proper way to carry out a study of social context is to observe the living society. This is impossible with the Parables of Enoch: all we have is the text. We are thus thrown back onto trying to extract from the text sufficient information to reconstruct its presumed context. This itself creates a further difficulty: since one of the reasons for constructing a social context is to better understand the text itself, this leads to a circular process. Unfortunately, historical reconstruction as such cannot avoid a certain amount of circularity: the most one can do is to be clear about it and to keep it carefully controlled.

Our aim is simple: to try to determine the world within the text, the world implied by the text. What sort of society or segment of society might be implied by the textual contents? What are its interests? What is important to it? What explicit references are there? What implicit references are there? It is important to consider several methodological principles when trying to analyze texts for the purpose of determining social context.

a. We need to be careful about assuming that the explicit contents of the text show the things that were most important to the author(s). Important things — or even the most important things — may be assumed by the text rather than talked about. But it is a reasonable inference that the contents will show *some* of the issues important to the author(s).

b. The matter is somewhat more complicated in traditional literature that has grown up over a long period of time. Sometimes "fossils" get into the text and remain there, despite redaction. Although the redactor might have taken the view that the contents were not contrary to his views, he might have overlooked or misunderstood various sections of the text. Thus, some traditions might reflect the main concerns or interests not of the final compiler(s)/redactor(s) of the book but of the original authors of the particular tradition in question.

c. Caution should be exercised about equating theology with sociology: beliefs are often inherited. They may be passed on from a group with a particular social structure to one with a quite different origin and structure. Also, a group might change certain beliefs while keeping their original structure, mission, and essential ethos. The question is how important a particular belief is to the existence of the group. Ultimately, the researcher must determine whether the set of beliefs implies a single social context or possibly several.

d. Care should be taken about drawing conclusions from omissions, especially in short texts. An author will not necessarily put all his concerns in every text he writes or edits.

e. The variety of possible social contexts has to be considered and the possibilities weighed as to which are more probable and which less so.

## Content

As noted above, to make a credible attempt to give a context to the Parables, one has to try to determine the world within the text. What are its interests? What is important to it? The following themes are some of the main ones in the text:

Lester L. Grabbe

## Wisdom

The Book of Parables has the heading that it is a "vision of wisdom" (1 En 37:1). Wisdom language is found throughout the book. A myth about wisdom (that wisdom could find no abode on earth and took her place in heaven) in 42:1-2 has parallels to Ben Sira (24:4-12), in which wisdom found a place in Israel. The righteous drink from fountains of wisdom (1 En 48:1). A spirit of wisdom is one of the characteristics of the Chosen One (49:3).

## Cosmology

As with other sections of 1 Enoch, the Book of Parables is very interested in cosmology. The subject comes up a number of times, and not just in passing; it is clear that the divine ordering of the natural phenomena is important to the author: 41; 43–44; 59; 60:11-23. The heavenly bodies are preserved in their ordered way through oaths (69:16-25). As with wisdom, cosmology might have been the concern of various circles by this time, but cosmic speculation was more likely the preserve of a scribal class with the leisure to think about such matters. Through much of the Second Temple period the priesthood had the resources and leisure to pursue such matters. The cosmological sections show no advance on the treatment elsewhere in 1 Enoch, such as the Astronomical Book. It is thus possible that the passages in the Parables are more or less borrowed from other sections of the Enoch tradition. Yet it is more likely that an interest in discussing these in detail lay with a particular sort of group. For example, in the section where the course of the natural phenomena is preserved through an oath, this could have been stated fairly concisely if the point was the oath, yet the passage goes through a lot of unnecessary cosmological detail. Such a detailed interest suggests a group that considered such matters important for their own sake. Interestingly, though, this cosmological speculation is not accompanied by any calendar interest, and there is no suggestion of use of a solar calendar.

## Daniel 7

The relationship of the Parables to Daniel is not altogether clear. The Book of Parables draws on a scenario of the Ancient of Days and the Son of Man very similar to that in Dan 7:9-14. The question is whether Parables used Daniel directly or drew on another source. That is, an argument can be made that Dan 7

*The Parables of Enoch in Second Temple Jewish Society*

itself draws on an older tradition and that the imagery of the Ancient of Days and one like a son of man might have been around in earlier sources that Daniel itself drew on. Although this cannot be ruled out, the details displayed by the Parables match closely those in Dan 7 and are most likely taken from it. Thus, the Book of Parables was written at a time when Daniel had become available (i.e., post–165 B.C.E.), and the author(s) regarded the book as at least containing useful information, if not authoritative.

### The Son of Man/the Chosen One/the Messiah

The concept of the Messiah in the Parables (1 En 45–46; 48–51; 61:5-10; 62; 69:26-29) stands out from what seems the most widespread concept in Second Temple Judaism.[1] Although there is a variety of messianic types, most are not heavenly figures. Instead of an earthly (if perhaps larger than life) conqueror and champion of the Jews, the Book of Parables puts forward a heavenly messiah, hidden from before creation but revealed to the righteous (48:6-7). This individual is called by a number of titles in the writing: "Son of Man," "Chosen One," "Holy One" (37:2), "Righteous One" (38:2; 53:6), "Chosen One of righteousness" (39:6).[2] One could argue (as did an older scholarly generation) that these were originally separate figures, perhaps coming from separate sources, that only later became assimilated to one another.[3] Whether this is the case or not, chap. 48 seems to identify them by referring to the Son of Man as the Chosen One (48:6) and the Messiah (48:10). The present form of the book appears to be thinking of a single figure, and the centrality of this figure to the Parables is evident.

### The Book of Noah

It has long been argued that a book of Noah underlies certain sections of the Parables (as elsewhere in 1 Enoch), especially chaps. 60, 65, and 67–68. This is a reasonable suggestion, except that the extracts might have come not from a

---

1. For a survey, with literature, see L. L. Grabbe, *Judaic Religion in the Second Temple Period: Belief and Practice from the Exile to Yavneh* (London and New York: Routledge, 2000), 271-91.

2. Michael Knibb's edition has the plural; see M. A. Knibb, *The Ethiopic Book of Enoch: A New Edition in the Light of the Aramaic Dead Sea Fragments,* 2 vols. (Oxford: Clarendon, 1978), 2:126.

3. See the discussion in R. H. Charles, *The Book of Enoch* (Oxford: Clarendon, 1913), 64-65.

"book of Noah" but from a version of "rewritten Genesis." We know that the Genesis Apocryphon covered some of the pre-Abraham events, including the life of Noah, but it is presently too difficult to read for much of the pre-Abraham story. The implication of this is that whoever wrote the Parables considered such a book authoritative in some sense and may have had connections with the author(s) of the Epistle of Enoch, who also made use of this book.

### Kings and Rulers

Charles argues that these are the "unbelieving native rulers [i.e., Hasmoneans] and Sadducees [their alleged supporters]";[4] however, despite his certainty, this seems nothing but unsupported guessing. Charles has *assumed* that any group responsible for the Parables must be in opposition to the state administration; i.e., the "rulers" must be Jewish. But there is nothing about the frequent references to rulers to indicate that they are Jewish, for in many passages the impression is that the reference is generic. One passage includes the statement that these individuals have "gods that their hands have made" (46:7).

### Eschatology

This is an important theme in the book, but there are various sorts of eschatology. Here are some of the main points of its eschatology:

- A judgment is often referred to or presupposed, but the time and place are rather vague (47:3; 53:1–54:6; 55:3–56:4).
- Judgment is executed by the Chief of Days (47:3) and the Chosen One (61:8).
- One passage suggests a one-off event, a resurrection, rather than just a judgment of the righteous and wicked in general (51).
- Righteous and chosen dwell on earth (38:1-2; 51:5).
- Some of the righteous dwell in the garden of life (61:12), under the wings of "the Lord of Spirits" (39; 45:3-6; 58), or elsewhere (61:12).
- Judgment is passed on the wicked and rulers who dwell on earth, and they are driven from the earth (38:1-2, 4; 62:1-12; 63; 67:8-12).
- The dwelling place of the righteous and the holy ones is in heaven (39:1-5; 41:2; 47:2; 58:5).

4. Charles, *The Book of Enoch*, 72 (on 1 En 38:5).

- Heaven and earth will be transformed for the righteous, but the wicked will be excluded (45:1-6).
- Valleys of judgment for the wicked are mentioned in one passage (53–54).
- The righteous do not seem to have a function in the judgment and punishment of the wicked, with the execution of judgment carried out by the Lord of Spirits, the Son of Man, and the angels. Only 48:9 mentions that the wicked will be "given into the hands" of the chosen and be like straw in the fire. But no specific actions by the righteous are enumerated, and the "chosen ones" might be the angels. The overwhelming emphasis is that the righteous passively receive and witness the actions of their supernatural overlords.

In sum, there will be a judgment, but its exact location and time are left vague. No attempt is made to calculate when the end-time is. The righteous will be vindicated and rewarded and the wicked punished, but there does not appear to be any cosmic cataclysm. The central focus of the Parables is on the eternal life of the righteous under the "wings of the Lord of Spirits" (39:7), praising him, with the Son of Man/Chosen One ruling among them (51; 62:13-16). The cosmic cataclysm known from a number of Jewish writings (Zech 14; 2 Bar 70; 4 Ezra 5:1-13; 6:18-28; 13; Rev 6; 8–9; 15–20; the Gospel Apocalypse [Mark 13//Matt 24//Luke 21]) does not appear to be a part of its thinking.

### Invasion of the Parthians and Medes

The reference to the Parthians and Medes in 56:5–57:2 is often taken to be to the invasion of the Parthians in 40 B.C.E., in which Jerusalem was taken, Aristobulus was put in control, and Herod escaped to Rome. The problem is that the wording of the passage suggests that Jerusalem was not taken and that the invaders fought among themselves and were destroyed (56:7-8). In addition, a second invasion from the east seems to be envisaged (57:1-2). Needless to say, none of this happened. Whatever the historical reality, this passage seems to be a metaphor for an eschatological defeat of Jerusalem's enemies.

### Angelology

Like the rest of 1 Enoch, the Book of Parables is pervaded by a view of an extensive angelic realm, comprised of both good and fallen angels. The four archangels are mentioned several times (1 En 40:9; 71:9, 13: Michael, Gabriel, Raphael,

Phanuel), though the fourth member is different from some lists elsewhere (9:1 [Greek]: Uriel). Various categories of good angels are mentioned, including cherubim, seraphim, and ophanim (61:10; 71:7). Fallen angels who lead men astray are taken for granted and mentioned several times in passing, but the fallen angels myth does not seem to have a very important place in the thinking of the writer. Some of those leading men astray are named (69:2-15), but such a focus on the angels themselves is unusual. There are also angels of punishment for the wicked angels and humans (53:3-5; 62:11-12; 66). Azazel and the other fallen angels will be punished (54:3-6; 55:3–56:4; 64; 67:4-13). In distinction from the rest of 1 Enoch, a number of passages mention "satans" (40:7; 53:3; 54:6; 69:4, 6).

### Knowledge of Secret Things

This is a two-sided coin: on the one side is the negative view about secret things, illicit knowledge taught to humans by fallen angels, including technological knowledge (65:6-11; 69:6-10). These secrets include not only the knowledge of making instruments of war (69:6) but also the working of metals and even writing with pen and ink (65:6-8; 69:9-10). A point is made that Noah has not been corrupted by knowledge of the secrets (65:11-12). The other side of the coin is that knowledge of secrets is a future reward for the righteous and even a gift in the present: the Chosen One teaches secrets of wisdom (46:2-3; 51:3). Noah (the text has Enoch but is probably in error) is shown the secret things in heaven and earth (60:11-23) and then receives a book containing all the secrets (68:1). Michael also shows Enoch all the secrets from the extreme ends of the heavens (71:3-4).

## Analysis

The first question we have to ask is whether the Book of Parables was written as an independent unit or composed from the first to be a part of 1 Enoch. J. T. Milik argued that the "pentateuch" of 1 Enoch did not originally contain the Parables but the Book of Giants.[5] He maintained that the Book of Giants was later displaced by the Parables, an argument based on the lack of the Parables at Qumran in contrast to the evident popularity both of the other parts of

---

5. J. T. Milik, *The Books of Enoch: Aramaic Fragments of Qumrân Cave 4* (Oxford: Clarendon, 1976), 4.

1 Enoch and also of the Book of Giants. One could ask why such a fundamental text as the Book of Giants should be removed. But for our purposes, the important fact is the absence of the Parables at Qumran despite the evident popularity of other parts of 1 Enoch. This is a strong argument for saying the Book of Parables was not originally a part of 1 Enoch. Yet this does not answer the question, since the book could have been written to add to the other four parts of 1 Enoch.

It seems obvious that the Book of Parables drew on the Enoch tradition and was influenced by themes in other sections of 1 Enoch. Yet a number of indications argue that it was composed to be a text that could be read on its own, even if written with an eye to including it as another section of 1 Enoch. First is the fact that the Book of Parables has a heading, a body made up mainly of three "parables," and a conclusion. As well as terms known from other parts of Enoch, it contains terminology unique to itself, such as "Lord of Spirits," "Son of Man," "Messiah." These are some of the reasons that the Book of Parables should be interpreted as an autonomous writing with its own coherence and unity, whatever traditions were used by the author(s) and even if it was intended from the beginning to be included with the other parts of Enoch to form a whole.

Several of the themes within the book show a connection with other sections of Judaism but not with any specific group. Concern for wisdom and the use of wisdom language were no longer indicative of a specific "wisdom tradition": wisdom had long become the general heritage of all Judaism. Similarly, an eschatology in which the righteous eventually lived in a transformed heavens and earth from which the wicked were excluded was widespread, even if the exact path by which they got there (whether end-time upheaval, resurrection, messianic rule, or individual postmortem judgment) may have differed from group to group.

A central role is played by the tradition known primarily from Dan 7:9-14. This is interesting for several reasons. The first one is that Daniel as a whole seems to play little or no role in the Parables. Earthly kingdoms, calculations of the end-time, prophecies of the future, and other parts of Daniel are absent. The writer is interested in two things from these few verses, the Ancient of Days and the one like a son of man. The first seems identified with the Lord of Spirits who plays an important role within the writing. Yet it is fair to say that the writer is somewhat more preoccupied with the Son of Man, whether called by this title or others such as "Chosen One."

Mention of "Parthians and Medes" in 1 En 56:5-8 is often taken to refer to the Parthian invasion of 40 B.C.E. This is a reasonable interpretation, but there are some difficulties. The main one is that none of the details in the account match that event. The Parthians were not destroyed, and Jerusalem did not provide a particular hindrance to the invaders. One might compare this with the *ex eventu* prophecies of Daniel that are commonly assumed to allow us to date the composition of the book of Daniel. The reason this dating is possible is that the prophecies correspond so closely to historical events in the first part but then suddenly go in a different direction at the end. But the reference to the Parthians and the Medes gives no particular details. It is so vague that one could plausibly interpret it as a general reference to a potential invader, not a reference to an actual historical event. I am not denying that it might well refer to the historical Parthian invasion, but there is not enough precise information to allow much in the way of conclusions from this passage.

One of the points that should be considered is the absence of certain beliefs or topics. We need to be cautious because in some cases this may be accidental or have an explanation other than absence of the belief, but some instances do seem significant because if they were important, they would likely have been mentioned. Here are some absent concepts:

- Nothing is said about the temple or altar. This could possibly be because no temple existed in the time of Enoch (or Noah). Yet altars were certainly known, and an eschatological temple was common in Jewish writings of the Second Temple period. If the temple was important to the writer, we would expect some reference to it for the final judgment or life of the righteous for eternity.
- There is an absence of eschatological activity by the righteous/chosen. They seem to take a passive stance, waiting the intervention of the Chosen One or Lord of Spirits to exalt and reward them and give them an eternal dwelling. No mention is made of their taking part in judgment, defeating the wicked, or executing vengeance on their enemies. Theirs is essentially a pacifist position, or at least a passive one.[6]
- Little in the way of cosmic upheaval occurs in the Parables. There is no universal catastrophe, no destruction on earth or in heaven, no end-time cataclysm. There is judgment, but the timing is somewhat vague. The only

---

6. In discussion at the Third Enoch Seminar, it was pointed out by Adela Yarbro Collins and others that simply composing the writing could be an act of defiance. I fully agree that such can be the case, but this is beside the point: the point of my argument is that the righteous are not pictured as doing anything *in the eschaton*. Early Christians were also pacifist, apparently, but they were only waiting until the day that God granted them power (cf. 1 Cor 6:1-3; Rev 20:4-6). It seems to me astonishing that the writer does not look forward to the time that his group is in power and can take action. This seems to be significant, though I am not quite sure what conclusions to draw from it.

real instance of anything approaching the cosmic end-time event is the reference to death being given up by the earth, Sheol, and Abaddon (51). This might imply a resurrection; if so, it is the only such reference in the book. Furthermore, it seems to involve only the righteous, not all the dead, since nothing is said of a judgment on those raised up.

- There seems to be no attempt to calculate the end-time or survey history (whether under the scheme of successive empires or any other). This means that the Book of Parables is silent on most of Daniel, despite the clear importance of Dan 7:9-14.
- No discussion of calendar is found, and not even a hint that anyone is using a wrong calendar. If the group was using a calendar at odds with the rest of Jewish society, which was likely to have been a lunisolar calendar,[7] there is complete silence on the matter.
- Specific reference to the Jews, Israel, or the Gentiles is absent. There are the righteous/holy ones and the wicked (or the rulers/officials and owners), but nothing identifies either group with any ethnic or religious grouping known from the Second Temple period. This could be because of its setting in the time before Abraham and Israel or even before Noah's flood, but the important division for the writer seems to be between his group and everyone else, not Jew and non-Jew.

## Considerations for a Social Setting of the Parables of Enoch

Just to remind ourselves: to ask questions about society is to ask about how society works, and about how the various bits in society work — institutions, communities, groups, and even individuals, for ultimately every society is made up of individuals. Sociologists and anthropologists observe societies and then attempt to describe them; finally, they sometimes even go on to try to extrapolate rules of how societies work that might be predictive of human actions. This is often very difficult, though biblical scholars not infrequently pick up such rules and then proceed to treat them as if they were factual data. In reality, they are only hypotheses, to be examined, tried, tested, modified, or rejected.

The reason biblical scholars so eagerly seek out such sociological rules is that we have to proceed in the opposite direction from real sociologists and anthropologists, for ours is a historical task. We cannot observe in action the society we are most interested in. If we are lucky, we might have a very partial description of an ancient society by an observer with some actual knowledge of

---

7. For the arguments for this position, see Grabbe, *Judaic Religion*, 143.

the society. More often, though, we have only some products of that society in the form of artifacts (archaeology) or writings (literature, inscriptions). The question is whether they will answer sociological questions.

The Book of Parables makes up one such writing. There seems to be general — if not universal — agreement that it is the product of Second Temple Jewish society. Beyond that, things become less and less certain. Some of the things it tells us are described above, but how to interpret them is not so clear. Our analysis has to be sociological, not theological. Yet the theological views of a group or institution are a form of sociological data; the difficulty is to view them from a sociological point of view and to consider their use for sociological reconstruction. Theological beliefs can be slippery because they can change, whereas the structure and general mission of the group remain the same. Here is where some of the observations of the sociologist of religion Bryan Wilson might be helpful. In trying to come up with a means of differentiating religious sects or groups, he first studied modern Christian groups in the United Kingdom, later shifting to movements in a global and non-Christian context.[8]

In his initial work he noted a number of characteristics found among the various sects: their procedures for organization, the ways in which they originated, and the elements of the conditions under which they emerged.[9] Such are the sorts of things nonsociologists tend to latch on to and try to apply to a quite different context. But while the lists might be helpful in giving a context to sectarian origin and development, they do not constitute a definition and, as Wilson made explicit, they vary from group to group. He eventually developed a typology of groups based on "response to the world."[10] This seems to provide the most useful analytical tool because it involves a variety of characteristics, including belief and ideology, lifestyle, organization, form of association, social orientation, and action.[11] It includes the important element of salvation that encompasses a number of possible approaches: achieving personal redemption

---

8. B. R. Wilson, *Patterns of Sectarianism: Organisation and Ideology in Social and Religious Movements* (London: Heinemann, 1967); Wilson, *Religious Sects: A Sociological Study*, World University Library (London: Weidenfeld and Nicolson, 1970); Wilson, *Magic and the Millennium: A Sociological Study of Religious Movements of Protest among Tribal and Third-World Peoples* (London: Heinemann, 1973); Wilson, *The Social Dimensions of Sectarianism: Sects and New Religious Movements in Contemporary Society* (Oxford: Clarendon, 1990).

9. Wilson, *Patterns of Sectarianism*, 1-45.

10. Wilson's main criterion for defining the various sorts of sects was originally that of their "mission" (*Patterns of Sectarianism*, 25-26), but this could be misunderstood since it might imply recruitment to membership. This is why his final refinement discussed the different sectarian types in terms of "response to the world," which included the element of salvation (*Magic and the Millennium*, 18-28).

11. Wilson, *Magic and the Millennium*, 18-30.

for the individual in this life or a life to come, changing the world for the better, saving a group or race or even all mankind from destruction, fulfilling some sort of divine destiny. However, they all involve overcoming evil. Again, "evil" is used in a broad sense to mean anything that is negative or bad, not just evil in a moral or religious sense. All sects know that something is wrong and set out to correct it: this is salvation from evil; this is their response to the world.

Although we should recognize the hazards of inferring sociological data from a written text such as this, the results suggest that the group (or possibly an individual who wrote the Parables) had the following sorts of interests and concerns:

- Importance of wisdom and use of wisdom language.
- Use of the myth of the Ancient of Days and one like a son of man, probably from the book of Daniel, though apparently no interest in calculating the end-time, unlike many sections of Daniel.
- A messianic figure (called variously "the Son of Man," "the Chosen One," "the Messiah") that is central, but evidently a heavenly figure who functions only in the eschaton to reward the righteous and punish the wicked; no clear function as champion of the earthly Jewish community or a military leader.
- Centrality of the angelic world, including both good and bad angels, but no special preoccupation with the myth of the fallen angels (unlike the Book of the Watchers).
- Eschatological judgment in which the wicked — angels and humans — were punished and the righteous rewarded, both immediately (apparently after death) and at an unspecified future date.
- Final dwelling place of the righteous not limited to heaven but includes a renewed earth.
- Importance of cosmology and knowledge of how the heavens and natural phenomena work.
- The Book of Parables written either before or a good time after the Parthian invasion of 40 B.C.E., since the Parthians and Medes seem to be a type rather than a reference to a specific historical event.
- Apparently the lunisolar calendar used, as normative in Judaism at this time.
- Where worship described, apparently only prayer and praise involved; no temple or altar mentioned.
- Knowledge of the Enoch tradition, probably as contained in other sections of 1 Enoch, but also of Dan 7:9-14 and of a book of Noah (or perhaps something larger, such as a "rewritten Genesis").

Absence of the following concerns might be significant, though one should be cautious since more than one explanation for the lack of such mention are often possible:

- No evident concern for the fate of the Jews as such or distinction in treatment or action between the Jews and Gentiles.
- Neither sins to be avoided (by oneself) or condemned (in others) nor good actions or beliefs to be embraced are specified.
- No evidence of drawing on Greek knowledge or even that the Greek language was known.

What sort of group do these views characterize? The danger of relying on a theological description has been commented on above. Yet the impression we have is that the Book of Parables is the product of a Jewish sect of some sort. Wilson has noted that membership in a sect usually implies total commitment.[12] Unlike large communities (churches, nationalities, ethnic groups, and the like), membership is not just nominal and casual. Sect activity usually dominates the member's life. The Book of Parables was written by a movement or group (or an individual who more or less represented such a group) that was Jewish but saw their identity primarily not as Jews but as members of a particular group (and was not therefore particularly concerned about temple worship but found prayer and praise sufficient) that believed that the eschaton was the important goal in which members would be saved under the leadership of a heavenly figure known variously as the Chosen One or the Son of Man, while members themselves remained quiescent, awaiting divine deliverance. The group did not apparently represent a radical group that rejected the priestly establishment, the standard religious observances, or much of common Judaism, though they may not have considered many of these things very important. The real concentration was on the eschaton and salvation by the Lord of Spirits via the Son of Man, though what members have to do or believe to obtain that salvation is not clear. They considered kings and officials negatively, but it is not clear whether these were confined to Gentile rulers or included Jewish officials. In addition to eschatology, the group considered knowledge of how the heavens worked quite important. For authoritative writings they knew at least some of the Enochic writings and a book of Noah (or perhaps a "rewritten Genesis"); they probably also knew Daniel but did not find it interesting apart from Dan 7:9-14; beyond that it is difficult to know for sure what "scriptures" they used.

---

12. Wilson, *Patterns of Sectarianism*, 24; Wilson, *Magic and the Millennium*, 32-33.

Let's look at some of the possible groups that might have produced this writing:

## Qumran Community

The Book of Parables has much in common with writings possessed by the Qumran community (though it is not certain that any of the Enochic writings are the products of Qumran). Yet the absence of the Parables from Qumran seems to be decisive.

## Essenes

As with Qumran (which is often identified as Essene in some way), the Book of Parables seems to be compatible with what we know of the Essenes, who are said to have been interested in esoteric books. On the other hand, there seems to be nothing specifically Essene in the Parables.

## Sadducees

We should not assume that we know much about the Sadducees nor that a definitive description of their beliefs is possible.[13] Yet much within the Parables seems to go contrary to the main list of Sadducean beliefs that have so far been reconstructed. The emphasis on angels, both good and bad, is a belief apparently not in Sadducean favor. An afterlife, with heavenly existence for the righteous, is a major feature of the Parables but seems not to have been the general Sadducean view.

## Pharisees

It is often assumed that we know a lot about the Pharisees. In fact, we do not.[14] It is not inconceivable that a writing such as the Parables could have been

---

13. For a critical examination of what we know about both the Pharisees and the Sadducees, see L. L. Grabbe, "Sadducees and Pharisees," in *Judaism in Late Antiquity: Part Three. Where We Stand: Issues and Debates in Ancient Judaism, Volume 1*, ed. J. Neusner and A. J. Avery-Peck, Handbuch der Orientalistik: Erste Abteilung, der Nahe und Mittlere Osten 40 (Leiden: Brill, 1999), 35-62.

14. See previous note.

known to and used by the Pharisees, but the Book of Parables does not seem to reflect some of the main Pharisaic interests, at least as inferred by recent study. These would be the appeal to tradition, the concern with purity and with eating food that is ritually pure and properly tithed, proper observance of the Sabbath, and the like.

### "Enochic Judaism"

Much depends on whether one is convinced that there was a separate movement that can be called Enochic Judaism. Leaving that aside for the moment, one might assume that it was obvious that the Book of Parables would be the product of an Enochic Judaism, or at least used by such a group or movement. But this brings us back to the common use of many different traditions in Judaism by this time. Just as wisdom language was widespread, much of the content of the Parables might have been acceptable to various streams within Judaism. Thus, it is not a foregone conclusion that the Book of Parables was the product of the hypothesized Enochic Judaism.

### "Messianic" Groups

This is a catchall term for a number of diverse groups that were connected by a common belief in some sort of messiah but were actually quite different in aims and organization. A group that believed a messiah would come and deliver the Jews might well have produced a book like the Parables, since it seems to assume that the righteous themselves had only to wait passively. The more militant groups, however, had an ethos that was contrary to the Parables.

### Scribes

Our problem is to find a unified group known as "the scribes." The function of a scribe was to write, but scribes varied in quality of education and status from a record keeper in a warehouse — with perhaps minimal skills — to a minister of state who might deal with anything from treaties to calendar promulgation, to a preserver and interpreter of authoritative religious writings and even a composer of new literature. The writer of the Parables certainly belonged to scribal circles, but scribes seem to have belonged to a wide variety of groups and views.

## Priests

All priests and Levites evidently had a right to serve in the temple, though not all seem to have taken advantage of it. But even those serving in the temple did not all share the same interests or even beliefs (outside some central priestly rules and requirements that would have been necessary for a proper functioning of the temple and cultic system). With leisure and an assured income, the priests would have had the opportunity for theological discussion and speculation. It is especially the cosmological interest that argues for priestly authorship. I see nothing in the Parables that would have prevented a temple priest from using or even composing the document. The apparent lack of interest in the temple and altar could be variously explained, though one would expect a writing by a priest to envisage a heavenly or eschatological temple. This suggests that a temple priest did not compose it. But if not, a priest might still have read it and embraced its general teachings.

## Christians

If the Book of Parables were written in the first century C.E. or later, one has to reckon with the possibility that it was a Christian composition. This is what Milik concluded,[15] but there is nothing specifically Christian about any of its content. The only possible datum is the "Son of Man." There are naturally some resemblances between this figure and the image of Jesus in the NT, but there is nothing uniquely Christian about the Son of Man in the Parables. This figure looks rather like a predecessor to or model for references to the Son of Man of the Gospels. The Book of Parables is unlikely to be a Christian writing.

Not all these groups are mutually exclusive, since some (such as the scribes or priests) might also be members of particular sects or groups. But apart from the hypothesized "Enochic Judaism" — for which I have considerable reservations — no known group seems to capture the characteristics listed above. What we seem to have is a messianic group with its own identity but that has not necessarily withdrawn from Jewish society nor is seeking to establish God's kingdom by military means. It includes intellectuals (whether priests or scribes), though no evidence that the Greek language was known.

---

15. Milik, *The Books of Enoch*, 91.

Lester L. Grabbe

## Summary of Conclusions

The following are some of the main points made in the article:

1. Sociological study of a historical topic is not easy. In a writing such as the Parables of Enoch, the normal sociological data one expects to collect are unavailable. One must work backward from the content of the writing to see what is of interest to those who composed the writing and also what does not receive attention. A certain amount of circular reasoning is inevitable, but this should be made explicit and carefully controlled. Finally, the plurality of possible social contexts has to be recognized and the probability in each case carefully weighed.

2. Much is not known about the context of the Parables: time of writing, place of writing, original language, which groups used it. These important sets of data remain to be determined rather than built upon.

3. Some of the more important themes of the Parables are the Son of Man as a heavenly figure who will rule among the righteous, an eschaton apparently without cosmic upheaval, and a significant interest in cosmology. The book also has certain unique titles or terms, such as "Lord of Spirits."

4. Themes important elsewhere in 1 Enoch that seem to receive less attention or are even de-emphasized here are the myth of the fallen angels and trying to reckon the end-time.

5. These characteristics seem to describe a messianic group with its own identity but that has not necessarily withdrawn from Jewish society. Members are pacifist, or at least aiming to let God be the active one in their salvation, and are certainly not seeking to establish God's kingdom by military means. The group includes intellectuals (whether priests or scribes) with a strong interest in cosmology, though no evidence of knowledge of Greek exists.

# Spatiality in the Second Parable of Enoch

*Pieter M. Venter*

## Hermeneutical Constructs

We need heuristic constructs to read and interpret texts. The reconstruction of the probable historical background of a text is a construct often used to relate the contents of that text to a specific time of history and its circumstances. The text is read and understood in terms of what we know of that particular time.

In his contribution to the present volume, David Suter[1] comes to the conclusion that "other approaches than the use of historical analysis" are demanded by the text of the Book of Parables (1 En 37–71). He proposes a "multiphased approach." His proposal includes aspects like the study of the social context of the Parables, investigation into the affinities between the Parables and other contemporary literature, and identifying and dating traditions behind the Parables.

The historical allusions in Parables provide only restricted possibilities for reconstructing the context of the work. I would therefore like to propose the study of the spatial aspect of the text as *one more possibility* of a multiphased approach. The spatial representations found in the text are much more exhaustive than the depictions of events. Visionary literature,[2] as found in the Para-

---

1. See below, D. W. Suter, "Enoch in Sheol: Updating the Dating of the Book of Parables."
2. Cf. how many times the visionary aspect is expressed with terms of observing: "to see" (first parable: 39:4, 7; 40:1-2 ["and there I saw"]; 41:1-5; 43:1-2; second parable: 46:1; 47:3; 48:1; 52:2 ["There my eyes saw"]; 53:3 ["For I saw"]; 54:1 ["And I looked and turned . . . and I saw"]; 56:1; third parable: 59:2, 3 ["all the secrets . . . were shown to me"]; 61:1; 64:1; 67:5). Cf. also the expression "my eyes saw" (first parable: 39:5, 6, 13; 41:2, [3]; second parable: 52:2; 53:1; 54:3; third para-

bles, is well-known for its portrayal of space to articulate the author's ideological point of view.[3]

## Reconstruction of Ancient Space

The discipline of *critical spatiality* is a branch of social scientific research that seeks "to reintroduce spatiality in an ontological trialectic that includes historicality, sociality, and spatiality."[4] This study of the ideological meaning of space in society was initially started by Henri Lefebvre and theoretically refined by the geographer Edward Soja.

Critical spatiality investigates the spatial aspect of the biblical text and relates the constructed space in the text to the sociohistoric context in which it originated. It understands space in the framework of the social experience and ancient conceptualization of the physical space in which people lived. Space is not only perceived as concrete geophysical reality, but also in terms of the way in which this space was conceived and the way in which it was related to the ideology of the author and of the society to which he belonged. In critical spatiality the first level of *physical* space is called "perceived space" or "Firstspace."[5] The term used for the second level of *interpreted* space is called "conceived space" or "Secondspace." The third level, where space is understood in terms of the author's *ideology*, is called "Thirdspace." As a tool for social-historical reconstruction,[6] spatial analysis can relate a text to the specific idea world of the author who wrote the specific text.

---

ble: 59:1). All quotations from G. W. E. Nickelsburg and J. C. VanderKam, *1 Enoch: A New Translation* (Minneapolis: Fortress, 2004).

3. Cf. also the threefold pattern of Enoch seeing, asking the angel what the significance is, and the explanation provided by the angel, repeated eight times in 40:1-10; 43:1-4; 46:1-8; 52:1-9; 53:1-7; 54:1-6; 56:1-4; 61:1-5. Cf. above, M. A. Knibb's essay "The Structure and Composition of the Parables of Enoch."

4. J. W. Flanagan, "Ancient Perceptions of Space/Perceptions of Ancient Space," *Semeia* 87 (1999): 15-43 (here 26).

5. Cf. V. H. Matthews, "Physical Space, Imagined Space, and 'Lived Space' in Ancient Israel," *BTB* 33, no. 1 (2003): 12-20 (here 12).

6. Cf. C. V. Camp, "Storied Space, or Ben Sira 'Tells' a Temple," http://www.cwru.edu/affil/GAIR/Constructions.html, 2002.

## Spatiality and Apocalyptic Literature

This discipline can also be applied to apocalyptic literature. Both Pippin and Lopez presented papers on apocalyptic literature at different meetings of the Construction of Ancient Space Seminar of the Society of Biblical Literature.

During the 2003 meeting Tina Pippin indicated that spaces depicted in apocalyptic narratives are never innocent. They are "highly politically charged narratives."[7] Following space theorists like Henri Lefebvre (with his trialectic of spatial practice, representations of space, and representational spaces), Foucault (with his idea of heterotopia), and Edward Soja (with his concept of Thirdspace), Pippin interpreted the use of time and especially space in the book of Revelation in terms of the ideologies that produced it. The heavenly realm depicted in the Apocalypse of John represents "the pinnacle of Christian values and a return to the 'original' paradise."[8] From a hodgepodge of architectural styles (city walls and gates, throne room of the court, streets, gardens) imagined on a fantastic scale,[9] using an ideology of utopia, an imagined space is created to bring readers peace and hope. For Pippin this means that the "political center of Jews and Christians is refurbished and reconstructed as heavenly space."[10]

In her paper during the 2004 meeting, Kathryn M. Lopez followed a program of "reading the space created by apocalyptic."[11] She aimed to "uncover the maps of space that the Jewish apocalypses are creating"[12] in Daniel and Enoch. Apocalyptic communities were political groups committed to the transformation of their society. They therefore created narrative spaces that were in direct conflict with the definitions of space found among the other groups with whom they were vying for power. By studying these ideologically created spaces in apocalyptic narratives, access can be gained to the ideas of the apocalyptic groups that formed these apocalypses.

Having explicit political aims, apocalyptic writings should therefore be understood as strategies of resistance. In terms of Soja's notion of Thirdspace, these groups formed a space of resistance in their writings to oppose the dominating definition of Secondspace forced upon them by Hellenized Jewish lead-

---

7. T. Pippin, "The Ideology of Apocalyptic Space" (draft paper prepared for the Construction of Ancient Space Seminar, SBL, 2003), 14.

8. Pippin, "Ideology of Apocalyptic Space," 6.

9. Cf. Pippin, "Ideology of Apocalyptic Space," 8.

10. Pippin, "Ideology of Apocalyptic Space," 8.

11. K. M. Lopez, "Standing before the Throne of God: Critical Spatiality in Apocalyptic Scenes of Judgment" (presentation at the AAR/SBL Annual Meeting in San Antonio, Construction of Ancient Space Seminar, 2004), 9.

12. Lopez, "Standing," 2.

ership and a variety of external powers that controlled the region. In the journeys, heavenly as well as on earth, described in their writings, they created a "real-and-imagined"[13] space to resist the definitions of Israel placed upon them as colony. The Thirdspace they created strives to present their world as the real world in which they are to live in opposition to the imagined space they opposed. Lopez therefore argues that "the Thirdspace strategies of apocalyptic writings are an attempt to make those 'longed-for expectations' the lived space of groups who hold them."[14]

In terms of Foucault's notions of "utopia" and "heterotopia," apocalyptic writings are "effectively enacted utopian visions of the world,"[15] heterotopian lived-out space, a supernatural world in which the faithful will live, and already live to some extent. This world stands in opposition to the "illusions" of the world in which the society lives.

## Spatiality in Daniel 7 and 1 Enoch 46:1–51:5

The "politics of naming geographical spaces"[16] is a key to identifying groups that compete for power under the apocalyptic umbrella. The spaces created in apocalyptic writings, and the way they are depicted in the literature, correlate to the space from which this literature was imagined. Reading these apocalyptic spaces informs the reader on the apocalyptic community that created them and their way of thinking. For this purpose Dan 7:9-14 and 1 En 46:1–51:5 can be compared. In both of these sections the concept "Son of Man" is found.

### Daniel 7

Dan 7 belongs to the genre of revelatory literature presented in a narrative framework.[17] In these narratives character, space, and time are integrated to form the plot of the story. Space is presented as Thirdspace in Dan 7:1-28, conceptualized in global terms. The setting of the scene of judgment is not heaven,

---

13. Cf. E. W. Soja, *Thirdspace: Journeys to Los Angeles and Other Real-and-Imagined Places* (Cambridge: Blackwell, 1996).
14. Lopez, "Standing," 7.
15. Lopez, "Standing," 8.
16. Lopez, "Standing," 11.
17. Adela Yarbro Collins indicates "apocalypse" as a genre of revelatory literature disclosing a transcendent reality that is both temporal and spatial involving another, supernatural world; see A. Yarbro Collins, *Cosmology and Eschatology in Jewish and Christian Apocalypticism* (Leiden: Brill, 1996), 7.

but actually the earth.[18] This space is intended to interpret earthly realities. The central issue in this narrative is one of yielding power. The power is transferred from figures symbolized by mythic animal images who use their power to devour and demolish, to one like a human being having everlasting dominion, and eventually[19] to the holy ones of the Most High. This is facilitated by an ancient of days, served by innumerable multitudes of people, who acts as supreme judge in this narrative.

In this ideologically created space the idea that God's holy ones are to be dominated by overwhelming world powers is resisted and replaced by a heterotopian lived-out space in which the faithful can already live and be protected from the dangers they experience from these world powers in their everyday life. In this "real-and-imagined"[20] space of Dan 7, God's sovereign judgment is experienced in terms of God coming to earth and transferring dominion to one like a man and eventually to his holy people on earth.[21] God's fiery throne with its mobile wheels depicts God's judgmental activities as executable in this world. Although the one like a man has heavenly attachments (coming with the clouds of heaven), his dominion is on earth over all peoples, nations, and languages. In their reflections the group of Dan 7 expected a humanlike leader who would advance their interests by annihilating the negative effect foreign kings had on their lives.[22]

*1 Enoch 46:1–51:5*

The ideological space in Daniel can be compared to the space created in the second parable. Using "traditional Enochic material from the Book of the

---

18. Cf. Lopez, "Standing," 12. John Collins interprets the scene as belonging to the tradition of biblical throne visions. He states that the "location is unclear"; see J. J. Collins, *Daniel*, Hermeneia (Minneapolis: Fortress, 1993), 300. Although obvious parallels can be indicated with Enoch's ascent to heaven in 1 En 14, the scene here is not explicitly the heaven. W. S. Towner indicates that no final conclusion can be drawn as to whether the ascent or descent of the Son of Man is intended; see W. S. Towner, *Daniel* (Louisville: John Knox, 1984), 104.

19. Cf. the explanation of the vision in Dan 7:15-28.

20. Cf. Soja, *Thirdspace*.

21. J. J. Collin's view (*Daniel*, 310, 313-17), that "one like a human being" is to be identified with the angel Michael and that the "holy ones" are heavenly beings, focuses the interests of the visionary/ies on the mystical, i.e., the heavenly throne and the angelic world. Cf. also S. R. Miller, *Daniel* (Nashville: Broadman and Holman, 1994), 207-10, where three possible views on the meaning of "son of man" are discussed.

22. Especially the decree of Antiochus Epiphanes, who suppressed the cult and imposed pagan worship (cf. Dan 7:25).

Watchers and a source like the Astronomical Book, following to some extent the order of the Book of the Watchers" and reworking "non-Enochic (traditional interpretations of) biblical material about the Daniel son of man, the Davidic Anointed One (Ps 2 and Isa 11), and the Servant/Chosen One/Righteous One of Second Isaiah and perhaps material about preexistent Wisdom,"[23] the author(s) of the second parable constructed an ideological space onto which his/their ideological position is projected. In all three parables space is depicted in cosmic terms. The scenarios of the first two parables are mainly presented in terms of heaven as the dwelling place of God, his angels, and the holy ones. Especially in the second parable, space is envisaged in terms of beings living in each other's presence. Not much information is given on the appearance of the surroundings. Focus rather falls on the appearance and acts of these heavenly beings. Characterization is therefore used above all to present the narrator's ideological space.

While the space in Dan 7 is depicted in earthly terms, the space in 1 En 46:1–51:5 is conceptualized in terms of heaven.[24] Compared to the Daniel vision, the Enoch rendering gives much clearer hints to the world from which it was constructed. The heterotopian zone presented here provides escape from a world that is primarily experienced as one of oppression (cf. 46:8; 48:7; 49:2; 50:4).

This can especially be seen in what the "Son of Man" causes to happen in this scene.[25] God chose him and destined him to be victorious in uprightness (46:3).[26] This task concerns two areas.[27] Firstly he deposes kings from their

---

23. Quoted from G. W. E. Nickelsburg's contribution to this volume, "Discerning the Structure(s) of the Enochic Book of Parables."

24. In his essay, "The Structure and Composition of the Parables of Enoch," Michael Knibb reads this section as part of the second parable (chaps. 45–57). It consists of a series of vision reports and descriptive statements concerning the Son of Man and the events connected with the judgment. According to Knibb, chap. 46 is "a report of a vision of the Head of Days and the Son of Man that is manifestly based on the Son of Man vision of Dan 7 (see vv. 9-10, 13-14); it is presented in the threefold pattern of description [of what Enoch saw], question, and explanation, but it is the explanation from the angel (vv. 3-8), which describes the role of the Son of Man as eschatological judge, on which the emphasis falls."

25. Cf. Leslie W. Walck's first table on the characteristics of the Son of Man in his essay, "The Son of Man in the Parables of Enoch and the Gospels." This characterization should be studied in conjunction with the way space and time are used in these narratives.

26. In Dan 7 it is the Ancient of Days who strips kings of their power, while in 1 En 47:3 it is done by the Son of Man.

27. In his essay, "The Son of Man: The Evolution of an Expression," Sabino Chialà refers to the Son of Man's prerogatives having a "messianic" nature, which is totally absent from the book of Daniel. In his essay, Walck describes the Son of Man in the second and third visions and the epilogue of the Book of the Parables as one carrying "messianic overtones."

thrones and kingdoms.²⁸ The most obvious characteristic of these strong ones is their denial of God and disobedience to him. Although they congregate with the faithful ones in God's house, they are in fact devoted to gods of their own fashion. They are arrogant and judge the heavens. Their wealth brings them power. Oppression is their motto. These characteristics reflect the real enemies whom the faithful met in their lives. These created a space in their time filled with oppression and falseness. It is from this world of oppression that the faithful long to be freed.

The second aspect of the righteousness of the Son of Man is his support for the righteous ones. He will be the staff on which they can lean (48:4). He will be the light of the Gentiles and the hope for those who are sick in their hearts (48:4). The wisdom of the Lord of Spirits reveals him to the holy and righteous ones as the one preserving their portions (48:7). This wisdom comprises a positive as well as a negative aspect. Positively it has in store the vindication of those who resisted this world with its oppression and its ways of life (48:7). Negatively it brings the humiliation of those who oppressed them. These people who oppressed them are described as "the strong who possess the earth,"²⁹ the "mighty landowners"³⁰ (48:8) who will be humbled in countenance³¹ before the holy ones on account of what they did to them. Their power and evil deeds will be brought to a final end. The salvation of the righteous ones is therefore depicted in terms of the vindication of their oppressing opponents. Again, conceived/perceived Secondspace with its intrigue is projected onto Thirdspace where the problems experienced in the life of the group are solved and where they can experience deliverance from them.

In this "real-and-imagined"³² space created in this section, two figures play the central role. One is characterized in terms of time. To him belongs the time before time. He precedes time. He is of primordial days.³³ In parallel terms he is described as old: his head was white like wool. He is also called the "Head of Days,"³⁴ the "Before-Time"³⁵ (46:2; 48:2), and the "Antecedent of Time"³⁶

---

28. In his essay, Walck remarks that several themes in this passage have similarities with the taunt against the king of Babylon in Isa 14.
29. Nickelsburg and VanderKam, *1 Enoch*, 62.
30. J. H. Charlesworth, ed., *The Old Testament Pseudepigrapha*, vol. 1 (Garden City, N.Y.: Doubleday, 1983), 36.
31. Cf. Charlesworth, *The Old Testament Pseudepigrapha*, 36 n. 1.
32. Cf. Soja, *Thirdspace*.
33. Cf. Charlesworth, *The Old Testament Pseudepigrapha*, 34 (footnotes on 1 En 46:1).
34. Cf. Nickelsburg and VanderKam, *1 Enoch*.
35. Cf. Charlesworth, *The Old Testament Pseudepigrapha*, vol. 1.
36. Cf. Charlesworth, *The Old Testament Pseudepigrapha*, vol. 1.

(47:3). Mostly he is named the "Lord of the Spirits"[37] (46:3, 4, 7, 8, etc.). He sits upon the throne of his glory (47:3) and executes judgment in favor of the righteous ones.

The other figure is the Antecedent's "prototype"[38] (46:2). He is described as one "whose face was like a human being"[39] (46:1). He was born of human beings and was called "the Son of Man" (46:3, 4; 48:2).[40] In the same vein as the wisdom in Prov 8, he was given a name in the presence of the Lord of Spirits before the creation of the heavenly bodies. The Lord of the Spirits concealed[41] him in his presence prior to the creation of the world (48:6). He became the Chosen One (48:6), the Elect One/[42] Chosen One[43] (49:2, 4; 51:3), the Messiah of the Lord of the Spirits[44]/his Anointed One[45] (48:10).[46]

What is important in this case is that although two individuals are indicated, a high degree of identity exists between them. The Son of Man was chosen by the Lord to execute the Lord's wisdom and his righteousness (46:4; 48:7). He is the object of the Lord's choice and the instrument through which his wisdom and righteousness are put into practice. Righteousness, however, does not belong to the Lord only, but also to the Son of Man. It dwells with him (46:3). He is mighty in all the secrets of righteousness (49:2), and the spirit of wisdom

---

37. In his essay, "The Son of Man in the Parables of Enoch," Helge Kvanvig relates the epithet of the divinity to the name YHWH Seba'ot in the vision in Isa 6.

38. Cf. Charlesworth, *The Old Testament Pseudepigrapha*.

39. Cf. Charlesworth, *The Old Testament Pseudepigrapha*. Nickelsburg and VanderKam (*1 Enoch*, 59) translate: "whose face was like the appearance of man." See their note c on the same page: "Term *son of man* refers to the human appearance of a divine figure and does not designate humanness."

40. In his essay in this volume, Sabino Chialà describes the "scene" in 1 En 46:1-4 as based on the same structure as Dan 7 consisting of "two tableaux." When the character presented in the second tableau is presented, the metaphorical attribute used in Daniel to describe someone in the image of a man is developed into one of a character with a proper name. Chialà opts here for a development of the angelic being in Dan 10, rather than development of the metaphorical character in Dan 7. He is a higher being with the resemblance of a man. In his essay "Enoch and the Son of Man: A Response to Sabino Chialà and Helge Kvanvig," John Collins explicitly rejects Chialà's idea of "one like a son of man" as a corporate symbol. He reads the Parables as directly continuous with Dan 7 and identifies Dan 7's "one like a son of man" with the archangel Michael.

41. Cf. Charlesworth, *The Old Testament Pseudepigrapha*, 1:35n.

42. Cf. Charlesworth, *The Old Testament Pseudepigrapha*.

43. Cf. Nickelsburg and VanderKam, *1 Enoch*.

44. Cf. Charlesworth, *The Old Testament Pseudepigrapha*.

45. Nickelsburg and VanderKam, *1 Enoch*, 63.

46. In his essay, Kvanvig proposes that these various titles refer to the same eschatological figure who is seen as a representative of Israel.

dwells in him as well (cf. 49:3). He acts where the fountain of righteousness is surrounded by fountains of wisdom, and all who drink from this water are filled with wisdom. Not only is the Son of Man the Prototype[47] of the Lord, but his attributes are the same as those of the Lord. He shares not only wisdom and righteousness with him, but also the idea of existence before the creation of the heavenly bodies. He also could have had white hair like the Lord has.

The Son of Man is, however, not identical with the Lord. He receives his name in the Lord's presence. He acts on behalf of God against the kings and powerful ones who deny the name of the Lord of Spirits (46:7), and who also do not exalt and praise the Son of Man, or obey him as the source of their kingship (46:5). Their transgression is evaluated in terms of misbehavior both against the Lord and against the Son. To decline to praise the name of the Lord is exactly the same as deprecating the name of the Son. The Son of Man also shares with the Lord the homage paid by innumerable people. All who dwell upon the earth shall fall and worship before him and simultaneously glorify the name of the Lord of Spirits (48:5). The Lord sits upon his throne and vindicates the blood of the righteous that had been shed. The Son executes this judgment by revealing the wisdom of the Lord to the holy ones (48:7) and pushes the oppressive kings from their thrones.[48]

The physical world the author(s) of the Book of Parables lived in was experienced as a world of oppression in which not only kings but also social groups living among them acted as agents of unrighteousness.[49] This interpretation of their physical world (Firstspace) defined in their minds the Secondspace from which they wanted to escape. They therefore imagined a Thirdspace that was believed to be a reality, but was not yet part of their daily existence.[50] The way this

---

47. Cf. Charlesworth, *The Old Testament Pseudepigrapha*, 34.

48. The words of the angel to Enoch in 71:14 ("You are that son of man, who was born for righteousness, and righteousness dwells on you, and the righteousness of the Head of Days will not forsake you") gave rise to the idea that what "Enoch sees is the Son of Man as the supernatural double of himself." Enoch sees what he will become; see Kvanvig's essay in this volume. Kvanvig's thesis is that a new Enoch myth was created in the Book of Parables. Three kinds of traditions are interwoven here: the preexistence of wisdom, the portrait of Enoch in the Book of the Watchers, and the expectations of the coming chosen Son of Man. They are combined to form a new myth in which Enoch's earthly life on the one hand is a manifestation of the preexistent wisdom, and his heavenly ascent on the other hand is an indication that he is the Son of Man for whom the chosen ones have longed through the ages.

49. In his essay, Walck proposes that Herod the Great, the Romans, and their generals fit the characterization of the kings and mighty ones in the Book of Parables.

50. Walck quotes a very important remark made by Morna Hooker in 1967 that "apocalyptic (literature) by its very nature held together what was at once present and future, that which was already in existence, but yet still had to take place."

Thirdspace is depicted presents the key to their basic ideology. This ideological space is depicted mainly by the characterization of two heavenly figures. The main agent who will eventually change their world is a humanlike being who is sharing many characteristics with the "Lord of Spirits" but is not fully identical with him. In the later addition of 71:14, Enoch living in heaven is identified with this Son of Man.

## Conclusion

From this brief spatial analysis it can be concluded that two totally different apocalyptic groups are found here.

The Daniel group is concerned with world powers, while the group of the Parables is concerned with local groups. The Daniel group works with terrestrial space in which universal powers are in conflict with each other. Geographical references in Daniel to places like Susa (Dan 8:2), Jerusalem (9:16), the bank of the Tigris (10:4), Persia (11:2), and glorious land (11:41) indicate a terrestrial type of conceptualization. Everything is restricted to the earthly scene. Power politics on a universal scale is their first concern. Even God and the Son of Man coming on/from the clouds execute their rule on earth. Even if this Son of Man is an angel, he still looks like a man and acts in human terms vindicating the interest of the faithful against beastly imperial powers.

The "world" in Parables, on the other hand, is much more concerned with local groups and powers than with universal kingdoms. These are explicitly characterized as oppressors, unrighteous landowners, wealthy individuals, and people pretending to be believers but denying God. The liberator of this group is more celestial than terrestrial. In Parables the Son of Man shares much more in the identity of the Lord of Spirits than does Daniel's Son of Man with the Ancient One. Although not identical, the two main figures in 1 En 46:1–51:5 are much closer to each other than those in Dan 7. The "real-and-imagined" space of Parables is much more heaven orientated than the politically orientated Thirdspace in Daniel. It is in a supernatural world with heavenly liberators where this group finds their final answer to the oppressive world in which they live. Whether the view in Enoch represents a development in apocalyptic thinking since Daniel, or represents merely an alternative way of thinking, is difficult to tell.

PART SIX

# THE DATING

# Enoch in Sheol:
# Updating the Dating of the Book of Parables

*David W. Suter*

Nearly thirty years ago Josef Milik delivered what Matthew Black called a "rude shock"[1] to the world of Jewish messianism and New Testament Christology in connection with his publication of the Aramaic fragments of the book of Enoch from Qumran. The shock was his argument that the Book of Parables (1 En 37–71), absent from Qumran, was a Christian work, composed in Greek around 270 C.E. in dependence upon the New Testament and the Sibylline Oracles.[2] It was, he claimed, substituted for the Book of the Giants, newly identified by Milik among the Enochic literature at Qumran, as part of an Enochic pentateuch. Since the Book of Parables was pivotal to the discussion of the Son of Man sayings in the teaching of Jesus and the Christology of the New Testament, his conclusions captured widespread attention, but as both John Collins and Black have observed,[3] virtually no one was convinced. The effect, however, is that there is a tendency to date the Parables later than was the custom earlier in

---

1. M. Black, "The Parables of Enoch (1 Enoch 37–71) and the Son of Man," *ExpTim* 88 (1976/77): 5-8 (esp. 5).

2. J. T. Milik, *The Books of Enoch: Aramaic Fragments of Qumrân Cave 4* (Oxford: Clarendon, 1976), 89-98. See also Milik, "Problèmes de la littérature hénochique à la lumière des fragments araméens de Qumrân," *HTR* 64 (1971): 333-78.

3. M. Black, "The Messianism of the Parables of Enoch: Their Date and Contribution to Christological Origins," in *The Messiah: Developments in Earliest Judaism and Christianity,* ed. J. H. Charlesworth (Minneapolis: Fortress, 1992), 145-68 (esp. 161); J. J. Collins, "The Heavenly Representative: The 'Son of Man' in the Similitudes of Enoch," in *Ideal Figures in Ancient Judaism: Profiles and Paradigms,* ed. J. J. Collins and G. W. E. Nickelsburg, SCS 12 (Chico, Calif.: Scholars, 1980), 111-33 (esp. 111).

the twentieth century, with dates ranging between 50 B.C.E. to 117 C.E., and its role in the discussion of the teachings of Jesus and the Christology of the New Testament has undergone some perhaps not-so-subtle changes.

In a review article on the Parables in the wake of Milik's publication, I noted that the work had been omitted from the historical survey of messianism in the Vermes and Millar update of Schürer on account of its uncertain date.[4] Collins added to that its omission from E. P. Sanders's *Paul and Palestinian Judaism*.[5] My suggestion was that in the process, like "bright one, son of Dawn" in Isa 14, the work had been consigned to some scholarly Sheol. Now that the dust has settled, perhaps it is time to take a look to see where the matter stands. Can we speak of the Parables redivivus?

## Issues in the Dating of the Parables

Since the purpose of this essay is more to provide resources for a discussion among scholars than to put forth a particular solution to the problem, perhaps the best approach is to organize the presentation around a list of issues involved in the discussion of dating, rather than a scholar-by-scholar survey of the literature.[6] Given the almost universal rejection of Milik's arguments — probably the closest thing to a consensus that will emerge from this discussion — I will allow the individual contributions on that topic to speak for themselves and not seek to summarize them here.[7] In general, the conclusion is that the allusions in chap. 56 do not fit the circumstances of 270 C.E.; the original language appears to be Semitic rather than Greek on both stylistic and linguistic grounds; and the manuscript history of 1 Enoch seems too fluid to sustain Milik's Enochic pentateuch argument. Once the critiques of Milik's arguments are set aside, the issues behind the discussion of a date for the Parables as I see them are as follows:

4. D. W. Suter, "Weighed in the Balance: The Similitudes of Enoch in Recent Discussion," *RelSRev* 7 (1981): 217-21 (esp. 217). See E. Schürer, *The History of the Jewish People in the Age of Jesus Christ (175 B.C.–A.D. 135): A New English Version*, ed. G. Vermes, F. Millar, and M. Black, vol. 2 (Edinburgh: T. & T. Clark, 1979), 505, 520-21.

5. Collins, "The Heavenly Representative," 127 n. 6. See E. P. Sanders, *Paul and Palestinian Judaism: A Comparison of Patterns of Religion* (Philadelphia: Fortress, 1977), 346-48.

6. For a summary of approaches to dating the Parables prior to 1984, see S. Uhlig, *Das äthiopische Henochbuch*, in *JSHRZ* 6, ed. Werner G. Kümmel (Gütersloh: Gütersloher Verlagshaus Gerd Mohn, 1984), 574-75. Uhlig divides approaches to dating into those that treat the work as pre-Christian and those that argue that it arose in Christian times.

7. Perhaps one of the most thorough approaches is that of J. C. Greenfield and M. E. Stone, "The Enochic Pentateuch and the Date of the Similitudes," *HTR* 70 (1977): 51-65. See also G. W. E. Nickelsburg, review of *The Books of Enoch*, by J. T. Milik, *CBQ* 40 (1978): 411-19.

1. The absence of the Parables from Qumran.
2. Is 1 En 56:5-8 a historical reference or an apocalyptic myth?
3. Does 1 En 56:7 require a date before the destruction of Jerusalem?
4. Are the hot springs in 1 En 67:4-13 a reference to Herod the Great at Callirrhoe?
5. The identity of the kings and mighty.
6. The implications of social context for the question of date.
7. The affinity of the Parables to other literature.
8. The influence of the Parables upon the New Testament.
9. Identifying and dating traditions behind the Parables.

In what follows we will explore these issues one by one in order to update the dating of the Parables.

## The Absence of the Parables from Qumran

In general, the absence of the section from the Dead Sea Scrolls is likely to be treated as decisive if the scholar has additional grounds for supporting a late date, although it is not always clear which motivation came first. Michael Knibb argues that the absence of the Parables points toward a date after the destruction of the Qumran site, an argument he then supports by appealing to similarities between the messianism of the Parables and that of other Jewish literature of the post-70 period, notably 2 Baruch and 4 Ezra.[8] In a later article Knibb maintains his late dating for the Parables but concedes that an earlier dating is possible given the potential dependence of Matt 19:28 and 25:31 upon the Parables and the apparent lack of reference in it to the fall of Jerusalem, in contrast to 4 Ezra.[9] Related issues frequently cited in the discussion are the additional absence of the Parables from manuscripts of the Greek version and the lack of citations of it in patristic literature.[10]

---

8. M. A. Knibb, "The Date of the Parables of Enoch: A Critical Review," *NTS* 25 (1979): 345-59 (esp. 358-59).

9. M. A. Knibb, "Messianism in the Pseudepigrapha in Light of the Scrolls," *DSD* 2 (1995): 165-84 (esp. 171). Knibb continued to support a late date for the Parables in discussions at the Third Enoch Seminar at Camaldoli.

10. See Greenfield and Stone, "The Enochic Pentateuch," 60. One possible exception to the absence from patristic literature is to be found in Origen, *Contra Celsum* 5.52, where thermal springs are explained as the consequence of the tears of angels imprisoned in the earth, an explanation that may derive from 1 En 67:4-13. In his contribution to the present volume ("An Overlooked Patristic Allusion to the Parables of Enoch?"), Daniel Olson argues for an allusion to the Parables in Irenaeus, *Adversus haereses*.

Barnabas Lindars likewise appeals to the absence of the Parables from Qumran. In "Re-enter the Apocalyptic Son of Man" he assumes a date somewhere around the beginning of the first century C.E., commenting that the date of the section of 1 Enoch is unresolved and its relevance to New Testament Christology is therefore doubtful. Later, in "Enoch and Christology" and *Jesus Son of Man*, he changes his dating to the end of the first century, contemporary to 4 Ezra and the development of the New Testament. He observes that the point of the Parables is the *naming* of the Elect One/Son of Man, which takes place in chap. 71 with the announcement to Enoch that he is the Son of Man,[11] following the celebration over the naming in chap. 69. He then argues that there is no literary dependence between Jewish works like the Parables and the use of Dan 7 to develop the sayings in Christianity — and no Son of Man concept per se — but a common milieu (reflected also in 11QMelchizedek) that includes the possibility of a celestial messiah that can be identified with a human figure.[12]

Greenfield and Stone, however, argue that the absence of the Parables from the Scrolls cannot be used to date the work.[13] Were we to admit the argument from absence, for example, Esther would need to be treated as late. In addition, there may be features in the Parables, like the equal role given the sun

---

11. The status of the conclusion to the Parables — chaps. 70–71 — could potentially be listed as an additional issue that is at least tangential to the issue of dating. Some scholars have argued that either chap. 71 or chaps. 70–71 are later additions to the Parables, perhaps to counter Christian claims about Jesus as the Son of Man. Others have argued that the identification is consistent both with the presentation of the Elect One/Son of Man in the parables as a whole and with Enoch's own unique career as a seer and revealer. Of the latter, Maurice Casey has addressed the issue of the inconsistency between 1 En 70:1, which appears to distinguish between Enoch and "that son of man," and 71:14, which identifies Enoch as "the son of man who is born unto righteousness," by appealing to a reading in an early Ethiopic manuscript, manuscript U, that has the name of that son of man (presumably Enoch) exalted to the Lord of Spirits. See M. Casey, "The Use of the Term 'Son of Man' in the Similitudes of Enoch," *JSJ* 7 (1976): 11-29 (esp. 25). While Casey has been criticized for relying upon insufficient evidence for the reading, recently Daniel Olson, in preparing a new translation of 1 Enoch, has identified five unpublished early EMML manuscripts from the Hill Monastic Manuscript Library (at Collegeville, Minn.) that support the reading of U. See D. C. Olson, "Enoch and the Son of Man in the Epilogue of the Parables," *JSP* 18 (1998): 27-38; Olson, *Enoch: A New Translation* (North Richland Hills, Tex.: BIBAL, 2004), 22, 132-33.

12. B. Lindars, "Re-enter the Apocalyptic Son of Man," *NTS* 22 (1975): 52-72 (esp. 58-60); Lindars, "Enoch and Christology," *ExpTim* 92 (1981): 295-99 (esp. 297-99); Lindars, *Jesus Son of Man: A Fresh Examination of the Son of Man Sayings in the Gospels in the Light of Recent Research* (London: SPCK, 1983), 14.

13. Greenfield and Stone, "The Enochic Pentateuch," 51-65. See also Uhlig, *Das äthiopische Henochbuch*, 575. Cf. J. Coppens, *Le Fils d'homme vétéro- et intertestamentaire* (Leuven: Peeters, 1983), 152.

and moon in 41:5-8, that would be inconsistent with the perspective of the community that produced or collected the Scrolls and would consequently explain its absence from the Scrolls. In maintaining a date around 50 B.C.E., Bampfylde likewise rejects as a nonargument the absence of the Parables from Qumran.[14] Chrys Caragounis objects that the absence of the Parables from Qumran is a dubious reason to overturn the results of established scholarship, which has long concluded that the New Testament is dependent upon the Parables. He suggests that scholars have seized upon the absence as a part of a movement toward "anthropology" and away from Christology.[15]

Paolo Sacchi gives the argument a different twist: "This question [why the Book of Parables is not present in the Qumran library] is poorly formulated, because it does not fit with history. In fact, the problem is as to why all Apocrypha [and Pseudepigrapha] written after 100 BCE are lacking in the Qumran library."[16] He and Gabriele Boccaccini explain the absence of the Parables from Qumran not as an accident of history[17] but as the consequence of the parting of the ways between Enochic Judaism and Qumranic Essenism, with the Parables reflecting continuity with the later stratum of the Epistle of Enoch (1 En 92–105), the point to which they trace the parting of the ways between the two movements over the issue of predestination versus freedom of choice as well as other ideological conflicts.[18]

The issue of the absence of the Parables from Qumran seems to be the main part of Milik's position on the Parables that has survived as a part of the discussion, at least requiring scholars to address it in arguing for a dating during the life of the Qumran community. Its presence in the discussion undoubtedly leads to the current tendency to date the Parables during the first century C.E. or early second century and to treat the writing as largely irrelevant for the

---

14. G. Bampfylde, "The Similitudes of Enoch: Historical Allusions," *JSJ* 15 (1984): 9-31 (esp. 10).

15. C. C. Caragounis, *The Son of Man: Vision and Interpretation*, WUNT 38 (Tübingen: Mohr Siebeck, 1986), 84-94.

16. P. Sacchi, "Qumran e la datazione del Libro delle Parabole di Enoc," *Hen* 25 (2003): 149-66 (esp. 166); in English, "Qumran and the Dating of the Book of Parables," in *The Bible and the Dead Sea Scrolls*, ed. J. H. Charlesworth (Waco: Baylor University Press, 2006).

17. Here compare James Charlesworth, who reflects upon the probabilities that the manuscripts found at Qumran reflect the entire collection of the owners. See J. H. Charlesworth, "The Date of the Parables of Enoch (1 En 37–71)," *Hen* 20 (1998): 93-98 (esp. 94).

18. Sacchi, "Qumran e la datazione," 160-62, and G. Boccaccini, *Beyond the Essene Hypothesis: The Parting of the Ways between Qumran and Enochic Judaism* (Grand Rapids: Eerdmans, 1998), 144-49. On the ideological incompatibility between the Parables and the sectarian literature of Qumran, see also, below, J. H. Charlesworth, "Can We Discern the Composition Date of the Parables of Enoch?"

discussion of Son of Man in the New Testament (see below), even where scholars recognize that such a conclusion involves an argument from silence. One theory to emerge since the initial debates over Milik's dating of the Parables in the late 1970s to explain more fully the absence of the Parables from Qumran not as chance but as the product of ideological and sectarian development is that of Sacchi and Boccaccini. Their argument is anticipated by Greenfield and Stone in suggesting the possibility of ideological differences related to the roles of the sun and moon in the Parables, but Sacchi and Boccaccini expand the discussion by seeking to write a history of sectarian development in the Hellenistic and Roman eras through the construction of chains of documents based upon ideological considerations.

## 1 Enoch 56:5-8, Historical Reference or Apocalyptic Myth?

There is a striking contrast between scholars who wish to argue in some detail that the vague allusion to the Parthians and Medes in 1 En 56:5-8 fits into a specific historical circumstance and those who discount it, either as apocalyptic myth or as potentially an interpolation in the Parables. Some, who take the historical reference seriously, use it directly as an indication of date, while others find a vague reference to the Parthian invasion of Syria and Palestine of 40-39 B.C.E. and treat it as evidence for dating sometime during the first century C.E.

Of scholars who take the passage seriously as a reference to history, Hindley and Bampfylde provide an interesting juxtaposition. Both search the passage for details that might be related to a particular situation in history, and then seek a correspondence through a fairly detailed scrutiny of a broadly defined historical period. Hindley rejects the Parthian invasion of 40-39 B.C.E. as the setting for the allusions in 56:5-8, primarily because there are Jews who welcome the appearance of the Parthians at that time. He looks instead at the post-70 period and suggests that the allusions best fit Trajan's Parthian adventure of 113-117 C.E. Among other arguments, he cites the Nero redivivus legend and what he perceives as a Parthian appropriation of it as a pointer to the post-70 period as a time at which the Parthians would have raised concerns in the eastern part of the Roman Empire. In the process of advocating a post-70 dating, he is obliged to deal with the implication of 56:7 that Jerusalem is still standing. It remains in some sense a Jewish city, he claims, with the possibility of the continuation of sacrifice at the temple site, and the potential to be central to the purposes of the God of Israel.[19]

19. J. C. Hindley, "Toward a Date for the Similitudes of Enoch: An Historical Approach," NTS 14 (1968): 551-65 (esp. 553, 556-65).

Bampfylde rejects Hindley's late dating of the Parables. For him the phrase "the kings and the mighty" points toward the Parthian empire with its system of satraps, rather than the Roman Empire, and the Parthians are not a factor in the land of Israel after their invasion of 40-39 B.C.E. On the other hand, the reference to the "Parthians and the *Medes*" requires a date after the Medes are taken into the Parthian empire, which takes place after 164 B.C.E., as Mithridates I extends his rule. He dates the Parables to 51-50 B.C.E. at the time of Parthia's first invasion of Roman territory in Syria as the Roman Republic was about to be drawn into civil war. He rejects the invasion of 40-39 B.C.E. as the occasion for 56:5-8 only because at that time the Parthians were welcomed by the Jews. He finds other links to the period by relating the passages from the Parables that speak of the melting of metal mountains and the uselessness of metal weapons in 1 En 52 to the inferiority of Roman armor against the weapons of the Parthians, and by noting that the Parthian cavalry, while effective in the open, was unable to take walled cities.[20] His treatment of the melting of the metal mountains highlights a problem with the historical approach for both Hindley and Bampfylde, since Bampfylde's example of the inferiority of Roman armor against Parthian weapons does not come close to matching the eschatological significance of the passage. In addition, it is a problem for the choices of both Bampfylde and Hindley that in 51-50 B.C.E. and in 113-117 C.E. respectively the Parthians do not seem to present a direct threat to Jerusalem.

Sacchi represents a third alternative for the effort to find specific historical allusions behind 1 En 56:5-8. He establishes a terminus ad quem of 70 C.E., concluding that the fall of Jerusalem should have had a greater impact on the Parables were the work to come from the period after the event, and a terminus a quo of 40 B.C.E., arguing that the references to internecine warfare in the passage fit well with the civil war that erupts within Judaism in the wake of the Parthian invasion. He seeks to establish widespread influence of the Parables within the New Testament, including the letters of Paul, and argues that the Parables of Enoch is the intermediate step between Dan 7 and Mark in the development of "Son of Man" as a known messianic title. He suggests a date of 30 B.C.E. for the Parables, based upon what he understands as the immediacy of the memory of the consequences of the Parthian invasion of 40 B.C.E.[21] While Boccaccini's approach to the material is similar to Sacchi's, note that he accepts

---

20. Bampfylde, "The Similitudes of Enoch," 15-16, 22-28.
21. Sacchi, "Qumran e la datazione," 157-64. In support of Sacchi's view, see also, below, L. Arcari, "A Symbolic Transfiguration of a Historical Event: The Parthian Invasion in Josephus and the Parables of Enoch."

a date for the Parables around the turn of the era, based upon what he perceives as a growing consensus of scholars.[22]

Other scholars avoid seeking precise historical details in the allusions of 56:5-8. While on other grounds he agrees with dating the Parables in the early second century C.E., Knibb finds the historical arguments of Hindley unconvincing.[23] Greenfield and Stone believe that the passage alludes to the events of 40 B.C.E., but take that as evidence for composition sometime during the first century C.E., indicating that it is useless to seek objective history in what amounts to interpretation.[24] Adela Yarbro Collins cites the allusions to the Parthian invasion of 40 B.C.E. and Herod at Callirrhoe as reason to date the work in the first half of the first century C.E.[25] In *Tradition and Composition in the Parables of Enoch*, I followed Lars Hartman in arguing that the allusions of 56:5-8, with sons slaying fathers and angels hurling themselves upon the Parthians and Medes, were the motifs of apocalyptic myth rather than the substance of history.[26] In general it seems that efforts to identify precise historical allusions and absolute dates in 56:5-8 have not carried the day, while for the most part commentators assume that we are dealing with updated apocalyptic myth or a vague memory of the invasion of the Parthians in 40-39 B.C.E.

## Does 1 Enoch 56:7 Require a Date before the Destruction of Jerusalem?

The reference to "the city of my righteous ones" as a hindrance to the horses of the Parthians and the Medes has been taken by many as an indication that the city of Jerusalem is standing at the time of the composition of the Parables; however, the reference has not been a hindrance to those who would argue for a post-70 date. As we have noted, Bampfylde finds in the reference a historical allusion to the difficulty of the Parthian cavalry in taking walled cities in the mid-

---

22. Boccaccini, *Beyond the Essene Hypothesis*, 144.
23. Knibb, "Date of the Parables," 354.
24. Greenfield and Stone, "The Enochic Pentateuch," 58-60.
25. A. Yarbro Collins, "The 'Son of Man' Tradition and the Book of Revelation," in *The Messiah: Developments in Earliest Judaism and Christianity*, ed. J. H. Charlesworth (Minneapolis: Fortress, 1992), 536-68 (esp. 563-64).
26. D. W. Suter, *Tradition and Composition in the Parables of Enoch* (Missoula: Scholars, 1979), 12, 24, 176-77 n. 86. See L. Hartman, *Prophecy Interpreted: The Formation of Some Jewish Apocalyptic Texts and of the Eschatological Discourse in Mark 13 Par.*, trans. N. Tomkinson (Lund: CWK Gleerup, 1966), 188-91. Coppens (*Le Fils d'homme*, 151 n. 7) cites my argument with approval.

dle of the first century B.C.E.,[27] while Hindley discounts the idea that the reference requires that the walls of Jerusalem be standing.[28] Black rejects any effort to interpret "hindrance" metaphorically as unconvincing: the passage implies that Jerusalem is standing, requiring a pre-70 dating for at least some parts of the Parables.[29]

In general, the destruction of Jerusalem looms large in various ways in both Jewish and Christian literature from the last part of the first century C.E., and it would seem at least odd if the Parables were to come from that period and not include the destruction of the city and the temple in its symbolic purview in some way, even given the disfavor in which earlier examples of the Enoch literature held the Second Temple.[30] What may be decisive here is not so much the allusion in 56:7 as the general failure of the Parables to address the issue in dealing with the crimes of the kings and mighty.

## 1 Enoch 67:4-13, Hot Springs as a Reference to Herod the Great at Callirrhoe

Some scholars, including Darrell Hannah in his contribution to the present volume, have found in the references in 1 En 67:4-13 to thermal springs in which the kings and mighty sport a potential allusion to Herod the Great's visit toward the end of his life to the warm springs at Callirrhoe in search of healing, based upon the celebrity of the waters of those springs in the ancient world and the likelihood that people in the Jewish world would have been aware of the event.[31] In the Parables, the heated waters are the product of the punishment of the fallen Watchers and are said to heal the bodies of the kings and mighty but to destroy their souls. Greenfield and Stone accept the possibility of the reference as further indication of composition during the first century C.E., while Bampfylde argues that the passage is an interpolation dating from the end of Herod's life in 4 B.C.E.[32] This passage receives far less attention than the refer-

27. Bampfylde, "The Similitudes of Enoch," 24-25.
28. Hindley, "Toward a Date," 556.
29. M. Black, *The Book of Enoch, or, I Enoch: A New English Edition with Commentary and Textual Notes,* SVTP 7 (Leiden: Brill, 1985), 187.
30. Note that in the Animal Apocalypse (1 En 85–90) and the Apocalypse of Weeks (93:3-10; 91:11-17), the Second Temple either is treated as polluted or is strangely absent (see 89:73; 93:9).
31. Josephus, *Ant* 17.171. See below, D. Hannah, "The Book of Noah, the Death of Herod the Great, and the Date of the Parables of Enoch."
32. Bampfylde, "The Similitudes of Enoch," 28-30; Greenfield and Stone, "The Enochic Pentateuch," 60.

ence to the Parthians and the Medes, perhaps because it is difficult to connect it specifically to Herod's journey to Callirrhoe.[33] The use of hot springs as well as the bath may be more a characteristic of Roman culture in general,[34] providing a clue to the identity of the kings and the mighty (see the next issue).

## The Identity of the Kings and Mighty

For R. H. Charles, the identity of the kings and mighty was decisive in his dating of the Parables. He identifies them as the late Hasmonean princes and their Sadducean supporters and argues that the date could not have been earlier than 94 B.C.E., because the blood of the righteous had not been shed (1 En 47:1-4), and not later than 64 B.C.E., because Rome is not included among the world powers and the Sadducees did not support the Herodians.[35]

In recent years scholars have tended to assume that the kings and the mighty represent the global rule of the Romans since they are said to possess the earth, leading them to look for a date at some point during Roman rule in the land of Israel. For some, the choice of the Parthians as the enemy points toward the Romans. Hindley notes a continuing instability between Parthia and Armenia on Rome's eastern frontier, exacerbated by Rome in an effort to use Armenia to contain Parthia. His article is a search through the history of this Roman "eastern frontier policy" to find a time at which Parthia presented a perceptible threat to the people of Judea.[36] Knibb observes that throughout the Roman period the Parthians are a potential threat, making it natural that the Parables would regard them as the enemy.[37]

On the other hand, Bampfylde claims that the Parthians and Medes represent the enemy during the Maccabean period and dates the Parables at the end of Hasmonean rule, although a bit later than Charles allowed. He identifies the kings and the mighty as the Parthians and bases his case upon what he per-

---

33. See Nickelsburg's conclusion: "the punishment of the kings and the mighty in 1 En 67:8-13 may have as much to do with mythic geography in general as with Herod's treatment at Callirrhoe." See G. W. E. Nickelsburg, *Jewish Literature between the Bible and the Mishnah: A Historical and Literary Introduction* (Philadelphia: Fortress, 1981), 222.

34. See Suter, *Tradition and Composition*, 24, 174 n. 56. See also Coppens, *Le Fils d'homme*, 151 n. 8.

35. R. H. Charles, ed., *The Apocrypha and Pseudepigrapha of the Old Testament*, vol. 2, *Pseudepigrapha* (Oxford: Clarendon, 1913), 171. Charles assumes that the author is a Pharisee and therefore excludes the reign of Alexandra in 79-70 B.C.E. from his window for the composition of the work.

36. Hindley, "Toward a Date," 554.

37. Knibb, "Date of the Parables," 352, 355.

ceives to be the relation between the kings and mighty and the Oriental political organization of the Parthians with their satraps and councils of nobles or great men to advise the king.[38]

In *Tradition and Composition,* I argued that the kings and the mighty exemplified the problem of the king who challenged God (see 1 En 46:4-8; 63:4) and suggested that the crisis during the reign of Gaius Caligula could be an appropriate context for the composition of the Parables as the emperor sought to have his statue placed in the temple in Jerusalem.[39]

An alternative approach to dating the Parables through the identification of the kings and the mighty is that of James Charlesworth, who dates the work during the reign of Herod the Great. He relates the concern in the Parables for the moral analysis of poverty and riches to Herod's seizure of the estates of the Hasmoneans and other Jews and his heavy taxation, impoverishing the aristocracy and people.[40] Charlesworth's approach to dating is complementary to Sacchi's (noted above), who relates the reference in 1 En 56:7 to internecine warfare to the civil war that erupts within Judaism in the wake of the Parthian invasion of 40 B.C.E.

In general, aside from Bampfylde, current scholarship seems to implicate the Romans and their associates as the villains of the Parables, pointing to a date after the coming of the Romans in the mid–first century B.C.E. The problem that seems to be emerging is where within the period of 40 B.C.E. to 70 C.E. to locate the work. Resolution of the problem appears to demand other approaches than the use of historical analysis, to which we will turn below.

## The Implications of Social Context for the Question of Date

While the issue of the social context of the Parables is not a direct determinant of the date of the work, as a part of the issue of provenance it is closely associated with the issue of dating. Christopher Mearns suggests that the work is

---

38. Bampfylde, "The Similitudes of Enoch," 16.
39. Suter, *Tradition and Composition,* 23-32. Michel Jas dates the Parables to the same time on different grounds (for him, they reflect a polemic against the identification of Jesus as the Son of Man). See M. Jas, "Hénoch et le fils de l'homme: datation du Livre des Paraboles pour une situation de l'origine du Gnosticisme," *La revue réformée* 30 (1979): 105-19 (esp. 113). Other scholars with roughly similar dates for various reasons are Christopher Rowland and Christopher Mearns. See C. L. Mearns, "Dating the Similitudes of Enoch," *NTS* 25 (1979): 360-69 (esp. 369); C. Rowland, *The Open Heaven: A Study of Apocalyptic in Judaism and Early Christianity* (New York: Crossroad, 1982), 264-66.
40. Charlesworth, "Date of the Parables," 94-97. See now, below, his contribution to this volume, "Can We Discern the Composition Date of the Parables of Enoch?"

Jewish-Christian in origin, based upon the affinity of the exaltation of the righteous Enoch in the Parables to the exaltation of the Son of Man in the Gospels (see below).[41] If this claim could be demonstrated on the basis of some other evidence than the use of Dan 7 and "Son of Man," it would have some implications for the involvement of the Parables in the formative process behind the Son of Man Christology in the New Testament and therefore implications for the question of date.

On the other hand, the majority opinion at present is that the Parables of Enoch is Jewish in provenance. As I argued in *Tradition and Composition* and in "Weighed in the Balance," the world in which the work moves is Jewish, and more specifically, from the early layers of the Hekhalot tradition.[42] When Enoch arrives in heaven, he hears the chant of a variation of the *Qeduššah*, in a form echoed in 3 Enoch, rather than the Sanctus (see 1 En 39:9-14; 3 En 1:12; 20:2; 39:1-2).[43] There are also some similarities in the representation of the mystical ascent (cf. 1 En 39:10-14 with 3 En 1:10-12).[44] The angels mentioned in the work include the ophanim, the "wheels" of the *merkabah* or divine throne chariot (1 En 61:10 and 71:7). The book speaks of an oath that maintains the cosmos (1 En 69:13-25; 3 En 13:1; 41:1-4),[45] again a feature of the Hekhalot tradition. And whether we treat chap. 71 as a later appendix (with the possibility that it is designed to counter the identification of Jesus as the Son of Man)[46] or as an integral part of the Parables, the naming of Enoch as the Son of Man (which seems almost to anticipate his identification as Metatron in 3 En 4:1-10) is not likely to be a Christian feature and can only confirm that the work either originated or

---

41. C. L. Mearns, "The Parables of Enoch — Origin and Date," *ExpTim* 89 (1978): 118-19 (esp. 118).

42. Suter, *Tradition and Composition*, 14-23; Suter, "Weighed in the Balance," 218. See J. C. Greenfield, "Prolegomenon," in H. Odeberg, *3 Enoch or the Hebrew Book of Enoch* (reprint, New York: Ktav, 1973), xi-xlvii (esp. xvii).

43. See Odeberg, *3 Enoch*, 184. The *Qeduššah* combines Isa 6:3 (the Trisagion) with the MT of Ezek 3:12 ("Blessed be the glory of the Lord from his place"). 1 En 39:13 has as the response, "You are blessed, and blessed in the name of the Lord for ever and ever," which could be compared to "Blessed be the name of his glorious kingdom for ever and ever" in 3 En 39:2, one of the two forms that the *Qeduššah* takes in 3 Enoch.

44. Suter, *Tradition and Composition*, 18-19.

45. See also a passage from the Lesser Hekhalot cited in G. G. Scholem, *Jewish Gnosticism, Merkabah Mysticism, and Talmudic Tradition* (New York: Jewish Theological Seminary of America, 1965), 79.

46. See Jas, "Hénoch et le fils de l'homme," 113.

47. Coppens (*Le Fils d'homme*, 152) cites my argument with approval. See also J. R. Davila, *Descenders to the Chariot: The People behind the Hekhalot Literature* (Leiden: Brill, 2001), 151.

was passed down in a Jewish context. The work is proto-Hekhalot in character and needs to be studied and understood in the context of Judaism.[47]

In a recent book Andrei A. Orlov argues against the connection of the Son of Man in the Parables with the Enoch-Metatron material in 3 Enoch.[48] He notes that the terminology associated with the Son of Man in the Parables is not continued in 3 Enoch and maintains that in 1 En 71:14 Enoch is identified as *a* son of man rather than *the* Son of Man. Orlov is correct in observing the discontinuity between the language associated with the Son of Man in the Parables and the Enoch-Metatron figure in 3 Enoch. I note, however, that my connection of the Parables with the Hekhalot tradition (as described above) is more broadly based than the identification of Enoch as the Son of Man in 1 En 71:14. In addition, as will be noted below, Charles A. Gieschen argues for similarities in the attribution of the divine name to the Son of Man in the Parables and Metatron in 3 Enoch,[49] a link between the Son of Man in the Parables and Metatron that Orlov seems to have overlooked.

It is possible that the issue of social context holds important clues to the puzzle presented by the origin and preservation of the Parables. In "The Pseudepigrapha in Christianity," Robert Kraft makes the following observation: "We need to examine the literature as it has been preserved for us, attempt to recreate the conditions under which it was preserved and transmitted, and then perhaps we will be in a position to identify the sort of 'Jewishness' it might represent. For the most part, and with significant exceptions (e.g., at least part of 1 Enoch), this has not been the normal approach to the pseudepigrapha in recent decades."[50] The exception he cites for at least part of 1 Enoch is the section of my *Tradition and Composition* noted above dealing with the provenance of the Parables and its relation to the Hekhalot tradition.[51]

In thinking about Kraft's remark, it seems possible that the correct solu-

---

48. See A. A. Orlov, *The Enoch-Metatron Tradition*, TSAJ 107 (Tübingen: Mohr Siebeck, 2005), 76-85. Excerpts from his book with some additional notes are presented (above) as his contribution to the present volume.

49. See above, C. A. Gieschen, "The Name of the Son of Man in the Parables of Enoch."

50. R. A. Kraft, "The Pseudepigrapha in Christianity," in *Tracing the Threads: Studies in the Vitality of Jewish Pseudepigrapha*, ed. J. C. Reeves (Atlanta: Scholars, 1994), 55-86 (esp. 75).

51. Kraft, "The Pseudepigrapha in Christianity," 86 n. 68. See Suter, *Tradition and Composition*, 11-33. In personal conversation at the Third Enoch Seminar at Camaldoli, Kraft noted that the original version of "The Pseudepigrapha in Christianity" was written prior to the publication of my *Tradition and Composition*, and that the footnote referring to my work was added only later in preparation for publication in *Tracing the Threads*. In discussion at Camaldoli, Kraft continued to apply the method set forth in "The Pseudepigrapha in Christianity," suggesting that before settling for a Jewish provenance and a pre-70 dating, the possibility of a Gnostic context needed further exploration.

tion to the survival of the Parables in the Ethiopic Book of Enoch alongside its absence from Qumran, the Greek version, and quotation in patristic literature is a different line of transmission and preservation somewhere within the byways of the Hekhalot tradition in Judaism rather than in Christianity.[52] Such a transmission might also fit with the suggestion of Edward Ullendorff and Knibb that the Parables of Enoch is based on an Aramaic archetype rather than a Greek one.[53] Ullendorff's discussion of Hebraic and Judaic elements in Ethiopian Christianity in *Ethiopia and the Bible* also may be of significance for the possibility of the transmission of the Parables through Jewish rather than Christian channels into Ethiopia, although a part of these elements seems to be the consequence of the imitation of the Bible rather than more direct Jewish influence.[54] However, while working with the secondary Adam and Eve literature in the wake of the 1996 NEH Adam and Eve seminar at Hebrew University, it became apparent to me that there are points at which the boundaries between Jewish and Christian communities are permeable,[55] and the possibility of the transmission of the Parables through Jewish rather than Christian channels may be worth consideration. Although this suggestion is admittedly speculative, the proto-Hekhalot element of the Parables may hold the answer to the riddle of its origin, transmission, and preservation. It represents an alternative approach to that of Sacchi and Boccaccini (noted above) to explaining the absence of the Parables from the Greek versions and citation or quotation in patristic authors, although the two approaches are not necessarily at odds with each other.

In his contribution to the present volume,[56] Pierluigi Piovanelli has

52. Cf. Greenfield, "Prolegomenon," xvii-xviii.

53. M. A. Knibb, *The Ethiopic Book of Enoch: A New Edition in the Light of the Aramaic Dead Sea Fragments*, vol. 2, *Introduction, Translation, and Commentary* (Oxford: Clarendon, 1978), 37-46; E. Ullendorff, "An Aramaic 'Vorlage' of the Ethiopic Text of Enoch?" in *Atti del convegno internazionale di studi Etiopici* (Rome: Accademia Nazionale dei Lincei, 1960), 259-67; Ullendorff, *Ethiopia and the Bible* (London: Oxford University Press, 1968), 61-62. Ullendorff and Knibb actually argue that the entire translation of the Ethiopic Book of Enoch is based upon an Aramaic archetype.

54. See Ullendorff, *Ethiopia and the Bible*, 1-30, 73-115.

55. Here cf. S. Brock, "Jewish Traditions in Syriac Sources," *JJS* 30 (1979): 212-32 (esp. 225-32). Brock is interested in Jewish material and traditions that find their way into Christian literature in Syriac; however, some of the items he discusses also appear in Ethiopia. Ullendorff notes that in the fourth or fifth century Syrian Monophysite monks fleeing Byzantine persecution came to Ethiopia and were involved in the translation of the Bible into Ethiopic. They would be the ones capable of producing a translation of 1 Enoch from Aramaic into Ethiopic. See Ullendorff, "An Aramaic 'Vorlage,'" 262.

56. See above, P. Piovanelli, "'A Testimony for the Kings and the Mighty Who Possess the Earth': The Thirst for Justice and Peace in the Parables of Enoch."

sought to examine the social perspectives embedded in the text, concluding that the Parables represents a political shift from the earlier Enochic literature in that the barbs of the work are directed at the political leaders of the time, quoting my *Tradition and Composition* to argue that these leaders are out of sync with a God who stands for justice.[57] At the same time, the work does not seem to be sectarian in nature since it does not set up boundary markers against other groups of Jews. In Piovanelli's estimation the work addresses the whole of the Jewish people while targeting Herod the Great. He thus dates the work during the reign of Herod after the invasion of the Parthians in 40-37 B.C.E., and after Herod's visit to Callirrhoe, but before the death of the king.

Other approaches to the question of context come from the contributions of Charles Gieschen and Daniel Boyarin. Gieschen links the figure of the heavenly Son of Man in the Parables to his discussion of angelomorphic Christology,[58] while Boyarin argues that interpretation of Dan 7:13 continues to be implied in the rabbinic traditions about two powers in heaven,[59] material first studied by Alan Segal.[60] Gieschen relates the Son of Man in the Parables to what he argues are hypostases of God in the biblical tradition representing the visible presence of the divine, including the Angel of YHWH, the glory of YHWH, and the name of YHWH. He shows how the introduction of the Son of Man in 1 En 46:1-3 reflects language used of the glory of YHWH in Ezek 1:26-28 in addition to the "one like a son of man" and the "Ancient of Days" in Dan 7:13, and argues that the Son of Man in the Parables is represented as possessing the name, YHWH, through which all things are created.[61] As such, the Son of Man reflects a creative approach to monotheism relating the visible divine presence to the mystery of God, an approach found also in Jub 36:7, in the figure of Yahoel in TestAbr 10:3, 8; 11:2-3, and Metatron in 3 En 12:5, 13:1.[62] In contrast to studies by Johannes Theisohn and Leslie Walck (to be noted below), who identify special Matthean sayings as reflecting the influence of the Parables, Gieschen argues that the Gospel of John and Revelation are the parts of the New Testament that

---

57. See Suter, *Tradition and Composition*, 163-64.

58. See also C. A. Gieschen, *Angelomorphic Christology: Antecedents and Early Evidence*, AGJU 42 (Leiden: Brill, 1998), 156-57.

59. See above, D. Boyarin, "Was the Book of Parables a Sectarian Document? A Brief Brief in Support of Pierluigi Piovanelli."

60. See A. F. Segal, *Two Powers in Heaven: Early Rabbinic Reports about Christianity and Gnosticism* (Leiden: Brill, 1977). See pp. 202-5 for his discussion of the Parables.

61. 1 En 48:2-3; 69:27. See 69:14-25 for the oath through which the name works its creative powers.

62. See also Philo, *De confusione linguarum* 146.

come closest to the treatment of the Son of Man in the Parables since they ascribe the divine name to Jesus as the Son of Man.

Boyarin believes that rabbinic traditions reflect the continuation of speculation about a second power in heaven[63] similar to the portrayal of the Son of Man in the Parables. In advancing this argument he is responding to Piovanelli's claim that the Book of Parables is not a sectarian document but one that addresses the whole of Israel. Boyarin suggests that the Book of Parables is a document from strands of Judaism that will give birth to the rabbinic movement but are also intimately related to the Hekhalot tradition. In contrast to Segal,[64] he argues that the debate about two powers in heaven reflects an issue that arises at the center of the rabbinic movement echoing concerns about a divine mediator with the world that earlier led to the emergence of Christianity. He explains the presence of the idea in both Christian and early rabbinic tradition by noting that the Christian tradition is initially an integral part of Judaism, in contrast to the tendency in the Son of Man debate (as evidenced elsewhere in this paper) to treat the two as distinct.

As will become apparent in further discussion below, the positions of Gieschen and Boyarin suggest that the discussion of the Son of Man in the Parables and early Christianity has been construed too narrowly with a focus on the use of the title, Son of Man, when the real issue is the problem of the relation of the transcendent to the mundane world, solved in the continuing Jewish tradition with an appeal to Dan 7 in a way that suggests two powers in heaven. This form of speculation continues on, pointing toward a context in Judaism (including the Hekhalot tradition) or in Gnosticism for the Parables, with its second divine figure occupying the throne of God. A central methodological question is whether one studies the Son of Man in the Parables by seeking elsewhere the use of the phrase "Son of Man" from Dan 7:13 or by looking for the recurrence of forms of messianism or mediation inspired by the presentation of a second divine figure in the verse from Daniel. From the latter perspective, a context for the Parables after the end of the first century C.E. is not yet out of the question, since this sort of speculation seems to continue on for several centuries. The issue is ultimately one of focus, to borrow a turn of speech from Collins in a contribution to be discussed below. How the discussion plays out will depend upon the texts and traditions with which scholars choose to associate the Son of Man materials in the Parables, and the grounds they use to justify those associations.

---

63. See *Mekhilta d'Rabbi Ishma'el* to Exod 20:2; and *BT Ḥagiga* 14a, 15a.
64. See Segal, *Two Powers in Heaven*, 41, 55, 71.

## The Affinity of the Parables to Other Literature

Given the paucity and the ambiguity of historical references internal to the Parables, perhaps a promising approach to settling upon a date for the work is to look for affinities between it and other works of literature during the period.[65] We have already noted that Knibb, in expressing his reservations about Hindley's historical approach to dating, appeals instead to affinities to the messianism of the Parables in works like 2 Baruch and 4 Ezra, which come from the period after the Roman destruction of Jerusalem. What these works have in common with the Parables is that the messianic figure enters into the process of judgment of the wicked (see 2 Bar 40:1-2; 72:2-6; 4 Ezra 12:32-33; 13:37-38). He is also described as preexistent and hidden by God in 4 Ezra (see 12:32; 13:25-26, 51-52). In another approach to an argument from affinity, Bampfylde appeals to the Psalms of Solomon as a work with a similar perspective in arguing for a date of 50 B.C.E.[66]

So far, these various approaches to affinity seem to cancel one another out, since they point toward literature at either end of the window of time current scholarship considers possible for dating the Parables. In addition, the messianism of chap. 17 of the Psalms of Solomon is purely royal in character, exhibiting none of the distinctive characteristics of the interpretation of Dan 7:13 found elsewhere. Moreover, the affinity of the Parables to the works from the end of the first century C.E. is a matter of some discussion. In arguing for a date during the life of the Qumran sect, Greenfield and Stone observe that the use of "Son of Man" as a messianic designation is already "suppressed and reinterpreted" in 4 Ezra.[67] Something of what they have in mind here can be discovered in Stone's article "The Concept of the Messiah in IV Ezra," where he distinguishes between the vision in 13:1-13 and its interpretation in 13:25-51 and shows how the author has sought to suppress the cosmic element of the vision in the interpretation so that the "Man" becomes simply a symbol.[68] In his contribution to the present volume, Stone reiterates his analysis of the material in 4 Ezra, observing that the vision represents an earlier source for the Son of Man tradition. How much earlier, however, is impossible to determine.[69]

Christopher Mearns, however, offers an approach based upon affinity to

---

65. Here see Suter, *Tradition and Composition*, 24-25.
66. Bampfylde, "The Similitudes of Enoch," 25.
67. Greenfield and Stone, "The Enochic Pentateuch," 57.
68. M. E. Stone, "The Concept of the Messiah in IV Ezra," in *Religions in Antiquity: Essays in Memory of Erwin Ramsdell Goodenough*, ed. J. Neusner (Leiden: Brill, 1968), 295-312 (esp. 308-9).
69. See below, M. E. Stone, "Enoch's Date in Limbo; or, Some Considerations on David Suter's Analysis of the Book of Parables."

other literature that seems somewhat more compelling. He argues for an affinity of the Son of Man messianism of the Parables, in which the Son of Man is exalted to the throne of his glory in the scenes set in heaven, to an exaltation Christology broadly represented in the New Testament and reflecting a stage in primitive Christian theology prior to the development of doctrine of the resurrection. Mearns traces this development to the end of the first generation of primitive Christianity in the late 40s and assigns a corresponding date to the Parables.[70] He also argues that chap. 11 of the shorter recension of the Testament of Abraham, which he dates to the first half of the first century C.E., contains a polemic against the designation of Enoch as judge at the last judgment, a feature that he believes reflects the identification of Enoch as Son of Man in 1 En 71.[71] However, it is not absolutely clear that the reference to Enoch in the Testament of Abraham is to the role of Enoch in the Parables, nor is it possible to date either recension of the work with any certainty.

Maurice Casey has a position somewhat similar to Mearns's approach in seeing the Jewish and Christian use of Dan 7 as parallel processes, although for Mearns the two processes seem to be intertwined while for Casey they are separate and distinct, as they were for Lindars (see above). Casey's position is predicated upon the argument that there is no Son of Man concept in the Judaism of the period, that the phrase simply means "man," and that the conclusion of the Parables with the exaltation of Enoch and his identification as the son of man is consistent with the intent of the entire work. On dating the Parables he comments: "Hence our inability to date the Similitudes of Enoch accurately matters little. The important factor is the similarity of the situation of the Enoch circle to that of the early Christians, such that independent application of Dan 7:13 to their respective intermediary figures is readily comprehensible."[72]

Joseph Coppens likewise treats the Parables as part of a parallel process to the teaching of Jesus and the work of the early church. He rejects the argument of Michel Jas that the Parables represents a polemic against the recognition of Jesus as the Son of Man, because the work exhibits no sign of such a polemic, but agrees with Jas in dating the Parables to the first century, prior to 70 C.E., and sees the work as evidence for the milieu of Jesus and the early church.[73]

---

70. Mearns, "Dating the Similitudes," 365-67, 369. Rowland comes to a date of around 50 C.E. for somewhat similar reasons; see Rowland, *The Open Heaven*, 264-66.

71. Mearns, "Dating the Similitudes," 363-64. Caragounis offers a critique of Mearns's discussion of the Testament of Abraham; see Caragounis, *The Son of Man*, 91-92.

72. M. Casey, *Son of Man: The Interpretation and Influence of Daniel 7* (London: SPCK, 1979), 137. See also M. Casey, *From Jewish Prophet to Gentile God: The Origins and Development of New Testament Christology* (Cambridge: James Clarke, 1991), 87-88.

73. See Coppens, *Le Fils d'homme*, 152-55; Jas, "Hénoch et le fils de l'homme," 113.

*Enoch in Sheol*

The use of affinities to establish a date for the Parables is potentially more promising than the use of historical allusions; however, the procedure depends upon a high degree of subjectivity on the part of the scholar. Perhaps the danger can be mitigated if the search for affinities can rest on a broader basis than the one of messianic traditions. For example, several attempts have been made to compare the uranology of the Parables to similar material in the New Testament and elsewhere, with the argument that the elaboration of heaven or the heavenly scene is cruder or simpler than comparative presentations.[74] Here the approach of Boccaccini has potential value in locating the Parables in the context of Jewish literature of the Roman era, since it uses systemic analysis to construct chains of documents on the basis of a number of factors in their ideologies, in addition to their use of eschatological or messianic traditions.[75] In his contribution to the present volume, Boccaccini presents a fresh approach to the problem. By tracking the use and interaction of five "paradigms" in Second Temple Jewish literature: (1) the wisdom paradigm of revelation, (2) the apocalyptic paradigm of reversal, (3) the messianic paradigm of power, (4) the covenantal paradigm of Law, and (5) the Enochic paradigm of corruption, Boccaccini concludes that the Book of Parables "testifies to a stage in which the encounter and merging of the Sapiential, Messianic, and Apocalyptic Paradigms were still at their inception — a stage that parallels the earliest origins of the Jesus movement and is the logical premise for the theological developments in Paul and the later Christian tradition."[76]

## The Influence of the Parables upon the New Testament

In the *Son of Man Debate: A History and Evaluation*, Delbert Burkett claims that as a consequence of the work of R. H. Charles, scholars during the early part of the twentieth century treated the Parables as earlier than the beginnings of

---

74. Mearns compares 1 En 40 with Rev 4 and 1 En 62 with Matt 25, concluding that the formulations of the New Testament are more developed. He makes similar comparisons between the presentation of the Son of Man in the Parables and the more complex elaboration of the idea in the four Gospels. See Mearns, "Dating the Similitudes," 364-65. I have argued that the twofold uranology of the Parables must antedate the development of a sevenfold uranology that seems to emerge during the course of the first century C.E. See Suter, *Tradition and Composition*, 24-25. See also Coppens, *Le Fils d'homme*, 154.

75. See Boccaccini, *Beyond the Essene Hypothesis*, 8-11, 144-49. See also G. Boccaccini, *Roots of Rabbinic Judaism: An Intellectual History, from Ezekiel to Daniel* (Grand Rapids: Eerdmans, 2002), 28-32.

76. See above, G. Boccaccini, "Finding a Place for the Parables of Enoch within Second Temple Jewish Literature."

David W. Suter

Christianity and therefore evidence for an apocalyptic Son of Man concept in Judaism prior to Christianity.[77] Charles had successfully attacked the consensus of the nineteenth century that "Son of Man" was not a title in pre-Christian Judaism but a way of speaking of a human figure. Burkett argues that subsequent to Milik's original announcement in 1959 of the Parables' absence from the Dead Sea Scrolls fragments of 1 Enoch, the idea of a pre-Christian apocalyptic Son of Man came under attack from two additional directions: in 1966 Norman Perrin began an effort to deconstruct Son of Man as a coherent concept in the available sources, and beginning in 1967 Geza Vermes put forth a linguistic argument against the titular use of "Son of Man" in pre-Christian Judaism.[78] In reviewing Perrin's work, Paul Winter summed up the results in this way: "If P[errin]'s interpretation of the Son of Man sayings in the Synoptic Gospels is right — and it is supported by Vermes' . . . study of the linguistic use of the word 'bar-nash(a)' in Jewish Aramaic — then the place of origin of the [Son of Man] myth must be sought neither in Iran, nor in Judea, nor even in Ugarit, but in German universities."[79] In all fairness to our German colleagues, we should acknowledge that British and American academics have also in their own ways been obsessed with the Son of Man.

If one follows these approaches, the Son of Man sayings in the Gospels are the product of either Jesus or the early church, working directly with Dan 7, and it becomes necessary to ask at what point, if any, the Parables influenced the sayings in the Gospels. If a relationship between sayings and the Parables can be demonstrated, then some additional line of reasoning is necessary to demonstrate the direction of that relationship in order to establish the Gospels as a terminus ad quem for the existence of the Parables.

As the result of Johannes Theisohn's work, the prime candidates for such influence are Matt 25:31 and 19:28, which present the Son of Man as a judicial figure seated upon the "throne of his glory," reflecting the role and the mode of appearance of the messianic figure in 1 En 62–63.[80] In Matt 19:28 the twelve disciples are also seated on thrones judging Israel. In Daniel judgment takes place before the appearance of the "one like a son of man," and the figure is given dominion but is not seated on a throne. The first of the two scenes in Matthew also relates the messianic figure to his compatriots on earth and

---

77. D. Burkett, *The Son of Man Debate: A History and Evaluation* (Cambridge: Cambridge University Press, 1999), 68-70.

78. Burkett, *Son of Man Debate*, 68-76.

79. As quoted by Burkett, *Son of Man Debate*, 75-76.

80. J. Theisohn, *Der auserwählte Richter: Untersuchungen zum traditiongeschichtlichem Ort der Menschensohngestalt des Bilderreden des Äthiopischen Henoch* (Göttingen: Vandenhoeck & Ruprecht, 1975), 153, 182. See also Black, "Messianism of the Parables," 162-63.

makes that connection the key to the judgment of the nations, a feature that is similar to the relation of the Son of Man/Elect One and the elect on earth in the Parables, where it is the kings and mighty who are judged for their treatment of the elect. In his contribution to the present volume, Leslie Walck, like Theisohn, uses a classification of features of the Son of Man passages in the Parables to restrict the link between the Parables and the New Testament to the verses from Matthew.[81]

In *Jewish Literature between the Bible and the Mishnah,* George Nickelsburg adds to these two passages Matt 24:37-44//Luke 17:22-27, which establishes a typological connection between Noah's flood and eschatological judgment in relation to the coming of the Son of Man, a pattern that reflects the Parables.[82] To answer the question of direction of influence, he notes that "Son of Man" appears as an established title in the Gospels, while in the Parables one can trace the exegetical steps by which passages from Daniel, Isaiah, and Psalms are brought together, suggesting that in the Parables the development of such a messianic figure is a work in progress independent of other sources. He also appeals to a linguistic argument to establish the priority of the Parables: "The parables employ the more Semitic and original meaning of the term in a nontitular sense (= 'man'). It is unlikely that this usage is a secondary resemiticizing of the titular use of the term."[83] Note that Nickelsburg subsequently revises his approach to Son of Man in the Parables and the New Testament, a discussion to which we will return immediately below.

The distinctive sayings in Matthew may establish a terminus ad quem, but not necessarily an absolute date. As we proceed, it becomes apparent that a multiphased approach to dating is necessary.

## Identifying and Dating Traditions behind the Parables

If a date cannot be fixed through historical allusions, affinities, or use in other literature, one approach to establishing a place in time for the Parables is through the identification of messianic traditions underlying the work. In *The Son of Man Debate,* Burkett describes two such approaches in the late twentieth century, which he identifies as a "'common model' of a 'transcendent judge and deliverer' in Jewish eschatology of the first century CE" undertaken by Nickels-

---

81. See above, L. W. Walck, "The Son of Man in the Parables of Enoch and the Gospels."

82. Nickelsburg, *Jewish Literature,* 222. Note that 1 En 65:1–67:3, which deals with Noah and the flood, follows almost immediately upon the revelation of the Elect One/Son of Man as judge in 1 En 62 and the repentance of the kings and mighty in chap. 63.

83. Nickelsburg, *Jewish Literature,* 223.

*David W. Suter*

burg, and the identification of "'common assumptions' about the interpretation of Daniel 7 in the Judaism of the first century CE" undertaken by Collins.[84] Burkett treats these two approaches as efforts to counter the trend beginning with the work of Perrin to deconstruct an apocalyptic Son of Man tradition in first-century Judaism.

In his earlier work, *Jewish Literature,* Nickelsburg advances the argument that the Wisdom of Solomon and the Parables share traditional material that must have existed around the beginning of the first century C.E. even if the Parables itself did not. He appeals to Wis 2, 4–5, which speak of a "persecuted righteous man, who is exalted as judge over his enemies,"[85] and then observes that in 4:10-15 Wisdom treats Enoch as the righteous man's prototype, noting the similarity to the Parables, where in chaps. 70–71 the Elect One/Son of Man is identified as Enoch.[86] It should be observed that the comparison to traditions in Wisdom provides a somewhat wider window in time than the beginning of the first century, since a few pages earlier, in discussing that work, Nickelsburg admits the possibility of a date for it as late as the time of Caligula.[87]

A later work carries Nickelsburg's analysis further. In his "Son of Man" article in the *Anchor Bible Dictionary,* he surveys the Parables, Wis 1–6, 4 Ezra 11–13, and 2 Baruch, concluding that, without necessarily assuming literary dependence, these texts share traditions about a transcendent redeemer and exalted one with judicial functions going beyond Dan 7 and based upon the use of royal traditions from Ps 2 and Isa 11 combined with the Servant Songs of Second Isaiah. He argues that these texts give witness to a fluid but "common model" of a transcendent judge and redeemer that can provide a context for the study of the Son of Man material in the New Testament. In dating the tradition, he notes that, while 4 Ezra 13 indicates that this "common model" was known at the end of the first century C.E., its presence in the Wisdom of Solomon — to be dated at the latest to 40 C.E. — allows us to push the date for the traditions back to the first part of the first century C.E. He also notes that the model seems to be used in texts struggling with persecution and suffering, including the effort to come to grips with the destruction of Jerusalem in 70 C.E.[88] Nickelsburg systematically examines the Son of Man material in the New Testament begin-

---

84. Burkett, *Son of Man Debate,* 109.

85. Nickelsburg, *Jewish Literature,* 222.

86. For Nickelsburg's original treatment of this traditional material, see G. W. E. Nickelsburg, *Resurrection, Immortality, and Eternal Life in Intertestamental Judaism,* HTS 26 (Cambridge: Harvard University Press, 1972), 48-92. Note that he dates the tradition to the second century B.C.E. in his earlier discussion; see 70, 78.

87. Nickelsburg, *Jewish Literature,* 184.

88. G. W. E. Nickelsburg, "Son of Man," in *ABD* 6 (1992), 137-50 (esp. 138-42).

ning with the sayings in Q, and concludes that as early as Q the common model is reflected in some measure in the Christian traditions about the Son of Man.[89]

An interesting tension emerges in Nickelsburg's work over whether the features of the messianic figure in the Parables are the product of an exegetical process as in *Jewish Literature* or a traditional process as in his "Son of Man" article.[90] Although the two descriptions are not necessarily at odds, the appeal to an exegetical process in *Jewish Literature* suggests the immediacy of interaction in the employment of passages of Scripture to build up a portrait in the composition of the Parables, while the appeal to a common model of a transcendent judge and redeemer suggests a process that has deeper roots in the messianic traditions of Judaism in the Hellenistic and Roman periods.

In "The Son of Man in First-Century Judaism," Collins offers several considerations for dating the Parables prior to the fall of Jerusalem in 70 C.E.: absence from Qumran should not be taken as a reason for a later date since the Parables seems to come from a different conventicle; it is not likely that Jewish communities would have used "Son of Man" subsequent to its adoption by Christians; and the work appears to be presupposed by sayings in Matt 19:28 and 25:31.[91] He notes a consensus that "Son of Man" was not a commonly understood title in first-century Judaism but suggests that the debate "has been too narrowly focused." He then seeks, through an examination of Dan 7, the Parables, and 4 Ezra, to show (1) that Dan 7 is the source of the apocalyptic use of "Son of Man" in Judaism; (2) that the Parables and 4 Ezra are independent and distinct from each other — in the Parables, the Son of Man is a transcendent judge, the celestial counterpart of the earthly elect, while 4 Ezra presents us with a more militant messianic figure, yet transcendent and preexistent, who takes on the characteristics of the divine warrior[92] — but (3) that in spite of those distinctions, "by the first century CE" there are some "common assumptions" concerning the interpretation of the humanlike figure in Dan 7:13, although they may not add up to a "'Son of Man' concept."[93] Collins lists these common assumptions: (1) the figure of 7:13 is an individual, not a symbol for a collective; (2) in both the Parables and 4 Ezra the figure is identified as the Messiah; (3) the figure is preexistent and transcendent, incorporating in different ways imagery associated with God; and (4) both are more directly involved in

89. Nickelsburg, "Son of Man," 142-49.
90. Note that at one point in the "Son of Man" article, Nickelsburg does speak of a "common exegetical tradition"; see 140.
91. J. J. Collins, "The Son of Man in First-Century Judaism," *NTS* 38, no. 3 (1992): 448-66 (esp. 451-52).
92. J. J. Collins, "Son of Man," 459, 464.
93. J. J. Collins, "Son of Man," 449-50.

the defeat or judgment of the wicked than is the case in Daniel. It is also possible that both are related to Second Isaiah's Servant figure.[94]

While Collins complains that "the whole debate about titular usage has been too narrowly focused,"[95] Burkett critiques both Nickelsburg's "common model" and Collins's "common assumptions" by suggesting that in reaching their conclusions they have failed to distinguish adequately between 1 En 37–70 and 71 on one hand, and between the vision in 4 Ezra 13:1-13 and its interpretation in 13:25-52 on the other. When one makes those distinctions, he claims, the messianic figure turns out to be at one time a warrior and at another a judge, once transcendent and elsewhere earthly, causing the commonality of model or assumptions to disappear. While the degree of focus may be a matter of judgment, at least Nickelsburg's appeal to the affinity of Wis 2, 4–5 with the Parables has the potential to draw the Parables back to a point somewhere in the first half of the first century C.E.

The issue of focus raised by Collins emerged as a significant question even in this volume, although more indirectly than directly. Leslie Walck's essay develops a detailed catalogue of the characteristics of the Son of Man in the Parables and compares them to the Son of Man material in the New Testament.[96] His conclusion echoes that of Theisohn (noted above) in limiting the influence of the Parables to specific items in Matthew. On the other hand, the discussion of messianism or mediation in Second Temple Judaism, reflected in contributions by Gieschen and Boyarin (noted above), suggests that the type of mediation reflected in the Son of Man in the Parables is of wider significance than generally has been recognized hitherto in the discussion of the Son of Man, which has focused more narrowly upon the use of the phrase itself. As Boyarin notes, the type of mediation found in the Parables may survive in Judaism into the early rabbinic period in the controversy over two powers in heaven, opening a potential window for the later dating of the Parables. On the other hand, in opening a consideration of a common model or common assumptions behind the use of Son of Man in early Judaism, Nickelsburg and Collins have broadened their focus but have in the process selected a different set of texts to study than those examined by Gieschen and Boyarin (see above), leading at least in Nickelsburg's case to an earlier date for the Parables. The methodological issue of the appropriate focus, raised first by Collins, needs to be addressed as the discussion of the date of the Parables continues.

The perceptive reader will note that the issue of commonality between

---

94. J. J. Collins, "Son of Man," 464-65.
95. J. J. Collins, "Son of Man," 449.
96. See above, Walck, "The Son of Man in the Parables of Enoch and the Gospels."

the Parables and the late first-century apocalypses, 4 Ezra and 2 Baruch, has been with us from the beginning of this essay, with Knibb appealing to an affinity with those late works to support a date at the end of the century, and Greenfield and Stone arguing along the way that Son of Man messianism already shows signs of suppression and transformation in 4 Ezra, leading them to look for a date during the life of the Qumran community. As precarious and uncertain as the procedure may be, we will more likely get further in dating the Parables by establishing its place in relation to other literature and traditions than by relying upon the meager possibilities for historical allusion with which the work provides us. However, success may depend upon including factors in the comparison other than and in addition to messianic titles and concepts.

## Conclusions

While Milik's publication of the Enoch manuscripts from Qumran has raised the Book of the Watchers (1 En 1–36) to the heights of scholarly discussion, his "rude shock," in Black's words, noted at the beginning of this essay, has cast the Parables down from its seat among the clouds. Several commentators have noted that the Book of Parables has diminished in its importance for the discussion of Son of Man messianism and Christology. At the conclusion of his study of the Son of Man debate, Burkett observes that there seems to have been no unified Son of Man concept in pre-Christian Judaism and that the titular use of "Son of Man" in the New Testament is the consequence of the interpretation of Dan 7 by either Jesus or the early church. He argues that even if we could date the Parables to the early part of the first century C.E., its significance would be only secondary for efforts to solve the problem of the Son of Man.[97]

On the other hand, Black observes that assessments of the Parables "have certainly been hardening in favor of a basically Jewish work, composed around the turn of the millennium." He claims that as the consequence of Carsten Colpe's article on the Son of Man in the *TDNT*, "there has been a marked tendency . . . to 'play down' and minimize the relevance and contribution of the Parables to New Testament christology."[98] Black calls for a reassessment of the question of the influence of the Parables on the Gospels and indicates that he has committed himself to the proposition that there are pre-Christian Jewish

---

97. Burkett, *Son of Man Debate*, 121-24.
98. Black, "Messianism of the Parables," 162. See also M. Black, "A Bibliography on 1 Enoch in the Eighties," *JSP* 5 (1989): 3-16 (esp. 6-7). For the Colpe article, see C. Colpe, "'Ο υἱὸς τοῦ ἀνθρώπου," in *TDNT* 8:400-477 (esp. 429).

traditions in the Parables, including the Son of Man passages, that have exercised an influence on Christian usage, although we cannot also rule out Christian editing of those traditions. Even so, exercising an influence upon Christian usage is a far cry from being taken as prima facie evidence for the apocalyptic Son of Man in ancient Judaism, as the Book of Parables once was.

Where do I come out in the midst of all these opinions of esteemed scholarly colleagues? I do not believe that the absence of the Parables from Qumran (or from the Greek version and patristic literature) requires a date after 70 C.E. As I suggested above, the presence of proto-Hekhalot material in the work combined with its absence in various contexts could point to transmission and preservation somewhere within the Hekhalot movement in Judaism rather than in Christianity. In the past I have argued that the Parables as an apocalypse is most like the apocalypses of the end of the first century. Revelation and 4 Ezra use Dan 7 in messianic contexts, and the Leviathan-Behemoth traditions show up in the Parables (1 En 60), 4 Ezra (6:49), and 2 Baruch (29:4).[99] It might also be possible to appeal to some formal considerations in the comparisons, based upon my article "*Mašal* in the Similitudes of Enoch." There I seek to establish a connection between cosmological wisdom and eschatology in the theodicy presupposed by the Parables, a feature that one could identify also in 4 Ezra (note 6:1-6, for example).[100]

However, I am also convinced by the argument that some of the distinctive Son of Man sayings in Matthew are influenced by the Parables, and that the work comes from before the destruction of Jerusalem, which leaves me wanting to date it in the first century as close as possible to the fall of Jerusalem. In preparing this essay, I have also been struck by Greenfield and Stone's point about the suppression and transformation of Son of Man messianism in 4 Ezra and believe that such a consideration also suggests that the Parables is earlier than the apocalypses of the end of the century, antedating the fall of Jerusalem.

Thematically, in terms of kings who would be God and the implied threat to "the city of my righteous ones," I like the time of the crisis under Gaius Caligula but recognize in the process that such a conclusion is little more than

---

99. Note also Darrell Hannah's treatment of the Parables as unique in the literature of Judaism in placing the messianic figure on the divine throne, a feature paralleling Rev 3:21; 22:1, 3, and some other passages from early Christianity; see D. Hannah, "The Throne of His Glory: The Divine Throne and Heavenly Mediators in Revelation and the Similitudes of Enoch," *ZNW* 94 (2003): 68-96. He quickly surveys the issue of date and concludes that the Parables could not be later than the end of the first century C.E. He is also hesitant to claim literary dependence between Revelation and the Parables.

100. See D. W. Suter, "*Mašal* in the Similitudes of Enoch," *JBL* 100 (1981): 193-212 (esp. 204-8).

an educated guess. I note that my conclusion fits well with Mearns's argument for an affinity between the final chapters of the Parables and the exaltation of the Son of Man in the Christology of the early church, although I would disassociate myself from his treatment of the Parables as Jewish-Christian. To keep things interesting, I also like Nickelsburg's argument that the Parables shares common traditions about Enoch with Wisdom — again traditions that deal with the exaltation of a righteous person — but I also note that Nickelsburg offers us the time of Caligula as a possible date for Wisdom. I am also interested in Boccaccini's construction of Enochic Judaism as an explanation for the absence of the Parables from Qumran, but I would argue for a later date than Sacchi and Boccaccini suggest for the work. I regard the Parables as a parallel process to the formation of Christology in the early church and not as evidence for the use of "Son of Man" in the teaching of Jesus.

In taking stock at the end of my survey of the issue of the date of the Parables, I note that, beyond Burkett's argument that for many scholars the date of the work may be largely irrelevant for the study of the Gospels, two possible trends may be emerging. For Black, Collins, and Nickelsburg, the debate may well come down to whether we can identify pre-Christian traditional elements behind the Parables in order to preserve for that work a place of significance at the table in the Son of Man debate. On the other hand, Lindars, Mearns, Casey, and Coppens in one way or another think of parallel processes taking place in Judaism and early Christianity. In suggesting dates for the Parables or related traditions, the first group *tends* toward the turn of the millennium while the second group *tends* to choose the mid to late first century C.E.[101] While in 1981 I argued that "There seems to be a basic consensus that the Similitudes does not antedate the origins of the Christian movement and therefore does not provide direct evidence for a pre-Christian Jewish Son of Man,"[102] since that time Black, Collins, and Nickelsburg have opened a new front by raising the issue of traditions, models, or assumptions underlying the Parables and the Gospels and seeking to extend the parameters of the question of date back to the turn of the era or beyond.

Beyond those possibilities, I also note that Sacchi and Boccaccini have found a place for the Parables within Enochic Judaism, explaining its absence from Qumran as the consequence of the parting of the ways between that movement and Qumran Essenism. Sacchi dates the work to around 30 B.C.E., in a position to exercise an influence upon the development of Christianity,

---

101. Note that Collins prefers to work backward from 70 C.E., while Coppens dates the Parables between the turn of the era and 70 C.E. (see above).

102. Suter, "Weighed in the Balance," 218.

while Boccaccini notes a consensus tending toward a date around the turn of the era.[103]

In the meantime, while some of the dust has settled, Enoch is still in Sheol. Or perhaps we should say that the Parables of Enoch is caught in Limbo. For many, although not necessarily for all, it is no longer prima facie evidence for an apocalyptic Son of Man in Judaism or the development of the Son of Man sayings in the Gospels, but perhaps there is still hope for a resurrection and a renewed life for the work in the discussion of traditions behind it or in the construction of Enochic Judaism and its relation to the origins of Christianity.

## Afterword

The Third Enoch Seminar (Camaldoli, June 7-9, 2005) has underlined the complexity of the problem of dating the Parables. On the one hand, I must note that discussion tended to support an earlier date at the turn of the era or before, consistent with the observation above that with the work of Black, Collins, and Nickelsburg a new front has been opened. However, some significant voices pointed in another direction.

The methodological issue of the proper focus for the debate, first raised by Collins, may be the key to the future of the discussion of the date and context of the Parables of Enoch. The methodological divergence is in the process of the selection of texts to place the Son of Man passages from the Parables in context. Theisohn and Walck use a restrictive approach to identifying material dependent upon the Parables and constrict their set of texts to certain passages in the Gospel of Matthew, pointing to a date in the latter part of the first century C.E.[104] Nickelsburg defines a common model of a messianic figure, who is a transcendent judge and redeemer, and broadens his scope to draw in material from Q and Paul. To explain the widespread presence that he finds of the common model in the New Testament, he must assume its existence around the turn of the era.[105] In a similar conclusion to the question of context, Boccaccini

---

103. Another approach to Enochic Judaism is found in the work of Carsten Colpe. In discussing the identification of Enoch as the Son of Man at the end of the Parables, Colpe has already suggested that the work is the product of a group that gives Son of Man eschatology concrete form by identifying its hero, Enoch, as Son of Man and universal Judge, in a manner analogous to early Christianity. See Colpe, "'Ο υἱὸς τοῦ ἀνθρώπου," 427.

104. Theisohn, *Der auserwählte Richter,* and Walck, "The Son of Man in the Parables of Enoch and the Gospels."

105. Nickelsburg, "Son of Man."

examines the interaction of various paradigms in the context of ancient Judaism and Christianity and places the Parables parallel to the origin of the Christian movement, making it the presupposition for the theology of Paul.[106]

Other approaches to the selection of comparative texts place the Parables in contexts that open the door to possible dates beyond the destruction of Jerusalem in 70 C.E. Kraft's methodological principle, that investigation needs to begin with the process of preservation of the pseudepigraphic text, is fundamentally sound.[107] With regard to the Parables, it is particularly of relevance, since that section of 1 Enoch is preserved only in the Ethiopic version. Kraft recommends that we eliminate a context in Gnosticism before seeking one in pre-70 Judaism. His suggestion that a possible connection with Gnosticism should be investigated is worth pursuing by someone with the proper credentials.

Parallel to the suggestion of a context in Gnosticism is my argument that the Parables of Enoch belongs to the early stages of the Hekhalot tradition. That possibility is strengthened by the contributions of Gieschen and Boyarin. Gieschen uses a different model than Nickelsburg to place the Parables in the context of angelomorphic Christology, in which the second figure in the heavenly scene is taken as a visible hypostasis of the Transcendent. He treats the Son of Man passages in relation to Jubilees, the Testament of Abraham, and 3 Enoch.[108] Boyarin follows a similar approach, relating the Parables to the rabbinic debate over two powers in heaven.[109] Although linking the Parables to the Hekhalot tradition does not yield an absolute date, it does open a window of possibility to the period after the fall of Jerusalem.

While Milik's argument, that the Parables of Enoch is a Christian work composed in Greek in the third century C.E., has been soundly and unanimously rejected, and a clear majority of specialists argues for a date at the turn of the era, I maintain that we are not yet in a position to rule out a date after the destruction of Jerusalem. The nature of the evidence and the existence of divergent methodologies for its assessment are such that the appropriate date and context of the Parables continue to elude us.

---

106. Boccaccini, "Finding a Place for the Parables of Enoch within Second Temple Jewish Literature."
107. Kraft, "The Pseudepigrapha in Christianity."
108. Gieschen, "The Name of the Son of Man in the Parables of Enoch."
109. Boyarin, "Was the Book of Parables a Sectarian Document?"

# Enoch's Date in Limbo; or, Some Considerations on David Suter's Analysis of the Book of Parables

*Michael E. Stone*

In his essay in the current volume, David Suter offers a clear, balanced, and sensible analysis of the various arguments for dating the Parables of Enoch.[1] Overall, I am in agreement with his summary that the Book of Parables was written either toward the turn of the millennium or in the late first century C.E., which excludes R. H. Charles's argument for dating the document before the Roman period,[2] as well as Josef Milik's suggestion that the Book of Parables dates to the third century C.E.[3] As I argued together with the late Jonas Greenfield many years ago, I would probably tend to favor "the turn of the millennium," albeit with some hesitation.[4] Rather than rehashing or adding to my earlier study of this issue, I would like in the following essay to reflect on several key issues emerging from Suter's analysis.

1. See above, D. W. Suter, "Enoch in Sheol: Updating the Dating of the Book of Parables." All quotations from Suter refer to this essay.

2. R. H. Charles, "The Book of Enoch," in *The Apocrypha and Pseudepigrapha of the Old Testament*, vol. 2, *Pseudepigrapha*, ed. Robert Henry Charles (Oxford: Clarendon, 1913), 163-281. Charles's thesis has been more recently reiterated by G. Bampfylde, "The Similitudes of Henoch: Historical Allusions," *JSJ* 15 (1984): 9-31, and M. Black, *The Book of Enoch, or, I Enoch: A New English Edition with Commentary and Textual Notes*, SVTP 7 (Leiden: Brill, 1985).

3. J. T. Milik, *The Books of Enoch: Aramaic Fragments of Qumrân Cave 4* (Oxford: Clarendon, 1976), esp. chap. 3. His views were first aired in detail in J. T. Milik, "Problèmes de la littérature Hénochique à la lumière des fragments araméens de Qumrân," *HTR* 64 (1971): 333-78.

4. J. C. Greenfield and M. E. Stone, "The Enochic Pentateuch and the Date of the Similitudes," *HTR* 70 (1977): 51-65; reprinted in M. E. Stone, *Selected Studies in the Pseudepigrapha with Special Reference to the Armenian Tradition*, SVTP 9 (Leiden: Brill, 1991), 198-212.

## Explicit Historical References?

The first thought that occurs to me is that the dating of the Parables is such a central issue for only one reason: the title Son of Man and its occurrence in the Gospels. This is apparent, for example, in Paolo Sacchi's recent article on the date of the Parables,[5] as well as in Suter's presentation of the scholarly consensus. I wonder how we would approach this question if the title had not been used in the Gospels or, alternatively, if the Gospels were not the canonical writings of Christianity. Naturally, the transformation of the Hebrew/Aramaic expression and its application to a redeemer figure is a totally legitimate object of scholarly investigation. Yet, perhaps few would zealously attempt to reach chronological precision with such meager evidence had the title not occurred in the Gospels.[6] Such intellectual energy is not expended on the dating of the Testament of Job, the Paralipomena of Jeremiah, or the Greek Baruch. I also wonder if this quest for a precise date of the Parables has produced fruitful results.

The question of the Parthian invasion that ostensibly appears in 1 En 56:5-8 is a case in point. If the reference to the Parthians and Medes is a real historical reference, then 56:5-8 anchors us to a specific event that occurred in 40 B.C.E., which then becomes the date *post quem* for the Parables. I tend to think that this is the case, at least in general terms.[7] True, as Michael Knibb remarked, the Parthians were a major opponent, perhaps the major opponent, of the Roman Empire for some centuries.[8] So is it possible that the Parthians function here as a stereotypical enemy likely to come and wreak havoc in accordance with this or that eschatological expectation? This Enoch reference and Sib Or 4:124 and 5:438 are the only mentions of the name "Parthian(s)" in Charles's *Apocrypha and Pseudepigrapha of the Old Testament*. I am not familiar with other symbolic references to the Parthians, though there may be some. Nevertheless, Rome, once it emerged on the scene, functioned as *the* great and stereotypical enemy. Thus it is likely (though not completely decisive) that the specific reference to the Parthians and Medes in the Parables is historically significant.[9] As I remarked

---

5. P. Sacchi, "Qumran e la datazione del Libro delle Parabole di Enoc," *Hen* 25 (2003): 149-66; in English, "Qumran and the Dating of the Book of Parables," in *The Bible and the Dead Sea Scrolls*, ed. J. H. Charlesworth (Waco: Baylor University Press, 2006).

6. The fact that the title occurs in the Gospels, of course, caused scholars to give priority to the study of this issue, but the results of that study may well have been the same.

7. Greenfield and Stone, "Enochic Pentateuch," in *Studies*, 205-6.

8. M. Knibb, "The Date of the Parables of Enoch: A Critical Review," *NTS* 25 (1979): 345-59.

9. On the expression "Parthians and Medes," see Greenfield and Stone, in *Studies*, 205.

elsewhere, "it may be futile to try to seek detailed historical references, for the use of biblical verses and the contrast between sinners and the elect in [56:] v. 8 clearly marked the section 56:5-8 not as objective history but as highly subjective interpretation of history."[10] So although I tend to view this as a historical allusion, I nevertheless remain somewhat skeptical.

As for King Herod at Callirrhoe, supposedly referred to in 1 En 67:4-13, if the date in the latter part of the first century C.E. is accepted on the basis of 56:5-8, then it may well be that Herod is referred to in 67:4-13.[11] On its own, however, this passage is not decisive for dating.

The absence of the destruction of Jerusalem does seem significant in a work predicting so much woe, but one can surely find works written indubitably after the destruction that do not refer to it (e.g., the Testament of Abraham). So much for explicit historical references.

### The Absence of the Parables from Qumran

The second main issue I wish to address is the absence of the Parables from Qumran, which some scholars have taken very seriously. Suter remarks that Sacchi and Gabriele Boccaccini "explain the absence of the Parables from Qumran not as an accident of history but as the consequence of the parting of the ways between Enochic Judaism and Qumranic Essenism."[12] Greenfield and I noted in 1977 that the absence of a document from Qumran *proves* nothing, certainly with regard to the date of the "missing" text.[13] The book of Esther is not there, nor is 2 Chronicles, but for a fragment. It seems doubtful whether the absence of a work reflects ideological or theological incompatibility between the views of the Qumran sect and the authors of the work.

Here I must add that just because a work has not been identified at Qumran, we should not immediately conclude that it did not exist there. Simple consideration of the number of unidentified fragments, running into the thousands, renders such an assertion dubious. Many works have simply not been identified. In general, then, the rule should be that absence from Qumran

---

10. Greenfield and Stone, in *Studies*, 206.

11. Greenfield and Stone, in *Studies*, 207, comparing Josephus, *Ant* 17.171-73; *War* 1.657-58. Cf. now, below, D. Hannah, "The Book of Noah, the Death of Herod the Great, and the Date of the Parables of Enoch."

12. Cf. Sacchi, "Qumran e la datazione del Libro delle Parabole di Enoc," and G. Boccaccini, *Beyond the Essene Hypothesis: The Parting of the Ways between Qumran and Enochic Judaism* (Grand Rapids: Eerdmans, 1998).

13. Greenfield and Stone, in *Studies*, 202.

proves nothing. Positive evidence, however, such as the *presence* of a work at Qumran, is certainly probative. Sacchi wonders "why all Apocrypha (i.e. Pseudepigrapha) written after 100 B.C.E. are lacking in the Qumran library."[14] Indeed, the absence of such works is intriguing. The question has relevance for numerous texts beyond the Parables, including the Psalms of Solomon, the present form of the Testament of Moses, the *Liber antiquitatum biblicarum* (i.e., Pseudo-Philo), among others. However, whether a supposed parting of the ways between Enochic and Qumranic Judaism offers a viable explanation is another matter. We simply do not know. Likewise, we could also ask why nonsectarian writings preserved only at Qumran are not transmitted in other Jewish and Christian channels.

The question of the provenance of the Parables within Jewish society of the Second Temple period is still debated. David Flusser observed many years ago that the Book of Parables, even if known, would not have been acceptable to the sectarians of Qumran because of the manner in which the sun and moon are treated in chap. 41, which accords equal status to both luminaries in contrast to the superiority of the sun in the various Qumran writings.[15]

If any weight is given to Flusser's observation, then the Parables did not originate within the Qumran sect, a view that accords with its absence from identified Qumran works (but note my caveats above about this argument). Greenfield and I noted that the Book of Parables employs sectarian terminology that seems to hint at a distinct social context.[16] Yet it is difficult to do more than speculate about the specific identity of that (sectarian?) context. The spread of Enoch traditions through the many streams of Second Temple Judaism indicates that we are dealing with a widespread phenomenon, both chronologically and geographically. For example, such diverse texts as Sir 44:6, the grandson's translation of the same, Pseudo-Eupolemus,[17] the Testament of Abraham, and the Slavonic Enoch all incorporate Enoch traditions. I am presently engaged in a study of Enoch traditions in early Armenian literature,

---

14. Sacchi, "Qumran e la datazione del Libro delle Parabole di Enoc."

15. D. Flusser, cited by J. C. Greenfield, "Prolegomenon," in H. Odeberg, *3 Enoch or the Hebrew Book of Enoch* (reprint, New York: Ktav, 1973), xi-xlvii (esp. xvii-xviii). Nathaniel Schmidt remarked that there seem to be no Byzantine quotations of the Parables and no surviving Greek text. He uses this to support the view that no Greek translation ever existed and that the Ethiopic was made directly from Aramaic. See N. Schmidt, "The Original Language of the Parables of Enoch," in *Old Testament and Semitic Studies in Memory of William Rainey Harper*, ed. Robert F. Harper et al. (Chicago: University of Chicago Press, 1908), 2:329-49. The issue is discussed in Stone, *Studies*, 207-8 (= Greenfield and Stone, "Enochic Pentateuch," 60-61).

16. Greenfield and Stone, "Enochic Pentateuch," in *Studies*, 202-3.

17. See also the remarks of B. Z. Wacholder, *Eupolemus: A Study of Judaeo-Greek Literature* (Cincinnati: Hebrew Union College, 1974), 74-77.

where very distinct and characteristic material is transmitted.[18] The spread of the Book of the Giants to Manichean circles is another indication of the broad familiarity with Enochic materials.[19]

## The Son of Man in the Parables and in 4 Ezra

A number of essays in this volume mention 4 Ezra 13 in connection with the development of the Son of Man ideas. In my doctoral thesis in 1965 and in a number of subsequent publications,[20] I proposed the hypothesis that a preexisting description of an expected cosmic human figure, whom we call the "Son of Man," was taken over by the author of 4 Ezra, who treated it as a symbolic vision and wrote an interpretation of it.[21] This was demonstrated by detailed textual and literary arguments. It is relevant to our discussion that the first part of the chapter, a preexisting tradition dealing with the Son of Man (13:1-11), was treated by the author of 4 Ezra (ca. 95 C.E.) as a symbolic vision to which he needed to write an interpretation.

The warrior "man" of the vision is described using ancient cosmic symbolism of the epiphanies of God, particularly his epiphanies as warrior. The interpretation suppressed the cosmic dimensions of the "man" and treated him as a symbol that needed explanation, just like "the lion" in 4 Ezra 12, or 2 Baruch's

---

18. Compare already the remarks by W. L. Lipscomb, *The Armenian Apocryphal Adam Literature*, University of Pennsylvania Armenian Texts and Studies 8 (Atlanta: Scholars, 1990), 99-101, who gives some fascinating preliminary indications. The matter is, however, much more complex.

19. It is not ad rem to survey this issue here, but I must mention John Reeves's excellent work and the brilliant pioneering paper of W. B. Henning. See J. C. Reeves, *Jewish Lore in Manichaean Cosmology: Studies in the Book of the Giants Traditions*, HUCM 14 (Cincinnati: Hebrew Union College, 1989); W. B. Henning, "The Book of the Giants," *BSOAS* 2 (1943): 52-74; and Henning, "Ein Manichäisches Henochbuch," *SPAW* 13 (1934): 27-35. The Qumran connection was recognized and first documented by J. T. Milik, "Turfân et Qumran. Livre des Géants juif et manichéen," in *Tradition und Glaube: Das frühe Christentum in seiner Umwelt*, ed. K. G. Kuhn et al. (Göttingen: Vandenhoeck & Ruprecht, 1971).

20. The thesis was submitted in 1965 but published after the conclusion of my Hermeneia Fourth Ezra commentary: M. E. Stone, *Features of the Eschatology of IV Ezra*, HSS 35 (Atlanta: Scholars, 1989). The analysis of chap. 13 was taken up again in M. E. Stone, "The Concept of the Messiah in IV Ezra," in *Religions in Antiquity: Essays in Memory of Erwin Ramsdell Goodenough*, ed. J. Neusner (Leiden: Brill, 1968), 295-312, and most recently in M. E. Stone, *Fourth Ezra: A Commentary on the Book of Fourth Ezra*, Hermeneia (Minneapolis: Fortress, 1990), 381-407.

21. In fact, the term "son of man" is found neither in the vision nor in the interpretation. I have argued, however, that it is most reasonable to hypothesize that this human figure was the anticipated Son of Man.

"light and dark waters." Moreover, the elements the interpretation adds in its presentation of the redeemer figure are precisely those that have close connections with the rest of 4 Ezra.

The implications of this analysis for our present concern are the following.

1. The vision of chap. 13 is older than 4 Ezra, although we do not know how much older. If the identification of the "man" in this vision with the Son of Man is accepted, then the vision should be treated as a separate source featuring this figure, quite distinct from the interpretation offered by the author of 4 Ezra. It cannot be treated as a product of the late first-century author of 4 Ezra, nor should it be exegeted in light of that book.
2. It seems to me that the interpretation could have treated the man of the vision as a symbol only at a time when the Son of Man concept no longer dictated its own meaning, at least in the circles that produced 4 Ezra. After all, the interpretation plays down or removes all the special, cosmic features of the figure. This implies that, at the end of the first century C.E., the expected eschatological human figure was no longer readily recognized.

To conclude, I would add, as Suter did, that there is something to be said for establishing a relative typology on the basis of the development of religious ideas. Certain of our number do exactly this with the Son of Man. The establishment of such a developmental series involves all sorts of presuppositions, which must be anchored in textual and literary critical study. The treatment of the Son of Man in the interpretation of 4 Ezra is typologically later than the Parables and the Gospels. Is this difference to be explained chronologically, assuming a more or less direct genetic relation, or is it to be explained by social (or even geographical) differences?

The date of the Parables may remain in limbo, then, as Suter rightly remarks, but in my judgment we will not be far wrong if we put it in the latter part of the first century B.C.E., or somewhat later. What sort of Judaism the Book of Parables represents, however, is another mystery.

# Can We Discern the Composition Date of the Parables of Enoch?

*James H. Charlesworth*

## Purpose

The purpose of this essay is to seek to discern the date when the Book of Parables of Enoch was most likely composed. In the process I shall introduce a new argument for dating this challenging work.

## Preliminary Observations

### The Unity of 1 Enoch 37–71

Many experts in Second Temple Judaism have assumed that Robert H. Charles, in 1893, correctly judged chap. 71 to be "most certainly a later addition" and that the "title 'Son of Man' is used in an absolutely different sense in this chapter."[1] Years later, in the second edition of his work, Charles changed his mind. He correctly concluded that chap. 71 is not an addition: "LXXI. This chapter seems to belong to the Parables, though in the first edition I thought otherwise."[2]

That the last chapters or the last chapter is an addition does not seem to be a tenable position. First, there is no manuscript evidence for an addition. Second, Charles saw reasons to abandon his first suggestion. Third, if the elevation of Enoch in chaps. 70–71 is foreshadowed in chaps. 37–69, then 1 En 70 and

---

1. R. H. Charles, *The Book of Enoch* (Oxford: Clarendon, 1893), 183.
2. R. H. Charles, *The Book of Enoch*, 2nd ed. (Oxford: Clarendon, 1912), 142.

71 must have been intended by the author when he supplied foreshadowing while composing chaps. 37–69.³

## Who Is the Son of Man?

Charles offered a translation that was the vade mecum of scholars from about 1913 until 1983: "This is the Son of Man who is born unto righteousness...."⁴

How could Charles obtain such a misleading translation? He claimed that he had "restored" the text. Yet, almost a century later, with a considerable increase in manuscript evidence for 1 Enoch, no manuscript has been discovered that can support such a restoration.

Why did Charles's advice darken counsel? It was because scholars were misled. They assumed that chap. 71 might be a later addition and that in this chapter Enoch is urged to look toward some figure who is announced to be that Son of Man.

## Is the Document Known as the Parables of Enoch a Christian Composition?

Another savant of 1 Enoch also misled experts on Second Temple Judaism and Christian origins. For decades Josef Milik claimed to be able to demonstrate that the Aramaic fragments of Enoch found in the Qumran caves would prove that the Book of Parables was a Christian composition that considerably postdated the first century C.E. Note Milik's words: "In conclusion, it is around the year A.D. 270 or shortly afterwards that I would place the composition of the Book of Parables."⁵ Today many scholars incorrectly assume that the judgment that the Book of Parables is a Christian work is a consensus among the experts of Second Temple Judaism. Yet in 1977, during a congress of specialists on 1 Enoch, no one agreed with Milik that the work is Christian.⁶

---

3. I raised this point during the last sessions of the Third Enoch Seminar at Camaldoli, and all present seemed to agree, including some specialists — like John Collins — who in the past had argued that 1 En 70 and 71 are redactional.

4. R. H. Charles, ed., *The Apocrypha and Pseudepigrapha of the Old Testament in English* (Oxford: Clarendon, 1913), 237.

5. J. T. Milik, *The Books of Enoch: Aramaic Fragments of Qumrân Cave 4* (Oxford: Clarendon, 1976), 96.

6. See J. H. Charlesworth, "1977 (Tübingen; Eberhard-Karls Universität): The Books of Enoch" and "1978 (Paris; Châtenay-Malabry): 1 (Ethiopic) Enoch and Luke and the Dating of the Parables of Enoch," in *The Old Testament Pseudepigrapha and the New Testament*, SNTSMS

James H. Charlesworth

## Philology

One of the main problems in working on the Parables of Enoch is the fact that it is preserved only in Ethiopic and in late medieval copies. It seems obvious that this text derives from an earlier Aramaic text. Hence, one eye should be on the Ethiopic text and another on the putative Aramaic original.

The Aramaic *bar 'ĕnāš,* "the Son of Man" (or "the son of man"),[7] and *bar nāšâ,* which also means "the Son of Man" (or "the son of man"), possess virtually identical meanings in Aramaic documents and sometimes merely represent different dialectics. No morphological or grammatical key is provided to help translators or exegetes to discern if the words are intended generically for the human, a technical term, or a title. We have no proof that the words should be capitalized, since capitalization does not appear in Aramaic. How should scholars discern what is intended by the implied author? What philological or contextual evidence helps the scholar to comprehend that an expression has become a *terminus technicus* and then a title? These are questions that should be kept in mind as we continue.

## Seeking the Date of Composition for the Parables of Enoch

The Book of Parables reinterprets and expands on Daniel's vision of "one like a son of man." This document certainly reflects a significant development in the Jewish understanding of Dan 7.[8] The work is thus to be dated after 164 B.C.E., when Daniel reached its present form.

The Book of Parables constitutes the second vision of Enoch. The document is preserved in the books of Enoch, which are a library of books attributed to Enoch by a group of Jews living in Palestine, most likely in Galilee (as we shall see). The earliest portions of this work, especially chaps. 1–36, were

---

54 (Cambridge, U.K., and New York: Cambridge University Press, 1985), 102-10. For the Italian version, see *Gli pseudepigrafi dell'Antico Testamento e il Nuovo Testamento,* ed. and trans. G. Boccaccini, Studi Biblici 91 (Brescia: Paideia, 1990), 224-36.

7. In Aramaic the construct state indicates almost always determination. To denote indetermination of the first element in a genitive construction, an Aramaic scribe tended to indicate a circumlocution. See F. Rosenthal, *A Grammar of Biblical Aramaic,* rev. ed. (Wiesbaden: Otto Harrassowitz, 1963), 25. In Aramaic the emphatic or determined state is not simply identical to the meaning of the English noun with an article. In the Targumim and midrashim, as in Syriac, the emphatic state has sometimes lost its definite meaning.

8. See esp. G. W. E. Nickelsburg, *1 Enoch: A Commentary on the Book of 1 Enoch* (Minneapolis: Fortress, 2001).

*Can We Discern the Composition Date of the Parables of Enoch?*

composed about 300 B.C.E. This apparent and new consensus was announced recently.[9] The latest document in the Enoch corpus is clearly the Parables of Enoch. In the following pages I shall summarize why a date for the Parables of Enoch during the time of Herod the Great (40-4 B.C.E.) or the early decades of the first century C.E. is most plausible.

In 1 En 37–71 (the Parables of Enoch) we find references to the Elect One, the Righteous One, the Messiah or the Anointed One, and the Son of Man (if that is the proper translation of the Ethiopic). All these may be imagined by the implied author as the same figure, since the functions are virtually identical (cf. Black, VanderKam, and Nickelsburg).[10] In chap. 53 the Righteous One is clearly identified as the Elect One. In chap. 61 the Elect One is placed "on the throne of glory" by the "Lord of the Spirits," which is a unique name for God. This name for God is found only in the Parables of Enoch, and it appears there over one hundred times.

In chap. 62 the Elect One is shown seated on the heavenly throne. All the mighty on the earth are called to acknowledge and salute the enthroned Elect One. God is then disclosed to be "the One who hides himself." At this point, in chap. 62, we first hear about the Son of Man, although Enoch is a "son of man" who will know "hidden things" in 60:10. The Son of Man was hidden "from the beginning." He is thus introduced as sharing qualities with God, since both are said to be hidden. He is now revealed to the elect on earth. All, even mighty kings, will fall down and worship the Son of Man.

In the final days — the days of judgment — sinners will be ashamed before the Son of Man. In the third parable of Enoch, found in chap. 69, all judgment is given to the Son of Man. Eventually the Son of Man seats himself on "the throne of glory." He is thus either identified with the Elect One or revealed to be the Elect One. One may not be able to discern which meaning was intended by the implied author. It is certain, nevertheless, that subsequently many Jews would imagine that the Son of Man is the Elect One.

Enoch is a human — a "son of man" — according to 1 En 70:1. His name is raised up before the Lord of the Spirits. With the exception of chap. 71, during the writing and compiling of the compositions now found in 1 Enoch no person is identified as the Son of Man. No clear evidence is given that Enoch might be the Son of Man, even though his divine nature evolves through the centuries of speculation and reflection, and is clearly foreshadowed in chaps. 37–69.

---

9. Charlesworth, "The Books of Enoch or 1 Enoch Matters: New Paradigms for Understanding Pre-70 Judaism," in *Enoch and Qumran Origins: New Light on a Forgotten Connection*, ed. G. Boccaccini (Grand Rapids: Eerdmans, 2005), 437-54.

10. See their reflections in *The Messiah: Developments in Earliest Judaism and Christianity*, ed. James H. Charlesworth (Minneapolis: Fortress, 1992).

The elevation of Enoch continues and reaches its zenith in chap. 71. That is, the climax of the Book of Parables comes in the final chapter. He is greeted by "that angel," who seems to be Michael, who has come to Enoch along with "that Head of Days," Gabriel, Raphael, Phanuel, and countless other angels. Michael seems then to be the one who speaks to Enoch. Here are his words to him (1 En 71:14):

> You are the Son of Man who was born to righteousness,
> and righteousness remains over you,
> and the righteousness of the Head of Days will not leave you.
> (Knibb, 1978)[11]

> Tu sei il figlio dell'uomo nato per la giustizia
> e la giustizia ha dimorato in te
> e la giustizia del Capo dei Giorni non ti abbandonerà. (Fusella, 1981)[12]

> You, son of man, who art born in righteousness
> and upon whom righteousness has dwelt,
> the righteousness of the Antecedent of Time will not forsake you.
> (Isaac, 1983)[13]

> You are the Son of Man who is born for righteousness,
> And righteousness abides upon you,
> And the righteousness of the Chief of Days forsakes you not.
> (Black, 1985)[14]

> You are the Son of Man who is born to righteousness,
> and righteousness has remained with you.
> The righteousness of the Antecedent of Days
> will not forsake you. (Olson, 2004)[15]

---

11. M. Knibb, *The Ethiopic Book of Enoch: A New Edition in the Light of the Aramaic Dead Sea Fragments*, 2 vols. (Oxford: Clarendon, 1978), 2:166.

12. L. Fusella, in *Apocrifi dell'Antico Testamento*, ed. P. Sacchi (Turin: UTET, 1981), 1:571-72.

13. E. Isaac, in *The Old Testament Pseudepigrapha*, ed. J. H. Charlesworth (Garden City, N.Y.: Doubleday, 1983), 1:50.

14. M. Black, *The Book of Enoch, or, I Enoch: A New English Edition with Commentary and Textual Notes*, SVTP 7 (Leiden: Brill, 1985), 68.

15. D. Olson, *Enoch: A New Translation* (North Richland Hills, Tex.: BIBAL, 2004), 135.

## Can We Discern the Composition Date of the Parables of Enoch?

> You are that son of man who was born for righteousness,
> and righteousness dwells on you,
> and the righteousness of the Head of Days will not forsake you.
> (Nickelsburg and VanderKam, 2004)[16]

All the recent translations reveal that Enoch is the Son of Man (or that son of man). It is clear that Enoch is called to a higher celestial status than he had formerly not only as patriarch in the Hebrew Bible but also in the earlier, though not preceding, sections of 1 Enoch (the various books in Ethiopic Enoch are not arranged in chronological order). Enoch is now revealed to be the heavenly Man, the Son of Man.

Most likely, 4 Ezra also is important for understanding the reinterpretation of Dan 7. 4 Ezra 13 contains a reference to one like the figure of a man who comes out of the sea. He is revealed to be the Messiah. The original Hebrew text most likely mentioned "the Son of Man," but only Latin *(ille homo* and *vir)* and Syriac *(bar nasha* and *gabra)* manuscripts preserve this pseudepigraphon. It is also difficult to use this text for Jesus since it postdates 70 C.E. It is judicious not to base conclusions regarding the meaning of pre-70 Son of Man traditions on 4 Ezra, but it is also wise to keep this text in perspective since it clearly preserves traditions that antedate 70.

We may now revisit the conclusion that 1 En 37–71 is Jewish. There is no obvious "Christian" thought in these chapters. Jesus is never mentioned and there is no allusion to him. The Son of Man is certainly not Jesus. The Son of Man is revealed, in the final scene, to be none other than Enoch.

What date should be given, or imagined, for the Parables of Enoch? Does it antedate Jesus and the Evangelists? Five reasons disclose a dating of this work to the time of Herod and the Herodians: (1) the insignificance of the fact that no fragment has been identified of this work among the hundreds of thousands of fragments found in the Qumran caves; (2) the late composition of the document within 1 Enoch; (3) the fact that it was not composed at Qumran; (4) the reference to a Parthian invasion; and (5) the curse on the landowners.

First, one cannot claim this document was absent or unknown at Qumran. One may only point out that no fragment of the Parables of Enoch has been identified among the Qumran fragments. This fact may be insignificant for numerous reasons. Many compositions are not found there, including Esther, 1 Maccabees, and the Psalms of Solomon. Some biblical or ancient Jewish documents are clearly preserved in extremely minuscule, fragile fragments

---

16. G. W. E. Nickelsburg and J. C. VanderKam, *1 Enoch: A New Translation* (Minneapolis: Fortress, 2004), 95.

— some of these disintegrated before they were identified. Over one hundred fragments remain unidentified within the Qumran corpus (there are also fragments still unavailable to scholars [at least two of them belong to 1 Enoch and both are from chaps. 1–36]).

Significantly, less than 20 percent or conceivably 10 percent of what was placed in the Qumran caves in 68 C.E. is available for us to study. Let me illustrate this point that has not been adequately perceived by scholars, including Qumranologists. The Bedouin reportedly found in Cave 1 seven manuscripts, but the archaeologists recovered fragments from over seventy documents once hidden in this cave. From Cave 2 comes very little, and maybe there was once more in this cave. Cave 3, which was discovered by R. de Vaux, preserved a few documents, most notably the Copper Scroll. Cave 4 (which is two caves because they were found at the same time and de Vaux numbered both "Cave 4" since he knew it would be impossible to distinguish the provenience of a fragment) produced only thousands of fragments of what had been full scrolls. There may have been four hundred documents in those two caves, but it is conceivable that we have only about 2 percent of what had been placed there.[17] Caves 5, 6, 7, 8, 9, and 10, most of which had collapsed centuries before they were discovered, produced only minuscule fragments. We can only speculate how many manuscripts they once contained. From Cave 11 come some large scrolls, as from Cave 1, but certainly no expert will state that we have all of what was hidden in that cave. Near Cave 5 are at least two "caves" that collapsed centuries ago; thus, we cannot now know what documents may have been placed in them. Obviously, if Josephus was allowed by Titus to take some scrolls to Rome (as he mentions in his *Life*), he and others in the Roman army most likely took with them some scrolls that had been hidden in caves near Qumran that were then visible and most likely easily accessible with stairs and wooden bridges.

Cumulatively, perhaps we possess only about 10 to 20 percent of the manuscripts that were in the Qumran caves before, or in, June 68 C.E. Thus, the absence of identifiable fragments of the Parables of Enoch from Qumran is neither remarkable nor a viable reason for dating the composition.[18]

---

17. Not well-known are two facts. The Bedouin do not know the caves by number. They also began to report that all fragments they still possessed were from Cave 4, since these were now deemed more valuable.

18. J. C. Greenfield and M. E. Stone also rightly dismiss the argument that the absence of a book among the Qumran fragments is data for dating a book. See Greenfield and Stone, "The Enochic Pentateuch and the Date of the Similitudes," *HTR* 70 (1977): 51-66. To be jettisoned from their argument, however, is the claim that the calendar would not be at home at Qumran. We now know that mixed calendars were known at Qumran.

## Can We Discern the Composition Date of the Parables of Enoch?

Far more disconcerting for dating the Parables of Enoch to the Herodian period than the absence of identifiable fragments among the Qumran corpus is the absence of quotations of this document in the early scholars of the church. How can one explain this fact? This question is not easy to answer.

Perhaps the early scholars of the church considered the document polemical. For them the Book of Parables was most likely not a source for explaining the origins of the Christian affirmation that ancient prophecy proved the divinity and messiahship of Jesus of Nazareth. These scholars may have reasoned that if Enoch is the Son of Man and identified as the Messiah, then it should not be translated from Aramaic to Greek or explored and mined for Christian kerygma and *didache*.

Second, if the Book of Parables was the latest composition in the corpus defined by 1 Enoch and was composed in Galilee, as seems evident now to many Enoch specialists, then the document might not have been known in Jerusalem or Judea before 68 C.E., and thence would not be expected to be present in the Qumran library.

Third, scholars agree that the Book of Parables was not composed at Qumran. It would have to be taken to Qumran by one who both was sympathetic to the ideas in the document and knew that its portrayal of Enoch would have been respected at Qumran. The ideas in the Rule of the Community are not conducive to the claim that the Messiah is to be identified as the Son of Man and, indeed, that these two are revealed by an archangel to be none other than Enoch. That would not fit with those who composed the pesherim and revered the Righteous Teacher. It would also not fit with the Davidic and Levitical concepts of the Messiah regnant at Qumran. The origin of Wisdom at Qumran, moreover, is not to be reduced to Enoch; recall that the Book of Parables identifies itself as "the vision of wisdom which Enoch . . . saw" (37:1).

Indeed, the manuscripts at Qumran that were not composed there and postdate the middle of the first century B.C.E. would have almost always been taken to Qumran by those who were close to Qumran theologies. The Parables of Enoch most likely would not have been a wise choice for someone coming to Qumran and seeking admission into the *Yaḥad*.

Why is that so? If the paleographical dating of the Qumran fragments of 1 Enoch is to be taken seriously, then the books of Enoch were important primarily for the early life of the Qumran community. More importantly, the Qumranites would not have agreed with the author's elevation of Enoch. Despite the diversity of thought at Qumran, it seems prima facie evident that the Qumranites would not have agreed with the claim that involved celebrating Enoch above Moses or the Righteous Teacher.

Fourth, the invasion mentioned in chap. 56 seems to refer to the Parthian invasion of 40 B.C.E.[19] Recall the passage in the Parables of Enoch: "the Parthians and Medes" will "come like lions from the lairs," and they will "trample upon the land of *my* chosen ones, and the land of *my* chosen ones will become before them a tramping-ground and a beaten track. But the city of my righteous ones (= Jerusalem) will be a hindrance to their horses" (56:6-7).

This invasion was lengthy and extensive, as we learn from Josephus in *Ant* 14. According to Josephus, Pacorus, the Parthian general and son of the Parthian king, assisted by Barzaphranes, the Parthian satrap, occupied Syria in 40 B.C.E. Meanwhile Judea was in a civil war, with the two rivals being Hasmoneans: Antigonus II and Hyrcanus II. The Parthians marched against Judea, with Pacorus proceeding along the coast and Barzaphranes invading the interior. Herod the Great and Phasael, his brother, were engaged in the battle. The Parthians around Jerusalem (*Ant* 14.344) put Hyrcanus and Phasael in chains but failed to trick and catch Herod. He and his family fled to Masada, and then the Parthians plundered Jerusalem and ravaged the countryside, even destroying Marisa (14.363-64). Eventually, the tide turned in favor of Herod.

Herod was declared "King of the Jews" by the Roman Senate in the same year (40). He had to fight against the Hasmoneans and the Parthians, who had invaded Palestine from the east and whom the Romans under Pompey and Antony never conquered. The Parthian invasion of 40 is now documented by recent excavations along the western littoral of the Dead Sea. While historians are left with the ambiguity of chap. 56, and the date of the Parthian invasion mirrored in the chapter, the most likely scenario, in light of Josephus's account and the archaeological excavations from Jericho to Ein Gedi, is the invasion in 40 B.C.E.[20] Thus the Parables of Enoch would postdate that event, but probably not

---

19. Paolo Sacchi contends rightly that 1 En 37–71 refers to an actual event, the Parthian invasion of 40 B.C.E., and that the Parables of Enoch should be dated shortly after that time. See P. Sacchi, "Qumran e la datazione del Libro delle Parabole di Enoc," *Hen* 25 (2003): 149-66; in English, "Qumran and the Dating of the Book of Parables," in *The Bible and the Dead Sea Scrolls*, ed. J. H. Charlesworth (Waco: Baylor University Press, 2006). See also, below, L. Arcari, "A Symbolic Transfiguration of a Historical Event: The Parthian Invasion in Josephus and the Parables of Enoch."

20. See A. Schalit, *König Herodes: Der Mann und Sein Werk*, SJ 4 (Berlin: De Gruyter, 1969), 74-80. Also see the evidence of this Parthian invasion in M. Mazar, T. Dothan, and I. Dunayevsky, *En-Gedi: The First and Second Seasons of Excavations, 1961-1962*, 'Atiqot English Series 5 (Jerusalem: Jerusalem Academic Press, 1966). The hoard of twenty bronze coins of Mattathias Antigonus (40-37 B.C.E.) discovered near the bathhouse and on the paved patio surrounding the swimming pools of the Hasmonean winter palace in Jericho are also, most likely, evidence of the Parthian invasion of 40 B.C.E. See E. Netzer, "Jericho — Exploration Since 1973," in *The New Encyclopedia of Archaeological Excavations in the Holy Land*, ed. Ephraim Stern (Jerusalem: Israel Exploration Society and Carta; New York: Simon and Schuster, 1993), 2:686;

by many years or decades, since, as with the reference to Pompey in PsSol 2, the crisis seems rather recent and still disturbing to the author, who seems to have remembered how the walls of Jerusalem had been "a hindrance to" the "horses" of the Parthians, who were famous for their skilled horsemanship. Thus, 1 En 56 may indicate that the Parables of Enoch should be dated within a generation of the Parthian invasion of 40 B.C.E.

Fifth, now let me introduce a final — and new — argument that may clinch the conclusion for dating the Parables of Enoch. Quite surprisingly, curses appear directed not only against kings and rulers but also against landowners. Note these excerpts (italics mine):[21]

> Those *"who possess the earth"* are the sinners who will be judged and condemned. (38:4)

> The "mighty kings" will be destroyed. (38:5)

> After a discourse on the desired place to dwell, the author notes that the Chosen One will make the ground a blessing so that the "chosen ones" may finally dwell on it. (45:5)

> When the Son of Man appears, he will destroy "the kings and the powerful from their resting-places," who along with "the strong" will be punished. (46:4)

> When the Son of Man appears, "the kings of the earth and *the strong who possess the dry ground* . . . will not save themselves." (48:8)

> At the time of judgment (presumably), "the kings and the powerful" will be thrown into a valley burning with fire. (54:1-2; cf. 55:4)

> The "kings and the mighty and *those who dwell upon the earth*" are the sinners and lawless ones who will be destroyed before the Lord of Spirit. (62:2)

> In that time of judgment, "all the kings and the mighty and the exalted, and *those who possess the earth*" or *"the land,"* will receive pain. (62:3-6)

---

Y. Meshorer, "Mattathias Antigonus," in *Ancient Jewish Coinage*, 2 vols. (New York: Amphora Books, 1982), 1:87-98; D. Hendin, "Mattathias Antigonus *(Mattatayah)*, 40 to 37 B.C.E.," in *Guide to Biblical Coins*, 3rd ed. (New York: Amphora Books, 1996), 93-99.

21. The translation is by Knibb, *The Ethiopic Book of Enoch*, vol. 2.

> At that time, "all the mighty kings, and the exalted, and *those who rule the dry ground*" will fall down and worship the Most High, setting their hopes now on the Son of Man. (62:9)
>
> "In those days *the mighty kings who possess the dry ground*" will beseech the angels of punishment, but they descend into the torments of Sheol. (63:1-10; cf. 63:12)

Among those condemned are kings and rulers. Well-known are the curses of kings and rulers in the Hebrew Bible. Notably, a king or kings are cursed in 1 Kings 21:10, 13; Isa 8:21; and Eccles 10:20. And, for example, a ruler or rulers are cursed in Exod 22:28 (cf. Lev 4:22; Prov 28:15). Most scholars rightly conclude that the words "the kings of the earth" in the Parables of Enoch clearly denote the Roman emperors. Are others also included for condemnation and final judgment?

It is clear that the Enochian community also suffered from those who were wealthy and oppressive. This phenomenon is not new in the Parables of Enoch. The suffering from the rich is also the case in earlier Enochic compositions. What is new in the Parables of Enoch and unrepresented in the earlier Enoch compositions?

According to the text of the Parables of Enoch, a new group is singled out for punishment. They are *the powerful or the strong that possess the land or "dry ground."* The Ethiopic word for "dry ground" can mean the division of the cosmos into the waters and the earth (or dry ground), but every good translator of the Ethiopic knows that one must keep in mind that the Ethiopic is a translation and the underlying Aramaic (or Hebrew) is not always accurately represented. Only to a certain extent does the expression "dry ground" reflect the Noah traditions that helped shape the final form of 1 Enoch; far more important is the sociological context of the text. Thus, the Ethiopic term for dry land should not be seen in terms only of creation or of Noah and the flood.

Sociologists have developed the insight that a text usually mirrors a social environment. Thus, those singled out for punishment are usually powerful people who have caused the author of a text, his group and related communities, to suffer. Studying the Parables of Enoch with historical and sociological imagination includes pondering who are the strong who control the *dry land* and cause Jews to suffer.

What is meant by the "dry ground" and who possesses or rules over it (48:8 and 63:1-10)?[22] Before the efforts of settlers in the nineteenth and early

---

22. Notably, in 1 En 62:1 some scribes changed "those who possess the earth" to "those

twentieth century to drain the swamps and marshes, Palestine was defined by two types of land: the dry land, and the swamps and marshes. Thus "the dry ground" in the Parables of Enoch most likely refers to the cultivatable land in distinction from the swamps. Where were swamps located? They defined the low country near the coast, the vast areas west of the Kinneret, and especially the land in the Hulah Valley. The latter was one long swamp that covered over thirty miles from Banias to Capernaum. One cannot imagine the area today when one looks down on the fertile valley below Rosh Pinna. The verdant area of Yesud HaMaʿala, north of Hazor and the Dishon stream, was until the last century a threatening swamp.

The dry ground was characterized by vineyards and farms that produced primarily grapes, wheat, and barley. The author of the Parables of Enoch laments that he and other Jews labor on such dry land and the strong, the sinners, eat of the produce of such land. The ground left to Jews would be the swamps — or nondry ground. These undesirable portions of the so-called Holy Land produced only snakes and insects. If one drained the swamp, it became dry ground and would be owned by the strong and mighty who "possess the dry ground" (48:8), who are also those who "rule the dry ground" (63:1-10). To the author these are sinners and lawless ones who will soon be judged and punished.

Note another translation of those who will be punished; they are "the mighty landowners" (48:8).[23] Perhaps with an intentional paronomasia, the author states that the landowners will be "like grass in the fire" so that they shall burn before the elect ones (48:9). Who are those who have caused the righteous to suffer? They seem to be those who have taken their land, since the "sinners" are the oppressors, and these are those who "eat all the produce of crime which the sinners toil for" (53:2). Who are those who eat the produce? It becomes clear at this point that those who toil for the produce of the land are the Jews who till the dry ground that is no longer theirs.

According to chap. 62 alone, the evil ones are "the kings, the governors, the high officials, and the landlords" (or "those who possess the earth").[24] In fact, this refrain appears no fewer than three times in this chapter (62:1, 3, 6). What stands out as an addition to a well-known topos (the cursing of kings and rulers) is the mentioning of "landlords." The formula appears again in 62:9, but this time the "landlords" are replaced by "those who rule the earth" (62:9). Who

---

who inhabit (or dwell on) the earth." See Nickelsburg and VanderKam, *1 Enoch*, 79. This alteration indicates that scribes did not understand the sociological meaning of taking and possessing the dry land, a setting now clarified by the present research.

23. See the translation by E. Isaac in *The Old Testament Pseudepigrapha*, vol. 1 (1983).
24. In *1 Enoch*, Nickelsburg and VanderKam prefer "those who possess the earth."

then are the "landlords" (Isaac), "those who possess the earth" (Knibb,[25] Nickelsburg, VanderKam), or "those who occupy the earth" (Olson)? It is clear that the author is thinking about those who would be punished in the eschatological judgment, since all of 1 En 62 is about the final judgment.

Such expectations not only fortify the hope of the oppressed, they also often mirror reality, especially disturbing conditions. Hence, we should explore further and seek to discern the author's vision. What is it?

The author dreams about being relieved of oppression, to be able to rise, to eat, and to rest with the Son of Man (62:14). The oppressors, the sinners, are the landowners who have taken food away from those who were promised the Land, the Jews. Soon these Jews, mirrored in the Parables of Enoch, will be able finally to rise, eat, and rest (62:14). We can imagine that many Jews in this Enochic community are obviously exhausted, hungry, and so oppressed that they can find no rest. The historian who is influenced by sociological research is trained to balance data and distinguish the conceivable from the probable. Who are the ones who rule the dry ground?

The answer becomes clearer in the next chapter. Note how chap. 63 ends: "And thus says the Lord of Spirits: 'This is the law and the judgment for the mighty and the kings and the exalted, and for those who possess the dry ground, before the Lord of Spirits'" (63:12; Knibb). The emphasis falls on the last-named: "the landlords" or "those who possess the dry ground." The Jews of the Enoch community have lost their land to others; they can no longer be landlords. Who are those who possess the dry land, and how does such identification help us date this document?

We have seen that *those cursed are landowners*. Who are those who are repeatedly singled out for judgment and condemnation? Who are the powerful or the strong that possess the "dry ground"? Who are "those who rule the dry ground"? Those who own the dry land are clearly condemned by those who desire the dry land and have lost it.

What sociological crisis explains this curse on landowners or those who possess the dry ground? The most plausible explanation is the disenfranchisement experienced by many wealthy Palestinian Jews. And among these are the wealthy Hasmoneans. During the time of Herod the Great primarily, but also during the rule of his sons and grandsons, Palestinian Jews were losing their farms and becoming tenant farmers.

Herod the Great seized the estates of the Hasmoneans, and taxed the Jews heavily to support his massive building projects. Along with this taxation from

---

25. In 1 En 62:1 Knibb has "those who dwell upon the earth." This translation is identical to Charles's rendering in the second edition of *The Book of Enoch*.

the Herodians and the increase in money demanded by the sacerdotal aristocracy in Jerusalem, many Jews lost their farms or estates. They lost all the dry land, the cultivatable land. The tax collectors and their collaborating investigators raised the land tax *(tributum)* and demanded excessive additional payments so that Jews were becoming landless. That is to say, many of the Jews lost their land to Herod and his aristocrats; not only the small landholders but also many of the estate owners lost their land to Herod and his hierarchy (*Ant* 17.304-14).

Most of these new landowners were not Jews and lived away from the land they owned; they even lived outside the Land, as is evident in Jesus' parable of the wicked tenant farmers. The demotion of Jews from landowners to tenant farmers was exceptional during Herod's reign. This crisis may also add historical insight into the story or legend that Hillel established the *prozbol* so Jews would not become bankrupt.[26] Through taxation and intrigue, Herod and his hierarchy controlled virtually two-thirds of the fertile land by the time he died.

Other causes than taxation undermined the ability of Jews to make a profit from farming. For example, the great famine of 25 B.C.E., about twelve years after Herod finally defeated his main rivals at the Arbel, stunned many farmers so they could not afford to pay their debts. They lost their land, becoming either laborers or tenant farmers on what had been their ancestors' land.

The acquisition of land from Jews was extreme during Herod's reign. Herod's finance minister, Ptolemy, owned a whole village named Arous. A wealthy Jerusalemite, named Eleazar, even owned 1,000 villages.

This aspect of the economy of Herod's reign — that is, how he exacerbated the land tax on Palestinian Jews — is too well-known to document here.[27] Herod's taxation system was sometimes so severe that he had to remit portions of the taxes (*Ant* 15.365; 16.64). Complaints against severe taxation undermined and ended Archelaus's reign, and Jewish delegates complained to

---

26. This judgment seems evident even if Hillel is not the author of the *prozbol*. See C. Safrai, in *Hillel and Jesus*, ed. J. H. Charlesworth and L. L. Johns (Minneapolis: Fortress, 1997), 312-13.

27. See especially the following: M. Rostovtzeff, *The Social and Economic History of the Roman Empire*, rev. P. M. Fraser, 2nd ed., 2 vols. (Oxford: Clarendon, 1957); J. Jeremias, *Jerusalem in the Time of Jesus*, trans. F. H. Cave and C. H. Cave (Philadelphia: Fortress, 1969); J. Klausner, "The Economy of Judea in the Period of the Second Temple," in *The Herodian Period*, ed. M. Avi-Yonah and Z. Baras, World History of the Jewish People (Jerusalem and New Brunswick, N.J.: Rutgers University Press, 1957), 180-205; S. Applebaum, "Economic Life in Palestine," in *The Jewish People in the First Century*, ed. S. Safrai and M. Stern, CRINT I (Assen and Amsterdam: Van Gorcum, 1976), 2:631-700; D. E. Oakman, *Jesus and the Economic Questions of His Day*, Studies in the Bible and Early Christianity 8 (Lewiston, N.Y., and Queenston, Ont.: Mellon, 1986).

Caesar that the taxation had led to the "loss of their property," which primarily meant their farmland.

It is obvious how the loss of land would impact any farmer, especially a Jew who believed that his farm or estate was part of the Land he inherited through God's promise to Abraham. The loss of one's own land would be unbearable when a Jew knew he could no longer control the land on which he had buried his ancestors, including conceivably his father and mother. Without any doubt most scholars would perceive that such shocking developments would have left an impact on a text composed by a Palestinian Jew during the crisis.

This catastrophic event — the loss of Jewish land and property to Herod and other Roman quislings — appears, in my judgment, mirrored in the Parables of Enoch. Thus, we perceive the reason for the appearance of a new topos — cursing the strong who control the dry land. Therefore, we have discerned another reason why the Book of Parables was most likely composed sometime between 37 and 4 B.C.E. — and conceivably up until the first two decades of the first century C.E.

Archaeological excavations strengthen this conclusion focused on texts. The recent excavations help us understand that two-thirds of the desirable land (the dry land) was lost to the Herodian dynasty from the end of the first century B.C.E. to the first two decades of the first century C.E. The appearance of large, sumptuous manor houses and palatial abodes witnesses to a new development in the Herodian period. Extreme wealth, as in imperial Rome, is evident in ancient Palestine. Elegant glass wine-pourers and beautifully crafted wineglasses have been discovered in Sebaste. Gold and silver jewelry appears in many places, including Jerusalem. Bronze lion-faced decorations for wooden chests have been found not only in Pompeii and Herculaneum but also in Jerusalem. The concentration and monopolization of vast wealth by a few is witnessed in a poignant and palpable fashion throughout ancient Palestine, from the Herodian palaces in Dan to the extravagances southward, especially at Ramat Hannadiv north of Caesarea Maritima, the coastal city of Caesarea, the Upper City of Herodian Jerusalem, and Herodian Jericho.

Almost all the new landlords were Romans and others who were considered pagans by Jews. When the Jewish author called them "the powerful" (1 En 46:4; 54–55), "the strong" (48:8), and "the mighty" (62:2), he revealed his feelings of impotence in a land that had been promised to him as a descendant of Abraham.

The author of the Parables of Enoch represents a Jewish community that yearns for another place, because of "those who rule the dry ground" (62:9 [Knibb]). The author hopes that "the Chosen One" will make the ground a blessing so that the "chosen ones" may finally dwell on it (45:5). While the

Qumran community and others yearned for the restoration of the Land promised to Abraham, the Enoch group finally suffered the loss of farming land, yearned for another place, and cursed those who stole the good land for farms and vineyards.

## Summary

The social condition mirrored by the author of the Parables of Enoch has become more clarified. It reflects more than many decades of Roman occupation. It probably best represents the period during the peak of King Herod's reign (20-4 B.C.E.), when more and more non-Jews are becoming landowners. What does that make Palestinian Jews? They are relegated to be tenant farmers.

"The kings of the earth" in the Parables of Enoch are clearly the Roman emperors, but some Jews may have included King Herod in that group since he was judged to be non-Jewish and perceived to be pro-Roman, even a Roman. Most scholars will have little difficulty perceiving that the Book of Parables is an anti-Herodian polemic. Herod the Great and his elite group have overtaxed the Jewish landowners and demoted them to tenant farmers.

The loss of land (and Land might be in the mind of the author and certainly some Palestinian readers of 1 En 37–71) would be monumentally significant for Jews who not only knew the promise to Abraham but also realized that their parents and forefathers were buried on the land, or vineyard, that they had once owned. This hatred and malice would have burned its way into our literature; most likely that sociological context shapes our text of the Parables of Enoch.

The cumulative result of recent research is monumental. The Book of Parables does not depend on the Gospels (as Milik claimed). Rather, the Evangelists either depend on this earlier Jewish apocalyptic work or are influenced by the traditions preserved in it. If the Gospels preserve echoes of Jesus' own words, and at times accurately preserve them, then "the Son of Man" is most likely an expression known to some Galilean Jews prior to Jesus' ministry in Galilee.

This conclusion seems to follow the probability that the provenience and origin of the books of Enoch is most likely in Galilee. For example, the Watchers do not descend on a spot in Judea. They descend on Mount Hermon in Upper Galilee. Moreover, the best location for those who live near swamps — nondry ground — and lament the loss of dry ground to the Herodians and their henchmen is the Hulah Valley, the large swampy area from Dan or Banias to Bethsaida or Capernaum.

*James H. Charlesworth*

## Prospect

If the Book of Parables is not only Jewish but re-presents the thought of some intellectually influential Jewish groups in Galilee, then we should revisit some allegedly closed debates among New Testament scholars. There seem to be reasons now to postulate that Jesus could have used the expression "Son of Man."

Interpretation of Jesus' sayings is the crucial issue and problem. We cannot discern if Jesus used the expression as a technical term or title. He may have chosen *bar nasha* ("Son of Man") because it was a vague concept and not a title. Thus, Jesus may have imagined that God was free to shape the Son of Man concept and define it. Hence, the term became a recognizable title only as Jesus' life was revealed to him and to those who witnessed to him.

In the Parables of Enoch the Son of Man is a celestial judge. It is significant that in the words attributed to Jesus, the Son of Man is assumed to be the judge at the end of times (cf. Mark 8:38; 13:24-27; esp. John 5:27). Is some relationship between the Jesus traditions and the Enoch traditions or texts revealed by this observation and perception?

As we seek to discern this possible link between the Parables of Enoch and the Gospels, it is helpful (perhaps imperative) to recognize the appearance of "the Son of God" at Qumran. Emile Puech told me in the Ecole Biblique de Jerusalem, as I was finalizing this paper, that he had become convinced that in the Qumran document entitled *An Aramaic Apocalypse* (or *Son of God* text), the person described as "the Son of God" is a messianic king. Like the Son of Man in the books of Enoch, the Son of God is primarily a judge. In the Gospels, Jesus is certainly portrayed both as the Son of God and the Son of Man. Despite advice to the contrary, neither refers to his human status. The Son of Man sayings in the Gospels frequently reveal the belief that Jesus, as the Son of Man, will serve as the cosmic judge at the day of judgment. To what extent are Jesus' traditions shaped here by Enoch traditions? Are the influences only on the later Evangelists?

Jesus is reputed to have said that the Son of Man has nowhere to lay his head (Matt 8:20; Luke 9:58; cf. Gos Thom Log. 86). That is, Jesus, using forms known from Wisdom literature (which can be found in the books of Enoch), is reported to have claimed that he cannot find a dwelling on earth. Moreover, he is reputed to have referred to himself as the Son of Man. It is significant, therefore, to perceive what the author of the Parables of Enoch states about Wisdom. This Jew presented as revelation the claim that "Wisdom could not find a place in which she could dwell" (42:1). Scholars will assess such parallels between Jesus and the books of Enoch differently. Some will see no relationship, many will appeal to common Jewish traditions, others will recognize some indirect influence, and perhaps a few will imagine that maybe Jesus knew this text or this

*Can We Discern the Composition Date of the Parables of Enoch?*

particular Enoch tradition. Perhaps Jesus discussed ideas, concepts, and terms with those in or related to the Enoch group.

## Conclusion

Five reasons disclose the most probable date for the Parables of Enoch. First, it is insignificant that no fragment of this document has been identified among the fragments found in the Qumran caves. Second, the Book of Parables is clearly the latest composition within 1 Enoch, and there are reasons to conclude it would not have sufficient time to make its way to Qumran. Third, the document was not composed at Qumran and contains concepts and perceptions that would not have been acceptable at Qumran. Fourth, the reference to a Parthian invasion makes best sense in light of what is known, from Josephus and archaeological research, about the invasion of 40 B.C.E. Fifth, the multitudinous curses on the landowners and those who monopolize the "dry land" make best sense during the period of the land grabbing by Herod and the Herodians. Cumulatively, then, dating the Parables of Enoch to the time of Herod the Great and the Herodians has become conclusive.[28]

The Book of Parables (1 En 37–71) appears to be a Jewish work that antedates Jesus, and the author seems to imagine a connection among the Messiah, the Righteous One, and the Son of Man. The work most likely took shape in Galilee, not far from where Jesus centered his ministry. He, thus, could have been influenced by this writing or the traditions preserved in the Parables of Enoch. In this case, his own self-understanding may have been shaped by the relationship between the Son of Man and the Messiah that is found only in the Parables of Enoch. If those in the Enoch group were known as the great scholars who had special and secret knowledge, and if they lived in Galilee, then Jesus would most likely have had an opportunity to learn firsthand about their teachings through discussions and debates.

Some of the Bultmannians (notably Hans Conzelmann) claimed that "the Son of Man" is a term and title that originates only in the post-Easter community. Conzelmann argued that all the Son of Man sayings in the words of Jesus are suspicious. They seem to be the creation of Jesus' post-Easter followers.[29] The Son of Man Christology is not linked to Jesus; it originated in "the

---

28. I note that this conclusion was shared by almost every leading specialist on 1 Enoch or Second Temple Judaism. It seems that M. Knibb remains unconvinced of this early dating and prefers a date sometime in the second half of the first century C.E.

29. H. Conzelmann, *Jesus,* trans. J. Reumann (Philadelphia: Fortress, 1973).

church," which — in my estimation — should be renamed (in order to avoid anachronisms) "the Early Palestinian Jesus Movement."[30] According to Conzelmann, in the early "church" the term "Son of Man" became a title and celebrated the earthly life and celestial origin of Jesus of Nazareth. The title reveals nothing about Judaism or the historical Jesus; it ushers us into the world after Jesus when "Christianity" can be declared distinct from Judaism. New Testament Christology does not flow from Jesus. As Conzelmann's professor, Bultmann, stressed, Jesus is not the foundation of New Testament theology. He is the presupposition of New Testament theology.[31]

These scholars, Bultmann and Conzelmann, were primarily trained in Greek and in the New Testament; they were not experts in Second Temple Judaism. If the preceding reflections are valid, then speaking personally, I would recast Bultmann's famous and influential dictum. He claimed that Jesus is the presupposition of New Testament theology. Far more likely, Jewish reflections on the Messiah and the Son of Man and Jewish conceptions of God's rule and the coming day of judgment are the presuppositions of Jesus' mind.

---

30. J. H. Charlesworth, *Jesus within Judaism*, ABRL (New York and London: Doubleday, 1988); see esp. 13, 20, 24, 31, 59, 89, 97, 103, 124, 142, 143, 167, 199, 233, 236.

31. R. Bultmann, *Theology of the New Testament*, 2 vols. (New York: Scribner, 1951, 1955), 1:3: "*The message of Jesus* is a presupposition for the theology of the New Testament rather than a part of that theology itself."

# The Book of Noah, the Death of Herod the Great, and the Date of the Parables of Enoch

Darrell D. Hannah

## The Problem

A number of interpreters have noted that "the kings and mighty and high ones" of 1 En 67:8-13 who repair to certain waters for "the healing of the body," which results only in the condemnation of their souls, call to mind Herod the Great's attempt to find a remedy, for what proved to be his fatal afflictions, in the waters of Callirrhoe (Josephus, *Ant* 17.168-72; *War* 1.656-58).[1] To be sure, scholars are usually cautious about concluding that we have here an actual allusion to Herod and his unsuccessful treatment at Callirrhoe. We know of other hot springs in Palestine, such as those in the vicinity of Machaerus (*War* 7.186-89) and at Tiberias (*War* 2.614; Pliny, *Natural History* 71), both of which were certainly used medicinally by members of the ruling classes. Moreover, some earlier interpreters of 1 Enoch found in this passage an allusion to the hot springs at the foot of Mount Vesuvius, to which Roman emperors and others of the senatorial and equestrian class repaired from time to time.[2] Thus, there existed

---

1. So, e.g., A. Dillmann, *Das Buch Henoch übersetzt und erklärt* (Leipzig: Vogel, 1853), 206; R. H. Charles, *The Book of Enoch,* 2nd ed. (Oxford: Clarendon, 1912), 134; M. Black, *The Book of Enoch, or, I Enoch: A New English Edition with Commentary and Textual Notes,* SVTP 7 (Leiden: Brill, 1985), 242; and A. Schalit, *König Herodes: Der Mann und sein Werk,* SJ 4 (Berlin: De Gruyter, 1969), 640 n. 200.

2. So E. Sjöberg, *Der Menschensohn im äthiopischen Henochbuch,* Skrifter Utgivna av kungl. Humanistika Vetenskapsamfundet i Lund 41 (Lund: Gleerup, 1946), 8, and A. Hilgenfeld (*Die jüdische Apokalyptik in ihrer geschichtlichen Entwicklung* [Jena: Friedrich Mauke, 1857], 161-63), who mentions the hot spring at Bajae in Campania (163 n. 2).

in antiquity a number of known hot springs whose waters were thought to have healing properties, and Herod cannot have been the only individual of note who unsuccessfully applied to one or another of them. So, unless precise reasons are forthcoming for connecting this passage with Herod and Callirrhoe, it would be unsafe to do so.[3]

## General Considerations

However, during a recent examination of the material usually thought to have been derived from a lost Noah apocryphon, and now found as interpolations within the text of the Parables, I stumbled on what I take to be cogent reasons for concluding that in 1 En 67 we do indeed encounter an allusion of Herod's ill-fated attempt at "taking the waters" at Callirrhoe. Before turning to those, two general considerations that also support such a conclusion, and are often overlooked, need to be mentioned. First, Callirrhoe must have been among the best-known thermal baths in the Roman east. Pliny, who clearly was interested in such matters, mentions only two sets of hot springs in his literary tour of Palestine, those at Callirrhoe and at Tiberias (*Natural History* 70-72),[4] but only with regard to the former does he speak of "the celebrity of its waters" (*aquarum gloriam*). Callirrhoe is also mentioned by two other ancient geographers, Ptolemy (*Geography* 15.6; [Nobbe: 16.9]) and Solinus Polyhistor (*De mirabilibus mundi* 35.4). While the latter is in all likelihood directly dependent upon Pliny, the witness of Ptolemy's *Geography* is highly significant, for he lists Callirrhoe as one of only five sites east of the Jordan. Callirrhoe was, thus, the location of hot springs repeatedly mentioned by Greco-Roman geographers. In addition, the rabbis frequently identified the Lasha of Gen 10:19 with Callirrhoe (*y. Meg.* 1.11, 71b; *Gen Rab* 37:6; *Targ. Ps.-Jon.* Gen 10:19; *Targ. Neofiti* Gen 10:19), a judgment picked up and repeated by Jerome (*Quaestionum hebraicarum liber in Genesim* on Gen. 10:19).[5] Since neither the rabbis nor Jerome ever uses this

---

3. 1 En 67:4-13 appears to have been alluded to by Celsus; cf. Origen, *Contra Celsum* 52-55. The difficulties surrounding Celsus's and Origen's knowledge of 1 Enoch are beyond the scope of this short paper. Cf. the discussion in J. C. VanderKam, "1 Enoch, Enochic Motifs, and Enoch in Early Christian Literature," in *The Jewish Apocalyptic Heritage in Early Christianity*, ed J. C. VanderKam and W. Adler, CRINT III.4 (Minneapolis: Fortress, 1996), 58-59, and below, D. C. Olson, "An Overlooked Patristic Allusion to the Parables of Enoch?"

4. Pliny omits any mention of the hot springs near Machaerus.

5. Eusebius does not, however, seem to know this identification. In his *Onomasticon*, he merely notes that *Lasan* is the boundary of the Canaanites in the territory of Sodom. Jerome, in his Latin translation of Eusebius's *Onomasticon*, does not repeat the insight, no doubt gained

## The Date of the Parables of Enoch

identification to support an exegetical or theological point, it would seem that its basis rests entirely on Callirrhoe's fame. *Targum Pseudo-Jonathan* adds a similar reference to Callirrhoe at Deut 1:7, while a marginal note in *Targum Neofiti* at Deut 2:32 identifies the Jahaz of that verse with our Callirrhoe. The principal reason for these two references would seem also to lie in Callirrhoe's prestige. At a later date, the sixth-century Madaba map eloquently attests the thermal baths' continuing importance.[6] Finally, archaeological evidence confirms that they were in use during Herod's reign, as the most significant of the remains of building structures, coins, and pottery found there are all clearly Herodian.[7] Thus, Callirrhoe offers an obvious candidate for any reference to unspecified hot springs within ancient Palestine.

Second, Herod's ill-fated visit to the famous thermal baths on the eastern shore of the Dead Sea could not but have been well-known in both Jewish and pagan circles. Herod's fame extended well beyond Palestine,[8] and the events surrounding his death, including the arrest of Jewish nobles with orders for their execution upon his death (Josephus, *War* 1.659-60; *Ant* 17.173-79) and the dispatch of Antipater (*War* 1.663-64; *Ant* 17.185-87), would have been matters of comment far and wide. The role the waters of Callirrhoe played in these fateful events must have been included in at least some of the rumors and stories that followed his demise. So even if a historical allusion to Herod in 1 En 67:8-13 cannot be strictly demonstrated, by no means should it be ruled out.

---

from Jewish sources, that Lasha is Callirrhoe. See E. Klostermann, *Eusebius: Das Onomastikon der biblischen Ortsnamen* (Hildesheim: Olms, 1966), 120-21.

6. On the northeastern shore of the Dead Sea, the words θερμὰ Καλλιρρόης (ΘΕΡΜΑΚΑΛΛΙΡΟΗ) above vignettes of three springs, one of which proceeds from a little building, and two palm trees are clearly visible. Cf. M. Avi-Yonah, *The Madaba Mosaic Map* (Jerusalem: Israel Exploration Society, 1954), 39-40, and the discussion in H. Donner, "Kallirrhoë: Das Sanatorium Herodes' des Großen," *ZDPV* 79 (1963): 59-89 (esp. 61-62).

7. C. Clamer, O. Dussart, and J. Magness, *Fouilles archéologiques de 'Aïn ez-Zâra/Callirrhoé* (Beirut: Institut Français d'archéologie du Proche-Orient, 1997). Cf. also A. Strobel and C. Clamer, "Excavations at Ez-Zara," *ADAJ* 30 (1986): 381-84; A. Strobel, "Zur Ortslage von Kallirrhoë: Ein Bericht," *ZDPV* 82 (1966): 149-62; and Donner, "Kallirrhoë."

8. Cf., e.g., (a) Josephus's admittedly exaggerated claim that Herod was Caesar Augustus's most trusted companion after Agrippa and Agrippa's after Caesar (*Ant* 15.361; *War* 1.400); (b) Strabo's assessment of Herod as "so superior to his predecessors . . . that he received the title of king" (*Geography* 16.2.46), as well as (c) Herod's patronage of many building projects outside of his kingdom. On all this see P. Richardson, *Herod: The King of the Jews and Friend of the Romans* (Minneapolis: Fortress, 1996), esp. 10-13, 174-202, 226-34.

*Darrell D. Hannah*

## The "Noachic" Interpolations

Turning to the text of the Parables of Enoch, chap. 67 presents us with certain difficulties. The first seven verses of this chapter have as good a claim, if not a better claim, to having been excerpted from a Noah apocryphon as any portion of the Parables. The narrative is in the first person with Noah as the speaker. He tells of God's antediluvian revelation (vv. 1-3), the building of the ark by angels (v. 2), the divine promise of the postdiluvian prosperity of Noah's descendants (v. 3), as well as the (postdiluvian?) incarceration of the Watchers in a valley, burning with fire, which Noah had previously been shown by his great-grandfather Enoch (v. 4). With vv. 8-13, however, we seem to be dealing with very different material. Here we encounter an abrupt introduction of "the kings, mighty ones and nobles who possess the earth" and a prophecy that in the future the water of the burning valley, in which the Watchers were incarcerated, will serve to punish these kings, mighty ones, and nobles.

After some study I have concluded, and hope in the future to publish my arguments in full, that passages from an otherwise lost Noah apocryphon were at some point in antiquity interpolated into the text of the Parables.[9] These Noachic passages should be regarded as interpolations rather than source material, because the longest such passage (1 En 64:1–69:25) interrupts the flow of 61:1–63:12 and 69:26-29. This is, by no means, a revolutionary proposal. Scholars who accept that portions of a "Book of Noah" have been either interpolated into the text of the Parables or have served as source material for the original composition of the Parables include both earlier commentators such as August Dillmann,[10] Heinrich Ewald,[11] Robert Henry Charles,[12] and François Martin,[13] and more recent scholars such as Albert-Marie Denis,[14]

---

9. D. D. Hannah, "Source Criticism (1): The 'Book of Noah' and the Composite Nature of the Similitudes" (unpublished chapter of a monograph in progress, *Enoch's Second Vision: Critical Issues in the Interpretation of the Similitudes of Enoch*).

10. Dillmann, *Buch Henoch*, xxxviii-xliii, and "Pseudepigraphen des Alten Testaments: Die Henoch- und Noah-Schriften," in *Real-Encyklopädie für protestantische Theologie und Kirche*, ed. J. J. Herzog, 2nd ed. (Leipzig: Hinrichs, 1883), 12:350-52.

11. H. Ewald, "Abhandlung über des äthiopischen Buches Henokh: Entstehung, Sinn und Zusammensetzung," *Abhandlungen der königlichen Gesellschaft der Wissenschaften zum Göttingen* 6 (1854): 107-78.

12. Charles, *The Book of Enoch*, xlvi-lvi.

13. F. Martin, *Le livre d'Hénoch: Documents pour l'étude de la Bible, traduit sur le texte éthiopien* (Paris: Letouzey et Ané, 1906), lxii-lxxxviii.

14. A.-M. Denis, "Le Livre grec d'Hénoch (éthiopien)," in *Introduction aux pseudépigraphes grecs d'Ancien Testament*, SVTP 1 (Leiden: Brill, 1970), 17.

George Nickelsburg,[15] Ephraim Isaac,[16] Siegbert Uhlig,[17] Matthew Black,[18] Florentino García Martínez,[19] and John Collins.[20] Thus, the existence of material from a Noah apocryphon within the text of the Parables continues to be widely recognized today, and probably represents the majority view, even though the extravagant claims made for source criticism, which held sway when Dillmann, Ewald, Charles, and Martin were active, are no longer in vogue. My research has led me to regard, at least, 1 En 54:7–55:2; 60:1-10, 24-25; and 65:1–69:25 as certainly deriving from a Noah apocryphon, and perhaps chap. 64 as well. However, the argument of this paper does not rest on an acceptance of my precise delimitation of Noachic material within the text of the Parables. One need only accept that chap. 67 cannot have been original to the author of the Parables and has been interpolated from Noachic material of some sort.

Once that is acknowledged, then the oddity of 1 En 67:8-13 immediately becomes apparent. For this is the only occurrence within the said Noachic material of "the kings, mighty ones and nobles who possess the earth," a theme constant throughout the Parables proper.[21] Moreover, within vv. 8-13 we also encounter other themes that are prominent in the Parables proper but rare in the Noachic material, such as the title "the Lord of Spirits" (vv. 8-9) and the phrases "for they have denied the Lord of Spirits" (v. 8; cf. 10) and "before the Lord of Spirits none shall utter a lying word" (v. 9). The presence of all this in the short compass of six verses could be taken as evidence that we have here returned to the Parables proper and have left Noachic material. However, the explicit connections with the immediately preceding 67:4-7, which is unambiguously Noachic, tell against this. Here, then, is a dilemma: 67:1-7 can only be described as Noachic material, while 67:8-13 seems more like material com-

---

15. G. W. E. Nickelsburg, *Jewish Literature between the Bible and the Mishnah* (London: SCM, 1981), 220-21.

16. E. Isaac, "1 (Ethiopic Apocalypse of) Enoch," in *Old Testament Pseudepigrapha*, ed. J. H. Charlesworth, vol. 1 (Garden City, N.Y.: Doubleday, 1983), 38 n. 54e (for 1 En 54:7–55:2) and 40 n. 60a (for 1 En 60).

17. S. Uhlig, *Das äthiopische Henoch*, in *JSHRZ* V.6, ed. H. Lichtenberger et al. (Gütersloh: Mohn, 1984), 599 (for 1 En 54:7–55:2) and 618 (for 65:1–69:25); cf. also 578 (for 39:1, 2a).

18. Black, *The Book of Enoch*, 225 (for 1 En 60) and 239 (for 1 En 64–69:25).

19. F. García Martínez, "4QMess Ar and the Book of Enoch," in *Qumran and Apocalyptic: Studies on the Aramaic Texts from Qumran*, STDJ 9 (Leiden: Brill, 1992), 1-44.

20. J. J. Collins, *The Apocalyptic Imagination: An Introduction to Jewish Apocalyptic Literature*, 2nd ed. (Grand Rapids: Eerdmans, 1998), 180.

21. I use the term "Parables proper" for material that derives from the author(s) of the Parables. In effect, it is the text of the Parables without the Noachic material and, perhaps, a few other passages such as chaps. 56 and 71.

posed by the author of the Parables proper. However, the many clear links between the two paragraphs point to their interdependence. There is, however, another explanation: the interpolator here "tips his hand." The individual who added the Noachic material to the Parables has himself authored the final paragraph of this chapter. In vv. 8-13 we have a text that comes directly from the interpolator's pen; he is here, as it were, updating his sources.

However, he has not entirely understood those sources. For the one sin of "the kings and mighty ones" singled out in the text of 1 En 67:8-13 is that of lust. This distinguishes this text from all the others concerning the kings and mighty ones in the Parables. In the Parables proper, "the kings and the mighty" are often accused of impiety, violence, persecution, and oppression (e.g., 46:4-5, 7-8; 48:10; 62:11; 63:1-4, 7, 10; cf. 47:1-4), but other than here we never hear of their licentiousness. In the whole of the Parables, what makes "the kings and the mighty" the villains is their oppression of the elect, righteous, and holy ones — except here. The elect, righteous, and holy ones are not even mentioned in this passage.

On the other hand, Herod and members of his family were infamous for their uncontrolled passions. Josephus, for example, can baldly assert that in the sexual arena Herod "had no qualms about living solely for his own pleasure" (*Ant* 15.319-22; cf. also *War* 1.477). Moreover, he reports that Mariamme "took full advantage of [Herod's] enslavement to passion" (*Ant* 15.219). To be sure, Josephus was quite critical of Herod, but before dismissing Josephus's portrait as a biased exaggeration, one should consider the likely reaction of pious Jews to Herod's ten wives (*War* 1.563; *Ant* 17.19),[22] to his concubines (*War* 1.511),[23] to

---

22. Polygamy itself was not unheard of and was even allowed within Second Temple Judaism: there are, of course, many examples in the Hebrew Bible; Josephus states that Jewish custom permitted it (*War* 1.477; *Ant* 17.15) and Tannaitic literature regulates concerning it (e.g., *m. Ketub.* 10.5; *m. Sanh.* 2.4; *t. Yebam.* 1.1-10). The Mishnah seemingly allows commoners as many as four wives (*m. Ketub.* 10.5), while regulating a maximum of eighteen for kings (*m. Sanh.* 2.4). However, the latter number is clearly an exegetical contrivance, interpreting Deut 17:17 by the example of David, multiplying his six wives (2 Sam 3:2-5) by those God would have added to him had he asked (2 Sam 12:8: lit. "I would added to you the like of these and the like of these"). See H. Danby, *The Mishnah* (Oxford: Oxford University Press, 1933), 384 n. 12. Nonetheless, there were also some Jews who opposed polygamy, notably the sectarians of Qumran; cf. CD 4:21; 11QTemple$^a$ (11Q19) 57:17-19. In any case, polygamy must not have been very common in Jewish society. Cf. J. Jeremias, *Jerusalem in the Time of Jesus*, trans. F. H. Cave and C. H. Cave (Philadelphia: Fortress, 1969), 369-70; S. Safrai, "Home and Family," in *The Jewish People in the First Century*, ed. S. Safrai and M. Stern, CRINT I.2 (Assen: Van Gorcum, 1987), 748-50; and S. Lowy, "The Extent of Jewish Polygamy in Talmudic Times," *JJS* 9 (1958): 115-38. My point is not that Herod had more than one wife at one time, but that he had *ten*.

23. This is the only explicit reference to a concubine of Herod in Josephus, but she could

his extravagant obsession with Mariamme (*Ant* 15.65-87, 207-46; *War* 1.435-44), to say nothing of his, and his son Alexander's, pederastic relations with eunuchs (*War* 1.488-89 par.; *Ant* 16.230-32; 17.44; cf. *War* 1.511).[24] In addition, there is also the accusation against Herod that he was in love with Glaphyra, Alexander's wife (*Ant* 16.206-12). While the accusation was not true, the ease with which it was believed speaks volumes concerning Herod's reputation.[25] D. J. Ladouceur has argued that Josephus's description of Herod's final illness in *Ant* 17.168-71 makes the very point that Herod was divinely chastised for his licentiousness.[26] Josephus does this by drawing on stereotypical suppositions regarding various sins and the diseases with which those sins are punished. Thus, it seems safe to conclude that Herod would have been widely regarded by pious Jews as a profligate and that his final illness was divine punishment — exactly the situation presumed of the royal figures in 1 En 67:8-13.

Thus, the second half of 1 En 67 can easily be understood as an allusion to Herod the Great's visit to the waters of Callirrhoe in the latter half of March 4 B.C.E.[27] Such a reading makes good sense of the data presented in the two parts

---

hardly have been the only one. As Nikos Kokkinos suggests, the very fact that Herod gave this one as a gift to Archelaus of Cappadocia implies the existence of others. See N. Kokkinos, *The Herodian Dynasty: Origins, Role in Society, and Eclipse* (Sheffield: Sheffield Academic, 1998), 143; cf. also 206.

24. *Ant* 17.44 has been interpreted differently by H. Clementz, *Des Flavius Josephus: Jüdische Altertümer* (Wiesbaden: Fourier, 1983), 444. He takes the eunuch Bagoas to be the subject of καὶ παιδικὰ ὄντα αὐτοῦ. This is grammatically possible and smoother than taking Herod as the subject. However, while eunuchs could be a παιδικά, they did not have them. Thus, only Herod can be the subject of the phrase in question. Cf. the translations of R. Marcus (LCL) and Whinston. For παιδικά in the technical sense of a "darling boy" or "favorite," the younger and passive member of a pederastic couple, cf. Philo, *De vita contemplativa* 59-61, and Plato, *Symposium* 178C-185A. For Jewish revulsion for pederasty and all forms of homoeroticism, cf. R. A. J. Gagnon, *The Bible and Homosexual Practice* (Nashville: Abingdon, 2001), esp. 159-83.

25. Is there another witness to this estimation of Herod in As Mos 6:2, where Herod is described as "a man bold and shameless" *(homo temerarius et improbus)*? The latter term, *improbus,* can have the connotation of "lewd" and "lascivious." If this is the intended meaning, then we have here an earlier witness than Josephus. A late witness to Herod's reputation for licentiousness appears in *b. B. Bat.* 3b-4a, where it is asserted that he committed necrophilia with Mariamme's corpse.

26. D. J. Ladouceur, "The Death of Herod the Great," *CP* 76 (1981): 25-34.

27. It is generally agreed that Herod died in late March of 4 B.C.E. So Richardson, *Herod*, xx; Schalit, *König Herodes*, 643; and esp. E. Schürer, *The History of the Jewish People in the Age of Jesus Christ*, trans. and rev. G. Vermes, F. Millar, M. Black, et al. (Edinburgh: T. & T. Clark, 1973-87), 1:326-28 n. 165. Since, according to Josephus, Herod died before Passover, which in 4 B.C.E. fell on April 11, and Herod's journey to Callirrhoe took place after the lunar eclipse, which occurred on the night of March 12/13, we know that the journey must be dated to the second half of March.

of 1 En 67, of Herod's reputation, and of the final events of his life. If this is accepted, then we have here important evidence for the dating of the interpolator's activity and indirect evidence for the date of the composition of the Noah apocryphon, as well as of the Parables themselves. The interpolator could have added this passage only after the fateful events of 4 B.C.E., but his allusion would have the most force if Herod's demise was a recent occurrence and still fresh in the memory. The material he was bringing up to date with this addition, however, would have to have been composed earlier. Both the Noah apocryphon and the Parables then must have been penned sometime before the death of Herod — perhaps well before.

## Possible Objections

If it is objected that the valley with which this text is concerned is explicitly said to be "in the west" *(ba-ʿārab)*[28] and so could not have been Callirrhoe, three responses can be made. First, this item appears in v. 4, which belongs to interpolated Noachic material, not the interpolator's updating. The interpolator may have missed this or simply ignored it. From the random nature of the interpolations, he does not appear to have been very concerned with details. Second, the Ethiopic word here rendered "west" is also the Ethiopic word for "Arabia," so we cannot tell whether the Greek *Vorlage* before the translator read ἐν δύσει/ ἐν δυσμαῖς or ἐν Ἀραβίᾳ. Moreover, Callirrhoe, east of the Jordan and virtually in Nabatean territory, could be thought of as in Arabia. Third, and most importantly, Genesis locates the Noah story not in Palestine, but east of Palestine, probably Mesopotamia. The Noah apocryphon may well have shared that perspective. And, of course, Callirrhoe is west of Mesopotamia. If the interpolator appreciated this fact, he would have known that the reference of the valley being in the west dovetailed with his purposes. While any one of these three explanations may be correct, I prefer the latter two.

Another possible objection concerns the particular nature of the hot springs in question. According to 1 En 67:6, they had the smell of sulfur *(ṣēnā tay)*, while Josephus (*War* 1.657; cf. *Ant* 17.171) informs us that the water of Callirrhoe was sweet. This objection was already noted by Charles, although his solution for it is inadequate, as he appeals to the sweet waters of Machaerus, which are too far away to be confused with the waters of Callirrhoe.[29] Again, it

---

28. This, after all, was the reasoning behind Hilgenfeld's and Sjöberg's argument that thermal baths at the foot of Mount Vesuvius were meant. See n. 2 above.

29. Charles, *The Book of Enoch*, 134. See esp. Donner, "Kallirrhoë," 62-65.

*The Date of the Parables of Enoch*

should be noted that the detail regarding the sulfurous waters appears in Noachic material, not in the interpolator's update. So again, he may have missed or ignored the apparent contradiction. In addition, he may not have known the precise makeup of the waters at Callirrhoe and so was unaware of the possible inconsistency. More importantly, it is unlikely that Josephus meant to assert that all the numerous springs of Callirrhoe contained only sweet water. We know that at least in the nineteenth century a variety of water types was found at Callirrhoe. H. B. Tristam reported about his 1872 journey there: "The plain is full of springs of hot water, sometimes sweet, but *for the most part slightly sulphurous.*"[30]

At the 2005 meeting of the Enoch Seminar it was stated by more than one member of the seminar that 1 En 67 can be of no help in dating the Parables, as the passage only alludes to a common practice of the Romans. Of course, it is true that the Romans made regular use of public baths and thermal springs. Such an objection, however, does not appreciate the nature of 1 En 67:8-13 as a late addition made when the Noachic material was added to the text of the Parables. It follows that if the interpolator went to the trouble to add such a paragraph, he must have had some reason for doing so. That he merely wished to take a swipe at Roman emperors and senators is perhaps possible, but not very probable. An allusion to some historical event is a much more likely explanation, and Herod's ill-fated visit to Callirrhoe is the best candidate for such an event.

## Conclusions

In conclusion, it must be admitted that this proposal depends on acceptance of the thesis that chap. 67 derives from Noachic material that has been interpolated into the text of the Parables. But then, the majority of interpreters who have written on the subject find the hypothesis of a Noah apocryphon the best explanation for Noachic material. The proposal of this essay, I would contend, makes the most sense of all the data. Moreover, any counterproposal would, of first importance, have to explain the combination of themes characteristic of the Noachic material and distinctive to the Parables proper, all within the short compass of 1 En 67:1-13 and, what is more important, the very different use of the "kings and mighty ones" theme in this chapter from the rest of the book.

---

30. Cited from Donner, "Kallirrhoë," 69, emphasis mine.

# A Symbolic Transfiguration of a Historical Event: The Parthian Invasion in Josephus and the Parables of Enoch

*Luca Arcari*

In a passage in the Parables of Enoch (1 En 56:5–57:3), the seer foresees a people from the East who become restless and leave their lands in order to trample the land of the elect ones. This invasion is dramatically described by the author of the Parables, who also seems to refer to a civil war after the invasion (56:7). Erik Sjöberg interpreted this narrative as an allusion to the Parthian invasion of 40 B.C.E.[1] J. C. Hindley countered Sjöberg's hypothesis, arguing that Josephus, the most important source on the Parthian invasion, treats this subject as an event considered positively by some Jews.[2] Michael Stone has correctly objected to Hindley's assessment that the author of the Parables was a member of a sectarian group and, thus, influenced by social motivations in the presentation of this event.[3]

---

1. E. Sjöberg, *Der Menschensohn im äthiopischen Henochbuch*, Skrifter Utgivna av kungl. Humanistika Vetenskapssamfundet i Lund 41 (Lund: Gleerup, 1946). Recently James Charlesworth and Paolo Sacchi defended this hypothesis: see J. H. Charlesworth, "From Jewish Messianology to Christian Christology: Some Caveats and Perspectives," in *Judaisms and Their Messiahs at the Turn of the Christian Era*, ed. J. Neusner et al. (Cambridge: Cambridge University Press, 1987), 225-64; P. Sacchi, "Qumran e la datazione del Libro delle Parabole di Enoc," *Hen* 25 (2003): 149-66.

2. J. C. Hindley, "Toward a Date for the Similitudes of Enoch: An Historical Approach," *NTS* 14 (1968): 551-65.

3. Jonas C. Greenfield and Michael E. Stone, "The Enochic Pentateuch and the Date of the Similitudes," *HTR* 70 (1977): 51-65; reprinted in M. E. Stone, *Selected Studies in Pseudepigrapha and Apocrypha with Special Reference to the Armenian Tradition* (Leiden: Brill, 1991), 198-212.

## A Symbolic Transfiguration of a Historical Event

### Josephus's Historical Narration and the Parables' Apocalyptic Vision

Josephus's presentation of the Parthian invasion gives prominence to some elements that can illuminate aspects of the description of this event in the Parables. Josephus mentions that the invasion was supported by Antigonus and that Herod was able to flee. On the other hand, Phasaelus and Hyrcanus were imprisoned and delivered to Antigonus. Antigonus then severed Hyrcanus's ears, rendering him unfit for the priesthood (*Ant* 14.330ff.; *War* 1.248ff.). As Antigonus and his supporters were ravaging Carmel, many of the Jews approached Antigonus, ready to support him by invading the country. So Antigonus sent them ahead to seize Drymus, whereupon a battle ensued between both Antigonus's and Hyrcanus's supporters. According to Josephus, Antigonus's allies successfully drove their enemy to Jerusalem, and as their numbers increased, they proceeded to the king's palace. Although Herod's party, "with a strong body of men," was able to resist the forces of Antigonus, and seemingly gain the upper hand in Jerusalem, ultimately the Parthians entered the city, transferred the power of government to Antigonus and took Hyrcanus as a prisoner to Parthia. Herod, of course, escaped, and after failing to receive assistance from Arabia, he appealed in person to Rome, where Antony and Caesar agreed to make him king.

The antithesis in Josephus between "many of the Jews" who joined Antigonus (*War* 1.250) and the "strong body of men" who defended Hyrcanus and Phasaelus (1:251) seems to support the notion in the Parables that "a man shall not know his brother, Nor a son his father or his mother" (56:7). But the apocalyptic narration of 1 En 56:5ff. appears to reflect an entirely different phase of the Parthian invasion. We can schematically represent both narratives in the following:

| Josephus (*War* 1.248ff.) | Book of Parables (1 En 56:5ff.) |
|---|---|
| Now two years afterward, when Barzapharnes, a governor among the Parthians, and Paeorus, the king's son, had possessed themselves of Syria, and when Lysanias had already succeeded upon the death of his father Ptolemy, the son of Menneus, in the government [of Chalcis], he prevailed with the governor, by a promise of a thousand talents, and five hundred women, to bring back Antigonus to his kingdom, and to turn Hyrcanus out of it. Pacorus was by | . . . and thrust themselves to the east at the Parthians and Medes. They will shake up the kings (so that) a spirit of unrest shall come upon them, and stir them up from their thrones; and they will break forth from their beds like lions and like hungry hyenas among their own flocks. . . . And they will go up and trample upon the land of my elect ones. . . . |

479

these means induced so to do, and marched along the sea-coast, while he ordered Barzapharnes to fall upon the Jews as he went along the Mediterranean part of the country; but of the maritime people, the Tyrians would not receive Pacorus, although those of Ptolemais and Sidon had received him; so he committed a troop of his horse to a certain cup-bearer belonging to the royal family, of his own name [Pacorus], and gave him orders to march into Judea, in order to learn the state of affairs among their enemies, and to help Antigonus when he should want his assistance.

| | |
|---|---|
| Now as these men were ravaging Carmel, many of the Jews ran together to Antigonus, and showed themselves ready to make an incursion into the country; so he sent them before into that place called Drymus [the woodland], to seize upon the place; whereupon a battle was fought between them, and they drove the enemy away, and pursued them, and ran after them as far as Jerusalem, and as their numbers increased, they proceeded as far as the king's palace. . . . Now when that festival which we call Pentecost was at hand, all the places about the temple, and the whole city, was full of a multitude of people that were come out of the country, and which were the greatest part of them armed also, at which time Phasaelus guarded the wall, and Herod, with a few, guarded the royal palace; and when he made an assault upon his enemies, as they were out of their ranks, on the north quarter of the city, he slew a very great number of them, and put them all to flight; and some of them he shut up within the city, and others within the outward | But the city of my righteous ones will become an obstacle to their horses. And they shall begin to fight among themselves; and (by) their own right hands they shall prevail against themselves. . . . |

## A Symbolic Transfiguration of a Historical Event

rampart. In the mean time, Antigonus desired that Pacorus might be admitted to be a reconciler between them; and Phasaelus was prevailed upon to admit the Parthian into the city with five hundred horse, and to treat him in an hospitable manner, who pretended that he came to quell the tumult, but in reality he came to assist Antigonus.

But now, when they were come to Galilee, they found that the people of that country had revolted, and were in arms, who came very cunningly to their leader, and besought him to conceal his treacherous intentions by an obliging behavior to them; accordingly, he at first made them presents; and afterward, as they went away, laid ambushes for them; and when they were come to one of the maritime cities called Ecdippon, they perceived that a plot was laid for them; for they were there informed of the promise of a thousand talents, and how Antigonus had devoted the greatest number of the women that were there with them, among the five hundred, to the Parthians; they also perceived that an ambush was always laid for them by the barbarians in the night time; they had also been seized on before this, unless they had waited for the seizure of Herod first at Jerusalem, because if he were once informed of this treachery of theirs, he would take care of himself; nor was this a mere report, but they saw the guards already not far off them.

A man shall not recognize his brother, nor a son his mother....

Nay, he found by experience that the Jews fell more heavily upon him than did the Parthians, and created him troubles perpetually, and this ever since

... until there shall be a (significant) number of corpses from among them. Their punishment is (indeed) not in vain.[4]

    4. English translation by E. Isaac in *The Old Testament Pseudepigrapha*, vol. 1, *Apocalyptic Literature and Testaments*, ed. J. H. Charlesworth (Garden City, N.Y.: Doubleday, 1983), 39.

he was gotten sixty furlongs from the
city; these sometimes brought it to a
sort of a regular battle. Now in the
place where Herod beat them, and
killed a great number of them, there he
afterward built a citadel, in memory of
the great actions he did there, and
adorned it with the most costly palaces,
and erected very strong fortifications,
and called it, from his own name,
Herodium.[5]

## Literary and Sociological Divergences

This narrative scheme enables us to understand the symbolic reinterpretation of the Parthian invasion by the Parables of Enoch. The seer presents the invasion from a transcendent perspective, which results from a particular ideological and sociological milieu. The ideological milieu is the same as that of the Book of Dream Visions:[6] the history is a symbolic process in which God controls everything. It is suggestive that we find the vision of the Parthian invasion immediately after the section dealing with the angels of punishment (1 En 56:1-4). The degenerating process of history was predetermined by God after the transgression of the Watchers; the Parthian invasion is a product of this degenerating process. The Parthian invasion is introduced in this manner: "In those days the angels[7] will assemble and thrust themselves to the east at the Parthians and Medes." This introduction is connected with 1 En 56:1, where we find "an army of the angels of punishment marching, holding nets of iron and bronze." Enoch says: "And I asked the angel of peace, who was walking with me, saying to him, 'To whom are they going, these who are holding (the nets)?' And he said to me: '(They are going) to their elect and beloved ones in order that they may be cast into the crevices of the abyss of the valley.'"

The sociological milieu is that of a group who consider themselves "the elect ones," where the noun "elect ones" is used as a term of belonging for Enoch, the authoritative figure who confirms the "truth" of the book. This is

---

5. Greek text in H. St. J. Thackeray, *Josephus*, vol. 2, *The Jewish War, Books I-III* (London and New York: William Heinemann; G. P. Putnam's Son, 1927), 114ff. The English translations are mine.

6. Regarding the place of the Parables in the previous Enochic tradition, see James VanderKam's contribution to this volume.

7. *'are'sti-homu*, literally "their heads," i.e., "their leaders."

evident not only in 1 En 56:6, where it says, "And they will go up and trample upon the land of His (my?) elect ones,"[8] and in 56:7, where it similarly states, "But the city of my righteous ones will become an obstacle to their horses," but also in the rest of the book, where the noun "elect ones" is parallel to "Elect One," one of the appellatives for defining the Messiah. The appellative in the second and third parable expresses a subordination of the motives of the elect ones to that of the Elect One. This subordination mirrors a sociological tendency to derive the ethos of a group from a leader who is interpreted as the speaker inspired by the divinity.[9]

| Elect One[10] | Elect Ones |
|---|---|
| 45:3a | 45:3b |
| 48:6 | 48:1 |
| 51:3-5 | |
| 53:6 | |
| 55:4 | |
| | 56:3 |

8. This verse is problematic in the manuscripts: in Tana 9 we find a first-person singular pronoun ("my"); some manuscripts have a third-person plural pronoun for the first occurrence and a third-person singular for the second occurrence; other manuscripts, however, have a third-person singular for both occurrences. The reading of Tana 9 seems acceptable because in v. 7 the manuscripts are unanimous in presenting a first-person singular possessive pronoun. See S. Chialà, *Libro delle Parabole di Enoc. Testo e commento* (Brescia: Paideia, 1997), 109 n. 115.

9. On leadership and the concept of ethos (in relationship with the formation of identity in a group), see J. J. Collins, "Ethos and Identity in Jewish Apocalyptic Literature," in *Ethos und Identität: Einheit und Vielfalt des Judentums in hellenistischen-römischen Zeit*, ed. M. Konradt and U. Steinert (Paderborn: Schöningh, 2002), 51-65.

10. On the motives of the Elect One and the elect ones, see J. C. VanderKam, "Righteous One, Messiah, Chosen One, and Son of Man in 1 Enoch 37-71," in *The Messiah: Developments in Earliest Judaism and Christianity*, ed. J. H. Charlesworth (Minneapolis: Fortress, 1992), 169-91. Concerning the appellative "Elect One" for defining the Messiah, Joseph Fitzmyer thinks it originates in the pronominal use of the singular בחיר, attributed to Moses (Ps 106:23), to David (Ps 89:4), to the servant of YHWH (Isa 42:1), and, collectively, to Israel (Isa 43:20; 45:4). But Fitzmyer also thinks that in 1 En 48:10; 52:4; 62:1-5 "it is apparent that the title 'the Elect One' was used interchangeably with 'Son of Man' and 'his Anointed'" ("The Aramaic 'Elect of God' Text from Qumran Cave IV," *CBQ* 27 [1965]: 348-72). I do not think it is possible to speak of "interchange" with regard to the use of messianic titles in the Parables; every title in the Parables is functional to a specific *sensus*. In the case of the "Elect One," it is in relationship with the elect ones. See also T. W. Manson, *Studies in the Gospels and Epistles* (Manchester: University Press, 1962), 140, although I find it problematic to interpret the Elect One in the Parables as a "corporate personality," as Manson seems to do. Against this interpretation, see M. Black, "The Messianism of the Parables of Enoch: Their Date and Contribution to Christological Origins," in *The Messiah*, 145-58.

Josephus has personal and ideological links with subjects in Parthia. The existence of Jews in large numbers in many of the regions beyond the Euphrates, seen as descending from the ten tribes taken into exile from Samaria (*Ant* 11.133), figured into the political consciousness of Jews during the Second Temple period.[11] Herod, anxious to create a new high priesthood that would be loyal to him, made an obscure Babylonian Jew, Ananel, his first high priest (*Ant* 15.22). The famed teacher Hillel was also said to have come from Babylon.[12] More explicit evidence is supplied by Philo, who in connection with opposition to Caligula's plan to put his own statue in the temple, invokes Jewish prominence not only in Babylon but also in many other satrapies. The potential power of these exiles is emphasized first in the deliberation ascribed to the Roman governor Petronius and then again in Agrippa I's letter to Caligula (Philo, *Legatio* 216; 218).[13]

Tessa Rajak supposes that the first edition of Josephus's *Jewish War* was an Aramaic edition of the work for Parthian readers.[14] Whether or not this is the case, Josephus's statement is still significant. It is remarkable that an author patronized by the Flavians freely admits involvement with the Parthians in a work consistently highlighting Roman activities and Roman concerns. This openness is connected by some scholars with the rapprochement between Rome and Parthia during the reign of Vespasian: Vologaeses offered 70,000 Parthian horses to assist the Romans in the Jewish War (Tacitus, *Historiae* 2.82; 4.51) and later sent Titus a golden crown to mark the victory in Judea. In 75 C.E., Vologaeses notoriously requested Roman help against the Alan invasion of Media (*War* 7.244-51; Suetonius, *Domitianus* 2.2; Dio, *Epitome* 66.11.3). Yet the Roman conception of Parthia and the Parthians remained largely negative, and, rather than promoting Flavian policy, it would seem that our historian was taking a risk. Josephus also uses Parthian material,[15] and he seems to identify himself with the Parthian Jews.[16] This is why, in my opinion, the presentation of the Parthian invasion in 40 B.C.E. is different from that of the Parables; both works mirror two different social and historical backgrounds.

But we must consider another element. In Josephus's narration Herod

---

11. On this topic see the "classic" work by G. Rawlinson, *Parthia* (London: T. Fischer Unwin, 1893), 246ff.

12. See J. Neusner, *A History of the Jews in Babylonia*, vol. 1, *The Parthian Period*, 2nd ed. (Leiden: Brill, 1969), 37ff.

13. On these topics see T. Rajak, "The Parthians in Josephus," in *Das Partherreich und seine Zeugnisse*, ed. J. Wiesehöfer (Stuttgart: Franz Steiner, 1998), 309ff.

14. Rajak, "The Parthians in Josephus," 310.

15. Rajak, "The Parthians in Josephus," 312ff.

16. Rajak, "The Parthians in Josephus," 323.

sailed for Rome, where he first went to his father's friend Antony to inform him of the numerous calamities he and his family had suffered and to request his assistance. In 39 B.C.E. Herod sailed from Italy and arrived at Ptolemais. After recruiting an army of foreigners and fellow countrymen, he marched through Galilee against Antigonus. Herod was assisted by Ventidius and Silo, who were persuaded by Dellius to allow Herod into the kingdom of Judea. Herod's forces increased daily as he continued toward Judea, and all Galilee, with few exceptions, joined him. Near the end of the war, the Roman legions also assisted Herod. In consequence, he was able to take Jerusalem by force and kill Antigonus. Caesar then confirmed Herod king, and in turn Herod presented to the emperor magnificent gifts. He also reinstated Hyrcanus as high priest in the temple of Jerusalem (*War* 1.276ff.).

In the symbolic vision of 1 En 57:1-3, the seer envisions soldiers coming from different regions. The text alludes to different *loci geographici* and seems to allude to Herod's actions in Rome and in Ptolemais. Specifically, the seer underscores the ample character of the military actions.[17] Herod called for help against Antigonus in Ptolemais and later in Rome. Thus the seer of the Book of Parables seems to point to Herod's mobilization of the army by referring to the soldiers coming from the east, west, and south. Obviously the apocalyptic symbolism of the Parables to a certain extent masks the historical events, so we cannot determine the exact events depicted by Josephus. Nevertheless, there are no compelling arguments against the supposition that the Parthian invasion of 40 B.C.E. stands behind this apocalyptic vision, and the possible presence of the chronological phases of this invasion strengthens this possibility.

## Toward a Conclusion

Based on our analysis of the historical narration of Josephus and the apocalyptic vision of the Book of Parables, we can conclude the following:

a. The *Grund* of the historical event of the Parthian invasion can be the basis for 1 En 56:5ff. because the essential chronological succession of the event is reflected in our apocalyptic text.

---

17. The interpretation of the Ethiopic noun *manfaqa 'alat* in 1 En 57:1 is not so simple. In Ethiopic the expression indicates the south. I do not accept Black's interpretation (the temporal character of the military action); see M. Black, *The Book of Enoch, or, I Enoch: A New English Edition with Commentary and Textual Notes*, SVTP 7 (Leiden: Brill, 1985), 223-24. Instead, I think the term recalls the LXX, where μεσημβρία occurs two times indicating the south (cf. Dan 8:4, 9 [LXX]); see Chialà, *Libro delle Parabole di Enoc*, 110 n. 119.

b. The divergences between Josephus and the Book of Parables are connected to the different formal and sociological milieu of each text, with the result that both texts represent two different perspectives on the same historical event.

c. Josephus's narration is influenced by a "Judaic" vision of the Parthians, who are considered an expression of the variegated "Judaic" world. The Book of Parables analyzes the same event from a different perspective, namely, from the vantage point of a group that considers itself the true interpreter of the Enochic traditions,[18] and thus human history is viewed by the seer (as in the Book of Dream Visions) as a degenerating process originating in the primordial angelic sin. So also the Parthian invasion is for the seer a mirror of this degenerative process.[19]

---

18. On the relationships between the Book of the Watchers and the Book of Parables, see Helge Kvanvig's contribution to this volume.

19. I am excluding the problem of the final chapters of the Book of Parables in this analysis (1 En 70–71), but I think some elements must be considered in spite of Daniel Olson's important article defending the originality of both chapters. See D. C. Olson, "Enoch and the Son of Man in the Epilogue of the Parables," *JSP* 18 (1998): 27-38. Regarding this problem and the use of the Abbadianus 55 manuscript, see Chialà, *Libro delle parabole di Enoc*, 288-91. Olson reviews and follows A. Caquot's arguments; see A. Caquot, "Remarques sur les chapitres 70 et 71 du livre éthiopien d'Hénoch," in *Apocalypses et théologie de l'espérance*, ed. L. Monloubou, LD 5 (Paris: Cerf, 1977), 111-22. Chialà has criticized Caquot's assessments, although Olson does not seem to be aware of Chialà's arguments in his article. Chialà concludes that chap. 70 (in its first part) is original and chap. 71 is posterior. On these problems, and on the literary stratification (or unity) of the Book of Parables, see the contributions of George Nickelsburg and Michael Knibb in the present volume.

# An Allusion in the Parables of Enoch to the Acts of Matthias Antigonus in 40 B.C.E.?

*Hanan Eshel*

A large portion of the scrolls found at Qumran was authored by members of a religious community who believed they were living at the end of days, on the eve of God's final judgment. Among the works that exhibit this worldview are a number of scrolls that contain contemporizing interpretations of biblical verses. This genre of commentary is referred to by scholars today as pesher. The method entails a citation of a certain verse by the author of the pesher, followed by the words "the pesher of the matter is about" or "its pesher is about," and an explanation of the cited verse. The pesher explanation presupposes the relevance of the verse beyond the era of the biblical prophet, to the time of the author of the pesher, which is to say, the Second Temple period. By interpreting biblical prophecies as applying to contemporary events, the authors of pesherim aimed to prove that salvation was imminent. Exegetical demonstrations of the fulfillment of biblical prophecies in the present time served to reinforce the belief that the entirety of the prophetic descriptions of divine salvation would soon be realized. Qumran yielded eighteen scrolls containing "continuous pesherim," which focus on individual biblical compositions, and "thematic pesherim," which discuss a specific idea recurring in verses gathered by the author from different biblical books. There are also pesher interpretations incorporated into other texts, particularly the Damascus Document.[1]

---

1. G. J. Brooke, "Qumran Pesher: Towards the Redefinition of a Genre," *RevQ* 10 (1980): 483-503; S. L. Berrin, "Pesharim," in *Encyclopedia of the Dead Sea Scrolls,* ed. L. H. Schiffman and J. C. VanderKam (Oxford: Oxford University Press, 2000), 644-47; J. H. Charlesworth, *The Pesharim and Qumran History* (Grand Rapids: Eerdmans, 2002); T. H. Lim, *Pesharim* (London: Sheffield Academic, 2002).

*Hanan Eshel*

Although pesherim of this sort are primarily recorded in the Qumran scrolls, they are also known from other Second Temple period writings. An example is the pesher written into the MT of Isa 9:13-14,[2] and that on Deut 32:21-22 at the end of Ben Sira (50:37-38).[3] There are also pesherim in the New Testament, the most notable being Acts 4:25-27, with its commentary on Ps 2:1-2.[4] Here I wish to propose that 1 En 56:5-7 incorporates a pesher to Deut 33:9, composed after 40 B.C.E., that interprets this verse as an allusion to certain acts of Matthias Antigonus.

The second parable of Enoch includes verses understood by many as referring to the Parthian invasion of Palestine in 40 B.C.E.[5] 1 En 56:5-7 reads:[6]

> [56:5] And in those days the angels will gather together, and will throw themselves towards the east upon the Parthians and Medes; they will stir up the Kings, so that a disturbing spirit will come upon them, and they will drive them from their thrones; and they will come out like lions from their lairs, and like hungry wolves in the middle of their flocks. [56:6] And they will go up and trample upon the land of my chosen ones, and the land of my chosen ones will become before them a tramping-ground and a beaten track. [56:7] But the city of my righteous ones will be a hindrance to their horses, and they will stir up slaughter amongst themselves, and their (own) right hand will be strong against them; and a man will not admit to knowing his neighbor or his brother, nor a son his father or his mother, until

---

2. See M. H. Goshen-Gottstein, "Hebrew Syntax and the History of the Bible Text: A Pesher in the MT of Isaiah," *Textus* 8 (1973): 100-106.

3. See M. Kister, "A Common Heritage: Biblical Interpretation at Qumran and Its Implications," in *Biblical Perspectives: Early Use and Interpretation of the Bible in Light of the Dead Sea Scrolls*, ed. M. E. Stone and E. G. Chazon, STDJ 28 (Leiden: Brill, 1998), 104.

4. See D. Flusser, "An Early Jewish-Christian Document in the Tiburtine Sibyl," in *Judaism and the Origins of Christianity* (Jerusalem: Magnes, 1988), 376.

5. For the association of this passage with the Parthian invasion of Judea in 40 B.C.E., see, for example, E. Sjöberg, *Der Menschensohn im äthiopischen Henochbuch*, Skrifter Utgivna av kungl. Humanistika Vetenskapssamfundet i Lund 41 (Lund: Gleerup, 1946); J. C. Greenfield and M. E. Stone, "The Enochic Pentateuch and the Date of the Similitudes," *HTR* 70 (1977): 58-60; M. A. Knibb, "The Date of the Parables of Enoch: A Critical Review," *NTS* 25 (1979): 354; A. Yarbro Collins, "The 'Son of Man' Tradition and the Book of Revelation," in *The Messiah: Developments in Earliest Judaism and Christianity*, ed. James H. Charlesworth (Minneapolis: Fortress, 1992), 563-64; J. H. Charlesworth, "The Date of the Parables of Enoch (1 En 37–71)," *Hen* 20 (1998): 93-98; G. Boccaccini, *Beyond the Essene Hypothesis: The Parting of the Ways between Qumran and Enochic Judaism* (Grand Rapids: Eerdmans, 1998), 144; P. Sacchi, "Qumran e la datazione del Libro delle Parabole di Enoc," *Hen* 25 (2003): 150-66.

6. Translation by M. A. Knibb, *The Ethiopic Book of Enoch: A New Edition in the Light of the Aramaic Dead Sea Fragments*, 2 vols. (Oxford: Clarendon, 1978), 2:140.

through their death there are corpses enough, and their punishment — it will not be in vain.

From these verses it follows that the angels will anger the Parthians and the kings of Medes, instigating them to invade Palestine, but that Jerusalem will be a hindrance to them. A civil war among the Jews will then break out, in which brothers, fathers, and sons will kill each other. V. 7 of the description is based on Deut 33:9: "Who said of his father and mother, 'I consider them not.' His brothers he disregarded, ignored his own children. Your precepts alone they observed, and kept Your covenant."[7] This verse appears in Moses' blessing to the Levites and hints at the acts of the Levites during the transgression involving the golden calf (Exod 32:26-28). The description of that incident tells of Levites showing no mercy on their blood relatives in their punishment of all who committed the sin of worshiping the golden calf. Moses had commanded them: "'Each of you put sword on thigh, go back and forth from gate to gate throughout the camp, and slay brother, neighbor, and kin.' The Levites did as Moses had bidden" (Exod 32:27-28).

The verse appearing in Moses' blessing — "Who said of his father and mother, 'I consider them not.' His brothers he disregarded, ignored his own children. Your precepts alone they observed, and kept Your covenant" (Deut 33:9) — would in the Second Temple period become a part of the description of the ideal priest. It seems as though this text, portraying the Levites as unwilling to grant special treatment to their relatives when they executed those who had sinned with the golden calf, had lost some of its original meaning, and was understood in the Second Temple period as referring to any priest who refrained from nepotism. One of the scrolls from Qumran (4QTestimonia) quotes these verses from Moses' blessings (Deut 33:8-11) when describing the ideal high priest who will serve at the end of days.[8] The verses are also cited in a fragmentary context in 4QFlorilegium, a scroll that describes the ideal temple at the end of days.[9]

In 40 B.C.E. the Parthian army capitalized on the civil war that had broken out in Rome and began a westward invasion, assuming control of large areas of Asia, as well as Syria and Palestine. They crowned Matthias Antigonus, son of

---

7. On the original version of this verse, see J. Strugnell, "Notes en marge du volume V des Discoveries in the Judaean Desert of Jordan," *RevQ* 7 (1970): 225-29.

8. On the historical significance of 4QTest, see H. Eshel, "The Historical Background of the Pesher Interpreting Joshua's Curse on the Rebuilder of Jericho," *RevQ* 15 (1992): 409-20.

9. On the importance of 4QFlor, see D. Dimant, "4QFlorilegium and the Idea of the Community as Temple," in *Hellenica et Judaica*, ed. A. Caquot, M. Hadas-Lebel, and J. Riaud (Leuven: Peeters, 1986), 165-89; M. O. Wise, "4QFlorilegium and the Temple of Adam," *RevQ* 15 (1991): 103-32; both articles include a large bibliography of works on this document.

Aristobulus II, as king of Judah. When the Parthians approached Jerusalem, Herod fled to Masada, then to the Nabateans and later to Rome. With Herod's retreat from Jerusalem, the Parthians gave Hyrcanus II, son of Alexander Jannaeus, over to his nephew — Matthias Antigonus. Antigonus had the ears of Hyrcanus II maimed so as to prevent him from continuing to serve as high priest.[10] According to Josephus's depiction in *War* 1.270, Antigonus bit off Hyrcanus's ear, while in *Ant* 14.366 he says Antigonus cut it off. In 38 the Romans were able to push the Parthians back to the eastern bank of the Euphrates, after which they could help Herod take control of Judah. Herod returned to rule over Judah in 37.[11]

If we adopt the accepted view that 1 En 56:5-7 describes the Parthian invasion of Judah in 40 B.C.E., then it can be supposed that the Deut 33:9 reference was an allusion to the acts of Matthias Antigonus. It should be noted that Hyrcanus II, son of Alexander Jannaeus, served as high priest until the Parthian invasion (i.e., 63-40 B.C.E.), with his nephew Matthias Antigonus succeeding him (40-37).[12] The two above-mentioned documents found in Qumran Cave 4 (4QTest and 4QFlor) attest that Moses' blessing to the Levites was used in the Second Temple period as an important element in the conception of the ideal priest untouched by corruption.

Based on the account in the Parables of Enoch, it seems as though the description in Deuteronomy of the Levites, who slew even their own relatives after the golden calf transgression, reminded various Second Temple period authors of the last Hasmonean ruler, Matthias Antigonus, who mutilated his uncle, Hyrcanus II, in order to prevent him from continuing as high priest. These authors would thus have returned to the original meaning of the verse in Deuteronomy, which spoke not of an incorrupt priest who refrains from nepotism, but of Levites who physically harmed their relatives. It is likely that one of these authors composed a pesher explaining Deut 33:9 as referring to the events of 40 B.C.E., when Matthias Antigonus maimed his uncle Hyrcanus II.[13] This pesher

---

10. See Lev 21:16-24, "Speak to Aaron and say: No man of your offspring throughout the ages who has a defect shall be qualified to offer the food of his God."

11. On these events see A. Schalit, "The End of the Hasmonean Dynasty and the Rise of Herod," in *The Herodian Period*, ed. M. Avi-Yonah, WHJP 7 (London: Allen, 1975), 59-70; E. Schürer, *The History of the Jewish People in the Age of Jesus Christ*, rev. and ed. G. Vermes and F. Millar, vol. 1 (Edinburgh: T. & T. Clark, 1973), 281-86.

12. J. C. VanderKam, *From Joshua to Caiaphas* (Minneapolis: Fortress, 2004), 345-93.

13. We cannot determine whether the author of this pesher would have supported politically Antigonus or Hyrcanus II or neither of them; exegetically he would have been interested in the fulfillment of this poetic text insofar as it describes nonrecognition of one's kin. I would like to thank S. L. Berrin for this insight.

appears to have been known by the author who wrote the Parables of Enoch, and thus he incorporated verses taken from Deut 33:9 into the section in which there is an allusion to the Parthian invasion.[14] If we accept this conjecture, then it follows that the above verses from the Parables of Enoch hint not only at the Parthian invasion, but also at the fact that Matthias Antigonus had maimed Hyrcanus II in 40 B.C.E.

14. On the hypothesis that around 40 B.C.E. the inhabitants of Qumran ceased writing pesherim on biblical verses, learning them only as oral traditions, see H. Eshel, "The Kittim in the *War Scroll* and in the Pesharim," in *Historical Perspectives from the Hasmoneans to Bar Kokhba in Light of the Dead Sea Scrolls,* ed. D. Goodblatt, A. Pinnick, and D. R. Schwartz, STDJ 37 (Leiden: Brill, 2001), 29-44. It should be emphasized that if we are correct in our estimation presented here, there is no reason to suppose that the pesher linking Deut 33:9 with the events of 40 B.C.E. was composed by an author from the Qumran sect. On the possible connection between the Book of Parables and the Qumran scrolls, see D. Dimant, "The Book of Parables (1 Enoch 37–71) and the Qumran Scrolls" (in Hebrew), *Meghillot* 3 (2005): 49-67.

# An Overlooked Patristic Allusion to the Parables of Enoch?

Daniel C. Olson

Discussions of the date and provenance of the Parables of Enoch sometimes take into consideration patristic use (or nonuse) of the booklet during the ante-Nicene period. While there are no explicit quotations of the Parables in early patristic sources, David Suter and Paolo Sacchi have recently drawn back to scholarly attention two of the more credible *allusions*.

David Suter mentions Origen, *Contra Celsum* 5.52 as a possible reference to 1 En 67:4-13.[1] Origen quotes a passage from Celsus's *True Discourse* (Ἀληθὴς Λόγος) that mentions sixty or seventy angels who came to earth, became wicked, and are now imprisoned underground and producing thermal springs with their tears. Just as interesting as the passage itself is Origen's reaction to it. He sees an allusion to the book of Enoch, but an inaccurate one, and he suggests that Celsus does not understand the book and does not seem, in fact, even to have read the relevant passages (5.54). He then ridicules the idea that hot springs are angelic tears, but without saying anything negative about a linkage per se between incarcerated angels and these waters (5.55). It is tempting to conclude that Origen is indeed evaluating Celsus's report against 1 En 67:4-13, especially since there is evidence elsewhere that Origen may have known the Parables. In his *Commentary on John*, Origen observes that "Jared was born to Maleleel, as it is written in the Book of Enoch" (6.25). As Birger Pearson has noted, this looks like a reference to 1 En 37:1.[2] In my view, it is a clearer allusion to the Parables than the better-known *Contra Celsum* passage.

---

1. See above, D. Suter, "Enoch in Sheol: Updating the Dating of the Book of Parables."
2. B. A. Pearson, "Enoch in Egypt," in *For a Later Generation: The Transformation of Tra-*

## An Overlooked Patristic Allusion to the Parables of Enoch?

A second passage has been highlighted by Paolo Sacchi, who maintains that Tertullian, *De cultu feminarum* 1.3 contains a "clear allusion" to the Parables.[3] But if this passage does contain such an allusion, it must be admitted that it is a very indirect one. Sacchi's claim rests on the supposition that Tertullian could not have found prophecies of Christ in the remainder of the Enochic corpus. But Christians had already found the parousia in 1 En 1:9 (Jude 14-15), and 1 En 90:37-38 is another text that looks ripe for the plucking. In light of Christian ingenuity in detecting such prophecies, I suspect that many critics would prefer to label *De cultu feminarum* 1.3 a *possible* allusion to the Parables rather than a *clear* one.[4] Nevertheless, as was the case with Origen, so also with Tertullian there are other passages that may suggest acquaintance with the Parables. In one place (*Adversus Marcionem* 5.11.8) Tertullian uses the phrase "Lord of Spirits" (*domino spirituum*) instead of "the Lord who is the Spirit" while quoting 2 Cor 3:18 from memory, and it has been suggested that familiarity with this title from the Parables could have influenced Tertullian's recollection.[5] In another place (*De resurrectione carnis* 32.1), Tertullian cites an otherwise unknown passage of "scripture": "Et mandabo piscibus maris et eructuabunt ossa quae sunt comesta, et faciam compaginem ad compaginem et os ad os" [And I will command the fish of the sea, and they will vomit up the bones that were eaten, and I will bring joint to joint and bone to bone]. Though I am not convinced, some have seen dependence on 1 En 61:1 in this quotation.[6] All in all, the case for acquaintance with the Parables is weaker for Tertullian than for Origen.

Origen, *Contra Celsum* 5.52, and Tertullian, *De cultu feminarum* 1.3 are the same two passages R. H. Charles put forward in 1912 as the clearest patristic allusions to the Parables, and so it could be argued that this part of the discussion

---

dition in Israel, Early Judaism, and Early Christianity, ed. R. A. Argall et al. (Harrisburg, Pa.: Trinity, 2000), 219.

3. See P. Sacchi, "Qumran e la datazione del Libro delle Parabole di Enoc," *Hen* 25 (2003): 149-66; in English, "Qumran and the Dating of the Book of Parables," in *The Bible and the Dead Sea Scrolls*, ed. J. H. Charlesworth (Waco: Baylor University Press, 2006).

4. See, e.g., the remarks of J. C. VanderKam, "1 Enoch, Enochic Motifs, and Enoch in Early Christian Literature," in *The Jewish Apocalyptic Heritage in Early Christianity*, ed. J. C. VanderKam and W. Adler, CRINT III.4 (Minneapolis: Fortress, 1996), 52.

5. F. F. Bruce, *The Canon of Scripture* (Downers Grove, Ill.: InterVarsity, 1988), 86.

6. E. Evans, *Tertullian's Treatise on the Resurrection* (London: SPCK, 1960), 266; J. Daniélou, *The Origins of Latin Christianity* (London: Darton, Longman and Todd, 1977), 166-67. See the evaluation of R. Bauckham, "Resurrection as Giving Back the Dead: A Traditional Image of Resurrection in the Pseudepigrapha and the Apocalypse of John," in *The Pseudepigrapha and Early Biblical Interpretation*, ed. J. H. Charlesworth and C. A. Evans, JSPSup 14 (Sheffield: JSOT Press, 1993), 288-89.

has advanced very little in almost a century.⁷ But other proposals have not been lacking. Besides the possible additional allusions in Origen and Tertullian, mentioned above, at least three others should be noted:

a. 2 Esd 2:44-47 (second-third century) may be inspired by 1 En 46:1-3, but the resemblance is too loose and imprecise to be certain.
b. The Ethiopic version of Apoc Pet 4, 13 (early second century) does seem to reflect 1 En 51:1, 61:5, and parts of chaps. 62–63;⁸ but despite the efforts of Dennis Buchholz to defend the Ethiopic text of the Apocalypse of Peter,⁹ his own comparison of the text with the Greek recensions makes it plain that the Ethiopic is an unreliable guide to details of the original wording,¹⁰ and it could be that it was only the Ethiopic translator who was under the influence of 1 Enoch.
c. Finally, James H. Charlesworth has argued for allusions to 1 En 48:2-10 in Odes Sol 36 (ca. 100 C.E.).¹¹ Charlesworth may be right, but the resemblances are, once again, more suggestive than conclusive.

There is another text that should, I think, be given serious consideration in this regard, a poem quoted by Irenaeus in his *Adversus haereses* as part of his polemic against the Valentinian teacher and theurgist Marcus. I quote the poem alongside the passage of the Parables to which it may allude:¹²

| 1 En 54:4-6 (trans. Nickelsburg/VanderKam) | Irenaeus, *Adversus haereses* 1.15.6 (trans. Unger/Dillon; ACW 55) |
|---|---|
| 4. And I asked the angel of peace who went with me, "for whom are these chains being prepared?" 5. And he said | Both rightly and fittingly, therefore, in view of your boldness, has the divinely inspired elder and preacher of the |

---

7. R. H. Charles, *The Book of Enoch or 1 Enoch* (Oxford: Clarendon, 1912), lxiv.

8. See G. W. E. Nickelsburg, "Enoch, Levi, and Peter: Recipients of Revelation in Upper Galilee," *JBL* 100 (1981): 575-600 (here 600).

9. D. Buchholz, *Your Eyes Will Be Opened: A Study of the Greek [Ethiopic] Apocalypse of Peter*, SBLDS 97 (Atlanta: Scholars, 1988), 376-424.

10. Buchholz, *Your Eyes*, 145-54.

11. See J. H. Charlesworth, "The Odes of Solomon," in *The Old Testament Pseudepigrapha*, vol. 2, *Expansions of the "Old Testament" and Legends, Wisdom and Philosophical Literature, Prayers, Psalms, and Odes, Fragments of Lost Judeo-Hellenistic Works*, ed. J. H. Charlesworth (Garden City, N.Y.: Doubleday, 1985), 732-33.

12. The translation of G. W. E. Nickelsburg and J. C. VanderKam is from *1 Enoch: A New Translation* (Minneapolis: Fortress, 2004), 68.

to me, "These are being prepared for the host of **Azazel**, that they might take them and throw them into the abyss of complete judgment . . . 6. . . . that the Lord of Spirits may take vengeance on them, for their unrighteousness in becoming servants of **Satan**, and **leading astray** *(wa-'aśhatewomu)* those who dwell on the earth."

Truth burst forth against you in the following poetic lines:

Marcus, maker of idols, observer of portents,
Skilled in astrology and in all arts of magic,
Whereby you confirm your erroneous doctrines.
Showing wonders to whomever you **lead into error** (πλανωμένοις),
Showing the works of the apostate Power,
Marvels which **Satan**, your father, teaches you always
To perform through the power angelic of **Azazel**,
Using you as the precursor of godless Evil.
Such are the words of the God-loving elder.

On the few occasions when *Adversus haereses* 1.15.6 has been cited as an allusion to 1 Enoch, it has been connected with chaps. 7–10 in the Book of the Watchers, because the poem associates "Azazel" with astrology and magic.[13] It seems to me that 1 En 54:4-6 is a better match. In both passages *Azazel acts as an instrument of Satan for the express purpose of leading humanity astray* (Ethiopian *'aśhata* = Greek *planaō*). This is a coherent and distinctive concept, and it is unique to these two documents, as far as I know. The figure of Satan (singular) appears only here in 1 Enoch, and so it is not surprising to find Christian interest in this passage. It might be objected that the poem mentions Azazel himself as Satan's agent, while 1 En 54:4-6 speaks of the "hosts of Azazel." But 1 En 55:4 suggests that Azazel himself is included with his "hosts," and the pur-

---

13. H. J. Lawlor, "Early Citations from the Book of Enoch," *Journal of Philology* 25 (1897): 196-97 ("*Enoch* vii.1, viii.1, &c."); Charles, *Book of Enoch*, lxxxiii ("8³," "8¹"); Charles, "Book of Enoch," in *The Apocrypha and Pseudepigrapha of the Old Testament in English*, vol. 2 (Oxford: Clarendon, 1913), 182 ("viii.1. Cf. also x.8"). J. C. VanderKam cites the poem as evidence that Irenaeus knew the Watcher story, but without citing any particular passages of 1 Enoch; see VanderKam, "1 Enoch, Enochic Motifs," 43. The mere mention of "Azazel" raises suspicion of an Enochic allusion, since this name is almost unknown in Greek and Latin patristics, the result of LXX ἀποπομπαῖος and Vulgate *caper emissarius* for עזאזל in Lev 16. Origen (*Contra Celsum* 6.43) once uses the name Azazel, but he tells the reader he is taking it from the Hebrew. I am not aware of any other occurrences in early patristic Greek or Latin.

pose of the allusion, in any event, is to imply that *Marcus* is acting like one of the "hosts of Azazel." The references to astrology and magic in the second line of the poem do seem to point back to the account in chaps. 7–10, but it may be noted that 1 En 54:4-6 itself points the reader back to those chapters as well (54:5-6; cf. 10:4-6). In the end, if it is accepted that *Adversus haereses* 1.15.6 alludes to 1 Enoch at all, then 1 En 54:4-6 provides the most satisfactory parallel.

The author of the poem in *Adversus haereses* 1.15.6, the "divinely inspired elder," is generally identified as Irenaeus's predecessor, Pothinus, the first bishop of Lyons and probably, like Irenaeus, a native of Asia Minor.[14] Pothinus died in the persecution of 177 (Eusebius, *Historia ecclesiastica* 5.1.29-31; 5.5.8), so his poem cannot be dated later than the mid-170s, making it one of our earliest and most direct patristic allusions to the Parables.

I append here the Greek text of the poem in Epiphanius, *Haereses* 1.15.6, as edited by Karl Holl:

εἰδωλοποιὲ Μάρκε καὶ τερατοσκόπε,
ἀστρολογικῆς ἔμπειρε καὶ μαγικῆς τέχνης,
δι' ὧν κρατύνεις τῆς πλάνης τὰ διδάγματα,
σημεῖα δεικνὺς τοῖς ὑπὸ σοῦ πλανωμένοις,
ἀποστατικῆς δυνάμεως ἐγχειρήματα,
ἃ σοὶ χορηγεῖ σὸς πατὴρ Σατὰν ἀεὶ
δι' ἀγγελικῆς δυνάμεως Ἀζαζὴλ ποιεῖν,
ἔχων σε πρόδρομον ἀντιθέου πανουργίας.[15]

---

14. D. J. Unger and J. J. Dillon, *St. Irenaeus of Lyons against the Heresies*, ACW 55 (New York: Paulist, 1992), 214; "Pothinus," in *Oxford Dictionary of the Christian Church*, ed. F. L. Cross and E. A. Livingstone, 2nd ed. (Oxford: Oxford University Press, 1983), 1113.

15. K. Holl, *Epiphanius II: Panarion haer. 34-64*, GCS (Berlin: Akademie-Verlag, 1980), 23.

# CONCLUSION

# The 2005 Camaldoli Seminar on the Parables of Enoch: Summary and Prospects for Future Research

*Paolo Sacchi*

Michael Stone is quite right when he wonders — obviously in a mental game, as one cannot draw a history of mere possibilities — how scholars would have approached the question of dating the Book of Parables if the title "Son of Man" had not occurred also in the New Testament.[1] The relationship between the Parables and the New Testament writings is much broader than the topic "Son of Man," which is only the most visible link. When we consider the precise relationship between the two, we face several different possibilities: (1) the Book of Parables is earlier than Jesus; (2) it dates after Jesus to the time of the earliest New Testament books; or (3) it is posterior to the entire corpus of the New Testament, or at least contemporaneous with its latest writings. There is a fourth possibility too: the composition of the Parables developed in several stages, so that the "book" actually reflects various chronological moments during the period in which Christianity arose.

It is important to solve at least some of these problems in order to describe an intellectual history of Judaism at the turn of the era, mainly because the Book of Parables may be the only extant document bearing witness to this particular form of Judaism. We cannot simply assume, however, that all its ideas originated with this book. Even if the specific theology of the author is essentially sui generis, it is very likely that the general outlines of his thought predate the Parables. It is certain that the book must be read and interpreted within the mainstream of Enochism, but the degree of innovation introduced

---

1. See above, M. E. Stone, "Enoch's Date in Limbo; or, Some Considerations on David Suter's Analysis of the Book of Parables."

by the author is still not entirely clear. Moreover, there is still uncertainty concerning the extent to which other Enochians accepted the many ideas found in the Parables. For example, what are the implications of VanderKam's and Ben-Dov's assertion that the astronomical knowledge of the Parables *did not* come from the Astronomical Book?[2] And how should we evaluate Piovanelli's argument that the Book of Parables is addressed to the whole of Israel?[3] Perhaps Boyarin's suggestion, building on Piovanelli's argument, that the ideology of the Parables represents in some fashion "the common religious heritage of much of Israel" is correct.[4] But this must be seriously tested, as it could drastically alter the image we have of Jewish society at the beginning of our era.

At any rate, we can only hope that in the future more attention will be given to the links between historical and sociological events on one hand and the history of ideas on the other. The intellectual developments of Enochism are deeply rooted in the social events of the Second Temple period.

The Camaldoli meeting and the essays included in this volume cover a variety of topics related to the study of the Parables of Enoch, and it would be impossible and unnecessary to address each of these individually. Therefore, I will focus here on two major issues that have been directly and indirectly addressed by all contributors in order to see how much our knowledge of the field has advanced. First, there is the problem of the dating of the document, and second, its compositional integrity, that is, whether the last chapter(s) where Enoch is identified as the Son of Man is integral to the original document or a secondary addition.

The two problems are not only complex on their own, but are also inextricably linked to one another. Any solution one may accept for one problem is certain to influence the other. For example, if we deem that the identification of Enoch with the Son of Man figure reverses the whole meaning of the book, then we are forced to see the last chapter(s) of the book as a secondary addition. If instead we feel that the final reversal is compatible with or even anticipated by the rest of the document, then the need for an interpolation theory disappears. Furthermore, the answer to these questions has profound implications on the problem of dating the Parables. If some kind of interpolation theory is accepted, then an argument taken from the first part of the book has no bearing on the final redactional context and vice versa.

2. See above, J. C. VanderKam, "The Book of Parables within the Enoch Tradition," and J. Ben-Dov, "Exegetical Notes on Cosmology in the Parables of Enoch."

3. See above, P. Piovanelli, "'A Testimony for the Kings and the Mighty Who Possess the Earth': The Thirst for Justice and Peace in the Parables of Enoch."

4. See above, D. Boyarin, "Was the Book of Parables a Sectarian Document? A Brief Brief in Support of Pierluigi Piovanelli."

## Two Books of Parables? A Review of Elements Supporting the Two-Stage Composition Theory

The scholars (Nickelsburg, Knibb, Stuckenbruck, Wright) who in the current volume dealt specifically with the form and structure of the Book of Parables all agreed on the basic structural elements of the book: an introduction, three parables, and a final addition.[5] Nevertheless, disagreement still remains on the nature of this final addition as well as some other minor passages. There was also some discussion on whether or not Nickelsburg's recent translation of the Parables is correct in displacing several verses from their traditional collocation.[6] Since this last case does not have any bearing on the general theme of this conference, I shall not address it here. However, the problems connected with the interpretation of the last two chapters of the Parables are absolutely critical for our understanding of the Son of Man figure in this text.

Both Nickelsburg and Knibb have offered important contributions to this issue. Nickelsburg stresses the literary and ideological links between the Parables and the Book of the Watchers. The author of the Parables generally follows and expands topics of the Book of the Watchers, but also refers to many passages of Scripture, particularly Isaiah's Servant Songs and the figure of Wisdom, whose preexistence is attributed to the Son of Man.

Nickelsburg argues generally for the compositional unity of the Parables. The three parables are clearly linked with one another, since the posterior parables always develop themes already present in the preceding ones. The Noachic materials form a coherent whole and seem to be additions or interpolations drawn from a separate text. Although it seems clear that the Noachic passages are copied from another text, the question of who inserted the Noachic narrative still remains. Was it the author of the entire text or a later scribe? Nickelsburg seems to think the latter, but not the same scribe who added the final chapters. Nickelsburg writes of an early stage of the Parables that more or less corresponds to the present form of the Parables without the so-called Noachic additions. But I wonder if such a book ever existed. In any case, we have no evidence of this earlier form of the book.

As Hannah's essay has shown, the links in chap. 67 between the Noachic

---

5. See above, G. W. E. Nickelsburg, "Discerning the Structure(s) of the Enochic Book of Parables"; M. A. Knibb, "The Structure and Composition of the Parables of Enoch"; L. T. Stuckenbruck, "The Parables of Enoch according to George Nickelsburg and Michael Knibb: A Summary and Discussion of Some Remaining Questions"; and B. G. Wright, "The Structure of the Parables of Enoch: A Response to George Nickelsburg and Michael Knibb."

6. See G. W. E. Nickelsburg and J. C. VanderKam, eds., *The Book of Enoch* (Minneapolis: Fortress, 2004).

text and the hand of a later interpolator who shared the main worldview of the Parables are very strong.[7] It is not an isolated case in the Parables, and in my opinion, the "interpolator" who shared this worldview cannot be but the author of the Parables. He modified in some cases the Noachic text for his aims, but there is no reason to think that he was an interpolator.

Since the Noachic passages fit contextually in the ensemble of the book, I think it is better to attribute the insertion of these passages to the author himself, who found in ancient texts passages useful for his intellectual construction. This is true even if the author included details that seem somewhat extraneous, since it was the text itself that was important for him, and not necessarily the particulars.

The method of Knibb's essay is more literary than that of Nickelsburg. He presents a masterful analysis of the Parables, and although the relationship between this text and the broader Enochic tradition is not central to his argument, he nevertheless offers some valuable insights. For Knibb, the Book of Parables is a continuation of the Book of the Watchers, as indicated in the phrase "second vision" at the beginning of the book. The book of Noah is also important for the Parables, and Knibb is convinced, like Nickelsburg, that the Parables is so full of "secondary passages" that "it is not possible to reconstruct a history of the text precedent to last writing." For example, 56:5–57:3a has peculiarities that make it "so out of character with the view of the rest of the Book of Parables that the passage would appear at the very least to have been taken over from elsewhere and may well have been added at a secondary stage."[8]

Knibb often speaks of blocks of materials that could have been introduced into the book in a second stage. He creates, so to say, the image of a book that continuously developed, so much so that I wonder from this vantage point if it is possible to identify the text of an author, because it is not clear if each passage was inserted by the author himself or added at a later stage. I think the simplest solution is to maintain that the loose connection of ideas belonged to the author himself: "loose connection" does not necessarily mean "no connection."

A particular case is that of the two final chapters. Knibb is conscious that the interpretation of these chapters raises many problems, even with regard to translation. Nevertheless, he can affirm with sufficient certainty that (1) chaps. 70–71 belong to a late stage in the formation of the Parables, and (2) these chapters contain the narration of the ascent of Enoch to heaven and his identification with the preexistent Son of Man. This means that the last two chapters,

---

7. See above, D. D. Hannah, "The Book of Noah, the Death of Herod the Great, and the Date of the Parables of Enoch."

8. Knibb, "The Structure and Composition of the Parables of Enoch."

though belonging to the text that tradition has handed down to us, *are not* the work of the same author of 1 En 37–69, and so the identification of Enoch with the Son of Man.

The word "addition" commonly used by scholars suggests that the appendix was written subsequent to the rest of the book. Thus, there is a glorification of Enoch in this so-called addition that the rest of the work does not know. The content of this addition cannot derive from a previous though now lost Enochic book, because it develops materials belonging to the Parables itself. Nevertheless, Enoch's identification with the Son of Man clashes with the Enoch who narrates details regarding this figure. Although there is no extended discussion of the dating of this addition, Nickelsburg does highlight some links with the figure of Enoch in the Slavonic Enoch, which, in its earliest form — the so-called recension B — could be contemporaneous.

Orlov, drawing on VanderKam, offers a different opinion on this issue.[9] Orlov cautiously considers the hypothesis that the final "addition" may have been written by the Parables' author. In this case, Enoch's identification with the Son of Man could be understood as integral to the author's theology in the light of the belief that a creature of flesh could have a double in heaven, an idea that is evident in the Prayer of Joseph. As Israel was the incarnation of an archangel, so Enoch was the incarnation of a still higher figure, that of the Son of Man. I think this is an interesting proposal, but I wonder if it really solves the main problem, namely, the difficulty of Enoch describing the Son of Man without perceiving that he is that figure.

As for the dating of the book, Nickelsburg has devoted much space to this topic and has concluded that Mark, the source Q, and Paul "knew a form of the son of Man tradition that we find in the Parables of Enoch but not in Daniel 7."[10] Thus, the dating of the Parables must be placed in the first decades of the first century, or a little before, if we consider that "there is perhaps further corroboration for this in the commonly held belief that 1 En 67:4-13 alludes to Herod the Great's retreat to the baths of Callirrhoe."[11]

Both Nickelsburg and Knibb point out some difficulties in chap. 42, where we find the figure of Wisdom, who cannot find her place among humanity and thus must return to heaven. While for Nickelsburg the problem concerns only the place of this passage within the whole of the work, for Knibb the problem concerns the authenticity of the passage itself. Thus, Nickelsburg

---

9. See above, A. A. Orlov, "Roles and Titles of the Seventh Antediluvian Hero in the Parables of Enoch: A Departure from the Traditional Pattern?"

10. See G. W. E. Nickelsburg, "Son of Man," in *ABD* 6:138-49.

11. Nickelsburg, "Discerning the Structure(s) of the Enochic Book of Parables." On this point, see also above, L. W. Walck, "The Son of Man in the Parables of Enoch and the Gospels."

solves the problem by displacing the block in order to obtain a more coherent reading, while Knibb leaves the problem open. For Knibb, the difficulty of the Wisdom pericope arises from the fact that it "does interrupt the natural sequence of the text and is widely regarded as misplaced."[12]

If Nickelsburg is correct and the problem is only that this passage is out of place, then this has no relevance for our understanding of the ideology of the author. But if it is an interpolation, then the theology of the author changes once we remove this text from consideration. I think Boccaccini is correct when he argues that the Wisdom figure is connected with the figure of the Son of Man as eschatological judge.[13] This image of Wisdom is thus perfectly confluent with the author's thought. As such, I maintain that Nickelsburg's solution is the most plausible.

In my opinion, little attention has been devoted to the actual compositional history of the Parables. At times one finds general assertions of an "earlier" form of the Parables — which of course we do not currently possess — minus the Noachic sections. For example, Kvanvig speaks of "the growth of the book" and Nickelsburg writes, "it is understandable that a redactor would interpolate Noachic materials into the Book of Parables with its heavy emphasis on the final judgment."[14] From this perspective, the Noachic material was added to a preexisting book and is thus considered interpolated material.

Although it is evident that the Noachic sections were copied from another book, this does not necessarily make this material a later interpolation. In fact, the Noachic passages fit nicely into the development of the author's thought. If an author copies some parts of a text and inserts them into his text, this material is only a copied source; it is no interpolation.

We can recognize an interpolation in a translated text such as the Ethiopic Enoch only through the analysis of the content, because the style is always that of the translator. This is the case in the last two chapters of the book, which at first glance do not appear continuous with the previous text. In this case we are faced with two options: (1) we suppose a discontinuity between the main text and the final two chapters and conclude that an interpolator intended to change the meaning of the work by inserting this material; or (2) we try to understand how this material may in fact serve the author's purpose, perhaps to surprise his readers, and conclude that the final chapters are not an interpolation but an integral part of the original document.

---

12. Knibb, "The Structure and Composition of the Parables of Enoch."

13. See above, G. Boccaccini, "Finding a Place for the Parables of Enoch within Second Temple Jewish Literature."

14. See above, H. S. Kvanvig, "The Son of Man in the Parables of Enoch"; and Nickelsburg, "Discerning the Structure(s) of the Enochic Book of Parables."

Herein lies the central problem: Is it possible that the same author depicts Enoch as a revealer of the Son of Man figure and later identifies Enoch with that figure? If yes, then more work should be devoted to the first chapters of the book to show how this is possible. However, in my opinion there still remains a major difficulty: How could Enoch, a figure born in time — as has been stressed in this seminar — be identified with the Son of Man, who was created before time? In light of this question, I think the most plausible explanation is that the final chapters are in fact an addition.

This statement includes some important consequences. It splits the problem of the date of the Parables into two distinct questions: When was the main text written and when was the final addition inserted? With this in mind, the conclusions in Boccaccini's essay, which considers the Parables a unity in the form it has reached us and tries to establish its date on the basis of the unfolding of the Jewish thought during a certain period, are valid only for the book as a whole, including its later parts.[15] So in considering the various arguments for dating the Parables, if the arguments are taken from chaps. 37–69, then they contribute only to the dating of the early stage of the book. But when the arguments are drawn from the last two chapters, then the results are valid for the final form of the book. Not surprisingly, Boccaccini's method leads to a little later date than that proposed by Arcari, Charlesworth, Chialà, Eshel, and others.[16]

This splitting of the question could have some interesting consequences for future research on the Parables. What we then have are "two" Parables of Enoch: the first presents the Son of Man as a heavenly being *created* before time, whose existence is revealed to Enoch; the second presents the Son of Man as both the preexisting, unnamed heavenly figure and the human-born revealer, Enoch.

## Enoch in Heaven? The Dating of the Book of Parables after the Camaldoli Meeting

As is well known, the dating of the Parables can be made only by internal criteria, because we have no external evidence from ancient sources about the Para-

---

15. See Boccaccini, "Finding a Place for the Parables of Enoch within Second Temple Jewish Literature."

16. See above, L. Arcari, "A Symbolic Transfiguration of a Historical Event: The Parthian Invasion in Josephus and the Parables of Enoch"; J. H. Charlesworth, "Can We Discern the Composition Date of the Parables of Enoch?"; S. Chialà, "The Son of Man: The Evolution of an Expression"; and H. Eshel, "An Allusion in the Parables of Enoch to the Acts of Matthias Antigonus in 40 B.C.E.?"

bles. This research can proceed in many different ways: (1) we can look for quotations in the patristic literature to obtain a terminus ante quem; (2) we can look for literary sources that could provide a terminus a quo; (3) we can analyze the ideology of the book itself to establish some ideological links between the Parables and other literary documents, which then help us determine what time period best fits the text; and (4) we can explore possible historical allusions in the text. This last approach is in my opinion the most secure, if and when it is possible. This method of dating has been applied to many other texts, such as the book of Daniel and the Book of Dream Visions, whose dating is reasonably deduced from the last known event recorded in each respective narrative.[17]

To these issues we can add the significance of the absence of the Parables in the Qumran library. It is appropriate to address this issue here, since some are inclined to use this absence as evidence for its later date. In fact, however, this has no relevance to the problem of the date of the Parables, as demonstrated in Charlesworth's essay. Specifically, he calculates that only a very small part of the texts hidden in the Qumran caves is available for analysis: "Cumulatively, perhaps we possess only about 10 to 20 percent of the manuscripts that were in the Qumran caves."[18] This is certainly a plausible explanation for the Parables' absence, but perhaps ideological tensions and the closure of the Qumran community from the rest of Israel, which occurred around 100 B.C.E., led to its exclusion. In fact, most Jewish works written after this date are missing at Qumran, which may indicate that such absences are not random or accidental. Boccaccini argues extensively for this explanation in his *Beyond the Essene Hypothesis*, which finds its origins in the Groningen hypothesis of García Martínez and van der Woude.[19]

Suter's essay nicely presents the *status quaestionis* on dating the Parables.[20] Specifically, he singles out and analyzes some of the major arguments utilized for dating the Parables. Of these I would like to consider several that

---

17. I have applied this method also to the author(s) who wrote that great history from the creation of man in Eden to the accession to the throne of Awil-Marduk, and I think it is a valid one to establish the date of some NT writings, such as the Acts of the Apostles and the Synoptic Gospels. See P. Sacchi, "I sinottici furono scritti in ebraico? Una valida ipotesi di lavoro," *Hen* 8 (1986): 67-78, and Sacchi, "Riflessioni metodologiche sulla critica biblica e soprattutto sul cosiddetto problema del Pentateuco," *Hen* 21 (1999): 179-84.

18. Charlesworth, "Can We Discern the Composition Date of the Parables of Enoch?"

19. G. Boccaccini, *Beyond the Essene Hypothesis: The Parting of the Ways between Qumran and Enochic Judaism* (Grand Rapids: Eerdmans, 1998); cf. F. García Martínez and A. S. van der Woude, "A Groningen Hypothesis of Qumran Origins and Early History," *RevQ* 14 (1990): 521-41.

20. See above, D. W. Suter, "Enoch in Sheol: Updating the Dating of the Book of Parables."

seem to shed light on the discussion. Suter's arguments are drawn from the academic discussions, and several new proposals based on new observations have been made in the current volume by the above-mentioned essays by Arcari, Charlesworth, Chialà, Eshel, Hannah, and in a particular way, Boccaccini.

Suter's conclusions are very cautious. On one hand he refuses Milik's third century C.E. dating, but on the other hand he is not convinced that the earlier dates proposed by many scholars are acceptable. He simply presents several possibilities without decisively accepting any one, from as early as the turn of the era to the middle of the first century or even later. With Johannes Theisohn and Leslie Walck, he is convinced that "some of the distinctive Son of Man sayings in Matthew are influenced by the Parables," and yet elsewhere he concludes that the development of the Parables is "a parallel process to the formation of Christology in the early church and [is not] evidence for the use of 'Son of Man' in the teaching of Jesus."[21] In the latter case (dating the book to the turn of the era, following Black, Nickelsburg, and Collins), the content of the Parables may have influenced not only early Christian theologies, but also Jesus' formative culture and teaching. In the former case, the Parables would have been parallel to the formation of the New Testament documents, and if there was any influence, it would have been on its writers but not on Jesus. Should we think that the title Son of Man was given to Jesus only by the Evangelists? The title or nickname Son of Man appears only on Jesus' mouth. If this phrase depended only on the Evangelists, then most likely it would have been used more frequently. I think this problem should be considered more carefully.

It seems to me that the most interesting aspect of the essays of both Suter and Stone is their attitude toward the problem of the dating of the Parables; their caution gives way to a methodological doubt that is evident even in their titles. For Suter, the problem of dating the Parables is "in sheol," and for Stone, who is apparently a bit more optimistic, "in limbo."[22] A similar uncertainty was also evident in several other scholars who attended the conference. Boyarin, after affirming his agreement with Piovanelli's essay, remarks that the Parables was probably written "sometime in the first century," an assertion not entirely consistent with Piovanelli's argument.[23] A consequence of this incertitude is that the Parables cannot be confidently used as a source for writing a history of

---

21. Suter, "Enoch in Sheol"; cf. J. Theisohn, *Der auserwählte Richter: Untersuchungen zum traditionsgeschichtlichem Ort der Menschensohngestalt der Bilderreden des Äthiopischen Henoch* (Göttingen: Vandenhoeck & Ruprecht, 1975); and Walck, "The Son of Man in the Parables of Enoch and the Gospels."

22. Compare Suter, "Enoch in Sheol," and Stone, "Enoch's Date in Limbo."

23. Boyarin, "Was the Book of Parables a Sectarian Document?" On this issue, see also above, L. Grabbe, "The Parables of Enoch in Second Temple Jewish Society."

the first century C.E. Indeed, as is well known, some scholars who deal with the history of ideas during this period have avoided using the Parables.

It is particularly noteworthy that Suter places the Parables in the prehistory of the Hekhalot movement, which would have already existed in the first century C.E.[24] Orlov likewise finds in the identification of Enoch with the heavenly Son of Man a signal "of a possible transition from Enochic to Metatron imagery."[25] This hypothesis really opens a new field of research, which perhaps could garner some attention in future meetings of the Enoch Seminar. I am not yet convinced that the Parables may be inserted into the same trajectory as the Hekhalot literature, but it does seem likely that some elements present in the Parables may be present in or have influenced the Gnostic movement. Keep in mind that the *Megale Apophasis* probably belongs to the first century B.C.E., which would make it contemporaneous not only with the Parables but also with some important Qumran texts.

Although Gieschen does not focus primarily on the date of the Parables, his essay is still worth mentioning in this context. Gieschen tries to understand what the figure of the Son of Man signified in the theological reflection of the Enochians of Jesus' time. His conclusion is profound and very stimulating: the Son of Man "shares the Divine Name of the Ancient of Days, the Tetragrammaton, which is a profound assertion that reflects a complex understanding of Jewish monotheism."[26] I am not yet certain that Gieschen has truly demonstrated his hypothesis, but such ideas should be considered carefully before they are accepted or refused. However, if Gieschen is correct, then he has uncovered a precedent to the form of monotheism we find more fully developed in Christianity some centuries later.

Other participants were more confident about the possibility of using the Parables for reconstructing an intellectual history of Second Temple Judaism. James Charlesworth dates the Parables to the time of Herod the Great, probably at the peak of his reign, that is, between 20 and 4 B.C.E.[27] The primary argument

---

24. Suter here takes up again a proposal he made in 1979, when he wrote that the Parables "belongs to an early stage of the Merkavah tradition. It might be better, perhaps, to classify the Parables as proto-Merkavah" (Suter, *Tradition and Composition in the Parables of Enoch* [Missoula: Scholars, 1979], 23). This suggestion has not been widely accepted, but I think it is worthy of careful consideration.

25. Orlov, "Roles and Titles of the Seventh Antediluvian Hero in the Parables of Enoch."

26. C. A. Gieschen, "The Name of the Son of Man in the Parables of Enoch." On this issue see also the important essay by G. Boccaccini, "Uomo, angelo o Dio? Alle radici del messianismo ebraico e cristiano?" in *Il messia tra memoria e attesa*, ed. G. Boccaccini (Brescia: Morcelliana, 2005), 15-48.

27. Charlesworth, "Can We Discern the Composition Date of the Parables of Enoch?"

for this dating is the interpretation of the invasion narrated in chap. 56 as the Parthian invasion. There is no reason to consider "Parthians" a symbolic nickname. Although apocalyptic literature does use this literary device, it would be unusual that one historical name was symbolically substituted for another equally historical name. Thus, when the author speaks of the Parthians, he really means the Parthians.

Luca Arcari also focuses on this issue by exploring how the apocalyptic writer transforms a historical event into a myth.[28] This is an important insight into an apocalyptic way of thinking — real events become understandable only if considered a manifestation or a sign of a superior reality. Arcari thus maintains the historical value of the name of the Parthians in a manner that is consistent with a distinctly apocalyptic mode of thought; reality always has the taste of myth, and earthly events always mirror events occurring in a higher world. He further shows that the narrative of chap. 56 follows the scheme of the event itself, at least as recorded in Josephus. The invasion detailed in the Parables was real for the author of this text.[29]

Charlesworth proposes a new argument for dating the Parables to the time of Herod. He accepts that the phrase "mighty of the earth" (according to Isaac's translation of the Parables) does not indicate the rulers of the earth, the kings and the rich, that is, all those having power, but indicates a third class of individuals, which he identifies, following Isaac's translation, as the "landowners." I have always been suspicious of such interpretations, primarily because they require more precision than the text typically allows. Nevertheless, in this case it seems to me that Charlesworth's proposal is worthy of consideration, since he has suggested a complex backdrop and has successfully pieced together so many particular details.

Several other participants also proposed new arguments supporting the dating of the Parables to Herod's time. Eshel's essay confirms the identification of chap. 56 with the Parthian invasion of 40 B.C.E.[30] According to Eshel, it is also likely that 56:7 contains an allusion to Matthias Antigonus, who bit off the ear of his uncle Hyrcanus to prevent him from serving as high priest. This is an intriguing hypothesis but perhaps a bit too complicated, as even Eshel is quite cautious in his presentation.

---

28. Arcari, "A Symbolic Transfiguration of a Historical Event."

29. I also argued for this method of dating the Parables at a Princeton meeting in 1997. See P. Sacchi, "Qumran e la datazione del Libro delle Parabole di Enoc," *Hen* 25 (2003): 149-66 [= "Qumran and the Dating of the Book of Parables," in *The Bible and the Dead Sea Scrolls*, ed. James H. Charlesworth (Waco: Baylor University Press, 2006)].

30. Eshel, "An Allusion in the Parables of Enoch to the Acts of Matthias Antigonus in 40 B.C.E.?"

Hannah's essay presents a careful interpretation of the Noachic interpolation of 67:1-13. According to Hannah, the second part of this passage, vv. 8-13, "can easily be understood as an allusion to Herod the Great's visit to the waters of Callirrhoe in the latter part of March 4 B.C.E."[31] Since he considers this interpolator later than both the text of the Parables and the text of the *Apocryphon of Noah*, it follows that this interpolator wrote after (but not much after) 4 B.C.E. and the original text obviously precedes this date. Even if this text was inserted into this place by the author of the Parables, as I suggested earlier, the argument still remains valid.

Another way to study the dating problem is to establish its terminus ante quem. Olson's analysis addresses the problem of the use (or not) of the Parables in the ante-Nicene period. While he confirms the assumption that there are no explicit quotations of the Parables at that time, he discusses two credible allusions that were recently highlighted by both Suter (*Contra Celsum* 5.52) and Sacchi (*De cultu feminarum* 5.3). According to Olson, these are only allusions and not quotations, especially that found in *De cultu feminarum*. In addition to these allusions, Olson proposes a possible quotation in *Contra haereses* 1.15.6, whose text probably originates with the "divinely inspired elder" who is generally identified as Pothinus. Pothinus died in 177 C.E., so the text must precede this date. If Olson is correct, then this is "one of our earliest and most direct patristic allusions to the Parables."[32] We can then conclude that the Fathers knew the Parables, even if they hesitated to quote it.

In sum, we may observe that those scholars who have directly addressed the problem of dating the Parables all agree on a date around the time of Herod. Other participants of the conference not addressing the problem directly nevertheless agree with this conclusion, namely, Chialà, Yarbro Collins, Nickelsburg, Piovanelli, and Walck.[33] We should also place Boccaccini in this group.[34] He has proposed a date in the first half of the first century C.E., but his main argument is based on the identification of Enoch with the Son of Man, and thus is relevant only for the dating of the last two chapters, which are later than the rest of the work.

It is interesting that those who have not accepted a date around the turn of the era do not propose any alternative date but instead focus on the many

---

31. Hannah, "The Book of Noah, the Death of Herod the Great, and the Date of the Parables of Enoch."
32. D. C. Olson, "An Overlooked Patristic Allusion to the Parables of Enoch?"
33. Besides the already mentioned essays, see above, A. Yarbro Collins, "The Secret Son of Man in the Parables of Enoch and the Gospel of Mark: A Response to Leslie Walck."
34. Boccaccini, "Finding a Place for the Parables of Enoch within Second Temple Jewish Literature."

possibilities and uncertainties in dating this text. In fact, no specific date other than the turn of the era was proposed at the conference. This lack of specificity on the part of some seems to have resulted in a scholarly impasse, since the two main positions represented at the conference are basically asymmetrical. Those offering concrete proposals on the date of the Parables are unable to assess alternative hypotheses that lack concrete elements for evaluation.

In his essay, Walck summarizes his position on the date of the Parables as follows:

> Most likely . . . the Book of Parables can be dated to the end of or shortly after the reign of Herod the Great, toward the end of the first century B.C.E. or early first century C.E. Herod, a vassal king of the Romans, the Romans, and their generals fit the characterization in the Parables of the kings and mighty ones. The Parthians' hand in Herod's accession and Herod's visit late in life to healing springs, probably Callirrhoe, also fit the allusions in the Parables. Further, the bloodshed, for which the righteous and elect desire vindication (1 En 47), fits the conflict of the times.

Earlier Walck remarked: "The dating of the Parables, while tentative, is important."[35] I think that after the Camaldoli meeting the adjective "tentative" should be dropped, given the impressive amount of evidence gathered in support of a pre-Christian origin of the document. The burden of proof has shifted to those who disagree with the Herodian date. It is now their responsibility to provide evidence that would reopen the discussion.

## Conclusion

In the essay I wrote for the second Enoch seminar in Venice, I proposed — on the basis of Boccaccini's ideas — a scheme of events for the second century B.C.E. that could clarify the emergence of Essenism as a combination of Enochic and Mosaic traditions, while the Enochic tradition continued in its distinctive autonomous path.[36] If the book of Jubilees was indeed at the origin of Essenism, what posterior books can be assigned to the tradition born from it? What was the form of Enochism and Essenism at Jesus' time? Here is a chapter

---

35. Walck, "The Son of Man in the Parables of Enoch and the Gospels."
36. P. Sacchi, "History of the Earliest Enochic Texts," in *Enoch and Qumran Origins: New Light on a Forgotten Connection,* ed. G. Boccaccini (Grand Rapids: Eerdmans, 2005), 401-7; cf. Boccaccini, *Beyond the Essene Hypothesis.*

of Jewish intellectual history yet to be written. Jesus' teaching took place in that historical context. Is it only by chance that Mark, who was the first to compose a narrative of Jesus, never put into Jesus' mouth the word "law"?

I think the Enoch Seminar could contribute to the start of what we might call the "fourth quest for the historical Jesus," which should begin with a careful study of Jesus' milieu. Through the ongoing research of the seminar participants, there is tremendous potential to describe the intellectual backdrop of the Jewish society in the century during which Jesus preached, the New Testament documents were composed, and many other Jews wrote in Greek. This is indeed an enormous task with profound implications even for the contemporary religious landscape. The search for Christian origins is also a search for the nature of both Christianity and Judaism and the origin and values of our modern society.

# The Parables of Enoch and the Messiah Son of Man: A Bibliography, 1773-2006

*Jason von Ehrenkrook*

Gabriele Boccaccini's introduction to the present volume divides the history of research on the Parables of Enoch into five major phases: (1) the initial exploration of the Parables made possible through the publication of the first editions and modern translations in the early part of the nineteenth century, following the "rediscovery" of 1 Enoch by James Bruce in 1773; (2) the publication of new translations and new critical editions of the Ethiopic text along with the first commentaries around the turn and into the first half of the twentieth century; (3) the years of "limbo" immediately following the discovery of the Dead Sea Scrolls and Josef Milik's announcement that the Book of Parables was missing from the Enoch fragments; (4) a gradual return to the question of the Parables' date and significance for Christian origins after the publication of the Aramaic fragments of 1 Enoch and the renewed interest in the Old Testament Pseudepigrapha in the 1980s; and (5) the current "renaissance" of studies on the Parables led by George Nickelsburg's work in the United States and Paolo Sacchi's in Europe, and fueled by a new awareness of the great diversity of messianic and intermediary figures in Second Temple Judaism. The following bibliography is organized chronologically to approximate this periodization.

In addition to studies focused on the Parables of Enoch, I have included works more generally devoted to the entire Enochic literature, on one hand, and on the other, to the problem of the Messiah Son of Man in Second Temple Judaism and the intellectual context of early Christology. The literature on these topics is of course immense, and an exhaustive bibliography of this research defies the limits of the present volume. I have limited my attention only to those works that more directly have affected, or were affected by, the research on the Book of Parables. Thus, the reader may wish to consult the bibliographies in Sabino Chialà's *Libro delle Parabole di Enoc* (1997) and Delbert Burkett's *The Son of Man Debate* (1999) as a supplement. The value of the ensuing bibliography resides mainly in its unique chronological arrangement, in the focus on the Parables within the broader context of *both* Enochic studies and studies on the Son of Man, and in the inclusion of the most recent research published after Chialà and Burkett.

## 1990-present

Alexander, Philip S. "From Son of Adam to Second God: Transformation of the Biblical Enoch." In *Biblical Figures outside the Bible*, edited by Michael E. Stone and Theodore A. Bergren, 87-122. Harrisburg, Pa.: Trinity, 1998.

Aufrecht, Walter E. "The Son of Man Problem as an Illustration of the Techne of New Testament Studies." In *Origins and Method: Toward a New Understanding of Judaism and Christianity*, edited by Bradley H. McLean, 282-94. JSNTSup 86. Sheffield: JSOT, 1993.

Bauckham, Richard. Review of *The Son of the Man in the Gospel of John*, by Delbert Burkett. *EvQ* 65 (1993): 266-68.

———. "The Throne of God and the Worship of Jesus." in *The Jewish Roots of Christological Monotheism*, edited by Carey C. Newman et al., 43-69. Leiden: Brill, 1999.

———. "Apocalypses." In *Justification and Variegated Nomism*, vol. 1, *The Complexities of Second Temple Judaism*, edited by D. A. Carson, Peter T. O'Brien, and Mark A. Seifrid, 149-51. Grand Rapids: Baker Academic, 2001.

Black, Matthew. "The Messianism of the Parables of Enoch: Their Date and Contribution to Christological Origins." In *The Messiah: Developments in Earliest Judaism and Christianity*, edited by James H. Charlesworth, 145-68. Minneapolis: Fortress, 1992.

Boccaccini, Gabriele. "Jewish Apocalyptic Tradition: The Contribution of Italian Scholarship." In *Mysteries and Revelations: Apocalyptic Studies since the Uppsala Colloquium*, edited by John J. Collins and James H. Charlesworth, 33-50. JSPSup 9. Sheffield: JSOT, 1991.

———. "E se l'essenismo fosse il movimento enochiano? Una nuova ipotesi circa i rapporti tra Qumran e gli esseni." *RSB* 7, no. 2 (1997): 49-67.

———. "Enochic Documents Unknown at Qumran; or, Enoch vs. Qumran." In *Beyond the Essene Hypothesis: The Parting of the Ways between Qumran and Enochic Judaism*, 131-49, esp. 144-49. Grand Rapids: Eerdmans, 1998.

———. "A Historian's Response to W. Wink's *The Human Being: Jesus and the Enigma of the Son of Man*." *Cross Currents* 53, no. 2 (2003): 270-75. With a response by Walter Wink, 276-78.

———. "Messianismo giudaico, messianismo cristiano: continuità e discontinuità." In *Gesù Cristo, Figlio di Dio e Signore,* edited by Vincenzo Battaglia and Carmelo Dotolo, 49-62. Bologna: Dehoniane, 2004.

———, ed. *Il messia tra memoria e attesa.* Brescia: Morcelliana, 2005.

———. "Uomo, angelo o Dio? Alle radici del messianismo ebraico e cristiano." In *Il messia tra memoria e attesa,* edited by Gabriele Boccaccini, 15-48. Brescia: Morcelliana, 2005.

Borsch, Frederick Houk. "Further Reflections on 'The Son of Man': The Origins and Development of the Title." In *The Messiah: Developments in Earliest Judaism and Christianity,* edited by James H. Charlesworth, 130-44. Minneapolis: Fortress, 1992.

Burkett, Delbert. *The Son of the Man in the Gospel of John.* JSNTSup 56. Sheffield: JSOT Press, 1991.

———. Review of *The Son of Man Tradition,* by Douglas A. Hare. *HeyJ* 33 (1992): 447-48.

———. "The Nontitular Son of Man: A History and Critique." *NTS* 40 (1994): 504-21.

———. *The Son of Man Debate: A History and Evaluation.* SNTSMS 107. Cambridge: Cambridge University Press, 1999.

Casey, Maurice. *From Jewish Prophet to Gentile God: The Origins and Development of New Testament Christology.* Cambridge: James Clarke; Louisville: John Knox/Westminster, 1991.

———. "Method in Our Madness and Madness in Their Methods: Some Approaches to the Son of Man Problem in Recent Scholarship." *JSNT* 42 (1991): 17-43.

———. "The Use of the Term (a) vn (a) rb in the Aramaic Translations of the Hebrew Bible." *JSNT* 54 (1994): 87-118.

———. "Idiom and Translation: Some Aspects of the Son of Man Problem." *NTS* 41 (1995): 164-82.

Charlesworth, James H. "The Date of the Parables of Enoch (1 En 37–71)." *Hen* 20 (1998): 93-98.

———. "Il Figlio dell'uomo, il primo giudaismo, Gesù, e la cristologia primitive." In *Il messia tra memoria e attesa,* edited by Gabriele Boccaccini. Brescia: Morcelliana, 2005.

———, ed. *The Messiah: Developments in Earliest Judaism and Christianity.* Minneapolis: Fortress, 1992.

Chialà, Sabino. *Libro delle Parabole di Enoc.* Brescia: Paideia, 1997.

Chilton, Bruce D. "The Son of Man: Human and Heavenly." In *The Four Gospels 1992: Festschrift Frans Neirynck,* edited by F. Van Segbroeck et al., 1:203-18. 3 vols. Leuven: Leuven University Press, 1992.

———. "The Son of Man: Who Was He?" *BRev* 12 (1996): 35-39, 45-47.

Collins, John J. "The Son of Man in First-Century Judaism." *NTS* 38, no. 3 (1992): 448-66.

———. "The Danielic Son of Man: Daniel 7, the Similitudes of Enoch, Fourth Ezra."

In *The Scepter and the Star: The Messiahs of the Dead Sea Scrolls and Other Ancient Literature*, 173-94. New York: Doubleday, 1995.

———. "The Similitudes of Enoch." In *The Apocalyptic Imagination: An Introduction to Jewish Apocalyptic Literature*, 177-93. Rev. ed. Grand Rapids: Eerdmans, 1998.

———. "Enoch, Books of." In *Dictionary of New Testament Backgrounds*, edited by Craig A. Evans and Stanley Porter, 313-18. Downers Grove, Ill.: InterVarsity, 2000.

Davila, James R. "Of Methodology, Monotheism and Metatron: Introductory Reflections on Divine Mediators and the Origins of the Worship of Jesus." In *The Jewish Roots of Christological Monotheism: Papers from the St. Andrews Conference on the Historical Origins of the Worship of Jesus*, edited by Carey C. Newman et al., 3-18. Leiden: Brill, 1999.

———. *The Provenance of the Pseudepigrapha: Jewish, Christian, or Other?* esp. 132-37. Leiden: Brill, 2005.

DiTommaso, Lorenzo. *A Bibliography of Pseudepigrapha Research, 1850-1999.* Sheffield: Sheffield Academic, 2001.

Fuller, Reginald H. Review of *Die Entchristologisierung des Menschensohnes*, by Rollin Kearns. *JBL* 109 (1990): 721-23.

Geay, Patrick. "L'ascension d'Hénoch: Imagination visionnaire et philosophie." *RSR* 80 (1992): 187-202.

Gieschen, Charles A. *Angelomorphic Christology: Antecedents and Early Evidence.* AGJU 42. Leiden: Brill, 1998.

Hampel, Volker. *Menschensohn und historischer Jesus: Ein Rätselwort als Schlüssen zum messianischen Selbverständnis Jesu.* Neukirchen-Vluyn: Neukirchener Verlag, 1990.

Hannah, Darrell. "The Throne of His Glory: The Divine Throne and Heavenly Mediators in Revelation and the Similitudes of Enoch." *ZNW* 94 (2003): 68-96.

Hare, Douglas R. A. *The Son of Man Tradition.* Minneapolis: Fortress, 1990.

Helyer, Larry R. *Exploring Jewish Literature of the Second Temple Period.* Downers Grove, Ill.: InterVarsity, 2002.

Himmelfarb, Martha. "Revelation and Rupture: The Transformation of the Visionary in the Ascent Apocalypses." In *Mysteries and Revelations: Apocalyptic Studies since the Uppsala Colloquium*, edited by John J. Collins and James H. Charlesworth, 79-90. JSPSup 9. Sheffield: JSOT, 1991.

———. *Ascent to Heaven in Jewish and Christian Apocalypses.* Philadelphia: University of Pennsylvania Press, 1993.

Jackson, David R. *Enochic Judaism: Three Defining Paradigm Exemplars.* London: T. & T. Clark, 2004.

Jennings, Theodore W., Jr. "The Martyrdom of the Son of Man." In *Text and Logos: The Humanistic Interpretation of the New Testament*, edited by Theodore W. Jennings, 229-43. Atlanta: Scholars, 1990.

Knibb, Michael A. "Messianism in the Pseudepigrapha in Light of the Scrolls." *DSD* 2 (1995): 164-84.

———. "The Translation of 1 Enoch 70:1: Some Methodological Issues." In *Biblical*

*The Parables of Enoch and the Messiah Son of Man: A Bibliography*

Hebrews, Biblical Texts: Essays in Memory of Michael P. Weitzman,* edited by Ada Rapaport and Gillian Greenberg, 340-54. JSOTSup 333. Sheffield: Sheffield Academic, 2001.

Koch, Klaus. "Messias und Menschensohn." In *Vor der Wende der Zeiten. Beiträge zur apokalyptischen Literatur,* 235-66. Gesammelte Aufsätze 2. Neukirchen-Vluyn: Neukirchener Verlag, 1996.

Lichtenberger, Hermann. "Messianische Erwartungen und messianische Gestalten in der Zeit des Zweiten Tempels." In *Messias-Vorstellungen bei Juden und Christen,* edited by Ekkehard Stegemann and Albert Friedlander, 9-20. Stuttgart: Kohlhammer, 1993.

Luz, Ulrich. "The Son of Man in Matthew: Heavenly Judge or Human Christ." *JSNT* 48 (1992): 3-21.

Martin de Vivies, Pierre de. *Jésus et le Fils de l'Homme: Emplois et significations de l'expression 'Fils de l'Homme' dans les Évangiles.* Lyon: Profac, 1995.

Miura, Nozomi. "A Typology of Personified Wisdom Hymns." *BTB* 34 (2004): 138-49.

Moule, Charles F. D. "'The Son of Man': Some of the Facts." *NTS* 41 (1995): 277-79.

Müller, Karlheinz. *Studien zur frühjüdischen Apocalyptic.* Stuttgart: Katholisches Bibelwerk, 1991.

Nickelsburg, George W. E. "Enoch, First Book of." In *ABD* 2 (1992), 508-16.

———. "Son of Man." In *ABD* 6 (1992), 137-50.

———. "The Books of Enoch at Qumran: What We Know and What We Need to Think About." In *Antikes Judentum und frühes Christentum. Festschrift für Hartmut Stegemann zum 65. Geburtstag,* edited by Bernd Kollmann, Wolfgang Reinbold, and Annette Steudel, 99-113. BZNW 97. Berlin and New York: De Gruyter, 1999.

———. *1 Enoch 1: A Commentary on the Book of 1 Enoch 1–36, 81–108.* Vol. 1. Hermeneia. Minneapolis: Fortress, 2001.

———. *Ancient Judaism and Christian Origins: Diversity, Continuity, and Transformation.* Minneapolis: Fortress, 2003.

———. *Jewish Literature between the Bible and the Mishnah.* Rev. ed. Minneapolis: Fortress, 2005.

Nickelsburg, George W. E., and James C. VanderKam. *1 Enoch: A New Translation.* Minneapolis: Fortress, 2004.

Oegema, Gerbern S. *Der Gesalbte und sein Volk: Untersuchungen zum Konzeptualisierungsprozess der messianischen Erwartungen von den Makkabäern bis Bar Koziba.* SIJD 2. Göttingen: Vandenhoeck & Ruprecht, 1994 [= *The Anointed and His People: Messianic Expectations from the Maccabees to Bar Kochba,* JSPSup 27 (Sheffield: Sheffield Academic, 1998)].

Olson, Daniel C. "Enoch and the Son of Man in the Epilogue of the Parables." *JSP* 18 (1998): 27-38.

———. *Enoch: A New Translation.* North Richland Hills, Tex.: BIBAL, 2004.

Orlov, Andrei A. *The Enoch-Metatron Tradition.* TSAJ 107. Tübingen: Mohr Siebeck, 2005.

Philonenko, Marc. "Le sang du juste (1 Hénoch 47,1.4; Matthieu 27,24)." *RHPR* 73 (1993): 395-99.
Reddish, Mitchell G. *Apocalyptic Literature*. Nashville: Abingdon, 1990.
Rhea, Robert. *The Johannine Son of Man*. Zürich: Theologischer Verlag, 1990.
Ricciardi, Alberto. "1 Henoc 70–71: ¿Es Henoc el Hijo del hombre?" *CuadT* 17 (1998): 129-46.
Ross, J. M. "The Son of Man." *IBS* 13 (1991): 186-98.
Rosso Ubigli, Liliana. "Gli Apocrifi (o Pseudepigrafi) dell'Antico Testamento: Bibliografia, 1979-1989." *Hen* 12 (1990): 259-321.
Rowland, Christopher. "Enoch." In *Dictionary of Deities and Demons in the Bible*, edited by Karel van der Toorn et al., 576-81. Leiden: Brill, 1995.
Russell, David M. *"The New Heavens and the New Earth": Hope for the Creation in Jewish Apocalyptic and the New Testament*, 102-5. Philadelphia: Visionary, 1996.
Sacchi, Paolo. *L'apocalittica giudaica e la sua storia*. Brescia: Paideia, 1990 [= *Jewish Apocalyptic and Its History*, JSPSup 20 (Sheffield: Sheffield Academic, 1997)].
———. *Storia del Secondo Tempio*. Turin: SEI, 1994 [= *The History of the Second Temple Period*, JSOTSup 285 (Sheffield: Sheffield Academic, 2000)].
———. "Formazione e linee portanti dell'apocalittica giudaica precristiana." *RSB* 7 (1995): 19-36.
———. "Enochism, Qumranism and Apocalyptic: Some Thoughts on a Recent Book." Review of *Beyond the Essene Hypothesis*, by Gabriele Boccaccini. *Hen* 20 (1998): 357-65.
———. *Gesù e la sua gente*. Cinisello Balsamo: San Paolo, 2003.
———. "Qumran e la datazione del Libro delle Parabole di Enoc." *Hen* 25 (2003): 149-66 [= "Qumran and the Dating of the Book of Parables," in *The Bible and the Dead Sea Scrolls*, edited by James H. Charlesworth (Waco: Baylor University Press, 2006)].
———. "Le figure messianiche superumane del Secondo Tempio e il Figlio dell'Uomo." In *Il messia tra memoria e attesa*, edited by Gabriele Boccaccini. Brescia: Morcelliana, 2005.
Schreiber, Stefan. "Henoch als Menschensohn: Zur problematischen Schlussidentifikation in den Bilderreden des äthiopischen Henochbuches (äthHen 71,14)." *ZNW* 91 (2000): 1-17.
Slater, Thomas B. "One Like a Son of Man in First-Century CE Judaism." *NTS* 41, no. 2 (1995): 183-98.
Tomasino, Anthony J. "Daniel and the Similitudes of Enoch." In "Daniel and the Revolutionaries: The Use of the Daniel Tradition by Jewish Resistance Movements of the Late Second Temple Period," 201-27. Ph.D. diss., University of Chicago, 1995.
Tuckett, Christopher. "The Son of Man in Q." In *From Jesus to John: Essays on Jesus and New Testament Christology in Honour of Marinus de Jonge*, edited by Martinus C. De Boer, 196-215. JSNTSup 84, Sheffield: JSOT Press, 1993.
VanderKam, James C. "Righteous One, Messiah, Chosen One, and Son of Man in

1 Enoch 37–71." In *The Messiah: Developments in Earliest Judaism and Christianity*, edited by James H. Charlesworth, 169-91. Minneapolis: Fortress, 1992.

———. *Enoch: A Man for All Generations*. Columbia: University of South Carolina Press, 1995.

———. "Messianism and Apocalypticism." In *The Encyclopedia of Apocalypticism*, vol. 1, *The Origins of Apocalypticism in Judaism and Christianity*, edited by John J. Collins, 193-228. New York: Continuum, 1998.

———. *An Introduction to Early Judaism*. Grand Rapids: Eerdmans, 2001.

Witherington, Ben. *The Christology of Jesus*, esp. 233-62. Minneapolis: Fortress, 1990.

Yarbro Collins, Adela. "The Apocalyptic Son of Man Sayings." In *The Future of Early Christianity*, edited by Birger A. Pearson, 220-28. Minneapolis: Fortress, 1991.

———. "The 'Son of Man' Tradition and the Book of Revelation." In *The Messiah: Developments in Earliest Judaism and Christianity*, edited by James H. Charlesworth, 536-68. Minneapolis: Fortress, 1992. Reprinted in Yarbro Collins, *Cosmology and Eschatology in Jewish and Christian Apocalypticism* (Leiden: Brill, 1996), 159-97.

———. "The Worship of Jesus and the Imperial Cult." In *The Jewish Roots of Christological Monotheism*, edited by Carey C. Newman et al., 234-57. Brill: Leiden, 1999.

## 1975-1989

Bampfylde, Gillian. "The Similitudes of Enoch: Historical Allusions." *JSJ* 15 (1984): 9-31.

Barker, Margaret. *The Lost Prophet: The Book of Enoch and Its Influence on Christianity*, esp. 91-104. 1988. Reprint, Nashville: Abingdon, 2005.

Bauckham, Richard. "The Son of Man: 'A Man in My Position' or 'Someone'?" *JSNT* 23 (1985): 23-33.

Berger, Klaus. *Die Auferstehung des Propheten und die Erhöhung des Menschensohnes*. Göttingen: Vandenhoeck & Ruprecht, 1976.

Bietenhard, Hans. "'Der Menschensohn' — ὁ υἱὸς τοῦ ἀνθρώπου. Sprachliche und religionsgeschichtliche Untersuchungen zu einem Begriff der synoptischen Evangelien. I. Sprachlicher und religionsgeschichtlicher Teil." In *ANRW* II.25.1, edited by Wolfgang Haase, 265-350. Berlin: De Gruyter, 1982.

Black, Matthew. "The Throne-Theophany Prophetic Commission and the 'Son of Man': A Study in Tradition History." In *Jews, Greeks, and Christians: Essays in Honor of William David Davies*, edited by Robert Hammerton-Kelly and Robin Scroggs, 57-73. Leiden: Brill, 1976.

———. "The Parables of Enoch (1 Enoch 37–71) and the Son of Man." *ExpTim* 88 (1976): 5-8.

———. "Jesus and the Son of Man." *JSNT* 1 (1978): 4-18.

———. "The Composition, Character and Date of the Second Vision of Enoch (The

Book of Parables)." In *Text, Wort, Glaube: Studien zur Überlieferung, Interpretation und Autorisierung bibl. Texte: Kurt Aland gewidmet*, edited by Kurt Aland and Martin Brecht, 19-30. Berlin: De Gruyter, 1980.

———. "The Twenty Angel Dekadarchs at I Enoch 6.7 and 69.2." *JJS* 33 (1982): 227-35.

———. "Aramaic bar nâshâ and the 'Son of Man.'" *ExpTim* 95 (1984): 200-206.

———. "Two Unusual Nomina Dei in the Second Vision of Enoch." In *New Testament Age: Essays in Honor of Bo Reicke*, edited by William C. Weinrich, 53-59. Macon, Ga.: Mercer University Press, 1984.

———. *The Book of Enoch, or, I Enoch: A New English Edition with Commentary and Textual Notes*. SVTP 7. Leiden: Brill, 1985.

Borgen, Peder. "Some Jewish Exegetical Traditions as Background for Son of Man Sayings in John's Gospel (Jn 3,13-14 and Context)." In *L'Evangile de Jean: sources, rédaction, théologie*, edited by Marinus de Jonge, 243-58. BETL 44. Gembloux: Duculot; Leuven: Leuven University Press, 1977.

Bowker, John. "The Son of Man." *JTS* 28 (1977): 19-48.

Bowman, John Wick. "David, Jesus Son of David and Son of Man." *Abr-Nahrain* 27 (1989): 1-22.

Brown, John Pairman. "The Son of Man: 'This Fellow.'" *Bib* 58 (1977): 361-87.

Bruce, Frederick F. "The Background to the Son of Man Sayings." In *Christ the Lord: Studies in Christology Presented to Donald Guthrie*, edited by Harold H. Rowden, 50-70. Leicester: Inter-Varsity, 1982.

Caquot, André. "Léviathan et Behémoth dans la troisième 'parabole' d'Hénoch." *Sem* 25 (1975): 111-22.

———. "Remarques sur les chapitres 70 et 71 du livre éthiopien d'Hénoch." In *Apocalypses et théologie de l'espérance*, edited by Louis Monloubou, 111-22. LD 5. Paris: Cerf, 1977.

———. "I Hénoch." In *La Bible: Écrits intertestamentaires*, edited by André Dupont-Sommer and Marc Philonenko, 463-625. Bibliothèque de la Pléiade. Paris: Gallimard, 1987.

Caragounis, Chrys C. *The Son of Man: Vision and Interpretation*. WUNT 38. Tübingen: Mohr Siebeck, 1986.

Casey, Maurice. "The Corporate Interpretation of 'One Like a Son of Man' (Dan. VII 13) at the Time of Jesus." *NovT* 18 (1976): 167-80.

———. "The Son of Man Problem." *ZNW* 67 (1976): 147-54.

———. "The Use of the Term 'Son of Man' in the Similitudes of Enoch." *JSJ* 7 (1976): 11-29.

———. *Son of Man: The Interpretation and Influence of Daniel 7*. London: SPCK, 1979.

———. "Aramaic Idiom and Son of Man Sayings." *ExpTim* 96 (1985): 233-36.

———. "The Jackals and the Son of Man (Matt. 8.20//Luke 9.58)." *JSNT* 23 (1985): 3-22.

———. "General, Generic, and Indefinite: The Use of the Term 'Son of Man' in Aramaic Sources and in the Teaching of Jesus." *JSNT* 29 (1987): 21-56.

Charlesworth, James H. "The Concept of Messiah in the Pseudepigrapha." In *ANRW* 19.1 (1979), 188-218.

———. *The Pseudepigrapha and Modern Research with a Supplement.* Chico, Calif.: Scholars, 1981.

———. "1977 (Tübingen; Eberhard-Karls Universität): The Books of Enoch" and "1978 (Paris; Châtenay-Malabry): 1 (Ethiopic) Enoch and Luke and the Dating of the Parables of Enoch." In *The Old Testament Pseudepigrapha and the New Testament: Prolegomena for a Study of Christian Origins,* 102-10. SNTSMS 54. Cambridge: Cambridge University Press, 1985.

———. *The Old Testament Pseudepigrapha and the New Testament: Prolegomena for a Study of Christian Origins.* Cambridge: Cambridge University Press, 1985.

———. *Jesus within Judaism: New Light from Exciting Archaeological Discoveries,* esp. 39-42. New York: Doubleday, 1988.

Ciholas, Paul. "'Son of Man' and Hellenistic Christology." *RevExp* 79 (1982): 487-501.

Coleman, Gillis B. "The Similitudes of I Enoch." In "The Phenomenon of Christian Interpolations into Jewish Apocalyptic Texts: A Bibliographical Survey and Methodological Analysis," 182-238. Ph.D. diss., Vanderbilt University, 1976.

Collins, John J. "Cosmos and Salvation: Jewish Wisdom and Apocalyptic in the Hellenistic Age." *HR* 17 (1977): 121-42. Reprinted in *Seers, Sibyls, and Sages in Hellenistic-Roman Judaism,* JSJSup 54 (Leiden: Brill, 1997), 317-38.

———. "The Jewish Apocalypse." *Semeia* 14 (1979): 21-59.

———. "The Son of Man Who Has Righteousness (1 Enoch 37–71)." In SBLSP 2 (1979), 1-13.

———. "The Heavenly Representative: The 'Son of Man' in the Similitudes of Enoch." In *Ideal Figures in Ancient Judaism: Profiles and Paradigms,* edited by John J. Collins and George W. E. Nickelsburg, 111-33. SCS 12. Chico, Calif.: Scholars, 1980.

———. *The Apocalyptic Imagination: An Introduction to the Jewish Matrix of Christianity.* New York: Crossroad, 1984.

———. "Apocalyptic Literature." In *Early Judaism and Its Modern Interpreters,* edited by Robert A. Kraft and George W. E. Nickelsburg, 345-70. Atlanta: Scholars, 1986.

Colpe, Carsten. "Neue Untersuchungen zum Menschensohn-Problem." *TRev* 77 (1981): 353-71.

Coppens, Joseph. "Le Fils d'homme dans le judaïsme de l'époque néotestamentaire." *OLP* 6-7 (1975/76): 59-73.

———. "Le Fils de l'homme dans l'Evangile johannique." *ETL* 52 (1976): 28-81.

———. "Où en est le problème de Jésus 'Fils de l'homme'?" *ETL* 56 (1980): 282-302.

———. *Le Fils de l'homme néotestamentaire.* BETL 55. Leuven: Peeters, 1981.

———. "Le Fils d'Homme dans les traditions juives postbibliques hormis le Livre des Paraboles d'Hénoch." *ETL* 57 (1981): 58-82.

———. *Le Fils d'homme vétéro- et intertestamentaire.* Leuven: Peeters, 1983.

Corriente, Frederico, and Antonio Piñero. "Libro 1 de Henoc." In *Apócrifos del*

*Antiguo Testamento I*, edited by Alejandro Díez Macho, 11-143. Madrid: Cristianidad, 1982.

Coughenour, Robert A. "The Wisdom Stance of Enoch's Redactor." *JSJ* 13 (1982): 47-55.

Davies, Philip R. "The Mythic Enoch: New Light on Early Christology." *SR* 13 (1984): 335-44.

Decock, Paul B. "Holy Ones, Sons of God, and the Transcendent Future of the Righteous in I Enoch and the New Testament." *Neot* 17 (1983): 70-83.

Delcor, Mathias. "Le livre des paraboles d'Hénoch éthiopien: le problème de son origine à la lumière des découvertes récentes." *EstBib* 38 (1979-80): 5-33.

Denis, Albert-Marie, ed. *Introduction à la littérature religieuse judéo-hellénistique*. 2 vols. Turnhout: Brepols, 2000.

Díez Macho, Alejandro. "La Cristologia del Hijo del Hombre y el uso de la tercera persona en vez de la primera." *ScrTh* 14 (1982): 189-201.

Dimant, Deborah. "The Biography of Enoch and the Books of Enoch." *VT* 33 (1983): 14-29.

Donahue, John R. "Recent Studies on the Origin of the 'Son of Man' in the Gospels." *CBQ* 48 (1986): 484-98.

Fitzmyer, Joseph A. "Another View of the 'Son of Man' Debate." *JSNT* 4 (1979): 58-65.

———. "The New Testament Title 'Son of Man' Philologically Considered." In *A Wandering Aramean: Collected Aramaic Essays*, 143-60. SBLMS 25. Missoula: Scholars, 1979.

Fuller, Reginald H. "The Son of Man: A Reconsideration." In *The Living Text: Essays in Honor of Ernest W. Saunders*, edited by Dennis E. Groh and Robert Jewett, 207-17. Lanham, Md.: University Press of America, 1985.

García Martínez, Florentino. "Enoch and the Figure of Enoch: A Bibliography of Studies, 1970-1988." *RevQ* 14 (1989): 149-76.

Geist, Heinz. *Menschensohn und Gemeinde: Eine redaktionskritische Untersuchung zur Menschensohnprädikation im Matthäusevangelium*. Würzburg: Echter Verlag, 1986.

Gerleman, Gillis. *Der Menschensohn*. Studia Biblica 1. Leiden: Brill, 1983.

Gese, Hartmut. "Wisdom, Son of Man, and the Origins of Christology: The Consistent Development of Biblical Theology." *HBT* 3 (1981): 23-57.

Girard, Marc. "Le semblant de Fils d'Homme de Dn 7, un personage du monde d'en haut: approche structurelle." *ScEs* 35 (1983): 265-96.

Glasson, Thomas Francis. "The Son of Man Imagery: Enoch XIV and Daniel VII." *NTS* 23 (1977): 82-90.

Greenfield, Jonas C., and Michael E. Stone. "The Enochic Pentateuch and the Date of the Similitudes." *HTR* 70 (1977): 51-65.

Grelot, Pierre. "Daniel 7,9-10 et le Livre d'Hénoch." *Sem* 28 (1978): 59-83.

Higgins, A. J. B. *The Son of Man in the Teaching of Jesus*. SNTSMS 39. Cambridge: Cambridge University Press, 1980.

Hooker, Morna D. "Is the Son of Man Problem Really Insoluble?" In *Text and Inter-*

pretation: Studies in the New Testament, Presented to Matthew Black,* edited by Ernest Best and Robert M. Wilson, 155-68. Cambridge: Cambridge University Press, 1979.
Horbury, William. "The Messianic Associations of 'The Son of Man.'" *JTS* 36 (1985): 34-55.
Isaac, Ephraim. "1 (Ethiopic Apocalypse of) Enoch." In *Old Testament Pseudepigrapha,* edited by James H. Charlesworth, 1:5-89. New York: Doubleday, 1983.
Jas, Michel. "Hénoch et le Fils de l'homme." *La revue réformée* 30 (1979): 105-19.
———. "Hénoch et le Fils de l'homme: datation du Livre des Paraboles pour une situation de l'origine du Gnosticisme." Ph.D. diss., Aix-en-Provence, 1979.
Kearns, Rollin. *Das Traditiongefüge um des Menschensohn.* Tübingen: Mohr, 1986.
———. *Die Entchristologisierung des Menschensohnes.* Tübingen: Mohr, 1988.
Kellner, Wendelin. *Der Traum vom Menschensohn: Die politisch-theologische Botschaft Jesu.* Munich: Kösel, 1985.
Kim, Seyoon. *"The 'Son of Man'" as the Son of God.* WUNT 30. Tübingen: Mohr, 1983.
Kingsbury, Jack Dean. "The Title 'Son of Man' in Matthew's Gospel." *CBQ* 37 (1975): 193-202.
Knibb, Michael A. *The Ethiopic Book of Enoch: A New Edition in the Light of the Aramaic Dead Sea Fragments.* 2 vols. Oxford: Clarendon, 1978.
———. "The Date of the Parables of Enoch: A Critical Review." *NTS* 25 (1979): 344-59.
———. "1 Enoch." In *The Apocryphal Old Testament,* edited by H. F. D. Sparks, 169-319. New York: Oxford University Press, 1984.
———. "The Ethiopic Book of Enoch." In *Outside the Old Testament,* edited by Marinus de Jonge, 26-55. Cambridge Commentaries on Writings of the Jewish and Christian World, 200 BC to AD 200, 4. Cambridge: Cambridge University Press, 1985.
Kümmel, Werner G. *Jesus der Menschensohn?* Stuttgart: Steiner, 1984.
Kvanvig, Helge S. "Henoch und der Menschensohn: Das Verhältnis von Hen 14 zu Dan 7." *ST* 38 (1984): 101-33.
———. *Roots of Apocalyptic: The Mesopotamian Background of the Enoch Figure and of the Son of Man.* WMANT 61. Neukirchen-Vluyn: Neukirchener Verlag, 1988.
Laperrousaz, Ernest-Marie. "Les Paraboles de l'Hénoch éthiopien." In *L'attente Du Messie en Palestine à la veille et au début de l'ère chrétienne,* 226-59. Paris: A. et J. Picard, 1982.
Legasse, Simon. "Jésus historique et le Fils de l'homme: aperçu sur les opinions contemporaines." In *Apocalypses et théologie de l'espérance: Congrès de Toulouse 1975,* 271-98. Paris: Cerf, 1977.
Leivestad, Ragnar. "Jesus — Messias — Menschensohn: Die jüdischen Heilandserwartungen zur Zeit der ersten römischen Kaiser und die Frage nach dem messianischen Selbstbewußtsein Jesu." In *ANRW* II.25.1, edited by Wolfgang Haase, 220-64. Berlin: De Gruyter, 1982.
Lindars, Barnabas. "Re-enter the Apocalyptic Son of Man." *NTS* 22 (1975): 52-72.

———. "Enoch and Christology." *ExpTim* 92 (1981): 295-99.
———. "The New Look on the Son of Man." *BJRL* 63 (1981): 437-62.
———. *Jesus Son of Man: A Fresh Examination of the Son of Man Sayings in the Gospels in the Light of Recent Research*. London: SPCK, 1983.
———. "Response to Richard Bauckham: The Idiomatic Use of Bar Enasha." *JSNT* 23 (1985): 35-41.
Marshall, I. Howard. *The Origins of New Testament Christology*. Downers Grove, Ill.: InterVarsity, 1976; 2nd ed. 1990.
Mearns, Christopher L. "The Parables of Enoch: Origin and Date." *ExpTim* 89 (1978): 118-19.
———. "Dating the Similitudes of Enoch." *NTS* 25 (1979): 360-69.
———. "The Son of Man Trajectory and Eschatological Development." *ExpTim* 97 (1985): 8-12.
Milik, Josef T. *The Books of Enoch: Aramaic Fragments of Qumrân Cave 4*, 89-98. Oxford: Clarendon, 1976.
Moloney, Francis J. *The Johannine Son of Man*. 2nd ed. Rome: LAS, 1978.
———. "The End of the Son of Man?" *DRev* 98 (1980): 280-90.
Müller, Mogens. "Über den Ausdruck 'Menschensohn' in den Evangelien." *ST* 31 (1977): 65-82.
———. *Der Ausdruck "Menschensohn" in den Evangelien: Voraussetzungen und Bedeutung*. Leiden: Brill, 1984.
———. "The Expression 'the Son of Man' as Used by Jesus." *ST* 38 (1984): 47-64.
Neusner, Jacob, et al., eds. *Judaisms and Their Messiahs at the Turn of the Christian Era*. Cambridge: Cambridge University Press, 1987.
Nickelsburg, George W. E. Review of *The Books of Enoch*, by J. T. Milik. *CBQ* 40 (1978): 411-19.
———. *Jewish Literature between the Bible and the Mishnah: A Historical and Literary Introduction*. Philadelphia: Fortress, 1981.
———. "I Enoch and Qumran Origins: The State of the Question and Some Prospects or Answers." In *SBLSP* 25 (1986), 341-60.
———. "Salvation without and with a Messiah: Developing Beliefs in Writings Ascribed to Enoch." In *Judaisms and Their Messiahs at the Turn of the Christian Era*, edited by Jacob Neusner et al., 49-68. Cambridge: Cambridge University Press, 1987.
Perrin, Norman. "The Son of Man." In *The Interpreter's Dictionary of the Bible: Supplement Volume*, 833-36. Nashville: Abingdon, 1976.
Pesch, Ruldolf, and Rudolf Schnackenburg, eds. *Jesus und der Menschensohn*. Freiburg: Herder, 1975.
Ricciardi, Alberto. "El elegido/hijo del hombre, vindicador de los oprimidos." *RevistB* 44 (1982): 207-32.
———. "La oración en las parabolas de Henoc." *RevistB* 47 (1985): 53-73.
———. "Algunos pasajes de las parabolas en recientes versiones del libro etiopico de Henoc." *RevistB* 50 (1988): 33-60.

———. "'Tradicción' y 'interpretación' en el Libro de las Parabolas de Henoc." *RevistB* 51 (1989): 219-31.
Rowland, Christopher. *The Open Heaven: A Study of Apocalyptic in Judaism and Early Christianity*. London: SPCK, 1982.
Sacchi, Paolo. "Henochgestalt/Henochliteratur." In *TRE* 15.1.2 (1985), 42-54.
———. "L'apocalittica del I sec.: Peccato e giudizio." In *Correnti culturali e movimenti religiosi del giudaismo: Atti del V Congresso internazionale dell' AISG. S. Miniato, 12-15 novembre 1984*, edited by Bruno Chiesa, 59-77. Rome: Carucci, 1987.
———. "Il messianismo ebraico dale origini al II sec. d.C." *Quaderni di Vita Monastica* 46 (1987): 14-38.
———. "L'eredità giudaica del cristianesimo." *Aug* 28 (1988): 23-50.
Sacchi, Paolo, and Luigi Fusella. "Libro di Enoc." In *Apocrifi dell'Antico Testamento*, edited by Paolo Sacchi, 1:413-667. Turin: UTET, 1981.
Sahlin, Harald. "Wie wurde ursprünglich die Benennung 'Der Menschensohn' verstanden?" *ST* 37 (1983): 147-79.
Sanders, E. P. "1 Enoch." In *Paul and Palestinian Judaism: A Comparison of Patterns of Religion*, 346-62. Philadelphia: Fortress, 1977.
Schimanowski, Gottfried. "Die Präexistenz des Messias in den Übersetzungen des AT, dem äthiopischen Henoch und anderen apokalyptischen Texten." In *Weisheit und Messias: Die jüdischen Voraussetzungen der urchristlichen Präexistenzchristologie*, 107-205. WUNT 2.17. Tübingen: Mohr Siebeck, 1985.
Schmithals, Walter. "Die Worte vom leidenden Menschensohn: Ein Schlüssel zum Lösung des Menschensohns-Problems." In *Theologia Crucis — Signum Crucis: Festschrift für Erich Dinkler zum 70 Geburtstag*, edited by Carl Andreson and Günter Klein, 417-45. Tübingen: Mohr, 1979.
Schürer, Emil, and Geza Vermes. "The Coming of the Messiah." In *The History of the Jewish People in the Age of Jesus Christ (175 B.C.–A.D. 135): A New English Version*, 2:517-25, esp. 520-21. Edinburgh: T. & T. Clark, 1979.
———. "The Ethiopic Book of Enoch." In *The History of the Jewish People in the Age of Jesus Christ (175 B.C.–A.D. 135): A New English Version*, 3.1:250-68, esp. 256-59. Edinburgh: T. & T. Clark, 1986.
Schürmann, Heinz. "Beobachtungen zum Menschensohn-Titel in der Redequelle: Sein Vorkommen in Abschluss- und Einleitungswendungen." In *Jesus und der Menschensohn*, edited by Ruldolf Pesch and Rudolf Schnackenburg, 124-47. Freiburg: Herder, 1975.
Schwarz, Günther. *Jesus "der Menschensohn": Aramaistische Untersuchungen zu den synoptischen Menschensohnworten Jesu*. BWANT 119. Stuttgart: Kohlhammer, 1986.
Schweizer, Eduard. "Menschensohn und eschatologischer Mensch im Frühjudentum." In *Jesus und der Menschensohn*, edited by Ruldolf Pesch and Rudolf Schnackenburg, 100-116. Freiburg: Herder, 1975.
Segal, Alan F. *Two Powers in Heaven: Early Rabbinic Reports about Christianity and Gnosticism*. Leiden: Brill, 1977.

Stone, Michael E. "Apocalyptic Literature." In *Jewish Writings of the Second Temple Period: Apocrypha, Pseudepigrapha, Qumran, Sectarian Writings, Philo, Josephus,* edited by Michael E. Stone, 383-441. Philadelphia: Fortress, 1984.

Suter, David W. "Apocalyptic Patterns in the Similitudes of Enoch." In SBLSP 13 (1978), 1-13.

———. "*Mašal* in the Similitudes of Enoch." *JBL* 100 (1981): 193-212.

———. "Weighed in the Balance: The Similitudes of Enoch in Recent Discussion." *RelSRev* 7 (1981): 217-21.

———. "The Measure of Redemption: The Similitudes of Enoch, Non-violence, and National Integrity." In SBLSP 22 (1983), 167-78.

———. *Tradition and Composition in the Parables of Enoch.* SBLDS 47. 1979. Reprint, Missoula: Scholars, 2006.

Svedlund, Gerhard. "Notes on *Bar nash* and the Detrimental Effects of Its Transformation into the Title of the Son of Man." *OS* 33-35 (1984-86): 401-13.

Theisohn, Johannes. *Der auserwählte Richter: Untersuchungen zum traditiongeschichtlichem Ort der Menschensohngestalt der Bilderreden des Äthiopischen Henoch.* Göttingen: Vandenhoeck & Ruprecht, 1975.

Tödt, Ilse. "Der 'Menschensohn' und die Folgen." In *Schöpferische Nachfolge: Festschrift für Heinz Eduard Tödt,* edited by Christofer Frey and Wolfgang Huber, 541-61. Heidelberg: Forschungsstätte der Evangelischen Studiengemeinschaft, 1978.

Tuckett, Christopher. "Recent Work on the Son of Man." *ScrB* 12 (1981): 14-18.

———. "The Present Son of Man." *JSNT* 14 (1982): 58-81.

Uhlig, Siegbert. *Das äthiopische Henochbuch.* In *JSHRZ,* edited by Werner G. Kümmel, 6:461-780. Gütersloh: Gütersloher Verlagshaus Gerd Mohn, 1984.

VanderKam, James H. "Some Major Issues in the Contemporary Study of I Enoch: Reflections on J. T. Milik's *The Book of Enoch: Aramaic Fragments of Qumran Cave 4.*" *Maarav* 3 (1982): 85-97.

———. *Enoch and the Growth of an Apocalyptic Tradition.* CBQMS 16. Washington, D.C.: Catholic Biblical Association of America, 1984.

Vermes, Geza. "The Present State of the 'Son of Man' Debate." *JJS* 29 (1978): 123-34.

———. "The 'Son of Man' Debate." *JSNT* 1 (1978): 19-32.

Villiers, Pieter G. R. de. "Revealing the Secrets: Wisdom and the World in the Similitudes of Enoch." *Neot* 17 (1983): 50-68.

———, ed. *Studies in 1 Enoch and the New Testament.* Stellenbosch: University of Stellenbosch Press, 1983.

Vögtle, Anton. "Bezeugt die Logienquelle die authentische Redeweise Jesu vom 'Menschensohn'?" In *Logia: les paroles de Jésus — the Sayings of Jesus,* edited by Joël Delobel, 77-99. BETL 59. Leuven: Peeters, 1982.

———. "Eine überholte 'Menschensohn'-Hypothese?" In *Wissenschaft und Kirche: Festschrift für Eduard Lohse,* edited by Kurt Aland and Siegfried Meurer, 70-95. Bielefeld: Luther-Verlag, 1989.

Vorster, Willen S. "1 Enoch and the Jewish Literary Setting of the New Testament: A Study in Text Types." *Neot* 17 (1983): 1-15.
Walker, William O. "The Origin of the Son of Man Concept as Applied to Jesus." *JBL* 91 (1972): 482-90.
———. "The Son of Man and the Synoptic Problem." *NTS* 28 (1982): 374-88.
———. "The Son of Man: Some Recent Developments." *CBQ* 45 (1983): 584-607.
Wilson, Frederick M. "The Son of Man in Jewish Apocalyptic Literature." *Studia biblia et theologica* 8 (1978): 28-52.
Wittlieb, Marian. "Die theologische Bedeutung von *Mashiach-Christos* in den Pseudepigraphen des Alten Testaments palästinischen Ursprungs." *BN* 50 (1989): 26-33.
Yarbro Collins, Adela. "The Origin of the Designation of Jesus as 'Son of Man.'" *HTR* 80 (1987): 391-407.
———. "The Son of Man Sayings in the Sayings Source." In *To Touch the Text: Biblical and Related Studies in Honor of Joseph A. Fitzmeyer, S.J.*, edited by Maurya P. Horgan and Paul J. Kobelski, 369-89. New York: Crossroad, 1989.

## 1950-1974

Agourides, Savvas. "The Son of Man in Enoch." *Deltion Biblikon Meleton* 2 (1973): 130-47.
Archibald, D. Y. "The Son of Man." *ExpTim* 62 (1951): 348-49.
Ashby, Eric. "The Coming of the Son of Man." *ExpTim* 72 (1961): 360-63.
Birdsall, J. Nevell. "Who Is This Son of Man?" *EvQ* 42 (1970): 7-17.
Black, Matthew. "The Eschatology of the Similitudes of Enoch." *JTS* 3 (1952): 1-10.
———. "The Servant of the Lord and the Son of Man." *SJT* 6 (1953): 1-11.
———. "The Son of Man Problem in Recent Research and Debate." *BJRL* 45 (1963): 303-18.
Borsch, Frederick Houk. "The Son of Man." *ATR* 45 (1963): 174-90.
———. *The Son of Man in Myth and History.* NTL. Philadelphia: Westminster, 1967.
———. "Mark XIV.62 and I Enoch LXII.5." *NTS* 14 (1968): 565-67.
———. *The Christian and Gnostic Son of Man.* SBT. London: SCM, 1970.
Braun, François-Marie. "Messie, Logos et Fils de l'homme." In *La venue du Messie*, edited by Edouard Massaux, 133-47. Bruges: Desclée de Brouwer, 1962.
Cambe, Michel. "Le Fils de l'homme dans les Evangiles synoptiques." *LumVie* 12 (1963): 32-64.
Campbell, John Y. "Son of Man." In *A Theological Wordbook of the Bible*, edited by Alan Richardson, 230-32. New York: Macmillan, 1950.
Cangh, Jean-Marie Van. "Le Fils de l'homme dans la tradition synoptique." *RTL* 1:411-19.
Caquot, André, and Pierre Geoltrain. "Notes sur le texte éthiopien des Paraboles d'Hénoch." *Sem* 13 (1963): 39-54.
Colpe, Carsten. "Der Begriff 'Menschensohn' und die Methode der Erforschung

messianischer Prototypen." *Kairós* 11, no. 4 (1969): 241-63; 12, no. 2 (1970): 81-112; 13, no. 1 (1971): 1-17; 14, no. 4 (1972): 241-57.

———. "'Ο υἱὸς τοῦ ἀνθρώπου." In *Theological Dictionary of the New Testament*, edited by Gerhard Friedrich, 8:400-477. Grand Rapids: Eerdmans, 1972.

Coppens, Joseph. "Le Fils d'homme daniélique et les relectures de Dan. VII, 13 dans les apocryphes et les écrits du Nouveau Testament." *ETL* 37 (1961): 5-51.

———. *De Menschenzoon-logia in het Markus-evangelie: avec un résumé, des notes et une bibliographie en français*. Brussels: Paleis der Academiën, 1973.

Coppens, Joseph, and Luc Dequeker. *Le Fils de l'homme et les Saints du Très-Haut en Daniel VII, dans les Apocryphes et dans le Nouveau Testament*. Gembloux: Duculot, 1961.

Cortés, Juan B., and Florence M. Gatti. "The Son of Man or the Son of Adam." *Bib* 49 (1968): 457-502.

Cruvellier, Jean. "La notion de 'Fils de l'homme' dans les Evangiles." *Etudes évangéliques* 15 (1955): 31-50.

Delorme, Jean. *Le Fils de l'homme*. Paris: Tournon, 1954.

Dhanis, Édouard. "De filio hominis in vetere Testamento et in judaismo." *Greg* 45 (1964): 5-59.

Dion, Hyacinthe-M. "Quelques traits originaux de la conception johannique du Fils de l'homme." *ScEc* 19 (1967): 49-65.

Eichrodt, Walther. "Zum Problem des Menschensohnes." *EvT* 19 (1959): 1-3.

Elliott, John H. "Man and the Son of Man in the Gospel according to Mark." In *Humane Gesellschaft: Beiträge zu ihrer sozialen Gestaltung*, 47-59. Zürich: Zwingli, 1970.

Emerton, John A. "The Origin of the Son of Man Imagery." *JTS* 9 (1958): 225-42.

Feuillet, André. "Le Fils de l'homme de Daniel et la tradition biblique." *RB* 60 (1953): 170-202, 321-46.

Ford, J. Massingberde. "'The Son of Man' — a Euphemism?" *JBL* 87 (1968): 257-66.

Formesyn, R. E. C. "Was There a Pronominal Connection for the 'Bar Nasha' Self-Designation?" *NovT* 8 (1966): 1-35.

Frost, Stanley B. "Enoch, Books Five and Two." In *Old Testament Apocalyptic: Its Origins and Growth*, 210-30. London: Epworth, 1952.

Gelston, Anthony. "A Sidelight on the 'Son of Man.'" *SJT* 22 (1969): 189-96.

Goppelt, Leonhard. "Zum Problem des Menschensohns: Das Verhältnis von Leidens- und Parusieankündigung." In *Mensch und Menschensohn: Festschrift für Bischof Professor D. Karl Witte*, edited by H. Sierig, 20-32. Hamburg: Wittig, 1963. Reprinted in Goppelt, *Christologie und Ethik: Aufsätze zum Neuen Testament* (Göttingen, 1969), 66-78.

Guillet, Jacques. "A propos des titres de Jésus: Christ, Fils de l'homme, Fils de Dieu." In Maurice Jourjon et al., *A la rencontre de Dieu: mémorial Albert Gelin*, 309-17. Le Puy: Mappus, 1961.

Hammerton-Kelly, Robert G. *Pre-existence, Wisdom, and the Son of Man: A Study of* the Idea of Pre-existence in the New Testament. SNTSMS 21. Cambridge: Cambridge University Press, 1973.

Harrison, Roland K. "The Son of Man." *EvQ* 23 (1951): 46-50.

Haufe, Günter. "Das Menschensohn-Problem in der gegenwärtigen wissenschaftlichen Diskussion." *EvT* 26 (1966): 130-41.

Henze, Clemens M. "Der Sohn des Menschen." *ThPQ* 104 (1956): 70-75.

Higgins, Angus J. B. "Son of Man — *Forschung* since 'The Teaching of Jesus.'" In *New Testament Essays: Studies in Memory of Thomas Walter Manson, 1893-1958*, edited by Angus J. B. Higgins, 119-35. Manchester: Manchester University Press, 1959.

———. *Jesus and the Son of Man.* Philadelphia: Fortress, 1964.

———. *Menschensohn Studien: Franz Delitzsch-Vorlesungen 1961.* Stuttgart: Kohlhammer, 1965.

———. "The Son of Man Concept and the Historical Jesus." *SE* 5 [= *TU* 103] (1968): 14-20.

———. "Is the Son of Man Problem Insoluble?" In *Neotestamentica et Semitica: Studies in Honour of Matthew Black,* edited by E. Earle Ellis and Max Wilcox, 70-87. Edinburgh: Clark, 1969.

Hindley, J. Clifford. "The Son of Man: A Recent Analysis." *IJT* 15 (1966): 172-78.

———. "Toward a Date for the Similitudes of Enoch: An Historical Approach." *NTS* 14 (1968): 551-65.

Hodgson, Peter C. "The Son of Man and the Problem of Historical Knowledge." *JR* 41 (1961): 91-108.

Hooker, Morna D. *The Son of Man in Mark: A Study of the Background of the Term "Son of Man" and Its Use in St. Mark's Gospel,* esp. 33-48. London: SPCK, 1967.

Jay, Eric G. *Son of Man, Son of God.* Montreal: McGill University Press, 1965.

Jeremias, Joachim. "Die älteste Schicht der Menschensohn-Logien." *ZNW* 58 (1967): 159-72.

Johnson, Sherman E. "Son of Man." In *The Interpreter's Dictionary of the Bible,* 4:413-20. Nashville: Abingdon, 1962.

Johnston, Leonard. "The Son of Man." *Scr* 6 (1954): 181-83.

Kertelge, Karl. "Die Vollmacht des Menschensohnes zur Sündenvergebung (Mk 2,10)." In *Orientierung an Jesus: Zur Theologie der Synoptiker,* edited by Paul Hoffmann et al., 205-13. Freiburg: Herder, 1973.

Ladd, George E. *A Theology of the New Testament,* 145-58. Grand Rapids: Eerdmans, 1974.

Leivestad, Ragner. "Der apokalyptische Menschensohn ein theologisches Phantom." *ASTI* 6 (1968): 49-109.

———. "Exit the Apocalyptic Son of Man." *NTS* 18 (1972): 243-67.

Lindeskog, Gösta. "Das Rätsel des Menschensohnes." *ST* 22 (1968): 149-75.

Longenecker, Richard N. "Son of Man as a Self-Designation of Jesus." *JETS* 12 (1969): 151-58.

———. *The Christology of Early Jewish Christianity.* SBT 17. London: SCM, 1970.

Maddox, Robert. "The Function of the Son of Man according to the Synoptic Gospels." *NTS* 15 (1968): 45-74.

———. "The Quest for Valid Methods in Son of Man Research." *ABR* 19 (1971): 36-51 [= "Methodenfragen in der Menschensohnforschung," *EvT* 32 (1972): 143-60].

———. "The Function of the Son of Man in the Gospel of John." In *Reconciliation and Hope: New Testament Essays on Atonement and Eschatology*, edited by Robert Banks, 186-204. Grand Rapids: Eerdmans, 1974.

Manson, Thomas Walter. "The Son of Man in Daniel, Enoch and the Gospels." *BJRL* 32 (1950): 171-95.

Marlow, Ransom. "The *Son of Man* in Recent Journal Literature." *CBQ* 28 (1966): 20-30.

Marshall, I. Howard. "The Synoptic Son of Man Sayings in Recent Discussion." *NTS* 12 (1965): 327-51.

———. "The Son of Man in Contemporary Debate." *EvQ* 42 (1970): 67-87.

Michel, Otto. "Der Menschensohn. Die eschatologische Hinweisung. Die apokalyptische Aussage. Bemerkungen zum Menschensohnverständnis des Neuen Testaments." *TZ* 27 (1971): 81-104.

———. "Der Menschensohn in der Jesusüberlieferung," *TBei* 2 (1971): 119-28.

———. "Ὁ υἱὸς τοῦ ἀνθρώπου." In *Theologisches Begriffslexicon zum Neuen Testament*, II 2:1153-66. Wuppertal: Brockhaus, 1971.

Milik, Josef T. "The Dead Sea Scrolls Fragment of the Book of Enoch." *Bib* (1951): 293-340.

———. *Ten Years of Discovery in the Wilderness of Judea*. SBT 26. London: SCM, 1959.

———. "Problèmes de la littérature Hénochique à la lumière des fragments araméens de Qumrân." *HTR* 64 (1971): 333-78.

Moe, Olaf. "Der Menschensohn und der Urmensch." *ST* (1960): 119-29.

Morgenstern, Julian. "The 'Son of Man' of Daniel 7:13f.: A New Interpretation." *JBL* 80 (1961): 65-77.

Moule, Charles F. D. "Neglected Features in the Problem of 'the Son of Man.'" In *Neues Testament und Kirche: Für Rudolf Schnackenburg*, edited by Joachim Gnilka, 413-28. Freiburg: Herder, 1974.

Mowinckel, Sigmund. *Han som kommer*. Copenhagen: GEC Gad, 1951 [= *He That Cometh: The Messiah Concept in the Old Testament and Later Judaism*, trans. G. W. Anderson (New York: Abingdon, 1956)].

Muilenburg, James. "The Son of Man in Daniel and the Ethiopic Apocalypse of Enoch." *JBL* 79 (1960): 197-209.

Müller, Karlheinz. "Beobachtungen zur Entwicklung der Menschensohnvorstellung in der Bilderreden des Henochs und im Buche Daniel." In *Wegzeichen: Festgabe zum 60 Geburtstag von Prof. Dr. Hermenegild M. Biedermann*, edited by Ernst C. Suttner et al., 253-61. Würzburg: Augustinus-Verlag, 1971.

Müller, Ulrich B. *Messias und Menschensohn in jüdischen Apokalypsen und in der Offenbarung des Johannes*. Gütersloh: Gütersloher Verlagshaus Mohn, 1972.

Neugebauer, Fritz. *Jesus der Menschensohn: Ein Beitrag zur Klärung der Wege historischer Wahrheitsfindung im Bereich der Evangelien*. Stuttgart: Calwer, 1972.

———. "Die Davidssohnfrage (Mark xii. 35-7 parr.) und der Menschensohn." *NTS* 21 (1974): 81-108.

Nickelsburg, George W. E. *Resurrection, Immortality, and Eternal Life in Intertestamental Judaism*. HTS 26. Cambridge: Harvard University Press, 1972.

Ory, Georges. "L'intrusion du Fils de l'homme dans nos Evangiles." *Bulletin du Cercle Ernest-Renan* 104 (1964): 1-3.

Perrin, Norman. "The Son of Man in Ancient Judaism and Primitive Christianity: A Suggestion." *BR* 11 (1966): 17-28. Reprinted with a postscript in *A Modern Pilgrimage in New Testament Christology* (Philadelphia: Fortress, 1974).

———. "The Creative Use of the Son of Man Traditions by Mark." *USQR* 23 (1968): 237-65. Reprinted with a postscript in *A Modern Pilgrimage in New Testament Christology* (Philadelphia: Fortress, 1974).

———. "The Son of Man in the Synoptic Tradition." *BR* 13 (1968): 3-25. Reprinted with a postscript in *A Modern Pilgrimage in New Testament Christology* (Philadelphia: Fortress, 1974), 57-83.

Preiss, Théo. *Le Fils de l'Homme*. Etudes théologiques et religieuses. Montpellier, 1951.

Proudman, C. L. J. "Remarks on the 'Son of Man.'" *CJT* 12 (1966): 128-31.

Rankin, Oliver S. "The Messianic Office in the Literature of Judaism and the New Testament." *ZAW* 63 (1951): 259-70.

Russell, David S. "The Son of Man." In *The Method and Message of Jewish Apocalyptic, 200 BC–AD 100*, 324-52. Philadelphia: Westminster, 1964.

Sanders, Ian L. "The Origin and Significance of the Title 'The Son of Man' as Used in the Gospels." *Scr* 10 (1958): 49-56.

Sandmel, Samuel. "Son of Man." In *In the Time of Harvest: Essays in Honor of Abba Hillel Silver*, edited by Daniel Jeremy Silver, 355-67. New York: Macmillan, 1963.

Schnackenburg, Rudolf. "Das kommende Reich Gottes und der Menschensohn." In *Gottes Herrschaft und Reich*, 110-22. Freiburg: Herder, 1959.

Schulz, Siegfried. *Untersuchungen zur Menschensohn-Christologie im Johannesevangelium*. Göttingen: Vandenhoeck & Ruprecht, 1957.

Schweizer, Eduard. "Der Menschensohn (Zur eschatologischen Erwartung Jesu)." *ZNW* 50 (1959): 185-209.

———. "The Son of Man." *JBL* 79 (1960): 119-29.

———. "The Son of Man Again." *NTS* 9 (1963): 256-61.

———. "Menschensohn." *Die Zeichen der Zeit* 22 (1963): 361-63.

Seethaler, Paula. "Kleine Studie über den 'Menschensohn.'" *BK* 11 (1956): 85-87.

Sidebottom, E. M. "The Ascent and Descent of the Son of Man in the Gospel of St. John." *ATR* 39 (1957): 115-22.

Sjöberg, Erik. "Ben 'adam und Bar 'enos im Hebräischen und Aramäischen." *AO* 21 (1953): 57-65, 91-107.

———. *Der verborgene Menschensohn in der Evangelien*. Lund: Gleerup, 1955.

Smalley, Stephen S. "The Johannine Son of Man Sayings." *NTS* 15 (1969): 278-301.

Stanley, David. "The Quest of the Son of Man." *Way* 8 (1968): 3-17.
Stauffer, Ethelbert. "Messias oder Menschensohn." *NovT* 1 (1956): 81-102.
Stott, Wilfrid. "'Son of Man' — a Title of Abasement." *ExpTim* 83 (1972): 278-81.
Sulzbach, Maria Fuerth. "Who Was Jesus? The Theology of the Son of Man." *Religion in Life* 30 (1961): 179-86.
Teeple, Howard M. "The Origin of the Son of Man Christology." *JBL* 84 (1965): 213-50.
Thompson, George H. P. "Son of Man: The Evidence of the Dead Sea Scrolls." *ExpTim* 72 (1961): 125.
———. "Son of Man — Some Further Considerations." *JTS* 12 (1961): 203-9.
Tödt, Heinz E. *Der Menschensohn in der synoptischen Überlieferung.* Gütersloh: Mohn, 1959 [= *The Son of Man in the Synoptic Tradition* (Philadelphia: Westminster, 1965)].
Ullendorff, Edward. "An Aramaic Vorlage of the Ethiopic Text of Enoch?" In *Atti del Convegno Internazionale di Studi Etiopici,* 259-67. Rome: Accademia Nazionale dei Lincei, 1960. Reprinted in *Ethiopia and the Bible* (London: Oxford University Press, 1968), 31-62.
Veilhauer, Philipp. "Gottesreich und Menschensohn in der Verkündigung Jesu." In *Festschrift für Günther Dehn,* edited by Wilhelm Schneemelcher, 51-79. Neukirchen: Erziehungsverein, 1957.
———. "Jesus und der Menschensohn: Zur Discussion mit Heinz Eduard Tödt und Eduard Schweizer." *ZTK* 60 (1963): 133-77.
Vermes, Geza. "Appendix E: The Use of *bar nash/bar nasha* in Jewish Aramaic." In *An Aramaic Approach to the Gospels and Acts,* edited by Matthew Black, 310-30. Oxford: Clarendon, 1967. Reprinted in Vermes, *Post-biblical Jewish Studies* (Leiden: Brill, 1975), 147-65.
Vilar Hueso, Vicente. "La recompense de los justos immediate a su muerte en IV Macabeos y en las parábolos de Enoc." *AnthA* 3 (1955): 521-49.
Weist, Ch. "Wer ist dieser Menschensohn? Die Geschichte der Exegese zum Menschensohn-Begriff." Ph.D. diss., Vienna, 1972.
Widengren, Geo. "Iran and Israel in Parthian Times with Special Regard to the Ethiopic Book of Enoch." *Temenos* 2 (1966): 139-77.
Zehrer, Franz. "Jesus, der Menschensohn." *BLit* 47 (1974): 165-76.

## 1880-1949

Abbott, Edwin A. *The Message of the Son of Man.* London: Black, 1909.
———. *"The Son of Man" or Contributions to the Study of the Thought of Jesus.* Diatessarica VIII. Cambridge: Cambridge University Press, 1910.
Appel, Heinrich. *Die Selbstbezeichnung Jesu: Der Sohn des Menschen.* Stavenhagen: Beholtz, 1896.
Bacon, Benjamin W. "The 'Son of Man' in the Usage of Jesus." *JBL* 41 (1922): 143-82.
Badham, F. P. "The Title 'Son of Man.'" *ThT* 45 (1911): 395-448.

## The Parables of Enoch and the Messiah Son of Man: A Bibliography

Baeck, Leo. "Der 'Menschensohn.'" *MGWJ* 81 (1937): 12-24.

Baldensperger, Wilhelm. *Das Selbstbewusstein Jesu im Lichte der messianischen Hoffnungen seiner Zeit*. Strasbourg: Heitz & Mündel, 1888; 2nd ed. 1892.

———. "Die neueste Forschung über den Menschensohn." *TRu* 3 (1900): 201-10, 243-55.

Bard, Friedrich. *Der Sohn des Menschen: Eine Untersuchung über Begriff und Inhalt und Absicht solcher Jesusbezeichnung*. Gütersloh: Bertelsmann, 1908; 2nd ed. 1915.

Bartlet, Vernon. "Christ's Use of the Term 'Son of Man.'" *Expositer* 4, no. 6 (1892): 427-43.

———. "Christ's Use of 'The Son of Man.'" *ExpTim* 4 (1892/93): 403.

———. "The Son of Man: A Rejoinder." *ExpTim* 5 (1893/94): 41-42.

Barton, George A. "Demons and Spirits (Hebrew)." In *Encyclopaedia of Religion and Ethics*, edited by James Hastings, 4:594-601. Edinburgh: T. & T. Clark, 1910.

———. "The Origin of the Names of Angels and Demons in Extra-Canonical Apocalyptic Literature to 100 AD." *JBL* 31 (1912): 156-67.

Beer, Georg. "Das Buch Henoch." In *Die Apokryphen und Psuedepigraphen des Alten Testaments*, edited by E. Kautzsch, 2:217-310. 1900. Reprint, Tübingen: Mohr Siebeck, 1921.

Billerbeck, Paul. "Hat die Synagoge einen präexistenten Menschensohn gekannt?" *Nathanael* 21 (1905): 89-150.

Black, Matthew. "Unsolved NT Problems: The 'Son of Man' in the Old Biblical Literature." *ExpTim* 60 (1948/49): 11-15.

———. "Unsolved NT Problems: 'The Son of Man' in the Teaching of Jesus." *ExpTim* 60 (1948/49): 32-36.

Bleibtreu, Walther. "Jesu Selbstbenennung als der Menschensohn." *TSK* 99 (1926): 164-211.

Bousset, Wilhelm. *Die jüdische Apokalyptic: Ihre religionsgeschichtliche Herkunft und ihre Beteudung für das Neue Testament*. Berlin: Reuther & Reichard, 1903.

———. *Kyrios Christos: Geschichte des Christusglaubens von den Anfangen des Christentums bis Irenaeus*. Gottingen: Vandenhoeck & Ruprecht, 1913 [= *Kyrios Christos: A History of the Belief in Christ from the Beginnings of Christianity to Irenaeus* (Nashville: Abingdon, 1970)].

———. *Die Religion des Judentums im späthellenistischen Zeitalter*. Edited by Hugo Gressmann. Tübingen: Mohr, 1926.

Bowman, John W. "The Background of the Term Son of Man." *ExpTim* 59 (1948): 283-88.

Brinkmann, Bernhard. "Die Lehre von der Parusie beim hl. Paulus in ihrem Verhältnis zu den Anschauungen des Buches Henoch." *Bib* 13 (1932): 315-34, 418-34.

Brückner, Wilhelm. "Jesus 'des Menschen Sohn.'" *JPT* 12 (1886): 254-78.

Bulcock, Harry. "Was the Double Use of 'Son of Man' a Factor in the Deification of Jesus?" *Congregational Quarterly* 17 (1945): 44-55.

Burkill, T. Alec. "The Son of Man: A Brief General Statement." *ExpTim* 56 (1944/45): 305-6.

———. "The Hidden Son of Man in St. Mark's Gospel." *ZNW* 52 (1961): 189-213. Reprinted in Burkill, *New Light on the Earliest Gospel: Seven Markan Studies* (Ithaca, N.Y.: Cornell University Press, 1977), 1-38.
Cadoux, Arthur T. "The Son of Man." *Interpreter* 18 (1929): 202-14.
Campbell, John Y. "The Origin and Meaning of the Term Son of Man." *JTS* 48 (1947): 145-55. Reprinted in *Three New Testament Studies* (Leiden: Brill, 1965), 29-40.
Carrairon, Emile. *Essai historique et critique sur le titre de Fils de l'homme*. Nîmes: Chastanier, 1886.
Charles, Robert Henry. "The Son of Man." *ExpTim* 4 (1892/93): 504.
———. *The Book of Enoch*. Oxford: Clarendon, 1893; 2nd ed. 1912.
———. *The Ethiopic Version of the Book of Enoch*. Oxford: Clarendon, 1906.
———. *The Book of Enoch, or I Enoch, Translated from the Editor's Ethiopic Text, and Edited with the Introduction, Notes, and Indexes of the First Edition Wholly Recast, Enlarged, and Rewritten*. Oxford: Clarendon, 1912.
———. "The Book of Enoch." In *The Apocrypha and Pseudepigrapha of the Old Testament*, vol. 2, *Pseudepigrapha*, edited by Robert Henry Charles, 163-281. Oxford: Clarendon, 1913.
Croskery, J. "Recent Discussions on the Meaning of the Title 'Son of Man.'" *ExpTim* 13 (1901/2): 351-55.
Derambure, Jean. "Le 'Fils de l'homme' dans les Evangiles." *RevAug* 13 (1908): 708-20; 14 (1909): 319-40.
Dieckmann, Hermann. "Ὁ υἱὸς τοῦ ἀνθρώπου." *Bib* 2 (1921): 69-71.
———. "'Der Sohn des Menschen' im Johannesevangelium." *Schol* 2 (1927): 229-47.
———. "De nomine 'Filius hominis.'" *VD* 8 (1928): 295-301.
Dix, Gregory H. "The Enochic Pentateuch." *JTS* 27 (1926): 29-42.
Driver, Samuel R. "Son of Man." In *A Dictionary of the Bible*, edited by James Hastings, 4:579-89. New York: Scribner, 1902.
Drummond, James. "The Use and Meaning of the Phrase 'The Son of Man' in the Synoptic Gospels." *JTS* 11 (1901): 350-58, 539-71.
Duncan, George S. *Jesus, Son of Man: Studies Contributory to a Modern Portrait*. London: Nisbet, 1947.
Dupont, Georges. *Le Fils de l'Homme: essai historique et critique*. Paris: Fischbacher, 1924.
Eaton, David. "Prof. Dalman on 'The Son of Man.'" *ExpTim* 10 (1898/99): 438-43.
Eerdmans, Bernardus D. "De Oorsprong van de uitdrukking 'Zoon des Menschen' als evangelische Messiastitel." *ThT* 28 (1894): 153-76.
Evans, Milton G. "The Title 'Son of Man.'" *BSac* 57 (1900): 680-95.
Feiers, F., and E. De Giovanni. "Il libro di Enoc." *Rivista delle riviste* 6 (1908): 297-319, 377-84, 412-19.
Feine, Paul. *Theologie des Neuen Testaments*, esp. 48-69. Leipzig: Hinrichs, 1910.
Fiebig, Paul. *Der Menschensohn: Jesu Selbstbezeichnung*. Tübingen: Mohr, 1901.
———. "Der 'Menschensohn' als Geheimname." *PM* 5 (1901): 333-51.
Flemming, Johannes. *Das Buch Henoch: Aethiopischer Text*. Leipzig: Hinrichs, 1902.

## The Parables of Enoch and the Messiah Son of Man: A Bibliography

Flemming, Johannes, and Ludwig Radermacher. *Das Buch Henoch.* Leipzig: Hinrichs, 1901.
Frey, Jean Baptiste. "Apocryphes de l'Ancien Testament." In *DBSup* 1 (1928), 357-71.
Gottsched, H. *Der Menschensohn.* Gütersloh: Bertelsmann, 1908.
Gry, Leon. "Le Roi-Messie dans Hénoch." *Mus* 24 (1905): 129-39.
———. "La composition littéraire des paraboles d'Hénoch." *Mus* 27 (1908): 27-71.
———. "Le messianisme des paraboles d'Hénoch." *Mus* 27 (1908): 319-67.
———. "Le messianisme des paraboles d'Hénoch et la théologie juive contemporaine." *Mus* 28 (1909): 143-54.
———. "Quand furent composées les Paraboles d'Hénoch?" *Mus* 28 (1909): 103-41.
———. *Les paraboles d'Hénoch et leur messianisme.* Paris: Picard, 1910.
———. "Mystique gnostique (juive et chrétienne) en finale des Paraboles d'Hénoch." *Mus* 52 (1939): 337-78.
Haupt, Paul. "Hidalgo and Filius Hominis." *JBL* 40 (1919): 167-70.
———. "The Son of Man — hic homo — ego." *JBL* 40 (1919): 183.
Headlam, Arthur C. *The Life and Teaching of Jesus the Christ,* esp. 297-306. New York: Oxford University Press, 1923.
Hertlein, Edouard. "Ὁ υἱὸς τοῦ ἀνθρώπου." *ZNW* 19 (1920): 46-48.
Hilgenfeld, Adolf. "Der Menschensohn-Messias." *ZWT* 35 (1892): 445-64.
———. "Noch ein Wort über den Menschensohn." *ZWT* 42 (1899): 149-51.
Holsten, Carl. "Die Bedeutung der Ausdrucksform ὁ υἱὸς τοῦ ἀνθρώπου im Bewußtsein Jesu." *ZWT* 8 (1891): 1-79.
Jansen, Herman Ludin. *Die Henochgestalt: eine vergleichende religionsgeschichtliche Untersuchung.* Oslo: Dybwad, 1939.
Joüon, Paul. "Appendice A: le Fils de l'homme." In *L'Evangile de Notre-Seigneur Jésus-Christ,* 601-4. Paris: Beauchesne, 1930.
Klöpper, A. "Der Sohn des Menschen in den synoptischen Evangelien." *ZWT* 42 (1899): 161-86.
Kraeling, Carl H. *Anthropos and Son of Man: A Study in the Religious Syncretism of the Hellenistic Orient.* Columbia University Oriental Studies 25. New York: Columbia University Press, 1927.
Kühl, Ernst. *Das Selbstbewusstsein Jesu,* esp. 65-87. Berlin: Runge, 1907.
Kuhnert, E. "Ὁ υἱὸς τοῦ ἀνθρώπου." *ZNW* 18 (1917/18): 165-76.
Lagrange, Marie-Joseph. *Le judaïsme avant Jésus-Christ.* 2nd ed. Paris: Gabalda, 1931.
Lietzmann, Hans. *Der Menschensohn.* Freiburg and Leipzig: Mohr, 1896.
———. *Zur Menschensohnfrage.* Freiburg: Mohr, 1899.
MacRory, Joseph. "The Son of Man." *ITQ* 10 (1915): 50-63.
Martin, François. *Le livre d'Hénoch: Documents pour l'étude de la Bible, traduit sur le texte éthiopien.* Paris: Letouzey et Ané, 1906.
McCown, Chester C. "Jesus Son of Man: A Survey of Recent Discussion." *JR* 28 (1948): 1-12.
McNaugher, John. "The Son of Man." *BSac* 88 (1931): 90-104.

Meloni, Gerardo. "Filius hominis." In *Saggi di Filologia Semitica*, 315-19. Rome: Casa Editrice Italiana, 1913.

Messel, Nils. *Der Menschensohn in der Bilderreden des Henoch*. BZAW 35. Giessen: A. Töpelmann, 1922.

Micklem, Nathaniel. "The Son of Man." *Queen's Quarterly* 36 (1929): 205-24.

Motso, Bacchisio. "Due scritti politico-religiosi del tempo di Cristo." *Religio*, 1920, 167-77. Reprinted in *Saggi di storia e letteratura giudeo-ellenistica* (Florence, 1924), 3-31, and in *Ricerche sulla letteratura e la storia giudaico-ellenistica*, edited by Fausto Parente (Rome: Centro Editoriale Internazionale, 1977), 427-55.

Mouren, J. *Le Fils de l'homme: étude historique et critique*. Lyons: Paquet, 1903.

Mowinckel, Sigmund. "Henog og Menneskesoennen." *NTT* 45 (1944): 57-69.

Muirhead, Lewis A. "The Name 'Son of Man' and the Messianic Consciousness of Jesus." *ExpTim* 11 (1899/1900): 62-65.

Oort, Henricus Lucas. *Die uitdrukking ὁ υἱὸς τοῦ ἀνθρώπου in het Nieuwe Testament*. Leiden: Brill, 1893.

Otto, Rudolf. *Reich Gottes und Menschensohn*. 2nd ed. Munich: Beck, 1934/1943; 3rd ed. 1954 [= *The Kingdom of God and the Son of Man: A Study in the History of Religion*, trans. Floyd V. Filson and Bertram Lee Wolf (London: Lutterworth, 1938; Boston: Star King, 1957)].

Parker, Pierson. "The Meaning of 'Son of Man.'" *JBL* 60 (1941): 151-57.

Patton, Carl S. "Did Jesus Call Himself the Son of Man?" *JR* 2 (1922): 501-11.

Peake, Arthur S. "The Messiah and the Son of Man." *BJRL* 8 (1924): 52-81. Reprinted in *The Servant of Yahweh* (Manchester: Manchester University Press, 1931), 220-37.

Preiss, Théo. "Le mystère du Fils de l'Homme." *Dieu Vivant* 8 (1947): 15-36.

Procksch, Otto. "Der Menschensohn als Gottessohn." *Christentum und Wissenschaft* 3 (1927): 425-43, 473-81.

Riessler, Paul. "I Enoch." In Riessler, *Altjüdisches Schrifttum ausserhalb der Bibel* (Heidelberg, 1928), 355-451, 1291-97.

Rose, Vincent. "Fils de l'homme et Fils de Dieu." *RB* 9 (1900): 169-99.

Roslaniec, Franciszek. *Sensus genuinus et plenus locutionis "Filius hominis" a Christo Domino adhibitae*. Rome: Typic Polygottis Vaticanis, 1920.

Ross, Alexander. "The Title Son of Man." *EvQ* 6 (1934): 36-49.

Sanday, William. "On the Title, 'Son of Man.'" *Expositor* 4, no. 3 (1891): 18-32.

Schmidt, Hans, and Gerhard Kittel. "Menschensohn." In *RGG*, 2nd ed., 3:2117-21. Tübingen, 1929.

Schmidt, Nathaniel. "Was בר נשא a Messianic Title?" *JBL* 15 (1896): 36-53.

———. "The Son of Man in the Book of Daniel." *JBL* 19 (1900): 22-28.

———. "Son of Man." In *Encyclopaedia Biblica*, edited by Thomas K. Cheyne and John Sutherland Black, 4:4705-40. London: A. & C. Black, 1903.

———. "The Original Language of the Parables of Enoch." In *Old Testament and Semitic Studies in Memory of William Rainey Harper*, edited by Robert F. Harper et al., 2:327-49. Chicago: University of Chicago Press, 1908.

———. "The Apocalypse of Noah and the Parables of Enoch." In *Oriental Studies*

*The Parables of Enoch and the Messiah Son of Man: A Bibliography*

Published in Commemoration of the Fortieth Anniversary (1883-1923) of Paul Haupt as Director of the Oriental Seminary of the Johns Hopkins University, edited by Cyrus Adler and Aaron Ember, 2:111-23. Baltimore: Johns Hopkins University Press, 1926.

———. "Recent Study of the Term 'Son of Man.'" *JBL* 45 (1926): 326-49.

Schmiedel, Paul Wilhelm. "Bezeichnet Jesus den Menschen als solchen durch 'Menschensohn'?" *PM* 2 (1898): 291-308.

———. "Der Name 'Menschensohn' und das Messiasbewußtsein Jesu." *PM* 2 (1898): 252-67.

———. "Die neusten Auffassungen des Namens 'Menschensohn.'" *PM* 5 (1901): 333-51.

Schodde, George Henry. *The Book of Enoch*. Andover: Draper, 1882.

Schweitzer, Albert. *Von Reimarus zu Wrede: eine Geschichte der Leben-Jesu-Forschung.* Tübingen: Mohr, 1906 [= *The Quest of the Historical Jesus* (New York: Macmillan, 1968)].

Sharman, Henry B. *Son of Man and Kingdom of God*. New York: Harper, 1943.

Sjöberg, Erik. "Kaenna 1 Henok och 4 Esra tanlen pae lidande Maenniskonsonen?" *SEÅ* 5 (1940): 163-83.

———. "Fregan om den lidande Maenniskonsonen in 1 Henok." *SEÅ* 7 (1942): 141-44.

———. *Der Menschensohn im äthiopischen Henochbuch*. Skrifter Utgivna av kungl. Humanistika Vetenskapssamfundet i Lund 41. Lund: Gleerup, 1946.

Skibniewski, St. de. *De bar našā Filio hominis*. Vienna: Méchitaristes, 1908.

Smith, David. "The Nickname 'Son of Man.'" *ExpTim* 18 (1906/7): 553-55.

Stanton, Vincent Henry. *The Jewish and Christian Messiah: A Study in the Earliest History of Christianity*. Edinburgh: Clark, 1886.

Stauffer, Ethelbert. *Die Theologie des Neuen Testaments*. Berlin: W. Kohlhammer Verlag, 1941 [= *New Testament Theology* (New York: Macmillan, 1955)].

Stephenson, T. "The Title 'Son of Man.'" *ExpTim* 29 (1917/18): 377-78.

Taylor, Vincent. "The 'Son of Man' Sayings Relating to the Parousia." *ExpTim* 58 (1946/47): 12-15.

Tillmann, Fritz. "Hat die Selbstbezeichnung Jesus 'der Menschensohn' ihre Wurzeln in Dan., VII,13?" *BZ* 5 (1907): 35-47.

———. *Der Menschensohn: Jesu Selbstzeugnis für seine messianische Würde*. Freiburg: Herder, 1907.

Torrey, Charles C. "Enoch." In *The Apocryphal Literature: A Brief Introduction*, 110-14. New Haven: Yale University Press, 1945.

Trenkle, F. S. *Der Menschensohn: Eine exegetisch-kritische Untersuchung*. Freiburg, 1888.

Usteri, Johann Martin. "Die Selbstbezeichnung Jesu als des Menschen Sohn." *Theologische Zeitschrift aus der Schweiz* 3 (1886): 1-23.

Völter, Daniel. *Jesus der Menschensohn; oder, Das Berufsbewußtsein Jesu*. Strasbourg: Heitz, 1914.

———. *Die Menschensohn-Frage neu untersucht*. Leiden: Brill, 1916.

Vosté, James M. "The Title 'Son of Man' in the Synoptic Gospels." *AER* 120 (1949): 310-26; 121: 18-33.
Wagner, Martin. "Der Menschensohn." *NKZ* 35 (1924): 345-78.
Weiss, Johannes. *Die Predigt Jesu vom Reiche Gottes*. Göttingen: Vanderhoeck & Ruprecht, 1892 [= *Jesus' Proclamation of the Kingdom of God* (Philadelphia: Fortress, 1971)].
Wellhausen, Julius. "Des Menschen Sohn." In *Skizze und Vorarbeiten*, 6:187-215. Berlin: Reimer, 1899.
Werner, Martin. *Die Entstehung des Christlichen Dogmas*. Bern: Haupt, 1941 [= *The Formation of the Christian Dogma* (London: Black, 1957)].
Wilson, William E. "The Coming of the Son of Man." *Modern Churchman* 36 (1946): 44-66.
Wrede, William. "Zum Thema 'Menschensohn.'" *ZNW* 5 (1904): 359-60.
Youtsi, Y. "Der Menschensohn." *Theologia Fennica* 2 (1940): 45-52.

## 1773-1879

Anger, Rudolf. *Vorlesungen über die Geschichte der messianischen Idee*. Edited by Max Krenkel. Berlin: Henschel, 1873.
Baur, Ferdinand Christian. "Die Bedeutungdes Ausdrucks: ὁ υἱὸς τοῦ ἀνθρώπου." *ZWT* 3 (1860): 274-92.
Böhme, Christian Friedrich. *Versuch das Geheimnis des Menschensohn zu enthüllen*. Neustadt: Orla, 1839.
Bruce, James. *Travels to Discover the Source of the Nile*. Edinburgh: Ramsay, 1790.
Brunet, Gustave. "Le livre d'Hénoch." In *Dictionnaire des Apocryphes*, edited by Jacques-Paul Migne, 1:393-514, 2:223-226. 2 vols. Paris: Migne, 1856, 1858.
Colani, Timothée. *Jésus-Christ et les croyances messianiques de son temps*. 2nd ed. Strasbourg: Treuttel et Wurtz, 1864.
Dillmann, August. *Liber Henoch aethiopice*. Leipzig: Vogel, 1851.
———. *Das Buch Henoch übersetzt und erklärt*. Leipzig: Vogel, 1853.
———. "1 Henoch." In *Real-encyclopädie für protestantische Theologie und Kirche*, edited by J. J. Herzog, 12:380-410. 22 vols. Hamburg: Besser, 1854-1868.
Dorner, Isaak August. *Entwicklungsgeschichte der Lehre von der Person Christi*. 3 vols. Stuttgart: Liesching, 1839; 2nd ed. 1845 [= *History of the Development of the Doctrine of the Person of Christ*, 5 vols. (Edinburgh: Clark, 1861-63)].
Drummond, James. *The Jewish Messiah*. London: Longmans and Green, 1877.
Ewald, Heinrich. *Commentarius in apocalypsin Johannis, exegeticus et criticus*. Leipzig: Hahn, 1828.
———. *Abhandlung über des Äthiopischen Buches Henokh*. Göttingen: Dieterich, 1854.
———. *Geschichte des Volkes Israel bis Christus*. Vol. 5, *Geschichte Christus' und seiner Zeit*. Göttingen: Dieterich, 1855; 2nd ed. 1857 [= *The History of Israel*, vol. 6, *The Life and Times of Christ* (London: Longmans, 1883), esp. 103-21, 230-31].

## The Parables of Enoch and the Messiah Son of Man: A Bibliography

Gass, Fr. Wilhelm. *De utroque Jesu Christi nomine in novo testamento obvio Dei filii et hominis.* Vratislavia: Friedländer, 1839.

Hilgenfeld, Adolf. "Das Buch Enoch." In *Der jüdische Apokalyptic in ihrer geschichtlichen Entwicklung,* 91-184. Jena: Mauke, 1857; Amsterdam: Rodopi, 1966.

Hoffmann, Andreas Gottlieb. *Das Buch Henoch.* 2 vols. Jena: Croeker, 1833, 1838.

Hofmann, Johann Christian Konrad von. "Ueber die Entstehungszeit des Buch Henoch." *ZDMG* 6 (1852): 87-91.

Holtzmann, Heinrich Julius. "Ueber den NTlichen Ausdruck 'Menschensohn.'" *ZWT* 8 (1865): 212-37.

Langen, Joseph. *Das Judenthum in Palästina zur Zeit Christi.* Freiburg: Herder, 1866.

Laurence, Richard. *The Book of Enoch.* Oxford: Parker, 1821.

———. *Libri Enochi prophetae versio aethiopica.* Oxford: Parker, 1838.

Less, Gottfried. *Nonnulla de Filio Hominis praefatus.* Göttingen: Rosenbusch, 1776.

Mangold, W. "Über die Bedeutung des Ausdrucks: ὁ υἱὸς τοῦ ἀνθρώπου." *Theologische Arbeiten aus dem rheinisch-wissenschaftlichen Predigerverein* 3 (1877): 1-25.

Nösgen, Karl Friedrich. *Christus der Menschen- und Gottessohn.* Gotha: Perthes, 1869.

Philippi, Ferdinand. *Das Buch Henoch, sein Zeitalter und sein Verhältniss zum Judasbriefe.* Stuttgart: Liesching, 1868.

Sacy, Silvestre de. Review of *The Book of Enoch,* by Richard Laurence. *Journal de savans* 7 (1822): 593-94.

Schenkel, Daniel. "Menschensohn." In *Bibel-Lexicon: Realwörterbuch zum Handgebrauch für Geistliche und Gemeindeglieder,* 4:170-75. Leipzig: Brockhaus, 1872.

Schmidt, Karl Christian Ludwig. "Ueber den Ausdruck ὁ υἱὸς τοῦ ἀνθρώπου im Neuen Testament." *Neues Magazin für Religionsphilosophie, Exegese und Kirchengeschichte* 2 (1798): 507-26.

Scholten, Wessel. *Specimen hermeneutico-theologicum: De appellatione ὁ υἱὸς τοῦ ἀνθρώπου, qua Jesus se Messiam professus est.* Trajecti ad Rhenum: Paddenburg & Schoonhoven, 1809.

Schulze, Ludwig. *Vom Menschensohn und vom Logos: Ein Beitrag zur biblischen Christologie.* Gotha: Perthes, 1867.

Sieffert, Friedrich. *De apocryphi libri Henochi origine et argumento.* Regimonti: Typis expressit Gruber et Longrien, 1867.

Tideman, Joannes. "De Apocalypse van Henoch en het Essenisme." *ThT* 9 (1875): 261-96.

Uloth, C. B. E. "De beteekenis van de uitdrukking 'Zoon des menschen.'" *Godgeleerde Bijdragen* 36 (1862): 467-78.

Vernes, Maurice. *Histoire des idées messianiques depuis Alexandre jusqu'à l'empereur Hadrien.* Paris: Sandoz et Fischbacher, 1874.

Volkmar, Gustav. "Beiträge zur Erklärung des Buches Henoch." *ZDMG* 14 (1860): 87-134, 296.

Weisse, Christian Hermann. *Die Evangelienfrage in ihrem gegenwärtigen Studium.* Liepzig: Breitkopft and Härtel, 1856.